New Frontiers in Regional Science: Asian Perspectives

Volume 2

More information about this series at http://www.springer.com/series/13039

Hirotada Kohno • Yoshiro Higano

Public Investment Criteria

Using an Interregional Input–Output Programming Model

Springer

Hirotada Kohno
University of Tsukuba
Professor Emeritus
Tokyo, Japan

Yoshiro Higano
University of Tsukuba
Tsukuba, Japan

ISSN 2199-5974 ISSN 2199-5982 (electronic)
New Frontiers in Regional Science: Asian Perspectives
ISBN 978-4-431-55220-8 ISBN 978-4-431-55221-5 (eBook)
https://doi.org/10.1007/978-4-431-55221-5

This Springer imprint is published by the registered company Springer Japan KK part of Springer Nature.
The registered company address is: Shiroyama Trust Tower, 4-3-1 Toranomon, Minato-ku, Tokyo 105-6005, Japan

This book is dedicated to the memory of
Professor Dr. Yasuhiko Oishi

Preface

When we were attached to the Institute of Socio-Economic Planning, University of Tsukuba, we desired to have a platform, with which our research results could be published without limit of pages. In that time, an article was generally forced to be published within 15–20 pages and we needed more than 40 pages because our works were based on an innovative simulation model of huge scale and their inputs as well as outputs were massive. It was a general current in regional science and related fields that scholars wrote shorter articles rigorously and published them in main stream of regional science journals. The implicit or explicit restriction set by journal editorship in that day was prohibitive for publication of the research results based on the philosophy, on which The Institute was newly established in the University of Tsukuba. It said that scholars do inter- and multi-disciplinary studies and return their research results for the society in order to, e.g., fix real issues and conflicts, make policy proposals, and eventually contribute for development of society. For this, we had requested Professor Dr. Jan Tinbergen to write a foreword through the good offices of Professor Dr. Peter Nijkamp. Then, a title of illusory journal ought to have been launched is *The Tokyo Journal of Large-scale Regional Modelling.*

It is a felicity for us that the monograph series *New Frontiers in Regional Science: Asian Perspectives* had been launched by the innovative undertaking of Springer Nature (Co.) in cooperation with the Japan Section of the Regional Science Association International (JSRSAI), having been admitted of the amazing conspicuous developments of JSRSAI during those 50 years.

In this volume of seven chapters, several studies which were kept within doors for more than 30 years now have been published to be able to see the light of day in the right way. Here, we express our sincere gratitude to Springer Nature above all.

During the 10 years from the latter half of the 1950s to the early 1960s (1957–1967), H. Kohno (one of the authors) had been attached to the Japan Highway Public Corporation and engaged mainly in the preparation of Loan Materials which had been submitted to the World Bank with the project of the Mei-shin (Nagoya-Kobe) Expressway and To-mei (Tokyo-Nagoya) Expressway. In other words, the preparation work was "Measurement of economic effects of public investment and the derivation of public investment criteria."

The former was dealt with in the first volume in this series, so this volume deals with topics focusing on the latter. What is public investment criterion? It is apt to be taken as a benefit–cost analysis in a conventional sense, which is still nowadays adopted by practitioners. However, it had been so often pointed out that the conventional benefit–cost analysis has many essential rudimentary defects and limits. For example, the conventional benefit–cost analysis neglects: the scarcity of allocated public fund, which means that the analysis has no idea of the opportunity cost of public fund; dynamic optimization of the streams of returns through re-investment of returns in the future, the scope of the economy by implementing several related projects, etc. So, from the first, our concern had been shifted to fix those defects inherent to the conventional benefit–cost analysis and to develop a more elaborate and sophisticated model, the second generation, based on what was initiated by Steiner=Marglin. It is dealt with in Chap. 3. The model is formulated as the maximization of an objective function being subject to resource fund allocation constraints.

Nevertheless, in Chap. 1, various themes are dealt with, i.e., superiority or inferiority of the benefit–cost *ratio* criteria vs. benefit–*less*–cost criteria, the present value method vs. internal rate of return method (Hirshleifer), and standardization of various criteria (Mishan). Chapter 1, in a sense, makes a comprehensive survey of the past studies on the benefit–cost analysis.

In Chap. 2, we will explain a typical process of applying the conventional benefit–cost analysis to the evaluation of Mei-Shin and To-Mei Expressway in the 1960s. It is still useful for readers who are in charge of the proposal of public investment projects of huge scale.

In Chap. 3, as mentioned above, the application of sophisticated Steiner=Marglin model to the public investment criteria of expressways in Japan is dealt with, in which built in are technical constraints such as preemptive right of public sector, incompatibility of location and transport modes, indivisibility, lumpiness, reflection of various opportunity costs of investments on the objective function (named as—supra-marginality), scheduling project implementation on the time horizon of multi-periods (evasion of fault due to myopic policy). The mode is formulated as an integer programming model. The solution to the model is obtained by application of the usual LP algorithm with the *combinatorial method.* In Chap. 3, however, the measurement of economic effects must be completed in advance and the values are given to the model that solves the optimal public investment criteria, on which investments shall be implemented with a scarce investment fund.

In the late 1960s, one of the urgent topics in the business world was how to determine optimal shares between investments into the public sector and the private sector. It was raised by the economic community because they realized that the social infrastructures, especially transportation infrastructures at that time were out-of-date, and the lack of social infrastructures of high quality would be serious bottlenecks for the economic growth which were expected in the 1970s. Also, motorization was about to start and optimal shares between investment into transportation infrastructures of railways, maritime, and roadways were urgent topics in the transportation economics association as well as among related departments of the central government.

In Chap. 4, the simulation model based on interregional input–output model of competitive-import type is formulated as a linear programming model. It was a cutting-edge model with the following features: "shipment activities" are formulated in order to simulate interregional trade patterns reflecting impacts of public projects such as expressway construction while it is different from Moses's model that transportation sectors explicitly specified in the input–output structure; and the public investment criteria is rightly embodied in the model to take into account imputed prices (or, opportunity costs) of injecting scarce public funds to possible investment targets. Imputed prices are critical indicators in order to pursue the optimality of solutions to a linear programming model based on the simplex algorithm. The model is applied to the above practical agendas. It is yet a static and prototype model, but the above-mentioned critical defects inherent to the conventional benefit–cost criteria were completely and consistently fixed. The measurement of economic effects and the identification of optimal investments targets are simultaneously solved by taking into account their impacts on the whole national economy through changes in interregional trade patterns. It was the first work in which the optimal investment shares are shown between the public sector and the private sector as well as between transportation infrastructures of railways, maritime, and roadways, based on the economic rationality of opportunity costs. Readers will confirm that the economic rationality is presented as the equalization of imputed prices that are associated with constraints, such as transportation infrastructure constraints, production capacity constraints, and scarce public fund allocation constraint, which could become bottlenecks for the economy to further grow, and can be directly fixed by the injection of scarce public funds, or indirectly fixed by, for example, changes in interregional trade patterns.

It can be said that the models developed in Chaps. 3 and 4 had achieved some success in that they are applicable to practical agendas of that day, and have shown quantitative (and objective) answers to the debated matters among related stakeholders qualitatively (and subjectively). However, the models had space for further improvements and developments. In Chap. 5, subjects for possible development and improvements of the models are discussed.

In Chap. 6, as one of the directions discussed in Chap. 5, the small-sized model of five regions, five industries, and three transport nodes developed in Chap. 4 is enlarged to incorporate ten regions, ten industries, nine means of transport. This was a practically useful model by taking advantage of the rapid development of computer architecture and software of the linear programming model. More minute and informative results can be obtained for policy proposals.

In Chap. 7, the dynamic interregional input–output programming model is shown, which is, however, a simple discrete linear model (not nonlinear). It looks like an extension of the DOSSO model, but the malleability of capital is completely denied (at least, it is not a sausage model); it is not focused on a steady-state rather on the transitional phase of transforming the economy in order to reply to practical agendas. It is applied to the evaluation of Asian Expressway construction investment project as a strategic variable for the Chinese economy to take off.

We owe many people who have assisted us in copywriting and preparation of materials, some of which laid gathering dust for a long time in a stockroom. Without their devotion, this book would not have been completed at this time. Firstly, to be praised is secretary to Dr. Takeshi Mizunoya' study room (and, to former Higano's study room), Ms. Hatsumi Uchimura, who has contributed to make a fair copy of manuscripts. Sasaki Publishing Printing Co. Tokyo Branch Office Editorial Adviser, Mr. Tatsuya Shimatai, contributed by advising us on how to compose difficult troublesome graphs; to publishing editor, Mr. Yutaka Hirachi, and editorial staff, Ms. Misao Taguchi, we express our deep and sincere gratitude.

Tokyo, Japan Hirotada Kohno
Tsukuba, Japan Yoshiro Higano
March 31, 2021

Contents

List of Figures

List of Tables

Chapter 1
Public Investment Criteria: A Tentative-Specific Survey on the Benefit–Cost Analysis in the Early Years

1.1 Underlying Fundamental Concepts of Public Investment Criteria: Significance and Necessity

1.1.1 Definition of Investment Criteria

Under the scarce total capital fund that is given in advance by the capital rationing through, for example, policy arguments between the alternative sets of investment targets such as the projects of road construction administered by the ministry of construction, the projects of the railway by the ministry of transportation, the projects of research and developments by the ministry of education, science and technology, and so on, the most concern, for example, the ministry of construction, which is in charge of planning and implementation of the projects of road, is to choose a set of projects of road to which the limited fund may be assigned. The ministry or the department in the ministry has to make a kind of selection between projects and determine a certain set of projects in a consistent manner by considering the accountability because it may usually not include all the projects which the department may implement even if the allocated fund through the capital rationing to the department were huge. The *static* investment criteria work as a sort of *Merkmal* (an indicator) in the choice of the optimal set of projects consistently in the sense that the additional total social surplus (the sum of consumer and producer surpluses = social benefits), which can be created in the whole national economy owing to the implementation of the optimal set of projects, is greater or at least is not less than the social surplus that is to be created by implementing other sets of projects created through the selection subject to the limited fund.

The essence of the public investment criteria is that: (1) the optimal set of projects, (2) the scale of projects in the optimal set to which the fund is to be allocated, and (3) the timing of implementation of projects in the optimal set if, for example, the total capital fund is given as an annual stream of budgets, and so on, are endogenously solved and simultaneously determined. The adoption of the public

H. Kohno, Y. Higano, *Public Investment Criteria*, New Frontiers in Regional Science: Asian Perspectives 2, https://doi.org/10.1007/978-4-431-55221-5_1

investment criteria in this manner will make efficient the allocation of the limited fund to the chosen and implemented projects in terms of the opportunity cost of the capital funds. This is critically different from the basic benefit–cost analysis principle in which typically the amount of allocated fund is predetermined and the project selection is made external to the principle, its scale and timing of implementation and so on are predetermined, and whether the increase in the social benefits, thanks to the project selected in advance, deserves the fund or not is the main concern in the analysis irrespective of how the allocation of the fund, the choice of the project, and so on were predetermined. However, in reality, the case in which the conventional benefit–cost analysis is yet adopted rather usually and even such cases are almost all with the public project management. Significance and necessity of the adoption of the public investment criteria in public investment management and the related topics are first taken in this chapter.

To apply the public investment criteria to the allocation of the limited fund to a limited number of public projects, which shall be implemented after choice among a set of potential investment targets[1] on *a certain criterion*, with respect to *each* potential public investment target (it is a public project) in the choice set, the sum of the increase (or decrease, that has a negative value) in the producers' surplus (profits) and consumer's surplus in the markets (including newly created) of the whole national economy, or, at least, a certain scope of the economy that is to be affected by the public investments in the choice set, are to be estimated focusing on the shifts of demand and supply curves in all the markets directly and indirectly affected by the public investment. The estimation is made over *the time horizon* of the public project, which means the time span in which impacts of the public investment continue. Finally, the time series of the sum of increases/decreases in producers' and consumers' surpluses over the time horizon are capitalized in terms of the value at the beginning of the initial period using a certain discounting ratio. The capitalized value (or, we sometimes call it—discounted value) is called the *benefits* or *economic effects* of the public investment, and it is an indicator of the increase in the welfare of the whole national economy owing to the public investment. In the case where the limited fund is very small compared to the total investment in the macroeconomic sense, as it is a usual case, it may be taken as the marginal benefits of the marginal public investment as far as the chosen public projects are independent of each other, which means that the created benefits by the chosen public project are independent of whether one or some of the other chosen public projects are implemented or not.

The ratio of the benefits to the cost[2] that is required for the implementation of the public project is calculated with respect to each public investment target, and it works as a marginal benefit indicator of public investment. Using the indicator, the optimal allocation of the limited capital fund to potential public investments targets and, therefore, the optimal set of chosen public projects that shall be implemented

[1]The set of public investment targets is called—the choice set.

[2]In case in which costs are required over the time horizon, the series of costs are capitalized, too.

using the limited capital fund is pursued to maximize the total capitalized benefits that are to be generated by the chosen public projects (Nakamura 1970, pp. 34–37).

The calculation of benefits to obtain the marginal benefit indicator and the solution process of the maximization stated above constitute the theory of *static* investment criteria.[3] However, there could be variations related to the maximization process depending on: (1) whether the conventional benefit–cost ratio or benefit-less-cost indicator is applied to the maximization process; (2) whether all the marginal benefit indicators are applied *in a lump sum manner* to the selection of the set of potential (feasible) public projects that shall be implemented with the limited fund; (3) the method applied to the calculation of the benefits that are critical components of the marginal benefit indicator; (4) to what extent *indirect* economic effects shall be included in the benefits; and (5) the scope of the economy with which the benefits created by the public project are to be calculated, and so on (Oishi 1960; Sasaki et al. 1965; Kohno 1974).

1.1.2 Significance of Public Investment Criteria

In the case of the business with the public utilities (whether they explicitly or implicitly exist in the economy does not matter), which utilize large-scale social infrastructures that are usually constructed through the public investment(s), (1) the control of the quantity (e.g., the traffic volumes on the expressway) in the short run through the price (fare) adjustment and (2) the control of the public investment to increase the capacity of the social infrastructures and, thus, control the quantity, are inconsistent with each other in the laissez-faire market, and results are *not* socially optimal because the decreasing marginal cost and, therefore, what the marginal cost is less than the average cost while it is decreasing with quantities produced is the pertinent characteristic to the public utilities (Negishi 1964, pp. 29–31). This means that we should not rely on the market mechanism with the quantity and/or investment adjustments through the price mechanism. In this case, (a) the control of the capacity of the social infrastructures shall be made through the application of the public investment criteria presuming the full utilization of the capacity by rather adopting the marginal cost pricing than the self-supporting accounting system that would damage the optimal organization of social infrastructures and (b) a possible deficit by the adoption of the marginal cost pricing (because the marginal cost cannot

[3]Here, only the public investment criteria will be discussed. Of course, the theory and measurement investigated here can be applied to the *private* (enterprise) investment criteria, also. The main difference between the two is that the benefits with the public project is "social benefits – economic effects created in a certain scope of the economy, typically the whole national economy" and the benefits with the private project is replace by "revenues in the private sense – revenues which only accrue to the firm which makes the investment." The concept of social discount rate is inherent to the public investment criteria. With the private investment criteria, it is replaced by the interest rate in the market.

cover the average cost) shall be compensated by, for example, using the government general/specific budget. This dichotomy is the kernel of Hotelling Theory that the public investment should be dealt with in a unitary manner focusing on the relation between the maximized total surplus (benefits) that are created by the investment and its necessary costs, namely, the benefit–cost criteria (Hotelling 1938). Here is the significance of the public investment criteria.

1.1.3 Adjustments with Product Quantity and Investment Quantity

Generally speaking, the market plays an important role truly with the short-run adjustment of product quantity through the price mechanism, but with the long-run adjustment of investment quantity, especially the public investment or construction of public facilities (infrastructures), it does not well perform as expected. Here, we would forward our arguments by introducing the following concepts:

1. Allocation objective and revenue objective.

   There are two objectives related to public utility activities. One is *allocative objective* and the other is *revenue objective*. The allocative objective is to attain the optimality of resource allocation (e.g., optimal capital fund allocation in the long run, the optimal degree of the rate of utilization to the capacity in the short-run in which the capacity of social infrastructure is fixed, etc.) in the light of the objective function of society, for example, the social welfare function, the sum of the social surpluses, and so on. On the other hand, the revenue objective is the maximization of revenues even if the allocative objective was not attained in the long run or in the short run. In relation to these concepts, we need to mention the pricing theories that are applied to, for example, the toll and fare charged by the public utilities.
2. Marginal cost pricing principle and average cost pricing principle.

   The allocation objective is surely attained by charging toll or fare, in conformity with the marginal cost pricing principle, on the users (consumers) of the goods (e.g., tap water) /services (e.g., expressway services) provided by the public utility, although the revenue objective may not be attained. On the other hand, the dependence on the average cost pricing principle assures the attainment of the revenue objective, but the allocative objective becomes imperfect (Table 1.1). The investment by private companies is essentially different from public investment. The decision-making of the former is simple compared to the public investment criteria (and still it is a tough business for the executive officers in the company) in the sense that when they apply a feasibility study, for example, based on internal rate of return or cap rate, they fairly can place reliance on the direction of the market now or in the near future as far as they have the capability of management. The latter has to involve a kind of forecast or prediction of the direction of the market in the long run to obtain the public investment criteria. The

Table 1.1 Summary of discussion in Sect. 1.1

Control mechanism for industries which produce under decreasing marginal cost	Objective	Private company (supply curve (= marginal cost curve) is increasing with the quantity produced)	Public utility (supply curve is decreasing with quantity produced)
Nothing (the laissez faire market)	Optimality of the quantity produced in the short run	Attained	Not attained (e.g., due to natural monopoly)
	Revenue objective in the short-run	Attained and socially optimal	Attained and not socially optimal
	Optimality of the resource allocation in the short-run (optimal utilization of the fixed amount of facilities)	Attained	Not attained (e.g., same reason in the above)
	Optimality of the resource allocation (=investment) in the long-run	Not attained (owe to feasibility study based on internal rate of return/cap rate, etc.)	Not attained (owe to feasibility study based on the public investment criteria)
The marginal cost pricing (MCP) principle in a unitary manner	Optimality of the quantity produced in the short-run	–(n/a)	Attained
	Revenue objective in the short-run	–(n/a)	Attained but deficit
	Optimality of the resource allocation in the short-run (optimal utilization of the fixed amount of facilities)	–(n/a)	Attained but deficit
	Optimality of the resource allocation (=investment) in the long run	–(n/a)	Not attained (owe to feasibility study based on the public investment criteria combined with MCP principle)
Average cost pricing (ACP) principle in a unitary manner	Optimality of the quantity produced in the short run	–(n/a)	Attained but not socially optimal
	Revenue objective in the short-run	–(n/a)	Attained but not socially optimal
	Optimality of the resource allocation in the short run (optimal utilization of the fixed amount of facilities)	–(n/a)	Attained but not socially optimal
	Optimality of the resource allocation (=investment) in the long run	–(n/a)	Not attained as far as ACP principle is adopted even if the public investment criteria is applied

raison dêtre of the public investment criteria and, therefore, the research field of the public investment criteria exist based on the reality that the social optimality of the resource allocation, that is, allocation objective in the long run is not attained through a la laissez-faire market mechanism (Table 1.1).

1.2 Benefit–Cost Criteria

1.2.1 Several Variations in Basic Benefit–Cost Criteria

The benefit–cost criteria and the public investment criteria are the formula for ordering objects (projects) based on a certain viewpoint, that is, in the light of the social efficiency of the project. And, the public investment criterion is used as a concept much broader than the benefit–cost criterion. Even if the concept of the criteria is limited to the *static* one,[4] there are several types of benefit–cost criterion and programming model. In the latter, the maximization problem subject to constraints is explicitly specified as shown in the next chapter. The most basic and primitive in the public investment criteria is what is called a theory of benefit–cost criteria. It is composed of benefit–cost ratio criteria, benefit–less–cost criteria, and the internal-rate-of-return criteria. The former two are called present-value criteria.

1.2.1.1 Benefit–Cost Ratio Criteria

The benefit–cost ratio is the ratio of the present valued benefit (=the capitalized value of the stream of benefits over the time horizon in terms of the value at the beginning of the initial period) to the cost (usually, it is the present valued cost, too, in case the expenditures were made before the beginning of the time horizon, and will be made over the time horizon).

A project that has the larger benefit–cost ratio is put the higher priority in the order of the implementation of projects with a limited capital fund. In case the capital fund has no limits, the project shall be selected while the benefit–cost ratio of the

[4]The static criteria are applied to the project choice that has no dimension of time, i.e. the choice has been done at once and therefore most of them have been implemented before the time horizon starts even if some of chosen projects will be implemented during the time horizon following the predetermined time schedule. The dynamic criterion means that it is applied to the project choice that may be made at any period in the time horizon. In this case, the state of the economy at any period in the time horizon must be dependent on the time series of chosen projects in the past, ceteris paribus. The dynamic criteria determine the time series of chosen projects over the time horizon in order to optimize the attained dynamic path of the economy, i.e. maximize the sum of the capitalized social benefits at the value of the beginning of the initial period over the time horizon. The dynamic criteria presume the forecast of the future economy endogenously dependent on the chosen projects, even if ceteris paribus condition holds.

chosen project is ≥1 (the last one thus chosen is called the marginal project). The following is a famous formula and the fundamental essence of Otto Eckstein (1958, pp. 55–57).

[Benefit–Cost Ratio]

The benefit–cost ratio is given by the following formula:

$$\text{The benefit–cost ratio} = \frac{V_B}{V_C} = \frac{B}{O + K\left[\sum_{t=1}^{T} \frac{1}{(1+i)^t}\right]^{-1}} \tag{1.1}$$

$$\text{Or, the benefit–cost ratio} = \frac{V_B}{V_C} = \frac{B}{O + a_{iT}K} \tag{1.2}$$

in which B = benefits created annually that are defined on the agency practice (it is assumed that B is constant over the time horizon), V_C = the present value of the costs, K = fixed investment costs in terms of the value at the beginning of the first period, O = operating, maintenance, and routine replacement costs incurred annually including interest on the capital, i = capitalization rate (discount rate), T = time horizon (amortization period) and

$$a_{iT} = \left[\sum\nolimits_{t=1}^{T} \frac{1}{(1+i)^t}\right]^{-1}. \tag{1.3}$$

The present value of the costs is given as follows:

$$V_C = \sum_{t=1}^{T} \frac{O}{(1+i)^t} + K. \tag{1.4}$$

The present value of the benefits is given as follows:

$$V_B = \sum\nolimits_{t=1}^{T} \frac{B}{(1+i)^t}. \tag{1.5}$$

The benefit–cost ratio is calculated as follows:

$$\frac{V_B}{V_C} = \frac{\sum_{t=1}^{T} \frac{B}{(1+i)^t}}{\sum\limits_{t=1}^{T} \frac{O}{(1+i)^t} + K}, \text{ or} \tag{1.6}$$

$$\frac{V_B}{V_C} = \sum\nolimits_{t=1}^{T} \frac{B}{(1+i)^t} \left[\sum_{t=1}^{T} \frac{O}{(1+i)^t} + K\right]^{-1}. \tag{1.7}$$

By dividing both the numerator and denominator of Eq. (1.7) by

$$\sum_{t=1}^{T} \frac{1}{(1+i)^t}, \tag{1.8}$$

we get the Eq. (1.1). Also, substituting Eq. (1.3) in Eq. (1.1), we obtain Eq. (1.2) (Eckstein 1958, p. 56).

The annual capital charge per one dollar of the investment at the beginning of the first year is a_{iT}, representing annual interest (in case K is financed by loan) plus amortization (as far as the going-concern hypothesis holds). Given i and T, the numerical value for a_{iT} can be obtained from a table, "Annuity whose present value is 1."[5] Eq. (1.2) is the formula that usually presents the benefit–cost ratio.

1.2.1.2 Benefit–Less–Cost

The criteria preferentially decide on the order of projects for selection: the project that creates the larger difference between benefits and costs shall be given higher priority in the selection of projects. It is given as follows:

[Benefit–less–cost (BLC) criterion]

$$\mathrm{BLC} = V_B - V_C = \sum_{t=1}^{T} \frac{B}{(1+i)^t} - \sum_{t=1}^{T} \frac{O}{(1+i)^t} - K. \tag{1.9}$$

Dividing Eq. (1.9) by Eq. (1.3) gives as follows:

$$\mathrm{BLC}\left[\sum_{t=1}^{T} \frac{1}{(1+r)^t}\right]^{-1} = B - O - K\left[\sum_{t=1}^{T} \frac{1}{(1+r)^t}\right]^{-1}, \tag{1.10}$$

and, equivalently, we get the following formula:

$$\mathrm{BLC}a_{iT} = B - O - a_{iT}K. \tag{1.11}$$

As a_{iT} is constant with varieties of projects as far as the same discount rate is applied, the right-hand side of Eq. (1.11) may be applied to the ordering of projects for selection in place of the original definition of the benefit–less–cost criterion, *BLC*.[6]

[5]This table is conveniently presented in *Mathematical Tables from Handbook of Physics and Chemistry* (Cleveland, Ohio: Chemical Rubber Publishing Company, 1948), pp.306–313, and in other collections of mathematical tables.

[6]Sometimes it should be reasonable to adopt different discount rates depending on a kind of the value judgement, e. g. the recovery projects in the regions damaged by an earthquake should have a lower discount rate. In that case, Eq. (1.9), or equivalently $BLC = a_{iT}B - a_{iT}O - K$, must be used, in which a_{iT} may change depending on the value of adopted discount rate, i, project by project.

1.2.1.3 Internal-Rate-of-Return Criteria

The internal-rate-of-return criteria decide on the order projects for selection: the project that produces the larger internal rate of return shall be given the higher priority in the ordering.[7]

[Internal rate of return]

It is the discount rate, r, which satisfies the following equation in terms of r:

$$K = \sum_{t=1}^{T} \frac{B - O}{(1+r)^t}, \text{ or}$$

$$K = \frac{(B - O)}{a_{rT}}, \tag{1.12}$$

in which:

$$a_{rT} = \left[\sum\nolimits_{t=1}^{T} \frac{1}{(1+r)^t}\right]^{-1}. \tag{1.13}$$

The solution of r is obtained as follows. Eqs. (1.12) and (1.13) gives the following:

$$B = a_{rT}K + O. \tag{1.14}$$

Substituting Eq. (1.14) into Eq. (1.2), we obtain as follows:

$$\frac{V_B}{V_C} = \frac{a_{rT}K + O}{O + a_{iT}K} \tag{1.15}$$

Solving Eq. (1.15) in a_{rT}, we obtain the following equation:

$$a_{rT} = \frac{\frac{V_B}{V_C}(O + a_{iT}K) - O}{K} = \frac{V_B}{V_C}\left(a_{it} + \frac{O}{K}\right) - \frac{O}{K}. \tag{1.16}$$

As a_{rT} increases as r increases, the internal rate of return r which meets Eq. (1.16) increases as the cost–benefit ratio increases as far as $\frac{O}{K}$ is held constant, which must mean that the value of annual benefit, B, increases. More drastically, we obtain the following equation:

---

[7]The internal rate of return, thus defined, should be called —*social* internal rate of return as it includes social benefits in place of the profits accrue to private company.

$$a_{rT} = a_{iT}\left(\frac{V_B}{V_C}\right), \tag{1.17}$$

in case the value of O, that is, operating, maintenance, and routine replacement costs incurred annually including interest on the capital, can be taken negligibly small compared to the value of K, fixed investment costs in terms of the value at the beginning of the time horizon. Eq. (1.17) means that the internal rate of return increases as the benefit–cost ratio increases. In case the benefit–cost ratio is equal to 1 (one), Eq. (1.17) implies $a_{rT} = a_{iT}$ and the internal rate of return is equated to the value of the discount rate (Eckstein 1958, p. 57).

1.2.2 Present Value Criteria vs. Internal-Rate-of-Return Criteria

1.2.2.1 Benefit–Cost Ratio Criteria vs. Benefit–Less–Cost Criteria

Before discussing the merits and demerits between the benefit–cost ratio and the benefit–less–cost criteria, we first compare the benefit–cost ratio criteria and benefit–less–cost criteria.

In the Green Book (1958), the benefit–less–cost criteria are dismissed by the reason that "the larger investment planning than the smaller one ought to be made more advantageous to." So, as to the criteria applied to the choice among many alternative projects, the superiority of the benefit–cost ratio criteria may be more admitted. On the other hand, P.O. Steiner et al. deny the result based on the benefit–cost ratio criteria by taking it as a "foolish solution" (e.g., Steiner 1959, p. 901).

As shown by the following example, it cannot be excluded that these two criteria result in different priority ordering. Assume two investment planning I_1 and I_2. The benefits and costs of I_1 are 2.0 billion JPY and 1 billion JPY, respectively. The benefits and costs of I_2 are 3.0 billion JPY and 1.8 billion JPY, respectively. The benefit–less–cost of I_1 is 1.0 billion JPY and that of I_2 is 1.2 billion JPY. Therefore, I_2 is a much more efficient project in terms of the benefit–less–cost criterion. On the other hand, the benefit–cost ratio is 2 for the I_1 and 1.667 for the I_2. Therefore, the two projects are preferentially chosen in different order depending on which criterion is applied. A defect of the problem and, therefore, the comparison is that it does not explicitly specify the constraint of the capital fund that can be allocated to the chosen project(s). To choose among two projects becomes an utterly different problem depending on whether the fund constraint is 1.0 billion JPY or 2.0 billion JPY. In the case in which the number of potential projects is larger compared to the amount of the limited fund, and the *divisibility* of project is admitted, the benefit–cost ratio criteria meet the higher efficiency, and, in this sense, it might be superior to the benefit–less–cost criteria. On the other hand, in the case in which the public investment must be implemented in a lump sum manner (Lorie and Savage 1955),

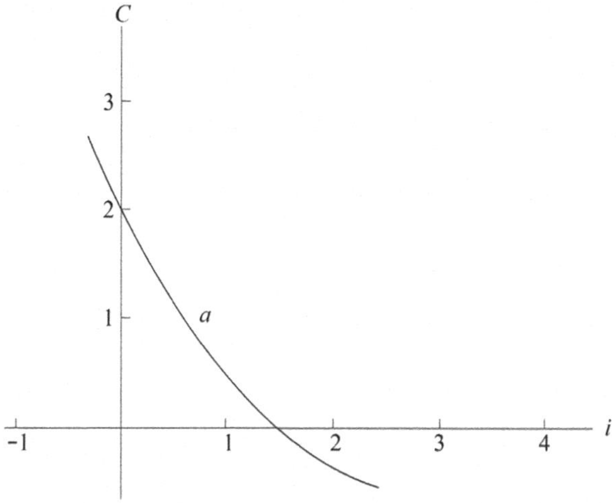

Fig. 1.1 Sketch of present value (*C*) of the option −1, 2, 1. Source: Hirshlifer (1958), p. 348

in a word, the criteria that maximize the net total benefits under the given fund constraint(s) and other constraints shall be most preferable. We cannot say more than that about superiority among the application of the two criteria so far as the divisibility, lumpiness, fund constraint, and so on are not taken into account in the problem with which the superiority is argued.

1.2.2.2 Present-Value Criteria vs. Internal-Rate-of-Return Criteria

It is not too much to say that the most valuable contribution to this theme has been done by J. Hirshleifer (1958), a part of which is quoted as follows (from the 25th line of page 347 to the 23rd line of page 348. Notes are added by the author):

For the investment option −1, 2, 1 considered above,[8] ρ is equal to $\sqrt{2}$, or 141.4%.[9] And, in fact, if the borrowing rate or the rate on the best alternative opportunity (whichever is the appropriate comparison) is less than $\sqrt{2}$, the investment is desirable. Figure 1.1[10] plots the present value C[11]of the option as a function of the discounting interest rate, *i*, assumed to be constant over the two discounting periods. Note that the present value of the option diminishes as *i* increases throughout the entire relevant range of *i*, from $i = -1$ to $i = \infty$. The internal rate of return ρ is that *i* for which the present value curve cuts the horizontal axis. Evidently, for any $i < \rho$, present value is positive; for $i > \rho$, it is negative.

[8] '−1, 2, 1' means the stream of *net* costs (negative) and net benefits (positive) created by or incurred in connection with the investment option at period 0, 1, and 2, respectively.

[9] ρ is a solution to Eq. (1.18).

[10] The figure number is changed by the author.

[11] The present value is calculated in terms of the value at the beginning of period 1 (the second period) and that coincides with the end of the period 0 (the first period).

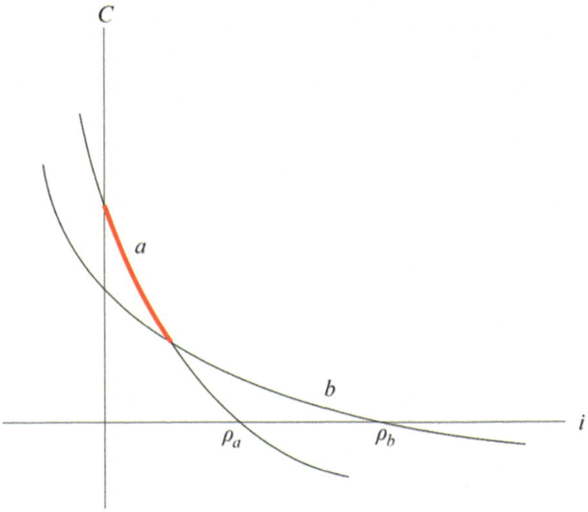

Fig. 1.2 Two alternative options. Source: Hirshlifer (1958), p. 348

However, the fact that the use of ρ leads to the correct decision in a particular case or a particular class of cases does not mean that it is correct in principle. And, in fact, cases have been adduced where its use leads to incorrect answers. Alchian (1955, p. 939) has shown that, in the comparison of two investment options which are alternatives, the choice of the one with a higher ρ is not in general correct—in fact, the decision cannot be made without knowledge of the appropriate external discounting rate. Figure 1.2[12] illustrates two such options, I being preferable for low rates of interest and II for high rates. The *i* at which the cross-over takes place is Fisher's rate of return on sacrifice between these two options. But II has the higher internal rate of return (that is, its present value falls to zero at a higher discounting rate) regardless of the actual rate of interest. How can we say that I is preferable at low rates of interest? Because its present value is higher, it permits the investor to move along a higher hyperplane to find the utility optimum attained somewhere on that hyperplane. If II were adopted, the investor would also be enabled to move along such a hyperplane, but a lower one. Put another way, with the specified low rate of interest, the investor adopting I could, if he chose, put himself in the position of adopting II by appropriate borrowings and lendings together with throwing away some of his wealth.

Although it is more or less duplicated, the essence of this theme is elucidated hereinafter. That is, as a weak point of the present-value criteria, it is mentioned that the intervention of the exogenous and subjective factor of social discounting rate is necessary to the unification (present valuation or capitalization) of each benefit and each cost formed in each period within the planning horizon to the present value (Eckstein 1958; Marglin 1963b). On the contrary, it is thought that this point, owing to the internal-rate-of-return criteria, will be apt "endogenously" dealt with. Which is

[12]The figure number is changed by the author.

the more valuable criteria? These problems have been discussed by Lorie and Savage (1955, p. 237), Solomon (1956, pp. 77–78), Turvey (1963, p. 97), Eckstein (1961, pp. 460–461), and Hirshleifer (1958, pp. 346–349), etc.

To give a conclusion first, as long as the perfect capital market does exist, the present-value criteria is universally right. On the other hand, it can be stated that the internal-rate-of-return criteria cannot give the right solution except for the case in which the present valuation or the capitalization is restricted to the time horizon of two periods. In case the time horizon includes more than two periods, it may not give the right solution.

Lets take up, as an example, the investment revenue stream that the investment equivalent to 100 million JPY is done at the period 0 (the first period), and the revenues of 200 million and 100 million JPY are formed at the periods 1 and 2, respectively, the internal rate of return is given as a solution to the following equation in ρ (This example was quoted from Hirshleifer (1958), in the middle of the right-hand side of p. 347):

$$\frac{-1}{(1+\rho)^0}+\frac{2}{(1+\rho)^1}+\frac{1}{(1+\rho)^2}=0. \tag{1.18}$$

The internal rate of return, ρ, thus obtained, is $\sqrt{2}=1.414$.[13]

A slight arrangement of terms in Eq. (1.18) and the replacement of ρ by i give the following:

$$\mathrm{NPV}=\frac{2}{(1+i)^1}+\frac{1}{(1+i)^2}-\frac{1}{(1+i)^0}. \tag{1.19}$$

This is the formula of the net present value (NPV) of the stream of costs and benefits capitalized in terms of the value at the beginning of period 1 (the second period) when the capitalization (discount) rate is i. NPV is the benefit–less–cost criterion in the sense of the definition in Sect. 1.2.1.2.

NPV is apparently monotonically decreasing function in i and the graph is drawn in Fig. 1.1 so that it is concave to the origin since the second derivative of NPV is a negative function in i. In case $i=0$, NPV $=2$. In case $i=\rho$, NPV $=0$ based on the definition of the internal rate of return. Namely, the value of i at the intercept of the axis i and the graph is the internal rate of return of the projects. Symbolize it as ρ_a. Of

[13] A same solution is given by solving the following equation: $\frac{-1}{(1+\rho)^1}+\frac{2}{(1+\rho)^2}+\frac{1}{(1+\rho)^3}=0$. This is a formula with the capitalization in terms of the value at the beginning of the first period (period 0). Eq. (18) presumes that the value, -1, is the capitalized value of all the costs incurred by the project till the end of the first period (period 0) including incurred costs before period 0. Actually, to get the internal rate of return with such simple formulation (static assumption), at which period the streams of benefits and costs are capitalized does not matter and the formula for discounting the net value at any period gives a same solution.

course, $\rho_a = \sqrt{2}$. With i such that $0 \le i \le \rho_a$, NPV is non-negative and it is a value on the part of the graph, which is named—curve a in Fig. 1.1.

In Fig. 1.2, the graph of NPV that is in the function of discount rate i with the stream of costs and benefits, $(-1, 2, 1)$ is drawn of which intercept with the axis i is ρ_a. In Fig. 1.2, we may draw another graph of NPV, which shows a lower value of NPV with a lower discount rate i $(\le \sqrt{2})$ and a higher NPV with a higher i $(\ge \rho_a)$ than NPV with the stream of $(-1, 2, 1)$. An example of the stream of such a graph is given by $(-0.4, 1.459966, 0.273367)$.[14] We call the project which gives the stream of $(-1, 2, 1)$ and $(-0.4, 1.459966, 0.273367)$ – project A and Project B, respectively. The internal rate of return of the project B, ρ_b, is $2\sqrt{2} = 2.828427 \cdot \left(> \rho_a = \sqrt{2} = 1.41421\right)$. The discount rate i with which both graphs intercept with each other is 0.6389692. We symbolize this value as ρ_f. The NPV of B in case $i = 0$ is 1.333.[*The first problem of the internal-rate-of-return criterion: it rejects the project of a higher NPV*]

As readers may see in Fig. 1.2 the project B is not necessarily superior to project A although the internal rate of return of the project B is greater than that of A $(\rho_b > \rho_a)$. Actually with the discount rate i such that $0 \le i < \rho_f$ NPV of B is less than NPV of A. As Hirshleifer says there is almost no reason why project A should not be chosen preferred to the project B when for example the interest rate in the capital market is now very low and it is expected that it continues fairly lower than ρ_a over the time horizon because project A possibly produces the net present value greater than B (a possible greater NPV of A is depicted as the part of the graph of A with a symbol a).[15] Here is the first problem of the internal-rate-of-return criterion (Hirshleifer 1958p. 348)

[*The second problem: the internal-rate-of-return may not be unique*]

In the case in which the investments are done after the period 0 a several times over the time horizon, the internal rate of return may have multiple values since the solution to the equation that equates the NPV of net benefits stream to the NPV of costs (negative) stream may have multiple solutions. (the number of solutions is equal to the number of reversals of sigh (+ −) in the *net* benefit stream) and, then, the internal rate of return is not unique (about the particulars of this problem, see, for example, Hirshleifer 1958, pp. 348–349).

[*The third problem: it is implicitly assumed that the endogenous internal rate of return is reproduced with the reinvestment in the future*]

Furthermore, a fundamental problem is related to the assertion itself that "the internal rate of return ρ is the purely internal rate" (Hirshleifer 1958, the upper part in the left-hand side of p.350). That is, it is a problem that the net revenue equivalent to

---

[14] This stream is given by the author which may draw the other graph in Fig. 1.2.

[15] In Fischer's sense, the opportunity cost of the choice of the project B based on the internal-rate-of-return criteria is higher than the NPV when the interest rate in the capital market (e.g., the interest rate for the loan which finance the initial (net) cost) is lower than ρ_f. With two examples in the text, the opportunity cost of the choice of the project B is 1.645 billion JPY (it is the value of NPV of the project A) while NPV of the project B is 1.153 billion JPY when the discount (interest) rate is 0.1.

200 million JPY formed on the way of the net benefit stream of (−1, 2, 1) produced by the project A mentioned above shall be obviously reinvested or consumed somewhere or other apart from this project. Usually, it is implicitly assumed that the reinvestment will again produce an internal rate of return that is the same as ρ_a, and in the light of the precise/pure meaning of the internal rate of return, an assumption does not work and what the internal rate of return of the reinvestment into other project(s) is ρ_a must be proved (Practically, this cannot be done as the chain of reinvestments continues forever in the future).

Because of such several defects pertinent to the internal-rate-of-return criteria, the decision of predominance is given in favor of "present-value criteria" (Hirshleifer 1958, pp. 349–351; Mishan 1967, pp. 777–778). A disputant being on the side of the internal rate of return is Mckean (1958). In the early stage, the emphasis was put on the point that the investment priority can be derived independent of the discount rate that must be given exogenously.

It seems that Eqs. (1.18) and (1.19) are almost the same. However, what is given by assuming an exogenous discount rate and what is given endogenously by assuming the completeness of the opportunities with which reinvestment can be made at the endogenously determined internal rate of return in the future have intrinsically different meanings in the application to the selection of investment projects.

1.3 Normalization of Various Benefit–Cost Criteria

1.3.1 Mishan's Theory of Normalization

As already seen in the previous subsection, in the controversy between the present-value-criteria and the internal-rate-of-return criteria, more or less intrinsic problems of the latter have been pointed out. Above all, after it had been pointed out that "the ultimate criteria is total wealth arising from investment by some terminal date" by E. Solomon (Solomon 1956, p. 127, Mishan 1967, note 1) of p. 779) with the criticism that "the idea that ρ is a purely internal rate is not true either," (Hirshlefer 1958, p. 350) (the third problem of the above), at length, the controversy was concluded by the esprit: "A proposed normalization procedure for public investment criteria," by Mishan (1967), which makes the priority ordering among the potential projects is mutually consistent between these variants of public investment criteria. Then, we will see the essence of the argument by Mishan.

First of all, it is indicated that the following four conditions necessarily hold to obtain a consistent ordering (Mishan 1967 pp. 778–779):

1. All benefits and outlays of any investment stream are to be compounded forward to yield a *terminal value, TV*, at some future date.
2. The maximum reinvestment potential is to be realized for each investment stream.

3. A capital outlay common to all the alternative streams under comparison is to be established.
4. The investment streams under comparison must be brought to a common period.

Then, the following is the core of the normalization of Mishan's Theory (Mishan 1967, pp. 781–783) (notes and the Eqs. (1.20) and (1.21) are added by the author):

The implications of this normalization procedure should be apparent. It enables us to transform the stream of benefits and outlays of any investment project A; $(b_o - c_o)$, $(b_t - c_t)$.... $(b_n - c_n)$, where b_t is the primary benefit and c_t the outlay in period t, into a stream, 0, 0...0, ...$(b^n - c^n)$, where b^n is the normalized terminal value of the benefits of the A stream, $TV^n(A)$, and c^n is the normalized terminal value of the outlays. Alternatively, if $B_t \equiv (b_t - c_t)$ we transform the stream $B_o, B_l, \ldots B_m$ into the stream 0, 0, ... 0, ... B^n, where B^n is the normalized terminal value of the net benefits of the A stream, $NTV^n(A)$, defined as $(b^n - c^n)$. It will be convenient, from now on, to denote the normalized terminal value of the outlays, c^n, as K, and therefore (1) to define $NTV^n(A)$ as $TV^n(A) - K$.

Having defined $TV^n(A)$ and $NTV^n(A)$, we are now in a position to define (2) $PV_i^n(A)$, (3) $NPV_i^n(A)$, (4) λ_A^n, these expressions corresponding to (2) the normalised present value of the benefits of the A stream discounted at any rate of interest i; (3) the normalised present value of the net benefits of the A stream, again discounted at any rate of interest i; and (4) the normalised internal rate of return.

$$PV_i^n(A) \text{ is defined as } \frac{TV^n(A)}{(1+i)^n} \tag{1.20}$$

$$NPV_i^n(A) \text{ is defined as } \frac{NTV^n(A)}{(1+i)^n}$$

$$\lambda_A^n \text{ is defined as } \sqrt[n]{\frac{TV^n(A)}{K^*}} - 1, \text{where } K^* = \frac{K}{(1+i)^n} \tag{1.21}$$

In other words, λ_A^n is defined as the discount rate which makes $TV^n(A)$, the normalised terminal value of the benefits of the A stream, equal to K^*, the normalised present value of the A outlays. Inasmuch as $TV^n(A)$ and K^* are positive, λ_A^n is single-valued and positive.

Recalling that normalisation requires, for each of the alternative investment projects, the same normalised terminal capital K, it is simple to prove that each of these three expressions, regarded as normalised criteria, will produce the same ordering for a group of projects as that resulting from the employment of $TV^n(A)$ and $NTV^n(A)$.

Given $TV^n(A) > TV^n(B)$,[16] we may infer each of the following:

[16] Symbol B in $TV^n(B)$ means a different B stream than the stream A, though it is confusing because the *net* stream of the stream A is symbolized as $B_0, B_l, \cdots, B_m$, etc.

(i) $TV^n(A) - K > TV^n(B) - K$,
Hence, by definition (1),
$NTV^n(A) > NTV^n(B)$ (I)

(ii) $\frac{TV^n(A)}{(1+i)^n} > \frac{TV^n(B)}{(1+i)^n}$,
Hence, by definition (2),
$PV_i^n(A) > PV_i^n(B)$ (II)

(iii) $\frac{TV^n(A)-K}{(1+i)^n} > \frac{TV^n(B)-K}{(1+i)^n}$,
Hence, by definition (3),
$NPV_i^n(A) > NPV_i^n(B)$ (III)

(iv) $(1+\lambda_A^n)^n K^* > (1+\lambda_B^n)^n \cdot K^*$,
and, therefore
$\lambda_A^n > \lambda_B^n$ (IV)

Finally, since normalisation requires that the alternative investment projects have the same K, or K^*, it is evident that the benefit–less–cost criterion gives the same ranking as the benefit–cost ratio criterion, whether benefit is measured as TV^n or, more commonly, as PV^n, and also whether benefit is measured net of capital outlay or not.

As to Mishan's theory of normalization above, some explanatory notes are made here. First, the definition of the internal rate of return λ_A^n, (4) gives:

$$(1+\lambda_A^n) = \sqrt[n]{\frac{TV^n}{K^*}}, \tag{1.22}$$

or equivalently

$$(1+\lambda_A^n)^n = \frac{TV^n}{K^*}. \tag{1.23}$$

Apparently, it has a single solution. The right-hand side of Eq. (1.23) shows what times the amounts of investment at the initial period, K^*, is the value at the terminal period of the stream, $TV^n(A)$. And, the left-hand side of Eq. (1.23) shows what growth rate per period is to attain the multiplicator through the compounding. Namely, it is the solution to the following:

$$(1+\lambda_A^n)^n \cdot K^* = TV^n(A). \tag{1.24}$$

Equation (1.24) can be rearranged as follows using Eq. (1.20):

$$(1+\lambda_A^n)^n \cdot K^* = (1+i)^n PV_i^n(A). \tag{1.25}$$

The discount rate i can be taken as the best return rate on the capital in the sense that the entity which is implementing the projects can produce it by considering all opportunities of business except for all the potential projects which should be now preferentially ordered. In case $PV_i^n(A) > K^*$, $\lambda_A^n > i$, which means project A produces a higher rate of return than i that is the opportunity cost of the capital K^* and it deserves to consider project A as one of the potential projects on which the capital K^* maybe invested. The concern is whether λ_A^n is the greatest value produced by the investment among all potential projects. In case, $PV_i^n(A) < K^*$, $\lambda_A^n < i$, which means project A does not deserve to be considered as one of the potential projects. The substance and ingenious point of the normalization are in the procedure that the benefit and cost or net benefit streams are once capitalized in terms of the value at the end of the time horizon using interest rate i at the capital market, and again it is discounted in the value of the beginning of the time horizon with an endogenous rate of return. Thus, the comparison can be made between the internal rate of return with the project and the interest rate (opportunity cost) in the capital market. The abovementioned criticism is resolved.

It appears that sum once via the capitalization all the net benefit streams in terms of the value at the end and discount it again to the value at the beginning using same interest rate i. However, the summation via capitalization takes into account the followings: with each period, (1) in case the net benefit is positive, yields which may be created by the best utilization of the positive benefit *forward* till the end of the time horizon and (2) in case the net benefit is negative, costs (negative *yields*) which ought to a loss by giving up the best utilization of the fund that is to be spent for making up the deficit (temporarily).[17] We see this more clearly. Eq. (1.24) give as follows:

$$\left(1+\lambda_A^n\right)^n \cdot K^* = TV^n(A) = \sum\nolimits_{t=0}^{n} (1+i)^{n-t} B_t. \qquad (1.26)$$

Equation (1.26) give as follows:

$$\left(1+\lambda_A^n\right)^n \cdot K^* = (1+i)^n \sum\nolimits_{t=0}^{n} (1+i)^{-t} B_t. \qquad (1.27)$$

In Eq. (1.26), $(1+i)^{n-t}B_s$ is the yield obtained by utilizing the net benefit B_s with the best opportunity for yielding having the yield rate i (i.e., the multiplication of the yield rate i and the net benefit is the net benefit plus the yield at the next period) from period s to the end of the time horizon, period n ($s = 0, 1, 2, \cdots, n$). Eq. (1.27) can be arranged into the following:

[17] B_t means the net benefit of the stream A at period t. Precisely speaking, the net benefit at period t is defined as the value of benefit at the beginning of period t by the definition. This means that streams of benefits which are created within period t with different timings (e.g., months) are capitalized in terms of the value at the beginning of period t using discount rate, e.g., i' per month that is equivalent to, e.g., per year, and so on.

$$\frac{1}{(1+i)^n}\left(1+\lambda_A^n\right)^n \cdot K^* = \sum_{t=0}^{n}\frac{1}{(1+i)^t}B_t \tag{1.28}$$

The right-hand side is the capitalized value of the net stream, $B_0, B_1, \cdots, B_n$ at the beginning of the initial period in terms of the definition in the conventional benefit–cost analysis given the discount rate i. This shows the clear difference between the internal rate of return in terms of the definition in the conventional analysis of the benefit–cost analysis and the definition by Mishan. Namely, as for. e.g., the public investment (project), the former equates the present value of the stream of net benefits of the public investment, which is defined as the capitalized value using that internal rate of return as the discount rate, to 0 (zero). Or, the former equates the present value of the stream of (gross) benefits of the public investment, which is defined as the capitalized value using that internal rate of return as the discount rate, to the present value of the costs of the public investment, which is the capitalized value of the stream of costs using that internal rate of return as the discount rate. On the other hand, the latter is the rate (λ_A^n) with which the present value of the capital fund (K^*) is operated for n years so that the present value of yields by the operation ($(1+i)^{-n}\left(1+\lambda_A^n\right)^n \cdot K^*$) is equal to the capitalized present value of the stream of net benefits ($\sum_{t=0}^{n}\frac{1}{(1+i)^t}B_t$) using discount rate i that is an opportunity cost of the business operation for the entity which implements the public project. In other words, it is an indicator in the sense that it shows, presuming the entity which implements the project produces the yields that were equivalent in value to the present value of the "project," which includes of course the project now examined as well as the business as the best opportunity for the entity with reinvestments of the streams of net benefits produced by the project, how much could be the rate of return to the capital fund K^* with the operation of (a virtual) business for n years. If the rate was less than the best return rate of business, which the entity has an opportunity to implement, namely, e.g., interest rate i in the capital market, the project incurs too expensive opportunity cost. In a sense, Mishan's theory of normalization well fixed the critics of the third problem above by taking into account the yields (losses) by the operation of the net benefit (net negative benefit) in the remaining periods till the end of the time horizon by explicitly casting a role to the interest i [18] to play a general opportunity cost indicator. The business opportunity cost for the entity is represented by the capitalization of the stream of net benefits to the value at the end of the time horizon with an opportunity cost of capital.

[18] Though the terminologies 'interest rate, discount rate, compound rate, etc.' are utilized here and elsewhere, it should be noted that they have a meaning of an opportunity cost. E.g., the yielding rate to the net benefit as the opportunity cost associated to the operation of the project (the attainable best rate of yielding to the net benefit with the operation of the business other than the potential public investments of which priorities are now examined).

Table 1.2 Numerical examples (1) and three criteria: without normalization

	t_0	t_1	t_2	t_3	t_4	(1) B	(2) K	(3) $B-K$	(4) $\frac{B-K}{K}$	(5) ρ
A	−110	75	80	0	0	134.30	110.00	24.298	0.221	0.259
B	−145	0	0	230	0	172.80	145.00	27.802	0.192	0.166
C	−40	345	−390	0	0	313.64	362.31	−48.678	−0.134	0.338
										6.287

Source: Calculated with numerical examples given by the author using Tables I and II (Mishan 1967) as references

Table 1.3 Numerical examples (2) and three criteria: without normalization

	t_0	t_1	t_2	t_3	t_4	(1) B	(2) K	(3) $B-K$	(4) $\frac{B-K}{K}$	(5) ρ
A	−110	75	80	0	0	134.298	110.000	24.298	0.221	0.259
B	−145	0	0	230	0	172.802	145.000	27.802	0.192	0.166
C	−44	168	−120	0	0	152.727	143.174	9.554	0.067	1.867

Source: Calculated with numerical examples given by the author using Tables I and II (Mishan 1967) as references

1.3.2 *Elucidation by the Example*

Mishan had tried to explain the essence of his theory of normalization, with which, as we see in the previous subsection, a consistent ordering with a set of potential projects is obtained with the application of the benefit–less–cost criteria, the benefit-cost-ratio criteria, and the internal-rate-of-return criteria in the definition of Mishan (1967, pp. 777–796). He assumes that the stream of *net* benefits (positive) and costs (negative) of three virtual projects are given over 5 periods (period 0, period 1, . . ., period 4; or, $t = 0, t = 1, \ldots, t = 4$, in which t is a running subscript indicating period t). He uses two Tables, i.e., Table I and Table II. The former is used to explain a possible inconsistency among the three criteria and Table II explains the consistency among the three criteria after the normalization. However, it seems that there are several miscalculations (and/or erratum), and we have considered that it may be very tough for readers to understand the essence of his theory of normalization based on these two tables. Therefore, the author tries to explain the essence of Mishan's theory of normalization using *new* Tables 1.2, 1.3, and 1.4 which are created by the author (but, the basic settings with which three numerical examples are created and the way of the explanation are almost same as what is adopted in his explanation).

In Table 1.2, the possible inconsistency between the three criteria is examined with three supposed (virtual) projects A, B, and C in case we apply the three criteria in a conventional way. The first five columns (headed by $t_0, t_1, \cdots, t_4$) show that the net benefit streams project by project at each period. Positive values mean that positive net benefits are created owing to the project, and the negative figures mean that costs are incurred by the project. It is assumed that the timing of the benefits and costs are counted in the following way:

Table 1.4 Normalized numerical example (3)

	t_0.	t_1.	t_2.	t_3.	t_4.	(1) B	(2) K	(3) $B-K$	(4) $\frac{B-K}{K}$	(5) λ
A	−110.00	75.00	80.00	0.00	0.00	196.625	161.051	35.574	0.221	0.156
B	−110.00	0.00	0.00	174.48	0.00	191.931	161.051	30.880	0.192	0.149
C	−33.81	129.07	−92.20	0.00	0.00	171.798	161.051	10.747	0.067	0.118

Source: Calculated with numerical examples given by the author using Tables I and II (Mishan 1967) as references

1. At the end of period t_0, costs are counted. They are costs, for example, incurred by the construction, management, investigation, and so on, which were implemented before the end of period t_0. The figures in the cells of the first column (t_0) are capitalized (compounded) values of thus incurred costs before and during the period t_0 into the values of the end of period t_0.
2. At the end of periods, t_1, t_2, t_3, and t_4, net costs (negative) and benefits (positive) are counted.

The column headed by "(1) *B*" shows the present value of the stream of net benefits at the value of the end of period t_0 (the beginning of period t_1) through the capitalization, presuming that the interest rate i is 10%.[19] For example, with project A, it is calculated as follows:

$$\frac{75}{(1+0.1)}+\frac{80}{(1+0.1)^2}=134.2975$$

The column headed by "(2) *K*" shows the present values of the stream of net costs at the value of the end of period t_0. For example, with project C, it is calculated as follows:

$$40+\frac{390}{(1+0.1)^2}=362.3140$$

The column headed by "(3) *B* – *K*" shows the present net values project by project. The column headed by "(4) (*B* – *K*)/*K*" shows the values of the benefits–cost ratios project by project. The last column headed by "(4) ρ" shows the internal rate of return in the conventional benefit–cost analysis. For example, with project C, it is a solution to the following equation in r:

$$40=\frac{345}{(1+r)}-\frac{390}{(1+r)^2}$$

The abovementioned equation has multiple solutions, $\rho = 0.3379990$ and 6.287001, of which the possibility rate of return in the conventional definition has been criticized.

Table 1.2 shows that the chosen projects shall be projects B, A, and C, respectively, following the benefit–less–cost, the benefit–cost ratio, and the internal-rate-of-return (in the conventional definition) criteria. These show the three criteria may produce an inconsistent ordering among the projects. Especially, the internal-rate-of-return criteria put first priority on project C that yields *negative* net benefits.

[19] It may be, again, confused with the symbol to the project B but the symbols to the present value of the stream of net benefits are *italicized*.

Using Tables 1.3 and 1.4, we next show how the normalization and Mishan's definition of the rate of return consistently works compared to the application of the three criteria without the normalization.

Table 1.3 creates another numerical example with the problem of the choice among project A, B, and C. The streams of net benefits and costs with the project A and B are same as shown in Table 1.2. The stream of net benefits and costs with project C is different from those in Table 1.2. In this numerical example, the stream of net benefit and costs makes the benefit–less–cost and therefore the benefit–cost ratio positive. However, the choice of the best projects is different between the three criteria.

Table 1.4 shows how the normalization by Mishan explained in the previous subsection works well to make a consistent ordering to the three projects, A, B, and C. First of all, following the normalization procedure 3) in the previous subsection, the total outlay to the project is equated presuming *divisibility* of the supposed projects B and C. It appeared in the column headed by "(2) *K*." The value of *K* is the capitalized value of the outlays at the value of the end of the last period t_4 following the normalization procedure (1) and values of *K* with projects B and C are equated with that of project A, namely, 161.051.[20] Thus, the streams of net benefits and costs of projects B and C are proportionally adjusted. The column "(1) *B*" is the value of the stream of net benefits compounded forward to the value of at the end of period t_4. The column headed by "(3) $B - K$, (4) $\frac{B-K}{K}$, and (4) λ " represent, repectively, the benefit–less–cost, the benefit–cost ratio, and the internal-rate-of-return criteria in Mishan's sense. Apparently, the three criteria decide on the choice of the best project uniquely, namely, the choice of project A, although the value of λ with all the projects is higher than the opportunity cost of the capital fund, namely 0.1 (10%). That means all the projects shall be implemented if there were a plenty amount of the capital fund of which opportunity cost is 10% interest.

By the way, readers may have thought that the column headed by t_4 has no meaning as no figures in the cells with the projects A, B, and C. This is related to the normalization procedure (4). Namely, the timing at which the capitalization made forward must be common to all potential projects. This may imply that the timing can be, e.g., at the end of *any* period. There may exist other project D which produces or incurred net benefit or cost at period t_4. In that case, we need the cell of t_4, and we just can only guess that Mishan would like to say the tables include a general case in which reinvestments shall be taken into account with whole the time horizon that is common to all potential projects following the procedures (2) and (4).

[20] In terms of the value at the end of period t_0, it becomes 110, of course.

1.4 Concluding Comments

1.4.1 Further Examination of the Grave Shortcomings of the Benefit–Cost Analysis

We have rather quickly tried to grasp the essence of the conventional benefit–cost analysis and Mishan's theory of normalization that had tried to fix the possible inconsistency in the analysis. To settle down to work in this field, in its own way, there are a lot of themes that should be investigated.

Although, in the earlier stage, the benefit–cost analysis had been done by the *Proposed Practices for Economic Analysis of River Basin Projects* (1950) (commonly called—Green Book 1958), as stated in the Margolis' review article (Margolis 1959), three books of Eckstein (1958), Krutilla and Eckstein (1958), and Mckean (1958) are now very excellent classics of the benefit–cost analysis, published on the same year of 1958.

Generally speaking, however, we are inclined to have a little bit negative view on the benefit–cost analysis with the conventional approach or Mishan's normalization approach, whatever, especially from the theoretical aspects of the public investment. Substantial reasons are: (1) it does not take into account any budget constraint on the capital fund, (2) it presumes that each possible project is independent of others in the sense that the stream of net benefits and costs of the project *A*, is not affected by whether other project, e.g., *B*, is implemented or not, and (3) it is a static analysis. These are *grave* shortcomings.

As we have already seen with Mishan's theory of normalization, to obtain a decision on the possible projects, namely, "accept" or "reject," by applying the criteria that are based on the benefit–cost analysis, the interest rate i must be given (or known in advance) with which *reinvestment* of the yields obtained at any period can produce returns till the end of the time horizon or the capital fund necessary to meet the outlays during the time horizon can be *financed*. As far as the capital market is perfect, and it is at an equilibrium state, we may refer to the capital market to know in advance the opportunity cost of the capital fund.[21] However, it is not reality. As for the public investment, which is usually large-scale and its impact is huge, which will diffuse through the whole markets for a long time. So, even if the market is at an equilibrium, the market adjustments must be started by the large-scale public investment till a new equilibrium is attained in the economy. Impacts of such a large-scale public investment will change the socioeconomic structure to improve the productivity of the economy. A good example is the high-standard expressway as shown in the next Chapter.

The essence of the economy in the dynamic context may be expressed as follows. The productivity of the economy in terms of GDP or the welfare of the people living there at period t_1 (e.g., present) must be dependent on the *investments* at period t_0

[21] Of course, even if it is admitted to presume the market is perfect in the dynamic sense.

($t_0 < t_1$), i.e., in the past. For a while, we take productivity in terms of GDP. More exactly, investments are categorized into private investments and public investments. Private investments mean increases in the capital stocks which industrial sectors (groups of firms categorized by kinds of products) can use for their production in the future. Public investments (called almost equivalently—public projects) mean increases in the social infrastructures (social capital) including software that all firms in the economy can use to increase their productivity *technically* as well as economically. In this sense, the productivity of the economy at period t_1 is dependent on how much investments were made into which industrial sectors and what public projects in the past (t_0 such as $t_0 < t_1$). In this sense, we use the expression the productivity of the economy must be dependent on the investments in the past.

The amount of investments at period t_1 is confined by the product (i.e., GDP) at period t_1, namely, GDP minus consumption is an investment in the macroeconomic sense as far as the economy is closed. In a more general and comprehensive analysis of the public investments, the capital fund allocated to the public investments must be competitive against the capital fund allocated to the private investments. However, for simplicity, we may assume the stream of the capital funds which can be allocated to the public investments of a certain specific category (e.g., social infrastructures for transportation) are exogenously given over the time horizon. Even, we may assume they are constant value (e.g., F_k) over the time horizon. This means that possible increases (decreases) in GDP at period t_3 ($>t_2$) may result in increases (decreases) in private investments and other public investments at period t_3.

It is a usual case that a set of public projects should be chosen among a set of potential public projects subject to limited amount (F_k) of a capital fund just same as the situation in which the application of the three benefit–cost criteria is considered in previous subsections. And, it is natural that not only the optimal set of chosen public projects among the potential public projects shall be pursued but also the optimal allocation of the capital fund (F_k) to the chosen projects by assuming the scale and/or extent of each potential public project is dependent on the allocated amount of capital fund to it, since still F_k must be huge and the scope of the economy is large in which socioeconomic structures can be covered by the public investments of F_k. Here are reasons for defects (1).

Even if we could admit this simplification, we need at least a dynamic forecast of the stream of net benefit and costs as far as we stick to try the application of the three benefit–cost criteria or its variants as a dynamic one to the optimization above. To conclude, the trial fails.

The productivity of an investment (say, *A*) using the allocated amount of capital fund (e.g., *C*) may be measured with the (capitalized) return (in any sense, e.g., profits, benefits, welfare, etc.) created by the investment (*C*). The return may be measured in profits as for the private investments and benefits, welfare, etc. as for the public investments using with-and-without method, namely, in terms of the difference of the profits, benefits, welfare, etc. between the economy in which the investment *A* is made and not. Here, there exists a shortcoming of the benefit–cost approach as impacts of projects A and B are not independent of each other, especially as for the public investments (the shortcoming (2) above). This means such with-and-without method does not work. However, this is not an essential shortcoming associated with the application of the benefit–cost analysis to the dynamic content. So, we dare to assume that they are independent of each other for a while.

The (private or social) marginal opportunity cost of an investment A using the capital fund C may be defined as the best (capitalized) stream of additional (private or social) returns that is obtained by other investment than A additionally using *unit* capital fund deducted from C.

To decide on the investment at period t, we need to know the *best* stream of net benefits and costs at period t ($t = t_2, \cdots, t_3, \cdots, t_n, \cdots$) that are additionally created by the public investment at period t_2. To know the best net benefits or least costs at period t_3, we need to decide on the best *re*-investment of the return that is created at period t_3 by the investment at period t_2 (i.e., in the past). Here, we have two inconsistencies. To know the net benefits and costs at period t ($t = t_2, \cdots, t_3, \cdots$), we must know the net benefits and costs at period s ($s = t_3, \cdots$). Logically, this holds with all periods t_2, t_3 such as $t_2 \leq t_3$ in the time horizon. This is a tautology as far as the benefit–cost analysis has no mechanism with which the investment at period t_2 and *re*-investment at period t_3, which are interrelated and dependent on each other, are *simultaneously* determined, since in order to decide on the investment at period t_2, we need to decide on the *re*-investment at period t_3 as it affects the productivity of the investment at period t_2 and to decide on the reinvestment at period t_3, we need to decide on the investment at period t_2 as it affects the productivity of reinvestment at period t_3. And, to calculate the opportunity cost of the capital fund which is utilized for the capitalization of the stream of net benefits and costs, we fall in the same kind of tautology.

It is a kind of *petitio principii* to suppose the stream of net benefits and costs in any manner and the interest rate (opportunity cost) with which the returns in the future is *capitalized* into the present value, etc., especially with its application to a large-scale public investment as far as a substantial dynamic mechanism is not built in the benefit–cost analysis. This means that the optimality of the choice of projects that are to be implemented must be decided on using the criterion (a kind of decision support model) in which investments at different periods are simultaneously determined by taking into account the recursive and nested mechanism of the economy in the dynamic context.

So, we would hold our target rightly and adopt an approach of programming model to establish the right variants of the benefit–cost analysis in the dynamic content.

1.4.2 Organization of the Chapters

First, the classical benefit–cost analysis is surveyed in this chapter. In Chap. 2, a good example is shown for the application of the conventional benefit–cost analysis.

The materials are submitted to the World Bank about 50 years ago related to the loan to the construction of Mei-Shin expressway. The analysis is fairly old and it is included in this book as a textbook of "feasibility study."

In Chap. 3, a fused model of: (1) Steiner (1959), in which are built authorities' pre-emptive right for investment fund allocation, incompatibility constraint among possible investment targets, lumpiness, and discreteness of investment projects, etc.; and (2) Marglin (1963a), in which is built the multi-period of benefit–cost analysis, is applied to the analysis of optimal investments into the expressway construction in Japan. The model is a generalized version of classical benefit–cost analysis in the sense that: (1) it embodies the essence of investment criteria discussed in the opening sentences and (2) inevitable arbitrariness with the selection of projects and the allocation of investment funds to selected projects, which is inherent to the application of benefit–costs analysis, is resolved by formulating a linear programming problem in which the optimality of: (a) the selection of projects among a set of alternative projects; (b) the fund allocation to the selected projects; and (c) the implementation timing of selected projects are consistently attained based on the opportunity cost criterion that is the essence of the simplex criterion. Eventually, projects having the best benefit–cost ratios are identified together with the best project implementation timing and the best fund allocation to the projects. This is the basic model to all the models in Chaps. 4, 6, and 7.

In Chap. 4, the interregional input–output programming model is treated, which is a static model and built in the optimal allocation mechanism of public investment. Interregional commodity flows and modes of transportation are explicitly specified in the model. It is useful and informative for comprehensive transport policy planning and decision-making. It first quantifies the discussion on the topic, which was an epoch-making achievement at that time, around 50 years ago. In Appendix 2, the interregional input–output model which is expanded by Moses with the ingenious concept of shipment activities is discussed together with the two basic concepts of input–output table at producers' price and purchasers' price.

In Chap. 5, the subjects for the development of model specifications are discussed in the light of comprehensive transport system policy and planning.

In Chap. 6, the model of Chap. 4 is extended to incorporate 10 regions, 10 industries, nine transport modes in responding to the subject raised in Chap. 5, namely, to be more informative for the practical agenda of government departments that are in charge of the comprehensive transport system at a nation-wide scale.

In Chap. 7, a full-scale dynamic interregional input–output programming model is shown and applied to the topic of making take-off China economy through the construction of Asian Expressway Network. The model is a certain measure of culmination in the sense that: (1) it is a dynamic model in its true sense so that investments to the private sectors as well as public sectors are endogenously and optimally determined; (2) transportation network is specified with links of transportation infrastructures; (3) public investments are optimized considering improvements in existing links as well as new links of which initial stock is zero; (4) optimal modal choice is made between different modes of transport and different routes as well as combination of plural modes presuming change of modes on the way;

(5) market flow conditions are specified using shipment activities so that the specification avoids issues inherent to input–output table at producers' price or purchasers' price, etc.

References

Alchian A (1955) The rate of interest, Fisher's rate of return over cost, and Keynes' internal rate of return. Am Econ Rev 45:938–943

Eckstein O (1958) Water resource development, the economics of project evaluation. Harvard University Press, Cambridge

Eckstein O (1961) A survey of the theory of public expenditure criteria. In: Buchanan JM (ed) Public finance: needs, source and utilization. Princeton University Press, Princeton, pp 439–504

Hirshleifer J (1958) On the theory of optimal investment decision. J Polit Econ 66(4):329–352

Hotelling H (1938) The general welfare in relation to problems of taxation and of railway and utility rates. Econometrica 6(3):242–269

Kohno H (1974) Economic effects of transport investment and investment criteria. In: Okano Y et al (eds) Treatise on transport economics. Seirin-Shoin Shinsha, Tokyo. (in Japanese)

Krutilla JV, Eckstein O (1958) Multiple purpose river development studies in applied economic analysis. The Johns Hopkins University Press, Baltimore

Lorie JH, Savage LJ (1955) Three problems in rationing capital. J Bus 28(4):229–239

Marglin SA (1963a) Approaches to dynamic investment planning. North-Holland Publishing Company, Amsterdam

Marglin SA (1963b) The social rate of discount and the optimal rate of investment. Q J Econ 77 (1):95–111

Margolis J (1959) The economic evaluation of federal water resource development: a review article. Am Econ Rev 49(1):96–111

Mckean RN (1958) Efficiency in government through systems analysis—with emphasis on water resources development. Wiley, New York

Mishan EJ (1967) A proposed normalization procedure for public investment criteria. Econ J 7 (308):777–796

Nakamura M (1970) Optimal investment allocation and the price mechanism. J Econ 35(4):24–51

Negishi T (1964) Theoretical study on the pricing policy of public utility enterprise. Research Q 5:17

Oishi Y (1960) Public investment. Expressway Autom Express Highway Res 3(7):38–41

Sasaki T, Kohno H, Kurashimo K (1965) Economic effects of road and investment criteria (traffic engineering). Gijutsu-Shoin, Tokyo. (in Japanese)

Solomon E (1956) The arithmetic of capital-budgeting decisions. J Bus 29(2):124–129

Steiner PO (1959) Choosing among alternative public investment in the water resource field. Am Econ Rev 49(5):893–916

Chapter 2
Economic Effects of Mei-Shin and To-Mei Expressways Based on the World Bank Formula of 50 Years Ago

Having ranged over the literature concerning Chap. 1, our eyes fell upon "The Economic Effects of Mei-Shin Expressway[1] (Sasaki et al. 1964)," and we felt that we met with a fossil as it was written 50 years ago and fairly kept out of sight so long. We found that it is a rudimentary report of project evaluation using quite old data in nature, and the system as a whole is yet well-ordered as the World Bank formula had discussed the indirect economic effects in a dignified manner. It was the document prepared and submitted to the World Bank to finance the Project.

We have begun to think that this format might be yet useful for people working at international organizations such as United Nations, World Bank, Asian Development Bank, and so on who are concerned with development works and for those who commit to preparatory documents of proposals to such organizations. Therefore, this format is included in the book.

It is desirable that readers will cast a glance at this chapter as a sort of well-balanced feasibility study without expecting a height. Chapters 3, 4, and 7 will be there as full-scale subjects of the public investment criteria.

By the way, the commemorative publications such as Mei-Shin Expressway Construction Archives have been published several times, at least, during the past 50 years, and there are no documents written comprehensively somehow or other concerning economic research. It is because the Japan Highway Public Corporation is a technology-oriented kingdom, so there is nowhere the economic research (office) is wanted (Exceptional was The Mei-Shin Expressway Construction Archives Editing Committee 1967e). In this sense, we are grateful that we are able

---

Even if we say "the World Bank formula" here, it was not what was given in advance by the World Bank as the rigid formula, but what was formed heuristically through trial and error among the persons in charge of the matter at the World Bank and the Japan Highway Public Corporation. As time goes on, it has seemed to be very precious, so···

---

[1] Mei-Shin is the abbreviation of Nagoya-Kobe, which is two names of cities where the expressway is starting (ending).

H. Kohno, Y. Higano, *Public Investment Criteria*, New Frontiers in Regional Science: Asian Perspectives 2, https://doi.org/10.1007/978-4-431-55221-5_2

Table 2.1 Outline of Mei-Shin expressway construction

		Whole line	Amagasaki–Ritto	Nishinomiya–Amagasaki and Ritto–Ichinomiya
Total length (km)		189.8	71.2	110.1
Number of traffic lanes		4	4	4
Number of interchanges		14	7	6
Time when construction was initiated		Sept. 1958	Sept. 1958	Nov. 1960
Prearranged time to be completed		Dec. 1964	July 1963	Sept. 1964
Construction costs (100 million JPY)		1164	447	666
Construction loans and funds		1164	447	666
Breakdown	World Bank (100 million yen)	288	144	144
	Domestic (100 million yen)	876	303	522

to write a chapter on The Economic Effects (of the Mei-Shin Expressway) over some spaces.

2.1 Preliminary Consideration

2.1.1 Concept of Economic Effects of the Expressway

The construction of the first real high-standard expressway of Japan, Mei-Shin Expressway, had been started with the budget of construction costs of 11,640 million Japanese Yen (JPY), among which 2880 million JPY was the loan by the World Bank (Table 2.1). At that time, it was said that the total costs including the other sundry costs are about 180 billion JPY, that is, 1.0 billion JPY/km.

In this chapter, it is intended that the economic meaning of Mei-Shin Expressway is made clear from the viewpoint of economic effects (= benefits).

The construction of the expressway brings about large economic and social impacts on the whole national economy as well as the local economy through the drastic improvement in locational and structural conditions for not only transportation but also all the other industries. First of all, the impacts of the expressway are summarized in brief from the economic viewpoint. The impacts of the expressway concretely arise from the benefits to the direct users and to the indirect users of the expressway; the former is called direct effects and the latter indirect effects.

2.1.2 *Direct Effects of Expressway Construction*[2]

Direct benefits are defined as the benefits that the motor car (automobile and truck) user directly and instantaneously enjoys by using the expressway. It has been said that the definition is most precise and definitive. They are categorized into the following:

1. Saving of running costs.

   Reduction in the maintenance and running costs: thanks to decrease in tire wear; decrease in fuel and oil consumption; extension of vehicle depreciable life; reduction in personnel expenses; and so on. Those effects are generated owing to the reduction in travel distance and improvement in the driving environment such as less traffic congestion, less fatigue, and so on, all of which are brought by expressway (high-standard highway) of compact pavement and curvature.

   The following items all quote Sasaki et al. (1964), (and see Sasaki et al. 1965; Sasaki 1961; Kohno and Kurashimo 1963; Kodan 1963a, b; Sasaki and Kurashimo et al. 1964; Adler 1963).
2. Reduction in traveling time.

   The traveling time (time spent for the trip) is reduced due to shortened travel distance and an increase in the average running velocity. The time spent on a trip is a kind of opportunity cost for expressway users, and, in this sense, saved driving time brings economic benefits to the users.
3. Fatigue reduction of driver.

   The mental and physical burden of vehicle drivers is reduced by using the high-standard expressway. Its structure is drastically improved compared to ordinal highways in various conditions, such as wider width, gentler gradient, less curve, compact pavement, no crossing, and so on.
4. Increase in the comfortableness of trip.

   A trip on the expressway (high-standard highway) makes it comfortable not only for the vehicle driver but also the passengers in the vehicle.
5. Decrease in damage on load and saving of packing cost.

   The shortened distance of travel and improvement in the driving conditions on high-standard highways contributes to a decrease in not only damage on load in transit but also packing cost through simple packing.
6. Decrease in traffic accident rates.

   The reduction in fatigue of drivers together with the improvements in the driving environment further makes less traffic accident rates.

[2]Usage of the terminology, expressway construction, means 'expressway placed in service.' Of course, the construction itself generates demand creation effects in Keynesian sense, which must be huge as the budget was huge. However, they can be taken as negligible compared to the scale of impacts after expressway is placed in service since the scope in space and time are critically different with which the whole national economy continues to be impacted by.

2.1.3 Indirect Effects of Expressway Construction

The construction of the expressway will influence the area along the expressway and its related areas linked by the expressway, too. These effects are named indirect effects. Direct effects occur and are usually enjoyed in a shorter term. On the other hand, indirect effects are formed over a longer term and diffused into the whole national economy through the effective and efficient generation, and diffusion of direct and indirect effects of expressway construction can be made through other related public investments into social infrastructures and private enterprise investments in parallel with and/or following the construction of the expressway.

1. Streamlining effects of production and logistics.

   The construction of expressways gives incentive to firms, which use carriers as a part of the logistics system, to adjust processes in production and logistics efficient and profitable due to reduction in traveling time, running costs, damage on loads, and so on accrues to the carriers that use the high-standard highway. And, transport carriers, too, make the provision of transport services efficient and profitable by the allocation of large-scale freight cars, thanks to the construction of high-standard highways and/or the expansion of the market area.

   Once such streamlining for production processes is made in manufacturing firms and transportation carriers, the inventory stock which must be made more or less can be reduced, and the inventory costs (interests and warehouse fees) can be saved. Thus, saved money can be used for other production activities and facilities, which may improve efficiency in production.
2. Effects of industrial development.

   Once the expressway goes through the areas where no high-standard highway went through before the construction, some of the areas may have competitive locational advantages, such as accessibility to the transportation network, labor supply with less wage, accessibility to scarce resources such as water, against existing other industrial areas. Such changes in locational conditions may induce the construction of new factories, in which advanced technologies are built-in, along the expressway. This enhances the dispersion of manufacturing and related industries.

   In case an expressway is constructed going through nearby existing factories, they have the opportunity to increase the capacity of production due to the streamlining effects of production and logistics scheduling and also brings scale effects to the firms.
3. Effects of resource development.

   The construction of the expressway will increase the market value of the resources existing along the constructed expressway such as latently unemployed labor, undeveloped sightseeing resources, and unused forest resources and mineral resources, which were untapped before the construction of the expressway due to, for example, prohibitively high access and development costs.
4. Dispersion effects of urban population.

   The highway makes the commuting time shorter to a large city like Tokyo. This induces the population movement into the suburbs and rural areas. This may increase the population of neighborhood cities around the large city, and a new town such as a garden city will be developed in the rural area. The dispersion of population from large cities may be enhanced by the dispersion of manufacturing factories.

5. Streamlining effects of distributional process.

   (a) Reduction in traveling time means a reduction in time spent for logistics of the firms, which use carriers that are used in the constructed expressway. The saving of running costs made by carriers possibly implies a reduction in logistics costs through the market of logistics services. Both induce streamlining in the distribution process. For example, traditionally, a typical distribution process is producer → intermediate wholesale dealer → retail dealer → consumer. This may change into producer → retail dealer → consumer, or, even simply, producer → consumer.
   (b) More drastic and decisive effects of the construction of expressways for both producers and consumers are brought by changes in the trade patterns between regions. For example, the producers of perishable goods in region A who used to ship the products to the market in the nearest city B may change the destination of shipment to the market in a remote city C, where the market price of the products is possibly higher than in the city B because such change in the destination becomes able to meet the timing for auction in the market in the city C in the same day of the shipment or next day due to the reduction in the time spent for the shipment. Same changes may occur with firms located in a city E that used to buy materials or parts from the factories located in the nearest city F. They can replace the materials and parts with those sourced in the markets in a further city G, which may further enhance the streamlining of the production and logistics processes involving other firms who have business relations with the firms, and so on.

6. Effects of expanding the market area.

   To change the view, the abovementioned effects by the streamlining of distributional and logistics processes expand the market area of producers located in region A and city G. This will occur in a competitive way involving the whole of the economy, namely, firms (producers) located in a city/region become competitive against firms located in another while they have expanded the market areas. Firms may expand the business having more management flexibility although the risk may increase. Or, firms may further agglomerate in specific cities/regions that have an advantage in location conditions over other cities/regions. Consumers living in the city, in which the shipment of perishable vegetables can be made from remoted regions, may enjoy varieties of goods irrespective of in- and off-season, and so on.

7. Effects of reducing traffic congestion on the competitive existing roads.

   In the case that expressway is constructed being parallel to the exiting road, the traffic congestion on the existing road may be reduced as some of the traffic volumes on the existing road will be diverted to the constructed expressway depending on the time values of the existing road users. An increase in the traffic velocity due to a decrease in traffic congestion decreases the running costs and traveling time born by users of existing roads, and so on.

2.1.4 *Impacts of the Expressway on the Whole National Economy: Observed Reality in 1970s Through 1980s in Japan*

As we saw earlier, economic effects of the expressway are first yielded by users like vehicle drivers (e.g., individuals who enjoy touring) or carrying companies that purchase the expressway services as intermediate inputs to produce delivery services. Those effects are named and categorized as direct benefits. Some of the direct benefits accrue to vehicle drivers/carrying companies and are enjoyed as an increase in utility or profit. Other remaining direct effects are *transferred* to the economic agents who have business relations and, therefore, trade relations with users of the expressway through adjustments in the markets in which the transactions are made. For example, firms that purchase services provided by carriers who substitute the former delivery route of existing roads with the new one using the constructed expressway may benefit from a decrease in the delivery price because it may occur as running, payroll costs, and so on of carriers decrease by using the expressway, and carriers may provide delivery services with lower price than the price with which delivery services were traded before the construction of the expressway. This may happen as a natural result of the equilibrium of competitive markets in the long run. The chain of transfer of *direct effects* is created through the market adjustments, and they diffuse into the whole national economy. They are enjoyed as an increase in utility or profit through the market adjustments, and they are eventually enjoyed as an increase in the welfare of the economy. For example, people living in a city, like Tokyo, can enjoy fresh and sometimes off-season vegetables/fruits once the expressway services are provided for carriers which enable carriers to transport goods with fewer damages on loads from far remoted sources, say Kochi Prefecture of Shikoku Island in Western Japan, where greenhouse cultivation of vegetables is a prosperous business. Firms that purchase parts produced by other firms that have trade with carriers may benefit from the decrease in the price of parts because the price of carrier service, which is a composition of the price of the part, may decrease due to the substitution in the delivery route after the construction of the expressway. Shareholders of those firms that may produce more profits through the chain of direct benefit transfer can enjoy an increase in dividends, and they as consumers may enjoy an increase in utility and so on.

Observing the miracle economic growth in 1970s and 1980s, which was initiated in 1960s and coincided with starting the expressway network construction projects, we cannot support the argument that the economic effects of the expressway are only composed of the direct benefits. The construction of the expressway had huge *technological* impacts on the whole national economy.

Technological impacts mean that the source of benefits generated by such impacts is *not* the direct benefits that are instantaneously generated by users of the expressway. Thus, the source (origin) is *not* in the chain of direct benefits transfer illustrated earlier. For example, benefits of the reduction in the traveling time due to decrease in the traffic congestion on the ordinary road that is parallel to the expressway are *only* enjoyed by the direct users of the ordinary road, and some of them diffused into the whole national economy through the chain of direct benefit transfer just same as the direct benefits generated on the expressway. Another example is the streamlining of the production and logistics schedule. For example, the high-standard expressway enables the carrier company to adopt a large motor truck, and the company may site a transport base near the interchange of the expressway. Such impacts must be taken as technical impacts by the expressway. Of course, the decrease in the traveling time on the express way is enjoyed by such a large motor truck (driver) or the carrier company, but the effects due to the adoption of a large motor truck and the new transportation base, which together makes the operation of the company efficient, cannot be attributed to and, therefore, are independent of the direct benefits of either the decrease in the traveling time or the decrease in the running cost on the expressway. The point is that the events that generate the indirect effects listed earlier should be attributed to the expressway since, for example, the development of tourism resources can be made only after the expressway is opened to traffic. In that sense, visitors to the developed tourism site and people living around the tourism site enjoy the decrease in the traveling time. They are categorized into direct benefits. However, there exist economic effects that are generated being independent of the effects that are enjoyed by the users (visitors) of direct benefits. For example, people living in the region where the tourism site is located may have an opportunity to have a new job, start a new business, and so on. Such events generate economic effects, at least some of which are independent of the direct benefits created on the expressway and, therefore, have the independent chain of benefit transfer, of which source (origin) is not on the chain of benefit transfer of direct benefits created on the expressway. Eventually, huge benefits independently exist that are not absorbed by the direct users of the expressway. When the assessment reports were submitted to the World Bank, no precise argument was made about the substance of indirect effects (benefits), and it is amazing that they had the concept of direct and indirect effects.

All or most of the indirect effects listed earlier are based on the technological impacts of the expressway. More or less, some of them are to be net indirect effects. With a comparison between the amount of investment into Meishin-Tomei Expressway and the increase in the GDP, all of which, of course, cannot be attributed to the construction of the expressway, it is a natural conclusion that the amount of net indirect effects is far larger than the amount of direct benefits.

It is true that we had experienced negative aspects of the construction of the expressway. Related to the abovementioned various (positive) effects, negative effects should be enumerated. As negative effects of the expressway construction, the following was stated concretely:

1. Public nuisance such as noise, exhaust gas, and so on, which are caused by auto cars, and trucks, and suffered by residents along the expressway.
2. Decrease in agricultural products due to the conversion of agricultural land to the road site of the expressway, disjuncture of agricultural land, and so on.
3. Decrease in the product volume of the existing factory that is caused by the construction of new industrial areas, and so on.

4. Disconnection of the supply chain with the firm which is less accessible to the newly organized logistics system, isolated from the main trade business of products, etc.
5. Social loss by the demolition of cultural assets, natural resources, especially sightseeing resources.

2.2 Basic Data of Various Reduced Direct Costs

Apart from the listed direct effects of the expressway in Sect. 2.1, basic data for the calculation of economic effects of the Mei-Shin expressway were collected with the following three categories. The main reason was that the calculation in monetary terms was easier at that time.

2.2.1 Basic Data for the Calculation of Saved Running Costs

When we use the Mei-Shin expressway, the traveling distance of automobiles is usually shortened compared to the case in which the expressway is not used (Table 2.2). For example, with the travel between Nishinomiya city and Ichinomiya city, the decrease in the traveling distance was estimated as 35.6 km.

As the expressway was of high standard compared to existing roads, the driving environment would be drastically improved as mentioned in Sect. 2.1. So, the user costs would be reduced, too. The saved running costs were calculated as follows:

$$\begin{bmatrix}\text{Saving of}\\\text{running costs}\end{bmatrix}=\begin{bmatrix}\text{running costs}\\\text{of ordinary road}\end{bmatrix}-\begin{bmatrix}\text{running costs}\\\text{of expressway}\end{bmatrix}+\begin{bmatrix}\text{running costs}\\\text{of access roads}\end{bmatrix}$$

The estimated running costs and the compositions per vehicle·kilometer with the route using only ordinary roads and the route via the expressway are shown in Table 2.3. It was supposed that "fuels, oils, and fats" and "tire, tube" costs increase by using the Mei-Shin expressway due to the high-speed driving. However, the total costs would be decreased since the costs such as repairing expenses, amortization costs of vehicle, personnel expenses, general management expenses, and so on would be decreased. As a result, it was estimated that the running cost of passenger car, small type of car, ordinary truck, small type of truck, bus for regular services, and bus for chartered services would be decreased by 9.28, 6.53, 15.08, 10.02, 15.52, and 16.95 JPY per vehicle·kilometer, respectively.

Parameters listed in Table 2.3, "Fuels, oils and fats costs," "Wear costs of vehicle (Tire, tube costs; Maintenance costs of vehicle)," and "Depreciation costs of vehicle," were neither estimated by the JHPC nor the Ministry of Construction of

Table 2.2 Decrease in traveling distance gained by utilization of the Mei-Shin expressway (unit: km)

Nishinomiya	Amagasaki	Toyonaka	Ibaraki	Kyoto	Ootsu	Ritto	Yokaichi	Hikone	Sekigahara	Oogaki	Ichinomiya
Nishinomiya	9.0	20.0	42.0	70.0	88.0	104.0	131.0	143.0	168.0	187.0	223.0
	10.0	20.3	27.2	54.9	63.6	84.7	107.3	126.5	150.9	168.7	187.4
	Δ 1.0	Δ 0.3	14.8	15.1	24.4	19.3	23.7	16.5	17.1	18.3	35.6
	Amagasaki	11.0	33.0	61.0	79.0	95.0	122.0	134.0	159.0	178.0	214.0
		14.3	21.2	48.9	57.6	78.7	101.3	120.5	144.9	162.7	181.4
		Δ 3.3	11.8	12.1	21.4	16.3	20.7	13.5	14.1	15.3	32.6
		Toyonaka	22.0	50.0	68.0	84.0	111.0	123.0	148.0	167.0	203.0
			21.9	49.6	58.3	79.4	102.0	121.2	145.6	163.4	182.1
			0.1	0.4	9.7	4.6	9.0	1.8	2.4	3.6	20.9
			Ibaraki	28.0	46.0	62.0	89.0	101.0	126.0	145.0	181.0
				30.7	39.4	60.5	83.1	102.3	126.7	144.5	163.2
				Δ 2.7	6.6	1.5	5.9	Δ 1.3	Δ 0.7	0.5	17.8
				Kyoto	18.0	34.0	61.0	73.0	98.0	117.0	153.0
					18.7	39.8	62.4	81.6	106.0	123.8	142.5
					Δ 0.7	Δ 5.8	Δ 1.4	Δ 8.6	Δ 8.0	Δ 6.8	10.5
					Ootsu	16.1	43.0	55.0	80.0	99.0	135.0
						28.1	50.7	69.9	94.3	112.1	130.8
						Δ 12.1	Δ 7.7	Δ 14.9	Δ 14.3	Δ 13.1	4.2
						Ritto	27.0	39.0	64.0	83.0	119.0
							32.8	52.0	76.4	94.2	112.9
							Δ 5.8	Δ 13.0	Δ 12.4	Δ 11.2	6.1
							Yokaichi	26.0	51.0	70.0	106.0
								27.2	51.6	69.4	88.1
								Δ 1.2	Δ 0.6	0.6	17.9
								Hikone	25.0	44.0	80.0

(continued)

Table 2.2 (continued)

Nishinomiya	Amagasaki	Toyonaka	Ibaraki	Kyoto	Ootsu	Ritto	Yokaichi	Hikone	Sekigahara	Oogaki	Ichinomiya
									28.4	46.2	64.9
									Δ 3.4	Δ 2.2	15.1
									Sekigahara	19.0	55.0
										21.8	40.5
										Δ 2.8	14.5
										Oogaki	36.7
											28.7
											8.0
											Ichinomiya

Note: (1) Upper line shows traveling distance via the existing road
(2) Middle line is the distance via the expressway.
(3) Lower line shows decrease (increase) in distance.
(4) Δ shows the case in which the traveling distance increases.
(5) decrease of running distance will be calculated by the the following equation (Fig. 2.1)
$\boldsymbol{S = H - (E + A_1 + A_2)}$.

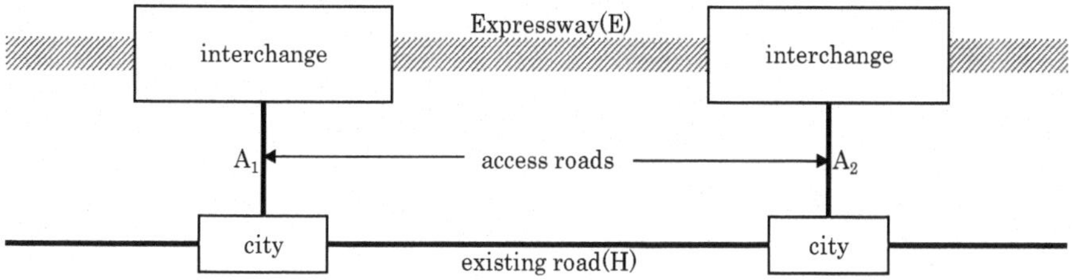

Fig. 2.1 Calculation of travelling distance: expressway vs. existing road. Source: The Japan Highway Public Corporation, Materials submitted to the World Bank – Written reply to the questionnaires related to the Second Loan, August 1961

Japanese Government. They were estimated by the road test that was taken by American Association of State Highway Officials (AASHO), Washington, D.C., USA (AASHO 1952; Sasaki et al., 1965, pp. 68–71). The situation had continued for a certain length of time and it can be said that the early history of the analysis of road users' benefits by, e.g., the Express Highway Research of Japan must have had relied on two sources, i.e., AASHO (1952) and Eckstein (1958).

2.2.2 *Basic Data for the Calculation of the Reduction in the Traveling Time*

Using the Mei-Shin expressway usually shortens the travel distance. Even if the travel distance increases, the traveling time decreases as the running speed of vehicles critically increases on the high-standard expressway. That is, it was assumed that the average running speed of passenger car and bus/truck would increase from 40 km/hour and 30 km/hour to 90 km/hour and 70 km/hour, respectively. The reduction in the traveling time was calculated as follows:

$$\left[\begin{array}{r}\text{Reduction in}\\ \text{traveling}\\ \text{time}\end{array}\right] = \left[\frac{\begin{array}{c}\text{Traveling distance}\\ \text{on the exiting road}\end{array}}{\begin{array}{r}\text{Average running}\\ \text{speed on}\\ \text{the existing road}\end{array}}\right]$$

$$-\left\{\left[\frac{\begin{array}{c}\text{Traveling distance}\\\text{on expressway}\end{array}}{\begin{array}{c}\text{Average running}\\\text{speed on the expressway}\end{array}}\right]+\left[\frac{\begin{array}{c}\text{Traveling distance of}\\\text{access road of both ends}\end{array}}{\begin{array}{c}\text{Average running speed}\\\text{on existing road}\end{array}}\right]\right\}$$

The estimated saved traveling time with passenger car and bus/truck are shown in Tables 2.4 and 2.5, respectively. For example, it was estimated that the saved time between Nishinomiya and Ichinomiya by using the expressway would be around 3 h and 25 min in a passenger car and 4 h and 40 min in bus/track, surprisingly.

2.2.3 *Basic Data for the Calculation of Decrease in Traffic Accident Rate*

The expressway is better than existing roads in terms of the driving environment. This reduces the traffic accident rate of vehicles using the expressway. The supposed traffic accident volumes per 100 million vehicle·kilometers on the expressway and existing roads are shown in Table 2.6. It was estimated that the number of traffic accidents would decrease from 688 with existing roads to 102 with the expressway. The number of deaths (injured persons) would decrease from 18.7 (468) persons with the route using only existing roads to 1.9 (76) persons with the expressway, respectively.

As we did not have the basic data for the estimation of the traffic accident rate on the expressway, the data in United States was used. According to the actual data, after the expressway services were provided, the number of traffic accidents was 277 cases, the number of deaths was 2.7 persons, and the injured were 136 persons between Amagasaki and Ritto. It was thought that these figures reflected that the driver of Japan was not yet accustomed to driving on the expressway as well as the whole expressway was not yet opened to traffic. Anyway, it was needed to collect actual traffic accident data on the expressway with a longer period to calculate more precise direct effects of the expressway in terms of decrease in the traffic accident rate.

2.3 Traffic Volumes of Mei-Shin Expressway

First, the supposed traffic volumes of the Mei-Shin Expressway are explained, on which the estimation of the direct effects by the construction of the expressway was to be based. Table 2.7 shows the supposed traffic volumes by section between interchanges and types of vehicle in the year 1964 when the whole line of the expressway was supposed to be opened to traffic and the section between

Table 2.3 Comparison of running costs of the ordinary road and the expressway (unit: yen/vehicle·kilometer)

Type of vehicle		By route	Fuels, oils and fats costs	Wear costs of vehicle		Depreciation costs of vehicle	Personnel costs	General administrative costs	Total	Amounts of saving
				Tire, tube costs	Maintenance costs of vehicle					
Auto car	Ordinary	Ordinary road	6.00	1.06	4.81	11.49	8.54	3.40	35.30	9.28
		Expressway	6.69	1.44	3.74	6.85	5.10	2.20	26.02	
	Small type of car	Ordinary road	3.88	0.90	2.35	5.51	7.97	3.40	24.01	6.53
		Expressway	4.33	1.22	1.80	3.30	4.79	2.04	17.48	
truck	Ordinary	Ordinary road	11.01	2.97	4.39	6.78	16.61	19.88	61.64	15.08
		Expressway	13.14	4.10	3.45	4.05	9.92	11.90	46.56	
	Small type of car	Ordinary road	4.58	1.00	2.00	5.38	9.86	11.80	34.62	10.02
		Expressway	5.44	1.39	1.57	3.23	5.92	7.05	24.60	
buss	Regular service	Ordinary road	9.63	3.53	4.64	15.60	11.21	16.84	61.45	15.52
		Expressway	11.37	4.87	3.66	9.32	6.70	10.01	45.93	
	Chartered buss	Ordinary road	10.48	3.54	4.64	16.83	13.08	16.84	65.41	16.95
		Expressway	12.37	4.82	3.66	9.80	7.80	10.01	48.46	

Source: The Japan Highway Public Corporation, Materials submitted to the World Bank—Written reply to the questionnaires related to the Second Loan–, August 1961

Table 2.4 Saved time by section between interchanges (passenger car) (unit: minute)

Nishinomiya	Amagasaki	Toyonaka	Ibaraki	Kyoto	Ootsu	Ritto	Yokaichi	Hikone	Sekigahara	Oogaki	Ichinomiya
Nishinomiya	13.5	30.0	63.0	105.0	132.0	156.0	196.5	214.5	252.0	280.5	334.5
	9.2	20.7	20.3	41.6	46.2	61.6	75.7	86.8	103.1	117.5	129.1
	4.3	9.3	42.7	63.4	85.8	94.4	120.8	127.7	148.9	163.0	205.4
	Amagasaki	16.5	49.5	91.5	118.5	142.5	183.0	201.0	238.5	267.0	321.0
		17.5	17.1	38.4	43.0	58.4	72.5	83.7	99.9	114.3	125.9
		Δ 1.0	32.4	53.1	75.5	84.1	110.5	117.3	138.6	152.7	195.1
		Toyonaka	33.0	75.0	102.0	126.0	166.5	184.5	222.0	250.5	304.0
			22.1	43.5	48.0	63.4	77.6	88.3	105.0	119.4	131.0
			10.9	31.5	54.0	62.6	88.9	95.7	117.0	131.1	173.5
			Ibaraki	42.0	69.0	93.0	133.5	151.5	189.0	217.5	271.5
				25.9	30.4	45.8	60.0	71.2	87.4	101.8	113.4
				16.1	38.6	47.2	73.5	80.3	101.6	115.7	158.1
				Kyoto	27.0	51.0	91.5	109.5	147.0	175.5	229.5
					19.6	35.0	49.1	60.2	76.5	90.9	102.5
					7.4	16.0	42.4	49.3	70.5	83.6	127.0
					Ootsu	24.0	64.5	82.5	120.0	148.5	202.5
						25.9	40.4	51.2	67.5	81.9	93.5
						Δ 1.9	24.4	31.3	52.5	66.6	109.0
						Ritto	40.5	58.5	96.0	124.5	178.5
							29.5	40.6	56.9	71.3	82.9
							11.0	17.9	39.1	53.2	95.6
							Yokaichi	39.0	76.5	105.0	159.0
								23.1	39.4	53.8	65.4
								15.9	37.1	51.2	93.6
								Hikone	37.5	66.0	120.0
									22.3	36.6	48.3

									15.2	29.4	71.7
									Sekigahara	28.5	82.5
										20.4	32.0
										8.1	50.5
										Oogaki	54.0
											26.6
											27.4
											Ichinomiya

Note: (1) Upper—Traveling time via the existing road
(2) Middle—traveling time required via the expressway.
(3) Lower—saved time.
(4) Δ sign shows the case in which the traveling time increases.
Source: The Japan Highway Public Corporation, Materials submitted to the World Bank—Written reply to the questionnaires related to the Second Loan, August 1961

Table 2.5 Saved time by section between interchanges (bus/truck) (unit: minute)

Nishinomiya	Amagasaki	Toyonaka	Ibaraki	Kyoto	Ootsu	Ritto	Yokaichi	Hikone	Sekigahara	Oogaki	Ichinomiya
Nishinomiya	18.0	40.0	84.0	140.0	176.0	208.0	262.0	286.0	336.0	374.0	446.0
	12.0	27.1	26.2	53.9	59.7	79.6	97.7	111.9	132.8	151.5	166.3
	6.0	12.9	57.8	86.1	116.3	128.4	164.3	174.1	203.2	222.5	279.7
	Amagasaki	22.0	66.0	122.0	158.0	190.0	244.0	268.0	318.0	356.0	438.0
		23.1	22.2	49.9	55.7	75.6	93.7	107.9	128.8	147.5	162.3
		Δ 1.1	43.8	72.1	102.3	114.4	150.3	160.1	189.2	208.5	265.7
		Toyonaka	44.0	100.0	136.0	168.0	222.0	246.0	296.0	334.0	406.0
			29.1	56.8	62.5	82.5	100.6	114.7	135.7	154.3	165.2
			14.9	43.2	73.5	85.5	121.4	131.3	160.3	179.7	240.8
			Ibaraki	56.0	92.0	124.0	178.0	202.0	252.0	290.0	362.0
				33.7	39.5	59.4	77.5	91.7	112.6	131.3	146.2
				22.3	52.5	64.6	100.5	110.3	139.4	158.7	215.9
				Kyoto	36.0	68.0	122.0	146.0	196.0	234.0	306.0
					25.7	45.7	63.8	77.9	98.9	117.5	132.4
					10.3	22.3	58.2	68.1	97.1	116.5	173.6
					Ootsu	32.0	86.0	110.0	160.0	198.0	270.0
						33.9	52.0	66.2	87.1	105.8	120.7
						Δ 1.9	34.0	43.8	72.9	92.2	149.3
						Ritto	54.0	78.0	128.0	166.0	238.0
							38.5	52.7	73.6	92.3	107.2
							15.5	25.3	54.4	73.7	130.8
							Yokaichi	52.0	102.0	140.0	212.0
								30.2	51.1	67.8	84.7
								21.8	50.9	70.2	127.3
								Hikone	50.0	88.0	160.0
									28.9	47.6	0.62.5

									11.1	40.4	97.5
									Sekigahara	38.0	110.0
										26.7	41.6
										11.3	68.4
										Oogaki	72.0
											34.9
											37.5
											Ichinomiya

Note: (1) Upper—transport time required via the existing road
(2) Middle—transport time required via the expressway.
(3) Lower—saved time.
(4) Δ shows the case in which the traveling time increases of saved time does not occur..
Source: The Japan Highway Public Corporation, Materials submitted to the World Bank—Written reply to the questionnaires related to the Second Loan—August 1961

Table 2.6 Comparison of the traffic accident rate per 100 million vehicle × kilometer between the route via the expressway and the route using only existing roads

	Ordinary road[1]		Expressway[2]	
The deaths	18.7	Persons	1.9	Persons
The injured persons	468	Persons	76	Persons
The number of traffic accidents	688	Cases	102	Cases
Sum of property damages due to traffic accident	18,500	1000 JPY		

[1]The traffic accident rate was estimated based on the data of the traffic accidents and the total traveling distance in vehicle•kilometer that were observed in the fiscal year of 1958 with vehicles using the part of the first-grade national highway no.1 and no.2 between Kusatsu and Amagasaki and with the industrial road between Osaka and Kyoto as they were to be paralleled to Mei-Shin expressway.
[2]As we had no expressway in Japan when the estimation was made, the traffic accident rate of *Full Control of Access* (USA) was used as the traffic accident rate with the expressway. It appeared in *Public Roads*, December 1957. However, as we did not have it and did not read it, we quoted the figure from the Ministry of Construction, Road Bureau (ed.), *Traffic accidents on the first-grade national highway no.1*, p.9, May 1961.

Nishinomiya and Ichinomya, almost the whole of Mei-Shin expressway was opened to traffic (July 1 in the next year, 1965, the whole line of the expressway was opened to traffic). The supposed volume of the traffic that uses the whole line of the expressway is 9760 vehicles per day on average, in which 68.8% of the traffic volumes is ordinary trucks, 11.3% is a small type of trucks, 8.6% is a small type of passenger cars, 6.5% is ordinary passenger cars, and 8.6% is a bus.

According to the figures by section, which is a part of the expressway line segmented by the nearest two interchanges, the biggest traffic volume was supposed with the section between Toyonaka and Ibaraki and it is 16,780 vehicles. The second was supposed between Ibaraki and Kyoto Minami, 15,364 vehicles. The third was between Kyoto Higashi and Ritto, 10,071 vehicles. It was supposed that the traffic volumes on these three sections would be only greater than the supposed volume of the traffic that would use the whole line of the expressway.

It was supposed that the traffic volume of the whole line of the expressway would be 28,791 vehicles in 1978—15 years later since the whole line of the expressway was supposed to be opened to traffic, which is 2.9 times the supposed volume in 1964. In these 15 years, it was supposed that the number of passenger cars of small type would rapidly increase, and it is around 10 times as much as what it would be in 1964. The vehicle components would change and 56.8% of the traffic volume would be trucks, 28.6% would be small type passenger cars, 6.1% would be small type trucks, 4.8% would be ordinary passenger cars, and 3.7% would be buses.

It was estimated that the volume of traffic that would use the whole line in 1974—11 years later since 1964—would be 25,085 vehicles and this is 2.6 times as much as what it would be in 1964 when the whole line of the expressway was supposed to open to traffic. It was forecasted that the traffic volume which would use the section between Ibaraki and Kyoto Minami would have reached the traffic capacity of 36,000 vehicles per day in 1974.

It was forecasted that the volume of the traffic which would use the section between Kyoto Minami and Ritto next would have reached the capacity in 1976. The traffic volume would have reached the capacity on the section between Ritto and Hikone and the section between Sekigahara and Ichinomia in 1978.

We have minute actual monthly data of the traffic volumes section by section with all the expressways in Japan. In 1963, the part of the expressway between Amagasaki and Ritto was opened to traffic. According to the actual data, the volume of the traffic that used through the expressway between Amagasaki and Ritto in 1963 was 8355 vehicles per day on average, which exceeds the supposed traffic volume, 7651 vehicles, by 8.7% though the section between Amagasaki and Ritto is just a part of the whole line of the expressway. There are five sections that are segmented by the nearest two interchanges between Amagasaki and Ritto (Table 2.7). The actual data have shown that the traffic volumes of the two sections between Kyoto Minami and Ritto exceeded the supposed traffic volumes, and the traffic volumes of the other three sections were 85.8–96.8% of the supposed traffic volumes. It was thought that it was caused by the regulation which substantially banned the large truck go through the bridges in Osaka.

In April 1964, the part of the expressway between Ritto and Sekigahara was opened to traffic. The actual data of the volume of the traffic that went through between Amagasaki and Sekigahara exceed the supposed traffic volume, 9760 vehicles per day on average by 4.9%. The actual data of the traffic volumes with the abovementioned three sections exceed the supposed traffic volumes by 69.1–142.6%.

The vehicle components show that the passenger car was 54.2% (51.9%), truck was 40.6% (41.6%), and bus was 3% (4.3%) of the traffic volume between Amagasaki and Ritto (Amagasaki and Sekigahara), respectively, which shows that the actual data of the component ratio exceed the supposed component ratio with passenger car and it was less than the supposed one with the truck. However, the traffic volume of trucks that used the two sections between Kyoto Minami, Kyoto higashi, and Ritto, on which no traffic regulation was done with truck, had increased at a fairly good rate. When we estimated the traffic volume, the most difficult type of vehicle was a truck. How to suppose the component ratio of the truck was a tough topic at that time.

2.4 Measurement of Direct and Indirect Effects of Mei-Shin Expressway

Based on the supposed basic data for the calculation of economic effects of Mei-Shin Expressway, the direct and indirect effects were estimated with the following items only, of which effects could be calculated in terms of monetary terms.

Table 2.7 Supposed traffic volumes of Mei-Shin expressway by section and types of vehicle (1964). Unit: vehicle/day

Section	Nishinomiya – Amagasaki	Amagasaki – Toyonaka	Toyonaka – Ibaraki	Ibaraki – Kyoto-Minami	Kyoto-Minami – Kyoto-Higashi	Kyoto-Higashi – Ritto	Ritto – Yokaichi	Yokaichi – Hikone	Hikone – Sekigahara	Sekigahara – Oogaki	Oogaki Ichinomiya	Ichinomiya – Komaki	Traffic volume through the whole line
Passenger car	897	892	1127	966	535	687	640	633	452	460	389	17	637
Small type of car	658	673	1796	1449	673	793	731	700	693	698	597	27	836
Bus	394	363	677	677	457	583	541	501	360	380	284	13	467
Ordinary truck	4340	5379	10,740	10,151	7081	7070	6367	6242	5713	5900	6111	274	6718
Small type of truck	1246	1445	2440	2121	884	938	802	724	695	724	1127	51	1102
Total	7535	8752	16,780	15,364	9630	10,071	9081	8800	7913	8162	8508	382	9760

Source: *Supposed traffic volumes of the Mei-Shin expressway*, The Japan Highway Public Corporation (ed.), May 1961

2.4.1 *Direct Effects*

2.4.1.1 Saved Amounts of Running Costs

First, the total running distance by vehicle type per day on average in vehicle·kilometer was obtained as the product of (1) the supposed traffic volume on the sections of the whole line of the expressway (Table 2.7) and (2) the length of the sections of the expressway. Next, the total saved amounts of running costs by vehicle type were obtained as the product of: (1) the total running distance by vehicle type per day on average in vehicle·kilometer and (2) saved running costs per vehicle·kilometer by type of vehicle (Table 2.3). Using the results of products, the total saved running costs per day on average were estimated as 25 million JPY. This is equivalent to 9.14 billion JPY per year (with the year 1964).

2.4.1.2 Saved Amounts of Traveling Time

First, the total saved traveling time by vehicle type and by section between interchanges per day in minute was obtained as the product of (1) the saved time by section between interchanges by vehicle type in minute (Table 2.4 with passenger car and Table 2.5 with truck/bus) and (2) the supposed traffic volumes of the expressway by section and types of the vehicle per day. Next, the total monetary value of the total saved traveling time by vehicle type and by section between interchanges per day in JPY was obtained as the product of (1) the total saved traveling time by vehicle type and by section between interchanges per day in minute and (2) the coefficient that converts saved time into monetary value in JPY per minute (Table 2.8). Finally, the total monetary value due to the reduction in the traveling time by vehicle type per day in JPY was obtained as the sum of the total monetary value of the total saved traveling time by vehicle type and by section between interchanges per day in JPY over all the sections between interchanges (Table 2.8).

The total monetary value of the saved traveling time in 1964 was estimated at about 7.2 billion JPY (Table 2.8), in which the amount accrues to the truck and those concerned would be 5.16 billion JPY (71.6% of the total), with small type of passenger car it would be 850 million JPY (11.7%), with small type of truck it would be 500 million JPY (7.0%), with bus it would be 380 million JPY (5.3%), and with ordinary passenger car it would be 320 million JPY (4.4%).

2.4.1.3 Effects of Decrease in Traffic Accidents

The decrease in traffic accidents (death, injury, property damage) due to the improvement in the driving environment by converting traffic volumes from ordinary roads to the expressway was estimated as follows:

Table 2.8 Time saved amounts by utilization of the Mei-Shin expressway (1964)

Vehicle type	Coefficient that converts saved time into monetary value (JPY per vehicle·minute)			Total monetary value due to reduction in running time (1000 JPY per day)	Total monetary value due to reduction in running time (million JPY per year)	%
	Saved money to vehicle	Saved money to freight and passenger	Total			
Ordinary truck	1.76	4.15	5.91	14,124.3	5155.4	71.6
Small type of truck	0.95	2.27	3.22	1371.4	500.6	7.0
Bus	1.32	27.6	28.92	1046.2	381.9	5.3
Ordinary Passenger car	–	–	10.00	869.2	317.3	4.4
Small type of car				2317.3	845.8	11.7
Total				19,728.4	7200.9	100.0

Note: Figures are rounded off and summations have round-off errors
Source: Supposed traffic volume of the Mei-Shin expressway, The Japan Highway Public Corporation (ed.), May 1961

$$\begin{bmatrix}\text{Decrease in}\\ \text{traffic accident}\end{bmatrix} = \sum_{\text{all sections}}\left\{\begin{bmatrix}\text{Traffic volume}\\ \text{on the expressway}\\ \text{by section between}\\ \text{interchanges}\\ \text{in vehicle}\end{bmatrix}\times\begin{bmatrix}\text{Running distance}\\ \text{on ordinary road}\\ \text{alternative to}\\ \text{section in kilometer}\end{bmatrix}\times\begin{bmatrix}\text{Traffic accident}\\ \text{per}\\ \text{vehicle}\bullet\text{kilometer}\\ \text{on ordinary road}\end{bmatrix}\right\} - \sum_{\text{all sections}}\left\{\begin{bmatrix}\text{Traffic volume}\\ \text{on the expressway}\\ \text{by section between}\\ \text{interchanges}\\ \text{in vehicle}\end{bmatrix}\times\begin{bmatrix}\text{Running distance}\\ \text{on the expressway}\\ \text{in kilometer}\end{bmatrix}\times\begin{bmatrix}\text{Traffic accident}\\ \text{per}\\ \text{vehicle}\bullet\text{kilometer}\\ \text{on the expressway}\end{bmatrix}\right\}$$

Precisely speaking, we needed to apply the accident rate of the railway to the traffic volumes converted from the railway. However, around 90% of the traffic

Table 2.9 Effects of decrease in traffic accidents on Mei-Shin expressway

	Decrease in traffic accidents[1] (person; case)	Valuation coefficient (1000 JPY/person; 1000 JPY/case)	Decreased loss (million JPY)
The number of deaths	172	6919	1190
The number of injured persons	3729	37	138
The number of traffic accidents[2]	5568		
Property damage		27[3]	150
Total			1478

[1]Calculated based on the formula in the above
[2]Includes all kinds of traffic accidents.
[3]The property damage per case was calculated on the following formula: property damage per case = total property damage/the number of cases, using data in Table 2.6.
Source: Kodan (1961a)

volumes on Mei-Shin expressway were supposed to be converted from the ordinary road, the abovementioned formula was adopted.

Table 2.9 shows the results of the estimation. The total effects in monetary terms due to a decrease in traffic accidents were estimated as 1478 million JPY in 1964. The most effects are a decrease in the deaths, and it is 1190 million JPY. The next is a decrease in property damages and is 150 million JPY. The decrease in injured persons is 138 million JPY.

2.4.2 *Indirect Effects*

1. Effects of streamlining production schedule and logistics: decrease in inventory stock.
   Those effects were calculated as saved interest on the working capital assigned for the inventory stock. The inventory stock can be decreased due to a decrease in the time necessary for shipment and receipt of commodities, thanks to a decrease in traveling time on the expressway. The amount of inventory stock was estimated as 2.89 billion JPY and the saved interest was 289 million JPY as the supposed interest rate was 10% in the year 1964 (Table 2.10).
2. Industrial development effects.
   Table 2.11 shows the land acquisition with industrial use around interchanges of the expressway with the year from 1956 to 1961. Table 2.12 shows the total land acquisition around interchanges of the expressway by the industrial sector during the years from 1959 to 1961. Assuming the capacity operation, the number of payrolls, operating costs, and shipment values were estimated based on the

Table 2.10 Decreases in inventory stock and saved interest (unit: million JPY)

		Converted amounts from railway	Converted amounts from ordinary road	Total
Decrease in inventory stock	Reserve supplies	400	2000	2400
	On the transport	440	50	490
	Total	840	2050	2890
Saved interest	Reserve supplies	40	200	240
	On the transport	44	5	49
	Total	84	205	289

Note: The supposed interest rate was 10%
Source: Kodan (1961b)

Table 2.11 Land acquisition with industrial use around interchanges of the expressway with the years from 1956 to 1961 (unit: ha)

Area along the Mei-Shin	1956	1957	1958	1959	1960	1961	Total
Nishinomiya Interchange	0.0	0.0	0.0	10.7	9.0	15.8	35.4
Amagasaki·Toyonaka Interchange	0.0	0.0	0.0	8.7	48.5	2.5	59.7
Ibaraki Interchange	6.0	30.6	9.5	77.5	332.4	17.8	473.7
Kyoto Interchange	0.0	0.0	2.5	35.1	36.8	0.0	74.4
Ootsu·Ritto Interchange	42.3	19.8	3.6	75.0	109.3	49.3	299.4
Yokaichi Interchange	0.0	0.0	0.0	9.9	52.3	287.6	349.8
Hikone Interchange	0.0	0.0	0.0	0.0	46.1	4.8	50.9
Sekigahara Interchange	0.0	0.0	0.0	12.4	1.7	0.0	14.1
Oogaki Interchange	0.0	0.0	0.0	4.9	19.6	37.8	62.3
Ichinomiya Interchange	0.0	0.0	0.0	28.5	45.3	89.7	163.5
Total	48.3	50.4	15.6	262.8	700.9	505.2	1583.2

Note: Figures are rounded off and summations have round-off errors
Source: The Japan Highway Public Corporation (ed.), *Economic Effects of Expressway,* September, 1962

area supposed to be developed for industrial use (Tables 2.11, 2.12). The total industrial development effects are summarized in Table 2.13. It was estimated that the total number of payrolls would be about 85,000 persons. The total shipment value would be about 163 billion JPY and the total value added would be about 56.5 billion JPY. Considering the additional public projects such as industrial and public water supply, construction and improvement of access road, and so on, around 17.0 billion JPY was supposed to be the industrial development effects in monetary term owing to the construction of expressway, which is around 30% of the total value added (Table 2.13).

Around Ibaraki and Yokaichi interchanges, the industrial development effects are prominent. It was considered that those effects were largely owing to the section of the expressway between Amagasaki and Ritto that was opened to traffic in July 1963.

Table 2.12 Land acquisition around interchanges of the expressway by industrial sector with the sum over the years from 1959 to 1961 (unit: ha)

Interchange	Iron and steel and metal	Machinery	Chemistry	Ceramics	Fiber	Timber · wooden articles	Paper pulp	Food and grocery	Miscellaneous	Total
Nishinomiya interchange	0.0	16.0	0.0	3.9	0.7	0.1	0.0	11.2	3.7	35.4
Amagasaki·toyonaka interchange	7.1	26.0	10.3	8.3	0.4	0.0	0.2	7.5	0.0	59.7
Ibaraki Interchange	98.4	113.7	80.0	9.5	80.4	0.9	7.0	37.2	0.7	427.7
Kyoto Interchange	5.9	30.4	3.5	15.9	0.4	0.8	1.6	13.4	0.0	71.9
Ootsu·Ritto Interchange	8.1	94.8	72.7	30.0	26.3	0.0	1.7	0.0	0.0	233.6
Yokaichi Interchange	0.0	241.3	64.5	44.0	0.0	0.0	0.0	0.0	0.0	349.8
Hikone Interchange	0.0	5.1	12.7	26.4	5.6	0.0	0.0	0.0	1.0	50.9
Sekigahara Interchange	0.0	10.8	0.0	0.0	3.3	0.0	0.0	0.0	0.0	14.1
Oogaki Interchange	0.0	16.5	1.7	8.8	33.6	0.0	1.7	0.0	0.0	62.3
Ichinomiya Interchange	18.5	18.2	4.1	2.6	91.5	1.7	0.0	23.5	3.3	163.5
Total	138.0	572.8	249.4	149.4	242.2	3.4	12.1	92.8	8.7	1468.9

Source: The Japan Highway Public Corporation (ed.), *Economic Effects of Expressway*, September, 1962

Table 2.13 Industrial development effects in the area along the Mei-Shin expressway (1959–1961) (unit: tsubo)

Interchange where industrial area was developed around	Site area	Employees	Working expense	Shipment amounts	Value added
Unit	ha	person	million JPY	million JPY	million JPY
Nishinomiya interchange	35.4	2199	4180	4108	1375
Amagasaki·Toyonaka interchange	59.7	4675	7034	8349	3008
Ibaraki interchange	427.7	25,709	50,446	54,735	17,696
Kyoto interchange	71.9	4555	8485	7892	2743
Ootsu·Ritto interchange	233.6	10,014	21,955	21,030	7639
Yokaichi interchange	349.8	23,049	41,269	40,678	15,962
Hikone interchange	50.9	2521	6006	4180	1558
Sekigahara interchange	14.1	935	1661	1518	578
Oogaki interchange	62.3	3040	7348	4932	1640
Ichinomiya interchange	163.5	8166	19,282	15,153	4320
Total	1468.9	84,863	167,666	162,575	56,519

Source: The Japan Highway Public Corporation (ed.), *Economic Effects of Expressway,* September, 1962

Setting factories into the area around Nishinomiya, Amagasaki, Toyonaka, and Ichinomiya interchanges had been matured in a sense and influenced by the growth of both Han-Shin (Osaka-Kobe) and Chukyo (Nagoya) industrial zones. Therefore, it was thought that it was difficult to differentiate the effects of the expressway from the effects of the existing matured industrial area, since they were competitive as well as complementary with each other in the industrial development. On the other hand, although effects of industrial development in the area around interchanges between Ibaraki and Oogaki were not so large because these areas were located in rural areas, it was thought that those effects were mostly due to the expressway. Although, as we see in the above, there could be differences between the effects of the industrial development depending on regions, the setting factories by machinery (39.0% in terms of land acquisition), chemistry (17%), and iron and steel and metal (9.4%) sectors characterized the industrial development owing to the expressway. It was expected that the industrial structures in Han-Shin and Chukyo industrial zones would dramatically change.

After the expressway was opened to traffic, land prices have risen and the acquisition of the factory site became economically difficult, and additional acquisition was hardly done. Irrespective of the situation, the land for the warehouse, truck terminal, and so on was acquired, for which the land is not so needed. It was taken as a recent trend (at that time) that the transition in the development from the secondary industries to the tertiary industries was about to begin.

2.4.2.1 Effects of the Decrease in the Traffic Congestion on the Competitive Ordinary Road

On the first-grade national highway no. 1, which was competitive against Mei-Shin expressway, considerable traffic congestion had occurred, with which the social loss was fairly big. It was supposed that, once Mei-Shin expressway is opened to traffic, a significant part of traffic volumes on the first-grade national highway no. 1 would be converted to the expressway and the traffic congestion on the national highway would be reduced to some extent, and the average running speed on the national highway would be increased. Therefore, the saving of running costs and the reduction in traveling time would be obtained. Such effects of the reduction in the traveling time on the national highway alone were estimated as 1.06 billion JPY per year.

The abovementioned items are the effects that were measurable in monetary terms. The following effects were mentioned as the indirect effects that were thought to be difficult to be measured in monetary terms.

2.4.2.2 Dispersion Effects of Urban Population

Table 2.14 shows the estimated increase in the population which would be induced by the industrial development into the area around interchanges of the expressway. It was supposed that the total increase in the number of payrolls due to the industrial development induced by the expressway would be 35,000 persons, and the increase in the population including his/her family would be 83,000 persons. It was supposed that such an increase in the population induces the development of commercial business in the area, and the increase in the number of payrolls in the commerce business would be 18,000 persons, then the total increases in the population would be 100,000 persons.

Due to the population movement, it was estimated that around 305 ha of residential land would be developed, and not only 3500 houses of apartments and 3500 detached houses but also about 1400 houses of "dwelling with shop" would be constructed (Table 2.15).

It was supposed that the decrease in the traveling time, furthermore, would technically expand the commuting area of the big cities, and it would induce the movement of population into the areas along Mei-Shin expressway. Thus, the construction of the expressway would induce the construction of a new (local) city, by which the dispersion of population would be enhanced.

2.4.2.3 Effects of Expanding the Area of the Market

For example, the marginal areas from which vegetables could be shipped to Osaka using the ordinary road network before the provision of expressway services were

Table 2.14 Estimates of moving-in population to the area along the Mei-Shin expressway

interchange	number of move-in workers (person)	move-in population (person)					commerce population			total (A + B) (person)
		number of the unattended	number of the householders	number of the family constituents except householder	sub total	(A) total (person)	(B) total (person)	number of commerce engaged	number of the family constituents of commerce engaged except householder	
Nishinomiya	924	388	536	1233	1769	2157	376	114	262	2533
Amagasaki·Toyonaka	1964	825	1139	2620	3759	4584	1435	435	1000	6019
Ibaraki	10,798	4535	6263	14,405	20,668	25,203	7900	2394	5506	33,103
Kyoto	1913	803	1110	2553	3663	4466	1016	308	708	5482
Ootsu·Ritto	4206	1767	2439	5610	8049	9816	1360	412	948	11,176
Yokaichi	9681	4066	5615	12,915	18,530	22,596	3232	949	2283	25,828
Hikone	1059	445	614	1412	2026	2471	343	104	239	2814
Sekigahara	393	165	228	524	752	917	155	47	108	1072
Oogaki	1277	536	741	1704	2445	2981	502	152	350	3483
Ichinomiya	3430	1441	1989	4575	6564	8005	1346	408	938	9351
Total	35,645	14,971	20,674	47,551	68,225	83,196	17,665	5323	12,342	100,861

Source: The Japan Highway Public Corporation (ed.), *Economic Effects of Expressway*, September, 1962

Table 2.15 Residential land development and the number of houses in the area along the Mei-Shin expressway

		residential house for exclusive use					residential house with store	
			apartment		separate houses			
interchange	total area of residential land (ha)	area (ha)	area (ha)	num. of houses	area (ha)	num. of houses	area (ha)	num. of houses
Nishinomiya	7.96	7.47	5.97	90	1.49	92	0.50	29
Amagasaki·Toyonaka	17.76	15.87	12.69	192	3.17	195	1.90	110
Ibaraki	97.68	87.23	69.79	1056	17.45	1070	10.45	605
Kyoto	16.80	15.46	12.37	187	3.09	190	1.34	78
Ootsu·Ritto	35.77	33.97	27.18	411	6.80	417	1.80	104
Yokaichi	82.48	78.21	62.57	946	15.64	959	4.27	248
Hikone	9.01	8.55	6.84	103	1.71	105	0.45	26
Sekigahara	3.38	3.17	2.54	38	0.63	39	0.20	12
Oogaki	4.37	10.32	8.25	125	2.06	127	0.66	38
Ichinomiya	29.49	27.71	22.17	335	5.54	340	1.78	103
Total	304.70	287.95	230.36	3483	57.59	3534	23.36	1353

Note: Figures are rounded off and summations have round-off errors

Shizuoka in Tokai area (Pacific coast) and Ishikawa in Hokuriku area (Japan Sea coast) at that time. It was supposed that it would be extended to Kanagawa near Tokyo and Toyama (next Ishikawa) by using the expressway route. It was also supposed that, in the same way, the area in which firms and consumers would purchase commodities produced in Osaka would be expanded.

2.5 Appraisal of the Mei-Shin Expressway Construction Project With the Estimated Direct and Indirect Effects

2.5.1 Profitability of the Mei-Shin Expressway as a Toll Road

The construction of Mei-Shin expressway as a toll road was subject to the institutional constraint of the self-supporting accounting system, that is, an entity, that would operate the provision of the expressway and related services using facilities of the Mei-Shin expressway (it was named Japan Highway Public Corporation (JH)—a government-affiliated public corporation[3] at that time) would be obliged to run the business on a standalone basis just like a private company. This means that the entity shall have redeemed all the investments in the construction of the expressway with streams of the business, which would be sourced to the toll revenue and other related business revenues, in the limited period[4] while it would be subject to a kind of regulation by the government authority as a public utility.

A certain level of the toll rate was supposed (actually, it could be guessed later on that it was supposed around 7.5 JPY per vehicle·kilometer with ordinary passenger car), and the profitability of the project was examined based on the basic data of the supposed traffic volumes by section between interchanges and so on. Table 2.16 shows basic data of the construction costs used for the profitability analysis of the expressway between Nishinomiya and Ichinomiya interchanges. According to this table, the project was taken as a very prosperous one since it was supposed that the redemption would be able to be done within 25 years (in 1987), which was far shorter than the economically reasonable and legally obliged period, that is, 50 years. For readers, it may look queer that no data of "toll revenues" is shown in the table. The reasons are now just guessed: (1) the staff in the Economic Research Room in JH did not pay notice to the stream of toll revenues because the matter related to the

[3]Later on, it had been dissolved in order that a several better independent administrative entities were to be formed. Mei-Shin expressway is now under the operation by three *private* companies: East Nippon Expressway Company Limited, Central Nippon Expressway Company Limited and West Nippon Expressway Company Limited.

[4]According to the law, it was 50 years since the year when the operation has been started (1964). Till the privatization had been done, the target year of the redemption had been postponed at the time when a new section of the expressway network was opened to traffic. The business of the amortization of loan and construction bond was succeeded by Japan Expressway Holding and Debt Repayment Agency when JH was privatized.

Table 2.16 Investment costs and depreciation conditions for Mei-Shin expressway (between Nishinomiya and Ichinomiya interchanges) (unit: million JPY)

Construction costs	110,650
Investigation costs	472
General administrative costs	5590
Interests of construction bond	11,307
Total	128,019
The supposed year when the expressway would be opened to traffic	1963
The estimated year of the redemption	1987
The target period of redemption	25 years

expressway toll system was investigated and controlled by another unit; (2) the estimated direct benefits would be quite large as we will see subsequently, based on which the toll could be charged to produce fairly good business profit, would enable the redemption in a fairly shorter period; and (3) the interests and mission of the Economic Research Room Section was the analysis of social usefulness of the expressway. It is a necessary condition that the construction of expressway is socially useful. This means that the sum of the direct and indirect benefits of the expressway, which would be directly and indirectly created based on the existence of the expressway, must be greater than the sum of the costs of the construction of the expressway and the maintenance and administration costs of the construction and the operation of the business with the expressway.

2.5.2 The Appraisal by Taking into Account Direct and Indirect Effects of the Expressway: The Viewpoint of the Whole National Economy

Generally speaking, profitability is one of the most decisive indicators for the private company that starts a new business. In the case of the expressway like Mei-Shin expressway, the profitability shall be examined based on the estimated length of the redemption period since the toll rate is controlled by the government authority. Roughly speaking, the toll revenue is the product of the toll rate (JPY/vehicle·kilometer) and the total traffic volumes (vehicle·kilometer) on the expressway. The profitability analysis which is mainly based on the toll revenue gives an advantage to the expressway that is to be provided to the regions, for example, Osaka, Kyoto, and Nagoya cities, where traffic volumes on the existing roads are large. On the other hand, the expressway has a disadvantage that is to be provided in the regions, for example, Hokkaido, Chugoku, Shikoku, Tohoku, Hokuriku, and so on (especially, more than 50 years ago), where traffic volumes on the existing roads are small, and we cannot expect that a good volume of traffic would be diverted to the expressway, irrespective of the effects of saved running cost and time, saved inventory costs, industrial development, and expanding market

Table 2.17 Economic effects of Mei-Shin expressway in 1964 (unit: million JPY)

	Item of effects	Monetary value
Direct effects	Saved running costs	9143
	Reduction in traveling time	7201
	Reduction in traffic accident	1478
	Subtotal	17,822
Indirect effects	Saved interests due to reduction in inventory stock	289
	Industrial development effects	16,962
	Effects of reduction in traffic congestion on ordinary roads	1063
	Subtotal	18,314
Total		36,136

Source: Sasaki et al. (1965), pp. 39–40

areas, and the diffusion of such direct and indirect effects into the whole national economy through the completion of the expressway network in the nationwide. To fairly justify and give the right decision on the project in such regions, the other approach should be adopted in which a kind of *social profitability* shall be taken as an indicator for the social accountability of the project in place of the (private) profitability. There could be many projects that are socially useful *and* less profitable in the sense of the private company, especially during the economic development phase in which the economy is rapidly growing. Whether we adopt or not such an approach must be critical when we consider an effective allocation of the limited amount of capital for alternatively and technically feasible projects. If it were not adopted, the foregone loss is an opportunity cost in the sense that we would lose what we ought to gain.

Table 2.17 shows the estimated direct and indirect effects in monetary terms in the year 1964 when the expressway was first opened to traffic. The direct effects measurable in terms of monetary value (17.8 billion JPY) alone were equivalent to 16.1% of the capitalized value of the construction costs (110.7 billion JPY in Table 2.16). The definition of effects, the methodologies adopted, and the basic data used in the estimation are explained in Sects. 2.2 and 2.3 with precise basic data and methodologies with several items of effects due to the limitation of pages. According to the table, the estimated direct effects were 17.82 billion JPY and the indirect effects were 36.14 billion JPY. Although Mei-Shin expressway would be located in the regions where economic activities were made in an active manner, it is remarkable that the indirect benefits were equivalent to and *not* less than the direct benefits, only on which the supposed toll revenues would have to be dependent (actually, it had been often said till the privatization of JH that the toll rate (fare) were adjusted to the amount with which around 60–70% of the direct benefits only could be taken as the source to the toll revenue considering JH was one of the public utilities).

The benefit–cost ratio analysis, which was developed and deepened by the water resource development research group in the United States, was a possible approach to the appraisal of the project from the viewpoint of the social profitability, that is, the welfare nationwide (Chap. 3 in Eckstein 1958, pp. 55–57):

$$\frac{B}{C} = \sum_{n=1}^{30} \frac{\left(B_n^1 + B_n^2\right)}{(1+i)^n} \left[\sum_{n=1}^{30} \frac{O_n}{(1+i)^n} + K\right]^{-1},$$

in which:

n is the running subscript ($n = 1, 2, 3, \cdot\cdot\cdot, 30$) and the first fiscal year ($n = 1$) means the fiscal year of 1964 (April 1, 1964–March 31, 1965);

B is the sum of benefits (=effects) capitalized at the beginning (April 1st) of the fiscal year of 1964 and it is calculated as $\sum_{n=1}^{30} \frac{\left(B_n^1+B_n^2\right)}{(1+i)^n}$;

C is the total cost capitalized at the beginning (April 1) of the first fiscal year, 1964, and it is calculated as $\sum_{n=1}^{30} \frac{O_n}{(1+i)^n} + K$;

B_n^1 is the sum of direct effects supposed to be obtained in the nth fiscal year;

i is the capitalization rate and it was supposed to be 5% per year;

O_n is the maintenance and administration costs in the nth fiscal year; and.

K is the total capitalized cost at the beginning of the fiscal year 1964 which includes all the expenses on the construction, land purchase, investigation, management, and interests of bond/loan till the beginning of the fiscal year of 1964, that is, all the costs through the preparation and construction periods till the expressway was opened to traffic.

Here, the time horizon over which the stream of benefits is capitalized into the value at the beginning of the fiscal year, 1964, was 30 years. This was a compromise between the supposed target of the redemption period, 25 years, from the view of private profitability and the longer economic life of the expressway as social infrastructure from the viewpoint of social profitability, reflecting a kind of sectionalism in JH in that day.

The calculation formulas used for the estimation of benefit in Table 2.17 were applied to the estimation of the benefits obtained for the other 29 years. Then, the sum of the capitalized streams of benefits (B) was estimated as 953,500 million JPY in monetary terms. The construction costs and maintenance management costs expended before the fiscal year 1964 were capitalized into the value at the beginning of the fiscal year 1964 (K), and it was 128,019 million JPY (Table 2.16). The capitalized value of the supposed streams of maintenance and administration costs, at the beginning of the fiscal year, 1964 ($\sum_{n=1}^{30} \frac{O_n}{(1+i)^n}$), was 12,700 million JPY. Using these estimated results, the benefit–cost ratio was obtained as follows:

$$\frac{B}{C} = \frac{953,500}{12,700 + 128,019} = 6.78$$

Although the benefits were summed up with only the items of direct and indirect effects which were able to be measured in monetary terms, and, therefore, the benefits in the abovementioned calculation were a part of the total benefits, and it turned out that the total benefits (measurable direct and indirect effects at that time) were about 6.8 times as much as the investment costs. Considering the ratio between the estimated direct and indirect benefits is 1:1 (Table 2.17), the *direct benefit*–cost ratio must be more than 3. Presuming that around 60–70% of the direct benefits can be taken as the toll charge base, the ratio of the cost to the toll revenue was around 2.0. This means it was supposed that the private profitability of the project was fairly good.

2.6 Consideration of Public Investment Criteria of Mei-Shin and To-Mei Expressway: Benefit–Cost Ratio and Difference Criteria

2.6.1 Benefits (Economic Effects) of To-Mei Expressway in the Year When it was Opened to Traffic

Table 2.18 shows the estimated direct and indirect effects of To-Mei expressway in the year when the expressway was opened to traffic, which was measurable in terms of monetary value ('To' means Tokyo and 'Mei' means Nagoya). The estimated direct effects between (1) Tokyo and Shizuoka and (2) Toyokawa and Komaki interchanges were 16.8 billion and 9.1 billion JPY, respectively. The estimated indirect effects between (1) Tokyo and Shizuoka and (2) Toyokawa and Komaki interchanges were 17.7 billion and 9.7 billion JPY, respectively. With the section of To-Mei between Tokyo and Shizuoka interchanges, the direct effects in terms of monetary value (16.8 billion JPY) alone were equivalent to 9.3% of the construction costs (180.0 billion JPY). With the section between Toyokawa and Komaki interchanges, the direct effects in terms of monetary value (9.1 billion JPY) alone were equivalent to 14.0% of construction costs (65.0 billion JPY). Considering that the direct benefits shall be the base for the toll revenues, the project of To-Mei Expressway was supposed to be a prosperous one.

Minute estimation of the streams of costs and economic effects (direct and indirect effects) was done anew to analyze the social usefulness (profitability) of both Mei-Shin and To-Mei Expressways by applying the public investment criteria. The estimated results are shown in Tables 2.19 and 2.20 which were the base for the analysis.[5] Table 2.19 is the growth rate that was calculated based on Table 2.20. It is incredible that the supposed growth rates of the benefits are far larger than the growth rate of the GDP at that time, which was more or less 7.2% (The main purpose of the national economic plan was to double everybody's income in 10 years). The growth rate itself diversifies dependent on the time and place.

[5]These two tables a little reflect changes in the economic situation at that time and the supposed future trend of the economy. Therefore, some of figures in these tables are not exactly same as the values in Tables 2.16, 2.17, and 2.18.

Table 2.18 Direct and indirect effects of To-Mei expressway in 1968 (unit: million JPY)

	Item of effects	To-Mei Expressway Tokyo–Shizuoka	To-Mei Expressway Toyokawa–Komaki
Direct effects	Saved running costs	8867	5863
	Reduction in traveling time	5390	2354
	Reduction in traffic accident	2573	858
	Subtotal	16,830	9075
Indirect effects	Saved interests due to reduction in inventory stock	220	172
	Industrial development effects	16,242	8726
	Effects of reduction in traffic congestion on ordinary roads	1266	823
	Subtotal	17,728	9721
Total		34,558	18,796
Remark	Opening year	1968	1968

Source: Sasaki et al. (1965), pp. 39–40

Table 2.19 Supposed growth rates of economic effects with Mei-Shin and To-Mei expressways (unit: billion JPY)

n	Mei-Shin expressway		To-Mei expressway Tokyo–Shizuoka		To-Mei expressway Toyokawa–Komaki	
	Capitalized economic effects at n = 1	Growth rate (%)	Capitalized economic effects at n = 1	Growth rate (%)	Capitalized economic effects at n = 1	Growth rate (%)
1	34.0	116.5	32.6	115.6	17.7	115.8
2	73.6	56.1	70.3	55.9	38.2	55.8
3	114.9	36.2	109.6	71.1	59.5	36.0
4	156.5		187.5	20.7	80.9	
5			226.3	16.9		
6			264.5			

Note: formed from the series of economic effects of Table 2.20
Source: calculated on Table 2.20

2.6.2 *Benefit–Cost Ratio Criteria*

The method applied to the measurement of economic effects and the list of various costs of To-Mei expressway was different from that applied to Mei-Shin expressway. The former was a little bit sophisticated than the latter as the former calculation was done later (Sasaki et al. 1965).

By adopting the measurable economic effects (≡ benefits) only, we consider the analysis of the social profitability of the expressway based on the public investment criteria (which incorporates the benefit–cost analysis) (quoted from Eckstein 1958, pp. 55–57).

Table 2.20 Analysis of the public investment criteria based on the benefit–cost ratio: Solutions to Problem: BBC Mei-Shin (Nishinomiya–Ichinomiya) (unit: million JPY)

t	Year	Benefits (b) (capitalized value at n = 1)			Costs (c) (capitalized value at n = 1)			
		Direct effects	Indirect effects	Accumulated sum (V_B^t)	Total investment for the construction (K)	Maintenance / administration	Accumulated sum (V_C^t)	$\frac{V_B^t}{V_C^t}$
1	1964	16,806	17,270	34,076	128,019	753	128,772	0.26
2	1965	17,289	22,295	73,660		692	129,464	0.57
3	1966	17,665	23,567	114,892		671	130,135	0.88
4 (=t*)	1967	18,208	23,413	156,513		615	130,750	1.20
To-Mei (section between Tokyo and Shizuoka interchanges)								
1	1969	15,871	16,720	32,591	218,928	1256	220,184	0.15
2	1970	16,177	21,524	70,292		1260	221,444	0.32
3	1971	16,540	22,746	109,578		1189	222,633	0.49
4	1972	16,928	22,593	149,099		1150	223,783	0.67
5	1973	16,595	21,850	187,544		1130	224,913	0.83
6	1974	17,679	21,029	226,252		1810	226,723	1.00
7 (=t*)	1975	18,131	20,073	264,456		1247	227,970	1.16
To-Mei (section between Toyokawa and Komaki interchanges)								
1	1969	8558	9167	17,275	72,654	475	73,129	0.24
2	1970	8723	11,752	38,200		466	73,595	0.52
3	1971	8919	12,412	59,531		441	74,036	0.80
4 (=t*)	1972	9057	12,327	80,915		429	74,465	1.09

Sources: Sasaki et al. 1965, p. 74.

Different from benefits (B) and costs (C) defined in Chap. 1, it was supposed that they would change with the lapse of time like $B_{1,}$, B_2, $\cdots$, B_T; C_1, C_2, $\cdots$, C_T. Thus, given supposed benefits and costs, the present value (V_B) of the stream of benefits (B_n, $n = 1, 2, \cdots, T$) was calculated with the following formula:

$$V_B = \frac{B_1}{(1+i)^1} + \frac{B_2}{(1+i)^2} + \cdots + \frac{B_T}{(1+i)^T} = \sum_{n=1}^{T} \frac{B_n}{(1+i)^n}$$

in which:

T is the time horizon of the stream of benefits and.

i is the discount rate ($\cong$ interest rate).

And, the present value (V_C) of the stream of costs was calculated with the following formula:

$$V_C = \frac{O_1}{(1+i)^1} + \frac{O_2}{(1+i)^2} + \cdots + \frac{O_T}{(1+i)^T} + K = \sum_{n=1}^{T} \frac{O_n}{(1+i)^n} + K$$

in which:

K is the total capitalized cost at the beginning of the first year, which included all the expenses on the construction, land purchase, investigation, management, and interests of bond/loan till the beginning of the first year, that is, all the costs through the preparation and construction periods till the expressway was opened to traffic.

Therefore, the benefit–cost ratio is given as follows:

$$\frac{V_B}{V_C} = \sum\nolimits_{n=1}^{T} \frac{B_n}{(1+i)^n} \left(\sum\nolimits_{n=1}^{T} \frac{O_n}{(1+i)^n} + K \right)^{-1} \tag{2.1}$$

The application of the benefit–cost ratio to the public investment criteria with the decision making whether the scarce capital fund should be allocated to, for example, the Mei-Shin Expressway project, from the view of social profitability, was to find out a value of t (lower case letter t), which was given as a solution to the following recursive problem:

[Problem: BBC].

Find out the minimum value of t among $t = 1, 2, \cdot \quad \cdot \quad \cdot, T$, which meets the following inequality:

$$\frac{V_B^t}{V_C^t} = \sum\nolimits_{n=1}^{t} \frac{B_n}{(1+i)^n} \left(\sum\nolimits_{n=1}^{t} \frac{O_n}{(1+i)^n} + K \right)^{-1} \geqq 1 \tag{2.2}$$

in which:

V_B^t is the capitalized value of the stream of benefits, B_n ($n = 1, 2, \cdots, t$) in terms of the value at the beginning of the period $n = 1$;

V_C^t is the capitalized value of the stream of costs, C_n $(n = 1, 2, \cdots, t)$ in terms of the value at the beginning of the period $n = 1$.

The solution to the problem, t^*, means that the project, that is, the construction of Mei-Shin expressway, can be redeemed within t^* years, which is less than the time horizon T that shall be given considering, for example, (1) the economic life of the expressway, (2) an obliged redemption periods in case a part of the construction costs is financed by a loan, (3) alternative public projects, in which the minimum redemption period in the above sense is around such and such years, and so on. The shorter t^* means the better project in terms of social usefulness.

The Problem: BBC was applied to the construction project of Mei-Shin expressway (the entire line) and the two sections of To-Mei (between Tokyo and Shizuoka interchanges and between Toyokawa and Komaki). Table 2.20 shows the results and the minimum redemption periods were 4, 7, and 4 years with Mei-Shin, To-Mei of Tokyo-Shizuoka, and To-Mei of Toyokawa-Komaki, respectively. It is incredible that the redemption period of Mei-Shin was far shorter than the target of the redemption period of 25 years focusing on the private profitability (Table 2.16).

2.6.3 *Benefit–Less–Cost (BLC) Criteria*

The benefit–less–cost criteria (benefit–cost difference criteria) based on the same data of the capitalized streams of benefits and costs was examined (Sasaki et al. 1965; pp. 74–77; and Sasaki 1961; Sasaki et al. 1965; Kodan 1963a, b). The value of the benefit–less–cost with the streams of benefits and costs over the time horizon T is calculated with the following formula (quoted from Eckstein 1958):

$$B - C = \sum_{n=1}^{T} \frac{B_n}{(1+i)^n} - \sum_{n=1}^{T} \frac{O_n}{(1+i)^n} - K \tag{2.3}$$

The logic for the application of Problem: BBC to the decision-making whether the scarce capital fund should be allocated to, for example, the Mei-Shin Expressway project, from the view of social profitability, can be applied to the BLC criteria. It was to find out a value of t (lower case letter t), which was given as a solution to the following recursive problem:

[Problem: BLC].

Find out the minimum value of t among $t = 1, 2, \cdots, T$, that meets the following inequality:

$$BLC_t = V_B^t - V_C^t = \sum_{n=1}^{t} \frac{B_n}{(1+i)^n} - \sum_{n=1}^{t} \frac{O_n}{(1+i)^n} \geqq \mathsf{K}, \text{ or}$$
$$BLC_t = \sum_{n=1}^{t} \frac{B_n - O_n}{(1+i)^n} \geqq \mathsf{K}, \tag{2.4}$$

in which:

$$V_B^t = \sum\nolimits_{n=1}^{t} \frac{B_n}{(1+i)^n},$$

and

$$V_C^t = \sum\nolimits_{n=1}^{t} \frac{O_n}{(1+i)^n}.$$

The results are shown in Table 2.21 and the minimum redemption periods were 4, 7, and 4 years with Mei-Shin, To-Mei (Tokyo–Shizuoka), and To-Mei (Toyokawa and Komaki), respectively. It was supposed that the construction costs per kilometer would be 610 million JPY for Mei-Shin; 800 million JPY for To-Mei (Toyokawa–

Table 2.21 Analysis of the public investment criteria based on the benefit–less–cost: solutions to problem: BLC Mei-Shin (Nishinomiya–Ichinomiya) (K = 128,019) (unit: million JPY)

		Benefits				
t	Year	Capitalized direct effects	Capitalized indirect effects	Total at t	Cost (V_C^t)	Accumulated amounts of benefit–cost difference (BLC_t)
1	1964	16,806	17,270	34,076	753	33,323
2	1965	17,289	22,295	39,584	692	72,215
3	1966	17,665	23,567	41,232	671	112,776
4 (= t^*)	1967	18,209	23,413	41,622	615	153,783
To-Mei (Tokyo–Shizuoka) (K = 218,928)						
1	1968	15,871	16,720	32,591	1256	31,335
2	1969	16,177	21,524	37,701	1260	67,776
3	1970	16,540	22,746	39,286	1189	105,873
4	1971	16,928	22,593	39,521	1150	144,244
5	1972	16,595	21,850	38,445	1130	181,559
6	1973	17,679	21,029	38,708	1810	218,457
7 (= t^*)	1974	19,131	20,073	39,204	1247	256,414
To-Mei (Toyokawa–Komaki) (K = 72,654)						
1	1968	8558	9167	17,725	475	17,250
2	1969	8723	11,752	20,475	466	37,259
3	1970	8919	12,412	21,331	441	58,149
4 (= t^*)	1971	9057	12,327	21,384	429	79,104

Source: Sasaki et al. 1965, p. 76

Komaki), and 1120 million JPY for To-Mei (Tokyo–Shizuoka), which was about twice of Mei-Shin. This was the main reason that the estimated redemption periods were longer than the others.

2.7 Summary

It has passed almost 60 years since one of the authors was deeply committed to the preparation of documents submitted to World Bank which gave loans to JH for the construction of Mei-Shin and Tomei expressway in 1960s. The project was one of the big and adventurous national projects which must have been successful as the main emphasis was still laid on the transportation by railway at that time. Arguments based on social profitability were strongly suggested in the so-called Watkins Report before the project was started. The documents did work in the sense that the methodologies adopted in the preparation of documents that were to be submitted to World Bank were far sophisticated than what World Bank ought to have presumed and requested and the loans were given to JH. At that time, the concepts of social profitability and even direct effects, as well as indirect benefits, were quite new and strange for people who were engaged in the transportation research mainly focusing on railway and marine transportation. They were inclined to discuss the amount of the toll revenues against the investment cost and that was all. It appears that even nowadays researchers in the field of transportation research pay less attention to the indirect benefits that are created being independent of the transfer process of direct benefits that are defined as the benefits directly enjoyed by users of, for example, the express way. Although the methodologies explained in this chapter may nowadays look nothing new for readers and in the opening of this chapter the documents were taken as fossil by the authors themselves, they are still new and useful for those who work with the project evaluation in the developing countries for loans by World Bank, Asian Development Bank, and so on.

Appendix 1 Estimation of the Traffic Volume on Mei-Shin Expressway

Opening the Door of Traffic Volume

The text of this chapter is the measurement of economic effects. It seemed sufficient for documents submitted to the World Bank. However, it is only one side of a coin. Whoever intends the economic appraisal of the huge transport project must recognize the necessity of traffic volume measurement (estimation), which is another side of the truth.

Everyone must start to examine the locational features of the proposed expressway. Namely, the location and line of the expressway may affect first the current and future traffic volumes[6] on the existing roads that are competitive to it with traffics between a certain pair of origin-region and destination-region by diverting some of them to the expressway. Next, the expressway may affect the total traffic volumes on the origin-destination (O-D) basis between regions on a nationwide scale by changing interregional trade patterns, developing new industrial areas and resources, and so on, and some of them may use the expressway in the long run. Finally, some of the traffic volumes of other modes than vehicles may be diverted to the traffic flow that uses the expressway. The O-D table of the current traffic volumes between widespread regions can be estimated using spot traffic volumes on the existing roads based on the observation by the traffic counter, statics of materials flows based on a social survey, other statistics such as car loading statics, and so on considering impacts of the expressway on the existing road, surrounding regions through which the expressway goes, widespread regions of which traffic potentially use the expressway, and so on. Based on the data, the diverted traffic volumes are estimated and, then, toll revenues, profitability, redeemability, and so on are examined.

The following brief explanation about the estimation is based on materials of the formal documents of The Mei-Shin Expressway Construction Archives Editing Committee (1967a, 1967b) and Sasaki and Kobayashi (1962).

What is the target of traffic volume estimation of Mei-Shin Expressway? It is to know numerically the traffic volumes that may use Mei-Shin expressway after it is placed in service. The direct/indirect economic effects (benefits) and toll revenues shall be estimated based on the numerical data of the traffic volume and (social and private) profitability, amortization period, and so on shall be examined based on them. It is useful if the estimation is made with each pairwise interchange of the expressway (or their surrounding regions/zones). Table 2.22 is an example that shows such basic data. It is data of traffic volumes of trucks on the O-D basis that was estimated by the O-D survey taken in 1957 and 1951 with the traffic volumes on the first-grade national highway which is parallel to the expressway. The figures in the cell of the row headed by "3 Toyonaka" and the column headed by "5 Kyoto," $T_{3,5}=2021$ means the traffic volumes of trucks that had origin (starting location of the trip) in the Toyonaka interchange region/zone and the destination of the trip that had in the Kyoto region/zone was 2021 vehicles per day according to the O-D survey taken in 1957. Generally, the figures in the cells can be represented by T_{rs} (r and $s = 0, 1, 2, 3, \cdots, 12$). The original source data of Table 2.22, which have been recently obtained at last, are included in the documents (Kodan 1958, 1959a, 1959b, 1961b). The source data are the results of the O-D surveys that were taken on the July 23, 1957 (first time), February 12, 1958 (second time), March 27, 1958 (third time), February 11, 1959 (fourth time), and March 14, 1961 (fifth time) with the

[6]The terminology "traffic volume" or "traffic volumes" presumes general mode of transportation, for example, vehicles, railway, ship, airplane, and so on. In the content of the traffic volume on the road, the traffic volume is equivalent to the "traffic vehicles."

Table 2.22 O.D. traffic volumes (truck) on the national first-grade national highways along Mei-Shin expressway by interchange section (unit: vehicle per day)

O(*i*)	*D*(*i*) 0 Nishinomiya and westward	1 Nishinomiya	2 Amagasaki	3 Toyonaka	4 Ibaraki	5 Kyoto	6 Ootsu	7 Ritto	8 Yokaichi	9 Hikone	10 Oogaki	11 Ichinomiya	12 Ichinomiya and eastward	Origin Total
0 Nishinomiya and westward	2	3	0	30	2	18	4	6	0	4	0	16	3	88
	0	0	60	684	15	55	2	9	0	3	4	14	11	857
1 Nishinomiya	4	646	0	4729	118	407	28	33	2	17	19	80	33	6116
	0	9840	1881	7510	440	863	36	55	2	13	23	31	48	20,742
2 Amagasaki	0	0	0	0	0	0	0	0	0	0	0	0	0	0
	16	1639	11	3	99	364	44	18	4	1	6	12	2	2219
3 Toyonaka	19	4470	0	152	1516	2021	150	163	25	105	51	391	161	9224
	709	7660	25	670	873	4844	416	282	23	129	90	483	285	16,489
4 Ibaraki	1	80	0	1380	218	255	20	11	2	3	2	3	13	1988
	27	417	102	584	2450	1057	56	116	1	2	2	6	4	4824
5 Kyoto	15	392	0	1751	265	595	1221	201	64	77	14	68	29	4692
	53	967	402	4554	1128	1695	1491	653	82	96	26	86	37	11,270
6 Ootsu	0	36	0	131	15	1245	4	23	26	37	8	14	1	1540
	3	63	19	234	53	1811	203	34	106	137	23	69	10	2765
7 Ritto	2	42	0	215	9	195	12	303	21	31	14	10	5	859
	15	90	22	509	130	639	49	783	96	113	56	52	15	2569
8 Yokaichi	0	6	0	26	3	71	15	10	0	60	11	8	1	211
	0	16	10	81	7	172	114	84	7	35	10	27	1	564
9 Hikone	3	31	0	124	2	62	25	38	48	183	29	57	1	603
	11	56	10	237	16	160	141	128	37	1437	117	297	49	2696
10 Oogaki	2	17	0	65	1	19	6	8	10	62	1748	591	20	2549
	9	42	16	178	7	66	27	44	17	123	4110	1802	71	6512
11 Ichinomiya	57	118	0	475	10	76	9	15	14	79	580	0	28	1461
	48	164	61	910	47	193	44	43	14	207	1704	0	0	3435
12 Ichinomiya and eastward	31	58	0	217	2	33	1	3	3	8	24	16	9	405

	89	139	14	674	36	94	5	8	4	63	35	0	0	1161
Destination	136	5899	0	9295	2161	4997	1495	814	215	666	2500	1254	304	29,736
Total	980	21,093	2633	16,828	5301	12,013	2628	2257	393	2359	6206	2879	533	76,103

Note: 1. Nishinomiya and westward includes the potential hinterland ranging over western Japan, e.g. Chugoku, Shikoku, and Kyushu Districts. Ichinomiya and eastward does Chubu, Kanto, Hokuriku and Tohoku Districts.

2. On the upper row, the results of the O-D survey taken on July 23, 1957, are shown. The lower row is the results of the O-D survey taken on the March 14th, 1961. Other O-D surveys were taken on: (1) February 12, 1958, (2) March 27, 1958, and (3) February 11, 1959. In the actual forecast of the traffic volumes in the O-D basis in the opening year of the expressway (1664), the average of the five surveys was used.

3. The totals are calculated by the author.

Source: Kodan (1961b), p. 11

traffic flows on the first-grade national highway that is parallel to the expressway. Besides these data, we have the O-D data based on the survey which was taken in 1951 by the Ministry of Construction (Kodan 1958). It was 14 years ago before the opening year of Mei-Shin Expressway. We just guess it was how far-reaching the proposed project!

To sort the traffic volumes on the first-grade national highway into the O-D basis, the origin and destination of each traffic volume were sorted in terms of the surrounding regions of interchanges (or spheres of influence in the sense that the interchange may be used as the one nearest the origin or destination if the traffic volume was diverted to the expressway although the traffics were mostly on the way). To multiply figures in each cell by the rates of diversion of traffic volumes from the existing roads to the expressway, the traffic volumes on Mei-Shin expressway were estimated on an O-D basis.

Taking a look at Table 2.22, it is realized that the O.D. traffic volumes from interchanges of (0) Nishinomiya and westward, (1) Nishinomiya (Kobe city), (2) Amagasaki, (3) Toyonaka (Osaka city), (4) Ibaraki, and (5) Kyoto, that is, from Kansai region to interchanges of (9) Hikone, (10) Ogaki, (11) Ichinomiya (Nagoya city), and (12) Ichinomiya and eastward, that is, Chukyo region and the reverse O-D traffic volumes were extremely few, notwithstanding that the two regions were each one of the four major industrial zones in Japan at that time. The total traffic volumes, $\sum_{r=0}^{12}\sum_{s=0}^{12}T_{rs}$, were 29,736 and 76,103 vehicles per day in 1957 and 1961 and, on the other hand, the total traffic volumes between the two regions, $\sum_{r=9}^{12}\sum_{s=0}^{5}T_{rs}+\sum_{r=0}^{5}\sum_{s=9}^{12}T_{rs}$, were 2492 and 4691 vehicles per day, respectively. They were just 6–8% of the total traffic volumes in both years. This was due to the actual situation that the first-grade national highway no.1, which was the main and important national highway connecting Kansai and Chukyo regions, was not going through Hikone, Sekigahara, and Ogaki but through the *Suzuka-toge* Pass, which is situated at the prefectural boundary between Shiga and Mie prefectures. More than half of the route of Mei-Shin expressway, which is the eastern section of the expressway to Chukyo region, was constructed far north to the first-grade national highway no.1 (Fig. 2.2). Along the eastern section of the expressway, the traffic volumes on the existing roads, which are parallel to the expressway, were very small at that time.[7]

It was a tough work to propose and plan such route of Mei-Shin expressway though it was a right proposal of the national project and the proposed route was perfect and ideal considering the current traffic volumes on the expressway which is now the main transportation artery from the view of the national land planning. Therefore, it was tried to complement the diverted traffic volumes with *induced or developed* traffic volumes without heavy dependence on the diverted traffic volumes

[7] Actually, as readers may see in Tables 2.22 and 2.24, Sekigahara, which is the most famous historic battlefield and located between Hikone and Ogaki, was not the survey station because there was nothing noticeable to affect the traffic volumes between Hikone and Ogaki.

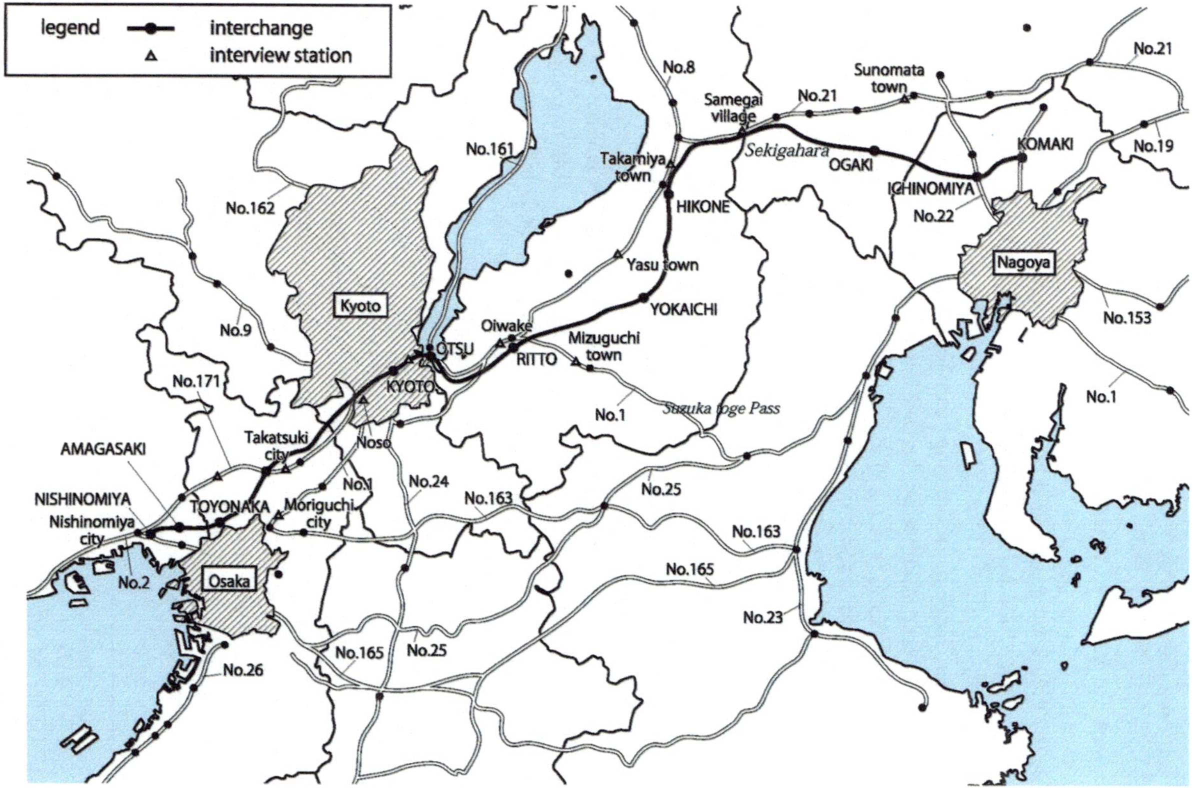

Fig. 2.2 Mei-Shin Expressway influence sphere block. Source: The Mei-Shin Expressway Construction Archives Editing Committee (1967c), pp. 63–64

when the social and private profitability was examined. The data referenced by such a trial was Kodan (1959a, 1959b). They were well-prepared data in its day.[8]

Other data for the analysis

By the way, we have had other data that may substitute Table 2.22 although we cannot have the data on the O-D basis as shown in Table 2.22.

Table 2.23 shows the estimated traffic volumes on each section between interchanges in the year 1964 in terms of the vehicle per day when Mei-Shin expressway would be opened to traffic.[9] Table 2.24 shows the estimated end traffic volumes (trip ends) at each interchange in the opening year. These data were to be calculated based on the estimated traffic volumes on the O-D basis in the year 1964.[10] The definition of trip ends is shown as T_r $(r = i, j, k)$ using Table 2.25, which is a so-called triangle table of the traffic distribution on the O-D basis presuming the traffic distribution is the diagonal line symmetry, that is, $T_{rs} = T_{sr}$ for all r and s such that $r, s = i, j, k$. T_i is the sum of figures in the cells of the row i (the first row), that is, $T_i = T_{ii} + T_{ij} + T_{ik}$; $T_{j,}$ is the sum of figures in the column j (representing an intermediate column) from the first cell to $(j - 1)$-th cell and figures in the row j (an intermediate row) from jth cell to the last cell, that is $T_j = T_{ij} + T_{jj} + T_{jk}$ and T_k is the sum of the figures in the cells of the column k (the last column), that is, $T_k = T_{ik} + T_{jk} + T_{kk}$. Readers may check the definition with Table 2.26.

Having the data of (1) trip ends at the opening year and (2) *current* O-D table (square or triangle table) based on the O-D survey, we were able to estimate the O.D. table (square or triangle) at the opening year (i.e., 1964) by using (3) Fratar Method. The O-D survey must have been conducted and the data of the O-D table above (2) must have been actual data at the point of time (day) when the survey was taken. The trip ends above (1) could be estimated statistically based on a numerical method using the economic data such as GRP, per capita income, industrial shipments of the prefectures where the origin and destination of the traffic volumes on the expressway may exist as well as the data calculated/estimated by the current O-D table. However, as it was difficult to estimate the traffic volumes on the O-D basis in the opening year (i.e., the figures in the cells of the O-D table except for trip ends), a technical calculation of the Fratar Method was adopted.

To examine social profitability (social benefits) and private profitability (toll revenues, redeemable years, etc.) of the expressway, the forecast of the traffic

---

[8]The original data included in Nihon Doro Kodan (1958, 1959a, 1959b, 1961a) have been difficult for the author to obtain so long time. We would express gratitude for Mr. Makoto Ueoka, Chief, Tokyo Head Office, NEXCO, West-Japan (Nishi-Nihon Expressway K.K) for his kind help with the collection of these data.

[9]The average of traffic volumes is the weighted average by the distance of sections between interchanges.

[10]Later on, we will see, the trip ends were firstly given and the traffic in the O-D basis was calculated using Fratar Method.

Table 2.23 Estimated traffic volume by type of vehicle and by section at the opening year (1964) (unit: vehicle per day)

Type of vehicle		Passenger car				Truck			
Section (interchange—interchange distance in km)		Ordinary	Small	Subtotal	Bus	Ordinary	small	Subtotal	Total
Nishinomiya–Amagasaki (7.0)		897	658	1555	394	4340	1246	5586	7535
Amagasaki–Toyonaka (4.8)		892	673	1565	363	5379	1445	6824	8752
Toyonaka–Ibaraki (12.8)		1127	1796	2923	677	10,740	2440	13,180	16,780
Ibaraki–Kyoto (23.9)		966	1449	2415	677	10,151	2121	12,272	15,364
Kyoto–Ootsu (13.3)		535	673	1208	457	7081	884	7965	9630
Ootsu–Ritto (16.3)		687	793	1480	583	7070	938	8008	10,071
Ritto–Yokaichi (23.7)		640	731	1371	541	6367	802	7169	9081
Yokaichi–Hikone (21.3)		633	700	1333	501	6242	724	6966	8800
Hikone–Sekigahara (23.9)		452	693	1145	360	5713	695	6408	7913
Sekigahara–Oogaki (14.5)		460	698	1158	380	5900	724	6624	8162
Oogaki–Ichinomiya (19.9)		389	596	985	284	6111	1127	7238	8507
Ichinomiya–Komaki (8.3)		17	27	44	13	274	51	325	382
Average over the whole line (the total distance is 189.7 km)		637	836	1473	467	6718	1102	7820	9760
Break–down	Traffic volumes diverted from the ordinary road	310	836	1146	103	6015	1102	7117	8366
	Traffic volumes diverted from the railway	327	0	327	364	703	0	703	1394

Note 1: figures under the hyphens are the distance between the interchanges in kilometer.
Note 2: the average over the whole line is the weighted one with distance between the interchanges. Due to the rounding, calculation errors exist.
Source: The Mei-Shin Expressway' Construction Archives Editing Committee (1967c, p. 169) and (1967e, p. 1553)

Table 2.24 Estimated end traffic volumes by interchange and type of vehicle at the opening year (1964). Unit: vehicle per day

Zone number	Type of vehicle / Zone name	Passenger car	Small type of car	Bus	Ordinary truck	Small type of truck	Other	Total
0	Beyond Nishinomiya	27	92	33	2803	460	50	3465
1	Nishinomiya	6653	20,818	219	16,090	32,689	1432	77,901
2	Amagasaki	810	2255	47	4682	5175	262	13,231
3	Toyonaka	3304	10,083	461	19,635	21,623	1980	57,086
4	Ibaraki	907	2908	126	6909	6295	367	17,512
5	Kyoto	1258	4469	616	10,298	14,494	1781	32,916
6	Ootsu	431	1000	586	1661	2486	383	6547
7	Ritto	244	548	437	2069	2916	72	6286
8	Yokaichi	23	177	56	751	833	60	1900
9	Hikone	29	81	33	1806	792	158	2899
10	Oogaki	527	2014	784	3702	5219	101	12,347
11	Ichinomiya	252	344	61	3873	2265	183	6978
12	beyond Ichinomiya	137	80	53	2533	437	61	3301
Total		14,602	44,869	3512	76,812	95,684	6890	242,369

Note: Total is calculated by the author
Source: The Mei-Shin Expressway Construction Archives Editing Committee (1967c, p. 165)

Table 2.25 Traffic distribution in O-D basis: Triangle O-D table

i	j	k	Total
T_{ii}	T_{ij}	T_{ik}	T_i
	T_{jj}	T_{ik}	T_j
		T_{ik}	T_k
			$\sum_{r\in\{i,j,k\}} T_r$

Source: The Mei-Shin expressway construction archives editing committee (1967c), p. 166

volume on the O-D basis in the opening year is essential. Namely, knowing the traffic volume (vehicles) that might have used the expressway (it was not yet opened for traffic) in the past (e.g., Table 2.22 as for truck) and data about the national and regional economic situation, figures which ought to be filled in all the cells with the framework of Table 2.22, must be forecasted with respect to the opening year (1964). Theoretically speaking, the tables in 1965, 1966, … were necessary for the analysis of the stream of benefits and revenues. Once the table in 1964 was known, the analysis can be developed without difficulty.

[11] The application of the Fratar Method is same as for a triangle O-D table as far as diagonal symmetry is presumed, that is, $T_{rs} = T_{sr}$ $(r,\ s = i, j, k, n)$.

Table 2.26 Diverted traffic volumes from railway in the O-D basis to Mei-Shin expressway in the opening year (all types of vehicle) (unit: vehicle per day)

Interchange	Nishinomiya	Amagasaki	Toyonaka	Ibaraki	Kyoto	Ootsu	Ritto	Yokaichi	Hikone	Sekigahara	Oogaki	Ichinomiya	trip ends
Nishinomiya		90	340	7	305	20	32	7	110	0	48	200	1159
Amagasaki			1	0	8	3	9	4	25	0	21	63	224
Toyonaka				0	39	7	75	22	301	0	144	300	1229
Ibaraki					16	1	5	2	3	0	3	9	46
Kyoto						0	0	0	0	0	0	0	368
Ootsu							1	9	60	0	82	176	359
Ritto								1	9	0	3	26	161
Yokaichi									1	0	3	11	60
Hikone										0	7	73	589
Sekigahara											4	71	75
Oogaki												51	366
Ichinomiya													980
Total													5616

Source: The Mei-Shin expressway construction archives editing committee (1967d), p. 180

Table 2.27 Traffic distribution in the origin-destination basis: Square O.D. table

D	i	j	k	n	Total
O					
i	T_{ii}	T_{ij}	T_{ik}	T_{in}	T_i
j	T_{ji}	T_{jj}	T_{jk}	T_{jn}	T_j
k	T_{ki}	T_{kj}	T_{kk}	T_{kn}	T_k
n	T_{ni}	T_{nj}	T_{nk}	T_{nn}	T_n
Total	T_i'	T_j'	T_k'	T_n'	$\sum_{r\in\{i,j,k,n\}} T_r$

Note: (1) The triangular table is prevailing, which can be made presuming the diagonal line symmetry, namely, $T_{rs} = T_{sr}$ $(r, s = i, j, k, n)$, as far as no special problems would be raised. However, theoretically, it is much better for us to grasp things with the square table
(2) The column heads are destination zone indices and the row heads are origin zone indices.
(3) Of course, the following holds: $\sum_{s\in\{i,j,k,n\}} T_r = \sum_{s\in\{i,j,k,n\}} T_s'$

Using the Fratar Method, the forecast of the traffic distribution on the origin and destination basis (e.g., the traffic distribution T_{rs}, $(r,\ s = i,\ j,\ k,\ n)$ in Table 2.27, which is a square O-D table)[11] in the target year, that is, in the opening year of the expressway (1964) was calculated so that: (1) the calculated trip ends (e.g., $\sum_{r\in\{i,j,k,n\}} T_{rs}$ $(s = i, j, k, n)$ in Table 2.27) are eventually equated with the statistically forecasted (estimated) trip ends (e.g., T_r, T_s' $(r, s = i, j, k, n)$ in Table 2.27) in the target year; and (2) a kind of the information loss due to the difference between (1) the forecasted traffic distribution on the O-D basis in the target year and (2) the actual traffic distribution observed by the O-D survey, for examplee.g., in 1961 is to be minimized.

In the sense above, the actual traffic distribution on the O-D basis (e.g., Table 2.22 as for truck) as well as the actual trip ends (the row sums and column sums in Table 2.22) and the estimated trip ends (Table 2.24) were critically important for the forecast of the traffic distribution on the O-D basis in the target year. According to Table 2.22, within 3.75 years, the total trip ends of the trucks had increased from 29,736 to 76, 103 vehicles per day, and its growth rate was around 28.5% per year.

According to Table 2.24, the forecasted total trip ends of the truck in 1964 is 172,496 vehicles per day. Roughly speaking, the estimated growth rate within 4 years after the last O-D traffic volume survey was taken was 31.4%. This was a fairly high growth rate although more than half the forecasted trip ends were induced and developed traffic volumes as well as the forecasted diverted traffic volumes from the railway (Table 2.23 and Table 2.26). On that day, the economy had rapidly grown and later on, it was realized that some of the forecasted traffic vehicles on the

[11]The application of the Fratar Method is same as for a triangle O-D table as far as diagonal symmetry is presumed, that is, $T_{rs} = T_{sr}$ $(r,\ s = i,\ j,\ k,\ n)$.

expressway were still underestimated although others were overestimated due to some reasons.

In Chap. 7, a more comprehensive appraisal of the public investment is developed. In terms of the O-D table in the sense above, the forecast of trip ends (e.g., T_r and T'_s ($r, s = i, j, k, n$) in Table 2.27) and traffic distribution in the O-D basis (e.g., T_{rs} ($r, s = i, j, k, n$) Table 2.27) are *simultaneously* and *endogenously* determined. This is critically different from the Fratar Method since it presumes that the amount of trip ends (e.g., T_r and T'_s ($r, s = i, j, k, n$) in Table 2.27) are predetermined and exogenously given before the application of the method. More technically speaking, the Fratar Method is an essential methodology in traffic engineering, and the O-D table obtained via the Fratar Method is a basic material for the traffic assignment to the transportation network links that is the main topic in the field of transportation engineering. Presuming that the traffic distribution of the O-D table is exogenously predetermined and, therefore, the data of the table are fixed, the traffic assignment to the transportation network links is done by making an optimal route search in minimization of the travel time with each pair of origin and destination. On the other hand, in the comprehensive analysis developed in Chap. 7, the growth of the regional economy (production and investment which generate trip ends at the origin and destination as derivative demand for the transportation services), optimal route search on the transportation network, traffic volumes on the transportation network links (subject to the capacity of links, which can be improved by the public investments over time, and the optimal route search in the short run), and the traffic distribution of the O-D table (the results of the endogenous trade patterns between the regions depending on, e.g., accessibility to the network, etc.)[12] are simultaneously and endogenously solved and determined. In terms of the terminologies of the traffic engineering, the trip ends, the traffic distribution of the O-D table, optimal route research, assignment of the traffic distribution to the transportation network links, the necessity of public investments for the improvement in the transportation network, and so on are all endogenously and optimally determined. However, it may be helpful for readers to briefly survey here the conventional transportation engineering approach to understand the essence of the innovative programming model developed in Chap. 7.

The explanation will be continued with the following topics:

1. O.D. survey method;
2. Method for the estimation of generated traffic volumes (e.g., trip ends T_r, T_r' ($r = i, j, k, n$) in Table 2.27), which become a kind of the total controls in the application of the Fratar Method;
3. Method for the estimation of the traffic distribution on the O-D basis (e.g., T_{rs} ($r, s = i, j, k, n$) in Table 2.27) in the future. It is the Fratar method that forecasts the traffic distribution of the O-D table in the future based on the traffic distribution of the current O-D table (usually it is based on a survey) and estimated trip

[12] As readers will see later on, the model developed in Chap. 7 has no explicit idea of "O-D table." It is eventually calculated and constructed over the time horizon based on results of the simulation.

ends (generated trips at the origin and attracted trips at the destination) in the future;

4. Method for the estimation of the diverted traffic volumes from existing road to the expressway, namely, how much of the current traffic distribution on the O-D basis (e.g., T_{rs} ($r, s = i, j, k, n$) in Table 2.27) will be diverted to the expressway. Or, more generally, the method for traffic assignment on the transportation network, the part of which is the expressway.

Method and Practice of O.D. Survey

Roadside Interview Method

To analyze the private and social profitability of Mei-Shin expressway, it was necessary to estimate/forecast the traffic volumes (i.e., direct users) on the expressway in the opening year. The estimation of the economic benefits and the toll revenues that are most important basic data for the analysis, they must be dependent on the minutes of estimated data of the traffic vehicles interchange by interchange. Namely, how many vehicles get on which interchange and come off from which interchange is important basic data, which must be forecasted/estimated based on the data observable (objectively).

The primary aim of the O-D survey is to know whether the capacity of existing roads is enough to meet the traffic volumes (users) on the road spot by spot. The results of the O-D surveys can be utilized to forecast/estimate the traffic volumes which may be diverted from the existing roads to Mei-Shin expressway on the O-D basis. For example, if the current route of the road which is used by the traffic between the origin region i and the destination region j is (partially) parallel to the expressway or competitive against the expressway in the sense that travel time with the current route can be much decreased by using the expressway, it is natural to presume that some of them are diverted to the expressway as direct users who get on such and such interchange and come off such and such interchange.

Mei-Shin expressway was just a road and addition of route to the existing transportation network although its capacity was far higher than the existing first-grade national highways. So, the interview stations (survey points), where the method of roadside interview was applied to the drivers of vehicles, of the O-D survey, which were taken with the purpose of project evaluation of Mei-Shin expressway, were not so many (Fig. 2.2).

The interview stations were 11 points on the existing roads which were taken parallel or competitive against the Mei-Shin expressway (the length is 189.7 km) (Table 2.28).

Figure 2.3 explains the character of cordon stations. The thick line symbolizes the route of the proposed expressway. Zones i and j symbolize regions along the expressway. Both ends are cordon stations (k and n are indices of the interview stations) in the sense that the traffic vehicle having the origin in the influence spheres

Table 2.28 National highway route no. 1 and interview station of the O-D survey

Grade of national highway	Route no.	Prefecture	Interview station
Second	21	Gifu	Sunomata town
Second	21	Shiga	Samegai village
Second	8	Shiga	Takamiya town
Second	8	Shiga	Yasu town
First	1	Shiga	Mizuguchi town
First	1	Shiga	Oiwake town
First	1	Kyoto	Noso village
First	1	Osaka	Moriguchi city
Second	171	Osaka	Takatsuki city
Second	171	Hyogo	Mino city
First	2	Hyogo	Nishinomiya city

Source: The Mei-Shin Expressway Construction Archives Editing Committee (1967c), p. 162
Note: interview stations are plotted on Fig. 2.2

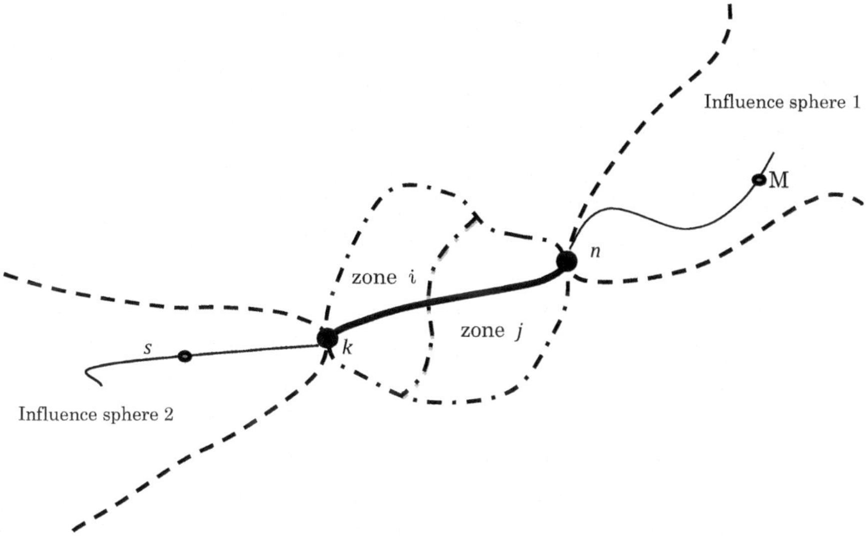

Fig. 2.3 Cordon station
Note: (1) *i*, *j*: inner zone indices where the proposed Expressway goes through
(2) *k*, *n*: indices for the cordon station, through which the traffic vehicle having the origin in the influence sphere (e.g., *S* or *M*) may get on the expressway wherever the destination is or the traffic vehicle on the expressway may come off to go to the destination in the influence sphere wherever the origin is
Source: Drawn by the author making reference to the figure in Sasaki and Kobayashi (1962), p. 67

1 (e.g., *M*) and 2 (e.g., S) may get on the expressway through interchange *n* and *k* as far as the destination of the traffic volume is in zone *i* or zone *j* or in the influence sphere 2 and 1, respectively.

For example, the traffic vehicle from Tokyo, Shizuoka, and so on to Osaka, Hiroshima, etc. may get on Mei-Shin expressway through Ichinomiya interchange, of which cordon station on the national highway was Sunomata town, and it may get off the expressway through Nishinomiya, of which cordon station on the national highway was Nishinomiya city. In the same manner, the traffic vehicle from Fukuoka, Hiroshima, etc. to Nagoya, Shizuoka, Tokyo, etc. may get on the expressway through Nishinomiya interchange and may get off the expressway at Ichinomiya interchange.

The interview survey was done with around 5000 vehicles for 24 hours at each of 11 survey stations (it was called—*roadside interview*). The following survey crews were assigned to each station (Sasaki and Kobayashi 1962, p. 48):

(a) Responsible person: 1 person.
(b) Traffic recorder: 2 persons.
(c) Interviewer: 6 persons.
(d) Flagman (Guiding person): 1–2 persons.
(e) Person directing traffic: 1–2 persons.

The interviewer first questioned the interviewee about the origin and destination and recorded the answer on the questionnaire (This was the most important matter).

With other items, the interviewer encircled the number corresponding to the answer by the interviewee. The interview was done at once with all the interview stations above. To avoid a duplicate count that the same vehicle is made to stop twice or more at different survey stations, *Finished Card*, a kind of pass, was issued.

As it was considered that one-time survey was insufficient, the same survey was done five times: on July 23, 1957; February 12, 1958; March 27, 1958; February 11, 1959; and March 14, 1961. The average of the five survey results was utilized for the calculation/estimation of the current traffic volumes on the O-D basis, that is, data of T_{rs} (r,$s = i, j, k, n$) in Table 2.27 (see The Mei-Shin Expressway Construction Archives Editing Committee 1967c, pp. 159–165).

Owner Interview Method

In addition to the roadside interview, a survey based on the *owner interview* method was done, too (Nagoya Area Owner Interview O.D. Survey Liaison Committee 1961; Kei-Han-Shin Area Owner Interview O.D. Survey Liaison Committee 1961). It is suitable for the estimation of traffic volumes on the O-D basis on the road where a fairly large flow of traffic vehicles is expected, for example, Mei-Shin expressway which was the first full-fledged intercity expressway in Japan in 1960s. Basically, there are two types of O-D surveys: an intra-regional survey and a survey outside the region. The roadside survey has both aspects of the survey. Namely, the roadside survey at interview stations on the roads that are parallel and competitive against the expressway are a sort of intraregional survey on the regions alongside the expressway but for the survey at cordon stations, in which the interviews are mostly categorized as a sort of the survey outside the region. The owner interview method is suitable for the intraregional survey, especially in a large city.

The objective of the owner interview is to investigate the vehicle trip within a day made by the vehicle owner living in the region. It starts with making sampling sets of vehicle owners. The necessary data for the sampling were available in the government agency in charge of the registration of vehicles and/or the agency in charge of the vehicle-related taxation. Sampling cards were prepared and the following items were filled in a sampling card with each interviewee (Sasaki and Kobayashi 1962, p. 26):

1. full name of the vehicle owner,
2. address of the vehicle owner,
3. business type of the vehicle owner (company),
4. registered number (vehicle identification number),
5. type of vehicle, manufacturing year,
6. loading capacity, deadweight, and the others.

The sampling rate of the intra-regional survey was given as follows:

	Sampling rate	
Population of the region (person)	Private passenger vehicle	Truck and taxi
50,000 or less	1/5	1/3
50,000–150,000	1/8	1/4
150,000–300,000	1/10	1/5
300,000–500,000	1/15	1/8
500,000–1000,000	1/20	1/10
1000,000 and over	1/25	1/13

Source: Sasaki and Kobayashi (1962), p. 26

On the other hand, the sampling rate adopted by The Chukyo Area Owner Interview O.D. Survey that was done by Chukyo Region Owners Interview O.D. Survey Liaison Council was 1/10 with the vehicle except for chauffeur-driven hired car and taxi; it was 1/50 with chauffeur-driven hired car and taxi (for minutes, see Sasaki and Kobayashi 1962, pp. 3–62, National Academy of Science 1956).

We have explained two types of the O-D survey which were actually applied to the collection of necessary data for the appraisal of Mei-Shin expressway. Furthermore, the survey was done to calculate/estimate the traffic volumes diverted from the railway on the O-D basis (Table 2.27).

Estimation of the Traffic Volumes on the Generation Basis

Table 2.29 is a triangular O-D table. It presumes $T_{rs} = T_{sr}$ for all $r, s = i, j, k, n$ with a square O-D table like Table 2.27. The traffic volumes in the generation basis, T_r $(r = i, j, k, n)$, are defined as follows:

Table 2.29 Traffic distribution in the origin–destination basis: Triangle O.D. table

Zones in the region alongside of the expressway and/or national highways		Zones outside the region (cordon stations)		
i	j	k	n	Trip ends
T_{ii}	T_{ij}	T_{ik}	T_{in}	T_i
	T_{jj}	T_{jk}	T_{jn}	T_j
		T_{kk}	T_{kn}	T_k
			T_{nn}	T_n
				$\sum_{s\in\{i,j,k,n\}} T_r$

$$T_i = \sum_{r\in\{i,j,k,n\}} T_{ir},$$

$$T_j = \sum_{r\in\{i,j\}} T_{rj} + \sum_{s\in\{k,n\}} T_{js},$$

$$T_k = \sum_{r\in\{i,j,k\}} T_{rk} + \sum_{s\in\{n\}} T_{sn},$$

$$T_n = \sum_{r\in\{i,j,k,n\}} T_{rn}.$$

It is easier to estimate the trip ends than T_{rs} $(r, s = i, j, k, n)$. That was the point.

The Economic Research Office, The Japan Highway Public Corporation, had adopted the following equation to estimate the trip ends in the generation basis (generated traffic volumes);

$$T_i = 12,140.42x_{1i} + 8.572x_{2i} - 244,827.242$$

in which:

T_i: generated vehicle trip volume in zone i (whole vehicle total),

x_{1i}: the number of households in zone i (unit: 1000 houses), and

x_{2i}: industrial shipment in zone i (unit: one million JPY).

The coefficients (and the constant) of the equation were estimated by the multiple regression analysis. Used data were obtained by the owner interview survey taken in Kei-Han-Shin (the area of Kyoto city, Osaka city, and Kobe city) and official statistics such as industrial statistics. The coefficient of correlation was 0.9975 (the determinant coefficient was 0.9950) and the fitting precision was fairly good. It is unbelievable that the constant was negative as it was expected that the trip ends would grow with a much higher growth rate than the households and industrial shipments, which reflected the car-oriented society just started. On a day of the year in 1965 in Osaka Prefecture, the generated end trips were 19,974,746 vehicles (with the whole vehicles) and the estimated one with the equation was 17,263,108 vehicles. With the country where the car-oriented society is matured, for example,

United States, such a linear equation might be well fit with the estimation of the generated trip ends. As for Japan at that time, the following nonlinear equation (linear in logarithms) might fit better:

$$T_i = a_0 x_{1i}^{a_1} x_{2i}^{a_2} \cdots x_{ni}^{a_n}.$$

Forecast of the Traffic Distribution on O-D Basis in the Target Year

Estimation of the Current Traffic Distribution on O-D Basis

It is ideal that the current traffic distribution on the O-D basis (e.g., T_{rs} (r, $s = i, j, k, n$) in Table 2.27) as well as the trip ends have been obtained with the square or triangle table by the O-D survey with the roadside interview method and the owner interview method (here, "current" means the date when the survey was taken). In the case in which some of the traffic distribution and/or the trip ends are not obtained, they must be estimated with the quantitative method derived by the statistical/ econometric analysis. The following gravity model was used for the estimation of the traffic distribution:

$$T_{ij} = T_i \cdot T_j \frac{k}{D_{ij}^n},$$

in which:

T_{ij}: traffic volumes (in vehicle) that have the origin in zone i and the destination in zone j;

T_i: traffic volumes having the origin in zone i (generated traffic volumes in zone i);

T_j: traffic volumes having the destination in zone j (attracted traffic volumes in zone j);

k: constant parameter (Table 2.30);

D_{ij}: distance (in kilometer)[13] between zones i and j; and

n : power of D_{ij} (Table 2.30).

[13]Precisely speaking, zone has an area with the space of two dimensions. A zone node is prespecified with a certain point (e.g., the center of gravity) in the space considering the distribution of population and economic activities over the space. The distance between two zones is defined with the distance (e.g., minimum distance with the road network and in the case in which this distance is used, the zone node is usually a link node (a connection point of different roads) of the network) between the two zone nodes. The zone node has another meaning in the sense that the generated and attracted traffic volumes are all get on and come off the road network at the zone node, respectively.

Table 2.30 Estimated parameters of gravity model

Vehicle type	Estimated k	Estimated n
All types of vehicles	$14{,}539 \times 10^{-10}$	1.6258
Passenger car	$159{,}926 \times 10^{-10}$	1.5490
Small truck	$558{,}625 \times 10^{-10}$	1.4319
Large truck	$52{,}560 \times 10^{-10}$	1.1607

Source: Sasaki and Kobayashi (1962), p. 72

The equation assumes that the traffic distribution between zones i and j is (1) proportional to the product of the generated traffic volumes in zone i and the attracted traffic volumes in zone j and (2) inversely proportional to the distance between zones i and j to the power of n. The parameters k and n used for the estimation are given by vehicle type in Table 2.30.

Forecast of the Traffic Distribution in the O-D Basis by the Fratar Method

To apply the Fratar Method, which is a kind of iterative process of calculation, to the forecast of the future (a target year) traffic distribution, the followings are prerequisites:

1. The square table of the current (the date on which the O-D survey was taken, or simply the date when the table was obtained based on the survey and the complementary numerical estimation) traffic distribution of vehicles in the O-D basis is known, which means the trip ends are known, too;
2. The future generated and attracted trip ends of vehicles are given by, for example, the numerical estimation/forecast method.

In case the traffic distribution is given as a triangle table, it is easy to extend it to the square one using, for example, the numerical method that might be used to complement the missing data in the O-D survey results, presuming diagonal line symmetry, etc.

[Fratar Method]

Being given the current O-D table in the following $m \times m$ matrix (m is the number of zones):

$$(T_{ij}),$$

in which:

T_{ij} is the number of the current traffic vehicles traveling from region i to region j, and being given the future generated and attracted trip ends, respectively, in the following m-dimension vectors:

$$\left(\widetilde{T}_i\right), \text{and } \left(\widetilde{T}_j\right),$$

in which $\widetilde{T}_i$ is the future generated trip ends in zone i and $\widetilde{T}_j$ is the future attracted trip ends in region j, the procedure of the Fratar Method at iteration n ($n = 0, 1, 2, 3, \cdots$) is given as follows:

(n.0) At the iteration n, given the $(n - 1)^{\text{th}}$ approximated O-D table in the following $m \times m$ matrix:

$$\left(\widetilde{T}_{ij}^{(n-1)}\right),$$

in which $\widetilde{T}_{ij}^{(n-1)}$ is the (i,j) element of the matrix, $\left(\widetilde{T}_{ij}^{(n-1)}\right)$, then

(n.1) firstly, the nth *tentative* O-D tables extended by the growth rate of the future *generated* trip ends and the future *attracted* trip ends against the generated trip ends and the attractive trip ends of the $(n - 1)$th approximated O-D table are, respectively, calculated as follows:

$$\widehat{T}_{ij}^{n} = \widetilde{T}_{ij}^{(n-1)} * g_i^n \quad (\mathrm{i,j} = 1, 2, \cdots, \mathrm{m});$$

and

$$\check{T}_{ij}^{n} = \widetilde{T}_{ij}^{(n-1)} * a_j^n \quad (i, j = 1, 2, \cdots, m),$$

in which:

$\widehat{T}_{ij}^{n}$ is the (i,j)-element of the nth tentative O-D table extended by the growth rate of *generated* trip ends, g_i^n;

$\check{T}_{ij}^{n}$ is the (i,j)-element of the nth tentative O-D table extended by the growth rate of *attracted* trip ends, a_j^n;

$$g_i^n = \frac{\widetilde{T}_i}{\sum_{\mathrm{s}=1}^{\mathrm{m}} \widetilde{T}_{is}^{(n-1)}} \quad (\mathrm{i} = 1, 2, \cdots, \mathrm{m});$$

and

$$a_j^n = \frac{\widetilde{T}_j}{\sum_{r=1}^{m} \widetilde{T}_{rj}^{(n-1)}} \quad (j = 1, 2, \cdots, m).$$

(n.2) Secondly, the difference rate matrix ($m \times m$) at iteration n, $\left(R_{ij}^{n}\right)$, is calculated as follows:

$$R_{ij}^{n} = g_{i}^{n} \times a_{j}^{n} \times \frac{(L_i + L_j)}{2} \quad (i, j = 1, 2, \cdots, m),$$

in which:

$$L_i = \frac{\sum_{s=1}^{m} \widetilde{T}_{is}^{(n-1)}}{\sum_{s=1}^{m} \widehat{T}_{is}^{n}} \quad (i = 1, 2, \cdots, m),$$

and

$$L_j = \frac{\sum_{r=1}^{m} \widetilde{T}_{rj}^{(n-1)}}{\sum_{r=1}^{m} \check{T}_{rj}^{n}} \quad (j = 1, 2, \cdots, m).$$

(n.3) Thirdly, the nth approximated O-D table, $\left(\widetilde{T}_{ij}^{n}\right)$, is calculated as follows:

$$\widetilde{T}_{ij}^{n} = \widetilde{T}_{ij}^{n-1} \times R_{ij}^{n} \quad (i, j = 1, 2, \cdots, m).$$

The forecasted future O-D table is obtained through the following iteration process:

(Step 0) Start with $n = 0$. The initial approximated O-D table, $\left(\widetilde{T}_{ij}^{0}\right)$, is equated to the current O-D table.[14]

(Step 1) Increase n by 1 (one) and calculate the nth approximated O-D table, $\left(\widetilde{T}_{ij}^{n}\right)$, following the above procedure, (n.0), (n.1), (n.2), and (n.3).

(Step 2) $n^* = n$. If the difference between the $(n-1)$th approximated O-D table, $\left(\widetilde{T}_{ij}^{n-1}\right)$, and the nth approximated O-D table, $\left(\widetilde{T}_{ij}^{n}\right)$, becomes negligibly small or, equivalently, all the element of the matrix, $\left(R_{ij}^{n}\right)$, are almost 1 (one), then go to Step 3. Otherwise, go back to Step 1.

(Step 3) Stop the iteration process. $\left(\widetilde{T}_{ij}^{n^*}\right)$ gives an approximation to the forecasted future O-D table, $\left(\widetilde{T}_{ij}\right)$.

[14] As mentioned in the note of Table 2.22, the average of the results of the O-D survey which was taken five times were used as the current O-D table in the preparation of documents submitted for World Bank.

By the Fratar method, the future trip ends at the generation and attraction basis is exactly equated with the forecasted trip ends exogenously given by the estimation based on, for example, the statistical regression model. The traffic distribution pattern (i.e., the rate of T_{ij} to T_i and/or T_j) is kept close to the current distribution pattern as much as possible. As far as the forecast by the exogenous estimation of the trip ends reflect changes in social and economic conditions, it can be said that the trip ends of the forecasted O-D table reflect the social and economic conditions to some degree. However, this does not necessarily mean that the traffic distribution reflects the changes in the social and economic conditions, especially impacts by, for example, the expressway construction which generates economic benefits, i.e., saving in travel time, decrease in cargo damages, industrial development alongside the expressway, etc. Practically, it was a powerful engineering technology to forecast the future traffic distribution considering that the project of Mei-Shin expressway is the first national big project of high-standard expressway in Japan, and we have no data which we could refer to in the forecast based on other numerical methods if any.

Estimation of the Allocated Traffic Vehicles

The next concern was how much traffic vehicles would use the Mei-Shin expressway. The forecasted future O-D table is the population of traffic vehicles, some of which would possibly be diverted to Mei-Shin expressway as direct users at the opening year (targeted year). The estimation of the allocated traffic vehicles to Mei-Shin expressway was done through the diversion rate method. The diversion rate is defined as the percentage of the diverted vehicles to Mei-Shin expressway, T_{ij}^E, to the population of traffic distribution $\widetilde{T}_{ij}$. The rate is to be calculated considering changes in the transportation network which consists of highway, expressway, railway, etc. and their impacts on the traffic distribution on the O-D basis. However, the inner zones in Table 2.22 and, therefore, the inner zones in the forecasted O-D table as the population of the traffic distribution are alongside Mei-Shin expressway and each internal zone corresponds to the interchange of Mei-Shin expressway, through which traffic vehicles generated and attracted in the zone get on and come off, respectively. So, the estimation of the allocation of traffic vehicles to Mei-Shin expressway is simple and directly done by multiplying the future forecasted O-D table by the diversion rate.

The studies on the diversion rate of traffic volumes or the allocation problem of traffic volume to the newly constructed expressway had been done intensively for a while in Japan. However, we will not refer to it anymore.

Estimated Traffic Volumes on Mei-Shin Expressway at the Opening Year

Estimated Traffic Volumes by Vehicle Type and Section of Interchange

Table 2.31 shows the estimated traffic vehicles on Mei-Shin expressway in 1964 in terms of vehicles per day. Table 2.22 had been obtained as the current traffic vehicles via the O-D survey and in the case in which some of T_{ij}, etc. were blank, they were made up with the estimated data given by the numerical method. Table 2.24 was the estimated trip ends in the year 1964 via the numerical method. As shown in Tables 2.23 and 2.26, the diverted traffic volumes from the existing roads as well as railway to the expressway in 1964 were estimated. This means that the traffic distribution on the O-D basis in 1964 was certainly forecasted by Fratar Method.

Actual Traffic Vehicles of Mei-Shin Expressway by Section of Interchange

Table 2.32 is an interesting data that show the actual traffic volumes on Mei-Shin Expressway with the period from July 1, 1965, to December 31, 1965.

The total actual inflows and outflows of traffic vehicles between Nishinomiya and Ritto interchanges to the planned one was 192%. On the other hand, the rate between Yokaichi and Ichinomiya (the east section of the expressway) was 76%. The average planned inflows and outflows between Nishinomiya and Kyoto-Higashi was 4200 vehicles per day and that between Yokaichi and Ichinomiya was 2900 vehicles per day. This means that the forecasted traffic vehicles between Nishinomiya and Ritto was far underestimated and that between Yokaichi and Ihcinomiya interchanges were overestimated. Since the year of the actual data was just 1 year or so later since the expressway was opened to traffic, it could be considered that the induced and developed traffic vehicles alongside the expressway between Yokaichi and Ichinomiya was not so large and the diversion from the first-grade national highway no.1, which was competitive against the expressway, was not so big at the initial phase as it might be expected.

Closing Comments

We have quickly reviewed the method and data used for the estimation of traffic volumes which ought to be prerequisite and complementary for the appraisal of Mei-Shin Expressway in terms of the economic effects. According to the information by the Asian Development Bank, facing huge varieties of potential developmental projects, what has been critically deficient is not the fund but 'the qualified proposal that ought to be submitted by the departments and agencies in charge of the

Table 2.31 Estimated traffic volume on Mei-Shin expressway by vehicle type and by section of interchange at the opening year (1964) (unit: vehicle/per day)

	Section												
Vehicle Type	Nishinomiya–Amagasaki	Amagasaki–Toyonaka	Toyonaka–Ibaraki	Ibaraki–Kyoto-Minami	Kyoto-Minami–Kyoto-Higashi	Kyoto-Higashi–Ritto	Ritto–Yokaichi	Yokaichi–Hikone	Hikone–Sekigahara	Sekigahara–Oogaki	Oogaki–Ichinomiya	Ichinomiya–Komaki	Average traffic volume through the whole length
Passenger car	897	892	1127	966	535	687	640	633	452	460	389	17	637
Small passenger car	658	673	1796	1449	673	793	731	700	693	698	597	27	836
Bus	394	363	677	677	457	583	541	501	360	380	284	13	467
Truck	4340	5379	10,740	10,151	7081	7070	6367	6242	5713	5900	6111	274	6718
Small Truck	1246	1445	2440	2121	884	938	802	724	695	724	1127	51	1102
Total	7535	8752	16,780	15,364	9630	10,071	9081	8800	7913	8162	8508	382	9760

Source: The Mei-Shin Expressway' Construction Archives Editing Committee (1967e), p. 1553

Table 2.32 Inflow and outflow of traffic vehicles on Mei-Shin expressway by interchange (Unit: vehicle)

Period	Days	Name of interchange	Nishinomiya	Amagasaki	Toyonaka	Ibaraki	Kyoto-Minami	Kyoto-Higashi	Ootsu	Ritto	Yokaichi	Hikone	Sekigahara	Oogaki	Ichinoomiya	Komaki	Total
July 1st to Dec 31st, 1965	184	Accumalted total	1,684,499	582,635	2,333,899	1,525,408	2,531,161	776,538	1,259,311	1,212,575	102,392	305,055	305,819	399,830	947,577	224,347	14,190,996
		Average per day (A)	9155	3166	12,684	8290	13,756	4220	6844	6590	556	1658	1662	2173	5150	1219	77,123
		Planned inflow and outflow (B)	8029	1516	11,799	2301	6416	1429	769	1375	702	1523	273	3302	8882	416	48,732
		A/B%	114.0	208.8	107.5	360.3	214.4	295.3	890.0	479.3	79.2	108.9	608.8	65.8	58.0	293.0	158.3

Source: The Mei-Shin Expressway' Construction Archives Editing Committee (1967c), p. 1487 public projects based on a well-designed feasibility study using an appropriate method and data. When one comes to be responsible for the planning, research, or implementation of a large-scale project of expressway construction, the reason why the state of things would not make steady progress is that the economic-oriented planners could not treat the traffic volume estimation or something like; on the other hand, with the engineering-oriented planners, the estimation of the economic effects or something like would be a tough work. Graduates in economics may well dispose of the estimation of economic effects one way or another, but they cannot well prepare for the O.D. survey, even if they have some basic knowledge of econometrics or statistics.

For graduates in economics, the estimation of the generated and attracted traffic volume, the distribution of traffic volume, and the allocation of traffic volumes would not be difficult works. They can do the estimation based on the knowledge of econometrics somehow. If they have experienced the O.D. survey work, it would give them a decisive advantage. In this sense, it is ideal that an expert in a field different from transportation engineering, that is, economics or management field, becomes able to plan and implement the O-D survey by actively expanding their research fields into a different field. It is ideal, too, that an expert in transportation engineering is able to estimate the economic effects of the expressway.[15]

References

Adler HA (1963) Economic evaluation of transport projects in less developed countries: theory and application. World Bank, Tokyo, Japan

American Association of State Highway Officials (AASHO) (1952) Road user benefit analysis for highway improvements, AASHO, Washington, D.C.

Eckstein O (1958) Water resource development: the economics of project evaluation. Harvard University Press, Cambridge, MA

Kei-Han-Shin Area Owner Interview O.D. Survey Liaison Committee (1961) Kei-Han-Shin area owner interview O.D. survey. The Japan Highway Corporation, Tokyo, Japan

Kodan ND (1958) Report on interzonal origin-destination traffic volumes survey along the proposed Nagoya-Kobe expressway route. The Japan Highway Public Corporation. Economic Research Office, Tokyo, Japan

[15]When one of the authors had worked at the Economic Research Office of the Japan Highway Public Corporation, he was inclined to study only the economics-oriented subjects. Mr. Yaichi Kobayashi, my senior by four or five, who was in charge of the estimation of the traffic volume in the economic research office, had doggedly performed his duty. Mr. Kobayashi had published an answer book on the estimation of road traffic volume (Sasaki and Kobayashi 1962) by making reference to Wilbur (1949). He had been sent to LAO several times and implemented the O-D traffic volume survey at Vientiane, metropolis of LAO, being transferred to another company. That is, he was acknowledged as a professional in the field of transportation engineering, especially in the O-D survey of traffic volume.

At that time (50–60 years ago), one of the authors could not fully understand the book by Mr. Kobayashi (Sasaki and Kobayashi 1962). This time, he has read it again, and begun to understand it. Using this opportunity, he would pay his respects for Mr. Kobayashi's endeavors.

Kodan ND (1959a) Traffic volume estimation on the proposed Nagoya-Kobe expressway: data 4, estimation of developed traffic volumes. The Japan Highway Public Corporation, Bureau of Mei-Shin expressway, Tokyo, Japan

Kodan ND (1959b) Calculation Process of Developed Traffic Volumes. The Japan Highway Public Corporation, Bureau of Mei-Shin Expressway, Tokyo, Japan

Kodan ND (1961a) Materials submitted to the world bank: written reply to the questionnaires related to the second loan. The Japan Highway Public Corporation, Tokyo, Japan

Kodan ND (1961b) Report on interzonal origin-destination traffic volumes survey along the proposed Nagoya-Kobe expressway route (III): The fifth O.D. survey. The Japan Highway Public Corporation, Economic Research Office, Tokyo, Japan

Kodan ND (1963a) Materials on toll traffic and economic benefits. In: III. Material on the Toyokawa–Komaki Expressway Project (prepared for World Bank for Reconstruction and Development). The Japan Highway Public Corporation, Tokyo, Japan

Kodan ND (1963b) Additional data. In: III. Material on The Toyokawa–Komaki Expressway Project (prepared for World Bank for Reconstruction and Development). The Japan Highway Public Corporation, Tokyo, Japan

Kohno H, Kurashimo K (1963) Public investment of the road: fundamental problem of road construction investment. In: Public investment in the transportation: 7 (annual report of 1963). Transportation Society, Tokyo, Japan

Nagoya Area Owner Interview O.D. Survey Liaison Committee (1961) Nagoya area owner interview O.D. survey. The Japan Highway Corporation, Tokyo, Japan

National Academy of Science (1956) Traffic assignment by mechanical method (Highway Research Board, Bulletin: 130). National Academy of Science, National Research Council, Washington, DC

Sasaki T (1961) Treatise on the economic effects of road: classification and measurement of economic effects (mimeograph)

Sasaki T, Kobayashi Y (1962) Road traffic volume estimation: manual for public officials. Kotsu Nihon Sha, Tokyo, Japan

Sasaki T, Kohno H, Kurashimo K (1964) Economic effects of the Mei-Shin expressway. Expressway Automobiles 7(9):49–64

Sasaki T, Kohno H, Kurashimo K (1965) Economic effects of the road and the public investment criteria. Gijutsu-shoin, Tokyo. (in Japanese)

Sasaki T, Kurashimo K (1964) Various problems on the economic valuations of the expressway construction: centering on the treatise of Mr. H. A. Adler. Express Highway Research Foundation of Japan, Tokyo, Japan

The Mei-Shin Expressway Construction Archives Editing Committee (1967a) The Mei-Shin expressway construction archives: general outline. The Japan Highway Public Corporation, Tokyo, Japan

The Mei-Shin Expressway Construction Archives Editing Committee (1967b) The Mei-Shin expressway construction archives: details. The Japan Highway Public Corporation, Tokyo, Japan

The Mei-Shin Expressway Construction Archives Editing Committee (1967c) Diverted traffic volume from road and railway. In: The Mei-Shin expressway construction archives: details. The Japan Highway Public Corporation, Tokyo, Japan, pp 159–187

The Mei-Shin Expressway Construction Archives Editing Committee (1967d) Traffic volume and toll revenue. In: The Mei-Shin expressway construction archives: details, the Mei-Shin expressway's construction archives editing committee. The Japan Highway Public Corporation, Tokyo, Japan, pp 1476–1487

The Mei-Shin Expressway Construction Archives Editing Committee (1967e) Ch. 13, economic effects of the Mei-Shin expressway. In: The Mei-Shin expressway construction archives. The Japan Highway Public Corporation, Tokyo, Japan

Wilbur Smith and Associates (1949), Mass Transportation Survey, 495 Orange Street, New Heavens, Conn. 200p.

Chapter 3
Generalized Benefit–Cost Criteria: Public Investment Criteria When Benefits Are Previously Measured

3.1 Genealogy of the Public Investment Criteria in the Field of Development Policy of Developing Countries

3.1.1 Public Investment Criteria: Definition 2

The definition in Chap. 1 can be taken as the criterion with which it can be examined whether the allocation of scarce public funds for public projects will achieve the golden rule of resource allocation, that is, the marginal rates of substitution/transformation shall be equated with the price ratios in the dynamic as well as spatial context. The topic of this chapter will play an important role in a practical setting as a positive version of the abstract and general investment criterion that examines the golden rule of resource allocation.

We can safely say that the research topic we investigate here is the fundamental problem of the public investment: (1) when; (2) in which way; (3) how much should we allocate scarce public investment funds to the construction of or the improvements in; (4) which public facilities such as expressway, water-storage dam; and so on to create economic effects in the whole of the economy in an appropriate and efficient way. The public investment criterion will solve these fundamental problems consistently.

3.1.2 Lineage of Typical Public Investment Criteria

The public investment allocation models by the water resource research group can be enumerated with Eckstein (1961), Steiner (1959), and Marglin (1963). Eckstein has integrated (1) the Marginal Social Productivity Criterion developed by R.F. Kahn and H.B. Chenery in the field of the development policy of developing countries, and (2) the Marginal Re-Investment Criterion by Hervey Leibenstein into the sophisticated general model that embodies the merit of both models. The model is

H. Kohno, Y. Higano, *Public Investment Criteria*, New Frontiers in Regional Science: Asian Perspectives 2, https://doi.org/10.1007/978-4-431-55221-5_3

mathematically formulated as a constrained optimization problem. The objective of the constrained maximization is the present value of the future consumption streams additionally created by the investment and reinvestment with a given time horizon. The constraints are given with the production function, the initial investment fund, and the reinvestment of earned profits on the way. Eckstein has solved the problem and obtained the investment criterion named as the *Marginal Contribution Rate to Growth* based on the necessary (marginal) conditions for the optimal solution. Eckstein's Model has been inherited by Steiner and Marglin of the same water resource research group in the sense that the explicit specification of production function is sidestepped, and it is replaced by the addition of concrete incompatibility, discreteness, and pre-emptive right constraints so that the model has become a more realistic and practical one.

3.2 Generalized Benefit–Cost Criteria Which We Should Rely On

3.2.1 Investment Choice Model of Steiner

The investment choice model, which denies the simple benefit–cost analysis, is proposed by Steiner. It is specified as a constrained optimization problem, too. There are two most important concepts with Steiner's Model. One is *the Sectors of the Economy* and the other is *the coding of the projects.* Without understanding the concepts clearly, nobody can understand the substance of the model. So, we would see the definitions of the two concepts and the explanations by Steiner (1959, pp. 897–900).

3.2.1.1 Sectors of the Economy and the Coding of the Projects

We directly quote the definition of the Sectors of the Economy by Steiner (1959):

The Public Sectors (*S1 and S3*). Sector 1 is defined to include the set of projects among which direct choice is to be made. It might include all water resources projects everywhere in the nation under the jurisdiction of the agencies selecting projects and allocating budgeted funds. It might be defined more broadly to include all public works projects, or it might be defined much more narrowly (quoted from Steiner 1959, p. 898, ll.9–14; the footnote is omitted by the author).

Sector 3 is viewed as the reservoir of such inchoate projects. If, because of a lack of meritorious projects in Sector 1, or because of lumpiness of discrete projects in Sector 1 there are extra funds, funds become available for expenditure in Sector 3. Consideration of Sector 3 thus serves two purposes: first, it requires that the yield of any project from Sector 1 included in the final program exceed the yield of any project not specifically considered, and second, it provides recognition of the fact that unutilized fund have some productive value (Steiner 1959, p. 898, ll. 25-33; the indent is by the author).

Sector 3 thus plays a role analogous to "slack activities" in linear programming and results in making the total expenditure from the restrained budget in the two public sectors definitionally equal to the amount of that budget. In what follows we assume, for simplicity, that the yield (to be defined) per dollar in Sector 3 is an estimable magnitude that can be represented by a constant, a_3 (Steiner 1959, p. 899, ll.1–6).

The Private Sectors (*S2 and S4*) Sector 2 consists of the relevant private projects that are alternative to the projects included in Sector 1 and that will thus be displaced if the public projects are undertaken. The *j*th project is the private alternative to the one or more public projects for providing the *j*th service (Steiner 1959, p. 899, ll. 7–11; the footnote is omitted by the author).

Sector 4 consists of what may be called the pool of marginal private investment opportunities. Need for this sector is due to the fact that the real opportunity cost of displacing a private project is the supramarginality of that project, not its total net benefits. For simplicity it is assumed that this sector consists of a homogeneous stock of investment opportunities whose yield per dollar can be represented by a constant, a_4 (Steiner 1959, p. 899, l.27 – p. 900, l. 2; the footnote is omitted by the author)

The coding of the projects is closely linked with the definition of the Sectors of the Economy. The direct choice by the agency, which is a certain jurisdiction selecting projects[1] and allocating budgeted funds, is made in the set of projects belonging to Sector 1. Therefore, the scope of Sector 1 and therefore the projects (as options) belonging to Sector 1 are dependent on the definition of the jurisdiction.

We define the set S_1 as follows:

$S_1 \equiv$ { the project *ij* that may be implemented by the agency through choice and assignment of the limited budget}.

The choice variable x^1_{ij} is defined by Steiner as follows[2]:

$x^1_{ij} = 1$ if the project *ij* in the set S_1 is chosen and, if not, it is 0 (zero).

$ij =$ index attached to the project in S_1. The double subscript is designated to recognize that a project involves the use of a certain facility ($i = 1, 2, \cdots, i^*$) for a certain purpose ($j = 1, 2, \cdots, j^*$) (footnote 11 in Steiner 1959, p. 898). Here, "purpose" may be interpreted as a certain service(s) (e.g., electric power), goods (e.g., irrigation water), and/or, broadly, the prevention against the flood, and so on.

Likewise, we define the set S_2 as follows:

[1] Here, they are just called - 'projects' and not 'public projects.' Later on, readers will see if the project is implemented by the agency, it may be called – public project because Steiner presumes possibility of the competitiveness that a certain project can be implemented by either an agency or a private company and they are exclusive with each other with the said projects when either an agency or a private company can implement it. Of course, still how to call it may be dependent on the definition of 'public' or the meaning of the initiative taken by an agency or a private company to implement the said project.

[2] The original symbol used by Steiner is x_{ij}. However, we add superscript 1 as it is the choice variable among S_1. It may be kind for unfamiliar readers. Analogically, we use x^2_j, x^3_p, and x^4_p with the choice variables among S_2, S_3, and S_4, respectively, which are later defined.

$S_2 \equiv \{$ the private project indexed by j ($j = 1, 2, \cdots, j^*$) that may be implemented by a private company to fulfill the purpose j alternatively to the projects ij in Sector 1, $S_1(i = 1, 2, \cdots, i^*$}.

We define the choice variable[3] x_j^2 among projects in Sector 2, S_2, as follows:

$x_j^2 = 1$ if the private project j is not displaced by the project ij in Sector 1 and if yes, it must be 0.

With the double index attached (as subscript) to a project belonging to S_1, Steiner presumes that: (1) a set of projects that may be generated by the combination of the types (including scales) of facility and purposes is to be taken into account when the agency decides on the choice; (2) the private project $\hat{j}$ is to be displaced, if it is implemented when the decision is made, by the choice of $x_{i\hat{j}}^1 = 1$ $(i = 1, 2, \cdots, \text{or } i^*)$.

We define the set S_3 as follows:

$S_3 \equiv \{$ the project indexed by p_3 ($p_3 = 1, 2, \cdots, p_3^*$)[4] that may be implemented by the agency but the maturity or probability of the project is low in the sense that the said project cannot be an element of Sector 1, S_1, due to the limited budget except for that if there exists an allowance in the limited budget, a project belonging to this set may be chosen depending on the net benefits of the said project}.

We define the choice variable (Steiner does not mention explicitly the number of projects in Sector 3 and any number works as far as projects belonging to this set has a reality in the sense that once it was chosen, it could be implemented without larger additional costs to the project costs that would be burden on the limited budget) $x_{p_3}^3$ $(p_3 = 1, 2, \cdots, p_3^*)$ as follows:

$x_{p_3}^3 = 1$ if project p_3 is chosen and if not, 0 $(p_3 = 1, 2, \cdots, p_3^*)$.

We define the set[5] S_4 as follows:

$S_4 \equiv \{$ the marginal private investment opportunities (projects) indexed by p_4 $(p_4 = 1, 2, \cdots, p_4^*)$ that may be implemented by a private company}.

We define the 'choice' variable[6] $x_{p_4}^4$ as follows:

$x_{p_4}^4 = 1$, always

---

[3] Actually, it is not a 'choice' variable. Steiner does not explicitly mention what value is taken by x_j and following his argument, it must be predetermined variables because the optimization problem is defined with only the selection of x_{ij}^3 among S_1 by the agency. We need it in order to take into account the opportunity cost with respect to the implementation of purpose j by Sector 1 (public sector) in place of a private company belonging to Sector 2. Later, more minute technical assumptions follow.

[4] The running subscript is changed by the author as the original one is confusing.

[5] The running subscript is changed by the author as the original one is confusing. As far as the content by Steiner goes, only one project belongs to this set. Anyway, the number of elements in the set S_4 does not matter and all have the same supramarginality of a_4.

[6] Actually, they are not choice variables. We need such variables in order to take into account the (possible) transfer from the private sector to the public sector (the said agency) through taxation or loan as an addition to the limited budget, which is later explained.

3.2.1.2 Forms of the Objective Function

Steiner first specifies the following objective function (Steiner 1959)[7]:

$$N = \sum\nolimits_{rs\in S_1} x_{rs}^1 G_{rs}^1 + \sum\nolimits_{s\in S_2} x_s^2 G_s^2 + \sum\nolimits_{r\in S_3} x_r^3 G_r^3 + \sum\nolimits_{r\in S_4} x_r^4 G_r^4, \tag{3.1}$$

in which:

We may interpret S_1, S_2, S_3, and S_4 as sets of indices attached to projects belonging Sector 1, Sector2, Sector 3, and Sector 4, respectively, without loss of generality; so, we may redefine S_1, S_2, S_3, and S_4 as follows:

$$S_1 \equiv \{rs : r = 1, 2, \cdots, i^*, s = 1, 2, \cdots, j^*); S_2 \equiv \{s : s = 1, 2, \cdots, j^*\}; S_3 \equiv \{r : r = 1, 2, \ldots, p_3^*\}; S_4 \equiv \{r : r = 1, 2, \ldots, p_4^*\}$$

G_{rs}^1 is the present value of the benefits over all costs incurred (except for the burden on the limited budget) ($\equiv$ the net present value) of the project belonging to the set S_1 $(r = 1, 2, \cdots, i^*, s = 1, 2, \cdots, j^*)$;

G_s^2 is the net present value of the project belonging to the set S_2 $\{s = 1, 2, \cdots, j^*\}$;

G_r^3 is the net present value of the project belonging to the set $S_3 \equiv \{r = 1, 2, \ldots, p_3^*\}$;

G_r^4 is the net present value of the project belonging to the set $S_4 \equiv \{r = 1, 2, \ldots, p_4^*\}$.

Steiner has shown that the objective function of (3.1) is substantially equivalent to the following in the sense that the optimal solutions are the same with each other with the objective functions (3.1) and (3.2):

$$Z = \sum_{ij\in S_1} x_{ij}^1 y_{ij}, \tag{3.2}$$

in which:

$$y_{ij} \equiv \left(G_{ij}^1 - a_3 k_{ij}\right) - \left(G_j^2 - a_4 k_j^2\right) - a_2 m_{ij}; \tag{3.3}$$

k_j^2: *the capital cost* of the private project j in Sector 4 as the burden on a limited amount of the funds for the investment in Sector 2 and 4;

m_{ij}: the amount of transfer to Sector 1 from Sector 2 (as the burden on Sector 2) through taxation or loan as a result of the choice of the project ij;

a_3 and a_4 are defined in the direct quotation earlier, namely, a_3 is *the yield* of the investment in the project in Sector 3 per the unit of the limited budget of the agency (a kind of imputed price for the allocation of the fund to the project in Sector 3) and

[7]The summation running subscripts are explicitly shown by the author.

a_4 is *the yield* of the investment in the project (investment opportunities) in Sector 4 per the unit of the limited amount of the funds for Sectors 2 and 4 (a kind of imputed price for the allocation of funds to the investment opportunities in Sector 4);

a_2 is *the yield* of the investment in the project in Sector 2 per the unit of the limited amount of the funds for Sectors 2 and 4 (a kind of imputed price for the allocation of fund to the project in Sector 2)[8];

k_{ij}: *the drain* of the project *ij* in Sector 1 as the burden to the limited budget of the agency and it is calculated as follows:

$$k_{ij} = \bar{k}_{ij} - m_{ij}; \tag{3.4}$$

$\bar{k}_{ij}$: the drain of the project *ij* in Sector 1 as the burden to the limited budget of the agency.

3.2.1.3 Constraints and the Proof of the Equivalence Between (3.1) and (3.2)

We try to show Eq. (3.1) is equivalent to Eq. (3.2) (conf. Mathematical Appendix in Steiner (1959), pp. 913–915).

[Budget constrain[9]] The agency is subject to the following:

$$\sum\nolimits_{r=1}^{i^*} \sum\nolimits_{s=1}^{j^*} x_{rs}^1 k_{rs} + \sum\nolimits_{r=1}^{p_3^*} x_r^3 k_r^3 = K, \tag{3.5}$$

in which:

k_r^3: *the capital cost* of project *r* in Sector 3 as the burden to the limited budget of the agency;

K: the amount of the limited budget which the agency is to allocate for projects among Sector 1 and Sector 3.

The private sector is subject to the following:

$$\sum\nolimits_{s=1}^{j^*} x_s^2 k_s^2 + \sum\nolimits_{s=1}^{p_4^*} x_s^4 k_s^4 = A - \frac{a_2}{a_4} \sum\nolimits_{r=1}^{i^*} \sum\nolimits_{s=1}^{j^*} x_{rs}^1 m_{rs} \tag{3.6a}$$

in which:

k_s^4: the capital cost of the private project *s* in Sector 4;

A: the (virtual and constant) limited amount of the capital fund in the capital market available in Sectors 2 and 4.

[8] Steiner does not give an explicit definition for a_2. He defines that $a_2 = \alpha a_4$ (α is a certain constant).

[9] Generally, the constraint must be an inequality ($\leq$). Here, it is assumed that at least one of the projects in Sector 3 has a divisibility.

In the mathematical appendix (Steiner 1959), the coefficient, $\frac{a_2}{a_4}$, in the second term of the right-hand side of Eq. (3.6a) abruptly appears with the definition: $a_2 = \alpha a_4$. It is a little bit difficult to interpret the term, $\frac{a_2}{a_4}$, and we try to make it as one of the possibilities.

In Eq. (3.6a), the appearance of the foregone benefits (yields) a_2 in Sector 2 and the investment opportunity (cost) a_4 in Sector 4 in the term of the burden of the transfer from Sector 2 to Sector 1 (a sort of *lien*) on the budget constraint of the private sector (i.e., the second term in the right-hand side) presumes that an allowance in the original budget for the projects in Sector 1 is competitive against investments into projects in Sector 2 and Sector 4.

Equation (3.6a) can be derived as follows. First, we formulate the following:

$$a_2 \sum_{s=1}^{j^*} x_s^2 \widetilde{k}_s^2 + a_4 \sum_{s=1}^{p_4^*} x_s^4 \widetilde{k}_s^4 = A' - a_2 \sum_{r=1}^{i^*} \sum_{s=1}^{j^*} x_{rs}^1 m_{rs}, \tag{3.6b}$$

$$\frac{a_2}{a_4} \sum_{s=1}^{j^*} x_s^2 \widetilde{k}_s^2 + \sum_{s=1}^{p_4^*} x_s^4 \widetilde{k}_s^4 = A'' - \frac{a_2}{a_4} \sum_{r=1}^{i^*} \sum_{s=1}^{j^*} x_{rs}^1 m_{rs}, \tag{3.6c}$$

in which:

$\widetilde{k}_s^p$: the drain cost of the investment in project s in Sector p $(p = 2, 4)$ (in the monetary term).

It can be considered that Eq. (3.6b) is the balance between a virtual *supply* (A') and demand in the capital market, which integrates the virtual capital markets for Sector 2 and Sector 4, which have different marginal opportunity (productivity) costs of investment. Equation (3.6c) is the balance between a virtual supply (A'') and demand in the capital market in terms of the marginal opportunity cost (foregone yields) of the project in Sector 4; and

$$A = A'' = \frac{1}{a_4} A'.$$

Making replacements as follows:

$$\frac{a_2}{a_4} \widetilde{k}_s^2 = k_s^2 \quad (s = 1, 2, \cdots, j^*);$$

$$\widetilde{k}_s^4 = k_s^4 \quad (s = 1, 2, \cdots, p_4^*);$$

and

$$A'' = A,$$

we obtain Eq. (3.6a). The value of A is the supply of the capital in the monetary term in Sector 4, and the value of A' is the supply of *the capital* in terms of the marginal opportunity of the project in Sector 4. The value of A, and therefore, the value of A' does not matter as far as they are constants. It looks unusual that the interpretation and the specification of the budget constraints presumes that the total yield which is targeted by investors in the capital market is fixed (A') only considering investments into Sector 2 (and Sector 4 as an opportunity cost). It can be taken that the capital market is stable, and investors would assign capital to public projects to the extent in which the capital assignment creates the same yields as what is created by the assigned capital before the assignment. Thus, the capital market is stable, again. Equations (3.6a) and (3.6c) can be taken as the potential function, a device, to arbitrage *the investment opportunities* of the capital assignment in the different sectors of the project in which the marginal productivities of the project are usually different.

[Incompatibility Constraints]

$$\sum_{r=1}^{i^*} x_{rs}^1 + x_s^2 = 1 \quad (s = (1, 2, \cdots, j^*) \tag{3.7}$$

This means that if a certain specific service s is provided by the choice of the project in Sector 1, the project s in Sector 2 is vanished (displaced by the project in Sector 1).

We define the (net) yield of the project r in Sector 3 per the unit of the budget, a_r^3, as follows:

$$a_r^3 = \frac{G_r^3}{k_r^3} \ \left(r = 1, 2, \cdots, p_3^*\right).$$

Also, the (net) yield of the project r in Sector 4 per the unit of the budget, a_r^4, is defined as follows:

$$a_r^4 = \frac{G_r^4}{k_r^4} \ \left(r = 1, 2, \cdots, p_4^*\right).$$

We may assume without loss of generality:[10]

$$a_r^3 = a_3 = \frac{G_r^3}{k_r^3} \text{ for all } r \ \left(r = 1, 2, \cdots, p_3^*\right); \tag{3.8}$$

$$a_r^4 = a_4 = \frac{G_r^4}{k_r^4} \text{ for all } r \ \left(r = 1, 2, \cdots, p_4^*\right). \tag{3.9}$$

Eq. (3.1) can be rewritten as follows:

[10] As for Sector 4, it is direct by definition. As for Sector 3, it plays a role of slack variables against the budget constraint of the agency and it goes without loss of generality that $a_3 = \max\{a_1^3, a_2^3, \cdots, a_{p_3^*}^3\}$.

$$N^{(1)} = \sum_{s=1}^{j^*} \left(\sum_{r=1}^{i^*} x_{rs}^1 G_{rs}^1 + x_s^2 G_s^2 \right) + \sum_{r=1}^{p_3^*} x_r^3 G_r^3 + \sum_{r=1}^{p_4^*} x_r^4 G_r^4 \tag{3.10}$$

By Eqs. (3.5) and (3.8), the following is derived:

$$\sum_{r=1}^{p_3^*} x_r^3 G_r^3 = a_3 \sum_{r=1}^{p_3^*} x_r^3 k_r^3 = a_3 \left\{ K - \sum_{r=1}^{i^*} \sum_{s=1}^{j^*} x_{rs}^1 k_{rs} \right\} \tag{3.11}$$

By Eq. (3.6a) and (3.9), we obtain the following equation:

$$\begin{aligned} \sum_{r=1}^{p_4^*} x_r^4 G_r^4 &= a_4 \left\{ \sum_{r=1}^{p_4^*} x_r^4 k_r^4 \right\} \\ &= a_4 \left\{ A - \frac{a_2}{a_4} \sum_{r=1}^{i^*} \sum_{s=1}^{j^*} x_{rs}^1 m_{rs} - \sum_{s=1}^{j^*} x_s^2 k_s^2 \right\} \end{aligned} \tag{3.12}$$

By substituting Eqs. (3.11) and (3.12) into Eq. (3.10), we can develop it as follows:

$$\begin{aligned} N^{(2)} &= \sum_{s=1}^{j^*} \left(\sum_{r=1}^{i^*} x_{rs}^1 G_{rs}^1 + x_s^2 G_s^2 \right) + \sum_{r=1}^{p_3^*} x_r^3 G_r^3 + \sum_{r=1}^{p_4^*} x_r^4 G_r^4 \\ &= \sum_{s=1}^{j^*} \left(\sum_{r=1}^{i^*} x_{rs}^1 G_{rs}^1 + x_s^2 G_s^2 \right) + a_3 \left\{ K - \sum_{r=1}^{i^*} \sum_{s=1}^{j^*} x_{rs}^1 k_{rs} \right\} \\ &\quad + a_4 \left\{ A - \frac{a_2}{a_4} \sum_{r=1}^{i^*} \sum_{s=1}^{j^*} x_{rs}^1 m_{rs} - \sum_{s=1}^{j^*} x_s^2 k_s^2 \right\} \end{aligned} \tag{3.13}$$

$$\begin{aligned} N^{(3)} &= \sum_{s=1}^{j^*} \sum_{r=1}^{i^*} \left(G_{rs}^1 - a_3\, k_{rs} - a_2\, m_{rs} \right) x_{rs}^1 + \sum_{s=1}^{j^*} \left(G_s^2 - a_4 k_s^2 \right) x_s^2 \\ &\quad + a_3 K + a_4 A \end{aligned} \tag{3.14}$$

By Eq. (3.7), Eq. (3.14) becomes as follows:

$$\begin{aligned} N^{(4)} &= \sum_{s=1}^{j^*} \sum_{r=1}^{i^*} \left(G_{rs}^1 - a_3\, k_{rs} - a_2\, m_{rs} \right) x_{rs}^1 \\ &\quad + \sum_{s=1}^{j^*} \left(G_s^2 - a_4 k_s^2 \right) \left(1 - \sum_{r=1}^{i^*} x_{rs}^1 \right) + a_3 K + a_4 A \\ &= \sum_{s=1}^{j^*} \sum_{r=1}^{i^*} \left(G_{rs}^1 - a_3\, k_{rs} - a_2\, m_{rs} - G_s^2 + a_4 k_s^2 \right) x_{rs}^1 + \sum_{s=1}^{j^*} G_s^2 \\ &\quad + a_3 K + a_4 A \end{aligned} \tag{3.15}$$

As the last three terms are constant, Eq. (3.10) is equivalent to the following with the optimal solutions:

$$N^{(5)} = \sum_{i=1}^{i^*} \sum_{j=1}^{j^*} \left(G_{rs}^1 - a_3\, k_{rs} \right) - \left(G_s^2 - a_4 k_s^2 \right) - a_2\, m_{ij} \} \, x_{ij} \tag{3.16}$$

[Steiner's Model] Maximize Eq. (3.16) with respect to the control variables, x_{ij} $(i = 1, 2, \cdots, i^*; j = 1, 2, \cdots, j^*)$,

Subject to:

Budget restraint (Steiner 1959, pp. 902–903):

$$\sum\nolimits_{ij \in S1} x_{ij} k_{ij} \leq K, \tag{3.17}$$

Discreteness.

$$x_{ij}, x_j = 0, 1 \quad \text{for all } ij, j, \tag{3.18}$$

Incompatibility constraints.

$$\sum\nolimits_i x_{ij} + x_j = 1, \text{ for all } j, \tag{3.19}$$

$$\sum\nolimits_j x_{ij} \leq 1; \text{all } i \tag{3.20}$$

3.2.2 Investment Choice Model Over the Multi-Periods: Marglin's Model

Marglin's Model is formulated as a constrained optimization model. The objective is to maximize the sum of the *net* present values of the streams of benefits created by the investment over the multi-periods after the said investment is made. The constraints are (1) the balance between the demand and supply of the investment funds at each period (the periods in which the investment can be made are predetermined), in which the cost incurred by the investment and the investment fund available at each period are adjusted for simplicity so that a kind of incompatibility constraint is substantially laid on the investment, that is, only one (kind of) investment can be made at each period; (2) with each investment, the sum of the discrete choice variables (which take values of 0 (zero) (if the decision is no with the investment associated to the choice variable) or 1 (decision is yes)) over the multi-periods must be equal to 1 (one) or less than 1, which means that the decision is yes or no with making an investment at a predetermined period, and once decision of yes made on a certain investment at a certain period, the said investment cannot be made at other periods; (3) nonnegativity conditions on the choice variable means that the decision of no with each investment can be optional (Marglin 1963, pp. 98–115). The point of Marglin's Model is that it definitely excludes the myopic decision that may cause a loss (foregone benefits).

By the way, for the choice among investments, there exist two types of choice: the static choice of substitution and the *postponement* choice over time. The former is dealt with by the almost completed format such as the golden rule of the equality between the marginal rate of substitution/transformation and price ratio in all sorts of static theories of economics, the opportunity cost criterion in the linear programming method, and so on. On the other hand, the importance of the latter has been pointed out by A.O. Hirschman (1968, pp. 134–135), and it comes into flower as a multi-period choice model by Marglin (1963). However, they did not advance to the analysis with the substantially dynamic model in the sense explained in Chap. 1.

We will expatiate on the arguments by Marglin concerning the possible fault that may be caused by the myopic decision since he has yet shown a good example that emphasizes the decision based on the dynamic context is "must" in the public investment even though his model is not a substantially dynamic one.

3.2.2.1 Evasion of Myopia Rule

We first quote the example shown by Marglin (1963, pp. 38–40); some of the figures are corrected as it looks that there exist round errors through the numerical calculation. However, the substance of the argument may not change by this

> In determining projects to be constructed in any period, this procedure, which we call the 'Myopia Rule', considers only the net gains for that period. It is thus essentially static; while it assigns to the first period the projects maximizing the net present value of outlay in the first period viewed alone, the complete assignment of projects to construction periods which it determines may not, as will shortly be shown, maximize overall net present value. The shortcoming of the Myopia Rule is a familiar one: it concentrates on the absolute advantage among projects within each period instead of looking at the comparative advantage among projects between periods (quoted from Marglin 1963, p. 38, ll. 6–15).

> The benefit data of Sect. 3.2.2 continue to apply to the uranium mine: potential benefits are \$10 per year from 1963 through 1982, then the demand for uranium is assumed to take a sudden spurt so that the potential benefits are \$100 per year from 1983 to infinity. The demand for textiles is assumed to remain constant over time, the potential benefits of the textile mill being \$25 per year from 1963 to infinity. These potential benefit rates are illustrated graphically in Fig. 3.1. For further simplicity we assume that the two projects cost the same amount, \$150, and that the available budgets are \$150 in 1962 and \$150 in 1967.
>
> As before, our goal is maximization of the overall net present value today from investment, future as well as present, 'today' once again taken to be 1962. Now, however, although the net present value of each project, viewed in isolation, is maximized for 1962 construction, the budget constraints, as we have set them, permit construction of only one project now, the other being forced to wait until 1967. The Myopia Rule tells us to construct the project in 1962 with the higher net present value for immediate construction. Straightforward computations reveal that construction of the uranium mine in 1962 – abbreviated (U, 1962) – yields a net present value of \$ 728.40, whereas immediate construction of the textile mill – (T, 1962) – yields a present value of only \$350.[1)] Accordingly, the Myopia Rule assigns U to 1962 construction, and residually assigns T to 1967. The net present value of (T, 1967) is \$274.23.[2)] Thus the Myopia Rule-determined sequence of (U,1962) and

(T.1967) gives an overall net present value of $1002.63 (quoted from Marglin 1963, p. 39, ll.11–21 – p. 40, ll. 1–13).

However construction of the uranium mine in 1967 yields a net present value of $718.61.[3)] Added to the net present value of construction of the textile mill in 1962, $350, this gives the alternative program of (T,1962) and (U,1967) an overall net present value of $1068.58, over $65 more than the Myopia Rule-determined program. The Myopia Rule clearly bats zero in this example: of the two possible sequences, it tells us to choose the inferior (quoted from Marglin 1963, p. 41, ll. 1–7).

Note:

1. The computations:
   For (U, 1962):

   (a) the present value of benefits from 1963 through 1982 is
   $10 \times 0.05^{-1} \times (1\text{-}1.05^{-20}) = 124.62$;
   (b) the present value of benefits from 1983 forward is
   $100 \times 0.05^{-1} \times 1.05^{-20} = 753.78$;
   (c) the present value of gross benefits, the sum of (a) and (b), is 878.40;
   (d) subtraction of the construction cost of $ 150 gives the net present value, 728.40.

   For (T, 1962):

   (e) the present value of benefits from 1963 forward is $25 \times 0.05^{-1} = 500$;
   (f) subtraction of the cost of 150 gives the net present value, 350

2. The computations:
   For (T, 1967)

   (a) the present value of benefits from 1968 forward is
   $25 \times 0.05^{-1} \times 1.05^{-5} = 391.76$;
   (b) the present value of the cost of 1967 construction is
   $150 \times 1.05^{-5} = 117.53$;
   (c) the net present value is the difference between (a) and (b), 274.23

3. The computations:
   For (U, 1967)

   (a) the present value of benefits from 1968 through 1982 is
   $10 \times 0.05^{-1} \times (1 - 1.05^{-15}) \times 1.05^{-5} = 81.33$;
   (b) the present value of benefits from 1983 forward is
   $100 \times 0.05^{-1} \times 1.05^{-20} = 753.78$;
   (c) the present value of gross benefits is the sum of (a) and (b), 835.11;
   (d) the present value of the cost of 1967 construction is $150 \times 1.05^{-5} = 117.53$;
   (e) the net present value, the difference between (c) and (d), is 717.58.
   Source: Marglin (1963), pp. 40–41.

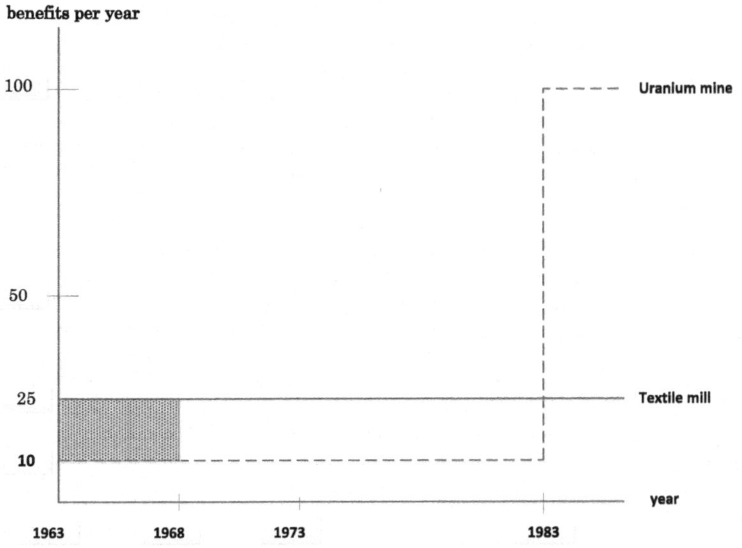

Fig. 3.1 Stream of the expected benefits by project (Ibid. Notes are added by the author) Source: made on Marglin (1963), p. 39.
Note: (1) Solid line shows stream of the benefits with textile mill. Broken line shows stream of the benefits with uranium mine.
(2) The shaded area is related to the foregone benefits due to the delay in the construction of textile mill until 1967. Or, equivalently, the shaded area is related to the opportunity cost for the choice of (U, 1962) (Precisely speaking, the shaded rectangle should be modified into five rectangles, of which one sides are 1 (one year) and the others are the differences between the present values of the annual benefits created by the textile mill and the uranium mine projects. Their areas are 14.286, 13.605, 12.958, 12.341, and 11.753, with the first, second, . . ., and fifth year, respectively. The total (the foregone costs) is 64.94).

3.2.2.2 Marglin's Model

Formally, the problem faced by the investor may be specified as follows:

[Marglin's Model] To maximize the following objective function:

$$728.40x_{U,1962} + 717.58x_{U,1967} + 350.00x_{T,1962} + 274.23x_{T,1967} \tag{3.21}$$

determine the value of $x_{U,\ 1962}$, $x_{U,\ 1967}$, $x_{T,\ 1962}$, and $x_{T,\ 1967}$ being subject to the following constraints:

[Budgetary Constraints (in Compatibility Constrains)]

$$150x_{U,1962} + 150x_{T,1962} \leq 150, \tag{3.22a}$$

$$150x_{U,1967} + 150x_{T,1967} \leq 150, \tag{3.22b}$$

[Incompatibility Constraints and No Decision May Be Optional][11]

$$x_{U,1962} + x_{U,1967} \leq 1 \tag{3.23a}$$

$$x_{T,1962} + x_{T,1967} \leq 1 \tag{3.23b}$$

[Nonnegativity and Discrete Choice Variable Constraints]

$$x_{U,1962}, x_{U,1967}, x_{T,1962}, x_{T,1967} = 0 \text{ or } 1 \tag{3.24}$$

The values of the coefficients of the objective function are given by Table 3.1 which are calculated *independent of* the solving procedure of the optimization problem. That is the point why Marglin's Model is not essentially a dynamic one because in the dynamic model, the benefits created by the decision on the investments over time shall be *endogenously determined* (the calculation mechanism is essentially built in the dynamic model) so that the additional (marginal) benefits in terms of the addition to the objective function created by the additional (marginal) investments to the *positive* investments[12] are equated with each other, and the equated value is the opportunity cost of the investment over time.

As already mentioned earlier, in the budget constraints, the adjustment of making the coefficients of the left-hand side of inequalities, (3.22a) and (3.22b), each equal to the right-hand side constants substantially laid a kind of incompatibility on the choice variables, $x_{i,\,j}$ $(i = U, T; j = 1962, 1967)$, namely, the choice (yes) is exclusive with each other among the options of the uranium mine and textile mill at any period. The constraints, (3.23a) and (3.23b), (with (3.24)), mean that neither the uranium mine nor the textile mill can be built more than once, and no decision (no) on either or both is optional. Thus, constraints (3.22a), (3.22b), (3.23a), (3.23b), and (3.24) together limit the substantial options—$(x_{U,\ 1962}, x_{U,\ 1967}, x_{T,\ 1962}, x_{T,\ 1967}) = (1, 0, 0, 1)$ or $(0, 1, 1, 0)$. We have already discovered by "trial and error" that $(0, 1, 1, 0)$ is optimal solution to the optimization problem of Marglin's Model (Marglin 1963, pp. 43–44).

By the way, here we would try to apply Mishan's normalization procedure to the decision in 1962 based on the benefit–cost criteria using the example earlier. In Marglin's example, the streams of benefits continue forever in both investment options, we set the end of the year of 2062 as the timing of period to which the capitalized value of the stream of benefits and costs are normalized.[13]

We use symbols in Chap. 1, Sect. 3.2.3.

---

[11] Marglin calls the constraints (3.23a), (3.23b), and (3.24) – physical constraints.

[12] Precisely speaking, as for an investment (in the sense of an option to construct/increase such and such facility, e.g., social infrastructure) of which value is 0 (zero), the additional benefit is equal to the equated value or less than it. More precisely, if the additional benefit is equal to the equated value, 0 (zero) is the optimal amount for the investment, i.e., the said investment is not made. If the additional benefit is less than the equated value, a minus figure were optimal for the investment and the investment must be 0 (zero) due to the nonnegativity condition.

[13] The discounting factor at 2062 with discount (interest) rate of 0.05 is 0.007604490, which means we may take the year of 2062 as the terminated year of both projects.

Table 3.1 Present value of the net benefits by choice (The caption is added by the author. Some of headings are changed.)

Project	Construction year	
	1962	1967
U	\$728.40	\$718.58
T	\$350.00	\$274.23

Source: made on Marglin (1963), pp. 41–42.

$$TV^{100}_{(U,1962)} = \frac{10}{0.05} \times (1+0.05)^{100} + \frac{90}{0.05} \times (1+0.05)^{80} = 115,510.8;$$

$$TV^{100}_{(T,1962)} = \frac{25}{0.05} \times (1+0.05)^{100} = 65,750.6;$$

$$K = 150 \times (1+0.05)^{100} = 19,725.2;$$

$$K^* = 150$$

$$\left(1+\lambda_{(U,1962)}\right)^{100} \cdot 150 = TV^{100}_{(U,1962)};$$

$$\lambda_{(U,1962)} = 0.068723$$

$$\left(1+\lambda_{(T,1962)}\right)^{100} \cdot 150 = TV^{100}_{(T,1962)};$$

$$\lambda_{(T,1962)} = 0.062718$$

These results constitute the following table. With adoption of any benefit–cost criterion, the uranium mine shall be chosen. It apparently shows that Mishan's normalization procedure is not perfect as far as the benefit–cost analysis is applied based on the conventional benefit–cost approach. As Marglin has pointed out, the conventional benefit–cost criteria, which are even integrated with Mishan's normalization procedure, may have a defect, namely, false due to myopic decision. In other words, the conventional benefit–cost approach substantially lacks a consistent mechanism with which a set of "projects" which are identified by scale, location and timing of implementation, and so on can be given investment priority levels correctly. However, by taking account investment fund constraints, incompatibility constraints, etc., we may construct a sub-set of the power set that is generated by the project set, to which the conventional benefit–cost criteria is to be applied (we may call it—expanded benefit–cost analysis approach) although the incompatibility constraints are very complicated, which may induce an error in the sub-set construction. Actually, if we take a set of uranium mine and textile mill projects implemented in 1967 and 1962, respectively, as a compound project, we can confirm that it is superior to a set of uranium mine and textile mill projects implemented in 1962 and 1967, respectively, in any benefit-cost criteria after the normalization.

	B	K^*	K	$B-K$	$\frac{B-K}{K}$	λ
(U, 1962)	115,510.8	150.0	19,725.2	95,785.6	4.85600	0.06872
(T, 1962)	65,750.6	150.0	19,725.2	46,025.4	2.33333	0.06272

The example given by Marglin earlier is simple, and the optimal decision is apparent by Fig. 3.1 because there cannot exist any reason why the project (T,1962) must wait until 1967 because the total benefits from 1968 forward are the same with either decision (U,1962) or (T,1962) and if the choice of (U,1962) was made, the foregone benefits are incurred between 1963 and 1968. However, it does not necessarily mean that a myopic decision is never made which results in a loss to the economy. Practically, the number of investments (as options) is huge, and the possibility of false increases if the conventional benefit–cost criteria, which are even normalized by Mishan's procedure, is applied to the decision-making on the choice among investment options that are minutely differentiated by the timing (when and in which manner), place (where), facility (which), and scale (how much funds and in which manner) and subject to compatibility constraints. The following constraints may highlight Marglin's idea of the cording variables in order to avoid the false due to the *myopic* decision (Marglin 1963, pp. 107–108):

[An example of the budget constraints]

$$\sum_{i=1}^{m}\sum_{j=1}^{n_i}\widehat{C}_{it}^{j}x_{it}^{j}+x_{st}=\overline{C}_t(t=1,2,3,\ldots,T) \tag{3.25}$$

An interpretation of the variable x_{i1}^{j} may help us to understand the false of myopic rule pointed out Marglin (1963):

x_{it}^{j}: choice variable (taking 0 or 1) for an investment option of type

$j\,(j=1,2,\cdots,n_i)$, that is implemented at location (zone) or, more specifically, a certain facility at a certain location, of which pair is given index $i\ (i=1,2,\cdots,m)$ and the period $t\ (t=1,2,\cdots,T)$,

$\widehat{C}_{it}^{j}$: drain due to the choice of $x_{it}^{j}=1$ on the budget at period $t\ (t=1,2,\cdots,T)$,

$\overline{C}_t$: the amount of the capital funds which may be allocated to the chosen projects at period $t\ (t=1,2,\cdots,T)$,

x_{st}: slack variable which exactly equates the total capital funds available $\overline{C}_t$ to the total amount of drains due to the choice of project at period $t\ (t=1,2,\cdots,T)$; we need it due to indivisibility of projects.

What is argued by Marglin using the simple example is that the timing of investment itself has meaning and is critical for the optimal choice of investments. Even if two projects are exactly the same in any sense, for example, with the place in which the projects are implemented, the scale, and so on, but the timing of the implementation, the two projects must be taken as different investment targets. Practically, the number of options exponentially increases as the number of periods, locations, and so on increases. The possibility of the false due to a kind of myopic decision increases if we adopt expanded benefit-cost analysis approach. The incompatibility constraints may be added to a certain set of choice variables with a certain location, period, facility, and so on. The programing model proposed by Marglin and others was a necessity to solve the complicated choice problem consistently whether the capability of computer and software could catch up with what was requested by the programing model on that day.

As already mentioned earlier, a defect of Marglin's approach is that the calculation of parameters that evaluate benefits and costs of projects is practically tough work as the number of timing, location, and so on is increasing. At all, the parameters that evaluate projects of different timing cannot be given as far as the calculation is not based on the substantially dynamic model. The amount of $\bar{C}_t$ is usually given based on a financial plan or construction plan that is predetermined politically or under a bureaucratic system and in that sense, the values may be fixed. However, logically or economically, the values cannot be given without the calculation based on the substantially dynamic model, which is just the same as the calculation of parameters for project evaluation because the capital fund available in the future must be dependent on what was decided in the past and now. If we could say that $\bar{C}_t$ is given logically in a right way, the assignment of the public funds to the projects was almost finished. Without knowing the dynamic opportunity cost of the investment funds, we cannot assign the public funds for each period logically in the right way. Ironically, it can be said that rather Marglin's model highlighted the importance of the dynamic approach to public investment decision-making (we already mentioned it in Chap. 1), since it suggested that the possibility of false increases due to the decision-making without the dynamic context. Readers must wait till the programing model is proposed in Chap. 7 in which the public investment as an important policy argument for the regional development is substantially dealt with in the dynamic context.

3.3 Application of Generalized Benefit–Cost Criteria

3.3.1 Setting Up of Our Problem to be Solved

We attempt to apply the above-mentioned Steiner=Marglin type of multiperiod investment choice model, which is a kind of the generalized benefit–cost criteria is built in, to the optimum allocation of scarce resources to public investment targets (projects) (hereinafter, based on Kohno 1974).

The problem of allocation of the scarce resource to and potentially feasible and/or optional economic activities, which is the root of the topics in this book, can be hierarchically classified into: (1) allocation of net national income between consumption and saving (=investment); (2) allocation of investment funds between public investment and private (nonpublic) industrial investment; (3) allocation of public investment funds by period, by region, and by project; and so on. Once getting into the problem (3), we cannot reply on the market to solve the problem.

Now, the problem (3) can be given a little bit practically as the fundamental problem of public investment, namely, "*When, where, how* (in which manner), and in *what* amounts the given public investment funds should be allocated to *which* projects among optional investment projects."

Taking the construction of expressway as an example of the targets (options) of the public investment, the problems may be given more concretely focusing on the following examples of main options:

A.	Congestion reducing policy	vs.	Development policy for the under-developed Area
or	Follow-up investment (investment running after burning)	vs.	Prior investment (investment prior to the issue anticipated)
B.	Mountainous route	vs.	Coastal route
C.	Construction by public authority	vs.	Construction by private company
D.	Construction with two stages at different periods	vs.	Construction en bloc
etc.			

Of course, problem (3) is not solved by only choosing among the options menitoned earlier. With each main chosen option, the more complicated and delicate problem of *when, where, how* (in which manner), and in *what* amounts the given public investment funds should be allocated to *which* projects among optional investment projects belonging to the said chosen option by taking account the opportunity cost of the public investment funds thus allocated to the chosen projects (investment targets) which meet the said chosen main option.

The objective function and constraints of the model, in which such various problems can be solved overall and consistently with the alternative combinations of *social discount rate* and *time horizon* are shown later on with data of budget constraint, construction costs, transport capacity, and economic effects. In this sense, the following is an empirical study which was done by applying and extending the procedure and method by Steiner=Marglin to derive the optimum allocation of the public investment funds, of which amount was given as the basic and of reality data by "53 Trillion JPY Highway Construction Planning Over the Periods of Twenty Years (from 1965 to 1985)" (hereafter, we call it – Highway Construction Planning) drawn up by the Ministry of Construction as the physical planning.[14]

3.3.2 *Code of Activity Variables*

First, the choice variables, ${}_{i}^{h}X^{p}_{j \cdot t}$, ${}_{i}^{h}X^{p}_{j \cdot tt'}$, are defined (*coded*) by making reference to the framework of the construction planning (The Ministry of Construction 1966). They are shown as follows:

[14]The Ministry of Construction (1967).

[Expressway/highway name][15]
h = suffix (left-superscript) of expressway/highway, and
$h = 1$ means Tohoku Expressway/highway;
$h = 2$ means Kan-Etsu Expressway/highway;
$h = 3$ means Tokyo–Gaikan Expressway/highway.

[Section of Expressway/Highway]
p = suffix (right-superscript) of sections of expressways ($p = 1, 2, \cdots, p(h)$; with $h = 1, 2, 3$) (explained later on).

[Route]
i = suffix (left-subscript) indicating inland (mountainous) route *vs.* seashore (built-up area) route, and
$i = 1$ means inland route;
$i = 2$ means seashore route.

[Grade of traffic lane and the way of construction]
j = suffix (the first right-subscript) indicating: (1) the number of traffic lanes and the grade of the traffic lane; and (2) the construction way either en bloc or with two stages at different periods, and

$j = 1$ means construction of six-lane expressway standard to be constructed en bloc;
$j = 2$ means four-lane expressway standard, en bloc;
$j = 3$ means two-lane expressway standard, en bloc;
$j = 4$ means two-lane highway standard, en bloc;
$j = 5$ means two-stage construction: the construction of two-lane expressway in the first period and two-lane expressway in the second period to expand the capacity of expressway; this is called—*two plus two-lane* stage construction of expressway,
$j = 6$ means four plus two-lane stage construction of expressway, and
$j = 7$ means construction of six-lane expressway by a nonpublic company in the construction way: (1) en bloc, or (2) four plus two.

Index $j = 7$ is the only possible option for $h = 3$, which means that the left-superscript, h, of the choice variable, of which right-subscript, j, is 7, must be always 3.

[Timing of the Construction En Bloc and the Two-Stage Construction]
1. In case the choice variable having the second right-subscript with only *one digit* is chosen, the construction is done en bloc,

   t = suffix (the second right-subscript) indicating timing of the construction, and

   $t = 1$ means the first period (1965–1968)
   $t = 2$ means the second period (1969–1972)
   $t = 3$ means the third period (1973–1976)
   $t = 4$ means the fourth period (1977–1980) and
   $t = 5$ means the fifth period (1981–1984).

[15] As historical fact, all the arterial roads were constructed as expressways. As readers may see below, there existed a possibility that some of which were constructed as high-grade highway.

The time horizon is defined by dividing the 20 years from 1965 to 1984 into five periods of 4 years. It is assumed that the expressway/highway is open for traffic in the first year of the next period, which is taken into account when the benefits (coefficients of the objective function) are estimated.

2. In case the choice variables having second right-subscript with *two digits*, namely, like $t\ t'$, is chosen, the construction is done with two stages. This means that the first right-subscript j of the choice variable, of which the second right-hand subscript is two digits, must be always 5, 6, or 7, and

   (a) The ten's digit (the left digit) of $t\,t'$ means an index for the period in the sense of (i) above in which the first stage of the construction is done, and

   (b) the one's digit (right digit) of $t\,t'$ means the period in which the second stage of the construction is done.

Readers will see it is not necessary that t and t' are continuous integers, such as 12, 23, 34, and so on. We call indices h, i, p, j, and the first and the second period of the two-stage construction generally—*attributes*.

3.3.2.1 Formulation of the Optimization a la Steiner=Marglin

Using the definition of code for the choice variables, ${}^{h}_{i}X^{p}_{j\cdot tt'}$, in the previous sub-section, we specify the optimal allocation of the investment funds for the construction of expressways/highways, which correspond to the plans in Highway Construction Planning, as a Steiner=Marglin type of model.

[The Objective Function] The objective is to maximize the following function in the choice variables:

$$Z \equiv \sum_{t=1}^{5}\left\{\sum_{h=1}^{3}\sum_{p=1}^{p(h)}\sum_{i=1}^{2}\sum_{j=1}^{4} {}^{h}_{i}\varepsilon^{p}_{j\cdot t}\times {}^{h}_{i}x^{p}_{j\cdot t}+\sum_{h=3}^{3}\sum_{p=1}^{p(h)}\sum_{i=1}^{2}\sum_{j=7}^{7} {}^{h}_{i}\varepsilon^{p}_{j\cdot t}\times {}^{h}_{i}x^{p}_{j\cdot t}\right\}$$

$$+\sum_{t=1}^{4}\sum_{h=1}^{3}\sum_{p=1}^{p(h)}\sum_{i=1}^{2}\sum_{j=5}^{6}\sum_{t'=t+1}^{5} {}^{h}_{i}\varepsilon^{p}_{j\cdot tt'}\times {}^{h}_{i}x^{p}_{j\cdot tt'}+\sum_{t=2}^{5}\sum_{h=1}^{3}\sum_{p=1}^{p(h)}\sum_{i=1}^{2}\sum_{j=5}^{6}\sum_{s=1}^{t-1} {}^{h}_{i}\varepsilon^{p}_{j\cdot st}\times {}^{h}_{i}x^{p}_{j\cdot st}$$

$$+\sum_{t=1}^{4}\sum_{h=3}^{3}\sum_{p=1}^{p(h)}\sum_{i=1}^{2}\sum_{j=7}^{7}\sum_{t'=t+1}^{5} {}^{h}_{i}\varepsilon^{p}_{j\cdot tt'}\times {}^{h}_{i}x^{p}_{j\cdot tt'}+\sum_{t=2}^{5}\sum_{h=3}^{3}\sum_{p=1}^{p(h)}\sum_{i=1}^{2}\sum_{j=7}^{7}\sum_{s=1}^{t-1} {}^{h}_{i}\varepsilon^{p}_{j\cdot st}\times {}^{h}_{i}x^{p}_{j\cdot st} \quad (3.26)$$

in which:

${}^{h}_{i}\varepsilon^{p}_{j\cdot t}$: the evaluation coefficient associated with the choice variable of the construction en bloc, ${}^{h}_{i}x^{p}_{j\cdot t}$,

${}^{h}_{i}\varepsilon^{p}_{j\cdot tt'}$, ${}^{h}_{i}\varepsilon^{p}_{j\cdot st}$: the evaluation coefficients associated with the choice variable of two-stage construction, ${}^{h}_{i}x^{p}_{j\cdot tt'}$ and ${}^{h}_{i}x^{p}_{j\cdot st}$; the evaluation coefficient, ${}^{h}_{i}\varepsilon^{p}_{j\cdot tt'}$, is the same value for all $t' = t + 1, \cdots, 5$ and ${}^{h}_{i}\varepsilon^{p}_{j\cdot st}$ is the same value for all $s = 1, 2, \cdots, t-1$, as far as other attributes are same. So, we may express the same values as ${}^{h}_{i}\varepsilon^{p}_{j\cdot t*}$ $(t = 1, 2, 3, 4)$ and ${}^{h}_{i}\varepsilon^{p}_{j\cdot *t}$ $(t = 2, 3, 4, 5)$, respectively.[16]

The evaluation coefficients are exogenously given, and the estimated present values of the net benefits that are created by the investment to the construction. So, if the period in which the construction is made is only different though other attributes are all same, the evaluation coefficient is different. As for the two-stage construction, the evaluation coefficient is split into two parts depending on the periods in which the first and second construction are made. The evaluation coefficient of the first (second) stage construction is not dependent on the period in which the second (first) stage construction is done as far as other attributes are same, respectively. Therefore, the coefficients of ${}^{h}_{i}x^{p}_{j\cdot rs}$ eventually becomes: ${}^{h}_{i}\varepsilon^{p}_{j\cdot r*} + {}^{h}_{i}\varepsilon^{p}_{j\cdot *s}$ for $(h = 1, 2, 3; p = 1, 2, \cdots, p(h); i = 1, 2; j = 5, 6; r = 1, 2, \cdots, 4; s = 2, \cdots, 5)$, and $(h = 3; p = 1, 2, \cdots, p(h); i = 1, 2; j = 7; \quad r = 1, 2, \cdots, 4; s = t + 1, \cdots, 5)$.

Actually, in Eq. (3.26), ${}^{h}_{i}x^{p}_{j\cdot rs}$ is appearing twice as for $(h = 1, 2, 3; p = 1, 2, \cdots, p(h); i = 1, 2; j = 5, 6; r = 1, 2, \cdots, 4; s = 2, \cdots, 5)$, and $(h = 3; \quad p = 1, 2, \cdots, p(h); i = 1, 2; j = 7; \quad r = 1, 2, \cdots, 4; s = t + 1, \cdots, 5)$.

[Budgetary Constraints]

$$\begin{aligned}
&\sum_{h=1}^{3}\sum_{p=1}^{p(h)}\sum_{i=1}^{2}\sum_{j=1}^{4}{}^{h}_{i}C^{p}_{j\cdot t} \times {}^{h}_{i}x^{p}_{j\cdot t} + \sum_{h=3}^{3}\sum_{p=1}^{p(h)}\sum_{i=1}^{2}\sum_{j=7}^{7}{}^{h}_{i}C^{p}_{j\cdot t} \times {}^{h}_{i}x^{p}_{j\cdot t} \\
&\quad + \sum_{h=1}^{3}\sum_{p=1}^{p(h)}\sum_{i=1}^{2}\sum_{j=5}^{6}\left\{\sum_{t'=t+1}^{5}{}^{h}_{i}C^{p}_{j\cdot tt'} \times {}^{h}_{i}x^{p}_{j\cdot tt'} + \sum_{s=1}^{t-1}{}^{h}_{i}C^{p}_{j\cdot st} \times {}^{h}_{i}x^{p}_{j\cdot st}\right\} \\
&\quad + \sum_{h=3}^{3}\sum_{p=1}^{p(h)}\sum_{i=1}^{2}\sum_{j=7}^{7}\left\{\sum_{t'=t+1}^{5}{}^{h}_{i}C^{p}_{j\cdot tt'} \times {}^{h}_{i}x^{p}_{j\cdot tt'} + \sum_{s=1}^{t-1}{}^{h}_{i}C^{p}_{j\cdot st} \times {}^{h}_{i}x^{p}_{j\cdot st}\right\} \\
&\quad \le \overline{C}_t \text{ for all } t\ (t = 1, 2, 3, 4, 5)
\end{aligned} \tag{3.27}$$

in which:

$\overline{C}_t$: amount of the capital funds available for the investments at period $t\ (t = 1, 2, 3, 4, 5)$,

---

[16] Other attributes with which the two-stage construction can be made are confined and no need to specify as far as no confusion.

${}^{h}_{i}C^{p}_{j\cdot t}$: the coefficient of the drain on the capital fund associated with the choice variable of the construction en bloc, ${}^{h}_{i}x^{p}_{j\cdot t}$,

${}^{h}_{i}C^{p}_{j\cdot tt'}$, ${}^{h}_{i}C^{p}_{j\cdot st}$: the coefficients of the drain on the capital fund associated with the choice variable of two-stage construction, of which first construction is made at period t (s) and second construction is made at period t' (t). The drain coefficient of the first (second) stage construction is not dependent on the period in which the second (first) stage construction is done as far as other attributes are the same, respectively. The value of ${}^{h}_{i}C^{p}_{j\cdot tt'}$ is the same for all $t' = t+1, \cdots, 5$ and ${}^{h}_{i}C^{p}_{j\cdot st}$ is the same for all $s = 1, \cdots, t-1$. We express them as ${}^{h}_{i}C^{p}_{j\cdot t*}$ and ${}^{h}_{i}C^{p}_{j\cdot *t}$, respectively. Therefore, if the two-stage construction is chosen, the drain on the investment fund appearing twice in the above budgetary constraints with different periods. Namely, if ${}^{h}_{i}x^{p}_{j\cdot rs}$ is chosen, the drain becomes burdens on the budget of capital funds at period r and s ($1 \le r < s \le 5$) as ${}^{h}_{i}C^{p}_{j\cdot r*}$ and ${}^{h}_{i}C^{p}_{j\cdot *s}$, respectively.

[Incompatibility Constraints]

(1) Section Incompatibility

It means that if the segment is constructed it is only once through the time horizon.

(a) As for routes 1 and 2 (public construction only)

$$\sum_{i=1}^{2}\sum\nolimits_{j=1}^{4}\sum\nolimits_{t=1}^{5}{}^{h}_{i}x^{p}_{j\cdot t}+\sum_{i=1}^{2}\sum\nolimits_{j=5}^{6}\sum\nolimits_{t=1}^{4}\sum\nolimits_{t'=t+1}^{5}{}^{h}_{i}x^{p}_{j\cdot tt'}$$
$$\le 1 \text{ for all } h\ (h=1,2) \text{ and all } p\ (p=1,2,\cdots,p(h)), \tag{3.28a}$$

(b) As for route 3 (public and private construction)

$$\sum_{i=1}^{2}\sum\nolimits_{j=1}^{4}\sum\nolimits_{t=1}^{5}{}^{h}_{i}x^{p}_{j\cdot t}+\sum_{i=1}^{2}\sum\nolimits_{j=5}^{7}\sum\nolimits_{t=1}^{4}\sum\nolimits_{t'=t+1}^{5}{}^{h}_{i}x^{p}_{j\cdot tt'}$$
$$+\sum_{i=1}^{2}\sum\nolimits_{j=7}^{7}\sum\nolimits_{t=1}^{5}{}^{h}_{i}x^{p}_{j\cdot t}$$
$$\le 1 \text{ for } h=3 \tag{3.28b}$$

(2) Route (in)Compatibility Condition

It means that if the segments are constructed, they must be able to be connected with a certain route i. It is difficult to specify the condition with linear equations. With the empirical example shown later, the route is uniquely determined and the condition is unnecessary. With a general case, we try to specify the condition in nonlinear functions, to which a currently available mathematical optimization software may be able to be dealt with, thanks to incredibly dramatic progress in the computer capacity and ubiquitous prevalence.

For simplicity, we firstly define several functions in the choice variables. With respect $r = 1, 2$ and $h = 1, 2$,

$$ {}^{h}_{r}\overline{D} \equiv \sum_{p=1}^{p(h)} \sum_{i \neq r} \sum_{t=1}^{5} \sum_{j=1}^{4} {}^{h}_{i}x^{p}_{j \cdot t} + \sum_{p=1}^{p(h)} \sum_{i \neq r} \sum_{t=1}^{4} \sum_{t'=t+1}^{5} \sum_{j=5}^{6} {}^{h}_{i}x^{p}_{j \cdot tt'} \tag{3.29a} $$

With respect $r = 1, 2$ and $h = 3$,

$$ {}^{h}_{r}\overline{D} \equiv \sum_{p=1}^{p(h)} \sum_{i \neq r} \sum_{t=1}^{5} \sum_{j=1}^{4} {}^{h}_{i}x^{p}_{j \cdot t} + \sum_{p=1}^{p(h)} \sum_{i \neq r} \sum_{t=1}^{5} \sum_{j=7}^{7} {}^{h}_{i}x^{p}_{j \cdot t} + \sum_{p=1}^{p(h)} \sum_{i \neq r} \sum_{t=1}^{4} \sum_{t'=t+1}^{5} \sum_{j=5}^{7} {}^{h}_{i}x^{p}_{j \cdot tt'} \tag{3.29b} $$

If ${}^{h}_{r}\overline{D} \neq 0$, the construction of highway/expressway h ($h = 1, 2, 3$) was done with at least one section of the route other than r.

With respect $r = 1, 2$ and $h = 1, 2$,

$$ {}^{h}_{r}D \equiv \text{the right-hand side of Eq.(3.29a)but all the operations of summation, } \sum_{i \neq r}\text{, be replaced by the operation of summation, } \sum_{i=r}^{r} \tag{3.30a} $$

With respect $r = 1, 2$ and $h = 3$,

$$ {}^{h}_{r}D \equiv \text{the right-hand side of Eq.(3.29b) but all the operations of summation, } \sum_{i \neq r} \text{ be replaced by the operation of summation, } \sum_{i=r}^{r} \tag{3.30b} $$

If ${}^{h}_{r}D = 1$, the construction of highway/expressway h ($h = 1, 2, 3$) was done with at least one section of the route r.

If ${}^{h}_{r}D = 1$, we define it is true and it is false otherwise. If ${}^{h}_{r}\overline{D} = 1$, we define it is true and it is false otherwise. The route compatibility is attained by adding the following function to the objective function as it is only attained when the logical conjunction is false:

$$ L = \sum_{h=1}^{3} \sum_{s=1}^{2} \gamma \times {}^{h}_{s}D \times {}^{h}_{s}\overline{D}, \tag{3.31} $$

in which γ is a negative constant of which absolute value is quite large. As the loss to the objective function is too large due to Eq. (3.31) if ${}^{h}_{s}D = 1$ and ${}^{h}_{s}\overline{D}=1$, which means the construction is done with segments of different routes, the case ${}^{h}_{s}D \times {}^{h}_{s}\overline{D} = 1$ is excluded from the optimal solution to the problem, which means the route incompatibility holds. We can analogically formulate compatibility constraints with *grade and/or way of construction*. However, such a constraint would apparently induce wasteful drain on the budget since it must sometimes neglect inefficient section valuation coefficients, which results in decrease in the maximized objective function value. We skip the formulation.

(3) Completeness of two-stage construction

It means that if two-stage construction is chosen, the first and second construction must be completed within the time horizon. With the coding above, the definition of ${}^{h}_{i}x^{p}_{j\cdot tt'}$ is already meet this condition since t and t'satisfy $1 \leq t < t' \leq 5$. In case it is admitted that the second stage construction is not completed in the time horizon, we additionally need the definition of two different variables such that ${}^{h}_{i}x^{p}_{j\cdot t*}$ and ${}^{h}_{i}x^{p}_{j\cdot *t'}$. The former can be 0 or 1 and the latter can be 1 if the former is 1, otherwise always 0. Of course, all the specifications must be changed, accordingly, and it is no further treated here.

(4) Construction order constraint

It should be dependent on the planning concept and in case there is a certain predetermined priority (order) with the construction timing of expressway/highway sections. In that case, the index attached to segments (of course ascending order) must follow the descending order priority. Generally, the section that creates larger benefits should be given high priority and constructed earlier. However, sometimes it is not necessarily a reality due to several reasons. It is very difficult to specify the construction order constraint in linear constraints, too. We try to specify it in nonlinear constraints with the same idea above.

For simplicity, we define a several functions in the choice variables.[17]

With respect to $h = 1, 2$ and $p = 1, 2, \cdot\cdot\cdot, p(h)$, $t = 2, 3, 4, 5$

$$
\begin{aligned}
{}^{h}F^{p}_{t} \equiv\ & \sum_{s=1}^{p-1} \sum_{i=1}^{2} \sum_{j=1}^{4} \sum_{k=1}^{t} {}^{h}_{i}x^{s}_{j\cdot k} \\
& + \sum_{s=1}^{p-1} \sum_{i=1}^{2} \sum_{j=5}^{6} \sum_{k=1}^{t} \sum_{t'=k+1}^{5} {}^{h}_{i}x^{s}_{j\cdot kt'}
\end{aligned}
\tag{3.32a}
$$

With respect to $h = 3$ and $p = 1, 2, \cdot\cdot\cdot, p(h)$,

[17] We may postulate that $\sum_{i=s}^{r} X = 0$ with whatever X if $s > r$ for simplicity of the specification.

$$
\begin{aligned}
{}^{h}F_t^p \equiv\ & \sum_{s=1}^{p-1} \sum_{i=1}^{2} \sum_{j=1}^{4} \sum_{k=1}^{t} {}^{h}_{i}x^{s}_{j\cdot k} \\
& + \sum_{s=1}^{p-1} \sum_{i=1}^{2} \sum_{j=7}^{7} \sum_{k=1}^{t} {}^{h}_{i}x^{s}_{j\cdot k} \\
& + \sum_{s=1}^{p-1} \sum_{i=1}^{2} \sum_{j=5}^{7} \sum_{k=1}^{t} \sum_{t'=k+1}^{5} {}^{h}_{i}x^{s}_{j\cdot kt'}
\end{aligned} \tag{3.32b}
$$

If ${}^{h}F_t^p = p-1$, it implies that the construction of the sections $1, 2, \cdots, p-1$ of the expressway/highway h is completed by the end of the period t with route $i = 1$ only or $i = 2$ only due to the route incompatibility. Only in this case, the section p of the expressway/highway h (with already determined route) can be (chosen to be) constructed at the period t, otherwise not.

With respect $r = 1, 2$ and $h = 1, 2$,

${}^{h}G_t^p \equiv$ the right-hand side of Eq. (3.32a) but all the operations of summation,

$$
\sum_{s=1}^{p-1}, \text{ be replaced by the operation of summation, } \sum_{s=p}^{p} \tag{3.33a}
$$

With respect $r = 1, 2$ and $h = 3$,

${}^{h}G_t^p \equiv$ the right-hand side of Eq. (3.32b) but all the operations of summation,

$$
\sum_{s=1}^{p-1} \text{ be replaced by the operation of summation, } \sum_{s=p}^{p}. \tag{3.33b}
$$

${}^{h}G_t^p$=0 means that the construction of the segment p is not made (with already predetermined route due to the route incompatibility constraint). If ${}^{h}G_t^p$=1, it means that the segment p of the expressway/highway h is constructed at the period t. With the same logic above, the construction order constraints are satisfied by adding the following function to the objective function:

$$
W = \sum_{h=1}^{3} \sum_{p=1}^{p(h)} \sum_{t=2}^{5} \gamma \times {}^{h}G_t^p \times \left\{ {}^{h}F_t^p - \left(\sum_{s=1}^{p-1} 1 \right) \right\} \tag{3.34}
$$

(4) Other constraints

(a) Nonnegative discrete variables

${}^{h}_{i}x^{s}_{j\cdot t}$ is 0 or 1.

${}^{h}_{i}x^{s}_{j\cdot tt'}$ is 0 or 1.

(b) Capacity constraints

As a preempt right, a certain segment may have a certain capacity in terms of traffic volumes by a certain period. For example, as for $h = 1$ and $p = 4$, the capacity be ${}^{1}K_t^4$ by (the end of) the period t with either route $i = 1$ or $i = 2$. The following constraint expresses the requirement:

$$\sum_{i=1}^{2}\sum_{s=1}^{t}\sum_{j=1}^{4}{}_{i}^{1}\Delta_{j}^{4}\times{}_{i}^{1}x_{j\cdot s}^{4}+\sum_{i=1}^{2}\sum_{s=1}^{t}\sum_{j=5}^{6}\sum_{k=s+1}^{5}{}_{i}^{1}\Delta_{j\cdot sk}^{4}\times{}_{i}^{1}x_{j\cdot sk}^{4}$$
$$+\sum_{i=1}^{2}\sum_{s=2}^{t}\sum_{j=5}^{6}\sum_{k=1}^{s-1}{}_{i}^{1}\Delta_{j\cdot ks}^{4}\times{}_{i}^{1}x_{j\cdot ks}^{4}$$
$$\geq {}^{1}K_t^4, \tag{3.35a}$$

in which:

${}_{i}^{1}\Delta_{j}^{4}$: increase in the capacity of the expressway/highway ($h = 1$, section 4 ($p = 4$)) at period t thanks to the construction at period s, ${}_{i}^{1}x_{j\cdot s}^{4} = 1\ \ (s = 1, 2, \cdots, t)$,

${}_{i}^{1}\Delta_{j\cdot st'}^{4}$: increase in the capacity of the expressway/highway ($h = 1$, section 4 ($p = 4$)) at period t thanks to the first stage construction at period s, ${}_{i}^{1}x_{j\cdot st'}^{4} = 1\ \ (s = 1, 2, \cdots, t; t' = s + 1, \cdots, 5)$,

${}_{i}^{1}\Delta_{rs}^{4}$: increase in the capacity of the expressway/highway ($h = 1$, section 4 ($p = 4$)) at period t thanks to the second stage construction at period s, ${}_{i}^{1}x_{j\cdot rs}^{4} = 1\ \ (r = 1, 2, \cdots, t-1; s = r + 1, \cdots, t)$.[18]

An alternative way to specify the above constraint, Eq. (3.35a), is first to specify a kind of stock variable,

$${}^{1}KC_t^4 = {}^{1}K_{t-1}^4 + \sum_{i=1}^{2}\sum_{j=1}^{4}{}_{i}^{1}\Delta_{j}^{4}\times{}_{i}^{1}x_{j\cdot t}^{4} + \sum_{i=1}^{2}\sum_{j=5}^{6}\sum_{s=1}^{t-1}{}_{i}^{1}\Delta_{j\cdot st}^{4}\times{}_{i}^{1}x_{j\cdot st}^{4}$$
$$+\sum_{i=1}^{2}\sum_{j=5}^{6}\sum_{r=t+1}^{5}{}_{i}^{1}\Delta_{j\cdot tr}^{4}\times{}_{i}^{1}x_{j\cdot tr}^{4}\ \ (t = 1, 2, 3, 4, 5) \tag{3.35b}$$

Define ${}^{1}K_0^4 = 0$, Eq. (3.35a) can be expressed as follows:

$${}^{1}KC_t^4 \geq {}^{1}K_t^4 \tag{3.35c}$$

(5) Other Pre-Empt Right Condition

[18] Because of the section incompatibility, which means a certain route is uniquely determined, there is no calculation of $\Delta's$ over different route.

It might become complicated, and most of the preempt right conditions can be specified in the same way. Yet, some of the preempt conditions can be specified with the phase of the coding combined with the specification of the model. Actually, a private company can only bid for the construction of Tokyo-Gaikan ($h = 3$), and this causes a little bit complicated specification of the objective function and constraints above. Alternatively, we can specify as follows.

[PreEmpt Right Constraint: Example] Firstly, define the choice variables ${}^{h}_{i}x^{p}_{7\cdot t}$ and ${}^{h}_{i}x^{p}_{7\cdot tt'}$ for all h, i, $p(h)$, t ($t = 1,2,3,4$) and t' ($t' = 2,3,4,5$). The following constraints formulate preempt right of the public sector with the construction of expressway $h = 1$ and $h = 2$:

${}^{h}_{i}x^{p}_{7\cdot t} = 0$ for all $h = 1, 2$; $i = 1, 2$; $p = 1, 2, \cdots, p(h)$, and $t = 1, 2, 3, 4, 5$; and

${}^{h}_{i}x^{p}_{7\cdot tt'} = 0$ for all $h = 1, 2$; $i = 1, 2$; $p = 1, 2, \cdots, p(h)$, $t = 1, 2, 3, 4$; $t' = 2, 3, 4, 5$ ($t < t'$).

A merit of the formulation is that it makes the model specification simple. The demerit is that the no. of variables increases and it was critical considering the capacity of compute and software on that day.

3.3.3 Restrictions by the Computer Capacity Constraints

At the time when the work (Kohno 1968) was done, the calculation capacity (computation speed, memory, and precision) of the computer and the software with which the mathematical optimization problem can be solved are very limited. First of all, it caused the number of variables be less than 200 or so. Next, the number of constraints must be less than 50 or so.

Express the cases produced by index n which is running from n_1 to n_2 by $[n]^{n_2}_{n_1} = (n_2 - n_1 + 1)$. The number of variables, ${}^{h}_{i}x^{p}_{j\cdot tt'}$ produced by combination of t and t' with given set of i, h, p, and j is 10 (=5 × 4/2).

$[\mathrm{t}]^5_1\{\left([\mathrm{h}]^2_1 \times [\mathrm{i}]^2_1 \times [\mathrm{j}]^4_1 + [\mathrm{h}]^3_3 \times [\mathrm{i}]^2_1 \times [\mathrm{j}]^7_7\right) + [\mathrm{h}]^3_1 \times [\mathrm{i}]^2_1 \times [\mathrm{j}]^6_5 \times$ $10 + [\mathrm{h}]^3_3 \times [\mathrm{i}]^2_1 \times [\mathrm{j}]^7_7 \times 10\} \times [\mathrm{p}]^{10}_1 = 2200$

A rough calculation of the number of variables with the above coding indicates that the number of variables becomes more than 2200 if the no. of sections of the expressway/highway is 10 for each.

3.3.4 Confining the Investment Targets

Due to the limitation of the computer capacity above, the number of project targets must be decreased to 8:

Tohoku Expressway/highway ($h = 1$)

1. Tokyo–Iwatsuki ($h = 1; p = 1$)
2. Iwatsuki–Tatebayashi ($h = 1; p = 2$)
3. Sendai–Ichinoseki ($h = 1; p = 3$)
4. Towada–Aomori ($h = 1; p = 4$)
   Kan-Etsu Expressway/highway ($h = 2$)
5. Kawagoe–Maebash ($h = 2; p = 1$)
6. Nagano–Naoetsu ($h = 2; p = 2$)
   Tokyo–gaikan Expressway/highway ($h = 3$)
7. Dainikeihin-Chuo-do-Guchi ($h = 3; p = 1$)
8. Chuo-do-Guchi-Tohokudo-Guchi ($h = 3; p = 2$).

Only one route is specified for each target. As for $h = 1$ and 2, $i = 1$ and as for $h = 3$, $i = 2$. So, no variation exists with the route choice.

Finally, as for the grade of traffic lane and the way of construction, and periods, the following combination is predetermined ($|x|$ is the number of choice variable produced by the confinement of the indices):

1. Tokyo-Iwaki ($h = 1; p = 1$) $j \in \{1, 2, 5, 6\}$ $t = 1$, 2, 3,4,5 $|x| = 30$
   En bloc choice variables: $2 \times 5 = 10$
   Two stage construction: $2 \times (5 \times 4 \div 2) = 20$
2. Iwatsuki-Tatebayashi ($h = 1; p = 2$) $j \in \{1, 2, 5, 6\}$ $t = 1$, 2, 3,4,5 $|x| = 30$
   En bloc choice variables: $2 \times 5 = 10$
   Two stage construction: $2 \times (5 \times 4 \div 2) = 20$
3. Sendai-Ichinoseki ($h = 1; p = 3$) $j \in \{2, 5\}$ t=1,2,3,4,5 $|x| = 15$
   En bloc choice variables: $1 \times 5 = 5$
   Two stage construction: $1 \times (5 \times 4 \div 2) = 10$
4. Towada-Aomori ($h = 1; p = 4$) $j \in \{2, 3, 4, 5\}$ t=1,2,3,4,5 $|x| = 25$
   En bloc choice variables: $3 \times 5 = 15$
   Two stage construction: $1 \times (5 \times 4 \div 2) = 10$
5. Kawagoe-Maebash ($h = 2; p = 1$) $\{1, 2, 5\}$ t=1,2,3,4,5 $|x| = 30$
   En bloc choice variables: $2 \times 5 = 10$
   Two stage construction: $2 \times (5 \times 4 \div 2) = 20$
6. Nagano-Naoetsu ($h = 2; p = 2$) $j \in \{2, 3, 4, 5\}$ t=1,2,3,4,5 $|x| = 25$
   En bloc choice variables: $3 \times 5 = 15$
   Two stage construction: $1 \times (5 \times 4 \div 2) = 10$
7. Dainikeihin-Chuo-do-Gucchi ($h = 3; p = 1$) $j \in \{1, 7\}$ $t = 1$, 2, 3, 4, 5 $|x| = 15$
   (private and en bloc)
   En bloc choice variables: $1 \times 5 = 5$
   Two-stage construction: $1 \times (5 \times 4 \div 2) = 10$
8. Chuo-do-Guchi-Tohokudo-Guchi ($h = 3; p = 2$) $j \in \{1, 7\}$ $|x| = 15$
   (private and en bloc).
   En bloc choice variables: $1 \times 5 = 5$
   Two-stage construction: $1 \times (5 \times 4 \div 2) = 10$

Eventually, we had succeeded to confine the number of choice variables into 185.

The number of constraints is calculated as follows (|*EQ*| means the number of equations (constraints + objective functions):

1. Objective function $|EQ| = 1$
2. Budgetary constraints $|EQ| = 5$ (the number of periods)
3. Section incompatibility $|EQ| = 8$ (the number of sections)
4. Choice variables among 0 or 1 $|EQ| = 0$

   Theoretically, the choice variables are discrete variables and must be 0 or 1. However, when the work (Kohno 1968) was done, the software that would deal with an integer programming problem did not practically perform well. So, in place of using discrete variables, the choice variables are taken as continuous variables and have values between 0 and 1. The section incompatibility constraints request the continuous choice variables must be less than 1 (we will need to consider an interpretation of the continuous choice variables or alternative solution algorithm to the integer programming specification). As a default, the linear programming software requests all variables must be non-negative. So, no constrains are necessary for this category.
5. Capacity constraints $|EQ| = 8$

   Presuming the possibility to adopt the two-stage construction with all the sections, capacity constraints are confined:
   with h = 1, on section $p = 1$ at period 3 and 4
   with h = 2, on section $p = 2$ at period 3 and 4
   with h = 3, on section $p = 1$ at period 2 and 4
   on section $p = 2$ at period 4 and 5.

For example, as for $h = 1$ and $p = 1$ (Tokyo–Iwatsuki), the capacity of the expressway must be 36,000 vehicles/day or more than that by (the end of) period 3 and must be 67,000 vehicle/day by period 4. Eventually, the number of constraints becomes 21.

3.3.5 Valuation Coefficients

The valuation coefficients are calculated as follows. First, the stream of gross benefits and the construction costs are calculated for each choice variable in terms of the present values. As for calculation of the stream of benefits, there are three cases: Cases 1, 2, and 3. In cases 1, 2, and 3, the stream of the benefits created by the construction of expressway/highway till the years of 1994, 2004, and 2014, respectively, are capitalized at the present value (at the year of 1965) with three different discount rates: 5%, 4%, and 3%. The valuation coefficients are given as the net benefits of the choice variables, namely, the present value of the gross benefits minus the present value of the construction costs (Table 3.2) shows a part of such valuation coefficients).

Table 3.2 Valuation coefficients

	Consecutive number		1	2	3	4	5	6	7
Variant number	Cases	Social discount rate	${}_1^1\varepsilon_{1\cdot 1}^1$	${}_1^1\varepsilon_{1\cdot 2}^1$	${}_1^1\varepsilon_{1\cdot 3}^1$	${}_1^1\varepsilon_{1\cdot 4}^1$	${}_1^1\varepsilon_{1\cdot 5}^1$	${}_1^1\varepsilon_{2\cdot 1}^1$	${}_1^1\varepsilon_{2\cdot 2}^1$
I	Case 1	5%	26,064	25,379	21,317	13,776	4643	40,231	37,034
II		4%	35,229	32,966	27,306	17,822	6367	49,809	45,428
III		3%	46,432	42,416	34,878	23,036	8679	61,444	55,751
IV	Case 2	5%	40,632	39,948	35,886	28,345	19,212	54,799	51,603
V		4%	55,044	52,781	47,121	37,637	26,682	69,624	65,243
VI		3%	73,482	69,466	61,928	50,086	35,730	88,490	82,801
VII	Case 3	5%	49,576	48,892	44,830	37,289	28,156	63,743	60,547
VIII		4%	68,430	66,167	60,507	51,023	39,568	83,010	78,628
IX		3%	93,610	89,594	82,057	70,214	55,858	108,618	102,929
	Period t		1	2	3	4	5	1	2

Note: Case 1: the stream of benefits till 1994 are capitalized (the time span is 30 years)
Case 2: the stream of benefits till 2004 are capitalized (the time span is 40 years)
Case 3: the stream of benefits till 2014 are capitalized (the time span is 50 years)

Table 3.3 Capital funds (unit: million JPY)

Period t	1	2	3	4	5	
The last year of the period t	1968	1972	1976	1980	1984	Total
$\overline{C}_t$	105,000	206,800	46,300	52,600	12,300	423,000

Source: The author calculated based on The Ministry of Construction (1966)

3.3.6 *Budget Constraint*

The capital funds assignment must meet the budget constraints given at each period. The funds can be spent for any investment target within the period. The amount of the capital funds at period t, $\overline{C}_t$, are shown in Table 3.3

3.4 Solutions for the Optimization Problem

3.4.1 *Computer and Algorithm*

When the work (Kohno 1968) was done, the machine used for the calculation was HITAC8500. Considering the recent development in IT technologies, which is based on super-ultra-high-speed CPU, it looks that the machine lived in a dawn of Homo sapiens idaltu. The required run time was 1 h 13 min 17 s for Case 1 and 1 h 15 min and 53 s for Case 2. The run time meant the elapsing time from (1) the input of the paper tape, to which data of the algorithm and parameters are punched, to the machine to (2) the output by the machine on print sheets with a *line printer*. The so-called core memory was less than 524K bite of 32 bits. It must occupy a fairly big room.

The integer programming algorithm was available on that day, and it did not work well practically. The following combinatorial and iterative solution process was applied to manage it.

1. First, apply the ordinal linear programming software to solve the problem assuming that the choice variables are continuous between 0 and 1. The problem thus defined is called continuous optimization problem.
2. Second, assign 1 or 0 alternatively to all the non-zero optimal solutions (they are called *chosen variables*; other choice variables are called *non-chosen variables*) for the continuous optimization problem of above (1). Thus, a set that consists of the combinations of chosen variables of which values are 0 or 1 can be obtained, which is called – combinatorial set.
3. With the continuous optimization problem of above (1), set the chosen variables equal to 0 or 1 corresponding to an element of the combinatorial set. The optimization problem is called pseudo-integer optimization problem. Solve all the pseudo-integer optimization problems that correspond to elements in the combinatorial set. Find an element in the combinatorial set, which constructs a

feasible pseudo-integer optimization problem and attains the maximum maximorum objective function value among the feasible pseudo-integer optimization problems. If there still exist choice variables that are not chosen variables and have non-zero values with the pseudo-integer optimization problem that gives the maximum maximorum objective function value, go back to process (2) by expanding the set of chosen variables. The process will be recursively applied till the following holds.
4. If there are *no feasible* solutions that give non-zero values to non-chosen variables with all the pseudo-integer optimization problems, the process stops. The obtained maximum maximorum solution with the precedent pseudo-integer optimization problem can be taken as an approximate to the optimal solution to the original integer programming problem.

Since the capital funds assignment problem specified earlier is very simple, we were actually able to confirm that thus obtained optimal solution is the solution to the original integer optimization problem by looking at all possible combinations of choice variables that have 0 or 1.

3.4.2 Image of the Integer Programming Format

Table 3.4 shows an image of the integer programming format of the optimal capital fund allocation problem. The second row, $[\varepsilon]$, is a row vector of 206 elements that consists of the valuation coefficients with the choice variables of the en bloc construction. The first row, $[\varepsilon']$, consists of the valuation coefficients with the choice variables of the two-stage construction. We need it as the benefits are to be calculated twice which will be made by the first and second stage construction if a two-stage construction variable is chosen. The third row shows the activity number of choice variables from 1 to 206 including activities of slack variables. Rows indexed by row numbers from 1 to 21 indicate coefficients of the constraints specified above. Row 1 corresponds to the budgetary constraint at period 1. Non-zero elements are coefficients of the costs which are incurred if the choice variables are 1. Row 6 corresponds to the section incompatibility constraint. The rows 14, 15, 18, 19, 20, and 21 correspond to the capacity constraints. For example, the capacity of section $p = 1$ of expressway/highway $h = 1$ at period 3 must be ${}^{1}K_{3}^{1}$ or more than that. In place of specifying variables ${}^{1}K_{3}^{1}$, a same constraint is made by adjusting coefficients like $(\cdots, -67{,}000, -67{,}000, -67{,}000, 0, 0, \cdots)$. [19]The signs of minus $(-)$ are results of making the original inequalities of the capacity constraints which are open to the left to be open to the right by multiplying both sides with -1 for the coefficients of slack variables associated with the rows of capacity constraint

[19]The capacity of 6 lanes expressway per day is 67,000 vehicles per day. That of 4 lanes is 36,000 vehicles per day.

Table 3.4 Integer programing format of the optimal capital fund allocation problem

Column no.	1	2	3	4	5	6	7	8	9	10	$n-1$	n	$n+1$	m	r	184	185	205	206
$[\varepsilon']$:	0	0	0	0	0	0	0	0	0	0	${}^3_1\varepsilon^1_{7\cdot *5}$	${}^3_1\varepsilon^2_{7\cdot 2*}$	${}^3_1\varepsilon^2_{7\cdot *3}$	${}^3_1\varepsilon^2_{7\cdot *3}$	${}^3_1\varepsilon^2_{7\cdot *4}$	${}^3_1\varepsilon^2_{7\cdot *5}$	${}^3_1\varepsilon^2_{7\cdot *5}$	0	0
$[\varepsilon]$:	${}^1_1\varepsilon^1_{1\cdot1}$	${}^1_1\varepsilon^1_{1\cdot2}$	${}^1_1\varepsilon^1_{1\cdot3}$	${}^1_1\varepsilon^1_{1\cdot4}$	${}^1_1\varepsilon^1_{1\cdot5}$	${}^1_1\varepsilon^1_{2\cdot1}$	${}^1_1\varepsilon^1_{2\cdot2}$	${}^1_1\varepsilon^1_{2\cdot3}$	${}^1_1\varepsilon^1_{2\cdot4}$	${}^1_1\varepsilon^1_{2\cdot5}$	$\varepsilon^1_{7\cdot4*}$	${}^3_1\varepsilon^2_{7\cdot1*}$	${}^3_1\varepsilon^2_{7\cdot1*}$	${}^3_1\varepsilon^2_{7\cdot2*}$	${}^3_1\varepsilon^2_{7\cdot3*}$	${}^3_1\varepsilon^2_{7\cdot3*}$	${}^3_1\varepsilon^2_{7\cdot4*}$	0	0
$[X]$:	${}^1_1x^1_{1\cdot1}$	${}^1_1x^1_{1\cdot2}$	${}^1_1x^1_{1\cdot3}$	${}^1_1x^1_{1\cdot4}$	${}^1_1x^1_{1\cdot5}$	${}^1_1x^1_{2\cdot1}$	${}^1_1x^1_{2\cdot2}$	${}^1_1x^1_{2\cdot3}$	${}^1_1x^1_{2\cdot4}$	${}^1_1x^1_{2\cdot5}$	${}^3_1x^1_{7\cdot45}$	${}^3_1x^2_{7\cdot12}$	${}^3_1x^2_{7\cdot13}$	${}^3_1x^2_{7\cdot23}$	${}^3_1x^2_{7\cdot34}$	${}^3_1x^2_{7\cdot35}$	${}^3_1x^2_{7\cdot45}$	${}^3_{\square}S^2_4$	${}^3_{\square}S^2_5$
Row no.																			
1	${}^1_1C^1_{1\cdot1}$					${}^1_1C^1_{2\cdot1}$						${}^3_1C^2_{7\cdot1*}$	${}^3_1C^2_{7\cdot1*}$						
2		${}^1_1C^1_{1\cdot2}$					${}^1_1C^1_{2\cdot2}$					${}^3_1C^2_{7\cdot*2}$		${}^3_1C^2_{7\cdot2*}$					
3			${}^1_1C^1_{1\cdot3}$					${}^1_1C^1_{2\cdot3}$					${}^3_1C^2_{7\cdot*3}$	${}^3_1C^2_{7\cdot*3}$	${}^3_1C^2_{7\cdot3*}$	${}^3_1C^2_{7\cdot3*}$			
4				${}^1_1C^1_{1\cdot4}$					${}^1_1C^1_{2\cdot4}$		${}^3_1C^1_{7\cdot4*}$				${}^3_1C^2_{7\cdot*4}$		${}^3_1C^2_{7\cdot4*}$		
5					${}^1_1C^1_{1\cdot5}$					${}^1_1C^1_{2\cdot5}$	${}^3_1C^1_{7\cdot*5}$					${}^3_1C^2_{7\cdot*5}$	${}^3_1C^2_{7\cdot*5}$		
6 $[A\|I]$:	1	1	1	1	1	1	1	1	1	1									
13												1	1	1	1	1	1		
14	−67,000	−67,000	−67,000	0	0	−36,000	−36,000	−36,000	0	0									
15	−67,000	−67,000	−67,000	−67,000	0	−36,000	−36,000	−36,000	−36,000	0									
16																			
18											0								
19											−36,000								
20												−67,000	−67,000	−67,000	−67,000	−36,000	−36,000	1	
21												−67,000	−67,000	−67,000	−67,000	−67,000	−67,000		1

$[B]$ $[B]$

$$[X]=\begin{bmatrix}\bar{C}_1\\ \bar{C}_2\\ \bar{C}_3\\ \bar{C}_4\\ \bar{C}_5\\ {}^1_{\square}I^1\\ {}^1_{\square}I^2\\ {}^1_{\square}I^3\\ {}^1_{\square}I^4\\ {}^2_{\square}I^1\\ {}^2_{\square}I^2\\ {}^3_{\square}I^1\\ {}^3_{\square}I^2\\ -{}^1_{\square}K^1_3\\ -{}^1_{\square}K^1_4\\ -{}^2_{\square}K^2_3\\ -{}^2_{\square}K^2_4\\ -{}^3_{\square}K^1_2\\ -{}^3_{\square}K^1_4\\ -{}^3_{\square}K^2_4\\ -{}^3_{\square}K^2_5\end{bmatrix}=\begin{bmatrix}1050\\ 2068\\ 463\\ 526\\ 123\\ 1\\ 1\\ 1\\ 1\\ 1\\ 1\\ 1\\ 1\\ -36{,}000\\ -67{,}000\\ -12{,}000\\ -36{,}000\\ -36{,}000\\ -67{,}000\\ -36{,}000\\ -67{,}000\end{bmatrix}$$

$\max_{\{X\}}[\varepsilon+\varepsilon'][X]$

Subject to

$[A|I][X]=[B]$

become plus one (+1), which constitute diagonal elements of the identity matrix of $[A|I]$, following the standard procedure of the simplex algorithm that the slack variables become the initial feasible solutions (initial basis). Corresponding to this, the capacity required, ${}^{1}K_{3}^{1}$, appears in the resource vector, $[B]$, with a minus value, namely $-{}^{1}K_{3}^{1}$ appears in $[B]$. This treatment decreases the number of explicit variables and the number of activities (columns of $[A|I]$). This is a good example to show how to formulate the optimization problem is not unique.

3.4.3 *Optimal Solutions by the Two Methods*

Table 3.5 shows the optimal solution with the continuous optimization problem which is solved by the ordinal LP method and the solution of the discrete optimization problem which is solved by the combinatorial method. There exists quite a difference between the solutions, and the maximized value of the objective functions are very close with each other. It can be considered that the combinatorial solution well closely hits the optimal solution. The solutions by the combinatorial method are shown in Table 3.6 together with the physical planning by The Ministry of Construction (1966).

3.5 Discussion on the Results of the Optimization

3.5.1 *Case Setting and Characteristics of Target Expressway/Highway*

As shown in Table 3.2, the cases are given by combinations of different discount rates and the time spans with which benefits created by the construction expressway/highway in the future are measured. The solution with the lower discount rate will relatively put emphasis on the future benefits compared to the higher discount rate. It is emphasized when the lower discount rate is combined with the longer time span. So, a typical comparison can be made with Variant I (discount rate is 5% and the time span is 30 years) and Variant IX (3% and 50 years).

Tohoku Expressway starts from Tokyo (Kawaguchi in Saitama Prefecture and linked to Tokyo-Gaikan and Metropolitan Expressways) and terminates at Aomori, the northernmost prefecture in the main island. Section Tokyo to Iwatsuki expected to contribute for relieving the traffic congestion (on the first-grade national highway no. 4) in the suburb of Tokyo. Iwatsuki to Tatebayashi was expected to meet vehicle traffic demand in Greater Tokyo. Sendai-Ichinoseki and Towada-Aomori had intentions of strategically developing the Tohoku District.

Kanetsu Expressway consists of Niigata Expressway and Joetsu Expressway. The former starts from Tokyo (Nerima Ward), goes through Takasaki City in Gunma

Table 3.5 Comparison between combinatorial (β) and LP (α) solutions

No.	1	2	3	4	5	6	7	8	
	Tohoku expressway (h =1)				Kanetsu expressway (h =2)		Tokyo-Gaikan expressway (h =3)		
Expressway/highway and sections	Tokyo - Iwatsuki ($p = 1$)	Iwatsuki - Tatebayashi ($p = 2$)	Sendai - Ichinoseki ($p = 3$)	Tawada - Aomori ($p = 4$)	Mawagoe - Maebashi ($p = 1$)	Nagano -Naoetsu ($p = 2$)	Dainikeihin - Chuodo ($p = 1$)	Chuodo - Tohokudo ($p = 2$)	The maximized value of the objective function (million JPY)
Non-zero chosen variables with Variant I ρ = 0.05 and T = 30 years	Continuous optimization problem (α)								
	(2)	(33)	(37)	(84)	(101)	(127)	(181)	(162)	382,104
	${}_{1}^{1}x_{1\cdot2}^{1}$	${}_{1}^{1}x_{7\cdot14}^{2}$	${}_{1}^{1}x_{5\cdot25}^{3}$	${}_{1}^{1}x_{4\cdot4}^{4}$	${}_{1}^{2}x_{2\cdot1}^{1}$	${}_{1}^{2}x_{4\cdot2}^{2}$	${}_{1}^{3}x_{7\cdot1}^{1}$	${}_{1}^{3}x_{1\cdot2}^{2}$	
	1.000	1.000	0.118	1.000	1.000	0.103	0.837	1.000	
			(62)			(137)	(182)		
			${}_{2}^{1}x_{1\cdot2}^{3}$			${}_{1}^{2}x_{5\cdot25}^{2}$	${}_{1}^{3}x_{7\cdot2}^{1}$		
			0.182			0.896	0.162		
			(63)						
			${}_{2}^{1}x_{1\cdot3}^{3}$						
			0.402						
			(64)						
			${}_{2}^{1}x_{1\cdot4}^{3}$						
			0.295						
	Combinatorial solution algorothm (β)								
	(2)	(21)	(56)	(83)	(107)	(137)	(181)	(176)	377,105
	${}_{1}^{1}x_{1\cdot2}^{1}$	${}_{1}^{1}x_{2\cdot1}^{2}$	${}_{1}^{1}x_{5\cdot24}^{3}$	${}_{1}^{1}x_{4\cdot3}^{4}$	${}_{1}^{2}x_{5\cdot13}^{1}$	${}_{1}^{2}x_{5\cdot25}^{2}$	${}_{1}^{3}x_{7\cdot1}^{1}$	${}_{1}^{3}x_{7\cdot24}^{2}$	
	1.000	1.000	1.000	1.000	1.000	1.000	1.000	1.000	
Non-zero chosen variables with Variant IX ρ = 0.03 and T = 50 years	(1)	(22)	(42)	(74)	(101)	(118)	(182)	(162)	1,347,015
	${}_{1}^{1}x_{1\cdot1}^{1}$	${}_{1}^{1}x_{1\cdot2}^{2}$	${}_{1}^{1}x_{2\cdot2}^{3}$	${}_{1}^{1}x_{2\cdot4}^{4}$	${}_{1}^{2}x_{2\cdot1}^{1}$	${}_{1}^{2}x_{2\cdot3}^{2}$	${}_{1}^{3}x_{7\cdot2}^{1}$	${}_{1}^{3}x_{7\cdot2}^{2}$	
	1.000	1.000	1.000	1.000	1.000	1.000	1.000	1.000	

Note: (1) The digits in the parentheses indicate the activity number. They do not necessarily coincide with the activity number in Table 3.4.
(2) Variant I, and IX correspond to the variants in Table 3.2.
(3) The solutions of IX by LP which corresponds to combinatorial algorithm (β) is omitted.

Table 3.6 Comparison between capital funds allocation by model and physical planning

Expressway/ Highway	year	65	66	67	68	69	70	71	72	73	74	75	76	77	78	79	80	81	82	83	84	85
		1960's					1970's										1980's					
period (t)		1				2				3				4				5				
Sections of express./high.		Tohoku expressway ($h=1$)																				
1. Tokyo-Iwatuski ($p=1$)	$\bar{C}_1 =$ 56,000 million JPY				1,700	7,100	10,900	10,800	15,000	10,500												
	[hatched]					6 lanes ($j=1$)																
	[grey]	6 lanes ($j=1$)																				
2. Iwatsuki-Tatebayashi ($p=2$)	$\bar{C}_2 =$ 27,400 million JPY		800	1,500	2,400	5,800	6,100	4,600	2,600				900	900	900	900						
	[hatched]	4 lanes ($j=2$)																				
	[grey]					6 lanes ($j=1$)																
3. Sendai-Ichinoseki ($p=3$)	$\bar{C}_3 =$ 50,700 million JPY			1,300	2,200	6,400	7,800	8,000	7,200	2,500						5,100	5,100	5,100				
	[hatched]					2 lanes ($j=5$; $tt'=24$)								2 lanes								
	[grey]					4 lanes ($j=2$)																
4. Towada-Aomori ($p=4$)	$\bar{C}_4 =$ 51,000 million JPY					1,100	3,300	5,500	9,300	10,100	6,400						5,100	5,100	5,100			
	[hatched]									2 lanes ($j=4$)												
	[grey]													4 lanes ($j=2$)								
		Kanetsu exprssway ($h=2$)																				
5. Kawagoe-Maebashi ($p=1$)	$\bar{C}_5 =$ 47,600 million JPY			300	2,500	8,500	8,600	11,900	10,500	5,300												
	[hatched]	2 lanes ($j=5$; $tt'=13$)								2 lanes												
	[grey]	4 lanes ($j=2$)																				
6. Nagano-Naoetsu ($p=2$)	$\bar{C}_6 =$ 39,000 million JPY												800	2,500	5,500	6,600	7,800	4,100	3,900	3,900	3,900	
	[hatched]					2 lanes ($j=5$; $tt'=25$)												2 lanes				
	[grey]									4 lanes ($j=2$)												
		Tokyo-Gaikan expressway ($h=3$)																				
7. Dainikeihin-Chuodo ($p=1$)	$\bar{C}_7 =$ 57,300 million JPY	200	1,000	3,800	17,200	16,900	10,200	8,000														
	[hatched]	6 lanes ($j=7$; en bloc)																				
	[grey]					6 lanes ($j=7$; en bloc)																
8. Chuodo-Tohokudo ($p=2$)	$\bar{C}_8 =$ 94,000 million JPY						2,700	7,400	8,800	25,500	29,600	20,000										
	[hatched]					4 lanes ($j=7$; two stage $tt'=24$)								2 lanes								
	[grey]					6 lanes ($j=7$; enbloc)																
$\sum_{i=1}^{8} \bar{C}_i =$	423,000	34,900				205,000				111,600				40,400				31,100				
$\sum_{t=1}^{5} \bar{C}_t =$	423,000	$\bar{C}_1 = 105{,}000$				$\bar{C}_2 = 206{,}800$				$\bar{C}_3 = 46{,}300$				$\bar{C}_4 = 52{,}600$				$\bar{C}_5 = 12{,}300$				

Notes are in the tetx.

Note: (1) The symbols ⟷ show the timing of the construction of expressway/highway and the digits above are the annual budgets of construction costs presumed in the physical planning of The Ministry of Construction (1966)
(2) The symbols ←---→ show the timing of the second-stage in case the two-stage construction is adopted. If the two-stage construction is not adopted, it is assumed that the capital funds which ought to be allocated to the second-stage is included in the capital funds which is to be used for the construction en bloc
(3) The symbols [hatched bar] show results of the construction timing of the expressway/highway in Variant I and [grey bar] shows that of in Variant IX. 'Digit lanes' above the symbols mean the grade of the highway/expressway constructed with that timing. When the symbols [hatched bar] appear twice in different periods, the expressway/highway is opened for traffic with the two-stage construction

Prefecture, and terminates at Nagaoka City in Niigata Prefecture. It goes to Niigata City through Hokuriku Expressway. Joetsu Expressway starts at Fujioka City (Gunma) and terminates at Joetsu City (Niigata). Both had an intention to connect the regions in the Pacific and Japan Seasides. Kawagoe-Maebashi was expected to meet vehicle traffic demand in Greater Tokyo. Nagano-Naoetsu intended to strategically develop the developing regions in Nagano and Niigata Prefectures.

Tokyo-Gaikan Expressway had an intention to connect all the expressways that start Tokyo and extend to the north-east (Tohoku Expressway), north (Kanetsu Expressway), west-north (Chuodo Expressway), west (To-Mei Expressway), and so on. It was expected to relieve the traffic congestion in the Tokyo Metropolitan Area that would be intensified by trips from the north to the west through Tokyo or from west to North, and so on by diverting the trips to the circumferential route (of the beltline).

As for the construction costs, it can be assumed that the costs are basically depending on the grade of the expressway, namely the number of lanes but the land purchase costs are quite different among the regions. Especially, in the suburb of Tokyo.

3.5.2 Meeting Vehicle Traffic Demand in the Suburb of Tokyo

Considering the absolute volume of vehicle traffic demand in 1960s, the first priority should be put on the construction of the segment, Tokyo-Iwatsuki, of Tohoku-Expressway. However, the construction at the first period is made with Iwatuski-Tatebayashi of Tohoku Expressway, Kawagoe-Maebashi of Kanetus Expressway, and Dainikeihin-chuodo of Tokyo-Gaikan Expressway. The former two were expected to contribute to the relief in the traffic congestion, which was rapidly intensified due to the rapid increase in the population in the suburb of Tokyo in 1960s. Relatively speaking, in the expanding suburb of Tokyo, the road condition was not good compared to the surrounding area of the core of Tokyo and, therefore, relatively large benefits can be expected by the construction of the two segments. With the same reason, the segment of Dainikeihin-Chuodo was chosen as larger benefits can be expected by the impacts of relieving the traffic congestion in the west of the core area of Tokyo Metropolitan, where the road condition was not good compared to other core area.

As the discount rate becomes lower and the time span becomes longer (comparison between Variants I and IX), the grade of the expressway increases with both segments of Tokyo-Iwatsuki and Kawagoe-Maebashi. However, as for Kawagoe-Maebashi, the timing of the construction is delayed by one period. It can be considered that since the construction timing becomes earlier for Tokyo-Iwatsuki and Kawagoe-Maebashi (grade increases, too), the budget constraint becomes more bound, so some project must be delayed considering comprehensively the total capitalized benefits created in the long run with the lower discount rate.

3.5.3 Strategic Investments in the Developing Regions

Sections of Sendai-Ichinoseki, Towada-Aomori, and Nagano-Naoetsu had an intention to invest in the developing regions. In case where the discount rate is higher and the time span is shorter, the provision of expressway services should be basically done with the two-stage construction. With Towada-Aomori, the construction is done with a grade of two lanes only. Considering the difference in periods of the second stage of the two-stage construction (the first stage is same), it can be said that Sendai-Ichinoseki will create more benefits than the section of Nagano-Naoetsu. One possible reason is that Sendai city, as a local core city, is bigger than Nagano city.

As the discount rate is decreased and the time span with which benefits are measured is extended, the two-stage construction becomes en bloc construction. Considering Variant IX has an intention to invest in the developing regions, the results were expected ones. As for Sendai-Ichinoseki, the construction timing is the same as the first stage of the two-stage construction. On the other hand, Nagano-Naoetsu and Towada-Aomori are delayed by one period. These are also consistently interpreted with the same reasons in the case of the higher discount rate and shorter time span.

3.5.4 Tokyo-Gaikan Expressway

As already explained earlier, the two sections of Dainikeihin-Chuodo and Chuodo-Tohokudo have different characteristics than sections other two Expressways. Expected benefits were larger than others, and most of them are due to the diverted vehicle traffic from existing roads which were utilized with fairly less traffic jams compared to the existing roads competitive against other expressways. So, net benefits were not so big compared to the requested number of lanes (6 lanes and the necessary construction costs).

In Variant I, the construction timing of Dainikeihin–Chuodo is at period 1. In Varian IX, it is rather delayed by one period. As for the construction of Chuodo-Tohokudo, the construction is done by a private company, which had a meaning that the public investment project could be privatized technically and should have no problem though nobody thought the possibility was high because the public sector had no issues of financing during the economic growing era. It adopts the two-stage construction of 4 plus 2, and the first stage is in period 2 in Variant I. In Variant IX, it adopts en bloc construction and the timing of the construction is the same as the first stage of the two-stage construction in Variant I. Sections of Tokyo-Gaikan were critically important expressways in the suburb of Tokyo in the sense that plenty of vehicles would use it, and the results show that the priority is not necessarily laid on the construction of these sections. Especially, in Variant IX, the construction timing is the second period though en bloc construction is adopted. This can be considered as result of the relatively small net benefits because the expected users were diverted ones and the land purchasing costs were huge compared to sections of other expressways.

3.5.5 Comparison with Physical Planning of the Ministry of Construction

Basically, there are no big differences between the timings of the optimization results and Physical Planning but sections of Towada-Aomori and Nagano-Naoetsu. The Physical Planning laid more emphasis on Towada-Aomori, a kind of strategic investment, than the optimization, which means the construction timing is earlier with the Physical Planning than the optimization results. On the other hand, Physical Planning laid less emphasis on Nagano-Naoetsu. Perhaps, it can be considered that a political situation was reflected on the planning.

3.5.6 Total Benefit–Cost Analysis

The solution given by the optimization reflects the conventional benefit–cost analysis *comprehensively* in the sense that it takes into account the present value of all the possible future stream of benefits and costs with all possible investment targets, which take into account scale, way and timing of construction, and it maximizes the value of the objective function in terms of the present value of net benefits created by the investments using a limited amount of capital funds. So, it should have no meaning that we will do again the conventional benefit–cost analysis because it has been done endogenously through optimization. The optimization has an advantage as it avoids errors resulting in the lower levels of optimality attained by the construction of expressways section by section due to pre-determined allocation of the capital funds for each section of expressways, myopic decision-making due to no consideration of the opportunity cost of the capital fund allocated, and so on. However, it may have a meaning to apply the benefit–cost analysis to the set of the optimal solutions by taking it as one package project, which might be competitive against other packaged projects given through the same process of the optimization, for example, allocation of capital funds to the construction of education facilities.

(1) Variant I

The present value of the capital funds in Table 3.4 is given as follows:

$$
\begin{aligned}
C_0^5 &= \frac{105,000}{(1+0.05)^4} + \frac{206,800}{(1+0.05)^8} + \frac{46,300}{(1+0.05)^{12}} + \frac{52,600}{(1+0.05)^{16}} + \frac{12,300}{(1+0.05)^{20}} \\
&= 280,868 \ (\textit{million JPY})
\end{aligned}
$$

The maximized present value of the net benefits, NPV_0^5, is given in Table 3.5.

$$NPV_0^5 = 382,104 \text{ (million JPY)}$$

Therefore, the benefit–cost ratio is calculated as follows:

$$R = \frac{(280,868 + 377,105)}{280,868} = 2.343$$

(2) Variant IX

$$
\begin{aligned}
C_0^3 &= \frac{105,000}{(1+0.03)^4} + \frac{206,800}{(1+0.03)^8} + \frac{46,300}{(1+0.03)^{12}} + \frac{52,600}{(1+0.03)^{16}} + \frac{12,300}{(1+0.03)^{20}} \\
&= 328,604
\end{aligned}
$$

$$R = \frac{(328,604 + 1,347,015)}{328,604} = 5.099$$

Considering that the real economic growth rates variated between 5% and 15 % and the average was around 10% in the 1960s, the benefit–cost ratio of Variant I might be too low. There should be various reasons for the result and one implication may be that the time schedule of the public investments like the construction of expressways should be determined with the longer time horizon. In this sense, the necessity of the generalized benefit–cost analysis in the substantially dynamic content is suggested in which the effectiveness of the re-investments of the obtained benefits that accrue to the whole national economy are taken into account. An ideal dynamic model will be presented in Chap. 7 with a basically same topic but the scope of subjects is more expanded.

3.6 Closing Comments

The empirical analysis shown in this chapter is an application of the capital fund allocation problem analyzed by the water resource research group in the United States. It tried to analyze the optimal capital allocation to the construction schedule of expressways, which were actually planned as the national project on that day. The model formulated incorporates incompatibility of location and the construction timing of expressway facilities, indivisibility of the construction costs, different construction way of en bloc or two-stage at different periods, the supra-marginal opportunity cost of the capital funds, and so on. The model was, in a sense, an orthodox succession to nuggets of wisdom by Eckstein, Steiner, and Marglin. In another sense, we had shown the practical solution algorithm based on the combinatorial method to the integer programming model and clarified the practicality of their model.

One (H. Kohno) of the authors had written a paper based on the empirical analysis shown in this chapter and submitted as his Master Thesis to Graduate School of Economics, University of Tokyo, when he was a student while working at Japan Highway Public Corporation (JH). It was later on known by a young staff that the thesis was highly appraised by the faculty staff as it was the first empirical and practical study to generalize the idea of Eckstein, Steiner, and Marglin. However, they were afraid of an influence that induces other students not to write theoretical papers. So, it did come to a usual end that things should be moderate. For the person who engaged in the Economic Research Section of JH for almost 10 years, this kind of article was a very natural outcome. It was a faint memory.

References

Eckstein O (1961) A survey of the theory of public expenditure criteria. In: Buchanan JM (ed) Public finance: needs, source and utilization. Princeton University Press, Princeton, NJ, pp 439–504

Hirschman AO (1968) The strategy of economic development. Yale University Press, New Haven, CT

Kohno, H. (1968) Dynamic optimal programming of public investment. Presented at the 6th Annual Meeting of The Japan Section of Th Regional Science Association, International, Nagoya

Kohno H (1974) Economic Analyses of Public Investment. In: Kato H, Furuta S (eds) Lecture on public economics. Seirin-Shoin, Tokyo, Japan, pp 166–186

Marglin SA (1963) Approaches to dynamic investment planning. North-Holland Pub, Amsterdam

Steiner PO (1959) Choosing among alternative public investment in the water resource field. Am Econ Rev 49(5):893–916

The Ministry of Construction (1966) Investment planning for construction by route, by section, by year: 53 trillion JPY long-range highway construction planning over the period of 20 years (tentative), The Ministry of Construction, Road Bureau, Planning Section, Tokyo (mimeograph in Japanese)

Chapter 4
Optimum Allocation of the Capital Funds to the Transportation Infrastructures Using the Interregional Input–Output Programming Model (Part I): Specification with Five Regions, Five Industries, and Three Transport Modes

4.1 Public Investment Criteria Incorporating the Endogenous Measurement of the Benefits—Two Subjects

The application of the public investment criteria is made with two stages in the traditional benefit–cost analysis and its sophisticated development by the water resources research group in the United States represented by Eckstein, Steiner, and Marglin (e.g., Marglin 1963). Namely, (1) the calculation of the investment criteria, which is basically the benefit–cost difference, the benefit–cost ratio, or the internal rate of return, with each of investment targets or each of the combinations of investment targets using the discounted present values of costs and benefits that would be incurred and created by the investment target or the combination of investment targets by presuming that it was or they were implemented; and (2) decision on the choice of an optimal set of investment targets in the sense that the objective function in the present value of the net benefits created by the chosen set of investment targets is not less than the other sets of investment targets under the constraint of the limited capital funds that can be allocated for the chosen investment targets.

It can be said that the public investment criteria based on the conventional benefit–cost analysis adopt a kind of *dichotomy* for simplicity or practical convenience. They have tried to develop a consistent and generalized public investment criterion independently from the improvements in the measurement method of benefits, and their approach has missed the point that the investments including reinvestments of returns during the time horizon and the benefits created by the (re)

This chapter is based on Kohno (1968, 1969, 1970, 1975, 1991a, b, c, 1992, 1996) and Kohno et al. (1996). The model presented is basically based on the idea in the latter part of Kohno (1966a, b). The refinement and the empirical study have been done during the project research on the social overhead capital, granted by The Economic Planning Agency, the Composite Planning Bureau, and the project on the construction technology granted by The Ministry of Construction.

H. Kohno, Y. Higano, *Public Investment Criteria*, New Frontiers in Regional Science: Asian Perspectives 2, https://doi.org/10.1007/978-4-431-55221-5_4

investments are interdependent with each other dynamically as stated elsewhere in Chaps. 2 and 3.

In this chapter and following chapters, we will deal with and improve the methods (models) with which the measurement of economic effects (benefits) that would be created by the potential investment targets and the decision on the investments, which are chosen among potential investment targets, and to be implemented, are endogenously and, therefore, simultaneously made consistently. It looks that the benefit calculation is made only once with the method. However, all possible set of investments targets, which are feasible to be implemented under the capital fund constraint, are taken into account through the search of optimal solution, and the optimal set of investment targets is obtained as if it is done through the procedures: (a) the benefits were calculated with all possible sets of investments targets and (b) the comparison with the objective function values is made with all the pairs of feasible sets of investments targets. *The optimality criterion* built in the method assures that the chosen set of investment targets is optimal in the sense above (2).

The point is that we are able to decide on the set of investment targets that shall be implemented and the chosen set is rightly the optimal one among all possible sets of investments. It does not matter if we actually measure benefits and costs and do the benefit–cost analysis with all the possible sets of investments in order to find out the right and optimal set of investments. Also, here, note that the optimality or rightness in the statement above never means that value judgment if any, which is implicitly presumed through the model specification, is the right one or appropriate one. Such a sort of value judgment must be given exogenously, that is, through a political process.

Readers may think that without any value judgment, nothing will start with the method (model) because it is not easy to say that this is the value judgment on which we (e.g., committee members) do discussion and decision-making on the investments. However, the model is rather suitable for presuming that such difficulties may happen in reality. The models we will present in this book are general one and flexible to be able to deal with institutional issues, political issues, or any non-reasonable or irrational arguments if they have to be taken into account through the decision-making. We can say here only in abstract manners. The model can incorporate such issues and arguments by, for example, alternatively adjusting the objective function, on which the optimality and rightness of chosen set of investment targets are fatally determined, by incorporating special preempt variables and constraints into the model, and so on. We can expect that a feedback process works by presenting: (i) the optimal (sometimes biased by the institutional issues) set of investments together with (ii) special treatments in the model specification that critically caused the chosen set of investments be optimal, and so on.

4.2 Basic Assumptions and Model Structures with the Economy

First, we propose the model with which all the direct and indirect economic effects (benefits) created by the investments through the whole of the national economy can be grasped and measured. Second, the mechanism will be built in the model with which the two subjects can be solved consistently based on the optimality criteria. We start with a description of the economy with which the model is specified.

1. Regions

   It is assumed that the economy consists of r regions.[1]
2. Industries, goods, commodities and services, and shipment to other regions

   The economy of each region is composed of n industries (sectors). The first k_n sectors produce non-service goods and that last $(n - k_n)$ sectors are service sectors including transportation sectors. It is assumed that services cannot be shipped (exported) to other regions.[2]
3. Competitiveness between imported and produced goods

   The goods i produced in the region p and the goods i produced in region q and shipped into the region p are competitive with each other in terms of the market flow conditions, namely the goods have no name of "region" where it is produced $(p, q = 1, 2, \ldots, r, p \neq q; i = 1, 2, 3, \ldots, k_n)$.
4. Intra-regional shipment of goods

   Goods i produced in region p and used for the intermediate inputs and the final consumption in region p are taken as the shipment of goods i from region p to region p $(i = 1, 2, \ldots, k_n; p = 1, 2, \ldots, r)$.
5. Flow condition of the markets

---

[1]We call assignment of natural numbers to sectors, regions, modes, etc.—coding. Alphabet in English, Greek, etc. which show the natural numbers assigned to sectors, etc. are called—indices. Indices are attached to variables, parameters, equations, etc., which are defined and formulated to construct the model, as right- or left- superscripts, or subscripts. Sometimes a summation is made like $Y = \sum_{k=1}^{n} X_k$. The right-subscript k of X only has a meaning in the sense that X_k should have a meaning following the coding, i.e., $k = 1, 2, \ldots, n$, e.g., X_1 is the production of goods 1, X_2 is the production of goods 2, etc. The right-subscript k itself has no special meaning, i.e., k can be replaced by p in the summation provided that special meanings are not given to alphabets k and p while construction of the model. Alphabets k and p can be used as the indices for the summation, specifying equations, etc. Such indices are called—running indices. If the indices are attached to variables as subscripts, they are called—running subscripts. In the coding, the point is: what is meant by natural numbers when they are attached to variables, parameters, equations, etc., as subscripts or superscripts, of which definition are given while construction of the model; and in which range the indices are running. In this sense, the coding is very important and it must be made consistently and generally to leave flexibility for the expansion of the model.

[2]We will see later on that CIF is assumed and the transportation services required for the shipment of commodities are satisfied by the transportation services produced in the origin region of the shipment. It can be taken that, in a sense, the transportation services are exported to other regions.

In the economy of each region, the demand of the goods i must be equated with (or less than) the supply of goods i ($i = 1, 2, \ldots, n$).

The supply of goods i in region p is the sum of the shipments of goods i from region q into region p ($p, q = 1, 2, \ldots, r; i = 1, 2, \ldots, k_n$). As for services ($i = k_n + 1, \ldots, n$), the shipment into region p is only intra-regional "shipment" from region p to region p ($p = 1, 2, \ldots, r$).

The demand of goods i in region p is the sum of the intermediate demand against goods i by the industries in the region p and the shipment of goods i from region p to *other* regions q, and the final demand of goods i in region p ($p, q = 1, 2, \ldots, r, q \neq p; i = 1, 2, \ldots, k_n$).

The demand against services in region p is the sum of the intermediate demands if any, the derivative demands that are induced by the shipments of goods i from region p to region q including intra-regional shipment from region p to region p ($p, q = 1, 2, \ldots, r; i = 1, 2, 3, \ldots, k_n$), and the final demand against services in region p, which means that the demand against services induced by the shipments of goods from region p to region q and, for example, leisure trips of which origin is located in region p must be satisfied with the supply of the said services produced in region p. This is a kind of cost, insurance, and freight (CIF) assumption with the logistics costs, which is required to be made (not necessarily) as the transportation services are not shipped to other regions.

6. Transportation sector and modes of transportation

   The shipments of goods between regions are made through the three transportation modes that each connects all the regions with each other: railway ($h = 1$), shipping ($h = 2$), and highway ($h = 3$). More precisely, the mode of railway implies: (a) railroad lines and related facilities as social infrastructures and (b) a sector which provides railway transport services as a constituent of the transportation service sector. The mode of shipping implies: (c) port and related facilities as social infrastructures; and (d) a sector that provides marine transport services as a constituent of the transportation service sector. The mode of highway implies: (e) highway/expressway and related facilities as social infrastructures; and (f) a sector that provides motor-vehicle transport services as a constituent of the transportation service sector. Namely, the goods produced by the transportation service sector are composite goods that can meet the demand by the three modes in the sense of (b), (d), and (f) above, and final demand against transportation services (e.g., leisure trip).

7. Social infrastructures for the transportation service sector

   It is assumed that virtual transportation networks exist in the economy with railway, shipping, and highway transportation services, and they each connect the regions with each other. The social infrastructures that sustain the transportation services are railroad lines (virtual railroad lines and related facilities), ports, and roads (virtual highway composed of the first-grade and second-grade highway and related facilities).

   It is assumed that railroad lines and roads exist within each region, which sustains intra-regional shipment of goods, as well as between regions, which sustain the shipment of goods between different regions. Ports exist in each region, which sustains the shipment of goods.

8. Route of the transportation services for the shipment

   It is assumed that the transportation mode will not change while the shipment of goods. A several routes for the shipments of goods are assumed with each transportation mode. The routes consist of: (a) intra- or interregional social infrastructures for the transportation services associated with the shipments of the goods and (b) the transportation modes. The route that sustains the transportation services for the intra-regional shipment of goods (henceforth called—the route of the intra-regional shipment of goods) uses the intra-regional social infrastructures associated with the transportation modes and the routes. The route that sustains the transportation services for the interregional shipment of goods (henceforth called—the route of the interregional shipment of goods) uses the interregional social infrastructures, which are associated with the transportation modes and the routes.
9. Loads on the social infrastructures of the transportation services

   Intra-regional shipments induce demand against transportation services within the region (5. above) and the induced transportation services cause loads on the intra-regional social infrastructures associated with the transportation modes and the route. Interregional shipments of goods induce demand against transportation services in the origin region of the shipment (5. above) and cause loads on the interregional social infrastructures associated with the transportation modes and the routes.
10. Capacities of the social infrastructures of transportation services

    The sum of the loads caused by the intra- and interregional shipments of goods must be less than the capacity with respect to each of the intra- or interregional social infrastructures of transportation services associated with the routes and the modes. The capacities of social infrastructures for the transportation services can be increased by the allocation of capital funds to the improvement in the social infrastructures associated with the transportation mode.
11. Capacities of the industries (sectors)

    The production of goods (=the supply of goods) is dependent on the production facilities (capital stocks; henceforth we call—the production capacities) of which amounts are given sector by sector and region by region. The production capacities are not mobile between the sectors and regions and can be increased by using the allocation of capital funds to the improvement in the production capacity, which is competitive against the outlay for the increase in the capacities of the social infrastructures.
12. Interregional input–output structure

    It is assumed that the goods are produced via an input–output structure in each region. The demand and supply in each region can be satisfied with the goods produced in the whole national economy but for the demand against transportation services which are induced by the intra- and interregional shipments of goods, and must be satisfied by the transportation services produced in the origin region of the shipment, presuming the competitiveness with the import and export of goods in the market flow conditions (see 5. above).

13. Other constraints
    (a) Labor constraint
    The production of goods is dependent on the amount of labor (workers) region by region and sector by sector. The amount of labor available is basically exogenously given region by region and it is immobile among regions. However, the labor available in each region can be increased by allocating the expected fixed increment in the total labor.
    (b) Water resource constraint
    The production of goods is dependent on the amount of water resource region by region and sector by sector. The amount of water resource available in each region is basically given and it is immobile among regions. However, the water resource available in each region can be increased by allocating the capital funds in order to develop the water resource available in the region.

4.3 Model

4.3.1 Explicit Specification of the Transportation Sector Using Shipment Activities of Moses Model

First of all, we construct our basic model using the concept of shipment activity which was first defined by Moses (1960).[3] The flow conditions of the market can be written as follows:

1. $i \neq n$,

$$\sum_{q=1}^{r} x_i^{qp} \geq \sum\nolimits_{j=1}^{n} a_{ij}^{p} x_j^{pp} + \sum\nolimits_{j=1}^{n-1} \sum_{q \neq p} v_{ij}^{pq} x_j^{pq} + F_i^p (i = 1, 2, \ldots, n-1; p = 1, 2, \ldots, r) \tag{4.1}$$

2. $i = n$,

$$x_i^{pp} \geq \sum\nolimits_{j=1}^{n} a_{ij}^{p} x_j^{pp} + \sum\nolimits_{j=1}^{n-1} \sum_{q \neq p}^{r} v_{ij}^{pq} x_j^{pq} + F_i^p (i = n; p = 1, 2, \ldots, r), \tag{4.2}$$

in which:

---

[3]Our model is different from Moses (1960) in that the transportation sector is not explicitly specified in his model. Of course, he assumes implicitly the transportation sector which needs intermediate inputs in order to produce delivery services for shipment of products from region where goods are produced and to region where goods are demanded.

r: the number of regions

n: the number of sectors and the number of goods (common to the regions); We assume that the $n - th$ sector is the transportation service sector and no more service sector for simplicity (i.e., $k_n = n - 1$)

x_i^{qp}: the product of goods i produced in region q and shipped (exported) to region i

a_{ij}^p: input coefficients of the input–output structure in region p (it is assumed that $a_{nn}^p = 0$ for all p $(p = 1, 2, \ldots, r)$

v_{ij}^{pq}: the coefficient of intermediate input of goods i in order to make a unit shipment of goods j $(j \neq n)$ from region p to region q

F_i^p: final demand of goods i in region p which is exogenously given

The left-hand side of Eq. (4.1) is the total supply of goods i in region p, which is the sum of the production of goods i produced in region p and shipped into region p (*the production for intra-regional demand*) and import of goods i from other regions (*the production for the demand outside the region* from the view point of the region, which makes the shipment). The left-hand side of Eq. (4.2) is the total supply of the transportation services in region p (the production in order to meet intra-regional demand only).[4]

The first terms of the right-hand side of Eqs. (4.1) and (4.2) are the usual intermediate demand against goods i which are induced by the production of goods j in region p (the production in order to meet intra-regional demand). The second term of Eq. (4.1) is the intermediate demand against goods i induced by the interregional shipment of goods j $(j \neq n)$. The second term of Eq. (4.2) is the demand against the transportation services, which are induced by the interregional shipment of goods j $(j \neq n)$.

We try to express Eqs. (4.1) and (4.2) in a matrix form. First, define the column vector $X = (x_i^{qp})$ as follows:

$$
\begin{aligned}
X' = \big[&x_1^{11}, x_1^{12}, x_1^{13}, \cdots, x_1^{1r}; x_2^{11}, x_2^{12}, x_2^{13}, \cdots, x_2^{1r}; \cdots; x_{n-1}^{11}, x_{n-1}^{12}, x_{n-1}^{13}, \cdots, x_{n-1}^{1r}; x_n^{11}; x_1^{21},\\
&x_1^{22}, x_1^{23}, \cdots, x_1^{2r}; x_2^{21}, x_2^{22}, x_2^{23}, \cdots, x_2^{2r}; \cdots; x_{n-1}^{21}, x_{n-1}^{22}, x_{n-1}^{23}, \cdots, x_{n-1}^{2r}; x_n^{22}; x_1^{31}, x_1^{32}, x_1^{33}, \cdots,\\
&x_1^{3r}; \cdots; x_{n-1}^{31}, x_{n-1}^{32}, x_{n-1}^{33}, \cdots, x_{n-1}^{3r}; x_n^{33}; \cdots, x_1^{r1}, x_1^{r2}, x_1^{r3}, \cdots, x_1^{rr}; x_2^{r1}, x_2^{r2}, x_2^{r3}, \cdots, x_2^{rr}; \cdots;\\
&x_{n-1}^{r1}, x_{n-1}^{r2}, x_{n-1}^{r3}, \cdots, x_{n-1}^{rr}; x_n^{rr}\big],
\end{aligned}
\tag{4.3}
$$

in which: variable x_i^{pq} is located as an element of vector X as follows:

[4]See note 3 in Sect. 4.2.

1. if $i \neq n, x_i^{qp}$ is the $J_i^{qp} - th$ element of X, in which:

$$J_i^{qp} = (q-1) \times \{(n-1) \times r + 1\} + (i-1) \times r + p; \text{and} \tag{4.4}$$

2. if $i = n$, x_n^{pp} is the $J_n^{pp} - th$ element of X, in which:

$$J_i^{pp} = p \times \{(n-1) \times r + 1\}. \tag{4.5}$$

Therefore, the dimension of vector X is $1 \times J_n^{rr}$.

We define $I_i^p \equiv (p-1) \times n + i$. Consider a matrix M of $I_n^r \times J_n^{rr}$, with which Eqs. (4.1) and (4.2) can be expressed as follows:

$$\boldsymbol{MX} \geq \boldsymbol{F}, \tag{4.6}$$

in which:

$$\boldsymbol{F}' = \left[F_1^1, F_2^1, F_3^1, \ldots, F_n^1; F_1^2, F_2^2, F_3^3, \ldots, F_n^2; F_1^3, \ldots, F_n^3; \cdots; F_1^{r-1}, \ldots, F_n^{r-1}; F_1^r, \ldots, F_n^r\right]. \tag{4.7}$$

The value of J_i^{qp} indicates the location of the column vector in $\boldsymbol{M}$, which represents shipment of goods i ($\neq n$) or transportation services ($i = n$) from region q to p (if $i = n, p = q$). The value of I_i^p indicates the location of the row vector in $\boldsymbol{M}$, which represents the flow condition of the market with goods i in region p. Expressing (k, l)-element of $\boldsymbol{M}$ as m_{kl}, the value of k and l is calculated as follows once the values of i, j, p, s, and t are specified:

$$k \equiv I_i^p = (p-1) \times n + i; \tag{4.8}$$

1. if $j \neq n$,

$$l \equiv J_j^{st} = (s-1) \times \{(n-1) \times r + 1\} + (j-1) \times r + t; \tag{4.9}$$

2. if $j = n$,

$$l \equiv J_j^{ss} = s \times \{(n-1) \times r + 1\}. \tag{4.10}$$

The (k, l)-element of $\boldsymbol{M}$, m_{kl}, is defined as follows:

1. if $p \neq s$ and $p \neq t$,

$$m_{I_i^p J_i^{st}} = 0, \tag{4.11}$$

2. if $i \neq n$,

   (a) if $p = s = t$,

   - if $i = j$,

$$m_{I_i^p J_i^{pp}} = 1 - a_{ii}^p, \tag{4.12}$$

   - if $i \neq j$,

$$m_{I_i^p J_j^{pp}} = -a_{ij}^p, \tag{4.13}$$

   (b) if $p = s$ and $s \neq t$,

$$m_{I_i^p J_j^{pt}} = -v_{ij}^{pt} \tag{4.14}$$

   (c) if $p \neq s$ and $p = t$,

   - if $i = j$

$$m_{I_i^p J_i^{sp}} = 1, \tag{4.15}$$

   - if $i \neq j$,

$$m_{I_i^p J_j^{sp}} = 0. \tag{4.16}$$

3. if $i = n$,

(a) if $p = s = t$,

   - if $j = n$,

$$m_{I_n^p J_n^{pp}} = 1, \tag{4.17}$$

[5] The value of a_{nj}^p ($j = 1, 2, \ldots, n-1$) is defined as input of transportation service into a unit intra-regional shipment of goods i in region p. A^P is taken as input–output coefficient matrix if the economy of region p were closed. Later on, it is expressed as V^{pp}.

- if $j \neq n$,

$$m_{I_n^p J_j^{pp}} = -a_{nj}^p. \tag{4.18}$$

(b) if $p = s$ and $s \neq t$,

$$m_{I_n^p J_j^{pt}} = -v_{nj}^{pt} \left(v_{nn}^{pt} = 0 \right), \tag{4.19}$$

(c) if $p \neq s$ and $p = t$,

$$m_{I_n^p J_j^{sp}} = 0. \tag{4.20}$$

Here, we may rewrite Eqs. (4.1) and (4.2) in other expression.

Define a column vector, $X^{st} = \left[x_1^{st}, x_2^{st}, \cdots, x_n^{st} \right]'$, in which $x_n^{st} = 0$ for all s and t such that $s \neq t$. Eqs. (4.1) and (4.2) can be expressed as follows:

$$\sum\nolimits_{k=1}^{r} X^{kp} \geq A^p X^{pp} + \sum_{k \neq p} V^{pk} X^{pk} + F^p \; (p = 1, 2, \ldots, r), \tag{4.21}$$

in which:

A^p: input coefficients in region p and $A^p = \left(a_{ij}^p \right)$ and $a_{nn}^p = 0$,[5]
V^{pk}: a matrix of which (i,j)-element is v_{ij}^{pk} and v_{nn}^{pk} =0, and
F^p: a column vector of which i th element is F_i^p.

The total production in region p is given as follows:

$$X^p = \sum_{t=1}^{r} X^{pt}, \tag{4.22}$$

[5] The value of a_{nj}^p ($j = 1, 2, \ldots, n - 1$) is defined as input of transportation service into a unit intra-regional shipment of goods i in region p. A^P is taken as input–output coefficient matrix if the economy of region p were closed. Later on, it is expressed as V^{pp}.

in which X^{pp} is put in the production as intermediate inputs, the consumption or the investment, and the shortage if any is satisfied by shipment from other regions. So, X^{pp} is called – production for intra-regional demand. Rewrite Eq. (4.21) as follows[6]:

$$\sum_{k=1}^{r} X^{kp} \geq A^p X^p + \sum_{k \neq p} \left(V^{pk} - A^P\right) X^{pk} + F^p. \tag{4.23}$$

A natural interpretation of (V^{pk} – A^P) is from the first row to (n – 1)-th row, all the elements are zero and the last row's elements are *additional intermediate demand* against the transportation services induced by the shipment of goods from region p to other regions and are dependent on the type of goods, the distance between region p and k. Namely, the j th row of V^{pk} are j th row of A^P but n th row that are demand against the transportation services. Therefore, the value-added coefficients are associated with all the variables X^{pk}, with which the GRP/NRPs[7] are calculated in terms of the market price.

On the other hand, we may take A^p as a variant of V^{pk} and can express it as $V^{pp} = A^p$. So, we define $A(V)^{pk}$ as follows:

1. if $k = p$, $A(V)^{pk} = A^p$.
2. if $k \neq p$,
   (a) ith row is the ith row of A^P $(i = 1, 2, \ldots, n-1)$
   (b) nth row is the row vector $\left(v_{nj}^{pk}\right)$ and $v_{nn}^{pk} = 0$.

Making arrangement for the terms in Eq. (4.21), we obtain as follows:

$$(I - A(V)^{pp})X^{pp} - \sum_{k \neq p} A(V)^{pk} X^{pk} + \sum_{k \neq p} X^{kp} \geq F^p. \tag{4.24}$$

Or, equivalently,

$$\sum_{k=1}^{r} X^{kp} \geq \sum_{k=1}^{r} A(V)^{kp} X^{pk} + F^p. \tag{4.25}$$

The summation of Eq. (4.24) with p gives as follows[8]:

---

[6] More precisely, $\sum_{k \neq p} X^{kp} + X^{pp} + \sum_{k \neq p} X^{pk} \geq A^p X^p + \sum_{k \neq p} \left(V^{pk} - A^P\right) X^{pk} + \sum_{k \neq p} X^{pk} + F^p$. This is a balance between the left-hand: the sum of the goods shipped into region p from other regions and the products in region p (for intra- as well as inter-regional usage), namely the total goods available for utilization in region p and the right-hand: the usage of the goods as intermediate inputs, shipments to other regions (for usage by other regions), and the final demand. The third terms in both sides are cancelled each other.

[7] It is dependent on whether the value-added ratios are the gross value-added ratios or not.

[8] Of course, Eq. (4.27) is directly given by the summation of Eq. (4.25) over region p.

$$\sum_{p=1}^{r}(I-A(V)^{pp})X^{pp}+\sum_{p=1}^{r}\sum\nolimits_{k\neq p}\left(I-A(V)^{pk}\right)X^{pk}\geq\sum_{p=1}^{r}F^{p} \tag{4.26}$$

$$=\sum_{p=1}^{r}\sum\nolimits_{k=1}^{r}\left(I-A(V)^{pk}\right)X^{pk}\geq\sum_{p=1}^{r}F^{p}. \tag{4.27}$$

It can be said that Eq. (4.27) expresses the national economy by taking into account the intra- and interregional trades. The first term of the left-hand side in Eq. (4.26) is popular expression of Leontief system in each region, which satisfies final demand, and the second term can be taken as a la Leontief system, which satisfies *net* export of goods that is demand by other region.

It can be said that the *national input–output table* can be constructed by collecting data related to $\sum_{p=1}^{r}(I-A(V)^{pp})X^{pp}$, $\sum_{p=1}^{r}\sum\nolimits_{k\neq p}\left(I-A(V)^{pk}\right)X^{pk}$, $\sum_{p=1}^{r}F^{p}$, and so on and input–output coefficients can be calculated based on the table. However, of course, thus obtained input coefficients matrix $\widetilde{A}$ are not stable even if we may be able to assume no technological change or we may assume non-substitution theorem since the input–output coefficients of the transportation sectors are dependent on the intra- and interregional shipment X^{st} and trade patterns will usually change when the estimated I-O table is applied to a practical analysis. This is a reason why we must rely on an interregional input–output table even we analyze the national economy. Of course, a same comment can be made on the stability of the regional input–output coefficients by finding endless fault with the neglect of intra-regional shipments among subregions. This is a fate for regional scientists involved in the definition of *region*.

By the way, as for the treatment of the shipment variables and the induced demand against the transportation serves, it is worth to explain here another specification of the model (the specification is applied to the model in Chap. 7).

$$A^{p}Y^{P}+F^{p}+\sum_{k=1}^{r}\widetilde{V}^{pk}\widetilde{X}^{pk}-\sum_{k=1}^{r}\widetilde{X}^{kp}\leq 0, \tag{4.28}$$

$$\sum_{k=1}^{r}\widetilde{X}^{pk}\leq Y^{p}, \tag{4.29}$$

in which:

Y^{p}: vector of the total product in region p, which calculate the value-added in region p

$\widetilde{V}^{pk}$: $n\times n$ matrix of which nth row elements are v_{nj}^{pk} and others are all zero.

In the specification, the value-added coefficients are only associated with the variables of the vector Y^{P}. Variables $\widetilde{X}^{sp}$ are just the shipments of goods (n-th elements are zero with all $\widetilde{X}^{sp}$) and they only induce the demand against the transportation services (of the route between region s and region p in a more general model which has an idea of transportation network). We may assume $\widetilde{V}^{pp} = 0$ as the demand against the transportation services induced by the intra-regional shipment is counted in the input–output structure via A^p ($\widetilde{X}^{pp}$ is a part of Y^p). Therefore, Eq. (4.28) becomes:

$$A^p Y^P + F^p + \sum_{k \neq p} \widetilde{V}^{pk} \widetilde{X}^{pk} - \sum_{k=1}^{r} \widetilde{X}^{kp} \leq 0, \tag{4.30}$$

which is equivalent to Eq. (4.23) since $Y^P \geq \sum_{k=1}^{r} \widetilde{X}^{pk} = X^p$ (in terms of the amount shipped, $\widetilde{X}^{pk} = X^{pk}$ and it can be taken that $\widetilde{V}^{pk} = V^{pk} - A^P$). It may be sometimes confusing among peoples who define the variable of "shipment" in the sense of Moses (1960) and who defined shipment in $\widetilde{X}^{pk}$ although the shipment in Moses sense is still "shipment of goods."

4.3.2 Capacity Constraints and Modes of Transportation

The model by Moses has no idea of capacity constraints. In a sense, it was a natural assumption because the subject of Moses was to find out the optimal location for the new industrial districts in order to meet the (increased) demands in regions/cities. The capacity constraints can be taken as barriers if they are bound, which slow the economic growth down during the economy grows. One of the most critical capacity constraints is the capital stocks put into the production in the private sector. It must be increased as the production increases when the economy grows. The other one is the stock of the social infrastructures, which sustain the economic activities of private firms and daily life of the citizens. The typical is the transportation infrastructures, which sustain the commodity flows between regions induced by the trade among regions. Generally speaking, the trades between regions increase as the economy grows. In 1960s, the Japanese economy had taken off and started to grow with an incredibly high growth rate through 1970s. When the economy had taken off, there were two revolutionary changes in the socioeconomic structure. One was the transformation from the coal-based energy to oil. The other was the modal shift in the cargo transport from the railway to road. When we analyzed the public investments into the transportation infrastructures, it was "must" to deal with the modal shifts among the transportation modes.

4.3.2.1 Modes and Routes

First, we try to incorporate the modes of transportation services (see 6. in Sect. 4.2) into Eqs. (4.1) and (4.2). First, we divide the shipment of goods j ($j \neq n$) from region s to region t as follows:

$$x_j^{st} = {}^1x_j^{st} + {}^2x_j^{st} + {}^3x_j^{st}, \tag{4.31}$$

or more generally,

$$x_j^{st} = \sum_{h=1}^{m} {}^hx_j^{st}, \tag{4.32}$$

in which:

${}^hx_j^{st}$: the shipment of goods j ($j \neq n$) from region s to region t with the transportation mode (henceforth, we call – mode) h; h = 1 means railway, h = 2 means shipping, and h = 3 means roads (highways)

m: the number of modes and $m = 3$.

The shipments of goods with mode h can be made via several routes (see 8. in Sect. 4.2):

$$x_j^{st} = \sum_{h=1}^{m} \sum_{u=1}^{\theta(h,s,t)} {}^{hu}x_j^{st} \; (j = 1, 2, \ldots, n-1; s, t = 1, 2, \ldots, r), \tag{4.33}$$

in which:

${}^{hu}x_j^{st}$: the shipment of goods j ($j \neq n$) from region s to region t with the transportation mode h via route u

$\theta(h, s, t)$: the number of routes from region s to region t with mode h.

By substituting Eq. (4.33) into Eqs. (4.1) and (4.2), we obtain as follows:

1. $i \neq n$,

$$\sum_{s=1}^{r} \sum_{h=1}^{m} \sum_{u=1}^{\theta(h,s,t)} {}^{hu}x_i^{st} \geq \sum_{j=1}^{n} a_{ij}^t \sum_{h=1}^{m} \sum_{u=1}^{\theta(h,t,t)} {}^{hu}x_j^{tt} + a_{in}^t x_n^{tt}$$
$$+ \sum_{j=1}^{n-1} \sum_{s \neq t} v_{ij}^{ts} \sum_{h=1}^{m} \sum_{u=1}^{\theta(h,s,t)} {}^{hu}x_j^{ts}$$
$$+ F_i^t (i = 1, 2, \cdots, n-1; t = 1, 2, \ldots, r), \tag{4.34}$$

2. $i = n$

$$x_i^{tt} \geq \sum\nolimits_{j=1}^{n} a_{ij}^{t} \sum_{h=1}^{m} \sum_{u=1}^{\theta(h,t,t)} {}^{hu}x_j^{tt} + \sum\nolimits_{j=1}^{n-1} \sum_{s \neq t}^{r} \sum_{h=1}^{m} \sum_{u=1}^{\theta(h,s,t)} {}^{hu}v_{ij}^{ts}\, {}^{hu}x_j^{ts}$$
$$+ F_i^t (i = n; t = 1, 2, \ldots, r). \tag{4.35}$$

Here, we again define a column vector ${}^{H\Theta}X$ which is created as a variant of the vector X of Eq. (4.3) by replacing each element x_j^{st} ($s, q = 1, 2, \ldots, r; j = 1, 2, \ldots, n - 1$) with the following (see Eq. (4.31)):

$$\ldots {}^{11}x_j^{st}, {}^{12}x_j^{st}, \cdots, {}^{1,\theta(1,s,t)}x_j^{st}; {}^{21}x_j^{st}, \cdots, {}^{2,\theta(2,s,t)}x_j^{st}; \cdots; {}^{m-1,1}x_j^{st},$$
$$\cdots, {}^{m-1,\theta(m-1,s,t)}x_j^{st}; {}^{m,1}x_j^{st}, \cdots, {}^{m,\theta(m,s,t)}x_j^{st} \cdots \tag{4.36}$$

Using the extended vector of ${}^{H\Theta}X$, we may express Eqs. (4.34) and (4.35) as follows:

$$\boldsymbol{{}^{H\Theta}M\,{}^{H\Theta}X \geq F}, \tag{4.37}$$

in which:

${}^{H\Theta}M$: a matrix of which (k, l) element is given as ${}^{H\Theta}m_{k,\,l}$,

in which:

$$k = I_i^p = (p - 1) \times n + i; \tag{4.38}$$

if $j \neq n$,

$$l \equiv {}^{h\tau}J_j^{st}$$
$$= \sum_{k=1}^{s-1} \left\{ (n-1) \sum_{q=1}^{r} \sum\nolimits_{v=1}^{m} \theta(v,k,q) + 1 \right\}$$
$$+ (j-1) \sum\nolimits_{v=1}^{m} \sum\nolimits_{q=1}^{r} \theta(v,s,q) + \sum\nolimits_{v=1}^{m} \sum\nolimits_{q=1}^{t-1} \theta(v,s,q)$$
$$+ \sum_{v=1}^{h-1} \theta(v,s,t) + \tau, \tag{4.39}$$

if $j = n$[9]

$$l \equiv {}^{11}J_j^{ss} = \sum_{k=1}^{s} \left\{ (n-1) \sum_{q=1}^{r} \sum\nolimits_{v=1}^{m} \theta(v,k,q) + 1 \right\}. \tag{4.40}$$

The matrix element, ${}^{H\Theta}m_{k,\,l}$, is given as follows:

1. if $p \neq s$ and $p \neq t$,

$$ {}^{H\Theta}m_{I_i^p,\,{}^{h\tau}J_j^{st}} = 0. \tag{4.41}$$

2. if $i \neq n$,

(a) if $p = s = t$,

- if $i = j$,

$$ {}^{H\Theta}m_{I_i^p,\,{}^{h\tau}J_i^{pp}} = 1 - a_{ii}^p, \tag{4.42}$$

- if $i \neq j$,

$$ {}^{H\Theta}m_{I_i^p,\,{}^{h\tau}J_j^{pp}} = -a_{ij}^p, \tag{4.43}$$

(b) if $p = s$ and $s \neq t$,

$$ {}^{H\Theta}m_{I_i^p,\,{}^{h\tau}J_j^{pt}} = -{}^{h\tau}v_{ij}^{pt}, \tag{4.44}$$

in which: ${}^{h\tau}v_{ij}^{pt}$ is the intermediate inputs of goods i induced by the shipment of goods j from region p to region t via route τ of mode h,

(c) if $p \neq s$ and $p = t$,

- if $i = j$,

$$ {}^{H\Theta}m_{I_i^p,\,{}^{h\tau}J_i^{sp}} = 1, \tag{4.45}$$

- if $i \neq j$,

$$ {}^{H\Theta}m_{I_i^p,\,{}^{h\tau}J_j^{sp}} = 0. \tag{4.46}$$

[9]The variable, ${}^{11}X_1^{s+1,1}$, is next to the variable ${}^{11}X_n^{ss}$, i.e., l of ${}^{11}X_1^{s+1,1}$ is larger than that of ${}^{11}X_n^{ss}$ by one (1). Readers may confirm this by substituting s, t, h, τ, and j by $s+1$, 1, 1, 1, and 1, respectively, in Eq. (4.39).

3. $i = n$,

(a) if $p = s = t$,

- if $j = n$,

$$^{H\Theta}m_{I_n^p,\, ^{h\tau}J_n^{pp}} = 1, \tag{4.47}$$

- if $j \neq n$,

$$^{H\Theta}m_{I_n^p,\, ^{h\tau}J_j^{pp}} = -a_{nj}^p. \tag{4.48}$$

(b) if $p = s$ and $s \neq t$,

$$^{H\Theta}m_{I_n^p,\, ^{h\tau}J_j^{pt}} = -^{h\tau}v_{nj}^{pt}\left(^{h\tau}v_{nn}^{pt} = 0\right), \tag{4.49a}$$

(c) if $p \neq s$ and $p = t$

$$^{H\Theta}m_{I_n^p,\, ^{h\tau}J_j^{sp}} = 0. \tag{4.49b}$$

Analogically, we may derive the equations which correspond to Eq. (4.21). Define column vector, $^{h\tau}X^{st}$, as $\left[^{h\tau}x_1^{st}, {^{h\tau}x_2^{st}}, \ldots, {^{h\tau}x_n^{st}}\right]'$ and we rewrite column vector, X^{st}, as follows:

$$X^{st} = \sum_{h=1}^{m} \sum_{\tau=1}^{\theta(h,s,t)} {^{h\tau}X^{st}}, \tag{4.50}$$

in which: $^{h\tau}x_n^{st} = 0$ for all s, t, h, and τ but $^{m\theta(m,s,s)}x_n^{ss} \equiv x_n^{ss}$.[10] Substituting Eq. (4.50) into (4.21), we obtain as follows:

$$\begin{aligned}\sum_{k=1}^{r}\sum_{h=1}^{m}\sum_{\tau=1}^{\theta(h,k,p)} {^{h\tau}X^{kp}} \geq \sum_{h=1}^{m}\sum_{\tau=1}^{\theta(h,p,p)} {^{h\tau}A^p}\, {^{h\tau}X^{pp}} \\ + \sum_{k\neq p}\sum_{h=1}^{m}\sum_{\tau=1}^{\theta(h,p,k)} {^{h\tau}V^{pk}}\, {^{h\tau}X^{pk}} \\ + F^p (p = 1, 2, \ldots, r),\end{aligned} \tag{4.51}$$

in which: $^{h\tau}A^p$ is input–output coefficient matrix of region p but $^{h\tau}a_{nj}^p$ is input of transportation service into a unit intra-regional shipment of goods j with mode h and route τ (it is assumed that $^{h\tau}a_{nn}^p = 0$); $^{h\tau}V^{pk}$: a matrix of which (i,j)-element is $^{h\tau}v_{ij}^{pk}$ and $^{h\tau}v_{nn}^{pk}$ =0.

[10] This is a treatment for convenience.

Rewrite Eq. (4.51) as follows:

$$\begin{aligned} &\sum_{h=1}^{m} \sum_{\tau=1}^{\theta(h,p,p)} {}^{h\tau}X^{pp} + \sum_{k \neq p}^{r} \sum_{h=1}^{m} \sum_{\tau=1}^{\theta(h,k,p)} {}^{h\tau}X^{kp} \\ &\geq \sum_{h=1}^{m} \sum_{\tau=1}^{\theta(h,p,p)} {}^{h\tau}A^{p}\, {}^{h\tau}X^{pp} + \sum_{k \neq p} \sum_{h=1}^{m} \sum_{\tau=1}^{\theta(h,p,k)} {}^{h\tau}V^{pk}\, {}^{h\tau}X^{pk} + F^{p} \end{aligned} \tag{4.52}$$

$$\begin{aligned} &\sum_{h=1}^{m} \sum_{\tau=1}^{\theta(h,p,p)} \left(I - {}^{h\tau}A^{p}\right) {}^{h\tau}X^{pp} + \sum_{k \neq p}^{r} \sum_{h=1}^{m} \sum_{\tau=1}^{\theta(h,k,p)} {}^{h\tau}X^{kp} \\ &- \sum_{k \neq p} \sum_{h=1}^{m} \sum_{\tau=1}^{\theta(h,p,k)} {}^{h\tau}V^{pk}\, {}^{h\tau}X^{pk} \\ &\geq F^{p} \end{aligned} \tag{4.53}$$

Considering ${}^{h\tau}A^{p}$ can be written as ${}^{h\tau}V^{pp}$ and summing up Eq. (4.53) over p, we obtain the following:

$$\sum_{p=1}^{r} \sum_{k=1}^{r} \sum_{h=1}^{m} \sum_{\tau=1}^{\theta(h,p,k)} \left(I - {}^{h\tau}V^{pk}\right) {}^{h\tau}X^{pk} \geq \sum_{p=1}^{r} F^{p}, \tag{4.54}$$

or equivalently, we obtain as follows:

$$\sum_{p=1}^{r} \sum_{k=1}^{r} \sum_{h=1}^{m} \sum_{\tau=1}^{\theta(h,p,k)} \left(I - {}^{h\tau}A(V)^{pk}\right) {}^{h\tau}X^{pk} \geq \sum_{p=1}^{r} F^{p}, \tag{4.55}$$

in which ${}^{h\tau}A(V)^{pk}$ is ${}^{h\tau}V^{pk}$ and it is the same as A^{p} (input–output coefficient matrix of region p) but nth row is given as follows:

$$\left[{}^{h\tau}v_{n1}^{pk}, {}^{h\tau}v_{n1}^{pk}, \ldots, {}^{h\tau}v_{n1}^{pk}, 0\right], \tag{4.56}$$

in which: ${}^{h\tau}v_{n1}^{pk}$ is input of transportation service in region p in order to deliver a unit jth goods to region k with mode h of route τ. The discussion in Sect. 4.3.1 can be done analogically with Eq. (4.55) and here we skip it.

4.3.2.2 Production Capacity Constraints

In the economy, production is dependent on the capital stock and labor. Assuming Leontief type of the production function, it can be expressed as follows:

$$\alpha_j^p \sum_{k=1}^{r} \sum_{h=1}^{m} \sum_{\tau=1}^{\theta(h,p,k)} {}^{h\tau}x_j^{pk} \le \overline{K}_j^p, \tag{4.57}$$

or

$$\sum_{k=1}^{r} \sum_{h=1}^{m} \sum_{\tau=1}^{\theta(h,p,k)} {}^{h\tau}x_j^{pk} \le \frac{\overline{K}_j^p}{\alpha_j^p}, \tag{4.58}$$

in which:

α_j^p: the coefficient (capital-output ratio) which converts a unit of the capital in JPY into a unit of product in sector j in region p

$\overline{K}_j^p$: the capital stock available at the initial period for sector j in region p.

Assuming mobility of labor between non-agricultural sectors within the region,[11] we can specify the labor constraints on the production as follows:

$$\sum_{j=1}^{n_L(1)} \sum_{k=1}^{r} \sum_{h=1}^{m} \sum_{\tau=1}^{\theta(h,p,k)} \beta_j^p \, {}^{h\tau}x_j^{pk} \le \overline{L}_1^p, \tag{4.59}$$

$$\sum_{j=n_L(1)+1}^{n} \sum_{k=1}^{r} \sum_{h=1}^{m} \sum_{\tau=1}^{\theta(h,p,k)} \beta_j^p \, {}^{h\tau}x_j^{pk} \le \overline{L}_2^p, \tag{4.60}$$

in which:

β_j^p: reciprocal of the coefficient which converts a unit of labor into a unit of the product in agricultural sector j ($j = 1, 2, \ldots, n_L(1)$) in region p

β_j^p: reciprocal of the coefficient which converts a unit of labor into a unit of the product in non-agricultural sectors j ($j = n_L(1) + 1, \ldots, n$) in region p

$\overline{L}_1^p$: the amount of labor available at the initial period for the agricultural sectors in region p

$\overline{L}_2^p$: the amount of labor available at the initial period for the nonagricultural sectors in region p.

It is also assumed that the production in each region is constrained by water resources.

$$\sum_{k=1}^{r} \sum_{h=1}^{m} \sum_{\tau=1}^{\theta(h,p,k)} {}^{h\tau}x_j^{pk} \le \frac{\overline{W}_j^s}{\omega_j^p}, \tag{4.61}$$

in which:

[11] This is an assumption in order to decrease the number of constraints.

ω_j^p: the coefficient which converts a unit of the water resources into a unit of product in sector j in region p

$\overline{W}_j^s$: the amount of water resources available at the initial period for the sector j in region p.

The model has multiple resource constraints and the non-substitution theorem does not hold, which means it has a meaning to consider several alternative technologies in each sector. However, here we do not explicitly take account substitution between different production technologies (cf. Moses 1960). In a sense, it can be taken that the combination of the production (supply) and the demand (intermediate demand, final demand, etc.) in different regions is a kind of substitution of technologies through the shipment of goods by pursuing the efficiency in the utilization of scarce resources and the produced materials from the viewpoint of the national economy as a whole. Therefore, those direct constraints on the production can be a bottleneck for the economic growth not only in a certain region where the supply of resources is scarce but also in other regions which demand the goods produced in that region and, thus, can be the bottleneck for the economic development of the whole national economy. That is one of the reasons why the shipments of goods are explicitly dealt with in the model.

The constraint of water resources on the production has a specific meaning for regional science. In some sense, we may assume mobility of the capital and labor in the long run. The capital stock is depreciated and replaced by new one through the investment in order to continue the production. Due to retirement, some must quit the labor market and new graduates enter into the market. The regions can be different where the capital is depreciated and the investment is made, which is sustained by the population movement (at least, in the same sectors) as well as by the new graduates who replace the retired peoples (in the same and different sectors). However, the amount of water resources is specific to each region in the sense that the currently available water resources as well as the potentially available water resources by the development are eccentrically located at certain regions. The geographical distribution of water resources may confine the geographical development pattern of the national economy. Other examples are sites suitable for a good harbor and airport, spacious hinterlands around the existing cities, and so on.

4.3.2.3 Capacity Constraints of the Transportation Infrastructures

The transportation sector is directly constrained by the own capital stock specified above as well as the conditions of the transportation infrastructures. For example, cargo transport services by truck, which is induced by the shipment of goods from regions s to t, use highways/roads which connect regions s and t. If the shipment of goods by cargo truck is prohibitively too large compare to the capacity of the road links between regions s and t, the shipments of goods from region s to region t may be caused additional costs due to traffic congestion, for example, larger time costs than usual, missing timely arrival of materials, and so on, which may induce roundabout shipment using different route than usual and further incur additional costs to the original users of the roundabout route. Thus, the overloaded transportation infrastructures can be indirectly a bottleneck for the growth of the economy as a whole.

We may define the constraints on the transportation infrastructures as follows:

$$\sum_{j=1}^{n-1}\sum\nolimits_{s=1}^{r}\sum\nolimits_{t=1}^{r}\sum\nolimits_{h=1}^{m}\sum_{\tau=1}^{\theta(h,s,t)} {}^{h\tau}\delta^{st}(k)\cdot{}^{h}\xi_{j}\cdot{}^{h\tau}x_{j}^{st}$$
$$\leq \overline{T}^{k}\ \left(k=1,2,3,\ \ldots,n^{\mathrm{T}}\right), \tag{4.62}$$

in which:

$\overline{T}^{k}$: capacity of the transportation infrastructure k in terms of 1000 ton/year at the initial period

n^{T}: number of the infrastructures

${}^{h}\xi_{j}$: coefficient that converts the amount of goods in JPY/year into the weight in ton/year as a load on the transportation capacity of the mode h (1000 ton/100 million JPY)

${}^{h\tau}\delta^{st}(k)=1$ if the shipment of goods from region s to region t uses the route of τ of the mode of h, if not it is equal to 0 (zero).

4.3.2.4 Value-Added and GRP/NRP

The total value added in terms of the market price is given as follows:

$$\mathrm{VAD}^{p}=\sum_{k=1}^{r}\sum_{j=1}^{n}\sum\nolimits_{h=1}^{m}\sum\nolimits_{\tau=1}^{\theta(h,k,p)} {}^{h\tau}\varphi_{j}^{pk}\,{}^{h\tau}x_{j}^{pk}\ (p=1,2,\ \ldots,r), \tag{4.63}$$

in which:

${}^{h\tau}\varphi_{j}^{pk}$: value-added ratio of (the production for) the shipment of goods j from region p to k via route τ of mode h; it satisfies the following identity: $\sum_{i=1}^{n}{}^{h\tau}v_{ij}^{ps}+{}^{h\tau}\varphi_{j}^{ps}=1$; therefore, the difference between ${}^{h\tau}\varphi_{j}^{pp}$ and ${}^{h\tau}\varphi_{j}^{pk}$ is the additional transportation costs incurred by the shipment of goods j from region p to region k via route τ of mode h

VAD^{p}: the total value-added in region p and it is defined as the GRP/NRP in region p.

The GDP of the economy is defined as follows:

$$\mathrm{GDP}=\sum_{p=1}^{r}\mathrm{VAD}^{p}. \tag{4.64}$$

4.4 Interregional Input–Output System of Noncompetitive and Competitive Import Types

4.4.1 System of Regional Account and SNA

We may have the following data within a certain one year with region p ($p = 1, 2, \ldots, r$):

Z_{ij}^{st}: sales of goods i produced in region s to sector j in region t (in JPY value unit[12]) $i, j = 1, 2, \ldots, n; s, t = 1, 2, \ldots, r; Z_{nj}^{st} = 0$ for all j if $s \neq t$)
Z_j^p: total products of goods j in region p
C_j^{sp}: goods j produced in region s, and consumed in region p
INV_j^{sp}: goods j produced in region s and utilized for the *gross* investment (capital stock formation) in region p (including changes in the inventory)
M_j^p: purchases (imports) of goods j from abroad ($j \neq n$) in region p
E_j^p: sales (exports) of goods j to abroad ($j \neq n$) from region p
NVD_j^{ps}: net value-added earned in sector j in region p and distributed to region s
D_j: depreciation costs of the capital in sector j.

Presuming that the values of all the variables are in terms of market prices, basically, the following identities hold[13]:

$$Z_i^p = \sum_{s=1}^{r} \sum_{j=1}^{n} Z_{ij}^{ps} + \sum_{s=1}^{r} C_i^{ps} + \sum_{s=1}^{t} \mathrm{INV}_i^{ps} + E_i^p - M_i^p (i = 1, 2, 3, \ldots, n; p = 1, 2, 3, \ldots, r), \tag{4.65}$$

$$Z_j^p = \sum_{s=1}^{r} \sum_{i=1}^{n} Z_{ij}^{sp} + \sum_{s=1}^{r} \mathrm{NVD}_j^{ps} + D_j \, (j = 1, 2, 3, \ldots, n; p = 1, 2, 3, \ldots, r). \tag{4.66}$$

The summation of Eq. (4.65) over i ($i = 1, 2, 3, \ldots, n$) and the summation of Eq. (4.66) with j must be equated with each other:

The summation of Eq. (4.65) over i ($i = 1, 2, 3, \ldots, n$) and p must be equal with the summation of Eq. (4.66) over j and p, which derives the following identity:

$$C + \mathrm{NINV} + E - M = \mathrm{NVD}, \tag{4.67}$$

in which:

[12]The physical amount of goods of which value is equal to, i.e., one million JPY is defined as a unit JPY-value. This is a genius device like date line and it enables the summation of elements of column vector in the I-O system.

[13]For simplicity, the import and export are counted in the total values.

C: total consumption in the economy
NINV: total net investment in the economy (the sum of private and public net investments)
NVD: total net value-added in the economy
E: total export to abroad from the economy
M: total import from abroad into the economy.

The following identities hold as for the distributed income:

$$\mathrm{NVD} = C + S, \tag{4.68}$$

in which:

C: total consumption in the economy.

Substituting Eq. (4.68) into Eq. (4.67) gives the following popular identities:

$$S - \mathrm{NINV} = E - M. \tag{4.69}$$

4.4.2 *Treatment of Interregional Shipments of Goods: Isard type*

The basic idea of the interregional input–output system of the Isard type is that: not only the purchase of goods i by sector j in region p but also the purchase of goods i by sector j in region p from sector i in other region s is proportional to the total product of sector j in region p. The interregional input–output table based on the idea is called—interregional input–output table of the *noncompetitive import type*. Namely, the product has the name of the place where it is produced and if the places where the goods are produced are different, they are taken as different goods even if they are produced in the sectors having the same "names."

For simplicity, we assume that the economy is closed hereafter and E^p and M^p are zero for all p. We define $F_i^{ps} \equiv C_i^{ps} + INV_i^{ps}$ for all i, p, and s ($F_n^{ps} = 0$ if $p \neq s$). The system Eq. (4.65) can be re-written as follows:

$$Z_i^p = \sum\nolimits_{s=1}^{r} \sum_{j=1}^{n} \tilde{a}_{ij}^{ps} Z_j^s + \sum_{s=1}^{r} F_i^{ps} \ (i = 1, 2, 3, \ldots, n; p = 1, 2, 3, \ldots, r) \tag{4.70}$$

in which:

$$\tilde{a}_{ij}^{st} = \frac{Z_{ij}^{st}}{Z_j^t} \ (i = 1, 2, \ldots, n; s, t = 1, 2, \ldots, r) \tag{4.71}$$

In a matrix form, Eq. (4.70) can be expressed as follows:

$$Z^s = \sum_{t=1}^{r} A^{st} Z^t + F^s \ (s = 1, 2, 3, \ldots, r) \tag{4.72}$$

$$(I - A^{ss})Z^s - \sum_{t \neq s} A^{st} Z^t = F^s (s = 1, 2, 3, \ldots, r) \tag{4.73}$$

$$(I - A)^{-1} Z = F, \tag{4.74}$$

in which:

$$A = \begin{pmatrix} A^{11} \, A^{12} & \cdots & A^{1r} \\ \vdots \, \vdots & \ddots & \vdots \\ A^{r1} \, A^{r1} & \cdots & A^{rr} \end{pmatrix}, Z = \begin{bmatrix} Z^1 \\ Z^2 \\ \vdots \\ Z^r \end{bmatrix}, Z^s = \begin{bmatrix} Z_1^s \\ Z_2^s \\ \vdots \\ Z_n^s \end{bmatrix}, F = \begin{bmatrix} F^1 \\ F^2 \\ \vdots \\ F^r \end{bmatrix}, A^{rs} =$$

$$\begin{pmatrix} \tilde{a}_{11}^{rs} \, \tilde{a}_{12}^{rs} & \cdots & \tilde{a}_{1n}^{rs} \\ \vdots \, \vdots & \ddots & \vdots \\ \tilde{a}_{n1}^{rs} \, \tilde{a}_{n2}^{rs} & \cdots & \tilde{a}_{nn}^{rs} \end{pmatrix}, F^s = \begin{pmatrix} \sum_{t=1}^{r} F_1^{st} \\ \vdots \\ \sum_{t=1}^{r} F_n^{st} \end{pmatrix}$$

, and I is an $rn \times rn$ identity matrix.

4.4.3 Interregional Input–Output System of Chenery=Moses Type[14]

The criticism against the interregional input–output system of Isard's type is mainly directed to the following points:

1. whether the coefficients, $\tilde{a}_{ij}^{st}$ $(s \neq t)$, are stable or not apart from the discussion on the stability of $\tilde{a}_{ij}^{pp}$
2. practically, huge materials are required for the construction of the system.

Resolving the criticism (2) above, Chenery (1953) and Moses (1955) have presented an interregional input–output model, which can be constructed with less materials than Isard's model. The most important definition is:

[14]This model is different from the inter-regional input–output model of Moses type explained in Sect. 4.3.1 and the next sub-section.

$$q_i^{ps} = \sum_{j=1}^{n} Z_{ij}^{ps} + F_i^{ps}, \tag{4.75}$$

in which:

q_i^{ps}: total demand by region s against goods i produced in region p.

$$Q_i^s = \sum_{p=1}^{r} q_i^{ps}, \tag{4.76}$$

in which:

Q_i^s: total demand in region s against goods i.

The data of q_i^{ps} and Q_i^s are easy to obtain than Z_{ij}^{st} and it could be considered that q_i^{ps} are more stable against Q_i^s. Presuming the stability in the ratio of q_i^{ps} to Q_i^s, the inter-regional trading pattern coefficient is defined as follows:

$$t_i^{ps} = \frac{q_i^{ps}}{Q_i^s}. \tag{4.77}$$

Of course, $\sum_{p=1}^{r} t_i^{ps} = 1$. Substituting Eq. (4.77) into (4.70), we obtain as follows:

$$Z_i^p = \sum\nolimits_{s=1}^{r} \left(\sum_{j=1}^{n} \widetilde{a}_{ij}^{ps} Z_j^s + F_i^{ps} \right) = \sum_{s=1}^{r} q_i^{ps} \tag{4.78}$$

$$= \sum_{s=1}^{r} Q_i^s \frac{q_i^{ps}}{Q_i^s} = \sum\nolimits_{s=1}^{r} \sum_{k=1}^{r} \left(\sum_{j=1}^{n} Z_{ij}^{ks} + F_i^{ks} \right) \frac{q_i^{ps}}{Q_i^s}$$

$$= \sum\nolimits_{s=1}^{r} \left\{ \sum_{k=1}^{r} \sum_{j=1}^{n} Z_{ij}^{ks} \frac{q_i^{ps}}{Q_i^s} + \sum_{k=1}^{r} F_i^{ks} \frac{q_i^{ps}}{Q_i^s} \right\}$$

$$= \sum_{s=1}^{r} \left\{ \sum\nolimits_{k=1}^{r} \sum_{j=1}^{n} \frac{Z_{ij}^{ks}}{Z_j^s} Z_j^s \frac{q_i^{ps}}{Q_i^s} + \sum_{k=1}^{r} F_i^{ks} \frac{q_i^{ps}}{Q_i^s} \right\}. \tag{4.79}$$

Defining $\widehat{a}_{ij}^s \equiv \frac{\sum_{k=1}^{r} Z_{ij}^{ks}}{Z_j^s}$, Eq. (4.79) becomes as follows:

$$Z_i^p = \sum_{s=1}^{r} \left\{ \sum_{j=1}^{n} \widehat{a}_{ij}^s \frac{q_i^{ps}}{Q_i^s} Z_j^s + \sum_{k=1}^{r} F_i^{ks} \frac{q_i^{ps}}{Q_i^s} \right\}$$

$$= \sum_{s=1}^{r} \left\{ \sum_{j=1}^{n} \widehat{a}_{ij}^s t_i^{ps} Z_j^s + \sum_{k=1}^{r} F_i^{ks} t_i^{ps} \right\}, \tag{4.80}$$

which implies:

$$\widetilde{a}_{ij}^{ps} = t_i^{ps} \widehat{a}_{ij}^{s}. \tag{4.81}$$

We try to express Eq. (4.80) in a matrix form.

$$\sum_{s=1}^{r} \left(\boldsymbol{T}^{ps} \widehat{\boldsymbol{A}}^{s} \boldsymbol{Z}^{s} + \boldsymbol{T}^{ps} \overline{\boldsymbol{F}}^{s} \right) = \boldsymbol{Z}^{p} \ (p = 1, 2, 3, \ldots, r), \tag{4.82}$$

$$\boldsymbol{T}\widehat{\boldsymbol{A}}\,\boldsymbol{Z} + \boldsymbol{T}\overline{\boldsymbol{F}} = \boldsymbol{Z}, \left(\boldsymbol{I} - \boldsymbol{T}\widehat{\boldsymbol{A}}\right)^{-1} \boldsymbol{Z} = \boldsymbol{F}, \tag{4.83}$$

in which: $\boldsymbol{I}$ is an $rn \times rn$ identity matrix, and

$$\boldsymbol{T}^{ps} = \begin{pmatrix} t_1^{ps} & \cdots & 0 \\ \vdots & \ddots & \vdots \\ 0 & \cdots & t_n^{ps} \end{pmatrix}, \boldsymbol{T} = \begin{pmatrix} \boldsymbol{T}^{11} & \cdots & \boldsymbol{T}^{1r} \\ \vdots & \ddots & \vdots \\ \boldsymbol{T}^{r1} & \cdots & \boldsymbol{T}^{rr} \end{pmatrix},$$

$$\widehat{\boldsymbol{A}} = \begin{pmatrix} \widehat{\boldsymbol{A}}^{1} & \cdots & \boldsymbol{0} \\ \vdots & \ddots & \vdots \\ \boldsymbol{0} & \cdots & \widehat{\boldsymbol{A}}^{r} \end{pmatrix}, \widehat{\boldsymbol{A}}^{p} = \begin{pmatrix} \widehat{a}_{11}^{p} & \cdots & \widehat{a}_{1n}^{p} \\ \vdots & \ddots & \vdots \\ \widehat{a}_{n1}^{p} & \cdots & \widehat{a}_{nn}^{p} \end{pmatrix},$$

$$\boldsymbol{Z} = \begin{bmatrix} \boldsymbol{Z}^1 \\ \boldsymbol{Z}^2 \\ \vdots \\ \boldsymbol{Z}^r \end{bmatrix}, \boldsymbol{Z}^s = \begin{bmatrix} Z_1^s \\ Z_2^s \\ \vdots \\ Z_n^s \end{bmatrix}, \overline{\boldsymbol{F}} = \begin{bmatrix} \overline{\boldsymbol{F}}^1 \\ \overline{\boldsymbol{F}}^2 \\ \vdots \\ \overline{\boldsymbol{F}}^r \end{bmatrix}, \overline{\boldsymbol{F}}^s = \begin{pmatrix} \sum_{k=1}^{r} F_1^{kp} \\ \vdots \\ \sum_{k=1}^{r} F_n^{kp} \end{pmatrix}.$$

The advantage of the Chenery=Moses type model of interregional input–output system is that the amount of data necessary for the construction of the interregional input–output table is far less than that required for Isard's Model. However, it is still fatally dependent on the stability of the coefficients, t_i^{ps}, even if it may be stable than the coefficients of $\widetilde{a}_{ij}^{rs}$. Although the interregional input–output table is categorized as the "competitive import type" in the sense that the goods once imported in region p can be used for any sector as intermediate inputs and for meeting the final demands (Eq. (4.75)), it is still substantial and shall be categorized as an interregional input–output table of the noncompetitive import type because there is no substitution (competitiveness) between the regions in terms of the supply of certain goods into a certain region. Rather, it may be said that Isard's model has a basis for the rigid connection between the sectors and regions based on the theory of the extended input–output system, although practically it is awkward to use and even useless.

4.4.4 Explicit Specification of the Transportation Sector Using Shipment Activities of Moses Model (Again)

Back to Eqs. (4.65) and (4.66), of which data we may assume to be able to collect, we will once again try to grasp the characteristics of Moses model (Moses 1960) with the more sophisticated model. We keep the assumption of the closed model (no international trades are made). The basic and substantial assumption is that the goods are not differentiated by the production place. Equations (4.65) and (4.66) may be rewritten in terms of market prices as follows ($Z_{nj}^{ps} = 0$ if $p \neq s$):

$$Z_i^p = \sum\nolimits_{s=1}^{r} \sum_{j=1}^{n} Z_{ij}^{ps} + F_i^p \ (i = 1, 2, 3, \ldots, n; p = 1, 2, 3, \ldots, r), \tag{4.84}$$

$$Z_j^p = \sum_{s=1}^{r} \sum_{i=1}^{n} Z_{ij}^{sp} + VAD_j \ (\ j = 1, 2, 3, \ldots, n; p = 1, 2, 3, \ldots, r), \tag{4.85}$$

The goods are of the competitive import type and we define the amount of goods j shipped from region p for the production and final demand in region s as follows:

$$\overline{Z}_j^{ps} = \sum_{k=1}^{n} Z_{jk}^{ps} + F_j^{ps} \ (\ j = 1, 2, \ldots, n; p, s = 1, 2, \ldots, r), \tag{4.86}$$

$$F_i^p = \sum\nolimits_{s=1}^{r} F_i^{ps} (i = 1, 2, \ldots, n; p = 1, 2, \ldots, r). \tag{4.87}$$

Most important definition of shipment activities in Moses sense is given as follows:

$$\overline{a}_{ij}^p = \left(\frac{\sum_{s=1}^{r} Z_{ij}^{sp}}{Z_j^p} \right) (i, j = 1, 2, \ldots, n), \tag{4.88}$$

$$\overline{a}_{ij}^{ps} = \overline{a}_{ij}^p \ (i \neq n; p \neq s; p, s = 1, 2, \ldots, r), \text{ and} \tag{4.89}$$

$$\overline{a}_{nj}^{ps} = v_{nj}^{ps} \ (p \neq s; p, s = 1, 2, \ldots, r). \tag{4.90}$$

Equations (4.89) and (4.90) mean that $\overline{a}_{nj}^{ps}$ is only dependent on where the good j is produced (i.e., region p) and where it is exported (i.e., region s), and $\overline{a}_{ij}^{ps}$ $(i \neq n)$ is only dependent on where the goods i is produced (i.e., region p). This point is critically different from Isard's model and Chenery=Moses model because in their model, $\widetilde{a}_{ij}^{ps}$ or $\widehat{a}_{ij}^{ps}$ is defined as being associated with the input–output structure in region s (the destination). The parameter, v_{nj}^{ps}, can be taken as the input coefficient of transportation services associated with the shipment of goods j from region p to region s. Dividing the shipments into intraregional shipments and interregional shipments, the n th row element of $\overline{a}_{ij}^{p}$ can be taken as an approximation to the input of transportation services into the intraregional shipment of goods j in region p. So, we may define $v_{nj}^{pp} = \overline{a}_{nj}^{p}$ as an approximation.[15] It is assumed that $\overline{a}_{nn}^{p} = 0$ in Sect. 4.3.1.

Equations (4.1) and (4.2) may be rewritten as follows:

1. $i \neq n$,

$$\sum_{q=1}^{r} x_i^{qp} \geq \sum\nolimits_{j=1}^{n} \overline{a}_{ij}^{p} x_j^{pp} + \sum\nolimits_{j=1}^{n-1} \sum_{q \neq p} \overline{a}_{ij}^{pq} x_j^{pq}$$
$$+ F_i^p \quad (i = 1, 2, \cdots, n-1; p = 1, 2, \cdots, r). \tag{4.91a}$$

2. $i = n$,

$$x_i^{pp} \geq \sum\nolimits_{j=1}^{n} \overline{a}_{ij}^{p} x_j^{pp} + \sum\nolimits_{j=1}^{n-1} \sum_{\substack{r \\ q \neq p}} v_{ij}^{pq} x_j^{pq} + F_i^p \quad (i = n; p = 1, 2, \cdots, r). \tag{4.91b}$$

The genius idea of Moses (1960) is that he takes each of the intra- and interregional shipments of goods as the production activities (variables) of the intraregional input–output model. This is apparently a departure and a drastic departure from the original input–output model developed by Leontief. Namely, with the model of the original input–output system or its variants (Isard's model, Chenery=Moses model, etc.), the matrix ($\boldsymbol{A}$ or $\boldsymbol{T}\hat{\boldsymbol{A}}$) must be a square matrix because it can give the Leontief inverse matrix or its variants, and a solution that satisfies the given final demands can be uniquely determined.

Equations (4.91a) and (4.91b) are equivalent to Eqs. (4.1) and (4.2); in Sect. 4.3.1, we take $\overline{Z}_j^{ps}$ as x_j^{ps}, which may be useful how to construct the interregional input–output system of Moses type starting from the same data usually available for other types of interregional input–output table.

---

[15] Precisely speaking, in order to obtain more reliable values of v_{nj}^{ps}, the total *volume* of the intra- and inter-regional shipments of goods i from region p to region s must be calculated, e.g., in terms of ton $\times$ kilometer. We symbolize the total volumes as φ_{nj}^{ps}. Allocate the total production of transportation services, $\sum_{j=1}^{n-1} Z_{nj}^{pp}$ (since only this data is usually available *before* the following adjustments if the basic table is not available), to each shipment activity as follows: $\overline{\overline{Z}}_{nj}^{ps} = \left(\sum_{j=1}^{n-1} Z_{nj}^{pp}\right) \varphi_{nj}^{ps} / \left(\sum_{s=1}^{r} \sum_{p=1}^{r} \sum_{k=1}^{n-1} \varphi_{nk}^{ps}\right)$ $(p, s = 1, 2, \ldots, r; j = 1, 2, \ldots, n)$. v_{nj}^{ps} is defined as $\overline{\overline{Z}}_{nj}^{ps} / \sum_{i=1}^{n} Z_{ji}^{ps}$.

A matrix form of the system of Equations (4.91a) and (4.91b) is given in the form of Eq. (4.6), and here we skip it. It must be pointed here that the system has several solutions unless a criterion that drives the activities in a certain direction is given to the system.

Here, it is better once to review the original model by Moses (1960). His objective is to find out an optimum assignment of the quantities of goods to be produced to several designated regions (West or East of US, etc.) to satisfy the given final demand at each region as well as intermediate demands by the whole national economy, being subject to the constraints of the capital stock and labor available in each region. The optimality of the production location and the trade patterns between the regions, which may induce shipments of goods, is pursued by minimizing the total transportation costs incurred by the shipments.

The essence of the original model by Moses (1960) is the following activity coefficient matrix that assumes three sectors and two regions:

$$\begin{pmatrix} \overline{a}_{11}^{1} & \overline{a}_{12}^{1} & \overline{a}_{13}^{1} & {}_{1}\overline{v}_{1}^{11} & {}_{1}\overline{v}_{1}^{12} & {}_{1}\overline{v}_{2}^{11} & {}_{1}\overline{v}_{2}^{12} & {}_{1}\overline{v}_{3}^{11} & {}_{1}\overline{v}_{3}^{12} \\ \overline{a}_{21}^{1} & \overline{a}_{22}^{1} & \overline{a}_{23}^{1} & {}_{2}\overline{v}_{1}^{11} & {}_{2}\overline{v}_{1}^{12} & {}_{2}\overline{v}_{2}^{11} & {}_{2}\overline{v}_{2}^{12} & {}_{2}\overline{v}_{3}^{11} & {}_{2}\overline{v}_{3}^{12} \\ \overline{a}_{31}^{1} & \overline{a}_{32}^{1} & \overline{a}_{33}^{1} & {}_{3}\overline{v}_{1}^{11} & {}_{3}\overline{v}_{1}^{12} & {}_{3}\overline{v}_{2}^{11} & {}_{3}\overline{v}_{2}^{12} & {}_{3}\overline{v}_{3}^{11} & {}_{3}\overline{v}_{3}^{12} \end{pmatrix}, \tag{4.92}$$

in which:

${}_{i}\overline{v}_{j}^{ps}$ is the amount of goods i required to transport a unit goods j from region p to region s.

In the original Moses model, the sector of transportation services, a sector that produces and provides transportation services, does not exist explicitly. However, the shipment of the commodity induces the derivative demands against goods that are necessary for the production of (i) the goods transported as well as (ii) the transportation services necessary for the shipment. Therefore, the system of Eq. (4.91a) becomes as follows:

$$\sum\nolimits_{s=1}^{r} \overline{Z}_{i}^{sp} = \sum\nolimits_{s=1}^{r} \sum_{j=1}^{n-1} \left(\overline{a}_{ij}^{ps} + {}_{i}\overline{v}_{j}^{ps} \right) \overline{Z}_{j}^{ps} + F_{i}^{p} \; (i = 1, 2, \ldots, n-1). \tag{4.93}$$

In our model, nth sector is explicitly treated as the transportation sector, and it may be built in the system as an endogenous sector using data of ${}_{i}\overline{v}_{j}^{ps}$ (or, the data used for the calculation of ${}_{i}\overline{v}_{j}^{ps}$) as follows:

$$\mathrm{IMD}_{in}^{ps} = \sum\nolimits_{j=1}^{n-1} {}_{i}\overline{v}_{j}^{ps} \overline{Z}_{j}^{ps}, \tag{4.94}$$

in which: IMD_{in}^{ps} is the intermediate input of goods i ($i = 1, 2, \ldots, n-1$) into the transportation sector ($j = n$) which delivers goods j (=1, 2, ..., $n-1$) from region p

to region s. Input coefficient of the transportation sector and coefficients of the derivative demand against transportation services, v_{nj}^{ps}, can be defined as follows:

$$\overline{\overline{a}}_{in}^{ps} = \frac{\text{IMD}_{in}^{ps}}{\sum_{j=1}^{n-1} Z_{nj}^{ps}} \quad (i = 1, 2, \ldots, n-1; p, s = 1, 2, \ldots, r). \tag{4.95}$$

$$\overline{\overline{v}}_{nj}^{ps} = \frac{\varphi_{nj}^{ps}}{\varphi} \frac{\left(\sum_{j=1}^{n-1} Z_{nj}^{pp} \right)}{\overline{Z}_{j}^{ps}} \quad (j = 1, 2, \ldots, n-1; p, s = 1, 2, \ldots, r), \tag{4.96}$$

$$\varphi = \sum_{s=1}^{r} \sum_{p=1}^{r} \sum_{k=1}^{n-1} \varphi_{nk}^{ps}, \tag{4.97}$$

in which: φ_{nj}^{ps} is the total volume of the intra- and interregional shipments of goods j from region p to region s which may be calculated, for example, in terms of ton × kilometer. By making the following replacements:

$$v_{nj}^{ps} = \overline{\overline{v}}_{nj}^{ps} \ (p \neq s), \tag{4.98}$$

$$\overline{a}_{in}^{ps} = \overline{\overline{a}}_{in}^{ps} \ (p \neq s), \tag{4.99}$$

$$\overline{a}_{nj}^{p} = \overline{\overline{v}}_{nj}^{pp} \ (i = 1, 2, \ldots, n-1), \tag{4.100}$$

$$\overline{a}_{in}^{p} = \overline{\overline{a}}_{in}^{pp} (i = 1, 2, \ldots, n-1), \tag{4.101}$$

$$\overline{a}_{nn}^{p} = 0, \text{ and} \tag{4.102}$$

$$\overline{a}_{nn}^{ps} = 0 \ (p \neq s), \tag{4.103}$$

we obtain the system of Equations (4.91a) and (4.91b) while others are defined by Eqs. (4.88) and (4.89).

4.5 Optimality Criteria Built in the Model

4.5.1 Problem Presentation

The problem we will now analyze and shall try to rightly give the solution is that: being given the current stage (1960) of the Japanese economy, making the economic structures at the beginning of the year 1971 most efficient in terms of the maximization of GDP/NNP by optimally allocating the capital funds for the capital formation in the private sectors as well as the public sectors, especially for the improvements in the transportation infrastructures of railway, harbor, and roads. In other words, how to maximize the economic growth of the Japanese economy within 12 years by optimally controlling the capital fund assignment between the private and the public sectors. This shall be a typical dynamic optimization problem of the Japanese economy. However, the model presented in this chapter is based on Kohno (1975) which was published based on the work conducted by one of the authors so long time since he was a student at the doctoral course while he was working at JHPC. At that time, due to the limited computer capacity and the capability of the software available, the model must be a constrained one in terms of the number of variables (activities in the sense of linear programming model) and other in structural equations (the number of rows). As a first step, the problem mentioned earlier must be replaced by the following: How to allocate the capital funds that are expected to be available in the 12 years for the capital accumulation in the private sectors and the public sectors to realize the most efficient Japanese economic structures at the beginning of the year of 1971. In other words, the GDP/NNP attained is maximized with the economic structures that are possibly realized in 1971 by allocating the capital funds for the private and public sectors. This problem implicitly assumes that stages of economic development which the Japanese economy is supposed to go through during the 12 years or more and a kind of inertia are neglected, namely, the economy can jump into the restructured one without costs. In reality, such a jump is impossible and not realistic. However, it is still worth knowing the ideal and most effective structures of the Japanese economy in terms of the economic growth, the economic balance between the regions, and the balance of the allocation of capital funds between the private and public sectors. It still provides us fruitful policy implications. It can be the next other problems how to realize it by spending more time and costs, what will be further costs to reach it as closely as possible, and so on. The model that can rightly reply to these questions is presented in Chap. 7 in a complete way.

4.5.2 *Bottleneck of the Development and the Measurement of the Investment Effects*

4.5.2.1 Necessity of the General Equilibrium Approach

The most important feature of the public investment is that its scale is quite large compared to the usual private investments in terms of the amount of capital funds, of course, as well as the scope space (regions and sectors) and the time span through which its impacts diffuse, and so on. Actually, in the given problem mentioned earlier, the amount of capital funds is huge. First of all, to rightly decide on the public investments (and the investments in the private sectors), the decision-aid method (the model) cannot assume the so-called *ceteris paribus*, which is typically made with the partial equilibrium analysis.

The structural model of Eq. (4.6) specified in Sect. 4.3.1 or one of the more practical variants, Eq. (4.37), has an advantage over the conventional benefit–costs measurement approach and is mostly suitable for the measurements of the impacts of the public investments. The economy specified in the model is consisting of several regions that may be on different stages of regional development, have different limited resources, and are economically linked with each other via transportation infrastructures that can be utilized for the shipments of goods induced by the trades between regions. The model is an interregional input–output model, and it has capability to capture and measure the indirect as well as direct benefits (economic effects) of the public investments.

4.5.2.2 Elimination of Economic Bottleneck and the Measurement of Its Effects

As the economy grows, it faces several bottlenecks. The private firms, which are bundled to be sectors in the model, product by product, first face a shortage in the supply of resources such as capital, labor, and other resources such as water resources and so on, As the economy grows, the demand for goods increase. For simplicity, we assume that the economy is closed and no government exists. Only the firms that are bundled into several sectors and the representative household exists. The economy can be represented as follows using the typical input–output system (symbols are defined for usage in this sub-section only):

$$(I - A)\,X = F, \tag{4.104}$$

$$V = l - l\,A\,X, \tag{4.105}$$

$$VAD = VX, \tag{4.106}$$

$$x_{ij} = a_{ij}\,X_j, \tag{4.107}$$

$$\widehat{\boldsymbol{\alpha}}X \leq K, \tag{4.108}$$

in which:

$X = [X_1, X_2, \ldots, X_n]'$, X_i is the total product of goods i; $F = [F_1, F_2, \ldots, F_n]'$, F_i is the final demand against goods i; $A = (a_{ij})$, a_{ij} is the input coefficient of goods i into sector j to produce a unit goods j; $V = [V_1, V_2, \ldots, V_n]$, V_i is the value-added ratio to the total product in sector i; $l = [1, 1, \ldots, 1]$, which is a row vector for the summation; x_{ij}: input of goods i into sector j:

$$\widehat{\boldsymbol{\alpha}} = \begin{pmatrix} \alpha_1 & \cdots & 0 & 0 \\ \vdots & \ddots & \vdots & \vdots \\ 0 & \cdots & \alpha_{n-1} & 0 \\ 0 & \cdots & 0 & \alpha_n \end{pmatrix},$$

α_i: the required amount of the capital in JPY in sector i to produce a unit goods i; $K = [K_1, K_2, \ldots, K_n]'$, K_i: the amount of the capital available for the production (henceforth, we call it—the capital stock) in sector i.

First, focus on the inequalities, (4.108), though they must hold with the exact equalities in the long-run equilibrium. Assuming that the constraints hold with exact inequality (<) for all sectors. Which means:

$$\alpha_j X_j < K_j \text{ for all } j. \tag{4.109}$$

As the economy grows, F increases to $F + \Delta F$ and X increases to $X + \Delta X$. Actually, the systems (4.104) and (4.105) are simultaneous equation systems. ΔF is induced by increases in V by ΔV, which is defined as $\Delta V = V\Delta X$. As far as the Eq. (4.108) holds, the economy can grow provided that other resources than capital stock are in abundant supplies. Eventually, Eq. (4.109) must hold with exact equality for a certain sector j^*.

This can be represented as follows:

$$\alpha_{j^*} X_{j^*} = K_{j^*}, \tag{4.110}$$

Once it happens, the economy cannot grow unless the capital stock K_i is increased. This is a so-called bottleneck for the economy to grow.

If K_{j^*} is increased to $K_{j^*} + \Delta K_{j^*}$, using the capital fund, the economy can grow till Eq. (4.108) holds with equality with a certain sector j. Define the amount of capital stocks K^* that is actually used for the production as follows:

$$\hat{\boldsymbol{\alpha}} (I - A)^{-1} F = K^* \le \overline{K}. \tag{4.111}$$

Any sector can be a bottleneck for the economy to grow, and it may be dependent on the composition of F.

$$\hat{\boldsymbol{\alpha}} (I - A)^{-1} (F + \Delta F) = K^* + \Delta K \le \overline{K}. \tag{4.112}$$

As far as ΔF and, therefore, ΔK is very small, Eq. (4.108) holds again with equality with only sector j^*.

$$B^1(\Delta K_{j^*}) = \sum\nolimits_{j=1}^{n} \Delta F_j \tag{4.113}$$

$B^1(\Delta K_{j^*})$ can be a first approximation to the effects of the investment ΔK_{j^*} in monetary terms. This must be taken as the impact of an increase in the capital stock only in sector j^*, since $K + \Delta K$ of other elements were idled before fixing the bottleneck and still idled after fixing it. Or, the effects of the investment of ΔK_{j^*} can be measured as follows[16]:

[16] Actually, in this system, $B^1(\Delta K_{j^*}) = B^2(\Delta K_{j^*}, \Delta F)$.

$$B^2(\Delta K_{j^*}, \Delta F) = V\Delta X.$$

B^2 is an increase in the total value added to the economy. The point here is that the *direct* impacts of ΔK_{j^*} is $BD^2(\Delta K_{j^*}, \Delta F) = V_{j^*}\Delta X_{j^*} = V_{j^*}\frac{\Delta K_{j^*}}{\alpha_{j^*}}$, which is apparently smaller than $B^2(\Delta K_{j^*}, \Delta F)$. With the conventional benefit–cost approach, it may be easy to calculate $BD^2(\Delta K_{j^*}, \Delta F)$, but it is difficult to calculate $B^2(\Delta K_{j^*}, \Delta F)$. The difficulty is like that in the conventional benefit–cost approach, we must know all the values of ΔX, which corresponds to ΔF, without knowing $(I - A)^{-1}$. This may well explain why we must rely on the mathematical model with which the direct and indirect economic effects of the investments can be measured in an overall and consistent way without leakages and double-counting with items of economic effects, and so on. As ΔX may be dependent on ΔF, the economic effects, $B^2(\Delta K_{j^*}, \Delta F)$, can be maximized with respect to ΔF. This may be a queer optimization problem in a sense, and this is just a simplicity for the explanation of direct and indirect effects.

4.5.2.3 Numerical Examples

The following is a simple numerical example:

$$A = \begin{pmatrix} 0.2 & 0.15 & 0.10 \\ 0.25 & 0.30 & 0.40 \\ 0.15 & 0.10 & 0.15 \end{pmatrix}, \hat{\boldsymbol{\alpha}} = \begin{pmatrix} 2.5 & 0 & 0 \\ 0 & 2.3 & 0 \\ 0 & 0 & 3.0 \end{pmatrix}, \overline{K} = \begin{bmatrix} 211 \\ 510 \\ 400 \end{bmatrix},$$

$$V = \begin{bmatrix} 0.40 \\ 0.45 \\ 0.35 \end{bmatrix}, \overline{F} = \begin{bmatrix} 30 \\ 50 \\ 72.319615 \end{bmatrix}, \text{and } \overline{C} = 5,$$

in which: $\overline{C}$ is the capital funds for investments.[17]

The abovementioned discussion can be described with the following optimal fund allocation problem. With an increment in the capital stock, $\Delta K = [\Delta K_1, \Delta K_2, K_3]'$, and adjustment of $\Delta F = [\Delta F_1, \Delta F_2, F_3]'$, solve the following problem:

[17] In order to show that the capital stock constraint is only bound in sector 1, the value of the final demand against goods 3 are so minutely adjusted.

$$\left[\begin{array}{l} \max\limits_{\{\Delta F, \Delta K\}} \ VAD = VX, \\ \text{subject to}: \left\{ \begin{array}{c} (I-A)\,X = \overline{F} + \Delta F \\ \widehat{\alpha} X \le \overline{K} + \Delta K. \\ (1, \quad 1, \quad 1)\Delta K = \overline{C}. \end{array} \right. \end{array}\right. \tag{4.114}$$

It is obvious that only ΔK_1 would have a positive value as far as the capital funds $\overline{C}$ is small. However, as a formal specification, the model, Eq. (4.114), is a right one. The point here is $\overline{F}$ is given. If $\overline{F} + \Delta F$ would be controllable, the problem becomes completely different and not suitable one for the explanation of elimination of bottlenecks. The solutions to (4.114) are given as follows:

$$\widehat{X} = \begin{bmatrix} \widehat{X}_1 \\ \widehat{X}_2 \\ \widehat{X}_3 \end{bmatrix} = \begin{bmatrix} 86.4000 \\ 175.4462 \\ 128.0308 \end{bmatrix}, \Delta F = \begin{bmatrix} 0 \\ 0 \\ 6.001923 \end{bmatrix}, \Delta K = \begin{bmatrix} 5 \\ 0 \\ 0 \end{bmatrix},$$

$$\widehat{\text{VAD}} = 158.3215, K^* = \begin{bmatrix} 216.0000 \\ 403.5262 \\ 384.0923 \end{bmatrix}, j^* = 1,$$

$$B^2\left(\Delta K_{j^*}, \Delta F\right) = 6.001923, BD^2\left(\Delta K_{j^*}, \Delta F\right) = 0.8000000,$$

while the solutions to Eq. (4.114) when $\overline{C} = 0$ are given as follows:

$$X = \begin{bmatrix} X_1 \\ X_2 \\ X_3 \end{bmatrix} = \begin{bmatrix} 84.40000 \\ 170.1385 \\ 119.9923 \end{bmatrix}, \text{VAD} = 152.3196, K^* = \begin{bmatrix} 211.0000 \\ 391.3185 \\ 359.9769 \end{bmatrix},$$
$$j^* = 1. \tag{4.115}$$

The amount of the direct effects by the increase in K_1 by 5 is 0.8. On the other hand, the total economic effects are $6.0019\cdots$ and the indirect economic effects are $5.2019\cdots$. The indirect economic effects are 6.50 times the direct economic effects. This simple example shows the necessity of the overall and consistent measurement method of the economic effects of the investments.

4.5.2.4 Allocation of the Capital Funds Between the Private and the Public Sectors of Water Resource Development

Using the numerical example earlier, we will show the essence mechanism of allocating capital funds for several investment targets. Assume that the production of sector 2 and sector 3 needs input of water resources and the additional constraint can be written as follows:

$$\Omega X \leq \overline{W}, \tag{4.116}$$

in which: $\Omega = [\omega_1 \quad \omega_2 \quad \omega_3]$;$\omega_i$: the amount of water required for a unit production of goods i and $\omega_1 = 0$;$\overline{W}$: the amount of water resources available for the production in sector 2 and sector 3.

We assume that the water resource can be developed by the public investment using the capital funds. The problem (4.114) is developed as follows:

$$\left[\begin{array}{l} \max\limits_{\{X,\Delta F,\Delta K,DW\}} \quad VAD = VX, \\ \left\{\begin{array}{ll} & (I-A)\,X = \overline{F} + \Delta F \\ \text{subject to :} & \widehat{\alpha}X \leq \overline{K} + \Delta K, \\ & \Omega X \leq \overline{W} + DW, \\ & (1,\quad 1,\quad 1)\Delta K + DW \leq \overline{C}, \end{array}\right. \end{array}\right. \tag{4.117}$$

in which: DW is increased in the water resources owing to the water resources development by using the capital funds. Assuming that $\Omega = (\omega_1 \quad \omega_2 \quad \omega_3) = (0 \quad 0.25 \quad 0.18333)$, $\overline{W} = 64.53322$, and other parameters are the same as above, the solution is given as follows[18]:

$$\widehat{X} = \begin{bmatrix} \widehat{X}_1 \\ \widehat{X}_2 \\ \widehat{X}_3 \end{bmatrix} = \begin{bmatrix} 85.68195 \\ 173.5406 \\ 125.1448 \end{bmatrix}, \Delta F = \begin{bmatrix} 0 \\ 0 \\ 3.847080 \end{bmatrix}, \Delta K = \begin{bmatrix} 3.204872 \\ 0 \\ 0 \end{bmatrix},$$

$$DW = 1.795128, \widehat{\text{VAD}} = 156.1667, \widehat{\alpha X} = K^* = \begin{bmatrix} 214.2049 \\ 399.1433 \\ 375.4343 \end{bmatrix}, j^* = 1,$$

[18] With $\overline{C} = 0$, therefore, with $\Delta K = 0$ and $DW = 0$, the solutions to the Eq. (4.117) are same as those to Eq. (4.114).

$$\varepsilon_w = 0.7694141,$$

$$B^2\left(\Delta K_{j^*}, \Delta F\right) = 3.847080,$$

$$BD^2\left(\Delta K_{j^*}, \Delta F\right) = V_1\Delta X_1 + \varepsilon_w DW = 0.5127796 + 0.7694141 \times 1.795128 = 1.893976,$$

in which: ε_w is the imputed price of the water resource. It is not sure whether the imputed price of the water resource shall be used for the calculation of the direct benefit (perhaps, "should not" because the partial analysis adopted by the conventional benefit–cost analysis cannot give its precise value). This shows the total benefits are more than twice of the direct benefits.

The capital funds of 5 are allocated to the private sector and public sector such as $\Delta K_1 = 3.205$ and $DW = 1.795$. The point of the numerical example is that there are two economic bottlenecks, that is, of the private capital in sector 1 and the supply of water resources which sectors 2 and 3 required to produce goods. The limited amount of capital funds is available for the elimination of the bottlenecks as well as further economic development. A natural question is how much should be allocated to the private sectors to increase their production capacity and how much allocated for the development of water resources as it is expected that the demand against the water resources increases due to the development of the private sectors induced by the allocation of capital funds. The numerical model is just to show how the model can work as the decision-aid system. Of course, the criteria must be exogenously given on which the optimality of the allocation of capital funds can be judged. Once it is given, the model gives useful information for the decision-making. Sometimes, the first priority is given to institutional constraints. For example, the shares between the private and public investments must be 3:2. In that case, the amount of 3 first allocated to $\Delta K_1 + \Delta K_2 + \Delta K_3$ and DW must be 2. Still, the same question is raised and the model suggests optimal shares between sectors 1, 2, and 3. Furthermore, the model will be able to drastically show the opportunity costs of such institutional constraints.

4.5.2.5 Capital Fund Allocation Matrix of Lefeber's Type

The simple numerical examples above are able to show the essence of the model presented in Sect. 4.3 in the sense that the substantial structures of the model are structured into the numerical model, and we may use it to explain how the model in Sect. 4.3 can solve the two subjects raised in Sect. 4.1. simultaneously and consistently without relying on the dichotomy that has to be adopted by the conventional benefit–cost approach.

By multiplying both sides of the second constraint of the problem Eq. (4.117) with $\widehat{\boldsymbol{\alpha}}^{-1}$, it can be written as follows:

$$X \le \widehat{\boldsymbol{\alpha}}^{-1}\left(\overline{K} + \Delta K\right). \tag{4.118}$$

This means that the capital stock of each sector can be measured in terms of the amount that is required for a unit production of goods i. Since usually the capital stock is measured in terms of JPY, the summation row vector, $(1, 1, 1)$, in the fourth constraint of Eq. (4.117), must be replaced by $(\alpha_1,\ \alpha_2,\ \alpha_3)$. The unit for the measurement of the water resources can be interpreted as the amount of water resources that can be developed by a unit of the capital funds, that is, cubic meter/100 million JPY. By making adjustment of units, the allocation mechanism can be written as follows:

$$[X_1,\quad X_2,\quad X_3,\ \Delta F_1, \Delta F_2, \Delta F_3, \Delta K_1, \Delta K_2, \Delta K_3, DW]$$

$$\begin{pmatrix} 1-a_{11} & -a_{12} & -a_{13} & -1 & 0 & 0 & 0 & 0 & 0 & 0 \\ -a_{21} & 1-a_{22} & -a_{23} & 0 & -1 & 0 & 0 & 0 & 0 & 0 \\ -a_{31} & -a_{32} & 1-a_{33} & 0 & 0 & -1 & 0 & 0 & 0 & 0 \\ 1 & 0 & 0 & 0 & 0 & 0 & -1 & 0 & 0 & 0 \\ 0 & 1 & 0 & 0 & 0 & 0 & 0 & -1 & 0 & 0 \\ 0 & 0 & 1 & 0 & 0 & 0 & 0 & 0 & -1 & 0 \\ 0 & \omega_2 & \omega_3 & 0 & 0 & 0 & 0 & 0 & 0 & -1 \\ 0 & 0 & 0 & 0 & 0 & 0 & \alpha_1 & \alpha_2 & \alpha_3 & 1 \\ V_1 & V_2 & V_3 & 0 & 0 & 0 & 0 & 0 & 0 & 0 \end{pmatrix} \begin{bmatrix} X_1 \\ X_2 \\ X_3 \\ \Delta F_1 \\ \Delta F_2 \\ \Delta F_3 \\ \Delta K_1 \\ \Delta K_2 \\ \Delta K_3 \\ DW \end{bmatrix} \begin{matrix} = \\ = \\ = \\ \leq \\ \leq \\ \leq \\ \leq \\ \leq \\ = \end{matrix} \begin{bmatrix} \overline{F}_1 \\ \overline{F}_2 \\ \overline{F}_3 \\ \overline{K}_1 \\ \overline{K}_2 \\ \overline{K}_3 \\ \overline{W} \\ \overline{C} \\ V \end{bmatrix}. \tag{4.119}$$

With the matrix in the left-hand side of Eq. (4.119), the right sub-sub-matrix of the following sub-matrix is called capital fund allocation matrix of Lefeber's type (Lefeber 1958):

$$[X_1\ \ X_2\ \ X_3\ \ \cdots\ \ \Delta K_1\ \ \Delta K_2\ \ \Delta K_3\, DW]$$

$$\begin{bmatrix} 1 & 0 & 0 & \cdots & -1 & & & \\ 0 & 1 & 0 & \cdots & & -1 & & \\ 0 & 0 & 1 & \cdots & & & -1 & \\ 0 & \omega_2 & \omega_3 & \cdots & & & & -1 \\ & & & \cdots & \alpha_1 & \alpha_2 & \alpha_3 & 1 \end{bmatrix} \cdots \begin{bmatrix} \overline{K}_1 \\ \overline{K}_2 \\ \overline{K}_3 \\ \overline{W} \\ \overline{C} \end{bmatrix} \tag{4.120}$$

This is simple and abstract as it is a matrix algebra and explains the essence of the mechanism of the capital funds allocation to eliminate economic bottlenecks. As the economy grows, the activity level of production (X) increases, and this needs increases in the inputs of capital and eventually the demand by, for example, sector 1 is constrained by the availability of capital stock, $\overline{K}$, namely, the growth of sector 1 must stop and the economy faces economic bottleneck to grow because the economy cannot further grow with the input–output structure (sectors are interdependent with each other). If the allocation of the capital funds for sector 1 could be approved by the criteria, the capital allocation activity, ΔK_1, has a positive value, for example, 10 (we say—the activity ΔK_1 starts to work) and the availability of the capital stock increases by 10 (the element -1 implies this amount must be added to $\overline{K}_1$ in the right-hand), and it incurs outlay on the capital finds by $\alpha_1 \times 10$, which is implied by the last row of the matrix (4.120). The availability of the capital funds becomes $\overline{C} - \alpha_1 \times 10$.

The usage of water resources is competitive among sectors 2 and 3. This is implied by the location of the coefficients, ω_2 and ω_2, on the same row, which is linked to the water resource availability, $\overline{W}$. By observing coefficients of the row and the column which has a common element of -1 in the matrix (4.120), we can say that: For example, by using α_1 amount of the capital fund, the capital stock in sector 1 can be increased by a unit, and it enables a unit increase in the production in sector 1 (if the shortage in the capital stock is only a bottle-neck in the economy) and directly increases the value added by $V_{1.}$ In the numerical example, $V_{1.} = 0.4$, and $\alpha_1 = 2.5$. Although it must be dependent on how much is the share allocated to dividends among the value-added, roughly speaking it takes around 10 years ($\alpha_1 \times 10 \div (V_1 \times \Delta X_1 \times 0.6) = 25 \div 2.4 = 10.4$) to depreciate the investment if the share is 0.6. If we use the capital fund of $\omega_2 = 0.25$, we can additionally produce a unit of goods 2, and it creates the value added of 0.45. It looks the investment in the water resources development is efficient, and it has no meaning of course to develop more than what is demanded.

It is still useful to see the matrix in Eq. (4.119). The trades of goods are simulated via the input–output structures (the first three rows). The trade is a result of the market in which the demand and the supply would be equated with each other, being given the final demands.[19] The production requires and induces increases in the supply of resources as the economy grows (as the final demand increases due to exogenous reasons). If the supply of resources and goods has to be stopped due to bottlenecks of shortage in the supply of the capital stocks, the capital funds allocation activities start to work. The amount of capital funds is limited, and the allocation matrix searches efficient allocation of the capital funds for eliminating bottlenecks (as there are possibly several ways to fix bottlenecks with the more practical models, e.g., direct allocation of capital fund to the capital formation in the bottleneck sector in a certain region vs. allocation of capital formation in the same sector in a different region, which increases interregional trades and may induce improvements in transportation infrastructures between the said two regions, etc.) by taking account of the efficiency of the direct effects induced by the allocation that can be confirmed by the rows and column which have crossing elements of -1 and 1 in the right-hand sub-sub matrix of (4.120) *as well as* the indirect effects that diffuse into the whole economy via the input–output structures. In this sense, it can be said that the model solves the two subjects raised in Sect. 4.1 simultaneously and consistently.

[19] With the model in this chapter, the final demands are exogenously given. However, a driving force (incentive for a kind of arbitrage) must be still given to the markets exogenously, which will be explained later on. By the way, the model in which final demands are treated endogenously in the markets will be shown in Chap. 7, to which a driving force must be given, too.

The optimality of the allocation of the limited funds for the elimination of bottlenecks is confirmed based on the opportunity cost criterion that is installed in the simplex criteria—solution algorithm for the linear programming problem.

4.5.2.6 Opportunity Cost Criteria—Simplex Criteria

Here, it is better to confirm why the following allocation of the capital funds is optimal, that is, most efficient (the best) in terms of the possible increase in the objective function:

$$\Delta K = \begin{bmatrix} 3.204872 \\ 0 \\ 0 \end{bmatrix}, \text{ and } DW = 1.795128.$$

A little bit technical argument follows, and readers who are not interested in technical matters may skip the following paragraphs as far as readers would admit that the allocation is obtained as solutions to the maximization problem, Eq. (4.117), and therefore, it is optimal allocation of the capital funds.

The linear programming problem (LP), Eq. (4.117), may be transformed into the following standard form of LP (see Appendix 4):

$$\left[\begin{array}{l} \max\limits_{\{X,\Delta F,\Delta K,DW,SX\}} \quad \mathrm{VAD} = VX, \\ \quad \left\{\begin{array}{l} \text{subject to :} \\ \qquad (I-A)\,X - \Delta F = \overline{F}, \\ \qquad \widehat{\boldsymbol{\alpha}}X - \Delta K + I\,SX_K = \overline{K} \\ \qquad \Omega X - DW + SX_W = \overline{W}, \\ \qquad (1,\ \ 1,\ \ 1)\Delta K + DW + SX_C = \overline{C}, \\ \qquad X, \Delta F, \Delta K, DW, SX \geq \mathbf{0}, \end{array}\right. \end{array}\right. \tag{4.121}$$

in which:

$SX = [SX_{K_1}, SX_{K_2}, SX_{K_3}, SX_W, SX_C]'$ is a column vector of slack variables that transforms inequalities to exact equalities. Slack variables, $SX_{K_1}, SX_{K_2}, SX_{K_3}; SX_W; SX_C$, are, respectively, associated with the constraints on the demand of capital stocks against the supply in sectors 1, 2, 3; the constraints of the demand of water resources against the supply; and the demand of capital fund allocation against the supply of capital funds. The optimal solution shows X_1, X_2, X_3, ΔF_3, ΔK_1, DW, SK_2, and SK_3 are the optimal basic activities. We obtain:

$$\boldsymbol{X_1} = [\, X_1, X_2, X_3, \Delta F_3, \Delta K_1, DW, SK_2, SK_3 \,],$$

$$\boldsymbol{A_1} = \begin{bmatrix} 1-a_{11} & -a_{12} & -a_{13} & 0 & 0 & 0 & 0 & 0 \\ -a_{21} & -a_{22} & -a_{23} & 0 & 0 & 0 & 0 & 0 \\ -a_{31} & -a_{32} & 1-a_{33} & -1 & 0 & 0 & 0 & 0 \\ \alpha_1 & 0 & 0 & 0 & -1 & 0 & 0 & 0 \\ 0 & \alpha_2 & 0 & 0 & 0 & 0 & 1 & 0 \\ 0 & 0 & \alpha_3 & 0 & 0 & 0 & 0 & 1 \\ 0 & \omega_2 & \omega_3 & 0 & 0 & -1 & 0 & 0 \\ 0 & 0 & 0 & 0 & 1 & 1 & 0 & 0 \end{bmatrix}, \tag{4.122}$$

$$\boldsymbol{C_1} = [\, V_1, V_2, V_3, 0, 0, 0, 0, 0 \,],$$

$$\boldsymbol{X_2} = [\Delta F_1, \Delta F_2, \Delta K_2, \Delta K_3, SK_1, SX_W, SX_C]$$

$$\boldsymbol{A_2} = \begin{bmatrix} -1 & 0 & 0 & 0 & 0 & 0 & 0 \\ 0 & -1 & 0 & 0 & 0 & 0 & 0 \\ 0 & 0 & 0 & 0 & 0 & 0 & 0 \\ 0 & 0 & 0 & 0 & 1 & 0 & 0 \\ 0 & 0 & -1 & 0 & 0 & 0 & 0 \\ 0 & 0 & 0 & -1 & 0 & 0 & 0 \\ 0 & 0 & 0 & 0 & 0 & 1 & 0 \\ 0 & 0 & 1 & 1 & 0 & 0 & 1 \end{bmatrix}, \tag{4.123}$$

$$\boldsymbol{C_2} = [\, 0, 0, 0, 0, 0, 0, 0 \,].$$

Therefore, the simplex criterion with the optimal solution is calculated as follows:

$$\boldsymbol{\delta} = \boldsymbol{C_2} - \boldsymbol{C_1}\boldsymbol{A_1^{-1}}\boldsymbol{A_2}$$
$$= [-1.917824, -0.04289588, -0.7694141, -0.7694141, -0.7694141, -0.7694141, -0.7694141.]$$

All the simplex criteria are negative, and the base matrix $\boldsymbol{A_1}$ is an optimal basic matrix, which gives the optimal solution. The imputed prices of resources are calculated as follows:

$$\boldsymbol{C_1}\boldsymbol{A_1^{-1}}$$

$$= [-1.917824, -0.04289588, 0.000000, 0.7694141, 0.000000, \\ 0.000000, 0.7694141, 0.7694141].$$

These prices calculate the opportunity cost of the inclusion of nonbasic activity into the (new) basic matrix by excluding one of the basic activities in the current basic matrix. For example, it must pay the opportunity cost of 0.7694141 = $\boldsymbol{C}_1\boldsymbol{A}_1^{-1}\boldsymbol{a}_4^2$ to include nonbasic activity $\boldsymbol{a}_4^2$ (the fourth column vector of $\boldsymbol{A}_2$) into the (new) basic matrix. Because the gain of the inclusion is 0 ($c_4^2 = 0$; the fourth element of $\boldsymbol{C}_2$), the opportunity cost is too high than the gain and the inclusion should not be made. The same logic holds for all nonbasic activities, so the current basic activities are the best and optimal basic activities.

4.5.3 Description of the Elimination of Economic Bottlenecks

It can be said that it is almost stated in the previous subsection using numerical examples. However, we once again confirm possible economic bottlenecks that are able to be predicted and how it can be eliminated most effectively using the model in Sect. 4.3 since the model is constructed in a more practical way.

4.5.3.1 Capital Stocks in the Private Sectors

First of all, it may be predicted that a shortage occurs in the capital stocks in the private sectors as the economy grows. In our model, the pressure against the markets is given by the final demands of which values are far bigger than the values in 1960 as the target years are 12 years later. There can be several ways to fix the bottlenecks. For example, following Eq. (4.58), we may assume the capital stock capacity constraints,

$$\sum\nolimits_{k=1}^{r} \sum_{h=1}^{m} \sum_{\tau=1}^{\theta(h,p,k)} {}^{h\tau}x_j^{pk} \leq \frac{\overline{K}_j^p}{\alpha_j^p}, \tag{4.58}$$

hold with exact equality with region p^* and sector j^*. This means as follows:

$$\sum\nolimits_{k=1}^{r} \sum_{h=1}^{m} \sum_{\tau=1}^{\theta(h,p^*,k)} {}^{h\tau}\widehat{x}_{j^*}^{p^*k} = \frac{\overline{K}_{j^*}^{p^*}}{\alpha_{j^*}^{p^*}}. \tag{4.124}$$

As the model assumes the interregional input–output system of the competitive import type, one possible way to eliminate the bottleneck is to increase import from other regions in which the capital stocks are in oversupply. The induced interregional trade patterns may be different from the conventional ones. As the economy, thus, further grows, shortages in the supplies of capital stocks will eventually occur in almost all regions and sectors. The bottleneck in the supply of capital stock can be eliminated by making investments into the private sectors to increase the production capacity.

4.5.3.2 Transportation Capacities in the Public Sectors

As the economy can grow further by the investment into the private sectors, the amount of goods will increase which are traded between regions with the conventional trade patterns as well as the induced new trade patterns. Eventually, a shortage in the capacity of the transportation infrastructures occurs. This means that Eq. (4.62) holds exact equality with a certain transportation infrastructure k^{*}:

$$\sum_{j=1}^{n-1}\sum\nolimits_{s=1}^{r}\sum\nolimits_{t=1}^{r}\sum\nolimits_{h=1}^{m}\sum_{\tau=1}^{\theta(h,s,t)} {}^{h\tau}\delta^{st}(k)\cdot{}^{h}\xi_{j}\cdot{}^{h\tau}x_{j}^{st}=\overline{T}^{k^{*}}. \tag{4.125}$$

There can be several ways to eliminate the bottleneck, too. Following coding of ${}^{h\tau}\delta^{st}(k)$, the shipment of ${}^{h\tau}x_{j}^{st}$ can be made from region s to region t by shifting the mode and/or route that provides transportation services for the shipment between region s and region t as far as the transportation capacity is oversupplied with the alternative mode and/or route. Thus, as the economy grows, the trade of goods increases by increasing trades and changing the trade patterns of goods between regions and among sectors. Eventually, all transportation infrastructures become in full operations, namely, Eq. (4.125) hold for all k.

The bottlenecks in the transportation infrastructures can be eliminated by making investments into the transportation infrastructures to increase the capacity of the transportation mode that is measured in terms of the amount of goods that can be transported.

4.5.3.3 Bottleneck due to Shortages in Other Resources

As for labor, water resources, and so on, the same story can be applied. As for labor, by assigning additional labor (e.g., new graduates) to the sectors and regions in which shortages in the supply of labor occur. As for water resources, the capital funds may be assigned to develop water resources and so on.

4.5.3.4 Built-in Resource Allocation Mechanism of Lefeber's Type

For simplicity, we may assume no alternative routes for all the modes of transportation services between regions. Therefore, $\theta(h, s, k) = 1$ for all h, s, and k.

Elimination of the Economic Bottlenecks and Allocation of the Capital Funds

Private Sectors

The production capacities of the private sectors can be increased by making allocation of the capital funds.

$$K_j^p = \overline{K}_j^p + \Delta K_j^p (\, j = 1, 2, \ldots, r; p = 1, 2, \ldots, n), \tag{4.126}$$

in which:

$\overline{K}_j^p$: initial amount of the capital stock in sector j in region p;
ΔK_j^p: increase in the amount of the capital in sector j in region p owing to the allocation of the capital funds.

Substituting K_j^p of Eq. (4.126) into Eq. (4.58) in place of $\overline{K}_j^p$, we obtain as follows:

$$\begin{aligned} &\sum\nolimits_{k=1}^{r} \sum_{h=1}^{m} \sum_{\tau=1}^{\theta(h,p,k)} {}^{h\tau}x_j^{pk} \leq \frac{\overline{K}_j^p + \Delta K_j^p}{\alpha_j^p}, \\ &\sum\nolimits_{k=1}^{r} \sum_{h=1}^{m} \sum_{\tau=1}^{\theta(h,p,k)} {}^{h\tau}x_j^{pk} - \frac{\Delta K_j^p}{\alpha_j^p} \leq \frac{\overline{K}_j^p}{\alpha_j^p}, \end{aligned} \tag{4.127}$$

By taking the measurement unit of the capital as the amount of the capital in JPY which is necessary for the production of unit goods, Eq. (4.127) becomes as follows:

$$\sum\nolimits_{k=1}^{r} \sum_{h=1}^{m} \sum_{\tau=1}^{\theta(h,p,k)} {}^{h\tau}x_j^{pk} - \Delta \widehat{K}_j^p \leq \overline{\widehat{K}}_j^p, \tag{4.128}$$

in which:$\overline{\widehat{K}}$: initial amount of the capital stock in sector j in region p in terms of the new measurement unit;$\Delta \widehat{K}_j^p$: increase in the capital stock in sector j in region p in terms of the new measurement unit.

Due to the transformation of the measurement unit of the capital, the load of outlay on the capital funds by $\Delta \widehat{K}_j^p$ becomes $\alpha_j^p \Delta \widehat{K}_j^p$.

Transportation Infrastructures

$$T^k = \overline{T}^k + \Delta T^k (k = 1, 2, \ldots, n^T), \tag{4.129}$$

in which:$\overline{T}^k$: initial amount of the transportation infrastructure k;ΔT^k: increase in the amount of transportation infrastructure k owing to the allocation of the capital funds.

Substituting T^k of Eq. (4.129) into $\overline{T}^{k^*}$ of Eq. (4.125), we obtain as follows:

$$\sum_{j=1}^{n-1}\sum\nolimits_{s=1}^{r}\sum\nolimits_{t=1}^{r}\sum\nolimits_{h=1}^{m}\sum_{\tau=1}^{\theta(h,s,t)} {}^{h\tau}\delta^{st}(k)\cdot{}^{h}\xi_j\cdot{}^{h\tau}x_j^{st} - \Delta T^k = \overline{T}^k. \tag{4.130}$$

Labor

$$L_j^p = \overline{L}_j^p + \Delta L_j^p \; (p = 1, 2, \ldots, r; j = 1, 2), \tag{4.131}$$

in which:$\overline{L}_j^p$: initial amount of labor in the agricultural sector ($j = 1$) and non-agricultural sector ($j = 2$);ΔL_j^p: an increase in the supply of labor in the agricultural sector ($j = 1$) and non-agricultural sector ($j = 2$) by assignment of new graduates.

Substituting L_j^p of Eq. (4.131) into $\overline{L}_j^p$ of Eqs. (4.59) and (4.60), we obtain as follows:

$$\sum_{j=1}^{n_L(1)}\sum\nolimits_{k=1}^{r}\sum_{h=1}^{m}\sum_{\tau=1}^{\theta(h,p,k)} \beta_1^p\,{}^{h\tau}x_j^{pk} - \Delta L_1^p \le \overline{L}_1^p, \tag{4.132}$$

$$\sum_{j=n_L(1)+1}^{n}\sum\nolimits_{k=1}^{r}\sum_{h=1}^{m}\sum_{\tau=1}^{\theta(h,p,k)} \beta_2^p\,{}^{h\tau}x_j^{pk} - \Delta L_2^p \le \overline{L}_2^p, \tag{4.133}$$

Water Resources

$$W_j^p = \overline{W}_j^p + DW_j^p \; (p = 1, 2, \ldots, r; j = 1, 2, \ldots, n), \tag{4.134}$$

in which: $\overline{W}_j^p$: initial amount of water resources available in sector j in region p; DW_j^p: increase in the amount of water resources in sector j in region p owing to the allocation of the capital funds.

Substituting W_j^p of Eq. (4.134) into $\overline{W}_j^p$ of Eq. (4.61), we obtain as follows:

$$\sum\nolimits_{k=1}^{r}\sum_{h=1}^{m}\sum_{\tau=1}^{\theta(h,p,k)} {}^{h\tau}x_j^{pk} \le \frac{\overline{W}_j^p + DW_j^p}{\omega_j^p},$$

$$\sum_{k=1}^{r} \sum_{h=1}^{m} \sum_{\tau=1}^{\theta(h,p,k)} {}^{h\tau}x_j^{pk} - \frac{DW_j^p}{\omega_j^p} \leq \frac{\overline{W}_j^p}{\omega_j^p},$$

$$\sum_{k=1}^{r} \sum_{h=1}^{m} \sum_{\tau=1}^{\theta(h,p,k)} {}^{h\tau}x_j^{pk} - D\widehat{W}_j^p \leq \overline{\widehat{W}}_j^p, \tag{4.135}$$

in which:

$\overline{\widehat{W}}_j^p$: initial amount of the water resources in sector j in region p in terms of the new measurement unit;

$\Delta\widehat{W}_j^p$: increase in the water resources available for sector j in region p in terms of the new measurement unit.

Limited Resource Allocation Mechanism of Lefeber's Type

Capital Funds

It is assumed that the total capital funds $\overline{C}$ is exogenously given, and it can be allocated for (1) the private sectors to increase the production capacity, (2) the public sectors to increase the transportation capacities, or increase the water resources available for the production sectors.

$$\sum_{k=1}^{n^T} \mu^k \Delta T^k + \sum_{p=1}^{r} \sum_{j=1}^{n} \alpha_j^p \Delta K_j^p + \sum_{p=1}^{r} \sum_{j=1}^{r} \eta_j^p DW_j^p \leq \overline{C}, \tag{4.136}$$

in which:μ^k is the coefficient which converts a unit of the capital funds into an increase in the capacity of the transportation infrastructure k;η_j^p: the amount of capital funds required for the development of a unit water resources available in sector j in region p.

Labor Assignment

$$\sum_{j=1}^{n_L(1)} \sum_{p=1}^{r} \Delta L_j^p \leq \overline{DL}_1, \tag{4.137}$$

$$\sum_{j=n_L(1)+1}^{n} \sum_{p=1}^{r} \Delta L_j^p \leq \overline{DL}_2, \tag{4.138}$$

in which:$\overline{DL}_k$: expected total increase in agricultural sectors ($k = 1$) and non-agricultural sectors ($k = 2$) in the economy at the target year.

4.5.3.5 Objective Function

The optimal allocation of the capital funds to the private sectors and the public sectors is given as an answer to the optimization problem that is specified as a linear programming problem. The objective function is:

$$\mathrm{NNP} = \sum_{p=1}^{r} \mathrm{NRP}^p, \tag{4.139}$$

in which:

$$\mathrm{GRP}^p = \sum\nolimits_{p=1}^{r} \mathrm{VAD}^p;$$

$$\mathrm{VAD}^p = \sum_{k=1}^{r} \sum_{j=1}^{n-1} \sum\nolimits_{h=1}^{m} {}^{h1}\varphi_j^{pk}\, {}^{h1}x_j^{pk} \ (p = 1, 2, \ldots, r).$$

The point here is that the maximization of the NNP is *not* the objective of the study in this chapter (and it is *not* yet in other chapters). The model structures are constructed taking into account the substance of the economy. One of the important features is that the economy must face and eliminate the bottlenecks to develop. In 1960s it is fairly predicted as the Japanese economy have rapidly taken off.

The model structure incorporates the logic for occurring economic bottlenecks and the possible way of varieties to eliminate the bottlenecks. The model incorporates the trades between regions and the possibility to change the trade patterns depending on the demand and supply between regions and the improvements by the anticipatory investments in the transportation infrastructures.

Only missing in the model so far explained is a kind of the driving force of the economy. As for the conventional input–output system of Leontief type and its variants, it can be considered that the calculation of the inverse matrix of a square matrix (Leontief matrix and its variants) simulates the general market equilibrium being given the final demand exogenously. The model is rigid (actually the solution is unique and it is only the solution regardless it is optimal or not) and no allowance for change. Our model is flexible, and there could be many solutions that satisfy the equations system.

Our argument is that the reality is originally flexible, and still we are induced to the direction which ought to be. The objective function can be taken as a kind of potential function to instill the driving force in the markets by maximizing it. Actually, with the numerical examples in Sect. 4.5.2, the same solutions are obtained by maximizing the sum of increases in the final demand, namely, $\sum_{i=1}^{3} \Delta F_i$. We refer to the *optimal* shares among the private investments and public investments because the model is specified as an optimization problem. However, at the same time, we can say that the shares are what ought to result in the markets in the long run.

4.5.4 *The Model with Capacity Constraints and the Funds Allocation of Lefeber's Type*

4.5.4.1 Formulation of the Model

Now, we can say that the structure of our model which describes the economy is the interregional input–output model with capacity constraints and the resource allocation of Lefeber's type. A driving force to the model markets is given by the maximization of the GDP/NNP. The maximization problem is formulated as a linear programming model.

It should be good for readers to imagine a huge matrix associated with our model, which corresponds to the matrix in the left-hand side of Eq. (4.119) in case of the numerical example, and the matrix $\boldsymbol{A}$ in Appendix 4.

$$\left[{}^{h\tau}X^{st},\quad \Delta T^{k},\ \Delta K^{s}_{j},\ DL^{s},\ DW,\qquad SX\right]$$

$$\begin{bmatrix} \left[{}^{H\Theta}m_{I^p_i,\,{}^{h\tau}J^{st}_j}\right] & \mathbf{0} & \mathbf{0} & \mathbf{0} & \mathbf{0} & -\boldsymbol{I} & \mathbf{0} & \cdots & \mathbf{0} & \cdots & \mathbf{0} & \mathbf{0} \\ \boldsymbol{L_K} & \mathbf{0} & -\boldsymbol{I} & \mathbf{0} & \mathbf{0} & \mathbf{0} & \boldsymbol{I} & \cdots & \mathbf{0} & \cdots & \mathbf{0} & \mathbf{0} \\ \boldsymbol{L_T} & -\boldsymbol{I} & \mathbf{0} & \mathbf{0} & \mathbf{0} & \mathbf{0} & \mathbf{0} & \cdots & \mathbf{0} & \cdots & \mathbf{0} & \mathbf{0} \\ \boldsymbol{R_C} & \boldsymbol{\mu^T} & \boldsymbol{\alpha^K} & \mathbf{0} & \boldsymbol{\eta} & \mathbf{0} & \mathbf{0} & \cdots & \boldsymbol{I} & \cdots & \mathbf{0} & \mathbf{0} \\ \boldsymbol{L_L} & \mathbf{0} & \mathbf{0} & -\boldsymbol{I} & \mathbf{0} & \mathbf{0} & \mathbf{0} & \cdots & \mathbf{0} & \cdots & \mathbf{0} & \mathbf{0} \\ \boldsymbol{R_L} & \mathbf{0} & \mathbf{0} & \boldsymbol{I} & \mathbf{0} & \mathbf{0} & \mathbf{0} & \cdots & \mathbf{0} & \cdots & \boldsymbol{I} & \mathbf{0} \\ \boldsymbol{L_W} & \mathbf{0} & \mathbf{0} & \mathbf{0} & -\boldsymbol{I} & \mathbf{0} & \mathbf{0} & \cdots & \mathbf{0} & \cdots & \mathbf{0} & \boldsymbol{I} \\ \boldsymbol{V} & \mathbf{0} & \mathbf{0} & \mathbf{0} & \mathbf{0} & \mathbf{0} & \mathbf{0} & \cdots & \mathbf{0} & \cdots & \mathbf{0} & \mathbf{0} \end{bmatrix} \begin{bmatrix} {}^{h\tau}X^{st} \\ \Delta T^{k} \\ \\ \Delta K^{s}_{j} \\ DL_i \\ DW \\ SX \end{bmatrix} = \begin{bmatrix} \overline{F} \\ \overline{K} \\ \overline{T} \\ \overline{C} \\ \overline{L} \\ \overline{\Delta L} \\ \overline{W} \\ GDP \end{bmatrix}, \tag{4.140}$$

in which: $\left[{}^{H\Theta}m_{I^p_i,\,{}^{h1}J^{st}_j}\right]$: sub-matrix of $N^{H\Theta} \times M^{H\Theta}$; $N^{H\Theta} = rn$ and $M^{H\Theta} = r\{(n-1)rm + 1\}$; the elements are given in Sect. 4.3.2;L_K:sub-matrix of $rn \times M^{H\Theta}$; its $(I^p_i, {}^{h1}J^{st}_j)$-th element is 1 (one) if and only if $p = s$ and $i = j$. Otherwise, it is 0 (zero); I^p_i and ${}^{h1}J^{st}_j$ are calculated using Eqs. (4.38), (4.39), and (4.40) assuming $\theta(h, s, k) = 1$ for all h, s, and k;L_T:submatrix of $n^T \times M^{H\Theta}$; its $\left(k, {}^{h1}J^{st}_j\right)$-th element is ${}^{h1}\delta^{st}(k) \cdot {}^{h}\xi_j$; ${}^{h1}\delta^{st}(k)$ is given in Sect. 4.3.2;R_C= $\mathbf{0}$;L_L: sub-matrix of $2r \times M^{H\Theta}$; its $({}^{A}I^p_i, {}^{h1}J^{st}_j)$-th element is β^p_a if $p = s$ and $i = 1 = \phi(j)$; it is β^p_m if $p = s$ and $i = 2 = \phi(j)$; otherwise, it is 0 (zero); $\phi(1) = 1; \phi(2) = 2; \phi(3) = 2; {}^{A}I^p_i = (r-1) \times 2 + i$; $R_L = \mathbf{0}$;L_W: sub-matrix of $rn \times M^{H\Theta}$ dimension, of which $\left(I^p_i, {}^{h1}J^{st}_j\right)$-th element is ω^s_j if and only if $i = j$ and $p = s$;V: row vector of $M^{H\Theta}$ dimension, of which ${}^{h1}J^{st}_j$-th element is ${}^{h1}\varphi^{sk}_j$.μ^T: row vector of n^T dimension, of which k th element is μ^k;α^K: row vector of rn dimension, of which I^p_j-th element is α^p_j; the measurement unit of the capital in the private sectors are expressed in terms of the amount of the capital in JPY required for the production of a unit goods; Therefore, α^K is appearing in the capital allocation mechanism matrix of Lefeber's type;$\overline{F}$: column vector of nr dimension, of which I^p_j-th element is $\overline{F}^p_j$ (j is nested inside p) ;$\overline{K}$: column vector of nr dimension, of which I^p_j-th element is $\overline{K}^p_j$;$\overline{T}$: column vector of n^T dimension, of which k th element is $\overline{T}^k$;$\overline{L}$: column vector of $2r$ dimension, of which $\{2(p-1)+1\}$-th element is $\overline{L}^p_1$ and $2p$-th element is $\overline{L}^p_2$ ($p = 1, 2, \ldots, r$); $\Delta\overline{L}$: column vector, $(\overline{DL}_1, \overline{DL}_2)$; $\overline{W}$: column vector of rn dimension, of which I^p_j-th element is $\overline{L}^p_j$ (j is nested inside r);SX: slack variables associated to each row except for the last one that is the objective function to be maximized.

The optimization problem of linear-programing model is given as follows

$$\left[\begin{array}{l} \max\limits_{\{X,\Delta T^K,\Delta K,DL,DW,SX\}} \text{Eq.}(4.139), \\ \left\{\begin{array}{l} \text{subject to :} \\ \qquad \text{Eq.}(4.140), \text{and} \\ {}^{h\tau}X^{st}, \Delta T^k, \Delta K^s_j, DL_i, DW, SX \geq \mathbf{0}. \end{array}\right. \end{array}\right. \tag{4.141}$$

4.5.5 *Concrete Image of the Matrix A*

It may be helpful for readers who might be difficult to imagine a concrete image of Eq. (4.140) following the expressions of vectors and matrix, to expand Eq. (4.140) into a table by using an example. Readers who are not interested in the table may skip this sub-sub-section.

4.5.5.1 Coding

For simplicity, we assume three regions ($r = 3$), three sectors ($n = 3$), and three modes of transportation ($m = 3$).[20] The first sector belongs to the agricultural sector. The second and third sectors belong to the non-agricultural sector. The third sector is the transportation services sector. In this example, we still adopt Eq. (4.91b) of Moses type in the treatment of transportation services required for the shipments of

[20] This assumption is only for the example developed in this sub-sub-section.

goods. Namely, the sector of transportation services is explicitly specified to exist as a sector in the model.

The infrastructures of railway, shipping (ports), and road (highway/expressway) exist for the intraregional shipments of goods in all regions. Also, the infrastructures of railway, shipping (ports), and road (highway/expressway) exist for the shipment of goods between: (a) region 1 and region 2; (b) region 2 and region 3; (c) and region 3 and region 1. The shipping of goods becomes load on the port facilities in the origin region and destination region. The port facilities are differentiated for the intraregional shipping of goods and the interregional shipping.

There are no alternative routes with all the modes with all the shipments of goods. Namely, $\theta(h, s, k) = 1$ for all h, s, and k ($h = 1, 2, 3; s, k = 1, 2, 3$).

The capital funds are allocated to the private sectors to increase the production capacities or to the public sectors to increase the transportation capacity to eliminate economic bottlenecks explained above. The expected increase in the labor supply (the accumulated amount of the annual new graduates by the target year), who are mobile between regions and the region does not matter in which the increase occurs, are allocated to only non-agricultural sectors (this was a natural assumption at that time as agricultural workers were decreasing). Therefore $\Delta L_1^p = 0$ for all $p = 1, 2, 3$. There are no other resources that can be economic bottlenecks for the development of the economy. The objective function is the total (net) value-added of the economy, namely, NNP in terms of the market price. Following Moses model, all activities of shipments of goods may potentially contribute to GDP/NNP.

4.5.5.2 Definition of Variables

The definition of variables basically follows the definition of variables in our model of Eq. (4.140) by taking into account the coding above.

Shipments of Goods

${}^{h1}X_j^{st}$: shipment of goods j (=1, 2) from region s(=1, 2, 3) to region t(=1, 2, 3) using transportation mode of h (=1, 2, 3);

ΔT^k: increase in the capacity of the transportation infrastructure k (=1, 2, . . ., 12);

ΔK_j^s : increase in the production capacity of sector j in region s;

DL_2: expected increase in the labor supply to non-agricultural sectors.

Image with Tables

For simplicity, we exclude slack variables from the tables. Tables 4.16–4.30 are partitions of the huge table (abstracted by Table 4.15 in Appendix 1). The columns are variables that represent activities in the economy. The rows correspond to the structure of the economy. It is expressed as the system of equations[21] in the variables.

Shipment variables ${}^{h1}X_j^{st}$ are assigned from column 1 to column 57. Firstl, the mode index runs ($h = 1, 2, 3$), next the destination region index runs ($t = 1, 2, 3$), then the goods index run s ($j = 1, 2, 3$), and finally the origin index runs ($s = 1, 2, 3$). When the goods index is three ($j = 3$), the origin and destination combination is only $s = t$, namely, 11, 22, and 33 (e.g., X_3^{11} only appears in Table 4.19 as a variable related to sector (goods) 3 in region 1). By Eq. (4.40), the total number of columns is $r \times \{(n - 1) \times r \times m + 1\} = 57$ ($r = 3, n = 3, m = 3$).

The rows are first the market flow conditions. The final demand against goods j in region p are given exogenously and they are appearing in the right-hand side of Eq. (4.140). Therefore, it is useful to assign the final demand variable F_j^p to the row (see, e.g., cells of the fifth column and the first to 9th column (vectors) in terms of the consecutive number in the fifth row (the first to the ninth activity vectors of the matrix of the linear programing formulation—henceforth, we use the consecutive number in the fifth column in order to specify the location of column (vector) of the matrix) in Table 4.16). First, the sector (goods) index runs and next the region index runs. This sub-matrix of 9 × 57 corresponds to $\left[{}^{H\Theta}m_{I_i^p, {}^{h\tau}J_j^{st}}\right]$ in Eq. (4.140).

The tenth row to the 18th row in terms of the consecutive number in the fifth row corresponds to the production capacity constraint in the public sectors (henceforth, we use the consecutive number in the fifth row in order to specify the location of row (vector) of the matrix). Related variables are ${}^{h1}X_j^{st}$ which are explained above, $\overline{K}_j^s$ which are given exogenously in the right-hand side of Eq. (4.140), and ΔK_j^s which are located as the 74th column to the 82nd column. As the production constraint is expressed using Eq. (4.127), elements of the sub-matrix $\boldsymbol{L_K}$, of 9 × 57, consists of only 0 (zero) or 1 (one) element. The sub-matrix of $-\boldsymbol{I}$ located at the 74th column to the 82nd column and the 10th row to the 18th row converts the capital funds allocations for the capital formation (ΔK_j^s) to increases in the capital stocks, K_j^s, that is defined by Eq. (4.126) and implicit in the model. The 35th row is the constraints on the capital fund allocation and coefficients from the 74th column to 82nd column are α_j^s because they are used as denominators for the definition of new measurement unit of the capital. The labor is allocated with an analogically same mechanism, but the allocation of the new graduates, $\overline{DL_2}$, is made through the constraint located on the 42nd row.

The loads on the transportation infrastructure capacity are located on the 19th row to the 34th row. Related variables are ${}^{h1}X_j^{st}$ and ΔT^k. The sub-matrix $\boldsymbol{L_T}$ of 16 × 57 is ${}^{h1}\delta^{st}(k) \cdot {}^{1}\xi_j$ in Eq. (4.130). The sub-matrix of $-\boldsymbol{I}$ located at the 58th column to the 73rd column and the 19th row and the 34th row converts the capital funds allocations for ΔT^k to increases in the transportation capacities, T^k, that is defined by Eq. (4.129) and implicit in the model. In the 35th row, elements from the 58th column to the 73rd column are $\boldsymbol{\mu}^{\boldsymbol{T}}$ which converts the capital funds allocations for ΔT^k to increases in the transportation infrastructure capacities.

---

[21] Constraints are converted to equations by adding or subtracting a slack variable to or from each constraint (See 'Standard form of the Linear Programming Problem' in Appendix 4).

The exogenously given constants of the final demands, $\overline{\boldsymbol{F}}$, the initial capital stocks in the private sectors, $\overline{\boldsymbol{K}}$, the initial transportation capacities, $\overline{\boldsymbol{T}}$, the total capital funds, $\overline{C}$, the initial amount of labor, $\overline{\boldsymbol{L}}$, and the new graduates that can be increased in the labor employed at nonagricultural sectors, $\overline{\Delta L_2}$, are located at the right-hand side of the system.

The last row is the definition of the NNP in terms of the market price and it is the objective function to be maximized.

4.6 Preparation of Basic Data

4.6.1 Ad Hoc versus Proactive prescriptions

We have shown that the model can be utilized to express how the economic bottlenecks may occur and how it can be eliminated in the content of so-called ad hoc prescriptions in Sect. 4.5.3. On the other hand, our model can be applied to the proactive prescriptions to eliminate bottlenecks to the economic development as the numerical examples have shown in Sect 4.5.2.

It comes into its own in the application to the national projects such as highway/expressway construction, aviation policy, maritime policy, and so on, in the long run. It is called—the construction of optimal comprehensive transport system. It should be the essential and substantial topic in the transportation economics.

More concretely, we are able to give right answers to the following policy agendas (Kohno 1975, p. 62):

[A]. Optimal shares of the public capital funds allocation between highway/expressway, railway, and shipping (seaport)
[B]. Regional balance of the public investment funds allocation to transport facilities and the optimal shares in the sense above
[C]. Optimal shares between the capital funds allocation in the private sectors and the public sectors.

The agenda [A] is the main topic in this chapter. With the model developed in this chapter and the models developed in succeeding chapters in this book, minute answers to [B] and [C] can be examined in a consistent and overall way and, eventually, we can give a right answer to the main agenda, [A]. In reality, the shares are exogenously and arbitrarily given sometimes neglecting the demand by the markets. The costs for the economy in any sense become fatal if they decide on the investments based on such predetermined shares.

The shares originally should be determined as a result of the market equilibrium of the economy. However, it is too late to know the shares by the markets in the long-run planning. We must know the shares in advance in a right way and at least in a transparent way with which stakeholders and people can discuss and decide on the investment shares. It is very important what model we will use as well as how the decision is made on what base.

We will show the application of our model to the topics of the public transportation investments, [A], [B], and [C], which ought to be critical in the 1960s.

4.6.2 *Calculation of Input–Output Coefficients of the Competitive Import Type*

4.6.2.1 Interregional Input–Output Model of the Competitive Import Type

It is critically important whether we assume that the interregional trade pattern will change after the relative advantage of accessibility to markets between regions changes due to drastic improvements in transportation infrastructures, or not. In our model, it is assumed that the interregional trade patterns will change because changes in the relative advantage of accessibility to markets cannot be neglected, especially which will be caused by a huge public investment project. Especially, the topic of this book is the establishment of public investment criterion on which a limited capital fund allocation ought to be done by taking into account social benefits created by the investment. The public investment criterion is built in the interregional input–output model by formulating it as an optimization problem. In our view, the most important direct impacts of the investments into the construction/improvement in the transportation infrastructure are changes in geographical and time distance between regions (cities) and the policy incentive (agenda) of such a project ought to be an expectation that accessibility advantage of a certain set of regions to a certain market is improved and opportunities for better business chance are created for them. As a result, for example, a new region will ship products to the market in which it did not make the shipment at other times. This is a kind of substitution between production regions from the view of markets, that is, the market buys products from different regions than before, which means trade patterns are changed. This is a substantial reason why we adopt the interregional input–output model of the competitive import type (Moses 1955, 1960; Chenery 1953), which presumes that interregional trade pattern can change if it is a natural and reasonable result. In this sense, interregional input–output model of the noncompetitive type has a critical defect in order to measure social benefits of a huge public investment project such as expressway/highway construction projects.

First of all, we needed to construct so-called 1960 inter-regional input–output coefficients (table) of the competitive import-type of 5 regions and 5 sectors. We basically used materials of 1960 Interregional Input–Output Table of nine regions and ten sectors (The MITI 1966a). It includes: Regional Industrial Input–Output Table of 43 sectors with 9 regions (Districts of Hokkaido, Tohoku, Kanto, Tokai, Hokuriku, Kinki, Chugoku, Shikoku, and Kyushu) at producers' price (The MITI 1966b); 1960 Inverse Matrix Table of Regional Industrial Input–Output Table (The MITI 1966c); 1960 Interregional Input–Output Table (25 sectors, 9 regions) (The MITI 1966d); 1960 Inverse Matrix Table of Interregional Input–Output Table (25 sectors, 9 regions) (The MITI 1966e); and 1960 National Input–Output Coefficient Table (60 sectors) (The MITI 1966f). We were able to use data of '1960 inter-regional input-output table at *purchaser's price*,' which correspond to MITI (1960a) thanks to an official of MITI.

4.6.2.2 Inter-regional Input–Output Table at Purchasers' Price

Materials and tables obtained in The MITI (1966a) are all calculated and constructed at *producers' price*. Our model is formulated as a linear programming model, in which the objective function (e.g., GDP) gives driving force in the market through maximization (see Sect. 4.5.3.5). The model embodies the public investment criterion based on the interregional input–output table at *purchasers' price*. The formulation necessitates a tough data mining, which is one more necessary step to the formulation of the model.

Responding to changes in the relative advantage of accessibilities to markets, which mean the trade patterns can change as a result of the substitution between production regions through the market equilibrium, the delivery costs are dependent on where goods are produced, how goods are shipped to consumers with which transportation route and mode, and to which market (region). This means as a result of difference in the delivery costs, the value-added ratios of a certain sector in a certain region vary between regions, that is, the said region in which the goods is produced and the region to which the said goods is shipped (it is assumed that the law of one price holds, eventually). Even if the destination region is the same, the value-added ratios vary depending on transportation modes and routes with which goods are delivered to the destination. The objective of the linear programming model is to maximize the sum of gross value-added over regions, which means the trade patterns change depending on improvements in the transportation infrastructures and it can be assumed that the market equilibrium is made through quantity adjustment led by producers.

In the sense of the terminology of Moses model (in which there is no idea of transportation sector) and in the sense of the terminology of our model (in which transportation sector exists), it is essential to construct shipment activities. The point is whether we keep to use interregional input–output table (data) at producers' price or at purchasers' price in order to construct shipment activities.

The difference between input–output table at producers' price, which is most common with the analysis of the conventional input–output analysis, and input–output table at purchasers' price is in the formalities of dealing delivery services such as wholesale, retail, warehouse, insurance, transportation costs, and so on. According to the definition of the input–output table at purchasers' price, delivery costs are listed twice in the table. One is addition to the price, which is the total delivery cost of intermediate inputs from the supplying sector (factory) to the purchasing sector and households following a kind of CIF price rule. The total delivery cost is once paid by the supplying sector and forwarded to the purchaser. The other lists of delivery costs in the table are inputs of delivery services into sectors if any and the delivery services incurred by all the inputs of non-services goods, which are taken as intermediate inputs of delivery services into purchasing sector, and measured in terms of the delivery costs.

It is said that the input–output table at purchasers' prices has a problem in the sense that the input–output table has an aspect of the national economic accounting (Kohno 1991a, b). However, if we would acknowledge the conventional input–output analysis by being able to neglect implicit issue related to Proposition 2 (Appendix 2), the one-to-one correspondence between the predicted economy based on the input–output analysis and the real economy, which is grasped by the data used for construction of input–output table, consistently holds with both the input–output tables at producers' price and purchasers' price.

A kind of shipment activities (it should be called—purchase activities) at producers' price can be defined and constructed into our model specification based on the interregional input–output basic table. However, as a practical matter, the shipment activities of our model must be constructed based on the idea of purchasers' price. With shipment activities at purchasers' price, alternative activities correspond to alternative routes through which goods are delivered to purchasers. On the other hand, goods at producers' price have a kind of label which shows route and transportation mode with which goods are delivered to purchasers. So, as the number of non-service goods increases, the number of alternative shipment activities at producers' price exponentially increases. This is the reason why shipment activities must be constructed at purchasers' price. See Appendix 2 for minute illustration of input–output tables of purchasers' price versus producers' price and shipment activities at purchasers' price versus producers' price.

4.6.2.3 Construction of Shipment Activities at Purchasers' Price

In order to simplify the illustration, we may assume only one sector locates at each region and each sector only locates at one region. Also, we may assume final demand sector locates at one region which is different from the regions where sectors are located. Hence, we assume six regions as it is assumed in sub-subsection, Installment of the Transportation Network Dimension into the Interregional Input-Output Model, in Appendix 2.

When one of the authors had constructed shipment activities at purchasers' price, he was unable to use a basic table (basic trade table) of interregional input–output table at purchasers' price. This means he has to estimate, for example, $T\_basic\_org(11, j)$ $(j = 1, 2, 3, 6, 9, 10)$ in Table 4.38, which are transportation costs incurred by shipment from agriculture sector (region 1) to agriculture ($j = 1$; region 1), manufacturing ($j = 2$; region 2), wholesale ($j = 3$; region 3), retail ($j = 6$; region 4), transportation ($j = 9$; region 5), and final demand ($j = 19$; region 6) sectors. In the model in this chapter, the transportation sector only provides delivery services (a kind of composite goods) for the shipment of goods. So, neglect for a while other delivery service sectors of wholesale and retail in Table 4.38.

Using interregional input–output table at producers' price, the total production of transportation sector in each region is divided and assigned to shipments of goods to own and other regions. It might be confusing for readers that, with the illustration example using Table 4.41, the value of 625.6, $IO\_table\_pro(7, 5)$, must be divided into 146.1, 319.5, and 160, *IO_table_pur*(5,1), *IO_table_pur*(5,2), and *IO_table_pur*(5,6) in Table 4.40 in Appendix 2, respectively, as only one transportation sector exists in region 5. It can be considered that region 5 is a kind of marshaling yard that covers transportation services of the whole of the economy. However, transportation sector exists in each region with the usual interregional input–output table and the values, which ought to be, for example, in the cells of $IO\_table\_pur(5,1)$ and $IO\_table\_pur(5,2)$ in Table 4.40 in Appendix 2, are given by the total production of the transportation sectors in regions 1 and 2 in a usual interregional input–output table at producers' price, respectively (the total production of transportation sectors is the same with the tables at producers' and purchasers' price). This is a starting point for the construction of shipment activities of our model.

We illustrate the construction of shipment activity with agricultural sector in region 1 using the illustration example. First, focusing on, for example, transportation sector (service), we need to divide the value of 146.1, $T\_basic\_org(11,11)$ into 10.0, 20.7, 1.0, 6.9, 10.0, and 97.5, which are transportation costs incurred by shipments of agricultural products (goods of sector 1) to region 1 (agricultural sector), region 2 (manufacturing sector), region 3 (wholesale sector), region 4 (retail sector), region 5 (transportation sector), and region 6 (household), respectively (Table 4.38 in Appendix 2). Those figures, which are divided by shipments from region to region 1, 2, ..., and 6, respectively, and are arrayed in a row vector, is called – *transportation vector* (or, generally, logistics vector considering same vectors with other logistics costs). The transportation vector of agricultural sector (in region 1) is estimated as follows:

(a) obtain the amount of agricultural goods shipped from region 1 to regions 1, 2, 3, ..., 6, in ton unit (they are given by, e.g., the interregional commodity flow table)
(b) using a table of tariff, estimate the total amount of transportation costs incurred by shipments of agricultural goods from region 1 to regions 1, 2, 3, ..., 6
(c) using the result of (b), calculate the share of the total transportation costs incurred by shipment of agricultural goods (commodity flow) from region 1 to regions 1, 2, 3, ..., 6 to the grand total transportation costs which is the sum of the total transportation costs over region 1,2,3, ..., 6.

Before calculation of transportation vector,

(d) in case in which we cannot use basic table (and actually we could not), divide the total input of transportation service into (agricultural sector in) region 1, which is given by interregional input–output table, into two parts: (α) original[22] input of transportation service into (agricultural sector in) region 1 and (β) the amount of transportation costs (inputs of service), which is to be allocated to shipment of agricultural goods from region 1 to regions 1, 2, 3, ..., and 6, and is to give transportation vector of region 1. Allocate transportation cost (β) using the shares obtained at step (c). With step (a), 20, 36, 2, 12, 20, and 130 are shipments of agricultural goods from region 1 to regions 1,2, ..., 5 and 6 in tons, respectively, which can be estimated by, for example, the table of interregional commodity flow. With step (c), using fare rates of, for example, 0.40, 0.46, 0.40,

[22] 'Original' input means without it, the sector cannot produce any. With transportation service, an example is person trips for business and tour organized by the company as a welfare program for employees.

0.46, 0.40, and 0.60 in million JPY/ton for shipments of agricultural goods from region 1 to regions 1,2, . . ., 5, and 6, which may be estimated by fare rate table between regions with agricultural goods, 8.00, 16.56, 0.80, 5.52, 8.00, and 78.00 are estimated as total transportation costs incurred by shipments (commodity flows) of agricultural goods from region 1 to regions 1,2, . . ., 5, and 6, respectively. With step (d), the grand total transportation cost is calculated as 116.88 (=8.00 + 16.56 + 0.80 + 5.52 + 8.00 + 78.00) and shares of the shipments (commodity flows) of agricultural good from region 1 to regions 1,2, . . ., 5, and 6 are calculated as 0.06845 (=8.00/116.88), 0.14168, 0.00684, 0.04723, 0.06845, and 0.66735, respectively.[23] With the illustration example, original input of transportation sector is assumed to be zero (0) for simplicity. So, the value of $IO\_table\_pur(5,1)$, 146.1, is allocated using the shares and 10.0, 20.7, 1.0, 6.9, 10.0, and 97.5 are obtained as estimated inputs (costs) of transportation service incurred by shipments of agricultural goods from region 1 to regions 1,2, . . ., 5 and 6, respectively. As readers may see, processes (a) to (d) are analogically applied to all pairs of regions with all non-service sectors (products) in order to obtain the transportation vector by firstly knowing, e.g., figures of *T_basic_org* (11,11) with all non-service sectors and all pairs of regions.[24]

As readers may see, processes (a) to (d) are analogically applied to all pairs of regions with all non-service sectors (products) in order to obtain the transportation vector by firstly knowing, e.g., figures of *T_basic_org*(11,11) with all non-service sectors and all pairs of regions.

As for other delivery service sectors, for example, wholesale and retail sectors in region 1, input of wholesale and retail sectors, 55 and 161.7 into agricultural sector, is divided into original inputs[25] and shipment costs inputs (costs) of whole sale and retail sectors, respectively, using, for example, shares to the cost price based on sampling survey of original wholesale and retail services. Shipment costs of wholesale and retail services incurred by shipments of agricultural goods from region 1 to regions 1,2, . . ., 5, and 6 are calculated by using rates of margin of wholesale and retail services to shipments of agricultural goods in JPY unit from region 1 to regions 1,2 . . ., 6, which can be given by interregional input–output table at producers' price (e.g., the first row in Table 4.41 in Appendix 2). This estimation method is the same as the calculation method adopted for the construction of Table 4.38 in Appendix 2 (of course, the latter method is just to simplify the construction of Table 4.38 in

[23] Usually, the grand total transportation cost thus calculated with region 1 is not equal to the total production of transportation sector in region 1 that is given by inter-regional input–output table at producers' price.

[24] As a matter of practice, original inputs of transportation exist and we need to allocate the input of transportation service into person trips and commodity flows. This can be done by using table of inter-regional person trips and fare table of person trips between regions together with table of transportation costs incurred by inter-regional shipment of goods, a part of which is used in step (c).

[25] Typical example is market information which can be provided by only wholesale sector and retail sector (in case goods are traded with wholesale sector skipped).

Appendix 2. Originally, it must be constructed based on survey data with sampling or complete census data). Row vectors, of which p th elements are thus obtained wholesale and retail costs incurred by shipments of agricultural goods from region 1 to regions p ($p = 1, 2, \ldots, 6$), can be called—wholesale vector and retail vector, respectively. And, such vector must be constructed with other logistics services such as insurance, warehouse, and so on, in case sectors are minutely defined. We may generally call thus constructed row vector with each of logistics sectors—*logistics vector*.

Second, shipment activities of agricultural goods from region 1 to region p ($p = 1, 2, \ldots, R$) are estimated as follows:

(A) construct column vector (it is called as—Type I) of n dimension with region p, in which i th elements of the first k_n elements ($i = 1, 2, \ldots, k_n$) are all zero (0) and i-th element of other ($n - k_n$) elements ($i = k_n + 1, k_n + 2, \ldots, n$) are p th element of logistics vector correspond to logistics service of i-th sector ($i = k_n + 1, k_n + 2, \ldots, n$), for example $k_n = 2$, wholesale ($i = 3$), retail ($i = 4$), transportation ($i = 5$) with the illustration example
(B) divide column vector of Type I that is constructed with region p ($p = 1, 2, \ldots, 5, 6$) by the amount of agricultural goods shipped to regions 1,2, ..., 5, and 6 at purchaser's price, which is given by interregional input–output table at purchasers' price. Calculated column vector is named—vector of Type 1
(C) construct column vector (it is called as—Type II) of n dimension with region p, in which ith elements of the first k_n elements ($i = 1, 2, \ldots, k_n$) are same as input–output coefficients of ith sector in region p at purchasers' price and ith element of the other $n - k_n$ ($i = k_n + 1, k_n + 2, \ldots, n$) elements are the quotient of: (1) *original* input of i-th ($i = k_n + 1, k_n + 2, \ldots, n$) service to agricultural sector, which is estimated in step (d) above; and (2) the total product of i-th sector ($i = k_n + 1, k_n + 2, \ldots, n$) at purchasers' price; and
(D) add column vector of Type 1 and Type II region by region and pair by pair of regions between which shipments of goods are made (the direction from which region to which region has a meaning except for intra-regional shipment). Those are the shipment activities of Moses type but we have an idea of explicit transportation sectors.

With the illustration example, column vector of Type I from region 1 to region 1 ($\equiv {}^{I}V_1^{11}$) is given as follows (see Table 4.38 in Appendix 2):

$$ {}^{I}V_1^{11} = \begin{bmatrix} 0 \\ 0 \\ T\_basic\_org(9,1) \\ T\_basic\_org(10,1) \\ T\_basic\_org(11,1) \end{bmatrix} = \begin{bmatrix} 0 \\ 0 \\ 5.0 \\ 16.5 \\ 10.0 \end{bmatrix}. \tag{4.142} $$

Vector of Type 1 with region 1 ($\equiv {}^{1}V_1^{11}$) is given by dividing ${}^{I}V_1^{11}$ by 81.5 (IO_table_pur(1,1) in Table 4.40 in Appendix 2):

$$
{}^{1}V_1^{11} = \begin{bmatrix} 0 \\ 0 \\ T\_basic\_org(9,1)/IO\_table\_pur(1,1) \\ T\_basic\_org(10,1)/IO\_table\_pur(1,1) \\ T\_basic\_org(11,1)/IO\_table\_pur(1,1) \end{bmatrix} = \begin{bmatrix} 0 \\ 0 \\ 0.061349693251534 \\ 0.202453987730061 \\ 0.122699386503067 \end{bmatrix}. \tag{4.143}
$$

Vector of Type II from region 1 to region 1 ($\equiv {}^{II}V_1^{11}$) is given as follows (Tables 4.38 and 4.40 in Appendix 2):

$$
\equiv {}^{II}V_1^{11} = \begin{bmatrix} IO\_table\_pur(1,1)/IO\_table\_pur(1,7) \\ IO\_table\_pur(2,1)/IO\_table\_pur(1,7) \\ T\_basic\_org(7,1)/IO\_table\_pur(1,7) \\ T\_basic\_org(19,1)/IO\_table\_pur(1,7) \\ T\_basic\_org(20,1)/IO\_table\_pur(1,7) \end{bmatrix} = \begin{bmatrix} 0.089285714285714 \\ 0.243618536371604 \\ 0.027388255915863 \\ 0 \\ 0 \end{bmatrix}. \tag{4.144}
$$

With step (D), the following is obtained:

$$A_1^{11} = {}^{I}V_1^{11} + {}^{II}V_1^{11}$$

$$= \begin{bmatrix} 0 \\ 0 \\ 0.061349693251534 \\ 0.202453987730061 \\ 0.122699386503067 \end{bmatrix} + \begin{bmatrix} 0.089285714285714 \\ 0.243618536371604 \\ 0.027388255915863 \\ 0 \\ 0 \end{bmatrix}$$

$$= \begin{bmatrix} 0.089285714285714 \\ 0.243618536371604 \\ 0.088737949167397 \\ 0.202453987730061 \\ 0.122699386503067 \end{bmatrix}. \tag{4.145}$$

So, shipment activity of agricultural goods from region 1 to region 1 is given as follows:

$$\begin{bmatrix} v_{11}^{11} \\ v_{21}^{11} \\ v_{31}^{11} \\ v_{41}^{11} \\ v_{51}^{11} \\ va_1^{11} \end{bmatrix} = \begin{bmatrix} A_1^{11} \\ 1 - \sum_{j=1}^{5} v_{j1}^{11} \end{bmatrix} = \begin{bmatrix} 0.089285714285714 \\ 0.243618536371604 \\ 0.088737949167397 \\ 0.202453987730061 \\ 0.122699386503067 \\ 0.253204425942156 \end{bmatrix}. \tag{4.146}$$

With the model in this chapter, first MITI (1966a) was aggregated into tables of five regions and five sectors. Then, with step (a) interregional commodity flows were estimated using TRO (1965). With step (b), MOT (1964) was used and the shares were estimated in step (c). With step (d) (α), it was assumed that inputs of transportation services (original inputs of transportation services) are all related to person trips and total products of person trip sector in each region, which were calculated on MITI (1966d), were added to transportation sector of tables of five sectors assuming value-added ratio of person trip transportation activity is same as the commodity shipment activity in each region. This was a first approximation to the calculation of (commodity) shipment activities without data of basic interregional trade table.

Precisely speaking, the shipment activities can be estimated only with interregional trade of nonzero shipments in the manner illustrated previously. As a matter of practice, it may happen that new shipment of goods starts with a certain region to other certain region due to improvements in the transportation infrastructures. In that case, shipment activities may be estimated using type I column vector of same goods and Type II column vector (with $k_n + 1, k_n + 2, \ldots, n$ elements) among other regions and tariff table for interregional commodity flows, and so on.

4.6.2.4 Decomposition into Shipment Activities Mode by Mode

The model in this chapter, a focus is laid on changes in shares between transportation modes (highway, railway, marine) caused by improvements in the transportation infrastructures, thanks to public investments. Shipment activities must be constructed mode by mode in order to analyze, for example, optimal shares among transportation modes, and so on.

The decomposition was made following steps (a)–(d) as follows:

(e) calculate fare rates delivered region by delivered region and mode by mode with agricultural goods (they are called—modal fare rate of, e.g., railway)
(f) using fare rates obtained (e) delivered region by delivered region and mode by mode and fare rates obtained in step (c) (it is called—*total fare rate*), calculate rate of modal fare rate to total fare rate delivered region by delivered region and mode by mode (thus obtained rates delivered region by delivered region and mode by mode are called—*rates of fare* delivered region by delivered region and mode by mode (cf. Table 4.31 in Appendix 2 as for case of three regions, three sectors, and three modes))
(g) multiply rates of fare of shipment from region 1 to region p via mode q to the p th element of transportation vector. We assign symbol, ${}^{Iq}V_1^{11}$, to the product thus obtained
(h) replace p th element of transportation vector (logistics vectors) obtained in step (D), ${}^{I}V_1^{11}$ by ${}^{Iq}V_1^{11}$, which gives pth element of transportation vector (logistics vectors) with shipment of agricultural goods from region 1 to region 1 via mode q.

With step (e), we used data of TRO (1965), MOT (1963, 1964), Ministry of Transport Approval (1966), MTJNR (1967), MTMP (1972), MTMD (1969), and so on.

4.6.2.5 Estimation of Shipment Activities in the Target Year of 1971

Because the Japanese economy had experienced rapid economic growth with more than 10% during the 1960s and the economic structures and social infrastructures had been drastically changed by introducing innovative technologies, we need to forecast shipment activities that can be applied to the target year of 1971. In the first report of Economic Committee (ECEC 1967), input–output coefficients of 1971 with 60 sectors had been estimated based on RAS method of R. Stone. We had aggregated the estimated input–output coefficients into five sectors of our model and calculated ratios between 1960 input–output coefficients of five sectors and corresponding sectors of thus aggregated input–output coefficients. Based on the ratios thus calculated, 1971 shipment activities are estimated.

4.6.3 Birdeye View of Interregional Input–Output Model of Shipment Activities: Illustration by Three Regions, Three Sectors, and Three Transportation Modes (Again)

4.6.3.1 Shipment Activities in Region 1

We back to the basic equation of the model, (4.34) and (4.35), and explain again how shipment activities thus estimated are installed in the model using Tables 4.15 and 4.16–4.30. The tables are constructed by assuming $r = 3, n = 3, k_n = 2, m = 3$, and $\theta(h, s, t) = 1$ for all h, s, and t in Eqs. (4.34) and (4.35).[26] So, for example, Eqs. (4.34) and (4.35) are developed with $t = 1$ (east region) as follows:

$$\sum_{s=1}^{3}\sum_{h=1}^{3}\sum_{u=1}^{1} {}^{hu}x_i^{s1} \geq \sum\nolimits_{j=1}^{2} a_{ij}^1 \sum_{h=1}^{3}\sum_{u=1}^{1} {}^{hu}x_j^{11} + a_{in}^1 x_n^{11}$$

$$+\sum\nolimits_{j=1}^{2}\sum_{s\neq 1} v_{ij}^{1s} \sum_{h=1}^{3}\sum_{u=1}^{1} {}^{hu}x_j^{1s} + F_i^1 (i = 1, 2), \quad (4.147)$$

$$x_3^{11} \geq \sum\nolimits_{j=1}^{2} \sum_{s=1}^{3}\sum_{h=1}^{3}\sum_{u=1}^{1} {}^{hu}v_{3j}^{1s}\, {}^{hu}x_j^{1s} + a_{33}^1 x_3^{11} + F_i^1. \quad (4.148)$$

More minutely, Eqs. (4.147) and (4.148) are developed as follows:

$i = 1$

$$\begin{aligned} &{}^{11}x_1^{11} + {}^{21}x_1^{11} + {}^{31}x_1^{11} + {}^{11}x_1^{21} + {}^{21}x_1^{21} + {}^{31}x_1^{21} + {}^{11}x_1^{31} + {}^{21}x_1^{31} + {}^{31}x_1^{31} \\ &\geq a_{11}^1 \left({}^{11}x_1^{11} + {}^{21}x_1^{11} + {}^{31}x_1^{11}\right) + a_{12}^1 \left({}^{11}x_2^{11} + {}^{21}x_2^{11} + {}^{31}x_2^{11}\right) + a_{13}^1 x_3^{11} \\ &\quad +v_{11}^{12}\left({}^{11}x_1^{12} + {}^{21}x_1^{12} + {}^{31}x_1^{12}\right) + v_{11}^{13}\left({}^{11}x_1^{13} + {}^{21}x_1^{13} + {}^{31}x_1^{13}\right) \\ &+v_{12}^{12}\left({}^{11}x_2^{12} + {}^{21}x_2^{12} + {}^{31}x_2^{12}\right) + v_{12}^{12}\left({}^{11}x_2^{13} + {}^{21}x_2^{13} + {}^{31}x_2^{13}\right) + F_1^1, \end{aligned} \quad (4.149)$$

$i = 2$

$$\begin{aligned} &{}^{11}x_2^{11} + {}^{21}x_2^{11} + {}^{31}x_2^{11} + {}^{11}x_2^{21} + {}^{21}x_2^{21} + {}^{31}x_2^{21} + {}^{11}x_2^{31} + {}^{21}x_2^{31} + {}^{31}x_2^{31} \\ &\geq a_{21}^1 \left({}^{11}x_1^{11} + {}^{21}x_1^{11} + {}^{31}x_1^{11}\right) + a_{22}^1 \left({}^{11}x_2^{11} + {}^{21}x_2^{11} + {}^{31}x_2^{11}\right) + a_{23}^1 x_3^{11} \\ &\quad +v_{21}^{12}\left({}^{11}x_1^{12} + {}^{21}x_1^{12} + {}^{31}x_1^{12}\right) + v_{21}^{13}\left({}^{11}x_1^{13} + {}^{21}x_1^{13} + {}^{31}x_1^{13}\right) \end{aligned}$$

[26] This is also a simple example for illustration of our model.

$$+v_{22}^{12}\left({}^{11}x_2^{12}+{}^{21}x_2^{12}+{}^{31}x_2^{12}\right)+v_{22}^{12}\left({}^{11}x_2^{13}+{}^{21}x_2^{13}+{}^{31}x_2^{13}\right)+F_2^1, \tag{4.150}$$

$i=3$

$$\begin{aligned}x_3^{11} \geq\ & {}^{11}v_{31}^{1111}x_1^{11}+{}^{21}v_{31}^{1121}x_1^{11}+{}^{31}v_{31}^{1131}x_1^{11}\\ &+{}^{11}v_{31}^{1211}x_1^{12}+{}^{21}v_{31}^{1221}x_1^{12}+{}^{31}v_{31}^{1231}x_1^{12}\\ &+{}^{11}v_{31}^{1311}x_1^{13}+{}^{21}v_{31}^{1321}x_1^{13}+{}^{31}v_{31}^{1331}x_1^{13}\\ &+{}^{11}v_{32}^{1111}x_2^{11}+{}^{21}v_{32}^{1121}x_2^{11}+{}^{31}v_{32}^{1131}x_2^{11}\\ &+{}^{11}v_{32}^{1211}x_2^{12}+{}^{21}v_{32}^{1221}x_2^{12}+{}^{31}v_{32}^{1231}x_2^{12}\\ &+{}^{11}v_{32}^{1311}x_2^{13}+{}^{21}v_{32}^{1321}x_2^{13}+{}^{31}v_{32}^{1331}x_2^{13}+a_{33}^1x_3^{11}+F_3^1,\end{aligned} \tag{4.151}$$

in which it is assumed that $a_{33}^1=0$.

Eq. (4.149) is recalculated as follows:

$$\begin{aligned}&\left(1-a_{11}^1\right)\left({}^{11}x_1^{11}+{}^{21}x_1^{11}+{}^{31}x_1^{11}\right)+{}^{11}x_1^{21}+{}^{21}x_1^{21}+{}^{31}x_1^{21}+{}^{11}x_1^{31}+{}^{21}x_1^{31}\\ &+{}^{31}x_1^{31}-a_{12}^1\left({}^{11}x_2^{11}+{}^{21}x_2^{11}+{}^{31}x_2^{11}\right)-a_{13}^1x_3^{11}\\ &-v_{11}^{12}\left({}^{11}x_1^{12}+{}^{21}x_1^{12}+{}^{31}x_1^{12}\right)-v_{11}^{13}\left({}^{11}x_1^{13}+{}^{21}x_1^{13}+{}^{31}x_1^{13}\right)\\ &-v_{12}^{12}\left({}^{11}x_2^{12}+{}^{21}x_2^{12}+{}^{31}x_2^{12}\right)-v_{12}^{12}\left({}^{11}x_2^{13}+{}^{21}x_2^{13}+{}^{31}x_2^{13}\right)\\ &\geq F_1^1.\end{aligned} \tag{4.152}$$

In the same way, Eq. (4.150) gives as follows:

$$\begin{aligned}&\left(1-a_{22}^1\right)\left({}^{11}x_2^{11}+{}^{21}x_2^{11}+{}^{31}x_2^{11}\right)+{}^{11}x_2^{21}+{}^{21}x_2^{21}+{}^{31}x_2^{21}+{}^{11}x_2^{31}\\ &+{}^{21}x_2^{31}+{}^{31}x_2^{31}-a_{21}^1\left({}^{11}x_1^{11}+{}^{21}x_1^{11}+{}^{31}x_1^{11}\right)-a_{23}^1x_3^{11}\\ &-v_{21}^{12}\left({}^{11}x_1^{12}+{}^{21}x_1^{12}+{}^{31}x_1^{12}\right)-v_{21}^{13}\left({}^{11}x_1^{13}+{}^{21}x_1^{13}+{}^{31}x_1^{13}\right)\\ &-v_{22}^{12}\left({}^{11}x_2^{12}+{}^{21}x_2^{12}+{}^{31}x_2^{12}\right)-v_{22}^{12}\left({}^{11}x_2^{13}+{}^{21}x_2^{13}+{}^{31}x_2^{13}\right)\geq F_2^1.\end{aligned} \tag{4.153}$$

Also, Eq. (4.151) is recalculated as follows:

$$\begin{aligned}&x_3^{11}-{}^{11}v_{31}^{1111}x_1^{11}-{}^{21}v_{31}^{1121}x_1^{11}-{}^{31}v_{31}^{1131}x_1^{11}-{}^{11}v_{31}^{1211}x_1^{12}-{}^{21}v_{31}^{1221}x_1^{12}\\ &-{}^{31}v_{31}^{1231}x_1^{12}-{}^{11}v_{31}^{1311}x_1^{13}-{}^{21}v_{31}^{1321}x_1^{13}-{}^{31}v_{31}^{1331}x_1^{13}-{}^{11}v_{32}^{1111}x_2^{11}\\ &-{}^{21}v_{32}^{1121}x_2^{11}-{}^{31}v_{32}^{1131}x_2^{11}-{}^{11}v_{32}^{1211}x_2^{12}-{}^{21}v_{32}^{1221}x_2^{12}-{}^{31}v_{32}^{1231}x_2^{12}\\ &-{}^{11}v_{32}^{1311}x_2^{13}-{}^{21}v_{32}^{1321}x_2^{13}-{}^{31}v_{32}^{1331}x_2^{13}\\ &\geq F_3^1.\end{aligned} \tag{4.154}$$

Equations (4.152), (4.153), and (4.154), respectively, correspond to the first, second, and third row (with row numbering) of Tables 4.16, 4.19, 4.22, 4.25, and

4.28. Comparison between Eqs. (4.152), (4.153), and (4.154), and the first, second, and third rows of Tables 4.16, 4.19, 4.22, 4.25, and 4.28, respectively, confirms the following matrices:

$$ {}^{11}A(V)^{11} \equiv \begin{bmatrix} a_{11}^1 & a_{12}^1 & a_{13}^1 \\ a_{21}^1 & a_{22}^1 & a_{23}^1 \\ {}^{11}v_{31}^{11} & {}^{11}v_{32}^{11} & 0 \end{bmatrix} = \begin{bmatrix} 0.09387 & 0.12510 & 0.00005 \\ 0.30174 & 0.43012 & 0.34209 \\ 0.00822 & 0.01199 & 0 \end{bmatrix} $$

$$ \equiv A^1 \equiv \begin{bmatrix} a_{11}^1 & a_{12}^1 & a_{13}^1 \\ a_{21}^1 & a_{22}^1 & a_{23}^1 \\ a_{31}^1 & a_{32}^1 & a_{33}^1 \end{bmatrix}, $$

$$ {}^{21}A(V)^{11} \equiv \begin{bmatrix} a_{11}^1 & a_{12}^1 & a_{13}^1 \\ a_{21}^1 & a_{22}^1 & a_{23}^1 \\ {}^{21}v_{31}^{11} & {}^{21}v_{32}^{11} & 0 \end{bmatrix} = \begin{bmatrix} 0.09387 & 0.12510 & 0.00005 \\ 0.30174 & 0.43012 & 0.34209 \\ 0.01058 & 0.01498 & 0 \end{bmatrix}, $$

$$ {}^{31}A(V)^{11} \equiv \begin{bmatrix} a_{11}^1 & a_{12}^1 & a_{13}^1 \\ a_{21}^1 & a_{22}^1 & a_{23}^1 \\ {}^{31}v_{31}^{11} & {}^{31}v_{32}^{11} & 0 \end{bmatrix} = \begin{bmatrix} 0.09387 & 0.12510 & 0.00005 \\ 0.30174 & 0.43012 & 0.34209 \\ 0.00760 & 0.00936 & 0 \end{bmatrix}, $$

$$ {}^{11}A(V)^{12} \equiv \begin{bmatrix} a_{11}^1 & a_{12}^1 & a_{13}^1 \\ a_{21}^1 & a_{22}^1 & a_{23}^1 \\ {}^{11}v_{31}^{12} & {}^{11}v_{32}^{12} & 0 \end{bmatrix} = \begin{bmatrix} 0.09387 & 0.12510 & 0.00005 \\ 0.30174 & 0.43012 & 0.34209 \\ 0.02639 & 0.03985 & 0 \end{bmatrix}, $$

$$ {}^{21}A(V)^{12} \equiv \begin{bmatrix} a_{11}^1 & a_{12}^1 & a_{13}^1 \\ a_{21}^1 & a_{22}^1 & a_{23}^1 \\ {}^{21}v_{31}^{12} & {}^{21}v_{32}^{12} & 0 \end{bmatrix} = \begin{bmatrix} 0.09387 & 0.12510 & 0.00005 \\ 0.30174 & 0.43012 & 0.34209 \\ 0.01872 & 0.02720 & 0 \end{bmatrix}, $$

$$ {}^{31}A(V)^{12} \equiv \begin{bmatrix} a_{11}^1 & a_{12}^1 & a_{13}^1 \\ a_{21}^1 & a_{22}^1 & a_{23}^1 \\ {}^{31}v_{31}^{12} & {}^{31}v_{32}^{12} & 0 \end{bmatrix} = \begin{bmatrix} 0.09387 & 0.12510 & 0.00005 \\ 0.30174 & 0.43012 & 0.34209 \\ 0.08712 & 0.11543 & 0 \end{bmatrix}, $$

$$ {}^{11}A(V)^{13} \equiv \begin{bmatrix} a_{11}^1 & a_{12}^1 & a_{13}^1 \\ a_{21}^1 & a_{22}^1 & a_{23}^1 \\ {}^{11}v_{31}^{13} & {}^{11}v_{32}^{13} & 0 \end{bmatrix} = \begin{bmatrix} 0.09387 & 0.12510 & 0.00005 \\ 0.30174 & 0.43012 & 0.34209 \\ 0.03846 & 0.05672 & 0 \end{bmatrix}, $$

$$ {}^{21}A(V)^{13} \equiv \begin{bmatrix} a_{11}^1 & a_{12}^1 & a_{13}^1 \\ a_{21}^1 & a_{22}^1 & a_{23}^1 \\ {}^{21}v_{31}^{13} & {}^{21}v_{32}^{13} & 0 \end{bmatrix} = \begin{bmatrix} 0.09387 & 0.12510 & 0.00005 \\ 0.30174 & 0.43012 & 0.34209 \\ 0.02239 & 0.03331 & 0 \end{bmatrix}, $$

$$^{31}A(V)^{13} \equiv \begin{bmatrix} a_{11}^1 & a_{12}^1 & a_{13}^1 \\ a_{21}^1 & a_{22}^1 & a_{23}^1 \\ ^{31}v_{31}^{13} & ^{31}v_{32}^{13} & 0 \end{bmatrix} = \begin{bmatrix} 0.09387 & 0.12510 & 0.00005 \\ 0.30174 & 0.43012 & 0.34209 \\ 0.53895 & 0.18419 & 0 \end{bmatrix}.$$

Also, we may define the following column vectors:

$$^{11}X^{11} = \left[^{11}x_1^{11}, {}^{11}x_2^{11}, 0\right]^{\mathrm{T}}, {}^{21}X^{11} = \left[^{21}x_1^{11}, {}^{21}x_2^{11}, 0\right]^{\mathrm{T}}, {}^{31}X^{11} = \left[^{31}x_1^{11}, {}^{31}x_2^{11}, x_3^{11}\right]^{\mathrm{T}},$$

$$^{11}X^{12} = \left[^{11}x_1^{12}, {}^{11}x_2^{12}, 0\right]^{\mathrm{T}}, {}^{21}X^{12} = \left[^{21}x_1^{12}, {}^{21}x_2^{12}, 0\right]^{\mathrm{T}}, {}^{31}X^{12} = \left[^{31}x_1^{12}, {}^{31}x_2^{12}, 0\right]^{\mathrm{T}},$$

$$^{11}X^{13} = \left[^{11}x_1^{13}, {}^{11}x_2^{13}, 0\right]^{\mathrm{T}}, {}^{21}X^{13} = \left[^{21}x_1^{13}, {}^{21}x_2^{13}, 0\right]^{\mathrm{T}}, {}^{31}X^{13} = \left[^{31}x_1^{13}, {}^{31}x_2^{13}, 0\right]^{\mathrm{T}}.$$

Here it specified that transportation demand against services of railway, shipping, and truck depending on the level of shipment activities mode by mode are supplied by transportation services of "transportation sector," which means that JPY unit for transportation services of three modes is the same and it should be adjusted using, for example, rates of fare delivered region by delivered region and mode by mode (Table 4.31). In order to keep formality of $^{h\tau}X^{1q}$, supply by transportation sector, x_3^{11}, is placed in $^{31}X^{11}$ as the third element. Due to definition of $^{h\tau}A(V)^{1q}$, it may be alternatively placed in $^{11}X^{11}$ or $^{21}X^{11}$. In Chap. 6, transportation sectors are explicitly divided depending on the modes. Based on Eq. (4.51), the first three rows of Tables 4.16, 4.19, 4.22, 4.25, and 4.28 can be developed as follows:

$$\sum_{k=1}^{3}\sum_{h=1}^{3}\sum_{\tau=1}^{1} {}^{h\tau}X^{k1} \geq \sum_{h=1}^{3}\sum_{\tau=1}^{1} {}^{h\tau}A(V)^{11}\,{}^{h\tau}X^{11} + \sum_{k\neq 1}\sum_{h=1}^{m}\sum_{\tau=1}^{1} {}^{h\tau}A(V)^{1k}\,{}^{h\tau}X^{1k} + F^1,$$

$$\sum_{h=1}^{3}\sum_{\tau=1}^{1}\left(I - {}^{h\tau}A(V)^{11}\right){}^{h\tau}X^{k1} + \sum_{k\neq 1}\sum_{h=1}^{3}\sum_{\tau=1}^{1} {}^{h\tau}X^{k1} - \sum_{k\neq 1}\sum_{h=1}^{m}\sum_{\tau=1}^{1} {}^{h\tau}A(V)^{1k}\,{}^{h\tau}X^{1k} \geq F^1. \quad (4.155)$$

4.6.3.2 Shipment Activities in Regions 2 and Region 3

Analogically, fourth, fifth, and sixth row of tables, which are composed by Tables 4.16, 4.19, 4.22, 4.25, and 4.28 in Appendix 1, are, respectively, the market flow conditions with agricultural goods, other goods, and transportation services in region 2:

$$\sum_{h=1}^{3}\sum_{\tau=1}^{1}\left(I-{}^{h\tau}A(V)^{22}\right){}^{h\tau}X^{22}+\sum_{k\neq 2}\sum_{h=1}^{3}\sum_{\tau=1}^{1}{}^{h\tau}X^{k2}$$
$$-\sum_{k\neq 2}\sum_{h=1}^{m}\sum_{\tau=1}^{1}{}^{h\tau}A(V)^{2k}\,{}^{h\tau}X^{2k}\geq F^{2}. \tag{4.156}$$

Also, with region 3, we obtain as follows:

$$\sum_{h=1}^{3}\sum_{\tau=1}^{1}\left(I-{}^{h\tau}A(V)^{33}\right){}^{h\tau}X^{33}+\sum_{k\neq 3}\sum_{h=1}^{3}\sum_{\tau=1}^{1}{}^{h\tau}X^{k3}$$
$$-\sum_{k\neq 3}\sum_{h=1}^{m}\sum_{\tau=1}^{1}{}^{h\tau}A(V)^{3k}\,{}^{h\tau}X^{3k}\geq F^{3}. \tag{4.157}$$

4.6.3.3 Value-Added by Shipment (Production) Activities

Shipment activities have two sides: one is production and the other is intra- or interregional goods flow. So, all shipment activities contribute value-added. Value-added ratios per activity level are shown on the 43rd row (with row number) of Tables 4.18, 4.21, 4.24, 4.27, and 4.30 in Appendix 1. For example, using values of the first column of ${}^{11}A(V)^{11}$, the value-added ratio of intra-regional shipment of agricultural goods in region 1 with mode of railway is calculated as follows:

$$0.59617 = 1-(0.09387+0.30174+0.00822).$$

That of interregional shipment (${}^{31}x_2^{31}$) of the other goods from region 3 to region 1 with mode of truck is given as follows (see 50th column in Table 4.24):

$$0.27401 = 1-(0.07946+0.37458+0.27195).$$

4.7 Simulation Model: Interregional Input–Output Programming Model of Five Regions, Five Industries, and Three Transport Modes

4.7.1 Coding

There exist five regions ($r = 5$) in the economy: Hokkaido–Tohoku ($p = 1$), Kanto ($p = 2$), Chukyo ($p = 3$), Kinki ($p = 4$), and Chugoku–Shikoku–Kyushu ($p = 5$).

The economy is divided into five sectors ($n = 5$) in each region: agriculture ($i = 1$), fiber · chemistry ($i = 2$), metal · machinery ($i = 3$), others ($i = 4$), and transport services ($i = 5$) ($k_n = 4$). There are three modes of transportation: railway ($h = 1$), highway ($h = 2$), and marine (shipping) ($h = 3$) ($m = 3$).[27] Readers are easy to see the visual image of the huge table (matrix) of elements for the linear programming model format by taking a birds-eye view of Tables 4.16–4.30 in Appendix 1, which illustrates our model with three regions, three sectors, and three transportation modes for saving space.

There exist intra-regional transportation infrastructures of the three modes in each region. There also exist interregional transport infrastructures of railway and highway. The shipment with shipping makes loads on both of the ports (for interregional shipment) in the origin and destination regions. An alternative route using the Japan sea side exists between Hokaido · Tohoku and Kanto, Kanto and Chukyo, Chukyo and Kinki, Kinki and Chugoku – Shikoku – Kyushu. Also, mountainous routes exist between Kanto and Chukyo with railway and highway.

The capital funds can be allocated for increasing the capital stocks in the private sectors as well as for the transportation infrastructure investments. Other resources constraints are put on the labor supply and the water resources supply in Kanto, Chukyo, Kinki, and Chugoku–Shikoku–Kyushu regions. It is assumed that Hokkaido–Tohoku region is abundant in the supply of water resources for the agricultural sector. The new graduates are allocated to both agricultural and nonagricultural sectors.

Therefore, the number of constraints become 132:25 constraints with the flow conditions of the markets; 25 with the production capacity constraints; 67 with the transportation capacity constraints (for decreasing the number of constraints, it is taken that the shipments of ${}^{h\tau}X_j^{pq}$ and ${}^{h\tau}X_j^{qp}$ makes loads on the same transportation facility of mode h and rout τ which connects between regions p and q) and; 10 for the labor supply constraints; 1 (one) for the funds capital allocation constraint; 1 (one) for the labor allocation constraint; and 3 for the water resource supply constraint (nonagriculture in Kanto, Chukyo, and Kinki).

On the other hand, the number of shipments activities is calculated based on Eq. (4.40). Once again, it is written here:

if $j = n$

$$l \equiv {}^{h\tau}J_j^{ss} = \sum_{k=1}^{s}\left\{(n-1)\sum_{q=1}^{r}\sum\nolimits_{v=1}^{m}\theta(v,k,q) + 1\right\}, \qquad (4.158)$$

in which:

[27] Note that the order of highway and marine (shipping) is different from that in the example shown in Table 4.15 in appendix.

$$n = 5, s = 5, r = 5, \text{and } m = 3;$$

$\theta(v, k, q)$ is given in Tables 4.38 and 4.39 in Appendix 3.

As for $v = 1$ and 2, $\sum_{k=1}^{5} \sum_{q=1}^{5} \theta(v, k, q) = 47$ and $\sum_{k=1}^{5} \sum_{q=1}^{5} \theta(3, k, q) = 25$. Therefore, it is calculated as follows:

$$4 \times (47 + 47 + 25) + 5 = 481.$$

It is 67 (=26 + 26 + 15) as for the increments in the transportation capacities. It is 25 as for the increments in the capital stocks in the private sectors. It is 10 as for the assignment of new graduates to the agricultural and non-agricultural sectors. It is 132 as for the slack variables. Therefore, the number of variables (columns) of the matrix of Eq. (4.77) is 715 (481 + 67 + 25 + 10 + 132). Including the final row that is the objective function, the matrix of Eq. (4.140) becomes 132 $\times$ 716. This was a huge matrix and the limit one in the sense that it was well treated by the computer and the software of L-P in the 1970s. It was all manually done to make the input data of zero and nonzero elements of Eq. (4.140) based on the basic socioeconomic data and the parameters which were also processed manually, to put them into the computer memory in the application software format, and to arrange outputs of the calculation into tables and figures, and so on. Nowadays, usual personal computer calculates it for several minutes and the application software has a human-friendly interface which saves most of the days spent for the calculation in that day.

4.7.2 *Simulation Results*

4.7.2.1 Optimal Basic Variables

Among the optimal basic variables (see Appendix 4), the number of the shipment variables is 58 (Tables 4.1, 4.2, 4.3, 4.4, 4.5, and 4.6),[28] the number of capital stock increment variables is 14 (Table 4.7), the number of transportation infrastructure increment variables is 12 (Table 4.8), and the number of labor increment variables is 2 (Table 4.9). The remaining variables are 48 slack variables, among which four slack variables are associated with the flow conditions of the markets (Table 4.11), another six slack variables are associated with the production capacity constraints (Table 4.13), and others are all associated with the transportation capacity constraints (Kohno 1975, pp. 68–74).

[28] A several negligibly small figures are not shown in the tables.

Table 4.1 Optimal shipment pattern of goods: agricultural products (unit: 100 million JPY)

Destination region		Hokkaido–Tohoku 0.21312		Kanto 0.00563		Chukyo 0.22999		Kinki 0.08709		Chugoku·Shikoku·Kyusyu 0.0		Total export		Export to other regions	
Origin region	Mode	Japan seaside/mountainous route	Main	Japan seaside/mountainous route	Main	Japan seaside/mountainous route	Main	Japan seaside/mountainous route	Main	Japan seaside/mountainous route	Main	Japan seaside/mountainous route	Main	Japan seaside/mountainous route	Main
Hokkaido–Tohoku 0.21312	Railway		10,818									0	10,818	0	0
	Highway				4781							0	4781	0	4781
	Marine											0	0	0	0
Kanto 0.00563	Railway				7580							0	7580	0	0
	Highway											0	0	0	0
	Marine				7641							0	7641	0	0
Chukyo 0.22999	Railway											0	0	0	0
	Highway			2376	3229				51			2376	3280	2376	3280
	Marine											0	0	0	0
Kinki 0.08709	Railway								2051			0	2051	0	0
	Highway											0	0	0	0
	Marine											0	0	0	0
Chu–Shi–Kyushu 0.0	Railway										18,076	0	18,076	0	0
	Highway											0	0	0	0
	Marine											0	0	0	0
Subtotal	Railway	0	10,818	0	7580	0	0	0	2051	0	18,076	0	38,525	0	0
	Highway	0	0	2376	8010	0	0	0	51	0	0	2376	8061	2376	8061
	Marine	0	0	0	7641	0	0	0	0	0	0	0	7641	0	0
Total destination (G)		0	10,818	2376	23,231	0	0	0	2102	0	18,076	2376	54,227	2376	8061
Total import from other regions (E)	Railway	0	0	0	0	0	0	0	0	0	0				
	Highway	0	0	2376	8010	0	0	0	51	0	0				
	Marine	0	0	0	0	0	0	0	0	0	0	The whole economy			

(continued)

Table 4.1 (continued)

Destination region		Hokkaido–Tohoku 0.21312		Kanto 0.00563		Chukyo 0.22999		Kinki 0.08709		Chugoku·Shikoku·Kyusyu 0.0		Total export		Export to other regions	
Origin region	Mode	Japan seaside/mountainous route	Main	Japan seaside/mountainous route	Main	Japan seaside/mountainous route	Main	Japan seaside/mountainous route	Main	Japan seaside/mountainous route	Main	Japan seaside/mountainous route	Main	Japan seaside/mountainous route	Main
Total arrived (A = F + G)		10,818		25,607		0		2102		47,209		85,736			
Intermediate demand (B)		10,297		32,327		5936		8577		53,421		110,558			
Final demand (C = A − B)		521		−6720		−5936		−6475		−6212		−24,822			
Export to other regions (D)		4781		0		5656		0		0		10,437			
Total import from other regions (E)		0		10,386		0		51		0		10,437			
Production (B + C + D − E)		15,599		15,221		5656		2051		47,209		85,736			
Slack variable (F)		0		0		0		0		29,133		29,133			

Table 4.2 Optimal shipment pattern of goods: fiber·chemistry (unit: 100 million JPY)

Destination region		Hokkaido–Tohoku 0.30183		Kanto 0.09342		Chukyo 0.09327		Kinki 0.17322		Chugoku–Shikoku–Kyushu 0.29320		Total export		Export to other regions	
Origin region	Mode	Japan Sea side/ mountainous route	Main	Japan Sea side/ mountainous route	Main	Japan Sea side/ mountainous route	Main	Japan Sea side/ mountainous route	Main	Japan Sea side/ mountainous route	Main	Japan Sea side/ mountainous route	Main	Japan Sea side/ mountainous route	Main
Hokkaido–Tohoku 0.30183	Railway		5449									0	5449	0	0
	Highway		8232		28,342							0	36,574	0	28,342
	Marine											0	0	0	0
Kanto 0.09342	Railway					750						750	0	750	0
	Highway											0	0	0	0
	Marine											0	0	0	0
Chukyo 0.09327	Railway											0	0	0	0
	Highway								13,828			0	13,828	0	13,828
	Marine											0	0	0	0
Kinki 0.17322	Railway											0	0	0	0
	Highway											0	0	0	0
	Marine								33,000			0	33,000	0	0
Chu–Shi–Kyushu 0.29320	Railway										12,300	0	12,300	0	0
	Highway								30,825		46,710	0	77,535	0	30,825
	Marine											0	0	0	0
Subtotal	Railway	0	5449	0	0	750	0	0	0	0	12,300	750	17,749	750	0
	Highway	0	8232	0	28,342	0	0	0	44,653	0	46,710	0	127,937	0	72,995
	Marine	0	0	0	0	0	0	0	33,000	0	0	0	33,000	0	0
Total destination (A)			13,681	0	28,342	750	0	0	77,653	0	59,010	750	178,686	750	72,995
Total import from other regions (E)	Railway	0	0	0	0	750	0	0	0	0	0				
	Highway	0	0	0	28,342	0	0	0	44,653	0	0				
	Marine	0	0	0	0	0	0	0	0	0	0	The whole economy			

(continued)

Table 4.2 (continued)

Destination region		Hokkaido–Tohoku 0.30183		Kanto 0.09342		Chukyo 0.09327		Kinki 0.17322		Chugoku–Shikoku–Kyushu 0.29320		Total export		Export to other regions	
Origin region	Mode	Japan Sea side/ mountainous route	Main	Japan Sea side/ mountainous route	Main	Japan Sea side/ mountainous route	Main	Japan Sea side/ mountainous route	Main	Japan Sea side/ mountainous route	Main	Japan Sea side/ mountainous route	Main	Japan Sea side/ mountainous route	Main
Total arrived (A = F + G)		13,681		28,342		750		77,653		59,010		179,436			
Intermediate demand (B)		10,692		23,022		7894		58,687		54,845		155,140			
Final demand (C = A − B)		2989		5320		−7144		18,966		4165		24,296			
Export to other regions (D)		28,342		750		13,828		0		30,825		73,745			
Total import from other regions (E)		0		28,342		750		44,653		0		73,745			
Production (B + C + D − E)		42,023		750		13,828		33,000		89,835		179,436			

Table 4.3 Optimal shipment pattern of goods: metal–machine (unit: 100 million JPY)

Destination region		Hokkaido–Tohoku 0.03933		Kanto 0.15195		Chukyo 0.27457		Kinki 0.27740		Chugoku–Shikoku–Kyushu 0.37439		Total export		Export to other regions	
Origin region	Mode	Japan seaside/mountainous route	Main	Japan seaside/mountainous route	Main	Japan seaside/mountainous route	Main	Japan seaside/mountainous route	Main	Japan seaside/mountainous route	Main	Japan seaside/mountainous route	Main	Japan seaside/mountainous route	Main
Hokkaido–Tohoku 0.03933	Railway											0	0	0	0
	Highway											0	0	0	0
	Marine											0	0	0	0
Kanto 0.15195	Railway				13,928							0	13,928	0	0
	Highway		12,795		54,580							0	67,375	0	12,795
	Marine											0	0	0	0
Chukyo 0.27457	Railway			2127	7341		3202					2127	10,543	2127	7341
	Highway	2			16,543		54,249					2	70,792	2	16,543
	Marine				4318		1543					0	5861	0	4318
Kinki 0.27740	Railway								2263			0	2263	0	0
	Highway	0.2							40,179			0	40,179	0	0
	Marine				547							0	547	0	547
Chu–Shi–Kyushu 0.37439	Railway								7674			0	7674	0	7674
	Highway										48,015	0	48,015	0	0
	Marine										35,759	0	35,759	0	0
Subtotal	Railway	0	0	2127	21,269	0	3202	0	9937	0	0	2127	34,408	2127	15,015
	Highway	2	12,795	0	71,123	0	54,249	0	40,179	0	48,015	2	226,361	2	29,338
	Marine	0	0	0	4865	0	1543	0	0	0	35,759	0	42,167	0	4865
Total destination (A)		2	12,795	2127	97,257	0	58,994	0	50,116	0	83,774	2129	302,936	2129	49,218
Total import from other regions (E)	Railway	0	0	2127	7341	0	0	0	7674	0	0				
	Highway	2	12,795	0	16,543	0	0	0	0	0	0				
	Marine	0	0	0	4865	0	0	0	0	0	0	The whole economy			

(continued)

Table 4.3 (continued)

Destination region		Hokkaido–Tohoku 0.03933		Kanto 0.15195		Chukyo 0.27457		Kinki 0.27740		Chugoku–Shikoku–Kyushu 0.37439		Total export		Export to other regions	
Origin region	Mode	Japan seaside/ mountainous route	Main	Japan seaside/ mountainous route	Main	Japan seaside/ mountainous route	Main	Japan seaside/ mountainous route	Main	Japan seaside/ mountainous route	Main	Japan seaside/ mountainous route	Main	Japan seaside/ mountainous route	Main
Total arrived (A = F + G)		12,797		99,384		58,994		50,116		83,774		305,065			
Intermediate demand (B)		1220		53,188		39,006		23,020		64,241		180,675			
Final demand (C = A − B)		11,577		46,196		19,988		27,096		19,533		124,390			
Export to other regions (D)		0		12,795		30,331		547		7674		51,347			
Total import from other regions (E)		12,797		30,876		0		7674		0		51,347			
Production (B + C + D − E)		0		81,303		89,325		42,989		91,448		305,065			

Table 4.4 Optimal shipment pattern of goods: others (unit: 100 million JPY)

Destination region		Hokkaido–Tohoku 0.0		Kanto 0.16367		Chukyo 0.21234		Kinki 0.29488		Chu–Shi–Kyushu 0.37970		Total		Export to other regions	
Origin region	Mode	Japan seaside/ mountainous route	Main	Japan sea side/ mountainous route	Main	Japan seaside/ mountainous route	Main	Japan seaside/ mountainous route	Main	Japan seaside/ mountainous route	Main	Japan seaside/ mountainous route	Main	Japan Sea side/ mountainous route	Main
Hokkaido–Tohoku 0.0	Railway	346										346	0	0	0
	Highway											0	0	0	0
	Marine		1871									0	1871	0	0
Kanto 0.16367	Railway		8072									0	8072	0	8072
	Highway		11,583		183,292							0	194,875	0	11,583
	Marine											0	0	0	0
Chukyo 0.21234	Railway											0	0	0	0
	Highway						37,551					0	37,551	0	0
	Marine											0	0	0	0
Kinki 0.29488	Railway	96					8215					96	8215	96	8215
	Highway	0.0000					41,692					0	41,692	0	41,692
	Marine		4461									0	4461	0	4461
Chu–Shi–Kyushu 0.37970	Railway					346			82,028			346	82,028	346	82,028
	Highway										171,949	0	171,949	0	0
	Marine		2518		4703							0	7221	0	7221
Subtotal	Railway	442	8072	0	0	346	8215	0	82,028	0	0	788	98,315	442	98,315
	Highway	0	11,583	0	183,292	0	79,243	0	0	0	171,949	0	446,067	0	53,275
	Marine	0	8850	0	4703	0	0	0	0	0	0	0	13,553	0	11,682
Total destination (G)		442	28,505	0	187,995	346	87,458	0	82,028	0	171,949	788	557,935	442	163,272
Total import from other regions (E)	Railway	96	8072	0	0	346	8215	0	82,028	0	0				
	Highway	0	11,583	0	0	0	41,692	0	0	0	0				
	Marine	0	6979	0	4703	0	0	0	0	0	0	The whole economy			
Total arrived (A = F + G)		64,005		187,995		87,804		82,028		171,949		593,781			
Intermediate demand (B)		13,974		80,758		32,760		28,108		109,752		265,352			
Final demand (C = A − B)		50,031		107,237		55,044		53,920		62,197		328,429			
Export to other regions (D)		0		19,655		0		54,464		89,595		163,714			

(continued)

Table 4.4 (continued)

Destination region		Hokkaido–Tohoku 0.0		Kanto 0.16367		Chukyo 0.21234		Kinki 0.29488		Chu–Shi–Kyushu 0.37970		Total		Export to other regions	
Origin region	Mode	Japan seaside/ mountainous route	Main	Japan sea side/ mountainous route	Main	Japan seaside/ mountainous route	Main	Japan seaside/ mountainous route	Main	Japan seaside/ mountainous route	Main	Japan seaside/ mountainous route	Main	Japan Sea side/ mountainous route	Main
Total import from other regions (E)		26,730		4703		50,253		82,028		0		163,714			
Production (B + C + D − E)		37,275		202,947		37,551		54,464		261,544		593,781			
Slack variable (F)		35,058		0		0		0		0		35,058			

Table 4.5 Intra-regional goods flow (unit: million ton · km (railway and highway); 1000 tons (port))

Region→	Hokkaido–Tohoku			Kanto			Chukyo			Kinki			Chugoku–Shikoku–Kyushu		
mode →	Railway	Highway (road)	Shipping (port)	Railway	Highway (road)	Shipping (port)	Railway	Highway (road)	Shipping (port)	Railway	Highway (road)	Shipping (port)	Railway	Highway (road)	Shipping (port)
Goods (sectors) ↓															
Agriculture	2002														
Fiber	901														
Fiber		1362													
Others		206													
Agriculture				969											
Agriculture						33,673									
Metal				1278											
Metal					5010										
Others					13,985										
Metal							364								
Metal								6178							
Metal									4882						
Others								3556							
Agriculture										272					
Fiber												129,984			
Metal										214					
Metal											3812				
Agriculture													3107		
Fiber													1889		
Fiber														7175	
Metal														5925	
Metal															113,155
Others														17,641	
Total transported	2903	1568	0	2247	18,995	33,673	364	9734	4882	486	3812	129,984	4996	30,741	113,155

(continued)

Table 4.5 (continued)

Region→	Hokkaido–Tohoku			Kanto			Chukyo			Kinki			Chugoku–Shikoku–Kyushu		
mode →	Railway	Highway (road)	Shipping (port)	Railway	Highway (road)	Shipping (port)	Railway	Highway (road)	Shipping (port)	Railway	Highway (road)	Shipping (port)	Railway	Highway (road)	Shipping (port)
Total capacity T^k	5382	1568	5731	2247	18,995	33,673	364	9734	4885	486	3812	129,984	4996	30,741	113,155
Initial capacity $\overline{T}^k$	5382	1568	5731	2247	2196	11,421	364	830	4885	486	1236	13,819	4996	2686	32,121
Increase in the capacity ΔT^k	0	0	0	0	16,799	22,252	0	8904	0	0	2576	116,165	0	28,055	81,034

Table 4.6 Interregional goods flow (unit: million ton · km (railway and highway); 1000 ton (port))

Regions of O-D or region where ports are located		Hokkaido–Tohoku ↔ Kanto		Kanto ↔ Chukyo		Chukyo ↔ Kinki		Kinki ↔ Chugoku ·Shikoku–Kyushu		Hokkaido–Tohoku ↔ Chukyo (Japan Sea side)		Hokkaido–Tohoku ↔ Kinki (Japan Sea side)		Kanto ↔ Chukyo (mountainous)		Hokkaido–Tohoku	Kanto	Chukyo	Kinki	Chugoku ·Shikoku–Kyushu
Mode (facilities) →		Railway	Highway	Railway	Highway	Railway	Highway	Railway	Highway	Railway	Highway	Railway	Highway	Railway	Highway	Interregional shipment port facilities				
Goods	O-D ↓																			
Agriculture	Hokkaido–Kanto		11,420																	
Fiber	Hokkaido–Kanto		60,508																	
Metal	Hokkaido–Kanto		14,990																	
Other	Hokkaido–Kanto	11,371																		
Other	Hokkaido–Kanto		16,509																	
Agriculture	Kanto–Chukyo				5308															
Agriculture	Chukyo–Kinki						44													
Metal	Kanto–Chukyo			8503																
Metal	Kanto–Chukyo				19,525															
Metal	Kanto–Chukyo																13,664	13,664		
Metal	Kanto–Kinki																1731		1731	
Others	Hokkaido–Kinki															11,731			11,731	
Others	Chukyo–Kinki					4113														
Others	Chukyo–Kinki						32,159													
Fiber	Kinki–Kyushu								51,915											
Fiber	Kinki–Kyushu																		29,625	29,624
Metal	Kinki–Kyushu								8621											
Others	Hokkaido–Kyushu															7532				7531
Others	Kanto–Kyushu																12,368			12,367
Others	Kinki–Kyushu							41,070												
Others	Hokkaido–Chukyo									985										
Fiber	Kanto–Chukyo													1298						
Agriculture	Kanto–Chukyo														4598					
Metal	Hokkaido–Chukyo										2									
Metal	Kanto–Chukyo													2957						
Others	Hokkaido–Kinki											330								

(continued)

Table 4.6 (continued)

Regions of O-D or region where ports are located		Hokkaido–Tohoku ↔ Kanto		Kanto ↔ Chukyo		Chukyo ↔ Kinki		Kinki ↔ Chugoku ·Shikoku–Kyushu		Hokkaido–Tohoku ↔ Chukyo (Japan Sea side)		Hokkaido–Tohoku ↔ Kinki (Japan Sea side)		Kanto ↔ Chukyo (mountainous)		Hokkaido–Tohoku	Kanto	Chukyo	Kinki	Chugoku ·Shikoku–Kyushu
Mode (facilities) →		Railway	Highway	Railway	Highway	Railway	Highway	Railway	Highway	Railway	Highway	Railway	Highway	Railway	Highway	Interregional shipment port facilities				
Metal	Hokkaido–kinki												1.0							
Total transported		11,371	103,427	8503	24,833	4113	32,203	41,070	60,536	985	2	330	1.0	4255	4598	19,262	27,763	13,664	43,087	49,522
Total capacity T^k		11,371	103,427	8503	24,834	4113	32,203	41,070	60,536	985	2	330	1.0	4255	4698	19,262	27,763	13,364	43,087	49,529
Initial capacity $\overline{T}^k$		11,371	72	8503	7728	4113	2252	4484	145	985	2	330	1.0	4255	4698	19,262	27,763	13,364	43,087	49,529
Increase in the capacity ΔT^k		0	103,355	0	17,106	0	29,951	36,586	60,391	0	0	0	0	0	0	0	0	0	0	0

Table 4.7 Optimal allocation of the capital funds for the private sectors (unit: 100 million JPY)

Region	Industry	Capital increase (100 million yen)	Imputed price p^K	Construction costs/production capacity coefficient $\frac{1}{\alpha^K}$	Optimal allocation of investment funds (100 million JPY)					$\frac{\Delta NNP}{\Delta C}\left(\Delta K_j^q\right) = \frac{\Delta NNP}{\Delta K}\frac{\Delta K}{\Delta C} = p^T \div \frac{1}{\alpha^K}$
					Agriculture	Fiber chemistry	Metal machine	Others	Transport service	
Hokkaido–Tohoku	Fiber chemistry	38,855	0.0837	0.7921		30,777				0.1057
Kanto	Metal machine	34,388	0.0467	0.4422			15,207			0.1057
Kanto	Other	102,642	0.1061	1.0039				103,043		0.1057
Kanto	Transport service	4096	0.2526	2.3902					9791	0.1057
Chukyo	Agriculture	728	0.4628	4.3782	3188					0.1057
Chukyo	Metal machine	78,256	0.0467	0.4422			34,605			0.1057
Chukyo	Other	7354	0.1061	1.0039				7383		0.1057
Kinki	Fiber chemistry	15,939	0.0837	0.7921		12,626				0.1057
Kinki	Metal machine	11,856	0.0467	0.4422			5243			0.1057
Kinki	Other	2680	0.1061	1.0039				2691		0.1057
Chu-Shi-koku–Kyushu	Agriculture	1400	0.4628	4.3782	6130					0.1057
Chu–Shi-koku–Kyushu	Fiber chemistry	91,253	0.0837	0.7921		72,282				0.1057
Chu–Shi-koku–Kyushu	Other	210,236	0.1061	1.0039				211,056		0.1057

(continued)

Table 4.7 (continued)

Region	Industry	Capital increase (100 million yen)	Imputed price p^K	Construction costs/production capacity coefficient $\frac{1}{\alpha^K}$	Optimal allocation of investment funds (100 million JPY)					$\frac{\Delta NNP}{\Delta C}\left(\Delta K_j^q\right) = \frac{\Delta NNP}{\Delta K}\frac{\Delta K}{\Delta C} = p^T \div \frac{1}{\alpha^K}$
					Agriculture	Fiber chemistry	Metal machine	Others	Transport service	
Chu–Shi-koku–Kyushu	Transport service	5958	0.2526	2.3902					14,241	0.1057
					9318	115,685	55,055	324,173	24,032	Private-sector share
					0.01764	0.21899	0.10422	0.61366	0.04549	
					528,263					0.66709
										$\overline{C} = 791,892$

Table 4.8 Optimal allocation of the capital funds for the transport facilities

Region	Mode of transport facilities	Increase in the capacity (R.H: million ton-kilometer; S: thousand ton)	Inputted price associated with the capacity constraint p^T	(Construction costs)/(transport volumes) $\frac{1}{\mu^T}$	Optimum allocation of funds (100 million JPY)			$\frac{\Delta NNP}{\Delta C}(\Delta T^k) = \frac{\Delta NNP}{\Delta T^k}\frac{\Delta T^k}{\Delta C} = p^T \div \frac{1}{\mu^T}q$
					Rail	Highway	Marine (port)	
Kinki–Chu–Shi–Kyu	Railway	36,586	0.15495	1.46572	53,625			0.1057
Kanto intra	Highway	16,799	0.08779	0.83053		13,953		0.1057
Chukyo intra	Highway	8904	0.08779	0.83053		7396		0.1057
Kinki intra	Highway	2576	0.08779	0.83053		2140		0.1057
Chu–Shi–Kyushu intra	Highway	28,055	0.06783	0.64177		18,005		0.1057
Hokkkaido–Tohoku–Kanto	Highway	103,355	0.07781	0.73615		76,085		0.1057
Kanto–Chukyo	Highway	17,106	0.08780	0.83053		14,207		0.1057
Chukyo–Kinki	Highway	29,951	0.08778	0.83053		24,876		0.1057
Kinki–Chu–Shi–Kyu	Highway	60,391	0.07781	0.73615		44,457		0.1057
Kanto intra	Port	22,252	0.00428	0.04048			901	0.1057
Kinki intra	Port	116,165	0.00428	0.04048			4703	0.1057

(continued)

Table 4.8 (continued)

Region	Mode of transport facilities	Increase in the capacity (R.H: million ton-kilometer; S: thousand ton)	Inputted price associated with the capacity constraint p^T	(Construction costs)/(transport volumes) $\frac{1}{\mu^T}$	Optimum allocation of funds (100 million JPY)			$\frac{\Delta NNP}{\Delta C}(\Delta T^k) = \frac{\Delta NNP}{\Delta T^k}\frac{\Delta T^k}{\Delta C} = p^T \div \frac{1}{\mu^T} q$
					Rail	Highway	Marine (port)	
Chu–Shi–Kyushu intra	Port	81,034	0.003065	0.02899			3281	0.1057
					53,625	201,119	8885	Public sectors share
					0.20341	0.76289	0.03370	
					263,629			0.33291
								$\overline{C} = 791,892$

Table 4.9 Optimum Allocation of new graduates

Region	Industrial sector	Optimum allocation (1000 persons)	Share
Chugoku–Shikoku–Kyushu	Nonagricultural	11,634	0.9236
Kanto	agricultural	963	0.0764
		12,597	

4.7.2.2 Objective Function

We explain above the role of the objective function, a potential function to be maximized in the model. It is the net national product (NNP) in terms of the market price and it is worth to compare it with different sources. The maximized value (NNP) is 45.70 trillion JPY. The planned target of the GDP was 47.95 trillion JPY in 1971 according to ECEC (1968), which can be taken equivalent to NNP of 37.22–37.87 trillion, and the result is greater than the planned value as expected considering that it is a solution with the maximization of NNP.

The nominal NNP in 1971 was 65.91 trillion JPY and its real value was 36.70 trillion JPY in terms of the price in 1960. It is considered that further increase in the GDP/NNP is to be bound by the constraints of resources, namely by the constraint of water resources, labor, and the capital funds. The substantial impacts of the resource constraints on the increase in the GDP/NNP can be relieved by further disaggregation of the private sectors and the introduction of technological progress. The latter can be reflected in an improvement in the investment costs per unit capacity increase, which makes possible an effective capital fund allocation in the private sectors (we will see later the mechanism through which the capital fund allocation becomes efficient).

4.7.2.3 Shipment of Goods and the Flow Conditions of Market

The flows of goods are divided into four categories in our model: (1) interregional shipment of goods in the economy (Japan); (2) intra-regional shipment of goods in regions in Japan, (3) export from regions in Japan to other countries; and (4) import from other countries to regions in Japan. As it is assumed that the goods are of the competitive import type, the flows of goods (3) and (4) above can be expressed in terms of *net* import from other countries. The amount is exogenously given goods by goods and region by region. Net import from other countries is taken as one of the constituents of the final demand like consumption, investment, and so on and it is a negative (positive) term in the summation of the final demand when the import from other countries is larger (smaller) than the export to other countries. Sometimes, the final demand can be negative when the absolute value of the net import is larger than the sum of other items of the final demand like consumption, investment, and so on. This can happen with certain goods and a certain region where the demand is dependent on the imported goods from other countries.

We define the total goods j delivered at region s as follows:

$$\begin{pmatrix} \text{total goods } j \\ \text{delivered at region s} \end{pmatrix} \equiv \begin{pmatrix} \text{Sum of the shipments of goods } j \\ \text{from regions } p \text{ (including } s\text{)} \\ \text{in Japan to region } s \end{pmatrix}. \tag{4.159}$$

The following holds:

$$\begin{pmatrix} \text{total goods } j \\ \text{delivered at region } s \end{pmatrix} = \begin{pmatrix} \text{Intermediate demand} \\ \text{of goods } j \text{ in region } s \end{pmatrix} + \left[\begin{matrix} \text{Final demand} \\ \text{of goods } j \text{ in region } s \end{matrix} - \begin{pmatrix} \text{Net import of goods } j \\ \text{from other countries} \end{pmatrix} \right]. \tag{4.160}$$

$$\begin{pmatrix} \text{total product of} \\ \text{goods } i \text{ in region } s \end{pmatrix} = \begin{pmatrix} \text{Intermediate demand} \\ \text{of goods } i \text{ in region } s \end{pmatrix} + \left[\begin{matrix} \text{Final demand} \\ \text{of goods } i \text{ in region } s \end{matrix} - \begin{pmatrix} \text{Net import of goods } i \\ \text{from other countries} \end{pmatrix} \right] + \begin{pmatrix} \text{export of goods } i \\ \text{to other regions} \end{pmatrix} - \begin{pmatrix} \text{import of goods } i \\ \text{from other regions} \end{pmatrix}. \tag{4.161}$$

Tables 4.1, 4.2, 4.3, 4.4, 4.5, and 4.6 show the optimal shipments of goods. For example, the shipments of agricultural goods from Hokkaito–Tohoku to other regions are shown in the first row, which is headed by “Hokkaito–Tohoku,” mode by mode and route by route in Table 4.1. The figures written under the names of region, for example, 0.21312 as for Hokkaido in Table 4.1 (agricultural products) are imputed prices (optimal shadow prices) of the final demand in Hokkaido (Table 4.10). Hokkaito–Tohoku exports 4,781,100 million JPY of agricultural goods to Kanto using transportation mode of highway. As readers may see, the imputed price in the exporting region is higher than that of importing region with the goods traded. An increase in the export to other regions has the same meaning of an increase in the final demand with the flow condition of markets. So, the goods flow should be made from regions where the shadow prices are greater to the regions where the shadow prices are relatively smaller.

Table 4.10 Imputed price associated with final demand constraint (unit: 100 million JPY)

Region	Sectors	Imputed price	constrained constants
Hokkaido–Tohoku	Agriculture	0.21312	521.48
	Fiber chemistry	0.30183	2989.97
	Metal machine	0.03933	11,577.06
	Others	0.00000	50,031.27[a]
	Transport service	0.00000	2457.11[a]
Kanto	Agriculture	0.00563	−6720.20
	Fiber chemistry	0.09342	5320.06
	Metal ·machine	0.15195	46,196.02
	Others	0.16367	107,237.63
	Transport service	0.37251	11,788.37
Chukyo	Agriculture	0.22999	−5936.40
	Fiber chemistry	0.09327	6679.77
	Metal machine	0.27457	19,989.75
	Others	0.21234	55,044.77
	Transport service	0.00000	2829.11[a]
Kinki	Agriculture	0.08709	−6469.54
	Fiber chemistry	0.17322	5138.82
	Metal machine	0.27740	27,096.42
	Others	0.29488	53,920.86
	Transport service	0.22557	6329.18
Chugoku–Shikoku–Kyushu	Agriculture	0.00000	−6212.11[a]
	Fiber chemistry	0.29320	4165.29
	Metal machine	0.37439	19,532.64
	Others	0.37970	62,197.44
	Transport service	0.15514	3857.22

[a]Means sectors with which associated slack variables take positive values

The final demand against agricultural goods is negative in all regions but Hokkaido–TohokuKanto (Table 4.10). This means that Japan was heavily dependent on the imports from other countries with agricultural products in the 1960s. Therefore, the interregional shipments of agricultural goods were able to be made only from Hokkaido to Kanto, Chukyo to Kanto, and Chukyo to Kinki (Table 4.1). Exports to other regions are calculated in the last two columns region by region, mode by mode, and route by route. The last six rows in Tables 4.1, 4.2, 4.3, and 4.4 show the flow condition of markets holds, of course, with Eqs. (4.160) and (4.161). Also, it holds with the whole economy (the lower right-hand corner). It is summarized in Table 4.11, which also shows the production of the transportation services region by region, a part of which is used for the shipment of goods under the CIF assumption.

Table 4.11 Balance between the demand and supply goods by goods and region by region (unit: 100 million JPY)

Sector/ goods	Region	Total supply		Total demand				Balance	
				Demand of intra region					
		Import from other regions (A)	Production (B)	Intermediate (C)	Final demand (D)	Shipment to other regions (F)	Slack (taken as increment to final demand)	A + B	C + D + F
Agriculture	Hokkaido–Tohoku	0	15,599	10,297	521	4781	0	15,599	15,599
	Kanto	10,386	15,221	32,327	−6720	0	0	25,607	25,607
	Chukyo	0	5656	5936	−5936	5656	0	5656	5656
	Kinki	51	2051	8577	−6475	0	0	2102	2102
	Chugoku–Shikoku–Kyusyu	0	47,209	53,421	−6212	0	29,133	47,209	47,209
Agriculture	The economy	10,437	85,736	110,558	−24,822	10,437	29,133	96,173	96,173
Fiber chemistry	Hokkaido–Tohoku	0	42,023	10,692	2989	28,342	0	42,023	42,023
	Kanto	28,342	750	23,022	5320	750	0	29,092	29,092
	Chukyo	750	13,828	7894	−7144	13,828	0	14,578	14,578
	Kinki	44,653	33,000	58,687	18,966	0	0	77,653	77,653
	Chugoku–Shikoku–Kyusyu	0	89,835	54,845	4165	30,825	0	89,835	89,835
Fiber chemistry	The economy	73,745	179,436	155,140	24,296	73,745	0	253,181	253,181
Metal machine	Hokkaido–Tohoku	12,797	0	1220	11,577	0	0	12,797	12,797
	Kanto	30,876	81,303	53,188	46,196	12,795	0	112,179	112,179
	Chukyo	0	89,325	39,006	19,988	30,331	0	89,325	89,325
	Kinki	7674	42,989	23,020	27,096	547	0	50,663	50,663
	Chugoku–Shikoku–Kyusyu	0	91,448	64,241	19,533	7674	0	91,448	91,448

Metal machine	The economy	51,347	305,065	180,675	124,390	51,347	0	356,412	356,412
Others	Hokkaido–Tohoku	26,730	37,275	13,974	50,031	0	35,058	64,005	64,005
	Kanto	4703	202,947	80,758	107,237	19,655	0	207,650	207,650
	Chukyo	50,253	37,551	32,760	55,044	0	0	87,804	87,804
	Kinki	82,028	54,464	28,108	53,920	54,464	0	136,492	136,492
	Chugoku–Shikoku–Kyusyu	0	261,544	109,752	62,197	89,595	0	261,544	261,544
Others	The economy	163,714	593,781	265,352	328,429	163,714	35,058	757,495	757,495
Transport services	Hokkaido–Tohoku	0	4176	1719	2457	0	908	4176	4176
	Kanto	0	16,413	4625	11,788	0	0	16,413	16,413
	Chukyo	0	4732	1903	2829	0	2188	4732	4732
	Kinki	0	8981	2652	6329	0	0	8981	8981
	Chugoku–Shikoku–Kyusyu	0	11,047	7190	3857	0	0	11,047	11,047
Transport services	The economy	0	45,349	18,089	27,260	0	3096	45,349	45,349
Total of the sectors in the economy		299,243	1,209,367	729,814	479,553	299,243	67,287	1,508,610	1,508,610

Table 4.12 Gross regional product (unit: 100 million JPY)

	Hokkaido–Tohoku	Kanto	Chukyo	Kinki	Chugoku–Shikoku–Kyushu	The economy
Total product (A)	99,073	316,634	151,092	141,485	501,083	1,209,367
Intermediate input (B)	37,902	193,920	87,499	121,044	289,449	729,814
GRP/GDP (C = A − B)	61,171	122,714	63,593	20,441	211,634	479,553
Maximized net value added (D)	–	–	–	–	–	457,010
Slack variable (E)	35,966	0	2188	0	29,133	67,287
Final demand (F)	67,575	163,821	64,781	99,836	83,540	479,553
Final demand (G) exogenously given constants	31,609	163,821	62,593	99,836	54,407	412,266
Δ Inventory/Δ consumption	35,966	0	2188	0	29,133	67,287

4.7.2.4 Gross Regional Product and the National Account of the Economy

We may confirm the economy in macro terms using results shown in Tables 4.1, 4.2, 4.3, 4.4, and 4.12. The national income + depreciation on the expenditure basis are 47.955 trillion JPY in terms of the price in 1960 (Final demand (F) in Table 4.12). It is the summation of: (1) the (gross) final demands (G) that are exogenously given in the model and (2) the slack variables (E) associated with the flow condition of the markets. The summation of gross regional product, namely the gross domestic product, is 47.955 trillion JPY (GRP/GDP (C = A − B) in Table 4.12), which is the same as the national income + depreciation on the expenditure basis.

4.7.2.5 Goods Flow Between Regions and Loads on the Transportation Infrastructures

The growth of the economy is induced by increases in the final demands in regions. In order to meet the demand pressure of the final demand, each region must produce more and it causes increases in trades of goods between regions via interindustrial and interregional dependency of the regional economies. The pressure possibly causes two bottlenecks: (1) shortage of the capital stock in the private sector and (2) shortage in the transportation infrastructure. The bottleneck (1) may be partially relieved by increasing imports of goods which is in short and the increase in the trade may cause more serious bottleneck of the transportation infrastructure. Bottleneck (2) may be relieved by increasing the production within the region where shortage in the supply of goods occurs and it may cause bottleneck of the production capacity in the private sector.

Thus, it is a natural way of consideration that the two types of bottleneck shall be simultaneously solved between different sectors in different regions and/or different transportation infrastructures connecting different pairs of regions. Readers may argue that the economy is not a planning economy and the investments in the private sectors shall be solved in the (financial) markets. The model does not intend to plan (control) the whole of the economy. It is just to know objectively the optimal and right shares of the private and public investments with the allocation of the limited capital funds.

In the 1960s in Japan, there actually existed many government-affiliated financial institutions which were politically established and did roles in the financial markets for the private sectors, for example, Industrial Bank of Japan, Limited; Development Bank of Japan Inc.; Norinchukin Bank; Agriculture, Forestry and Fisheries Finance Corporation; Government's loan and Investment Programs financed by Postal-office Savings; Japan Finance Corporation for Small Business; The Shoko Chukin Bank, Ltd.; People's Finance Corporation; Environmental Sanitation Business Finance Corporation; Export–Import Bank of Japan; Japan Development Bank; Hokkaido Takushoku Bank, Limited; Hokkaido–Tohoku Development Finance Public Corporation; and so on (as abundant as stars!) Therefore, it must be informative to know not only the optimal shares of the capital funds allocation between the private and public sectors but also the optimal investments targets in private sectors region by region (at that time).

Tables 4.5 and 4.6 show intra- and interregional goods flow and loads on the transportation infrastructures. The transportation infrastructures of no loads are not listed on the tables. This means that no shipments of goods are made by the transportation infrastructures which are not listed. These tables are organized based on Tables 4.1, 4.2, 4.3, and 4.4 by converting the intra- and interregional shipments of goods in monetary terms into the volume in terms of ton · km. The results shown in the last four rows (Tables 4.5 and 4.6) show practical usefulness and, therefore, are informative for policy makers and planners.

"Total transported" shows the loads on the transportation infrastructure in terms of ton · km. The loads are the sum of loads of the shipments of goods that use the said facility. For example, the shipments of goods are made between Kinki and Chukyo with agricultural goods and others, which can be confirmed in Tables 4.1 and 4.4. The total load on highway is 32,203 ton km and it is beyond the initial transportation capacity of highway ($\overline{T}^k$) that is 2,252 ton km. It is a bottleneck of the economy and the capacity is increased by the gap, 29,951 ton km by allocating the capital funds. Of course, there could be an alternative solution to eliminate the bottleneck, namely it could be substituted by converting transportation mode from highway to railway in order to ship goods of others, 41,692,100 million JPY, from Kinki to Chukyo (in Table 4.4). Perhaps, it causes another bottleneck with the capacity of railway. Or, by allocating the capital funds to investments in the private sector of others in Chukyo in order to increase the production capacity to produce goods of others more, which makes the economy of Chukyo independent from Kinki in terms of goods of others. The optimality criteria chooses investment in highway (to expand the capacity of highway) among several alternative resolutions. We will explain why it is optimal in the next subsection.

4.7.2.6 Investments for Increments in Transportation Capacities

Table 4.8 summarizes the optimal solutions with the allocation of the capital funds for the transport facilities. The allocation of the capital funds for improvements of the transportation capacities is based on the elimination of bottlenecks due to the overloads of the intra- and interregional shipments of goods explained previously. However, we still need to know why have been chosen these improvements in the transportation infrastructures. The right answer is given by examining the imputed prices.

The imputed prices (p^T) are shown in the second column in Table 4.8. The imputed prices are associated with the transportation capacity constraints. They each imply an increment in the objective function by increasing a unit of the transportation capacity which the imputed price is associated with. Namely, the following holds:

$$p_k^T = \frac{\Delta \text{NNP}}{\Delta T^k}, \tag{4.162}$$

in which: p_k^T: imputed price associated with the transportation capacity constraint of $\overline{T}^k$; ΔT^k: unit increase in the transportation capacity of $\overline{T}^k$; ΔNNP: increase in the objective function (the net national product) due to increase in the transportation infrastructure by ΔT^k.

Since ΔT^k is owing to the allocation of the capital funds, the following holds:

$$\frac{\Delta T^k}{\Delta C} = \mu_k^T, \tag{4.163}$$

in which:ΔC: unit increase in the allocation of the capital funds; μ_k^T: coefficient which converts unit outlay of the capital funds ΔC into an increase in the transportation capacity of T^k.

Therefore, increase in the objective function can be expressed in terms of unit outlay of the capital funds:

$$\frac{\Delta \text{NNP}}{\Delta T^k} \times \frac{\Delta T^k}{\Delta C} = \frac{\Delta \text{NNP}}{\Delta C}\left(T^k\right) = p_k^T \times \mu_k^T. \tag{4.164}$$

The result of Eq. (4.164) is shown in the last column of Table 4.8. As readers may confirm, it is 0.1057 with all the capital fund allocation to the transportation infrastructure improvements. An allocation of ΔC to a certain object excludes an allocation to other targets since the total amount of the capital funds is limited and in that sense it has always opportunity cost. Equation (4.164) means that if a unit allocation is canceled with one of the allocations listed in Table 4.8 and the amount is additionally allocated to another transportation infrastructure listed in the table, the cancellation loses 0.1057 in terms of the objective function value as an opportunity cost and the addition gets 0.1057 in the same way. So, reallocation of the capital funds allocation would result in no loss and no gain among the listed transportation infrastructures. In this sense, the capital allocations are optimal as far as the listed infrastructures are concerned in terms of the listed facilities as well as the allocated amounts. We must examine if there are other investment targets that have greater values than $\frac{\Delta \text{NNP}}{\Delta C}(\Delta T^K) = 0.1057$. Such possibilities may exist with the investments into the private sectors.

4.7.2.7 Investments for Increments in Production Capacities

Table 4.7 summarizes the allocation of the capital funds to the private sectors. The last column is calculated based on the following equation:

$$\frac{\Delta \text{NNP}}{\Delta K_j^q} \times \frac{\Delta K_j^q}{\Delta C} = \frac{\Delta \text{NNP}}{\Delta C}\left(K_j^q\right) = p_{qj}^K \times \alpha_{qj}^K, \tag{4.165}$$

in which:p_{qj}^K: imputed price associated with the production capacity constraint of $\overline{K}_j^q$; α_{qj}^K: coefficient which converts an outlay of the capital funds into an increase in the production capacity of ΔK_j^q; $\frac{\Delta NNP}{\Delta C}\left(K_j^q\right)$: imputed price of the capital funds via allocation of the capital funds to increase K_j^q.

The results of Eq. (4.165) are shown in the last column in Table 4.7. As readers may confirm, it is 0.1057 with all the capital funds allocation to the private sectors. In Table 4.13, the imputed prices are shown with the production capacities in the private sectors. As for the agricultural sector in Kanto, the imputed price is 0.03535 and $\frac{\Delta \text{NNP}}{\Delta C}\left(K_1^2\right)$ is calculated as $\frac{0.003535}{4.3782} = 0.0081$ since $\frac{1}{\alpha_{qj}^K} = 4.3782$. This is a reason why the allocation of the capital funds is not made in the agricultural sector in Kanto notwithstanding the capital is used for the production and it is fully utilized, which is implied by the positive imputed price. A same logic above is applied and the listed production capacities and the allocated amounts to them are both optimal with the capital funds allocation to the public sectors and the private sectors.

Since there are no further possibilities to which the capital funds are allocated in the economy with larger imputed price than 0.1057, the capital allocation summarized in two tables must be optimal. This can be confirmed as the value of $\frac{\Delta \text{NNP}}{\Delta C}$ is 0.1057, which is the imputed price associated with the capital funds allocation constraint. This confirms that the listed set of targets have been optimally chosen as well as the allocations are optimally made. If the imputed price of the capital

Table 4.13 Imputed price associated with production capacity constraint (unit: 100 million JPY)

Region	Sectors	Imputed price p^K	Constrained constants	Increase in the capital	Construction costs/production capacity coefficient $\frac{1}{\alpha^K}$	Normalized inputted price $\frac{\Delta NNP}{\Delta C} \times \left(\Delta K_j^p\right) = \frac{\Delta NNP}{\Delta K} \frac{\Delta K}{\Delta C} = p^T \div \frac{1}{\alpha^K}$
Hokkaido–Tohoku	Agriculture	0.00000	16,296.10	0	4.3782	0.0000
	Fiber chemistry	0.08374	3169.40	38,855	0.7921	0.1057
	Metal machine	0.00000	6124.20	0	0.4422	0.0000
	Others	0.00000	30,165.10	0	1.0039	0.0000
	Transport service	0.14865	3268.90	0	2.3902	0.0622
Kanto	Agriculture	0.03535	15,222.30	0	4.3782	0.0081
	Fiber chemistry	0.00000	17,121.00	0	0.7921	0.0000
	Metal machine	0.04675	46,915.80	0	0.4422	0.1057
	Others	0.10613	100,305.90	102,642	1.0039	0.1057
	Transport service	0.25269	12,316.50	4096	2.3902	0.1057
Chukyo	Agriculture	0.46285	4928.80	728	4.3782	0.1057
	Fiber chemistry	0.00000	14,567.40	0	0.7921	0.0000
	Metal machine	0.04675	11,071.20	78,256	0.4422	0.1057
	Others	0.10613	30,196.60	7354	1.0039	0.1057
	Transport service	0.22644	2544.90	0	2.3902	0.0947
Kinki	Agriculture	0.00000	4270.60	0	4.3782	0.0000

	Fiber chemistry	0.08374	17,061.40	15,939	0.7921	0.1057
	Metal machine	0.04675	31,133.90	11,856	0.4422	0.1057
	Others	0.10611	54,464.70	2680	1.0039	0.1057
	Transport service	0.10613	6300.90	0	2.3902	0.0444
Chugoku–Shikoku–Kyushu	Agriculture	0.46285	16,676.60	1400	4.3782	0.1057
	Fiber chemistry	0.08374	12,406.80	91,253	0.7921	0.1057
	Metal machine	0.00125	19,930.30	0	0.4422	0.0028
	Others	0.10613	51,310.40	210,236	1.0039	0.1057
	Transport service	0.25269	5088.70	5958	2.3902	0.1057

Table 4.14 Allocation of the capital funds (unit: 100 million JPY)

	Mode/sector	Allocated amount	Share between modes/sectors	Total allocated amount	Share between public and private sectors
Public sectors	Railway	53,625	0.2034	263,629	0.3329
	Highway	201,119	0.7629		
	Marine (port)	8885	0.0337		
Private sector	Agricultural	9318	0.0176	528,263	0.6671
	Fiber chemical	115,685	0.2190		
	Metal	55,055	0.1042		
	Others	324,173	0.6137		
	Transportation	24,032	0.0455		
Capital funds				791,892	1.0000

funds, $\frac{\Delta NNP}{\Delta \overline{C}}$, is greater than 0.1057, some efficient targets are missed in the listed set. It cannot be less than 0.1057, of course.

4.7.2.8 Investment Shares Between the Transportation Infrastructures

The allocation of the funds is summarized in Table 4.14 (Kohno 1970, p. 69, 78), which is the main topic of this chapter. First of all, the shares are 0.3329:0.6671 between the public sectors and the private sectors. With the transportation infrastructures, the simulation shows that the shares should be 0.2034:0.7629:0.0337 between railway, highway, and marine (port). According to EPA (1967) and ECEC (1967), the shares between the public and private sectors are 0.2360:0.7640 and the shares between railway, highway, and marine are 0.3903:0.5306:0.0789. We can say that more allocation to the public sectors and more allocation to highway are suggested by the optimal solution (cf. ECEC 1967).

To argue which is right one is not important here. Originally, the allocation of capital funds having any objectives should be allocated based on the optimality criteria, which we have adopted, and is endogenously built into the model, that is, opportunity cost criteria.

When we apply the conventional benefit–cost approach, the benefit–cost ratio or its equivalents in Mishan's sense must be iteratively calculated to eventually find out that: (1) for example, the benefit–cost ratios are equated with each other with all elements in the set of investment targets which are chosen to be implemented among all possible investment targets by tentatively changing the allocation of capital funds to all the potential investments targets in the set; (2) and the equated benefit–cost ratio is maximum with alternative sets of investment targets which can be constructed by tentatively replacing an element or elements in the set with a possible investment target or targets out of the set. This process can be logically completed and it cannot as a matter of practice. The authors dare to say that such iterative application of the benefit–cost approach does not well work with the objective of this chapter, which is the ultimate topic in the transportation economics, namely to find out optimal share of the capital fund allocation between railway, highway, and marine (port).

4.7.2.9 Allocation of Labor

Table 4.9 shows the allocation of new graduates that occurs in agricultural sector in Kanto and nonagricultural sector in Chugoku–Shikoku–Kyushu. Kanto only imports agricultural product from other regions. The investments into nonagricultural sectors in Chugoku–Shokoku–Kyushu are more than 50% of the total investments into the private sectors. These may explain the allocation of new graduates although it is a little bit different from usual expectations (Kohno 1970, p. 69).

4.8 Conclusion

4.8.1 Superiority of the Model with the Endogenous Opportunity Cost Criteria

In a figurative sense, there are potential projects that are specified as increments in the transportation infrastructures and production capacities. The problem that must be solved by application of the benefit–cost approach is to allocate the limited amount of capital funds to 59 potential investment targets (34 as increments in transportation infrastructure capacities (Tables 4.5 and 4.6) and 25 as increments in production capacities of five sectors in five regions) in order to maximize the effects of the allocation and eventually decide on the optimal set of investment targets on which the allocation of (positive) capital funds is to be made and decide on the allocation of capital funds to them. It is almost impossible to solve it since the combinations of the sets become huge to which the allocation is made in any way and to which the allocation is not made even if we know the number of 26, in advance, namely, the number of chosen investment targets (Tables 4.7 and 4.8).

The superiority of the model is the opportunity cost criteria is systematically (endogenously) installed in the model, namely the equalization of $\frac{\Delta NNP}{\Delta C}\left(T^k\right)$, $\frac{\Delta NNP}{\Delta C}\left(K_j^q\right)$, and $\frac{\Delta NNP}{\Delta \overline{C}}$ with each other is pursued with all possible ΔT^k and ΔK_j^q such that $\Delta T^k > 0$ and $\Delta K_j^q > 0$; the equalization takes into account all the direct and indirect effects of the allocation of capital funds into the public as well as private sectors based on the simultaneous equations system of the general equilibrium of the economy including the intra- and interregional goods flow; therefore, we do not need to rely on any ceteris paribus assumption in the measurement of effects; and the specification of the model is flexible and systematically consistent so that it can be expanded to examine more practical and complicated problems of the capital funds allocation.

4.8.2 Historical Background and Sprit of Our Main Theme

To conclude this chapter, it should be better to refer to the spirit of the age and sense of the times related to our main themes because the research motivation and scientific as well as practical meaning of our model approach become clearer.

In the 1960s when one of the authors started the work, Mr. Kiyoshi Maeda, Researcher of the Federation of Economic Organizations, Japan, has published a book entitled—Treatise on Public Investment (Maeda 1961). The most concern shown in the book is the optimal ratio between the private and public investments. This means that it is the primary concern for the general headquarters of the big business community of Japan. In a sense, it is a surprise why the business association has shown interests in the optimality of the share between the public and private investments. In the 1960s, the private sectors have steadily grown leading by iron steel and electricity power industries. The reality was that improvements were delayed in the social overhead capitals, especially transportation infrastructures compared to the growth rate in the private sectors focusing on the coming car-oriented society. It is natural for the leading association of private sectors to pay attention to the public sectors since the capital accumulation in private sectors and public sectors should be made complementary in order to keep the economic growth of the Japanese economy which was about to takeoff after a decade has passed since the last Second World War. It can be taken that the leading association would like to implicitly request the government, which shall be mainly in charge of the matter of public investments, drastic improvements in the social overhead capitals and transportation infrastructures by knowing the optimal shares based on well-documented materials.

On the other hand, we should also refer to the keynote of thinking by peoples who were to take leading roles in improvements in the social overhead capitals, especially transportation infrastructures. Chronologically considering the transportation sector in the era of 1960s–1970s, it is taken as the time of transition from the modes of railway and marine to the modes of Shinkansen, expressway, and air transport with jumbo. However, the matters related to the transportation, especially to the ground transport, the emphasis was centered on the matters related to Japanese National Railways (JNR) since Meiji era through Taisho era and after the Second World War. Peoples leading JNR as a mono-transport reigned supreme just when the transition in the transportation sector was about to begin. The peoples were stick to the custom and convention as vested rights. It was a kind of inertia and it was a big challenge to advocate the transformation of transportation infrastructures against the keynote of that era.

Genpachiro Konno has firstly advocated a biggest paradigm shift in the transportation sectors after the Second World War. He had visited The Brookings Institution in the United States as a researcher and moved to Kiel University in Germany as a lecturer to have opportunities to minutely observe highway transportation policies in the car-oriented societies before the Second World War. His main books are Konno (1955, 1959), in which necessity of expressway network is argued with passion

(Higano 2020). During such keynote was prevailing in the academia as well as political and business establishment, his advocation of a paradigm shift was timely and therefore stood out in every sense although the national projects of inviting the investigation team led by Watkins was implemented in order to be given advise on the improvements in the expressway and highway transportation network in Japan (Watkins 1956). A paradigm shift of course means a drastic change in the transportation policy from railway and marine to road transportation focusing on the coming car-oriented society in the dynamic era. Generally speaking, the point was what should be roles of the national government in the mixed economic system. Konno advocated a departure from traditional roles such as a watchman state—that means that the government originally should indirectly assist the development of the private sectors and correct the market failure and more active commitment by the government to the investments in the public sectors.

Yasoshima (1964) firstly advocated the theory of comprehensive transportation system in which improvements in the infrastructures of railway, road, and marine (port) are considered with a consistent and unified criterion. The way of thinking of The Ministry of Transportation responding to Prof. Yasoshima's idea is shown in MTMD (1969) (and MTMP 1972). Though this was based on qualitative and descriptive argument, it was succeeded by the derivation of the quantitative shares given by EPA (1967) and ECEC (1967) (see Sect. 4.7.2.8). The shares were based on the summation of budget appropriation requests by the related divisions and sections of the government. On the other hand, our model derives the optimal shares based on the opportunity cost criterion and gives objective rationale for the allocation of capital funds to the transportation infrastructures consistently and comprehensively.

It can be said that the model had achieved two tough matters which were closely related with each other: (1) it had given peoples biased in mono-transport policy the final word who were stick to conventional and custom transportation policy based on the vested right; and (2) reminded peoples, who were concerned with the transportation infrastructure policies, of the importance of the comprehensive transport system planning approach in which focus is laid on effectiveness of the improvements in the system in the light of their impacts on the whole national economy. Those were achievements in the fields of regional development and transportation policies, which were firstly possible by adopting the quantitative approach of the cutting-edge programming model. Without quantitative results, nothing goes forward.

Appendix 1: BirdEye View of Interregional Input–Output Model of Shipment Activities: Illustration by Three Regions, Three Sectors, and Three Transportation Mode

Table 4.15 Plane view of Tables 4.16–4.30: three regions, three sectors, and three transport modes model (sample)

	1		*15*		*16*		*34*		*35*		*53*		*54*		*71*		*72*		*85*
1				1				1				1				1			
		4.16				**4.19**				**4.22**				**4.25**				**4.28**	
15				15				15				15				15			
	1		*15*		*16*		*34*		*35*		*53*		*54*		*71*		*72*		*85*
16				16				16				16				16			
		4.17				**4.20**				**4.23**				**4.26**				**4.29**	
34				34				34				34				34			
	1		*15*		*16*		*34*		*35*		*53*		*54*		*71*		*72*		*85*
35				35				35				35				35			
		4.18				**4.21**				**4.24**				**4.27**				**4.30**	
43				43				43				43				43			

Note: (1) Table 4.15 abstracted a huge (43×85) matrix, which corresponds to the matrix in Eq. (4.140) with Sect. 4.5.5.1. (2) For example, "4.23" means Table 4.23 represents the partition of the huge matrix abstracted by Table 4.15, in which its row no. starts with 16 and ends with 34, and its column no. starts with 35 and ends with 53. (3) With each of Tables 4.16–4.30, row no. and column no., which specify location of partitioned matrix in the huge matrix, are shown with consecutive integers in cells of certain column and row. For example, fourth column and fifth row in Table 4.16

Table 4.16 Three regions, three sectors, and three transport modes model (sample)

		Region to be delivered (destination) →			1 East			2 Central			3 West			1 East			2 Central		
		Goods to be delivered			Agriculture (primary)									The others					
		Variables			${}^{11}x_1^{11}$	${}^{21}x_1^{11}$	${}^{31}x_1^{11}$	${}^{11}x_1^{12}$	${}^{21}x_1^{12}$	${}^{31}x_1^{12}$	${}^{11}x_1^{13}$	${}^{21}x_1^{13}$	${}^{31}x_1^{13}$	${}^{11}x_2^{11}$	${}^{21}x_2^{11}$	${}^{31}x_2^{11}$	${}^{11}x_2^{12}$	${}^{21}x_2^{12}$	${}^{31}x_2^{12}$
	Region of production (origin) ↓	Mode for delivery			Railway	Shipping	Truck	Railway	Shipping	Truck	Railway	Shipping	Truck	Railway	Shipping	Truck	Railway	Shipping	Truck
		Input sector ↓			1	2	3	4	5	6	7	8	9	10	11	12	13	14	15
Production and shipment	1 East	1 Agriculture (primary)	1	$\overline{F}_1^1$	1–0.09387	1–0.09387	1–0.09387	−0.09387	−0.09387	−0.09387	−0.09387	−0.09387	−0.09387	−0.12510	−0.12510	−0.12510	−0.12510	−0.12510	−0.12510
		2 the others	2	$\overline{F}_2^1$	−0.30174	−0.30174	−0.30174	−0.30174	−0.30174	−0.30174	−0.30174	−0.30174	−0.30174	1–0.43012	1–0.43012	1–0.43012	−0.43012	−0.43012	−0.43012
		3 transport	3	$\overline{F}_3^1$	−0.00822	−0.01058	−0.00760	−0.02639	−0.01872	−0.08712	−0.03846	−0.02239	−0.53895	−0.01199	−0.01498	−0.00936	−0.03985	−0.02720	−0.11543
	2 Central	1 Agriculture (primary)	4	$\overline{F}_1^2$				1	1	1									
		2 the others	5	$\overline{F}_2^2$													1	1	1
		3 transport	6	$\overline{F}_3^2$															
	3 West	1 Agriculture (primary)	7	$\overline{F}_1^3$							1	1	1						
		2 the others	8	$\overline{F}_2^3$															
		3 transport	9	$\overline{F}_3^3$															
Production capacity	1 East	1 Agriculture (primary)	10	$\overline{K}_1^1$	1	1	1	1	1	1	1	1	1						
		2 the others	11	$\overline{K}_2^1$										1	1	1	1	1	1
		3 transport	12	$\overline{K}_3^1$															
		1 Agriculture (primary)	13	$\overline{K}_1^2$															

(continued)

Table 4.16 (continued)

		Region to be delivered (destination) →			1 East			2 Central			3 West			1 East			2 Central		
		Goods to be delivered			Agriculture (primary)									The others					
		Variables			${}^{11}x_1^{11}$	${}^{21}x_1^{11}$	${}^{31}x_1^{11}$	${}^{11}x_1^{12}$	${}^{21}x_1^{12}$	${}^{31}x_1^{12}$	${}^{11}x_1^{13}$	${}^{21}x_1^{13}$	${}^{31}x_1^{13}$	${}^{11}x_2^{11}$	${}^{21}x_2^{11}$	${}^{31}x_2^{11}$	${}^{11}x_2^{12}$	${}^{21}x_2^{12}$	${}^{31}x_2^{12}$
	Region of production (origin) ↓	Mode for delivery			Railway	Shipping	Truck	Railway	Shipping	Truck	Railway	Shipping	Truck	Railway	Shipping	Truck	Railway	Shipping	Truck
		Input sector ↓			1	2	3	4	5	6	7	8	9	10	11	12	13	14	15
	2 Central	2 the others	14	$\overline{K}_2^2$															
		3 transport	15	$\overline{K}_3^2$															

Table 4.17 Three regions, three sectors, and three transport modes model (sample)

					${}^{11}x_1^{11}$	${}^{21}x_1^{11}$	${}^{31}x_1^{11}$	${}^{11}x_1^{12}$	${}^{21}x_1^{12}$	${}^{31}x_1^{12}$	${}^{11}x_1^{13}$	${}^{21}x_1^{13}$	${}^{31}x_1^{13}$	${}^{11}x_2^{11}$	${}^{21}x_2^{11}$	${}^{31}x_2^{11}$	${}^{11}x_2^{12}$	${}^{21}x_2^{12}$	${}^{31}x_2^{12}$
					1	2	3	4	5	6	7	8	9	10	11	12	13	14	15
Production capacity	3 West	1 Agriculture (primary)	16	$\overline{K}_1^3$							1	1	1						
		2 The others	17	$\overline{K}_2^3$															
		3 Transport	18	$\overline{K}_3^3$															
Transportation capacity	Railway	East intra	19	$\overline{T}^1$	4.407									2.9575					
		Central intra	20	$\overline{T}^2$															
		West intra	21	$\overline{T}^3$															
		East–central	22	$\overline{T}^4$				4.407			4.407						2.9575		
		Central–west	23	$\overline{T}^5$							4.407								
	Shipping	East intra	24	$\overline{T}^6$		4.407									2.9575				
		Central intra	25	$\overline{T}^7$															
		West intra	26	$\overline{T}^8$															
		East inter	27	$\overline{T}^9$					4.407			4.407						2.9575	
		Central inter	28	$\overline{T}^{10}$					4.407									2.9575	
		West inter	29	$\overline{T}^{11}$								4.407							
	Highway	East intra	30	$\overline{T}^{12}$			4.407									2.9575			
		Central intra	31	$\overline{T}^{13}$															
		West intra	32	$\overline{T}^{14}$															
		East–central	33	$\overline{T}^{15}$						4.4070			4.4075						2.9575
		Central–west	34	$\overline{T}^{16}$									4.4075						

Table 4.18 Three regions, three sectors, and three transport modes model (sample)

					${}^{11}x_1^{11}$	${}^{21}x_1^{11}$	${}^{31}x_1^{11}$	${}^{11}x_1^{12}$	${}^{21}x_1^{12}$	${}^{31}x_1^{12}$	${}^{11}x_1^{13}$	${}^{21}x_1^{13}$	${}^{31}x_1^{13}$	${}^{11}x_2^{11}$	${}^{21}x_2^{11}$	${}^{31}x_2^{11}$	${}^{11}x_2^{12}$	${}^{21}x_2^{12}$	${}^{31}x_2^{12}$
					1	2	3	4	5	6	7	8	9	10	11	12	13	14	15
		Capital fund allocation	35	$\overline{C}$															
Labor force available	East	Primary	36	$\overline{L}_1^1$	0.0750	0.0750	0.0750	0.0750	0.0750	0.0750	0.0750	0.0750	0.0750						
		Nonprimary	37	$\overline{L}_2^1$										0.0450	0.0450	0.0450	0.0450	0.0450	0.0450
	Central	Primary	38	$\overline{L}_1^2$															
		Nonprimary	39	$\overline{L}_2^2$															
	West	Primary	40	$\overline{L}_1^3$															
		Nonprimary	41	$\overline{L}_2^3$															
	Whole country	Nonprimary	42	$\overline{DL_2}$															
		Rate of profit			0.41724	0.41488	0.41840	0.39907	0.40674	0.33834	0.38700	0.40307	0.28651	0.14886	0.14587	0.15149	0.12100	0.13365	0.04542
		Rate of value added	43		0.59617	0.59381	0.59679	0.57800	0.58567	0.51727	0.56593	0.58200	0.06544	0.43279	0.42980	0.43542	0.40493	0.41758	0.32935

Table 4.19 Three regions, three sectors, and three transport modes model (sample)

		3 West			1 East	1 East			2 Central			3 west			1 east			2 central		
		the others			transport	Agriculture (primary)									the others					
		$^{11}x_2^{13}$	$^{21}x_2^{13}$	$^{31}x_2^{13}$	x_3^{11}	$^{11}x_1^{21}$	$^{21}x_1^{21}$	$^{31}x_1^{21}$	$^{11}x_1^{22}$	$^{21}x_1^{22}$	$^{31}x_1^{22}$	$^{11}x_1^{23}$	$^{21}x_1^{23}$	$^{31}x_1^{23}$	$^{11}x_2^{21}$	$^{21}x_2^{21}$	$^{31}x_2^{21}$	$^{11}x_2^{22}$	$^{21}x_2^{22}$	$^{31}x_2^{22}$
		Railway	Shipping	Truck	Shipping	Railway	Shipping	Truck	Railway	Shipping	Truck	Railway	Shipping	Truck	Railway	Shipping	Truck	Railway	Shipping	Truck
		16	17	18	19	20	21	22	23	24	25	26	27	28	29	30	31	32	33	34
1	$\overline{F}_1^1$	−0.12510	−0.12510	−0.12510	−0.00005	1	1	1												
2	$\overline{F}_2^1$	−0.43012	−0.43012	−0.43012	−0.34209									1	1	1				
3	$\overline{F}_3^1$	−0.05672	−0.03331	−0.18419	1															
4	$\overline{F}_1^2$					−0.07946	−0.07946	−0.07946	1−0.07946	1−0.07946	1−0.07946	−0.07946	−0.07946	−0.07946	−0.06560	−0.12510	−0.12510	−0.12510	−0.12510	−0.12510
5	$\overline{F}_2^2$					−0.37458	−0.37458	−0.37458	−0.37458	−0.37458	−0.37458	−0.37458	−0.37458	−0.37458	−0.52635	−0.43012	−0.43012	1−0.43012	1−0.43012	1−0.43012
6	$\overline{F}_3^2$					−0.17324	−0.12292	−0.27195	−0.05192	−0.05416	−0.03778	−0.13235	−0.09515	−0.36394	−0.09093	−0.01199	−0.01498	−0.00936	−0.02720	−0.11543
7	$\overline{F}_1^3$											1	1	1						
8	$\overline{F}_2^3$	1	1	1																
9	$\overline{F}_3^3$																			
10	$\overline{K}_1^1$																			
11	$\overline{K}_2^1$	1	1	1																
12	$\overline{K}_3^1$				1															
13	$\overline{K}_1^2$					1	1	1	1	1	1	1	1	1						
14	$\overline{K}_2^2$														1	1	1	1	1	1
15	$\overline{K}_3^2$																			

Table 4.20 Three regions, three sectors, and three transport modes model (sample)

		${}^{11}x_2^{13}$	${}^{21}x_2^{13}$	${}^{31}x_2^{13}$	x_3^{11}	${}^{11}x_1^{21}$	${}^{21}x_1^{21}$	${}^{31}x_1^{21}$	${}^{11}x_1^{22}$	${}^{21}x_1^{22}$	${}^{31}x_1^{22}$	${}^{11}x_1^{23}$	${}^{21}x_1^{23}$	${}^{31}x_1^{23}$	${}^{11}x_2^{21}$	${}^{21}x_2^{21}$	${}^{31}x_2^{21}$	${}^{11}x_2^{22}$	${}^{21}x_2^{22}$	${}^{31}x_2^{22}$
		16	17	18	19	20	21	22	23	24	25	26	27	28	29	30	31	32	33	34
16	$\overline{K}_1^3$																			
17	$\overline{K}_2^3$																			
18	$\overline{K}_3^3$																			
19	$\overline{T}^1$																			
20	$\overline{T}^2$								4.4070									2.9575		
21	$\overline{T}^3$																			
22	$\overline{T}^4$	2.9575				4.407									2.9575					
23	$\overline{T}^5$	2.9575										4.4070								
24	$\overline{T}^6$																			
25	$\overline{T}^7$									4.4070									2.9575	
26	$\overline{T}^8$																			
27	$\overline{T}^9$		2.9575				4.4070									2.9575				
28	$\overline{T}^{10}$						4.4070						4.4070			2.9575				
29	$\overline{T}^{11}$		2.9575										4.4070							
30	$\overline{T}^{12}$																			
31	$\overline{T}^{13}$										4.4070									2.9575
32	$\overline{T}^{14}$																			
33	$\overline{T}^{15}$			2.9575				4.4070									2.9575			
34	$\overline{T}^{16}$			2.9575										4.4070						

Table 4.21 Three regions, three sectors, and three transport modes model (sample)

		$^{11}x_2^{13}$	$^{21}x_2^{13}$	$^{31}x_2^{13}$	x_3^{11}	$^{11}x_1^{21}$	$^{21}x_1^{21}$	$^{31}x_1^{21}$	$^{11}x_1^{22}$	$^{21}x_1^{22}$	$^{31}x_1^{22}$	$^{11}x_1^{23}$	$^{21}x_1^{23}$	$^{31}x_1^{23}$	$^{11}x_2^{21}$	$^{21}x_2^{21}$	$^{31}x_2^{21}$	$^{11}x_2^{22}$	$^{21}x_2^{22}$	$^{31}x_2^{22}$
		16	17	18	19	20	21	22	23	24	25	26	27	28	29	30	31	32	33	34
35	$\overline{C}$																			
36	$\overline{L}_1^1$																			
37	$\overline{L}_2^1$	0.0450	0.0450	0.0450	0.0450															
38	$\overline{L}_1^2$					0.0875	0.0875	0.0875	0.0875	0.0875	0.0875	0.0875	0.0875	0.0875						
39	$\overline{L}_2^2$														0.0525	0.0525	0.0525	0.0525	0.0525	0.0525
40	$\overline{L}_1^3$																			
41	$\overline{L}_2^3$																			
42	$\overline{DL_2}$																			
		0.10413	0.12754			0.27583	0.32615		0.39715	0.39491	0.41129	0.31672	0.35392	0.08513	0.07125					
43		0.38806	0.41147	0.26059	0.65786	0.37272	0.42304	0.27401	0.49404	0.49180	0.50818	0.41361	0.45081	0.18202	0.31712	0.43279	0.42980	0.43542	0.41758	0.32935

Table 4.22 Three regions, three sectors, and three transport modes model (sample)

	3 West			2 Central	1 East			2 Central			3 West			1 East			2 Central		
	The others			Transport	Agriculture (primary)									The others					
	${}^{11}x_2^{23}$	${}^{21}x_2^{23}$	${}^{31}x_2^{23}$	x_3^{22}	${}^{11}x_1^{31}$	${}^{21}x_1^{31}$	${}^{31}x_1^{31}$	${}^{11}x_1^{32}$	${}^{21}x_1^{32}$	${}^{31}x_1^{32}$	${}^{11}x_1^{33}$	${}^{21}x_1^{33}$	${}^{31}x_1^{33}$	${}^{11}x_2^{31}$	${}^{21}x_2^{31}$	${}^{31}x_2^{31}$	${}^{11}x_2^{32}$	${}^{21}x_2^{32}$	${}^{31}x_2^{32}$
	Railway	Shipping	Truck	Railway	Railway	Shipping	Truck	Railway	Shipping	Truck	Railway	Shipping	Truck	Railway	Shipping	Truck	Railway	Shipping	Truck
	35	36	37	38	39	40	41	42	43	44	45	46	47	48	49	50	51	52	53
1		1			1	1	1												
2														1	1	1			
3																			
4	−0.12510	−0.12510	−0.12510	−0.00005				1	1	1									
5	−0.43012	−0.43012	−0.43012	−0.34209													1	1	1
6	−0.05672	−0.03331	−0.18419	1															
7					−0.09387	−0.09387	−0.09387	−0.09387	−0.09387	−0.09387	1−0.09387	1−0.09387	1−0.09387	−0.07946	−0.07946	−0.07946	−0.07946	−0.07946	−0.07946
8	1	1	1		−0.30174	−0.30174	−0.30174	−0.30174	−0.30174	−0.30174	−0.30174	−0.30174	−0.30174	−0.37458	−0.37458	−0.37458	−0.37458	−0.37458	−0.37458
9					−0.00822	−0.01058	−0.00760	−0.02639	−0.01872	−0.08712	−0.03846	−0.02239	−0.23895	−0.17324	−0.12292	−0.27195	−0.05192	−0.05416	−0.03778
10																			
11																			
12																			
13																			
14	1	1	1																
15				1															

Table 4.23 Three regions, three sectors, and three transport modes model (sample)

		${}^{11}x_2^{23}$	${}^{21}x_2^{23}$	${}^{31}x_2^{23}$	x_3^{22}	${}^{11}x_1^{31}$	${}^{21}x_1^{31}$	${}^{31}x_1^{31}$	${}^{11}x_1^{32}$	${}^{21}x_1^{32}$	${}^{31}x_1^{32}$	${}^{11}x_1^{33}$	${}^{21}x_1^{33}$	${}^{31}x_1^{33}$	${}^{11}x_2^{31}$	${}^{21}x_2^{31}$	${}^{31}x_2^{31}$	${}^{11}x_2^{32}$	${}^{21}x_2^{32}$	${}^{31}x_2^{32}$
		35	36	37	38	39	40	41	42	43	44	45	46	47	48	49	50	51	52	53
16	$\overline{K}_1^3$					1	1	1	1	1	1	1	1	1						
17	$\overline{K}_2^3$														1	1	1	1	1	1
18	$\overline{K}_3^3$																			
19	$\overline{T}^1$																			
20	$\overline{T}^2$																			
21	$\overline{T}^3$					4.4070						4.4070			4.4070					
22	$\overline{T}^4$																			
23	$\overline{T}^5$	4.4070				4.4070			4.4070						404,070			4.4070		
24	$\overline{T}^6$																			
25	$\overline{T}^7$																			
26	$\overline{T}^8$												2.9575							
27	$\overline{T}^9$						2.9575									2.9575				
28	$\overline{T}^{10}$		2.9575							2.9575									2.9575	
29	$\overline{T}^{11}$		2.9575				2.9575			2.9575						2.9575			2.9575	
30	$\overline{T}^{12}$																			
31	$\overline{T}^{13}$																			
32	$\overline{T}^{14}$							4.4070									4.4070			
33	$\overline{T}^{15}$			4.4070																4.4070
34	$\overline{T}^{16}$							4.4070			4.4070			4.4070			4.4070			4.4070

Table 4.24 Three regions, three sectors, and three transport modes model (sample)

		${}^{11}x_2^{23}$	${}^{21}x_2^{23}$	${}^{31}x_2^{23}$	x_3^{22}	${}^{11}x_1^{31}$	${}^{21}x_1^{31}$	${}^{31}x_1^{31}$	${}^{11}x_1^{32}$	${}^{21}x_1^{32}$	${}^{31}x_1^{32}$	${}^{11}x_1^{33}$	${}^{21}x_1^{33}$	${}^{31}x_1^{33}$	${}^{11}x_2^{31}$	${}^{21}x_2^{31}$	${}^{31}x_2^{31}$	${}^{11}x_2^{32}$	${}^{21}x_2^{32}$	${}^{31}x_2^{32}$
		35	36	37	38	39	40	41	42	43	44	45	46	47	48	49	50	51	52	53
35	$\overline{C}$																			
36	$\overline{L}_1^1$																			
37	$\overline{L}_2^1$																			
38	$\overline{L}_1^2$																			
39	$\overline{L}_2^2$	0.0525	0.0525	0.0525	0.0525															
40	$\overline{L}_1^3$					0.075	0.075	0.075	0.075	0.075	0.075	0.075	0.075	0.075						
41	$\overline{L}_2^3$														0.045	0.045	0.045	0.045	0.045	0.045
42	$\overline{DL_2}$																			
43		0.38806	0.41147	0.26059	0.65786	0.59617	0.59381	0.59679	0.57800	0.58567	0.51727	0.56593	0.58200	0.36544	0.37272	0.42304	0.27401	0.49404	0.49180	0.50818

Table 4.25 Three regions, three sectors, and three transport modes model (sample)

		3 West			3 West	Incremental variable activities													
		The others			Transport	Railway					Port						Road		
		${}^{11}x_2^{33}$	${}^{21}x_2^{33}$	${}^{31}x_2^{33}$	x_3^{33}	ΔT^1	ΔT^2	ΔT^3	ΔT^4	ΔT^5	ΔT^6	ΔT^7	ΔT^8	ΔT^9	ΔT^{10}	ΔT^{11}	ΔT^{12}	ΔT^{13}	ΔT^{14}
		Railway	Shipping	Truck		East intra	Central intra	West intra	East–central inter	Center–west inter	East intra	Central intra	West intra	East inter	Central inter	West inter	East intra	Central intra	West intra
		54	55	56	57	58	59	60	61	62	63	64	65	66	67	68	69	70	71
1	$\overline{F}_1^1$																		
2	$\overline{F}_2^1$																		
3	$\overline{F}_3^1$																		
4	$\overline{F}_1^2$																		
5	$\overline{F}_2^2$																		
6	$\overline{F}_3^2$																		
7	$\overline{F}_1^3$	−0.07946	−0.07946	−0.07946	−0.00005														
8	$\overline{F}_2^3$	1–0.37458	1–0.37458	1–0.37458	−0.34209														
9	$\overline{F}_3^3$	−0.13235	−0.09515	−0.36394	1														
10	$\overline{K}_1^1$																		
11	$\overline{K}_2^1$																		
12	$\overline{K}_3^1$																		
13	$\overline{K}_1^2$																		
14	$\overline{K}_2^2$																		
15	$\overline{K}_3^2$																		

Table 4.26 Three regions, three sectors, and three transport modes model (sample)

		${}^{11}x_2^{33}$	${}^{21}x_2^{33}$	${}^{31}x_2^{33}$	x_3^{33}	ΔT^1	ΔT^2	ΔT^3	ΔT^4	ΔT^5	ΔT^6	ΔT^7	ΔT^8	ΔT^9	ΔT^{10}	ΔT^{11}	ΔT^{12}	ΔT^{13}	ΔT^{14}
		54	55	56	57	58	59	60	61	62	63	64	65	66	67	68	69	70	71
16	$\overline{K}_1^3$																		
17	$\overline{K}_2^3$	1	1	1															
18	$\overline{K}_3^3$				1														
19	$\overline{T}^1$					−1													
20	$\overline{T}^2$						−1												
21	$\overline{T}^3$	2.9575						−1											
22	$\overline{T}^4$								−1										
23	$\overline{T}^5$									−1									
24	$\overline{T}^6$										−1								
25	$\overline{T}^7$											−1							
26	$\overline{T}^8$		2.9575										−1						
27	$\overline{T}^9$													−1					
28	$\overline{T}^{10}$														−1				
29	$\overline{T}^{11}$															−1			
30	$\overline{T}^{12}$																−1		
31	$\overline{T}^{13}$																	−1	
32	$\overline{T}^{14}$																		−1
33	$\overline{T}^{15}$																		
34	$\overline{T}^{16}$			2.9575															

Table 4.27 Three regions, three sectors, and three transport modes model (sample)

		${}^{11}x_2^{33}$	${}^{21}x_2^{33}$	${}^{31}x_2^{33}$	x_3^{33}	ΔT^1	ΔT^2	ΔT^3	ΔT^4	ΔT^5	ΔT^6	ΔT^7	ΔT^8	ΔT^9	ΔT^{10}	ΔT^{11}	ΔT^{12}	ΔT^{13}	ΔT^{14}
		54	55	56	57	58	59	60	61	62	63	64	65	66	67	68	69	70	71
35	$\overline{C}$					0.06	0.06	0.06	0.12	0.12	0.05	0.05	0.05	0.0700	0.0700	0.0700	0.0300	0.0597	0.0300
36	$\overline{L}_1^1$																		
37	$\overline{L}_2^1$																		
38	$\overline{L}_1^2$																		
39	$\overline{L}_2^2$																		
40	$\overline{L}_1^3$																		
41	$\overline{L}_2^3$	0.045	0.045	0.045	0.045														
42	$\overline{DL_2}$																		
						0.0	0.0	0.0	0.0	0.0	0.0	0.0	0.0	0.0	0.0	0.0	0.0	0.0	0.0
43		0.41361	0.41361	0.41361	0.41361	0.0	0.0	0.0	0.0	0.0	0.0	0.0	0.0	0.0	0.0	0.0	0.0	0.0	0.0

Table 4.28 Three regions, three sectors, and three transport modes model (sample)

Incremental variable activities																				
Road		Production facilities									Employment (nonagri)									
		Hokkaido–Tohoku (east)			Kanto–Chukyo–Kansai (central)			Chugoku–Shikoku–Kyushu (west)			East	Central	West							
ΔT^{15}	ΔT^{16}	ΔK_1^1	ΔK_2^1	ΔK_3^1	ΔK_1^2	ΔK_2^2	ΔK_3^2	ΔK_1^3	ΔK_2^3	ΔK_3^3	ΔL_2^1	ΔL_2^2	ΔL_2^3							
East–central	Central–west	Primary	Others	Transport	Primary	Others	Transport	Primary	Others	Transport					Constrained constant	Unit				
72	73	74	75	76	77	78	79	80	81	82	83	84	85							
														≧	653	100 Million yen/1971	$\overline{F}_1^1$	1	1 East	Final demand
														≧	55,391	〃	$\overline{F}_2^1$	2		
														≧	2179	〃	$\overline{F}_3^1$	3		
														≧	14,047	〃	$\overline{F}_1^2$	4	2 Central	
														≧	100,000	〃	$\overline{F}_2^2$	5		
														≧	18,095	〃	$\overline{F}_3^2$	6		
														≧	4556	〃	$\overline{F}_1^3$	7	3 West	
														≧	73,559	〃	$\overline{F}_2^3$	8		
														≧	3439	〃	$\overline{F}_3^3$	9		
		−1												≦	16,296	100 Million yen/1960	$\overline{K}_1^1$	10	1 East	Production capacity
			−1											≦	39,458	〃	$\overline{K}_2^1$	11		
				−1										≦	3268	〃	$\overline{K}_3^1$	12		
					−1									≦	24,420	〃	$\overline{K}_1^2$	13	2 Central	
						−1								≦	322,832	〃	$\overline{K}_2^2$	14		
							−1							≦	21,160	〃	$\overline{K}_3^2$	15		

Table 4.29 Three regions, three sectors, and three transport modes model (sample)

ΔT^{15}	ΔT^{16}	ΔK_1^1	ΔK_2^1	ΔK_3^1	ΔK_1^2	ΔK_2^2	ΔK_3^2	ΔK_1^3	ΔK_2^3	ΔK_3^3	ΔL_2^1	ΔL_2^2	ΔL_2^3							
72	73	74	75	76	77	78	79	80	81	82	83	84	85		Constrained constant	Unit				
								−1						$\leqq$	16,676	100 Million yen/1960	$\overline{K}_1^3$	16	3 West	Production capacity
									−1					$\leqq$	83,646	″	$\overline{K}_2^3$	17		
										−1				$\leqq$	5088	″	$\overline{K}_3^3$	18		
														$\leqq$	42,086	1000 ton km	$\overline{T}^1$	19	Railway	Transport facilities capacity
														$\leqq$	64,944	″	$\overline{T}^2$	20		
														$\leqq$	42,707	″	$\overline{T}^3$	21		
														$\leqq$	14,928	″	$\overline{T}^4$	22		
														$\leqq$	15,038	″	$\overline{T}^5$	23		
														$\leqq$	5732	″	$\overline{T}^6$	24	Port	
														$\leqq$	39,968	″	$\overline{T}^7$	25		
														$\leqq$	45,409	″	$\overline{T}^8$	26		
														$\leqq$	12,842	″	$\overline{T}^9$	27		
														$\leqq$	49,530	″	$\overline{T}^{10}$	28		
														$\leqq$	6421		$\overline{T}^{11}$	29		
														$\leqq$	142,575	″	$\overline{T}^{12}$	30	Highway	
														$\leqq$	676,898	″	$\overline{T}^{13}$	31		
														$\leqq$	260,833	″	$\overline{T}^{14}$	32		
−1														$\leqq$	343	″	$\overline{T}^{15}$	33		
	−1													$\leqq$	1563	″	$\overline{T}^{16}$	34		

Table 4.30 Three regions, three sectors, and three transport modes model (sample)

ΔT^{14}	ΔT^{15}	ΔK_1^1	ΔK_2^1	ΔK_3^1	ΔK_1^2	ΔK_2^2	ΔK_3^2	ΔK_1^3	ΔK_2^3	ΔK_3^3	ΔL_2^1	ΔL_2^2	ΔL_2^3							
72	73	74	75	76	77	78	79	80	81	82	83	84	85							
0.0530	0.0530	4.377	0.8609	2.3901	4.377	0.8609	2.3901	4.377	0.8609	2.3901				$\leqq$	800,000	100 Million yen/1961–1971	$\overline{C}$	35		Inv.
														$\leqq$	2340	1000 Person/1971	$\overline{L}_1^1$	36	East	Labor force available
											−1			$\leqq$	4220	1000 Person/1962	$\overline{L}_2^1$	37		
														$\leqq$	3050	1000 Person/1971	$\overline{L}_1^2$	38	Central	
												−1		$\leqq$	20,690	1000 Person/1962	$\overline{L}_2^2$	39		
														$\leqq$	2350	1000 Person/1971	$\overline{L}_1^3$	40	West	
													−1	$\leqq$	6450	1000 Person/1962	$\overline{L}_2^3$	41		
											1	1	1	$\leqq$	8660	1000 Person	$\overline{DL_2}$	42	Whole country	
0.0	0.0	0.0	0.0	0.0	0.0	0.0	0.0	0.0	0.0	0.0	0.0	0.0	0.0							
0.0	0.0	0.0	0.0	0.0	0.0	0.0	0.0	0.0	0.0	0.0	0.0	0.0	0.0					43		

Table 4.31 Rates of fare delivered region by delivered region and mode by mode: example of three regions, three sectors, and three modes

Sector ↓	Origin ↓	Mode ↓	Destination →	1 East	2 Central	3 West
Agricultural goods	1 East	Railway		0.95391	0.59871	0.57751
		Shipping		1.22696	0.42478	0.33621
		Truck		0.81913	0.97651	2.08629
	2 Central	Railway		0.59871	1.08257	0.65740
		Shipping		0.42478	1.12939	0.48551
		Truck		0.97651	0.78784	1.85711
	3 West	Railway		0.57751	0.65740	1.02937
		Shipping		0.33621	0.48551	1.08661
		Truck		2.08629	1.85711	0.88393
Other products	1 East	Railway		0.98983	0.65510	0.62050
		Shipping		1.23730	0.44728	0.36450
		Truck		0.77295	1.89762	2.01499
	2 Central	Railway		0.65510	1.11422	0.70695
		Shipping		0.44728	1.12875	0.50237
		Truck		1.89762	0.75712	0.79065
	3 West	Railway		0.62050	0.70695	1.08184
		Shipping		0.36450	0.50237	1.07657
		Truck		2.01499	0.79065	0.84167

Appendix 2: Input–Output Table at Purchasers' Price and Shipment Activities

Input–Output Table

General Definition

It is considered that the regional economy, which consists of industries (called—sectors), features its own industrial structures by making trades between industries inside and/or outside the region. It is also considered that the national economy consists of the regional economies, which are linked with each other through the trades. The sector typically purchases materials that are goods and services (materials) produced by other sectors inside or outside the region in order to produce new goods/services (outputs) through manufacturing the materials (inputs), and earn added values to sell the outputs to other sectors inside or outside the region.

The sectors, which constitute and characterize the regional economy and, thus, the national economy, are linked with each other through trades, and eventually provide goods and services for the final demanders (of consumption, investment, export, etc.). The input–output table summarizes the trades in a certain specific year in a matrix form. In terms of the production line of goods and services, which may be represented by a river and tributaries in the figurative sense, the final demanders are definitely located at a mouth of a river. A sector α is located down the stream and a sector β is upstream with the production of goods/services by sector α. However, a sector α can be located upper stream than a sector β with the production of goods/services of sector β. The complicated interindustrial relation, which features the regional economy, can be well understood by representing the trades in a matrix form.

Numerical Example

We explain the core feature of the input–output (I-O) table using Table 4.32. The trades are typical "flow" variables in the economic model. Therefore, the I-O table must have a dimension of period, which has a starting point of time and an ending point of time, within which the trade can be measured. The I-O table is constructed with the period of one calendar year (i.e., starting January 1st) which has the last digit of 0 (zero) or 5 (five) in Japan.

Focusing on the 3×3 matrix located at the upper-left corner, the column heads of the first three rows show names of the sector, which provides goods/services to sectors including itself. Sector 1 sells 20, 30, 20 million JPY to sectors 1, 2, and 3, respectively. Here, million JPY is a special unit with I-O table. It represents the volume of goods/services produced by sector 1 in terms of a measurement unit specific to the said goods/services (e.g., such and such tonnage of coal) that can be purchased with million JPY. It is called—million JPY value unit. It has dual meanings, that is, a unit for counting the volume of goods/services, as far as we know what is meant by million JPY value with each sector, and a unit for counting the value of goods/services in a monetary term. Thanks to the device of unit, it has a meaning to add up elements of column vector. The figure in each column can be interpreted as inputs of goods/services into the said sector. Sector 1 inputs 20, 45, and 20 million JPY goods/service produced by sector 1, 2, and 3, respectively, and the total input (purchase) cost is 85 million JPY (20 + 45 + 20). If inputs are tabled using physical units pertinent to goods/service, such as ton, cubic meter, and so on, the addition has usually no meaning (cannot make the addition). Another point here is "sector." Sector is a set of production units, that is, a set of firms, factories, shops, and so on. The production unit is defined being associated with the definition of goods/and service, with which the coverage of firms, factories, shops, and so on is aggregated into the production unit. The definition of sectors is internationally standardized for, for example, the purpose of meta-analysis. The definition is called—the industrial classification and there are several classifications depending on the minuteness of classification. The I-O tables with different industrial classifications are consistent with each other in the sense that a rough one is obtained by simply aggregating elements of sub-matrices of the I-O table constructed with a minute industrial classification. Sometimes, a specific industrial classification is used for a certain purpose of research which is consistent with I-O table with the international standard classification in the sense that it is made through simple aggregation/disaggregation of sub-matrices or elements of the I-O table constructed one of the standard industrial classifications. Eventually, the goods/service produced by sector i is defined as goods/service i and it is dependent on the adopted industrial classification.

Final Demand and Gross Value Added

It can be said that the economy eventually provides goods and services for the life of the constituents in the economy through production and trade. The figures in the fourth column of Table 4.32 are the amount of goods consumed, utilized for investments, exported, and so on. The column head is named—final demand sector. To see each row in Table 4.32, we can see the trade outlet of each sector. For example, sector 1 sells 20, 30, 20, and 70 million JPY to sector 1, sector 2, sector 3, and the final demand sector, respectively. It can be taken that the final demand is the difference between the total production and the total sale of goods/services to sectors for the production. Investment is a kind of consumption over time through the roundabout production process. Exports are directly or indirectly utilized for the consumption in other regional economies.

To see each column in Table 4.32, we can see inputs (we call—intermediate inputs) of goods/services for the production. For example, sector 1 purchases 20, 45, and 20 million JPY of goods/services produced by sectors 1, 2, and 3, respectively, in order to produce goods/service of 140 million JPY. The sum of intermediate inputs is the total cost for the production and it is 85 million JPY. Assuming the total products can be sold including addition to the inventory, the total sales of sector 1 is 140 million JPY. So, the gross value-added is 55 (=140 − 85) million JPY. The sum of the final demand over all the sectors is equal to the sum of the gross value-added over the all the sectors since: (1) the row sum and the column sum are equal to each other with each sector and (2) the upper-left 3×3 matrix is inclusive to the upper-left 4×4 matrix and the 3×3 matrix is common to the calculation of the final demand (the total products − the total sale for sectors) and value-added (the total sale of products − the total intermediate input costs). This is a logical result of the calculation. However, using macroeconomic terminologies, the equality between the total final demand and the total gross value-added must hold as an identity, thanks to the triangular equality of national incomes.

Primitive Input–Output Analysis

It is said that the input–output analysis was developed by W. Leontief. His motivation was laid on how much additional labor (skilled workers) and/or how much additional capital stock (investment) is necessary in order to meet unusually huge increases in the final demand in such and such sectors. In order to reply these questions, it is essential to know increase in the total production in each sector. His analysis presumes the final demand against each sector is exogenously given and the analysis is focusing on the total product of each sector, which meets the final demand exogenously given. Assuming that the output is linearly dependent on input in each sector, the core of the analysis is reduced to a simple matrix algebra. In order to save the space, we should stop here the explanation of the conventional input–output analysis because readers can refer to any textbook. However, the basic data is the interregional input–output table on which the model is specified and the simulation is conducted in this chapter. It is also the basic data for the analysis developed in Chap. 6. Therefore, we explain a little bit more about the matters which are linked to the construction of the interregional input–output table.

I-O Tables at Purchasers' Price and Producers' Price

Table of Explicit Trades via Commercial Sectors

It is explained in this chapter that there are several types of interregional input–output table and, therefore, several types of model specification using interregional input–output table. Here, it is shown that there could be several types of interregional input–output table depending on the treatment of service sectors, especially commercial and transportation sectors related with the expansion of the national input–output table into the interregional one.

Firstly, we assume a virtual national economy and Table 4.33 summarizes the trades between the sectors (the production units) in a certain year. The unit is million JPY and it is omitted in the explanation as far as there is no confusion. Basically, a cell filled with a symbol, "–," means that it should have no data (or 0). Zero (0) in the cell means that it may have a nonzero data and zero (0) is assumed with the cell for simplicity. Table 4.33 is an example of the data on which the I-O table should be compiled. It should contain various and minute data based on the social statistical survey, economic statistics of different sources, and so on, and it should be taken that the data reflect certain aspects of the real economy although the data must be subject to the data collection errors as usual.

Table 4.33 is constructed based on the following (virtual) records of trades:

(a) Agricultural sector sold the product (agricultural goods) to the sector of wholesale dealer (wholesale sector) and received 300 (million JPY) (the first row says)
(b) Manufacturing sector sold the product (manufactured goods) to wholesale sector and received 800 (second row)
(c) Wholesale sector sold agricultural goods and manufactured goods to the sector of retail (retail sector) and received 345.0 and 920.0, respectively (third and fourth rows)
(d) The fifth, sixth, seventh, and eighth rows, respectively, show sales of goods/service produced by wholesale, agricultural, manufacturing, and retail sectors to agricultural, manufacturing, wholesale, retail, transportation (they are so-called intermediate inputs), and final demand sectors;

(e) In the ninth row, the sales of transportation services: to wholesale sector in order to distribute agricultural goods (fourth column) and manufactured goods (fifth column) from the producers to retail sector through whole sector; and to retail sector in order to distribute agricultural (seventh column) and manufactured goods (eighth column) to the production sectors (agricultural, manufacturing, wholesale, retail, and transportation sectors) and the final demand sector (tenth column)
(f) It is assumed that sale of transportation services (intermediate inputs) to agriculture, manufacturing, wholesale, retail, and transportation sectors is 0 for simplicity (first, second, third, sixth, and ninth column, respectively)
(g) The gross value-added is calculated by the definition:
(h) Gross value-added = total sales − total costs.

For example, as for the wholesale sector (third column):

The total sales are the sum of the sales of dealt products, agricultural goods (third row), and manufactured goods (fourth row), which include the commercial service cost (it is henceforth called—"margin" though the margin in its usual sense is a part of the commercial service cost) of wholesale sector; and the transportation costs for distribution from the producers to retail sector that are born by the wholesale sector and passed forward to retail sector, and the sales of wholesale service as intermediate input for production units (fifth row):

$$345.0 + 920.0 + 20 = 1285.0$$

The total costs are the sum of intermediate inputs into the wholesale sector including margin and transportation costs (the cells of the third column and fifth, sixth, seventh, eighth, and ninth rows):

$$0.0 + 7.6 + 22.8 + 10.0 + 0.0 = 40.4,$$

the buying costs of agricultural goods (first row) and manufactured goods (second row) for the dealing:

$$300 + 800 = 1100, \text{and}$$

the transportation costs (ninth row and fourth and fifth columns) that are born by wholesale sector and pass forward to retail sector:

$$15 + 40 = 55.$$

(i) The gross value-added of wholesale sector is calculated as follows:

$$1285.0 - 40.4 - 1100 - 55 = 89.6$$

(j) The total shipment (product) with Table 4.33 is calculated as follows:

$$300 + 800 + 1285.0 + 1682.0 + 280 = 4347.0$$

Basic Trade Table

Table 4.34 is the so-called basic trade table and it is a direct table of the real trades in the sense that it is compiled on a simple aggregation of various statistical data collected. It is a starting point for the compilation of the I-O table although Table 4.33 may be friendly for most readers because the explanation above is rather close to the daily conversation. Table 4.33 should be constructed rather based on Table 4.34 if necessary. It must be tough to compile any basic trade table based on all kinds of social and economic statistics that are constructed, too, based on statistical sampling surveys of factory shipments, record documents of distance driven by trucks that are required for maintenance, and so on. With the numerical example, it would be easy to compile Table 4.34 being based on the *virtual* trades assumed in Table 4.33 by taking a retrograde step, since the followings are assumed for simplicity:

(a) The margin rate to the cost price is 0.1 and 0.2 for wholesale and retail sectors, respectively and
(b) The transportation cost ratio to the producer's (selling) price is 0.05 and 0.15 for wholesale and retail sectors, respectively.

Actually, we do not need to assume any linearity assumptions in order to construct the I-O table itself based on a basic trade table if the table contains minute data of the distribution costs sector by sector or goods by goods.

As for the trade between wholesale and retail sectors (the cells in first to eighth rows and fourth to eighth columns), it is decomposed into as follows (practically, the following results must be calculated based on minute trade data and distribution cost data obtained by survey and on other statistical sources):

(c) the cost price of agricultural and manufactured goods is 300 and 800, respectively (first and second row)
(d) the margin added by wholesale sector is 30.0 (=300 $\times$ 0.1) and 80(=800 $\times$ 0.1), respectively, with trade of agricultural and manufactured goods (fifth row)
(e) the transportation cost is 15 (=300 $\times$ 0.05) and 40 (=800 $\times$ 0.05) (sixth row)
(f) the intermediate input of wholesale service into retail sector is 5 (seventh row).

As for the trade between commercial sectors and agricultural sector (7th, 9th, 10th, 12th, and 13th row and first column), it is decomposed as follows:

(g) the intermediate input of wholesale services is 5 (seventh row)
(h) the cost price of the intermediate inputs of agricultural and manufactures goods are 50 and 80, respectively (ninth and tenth row)
(i) the margin added by wholesale and retail sectors, which are passed forward, is calculated as follows (11th row):

$$(50 \times 1.1 \times 1.2 - 50) + (80 \times 1.1 \times 1.2 - 80) = 41.6$$

(j) the intermediate input of retail service into agricultural sector is 0 (12th row)
(k) the transportation costs, which are born by wholesale and retail sectors, and passed forward, are calculated as follows (13th row):

$$(50 + 80) \times (0.05 + 0.15) = 26; \text{and}$$

(l) the intermediate input of transportation service into agricultural sector (e.g., business passenger trips) is 0 (15th row).

As for transportation service, the total production must be 280 (15th row) because it is the sum of:

(α) the total transportation costs incurred by the distribution of the goods (agricultural and manufacturing goods, 300 and 800) through wholesale and retail sectors to all the production units is:

$$(300 + 800) \times (0.05 + 0.15) = 220,$$

which is also shown in the total of the 13th row

(β) the final demand (such as leisure passenger trip), 60 (15th row); and
(γ) the intermediate inputs to production units (sectors), which are assumed to be 0 for simplicity (first, second, third, sixth, and ninth columns).

There exists no substantial difference between Tables 4.33 and 4.34. The total shipment is 4347.0 million JPY.

Table of Summarized Figures with Commercial Sectors

Table 4.35 is compiled by aggregating the fourth and fifth (seventh and eighth) columns into the third (sixth) column with Table 4.33, which becomes the third (sixth) column in Table 4.35, respectively. If the third, fourth, and fifth (sixth, seventh, and eighth) rows in Table 4.35 are aggregated into the third (fourth) row, respectively, in the new table, the input–output analysis may be developed based on the new table of 7×7 matrix, in which the interindustrial input–output structure of endogenous sectors correspond to the upper-left corner of 5×5 matrix. As far as technologies are stable in the economy, it should well work. However, it has several problems. The ratio of the sum of margin and transportation cost to the cost price of goods must be dependent on the distribution (commercial and transportation) system. It means that it is difficult to identify whether change in the input–output coefficients, which must be defined as the ratio of intermediate inputs to the total production, is due to change in the substantial technology of the production unit, or due to change in the distribution system.

Explicit Listing of Intermediate Inputs and Final Demand: Input–Output Tables at Purchasers' Price

The natural way to substantially minimize the problems above is to explicitly list intermediate inputs sector by sector. The idea for the construction of Table 4.36 is as follows:

(a) The goods/service sold to production unit (purchasing sector) through the distribution system is taken as intermediates input directly made by the production unit (selling sector), which produces the said goods/service to purchasing sector and it is listed in the I-O table with the value that is defined as the sum of the cost price and all the distribution costs from the factory (selling sector) to purchasing sector.

    The I-O table thus compiled is called—I-O table at purchasers' price and the way of listing above is customarily called—expression in terms of purchasers' price. According to the summation, the so-called JPY value unit must be defined. If the total product of agricultural sector is 150,000 in physical unit, namely ton, then agricultural product of 1 million JPY value unit is defined as 328.95 (=150,000 ÷ 456) ton of agricultural product as far as the idea above is kept through compiling the trades into I-O table. As far as users of the I-O table do not need to know (and it has no meaning to know) how much the total products expressed in JPY value unit is in the physical unit, they do not need to know how much agricultural products of JPY value unit is in the physical unit, for example, how much it is in ton, because "the physical unit" must be a virtual composite. Related with the model in Chaps. 4, 6, and 7, the point is to accept that the JPY value unit is something like a composite goods (including logistics services) and to focus on only "physical parts of the composition" if we are interested in the analysis in terms of physical units since the composition will not change[29] as far as the analysis is made by using the I-O coefficients calculated with the I-O table at purchasers' price to which the said JPY unit is associated.

(b) The goods/service sold to the final demand sector (purchasing sector) through the distribution system is listed in the table as the input to the final demand sector from the production unit (selling sector), which produces the said goods/service and it is listed in the I-O table at purchaser's price.

(c) The margin and transportation costs are listed in the I-O table as follows:

    (c-1) the wholesale, retail, and transportation services sold to production units (including those in the distribution system) are listed in the table as intermediate inputs made by the production units (selling sectors) to purchasing sector with no change (e.g., figures in fifth, eighth, and ninth rows for agricultural sector, which is appearing in the first column in Table 4.33).

[29] This is a basic foundation on which input–output coefficients are defined and they have operational meanings.

This is a natural treatment as the services are directly traded without an idea of logistics services.

(c-2) The commercial margins and transportation cost incurred by the distribution of goods (physical goods only in this numerical example) through the commercial sectors to the final purchasers (which process or consume the said goods) are listed in the table as additional intermediate inputs to (c-1) above from the commercial sectors and transportation sector, respectively, to the sector (selling sector) which produces the said goods (physical goods only).

As for agricultural sector, for example, the sum of (c-1) and (c-2) is decomposed into the following:

[wholesale margin]

The intermediate input of wholesale service into agricultural sector is 5 (seventh row and first column in Table 4.34). The amount of agricultural goods dealt by wholesale sector is 300 (first row and fourth column). Therefore, the figure which is filled in the cell of the third row and first column in Table 4.36 is calculated as follows:

$$5 + 300 \times 0.1 = 35,$$

in which "0.1" is the margin (distribution cost excluding transportation cost) ratio to the cost price (practically, the calculation must be made on minute basic trade table and the operation is basically only addition based on the basic trade).

[retail margin]

The intermediate input of retail service into agriculture is 0 (12th row and first column in Table 4.34). The amount of agricultural goods dealt by retail sector is 300 and it is distributed to production units including retail sector and the final demand sector (shown in the ninth row). Therefore, the figure that is filled in the cell of the fourth row and first column in Table 4.36 is calculated as follows:

$$0.0 + 50 \times 1.1 \times 0.2 + 90 \times 1.1 \times 0.2 + 5 \times 1.1 \times 0.2 + 10 \times 1.1 \times 0.2$$
$$+20 \times 1.1 \times 0.2 + 125 \times 1.1 \times 0.2 = 300 \times 1.1 \times 0.2 = 66,$$

in which: "0.2" is the assumed ratio of retail margin to the cost price including wholesale margin (its ratio is 0.1 to the cost price). Since the margin ratio of retail sector is the same with all the dealing irrespective of purchasers in the numerical example for simplicity, and the amount of agricultural goods dealt by retail sector is 300, the calculation of the second expression in the equation above is easy way to calculate the total retail margin. Usually, the margin ratio should be different among purchasers and the decomposition/inclusion of the commercial margin must go back to the basic trade table. In this sense, the basic trade table is informative and it must be 'basic' in its true sense.

[transportation cost]

The figure which is filled in the cell of the fifth row and the first column (as for agricultural goods) is calculated as follows:

$$0 + 300 \times (0.05 + 0.15) = 60,$$

in which "0.05" and "0.15" are assumed transportation cost ratios to the cost price without retail and wholesale margins, respectively.

The total shipment of goods/service is 2334.0 million JPY in Table 4.36, which is less than that of Table 4.33 (or, Table 4.34) by 2013.0 million JPY. In Table 4.33, the following is twice or thrice included into the total shipment:

1. the cost price of the goods dealt (thrice)

$$300 + 800 + 300 + 800 = 2200$$

2. wholesale margin (twice)

$$(300 + 800) * 0.1 = 110$$

3. transportation cost (wholesale thrice, retail twice)

$$(300 + 800) * (0.05 + 0.05 + 0.15) = 275$$

4. total which should be deducted from the total shipment in Table 4.33

$$2200 + 110 + 275 = 2585$$

On the other hand, the following is included twice in Table 4.36:

5. commercial margin (twice)

$$(300 + 800) \times (0.1 + 1.1 * 0.2) = 352.$$

6. transportation cost (twice)

$$(300 + 800) \times (0.05 + 0.15) = 220.$$

7. total which should be deducted from the total shipment in Table 4.36

$$352 + 220 = 572.$$

Therefore, the following equation holds:

$$4347 - 2585 = 2334 - 572 = 1762 \tag{4.166}$$

Communication Services and Electric Power

In the numerical example mentioned previously, commercial sectors and transportation sectors provide typical service in the sense that most demand against the service is a derivative demand as far as the objective of the demand is not the consumption of service itself which produces directly an increment in the welfare of consumer. Such and such sector needs (demands) input of goods produced by other sector and usually two sectors are spatially remoted from each other, which derives demand against transportation service. It is called—derivative demand. Another typical derivative demand is demand against insurance services.

The modern society is very complicated and there are many kinds of derivative demand. Other typical example is derivative demand against communication services. The communication (telecommunication, postal, transmission line [in case carrier is operated by other company], etc.) costs incurred by the negotiation with trades of goods/service should be listed in the input–output table just same as the listing of transportation costs although the communication costs incurred by the negotiation with which contract is not concluded must be attributed to other related contract concluded.

The electric power can be treated as usual physical goods in terms of listing the intermediate input and consumption of the electricity power in the I-O table. However, the business of power generation and transmission are operated by different companies and nowadays it becomes usual even in Japan. Precisely speaking, the derivative demand against the transmission service should be listed in the same way as the case of the derivative demand against commercial service and transportation service.

CIF (Cost, Insurance, Freight) Price and FOB Price

CIF is one of the trade terms that shall condition the price with which the goods exported is delivered to the dealer at the port (airport) in the importing country so that all the costs (e.g., purchase cost at the factory in the exporting country, insurance (risk), transportation costs from the factory to the imported country, etc.) shall be paid (born) by the exporter. The price with which the international trade is made under the trade term of CIF is called—CIF price.

FOB is one of the trade terms that shall condition the price with which the goods exported is delivered to the importing dealer at the exporting port (airport, etc.) after the embarkment of the goods on the ship or airplane, and so on, in the exporting country so that all the costs (e.g., purchase cost at the factory in the exporting country, insurance (risk), transportation costs from the factory to the exporting port, etc.) shall be paid (born) by the exporter and all the costs incurred by the transportation from the exporting port to the importing port, land transportation, risk, and so on, shall be paid (born) by the importing dealer. The price with which the international trade is made under the trade term of FOB is called—FOB price.

CIF and the I-O Table at Purchasers' Price

A same idea of the trade term, CIF, can be applied to the construction of the input–output table. To see a certain row in the I-O table, it can be assumed that purchasing sectors receive goods on-site under a kind of the trade term of CIF. All the distribution costs from the production units to the gates of factory or household are born by selling sectors and all the costs are passed forward to purchasers. It can be taken that the input–output table at purchasers' price explained previously is constructed based on the trade term of CIF.

Input–Output Table at Producers' Price and FOB

An idea of the trade term of FOB can be applied to the construction of input–output table (Table 4.37), too. To see a certain column in the I-O table, it can be assumed that purchasing sector (production unit or final demand sector) receives goods at the factory gates of selling sectors under a kind of the trade term of FOB. It implies that the cost price of goods for purchasing sector is the price at the gate of production unit where the said goods are delivered to the said purchasing sector under the rule of FOB, namely all the necessary distribution costs (commercial services, transportation cost, etc.) of goods from the gate of production unit where the said goods are delivered to purchasing sector are born by the said purchasing sector.

Assuming FOB trade rule, we may specify the way of listing trades in the input–output table as follows:

(a) The goods/service sold to production unit (purchasing sector) through the distribution system is taken as intermediate input made by the production unit of the said goods/service (selling sector) and it is listed in the I-O table with the value at the cost price.
(b) The goods/service sold to the final demand sector (purchasing sector) through the distribution system is listed in the table as input to the said purchasing sector from the production (selling sector) unit which produces the said goods/service.
(c) The margins and transportation cost are listed as follows:

  (c-1) the wholesale, retail, and transportation services sold to the production units (including those in the distribution system) are listed in the table as intermediate inputs into the said production units (purchasing sectors) with no change (e.g., in Table 4.34, the figures are in 7th, 12th, and 15th rows of the first column as for agricultural sector)
  (c-2) the commercial margins and transportation cost incurred by the distribution of goods (physical goods only in this numerical example) through the commercial sectors from production unit (selling sector) to the final purchasers (which process or consume the said goods) are listed in the table as intermediate inputs from the commercial sectors and transportation sector to the said purchasing sector, respectively, and they are added to (c-1) above.

As for agricultural sector, for example, the sum of (c-1) and (c-2) is decomposed into the following:

[wholesale margin]

The intermediate input of wholesale service into agricultural sector is 5 (seventh row and first column in Table 4.34). The amount of agricultural goods and manufactured goods purchased by agricultural sector is 50 (ninth row and first column in Table 4.34) and 80 (tenth row and first column in Table 4.34), respectively. Therefore, the total wholesale margin that is listed in the cell of the third row and first column in Table 4.37 is calculated as follows:

$$5 + (50 + 80) \times 0.1 = 18,$$

in which "0.1" is assumed margin (distribution cost excluding transportation cost) ratio to the cost price.

[retail margin]

The intermediate input of retail service into agriculture is 0 (12th row and first column in Table 4.34). Therefore, the total retail margin that is listed in the cell of the fourth row and first column in Table 4.37 is calculated as follows:

$$0 + (50 + 80) \times 1.1 \times 0.2 = 28.6,$$

in which: "0.2" is the assumed ratio of retail margin to the cost price including wholesale margin (its ratio is 0.1 to the cost price).

[transportation cost]

The figure that is filled in the cell of the fifth row and the first column in Table 4.37 (as for agricultural goods) is calculated as follows:

$$(50 + 80) \times (0.05 + 0.15) = 26,$$

in which "0.05" and "0.15" are assumed transportation cost ratios to the cost price with the delivery of goods: from factory to retail; and retail to purchaser without margins, respectively.

The total shipment of goods/service is 1762 million JPY, which is less than that of Table 4.36 by 572 million JPY. The difference is exactly equal to the sum of margins and transportation costs listed twice in Table 4.36 (See Eq. (4.166)).

As the total product of agricultural sector is 150,000 in physical unit, for example, ton as assumed above and JPY value unit with the I-O table at producers' price is calculated with agricultural products as follows:

$$150,000 \div 300 = 500 \text{ ton/million JPY}.$$

JPY value unit with the I-O table at purchasers' price is 328.95 ton/JPY million as calculated previously.

I-O Table at Purchasers' Price Versus Producers' Price

Numerical Example 2

Table 4.38 is another virtual numerical example in order to discuss the relation between the I-O table at purchasers' price and producers' price. Table 4.39 shows (average) rates of distribution costs to the amount of goods traded. For example, in Table 4.38 the cell in the intersection of fifth row and seventh column (it is henceforth expressed as— $T\_basic\_org(5,7)$) is 55.0 million JPY (henceforth, we omit "Million JPY" so far as no confusion) and it is the "distribution costs" (including margins in its true sense) taken by wholesale sector and forwarded to the retail sector with the trade of agricultural product ($T\_basic\_org(3,7)$= 550.0). There should be plural companies in the wholesale sector and their margins should be different among them. It was observed that the total agricultural products dealt by them were 550.0 and the total distribution costs taken by them were 55.0 in a certain specific year with the virtual economy. The figure in the cell of the intersection of first row and fourth column in Table 4.39 shows that the rate of the margin, which was taken by the wholesale sector and forwarded to retail sector, to the total amount of agricultural goods dealt by wholesale sector, which was all sold to retail sector, was 0.1 on average. $T\_basic\_org(6,7) = 82.5$ is the transportation cost related to the trade between the agricultural sector (seller) and retail sector (purchaser) and its rate to the total amount of agricultural goods at the cost price was 0.15, which is shown in the cell of fifth row and fourth column in Table 4.39.

$T\_basic\_org(8,2)$ = 90.0 is the amount of agricultural goods in terms of JPY unit which was sold by retail sector to manufacturing sector (as intermediate inputs of materials). $T\_basic\_org(9,2)$ = 9.0 is the amount of margin taken by wholesale sector and forwarded to retail sector, which must be 10% of the agricultural goods sold to manufacturing sector at the cost price. Here, we assume that all the goods once purchased by wholesale sector will be sold to retail sector for simplicity. Also, it is assumed that retail sector can purchase goods only through the trade with wholesale sector for simplicity. In reality, there should be many trades between companies belonging to wholesale sector and between companies belonging to retail sector. Those complicated trades can be simplified at the compilation of the basic trade table by aggregating margins, which are added and forwarded through the trades by assuming a virtual wholesale (retail) company. Anyway, even we may assume there are no such trades and the assumptions made in this appendix are not substantial for the discussion of topics here.

Thus, $T\_basic\_org(9,2)$ (= 9.0) is calculated as 90×0.1. $T\_basic\_org(10,2)$ shows margin taken by retail sector and forwarded to manufacturing sector (purchaser). It was 24.75 and its rate to the purchased price ($99 = 90 + 9$) of agricultural goods was 0.25, which is shown in the cell of third row and second column in Table 4.39, namely $99 \times 0.25 = 24.75$.$T\_basic\_org(11,2)$ (= 20.7) is the sum of transportation costs: (a) taken by wholesale sector in order to deliver agricultural goods from the producer to retail sector or warehouse located somewhere and (b) taken by retail sector and forwarded to purchasers for the delivery from wholesale sector (or warehouse) to purchasers. The former was 13.5 (= 90 × 0.15) and the latter must be 7.2 (90 × 0.08) on average. Practically speaking, it can be said that the rate of transportation cost taken by retail sector to the amount of agricultural goods traded between retail sector (sellers) and manufacturing sector (purchaser) was 0.08 (=7.2 ÷ 90) on average based on a basic trade table constructed with real data collected via survey, and so on, which is listed in the cell of seventh row and second column in Table 4.39. $T\_basic\_org(12,2)$ (= 54.45 = 9 + 24.75 + 20.7) is the sum of distribution cost taken by retail sector (seller) and forwarded to manufacturing sector (purchaser).

The transportation cost should be dependent on the haul and not on who is the purchaser. However, supposed variance in the transportation costs in Table 4.39 can well represent producers and consumers are located over the geographical space. Again, it must be noted that practically, Table 4.38 must be constructed based on the so-called basic trade table that is compiled based on various surveys and statistical data sources. It is obvious that we can construct a kind of Table 4.38 based on a basic trade table when it is available. It can be said that Table 4.38 shows a certain substantial aspect of the virtual economy in the sense that it can be linked to the basic trade table of the virtual economy which has more minute information of trades and shipments.

Tables 4.40 and 4.41 are I-O table at purchasers' price and producers' prices, respectively, which are constructed on the numerical example 2. For example, the figures listed in the cell of first row and second column (it is henceforth called as— $IO\_Table\_pur(1,2)$) are 144.45 and calculated as follows:

$$\begin{aligned}&T\_basic\_org(8,2)+T\_basic\_org(9,2)+T\_basic\_org(10,2)\\&\quad+T\_basic\_org(11,2)\\&\quad=T\_basic\_org(8,2)+T\_basic\_org(12,2)=144.45\end{aligned}$$

Also, for example, $IO\_table\_pur(4,2)$ (=309.225) is calculated as follows:

$$T\_basic\_org(19,2)+T\_basic\_org(15,11)=0+309.225=309.225$$

On the other hand, the figure listed in the cell of third row and first column in Table 4.41 (it is henceforth called as— $IO\_table\_pro(3,1)$) is 37.5 and it is calculated as follows:

$$T\_basic\_org(7,1)+T\_basic\_org(9,1)+T\_basic\_org(14,1)=37.5$$

Also, $IO\_table\_pro(5,2)$ (=92.7) is calculated as follows:

$$\begin{aligned}&T\_basic\_org(19,2)+T\_basic\_org(11,2)+T\_basic\_org(16,2)\\&\quad=0.0+20.7+72=92.7\end{aligned}$$

Tables 4.42 and 4.43 are input–output coefficients, which correspond to the input–output tables of Tables 4.40 and 4.41, respectively. Tables 4.44 and 4.45 are the Leontief inverse matrix, which corresponds to the input–output coefficients of Tables 4.42 and 4.43, respectively.

Importance of the Basic Trade Table

It can be considered that the input–output analysis abstracts the substance of the economy in terms of the input–output coefficient and the Leontief (inverse) matrix based on the basic trade table. It is well-known that the solvable condition holds if the input–output coefficient matrix is constructed based on the basic trade table of the actual economy. Due to the solvability condition, users of the I-O analysis have not paid much attention to the basic trade table once they obtain the input–output coefficient data. However, the input–output analysis makes the linearity assumption and presumes no technological changes in the production activities. As far as these assumptions are admitted, we should be able to construct the basic trade table which corresponds to the results of the input–output analysis given a new (nonnegative) final demand vector. In order to simplify the analysis, we define several terms.

[Original basic trade table] The basic trade table on which the input–output coefficients are calculated and the input–output analysis is developed for such and such study purposes.

[Original final demand vector] The final demand vector is constructed on the original basic trade table.

Our proposition and conjectures are as follows:

[Proposition 1] A basic trade table can be constructed based on the results of the input–output analysis with the original final demand vector at purchasers' (producers') price by keeping the listing rules of purchasers' (producers') table that includes constant distribution parameters, respectively. The basic trade tables thus constructed are the same as the original basic trade table.

It looks obvious and has no meaning but it is important in the sense that a possibility exists that a basic trade table can be constructed based on results of the input–output analysis with a final demand vector. Once a basic trade table can be constructed which corresponds to the results of the input–output analysis with a final demand vector at purchasers' (producers') price, the I-O table at producers' (purchasers') price can be constructed based on the basic trade table thus obtained and the same basic trade table can be constructed based on the results of the input–output analysis with the final demand vector at producers' (purchasers') price, respectively.

Here, it must be noted that we need "the basic trade table" in order to know the final demand vector at producers' (purchasers') price, which corresponds to an exogenously given (and independently given from the original basic trade table) final demand vector at purchasers' (producers') price, respectively.

Historically, it was argued which rule of listing table is superior, at purchasers' price or producers' price. It can be said that they are substantially the same and both sides of a coin if the basic trade table can be constructed on the input–output analysis with a given final demand vector since once it is constructed the input–output analysis with the final demand vector that is constructed with the other rule for listing table can be done and the same basic trade table can be constructed based on the results of input–output analysis with the other rule for listing table.

While writing this appendix, the author has conducted simulation with the original basic trade table shown in Table 4.38 and the rule for listing table: (1) sets of the rules listed in (a)–(c) in sections of "Explicit Listing of Intermediate Inputs and Final Demand: Input–Output Tables at Purchasers' Price" and "Input–Output Table at Producers' Price and FOB" above and (2) the specification of parameters of the distribution cost shown in Table 4.39. After conducting several cases of simulation with variants of the final demand vector, the author has obtained the following, which should be just conjectures at this moment. Deepening the analysis further is not directly related to the topic of this book, it should be done using other opportunities.

[Proposition (conjecture) 2] The basic trade table cannot necessarily be constructed based on the input–output analysis with a given (nonnegative) final demand vector by keeping the rules in any sense which are applied to the construction of basic trade table and I-O tables at producers' price and purchasers' price, respectively.

Proposition 2 is generally true because the composition of distribution services which are attributed to shipment sector as intermediate inputs of distribution services must be changed responding to the composition of final demand. This means we cannot find out a basic trade table which describes the new economy which is given by (and, reversely, sustains) a new final demand. This is a kind of inconsistency and it will be shown how it can be solved in Chap. 7.

[Proposition (conjecture) 3] Start with the input–output coefficient matrix at purchasers' price. If and only if the basic trade table (call it—Table_pur) can be constructed based on the results of the input–output analysis with an exogenously given final demand vector (at purchasers' price if it could be constructed), then the input–output table based on thus constructed basic trade table gives the input–output coefficients at producers' price, which are same as the input–output coefficients based on the original basic trade table. And, the basic trade table (call it—Table_pro) can be constructed based on the results of the input–output analysis with the input–output coefficients with the final demand vector at producers' price that is constructed based on Table_pur. Table_pur and Table_pro are equal to each other. Analogically, same as for starting with the input–output coefficients at producers' price.

[Proposition (conjecture) 4]

If and only if a nonnegative final demand vector can be exogenously given which is consistent with the listing rules of the basic trade table including distribution cost parameters, a basic trade table can be constructed based on the results of the input-output analysis with the given non-negative final demand.

Proposition 3 means that (if it is true) the comparison between the results of the input–output analysis with the input–output coefficient matrix at purchasers' and producers' price can be meaningful only if the results can give a basic trade table and, in that case, they have no difference. Due to the solvability condition, for example, Hawkins–Simon condition, actually we can have results of the input–

output analysis with any nonnegative final demand vector at purchasers' (producers') price. So, we would face a serious problem if we cannot construct a basic trade table because we cannot know what trades are made among sectors and how they are able to be traded in terms of a basic trade table. In that case, we even cannot know what is the final demand vector at producers' (purchasers') price which corresponds to the given final demand vector at purchasers' (producers') price, respectively.

Proposition 4, if it is true, raises a question of how we can understand the results of the input–output analysis with a given nonnegative final demand vector (it does not matter how and why it can be given) when a basic trade table cannot be constructed based on the results as far as we must keep the rule for listing basic trade table and input–output tables.

Treatment of Distributional Costs in the Interregional Input–Output Programming Model

The novelty of the model developed in this chapter is that potential improvements in the transportation network owing to the public investments is represented (evaluated) by installing alternative shipment activities, which reflect decreases in distribution costs of the intra- and interregional shipment of commodities and the conventional (rigid) interregional input–output model is extended to the programming model to be able to derive a set of optimal public investment targets in the transportation network. The installment is made by using the interregional input–output table at purchasers' price. We will show that the model construction must be based on the interregional input–output table at purchasers' price, especially at that time.

Installment of the Transportation Network Dimension into the Interregional Input–Output Model

Using Table 4.38, we explain briefly the installment of the alternative shipment activities at purchasers' price into the interregional input–output model. For simplicity of the analysis, we may assume that the five sectors and final demand sector (household) are located over space, which means that sectors can be taken as regions remoted from each other. It can be considered that the distance friction between the sectors causes different transportation and other distribution costs with the trade of physical goods. Further, we may assume later on, for simplicity of the analysis, that the transportation costs only vary with the improvements in the transportation network, thanks to public investments, of which optimality is the main topic of this book.

In terms of Table 4.40, we first decompose the activities of agricultural and manufacturing sectors into shipment activities using: (a) Tables 4.40 and 4.41; (b)

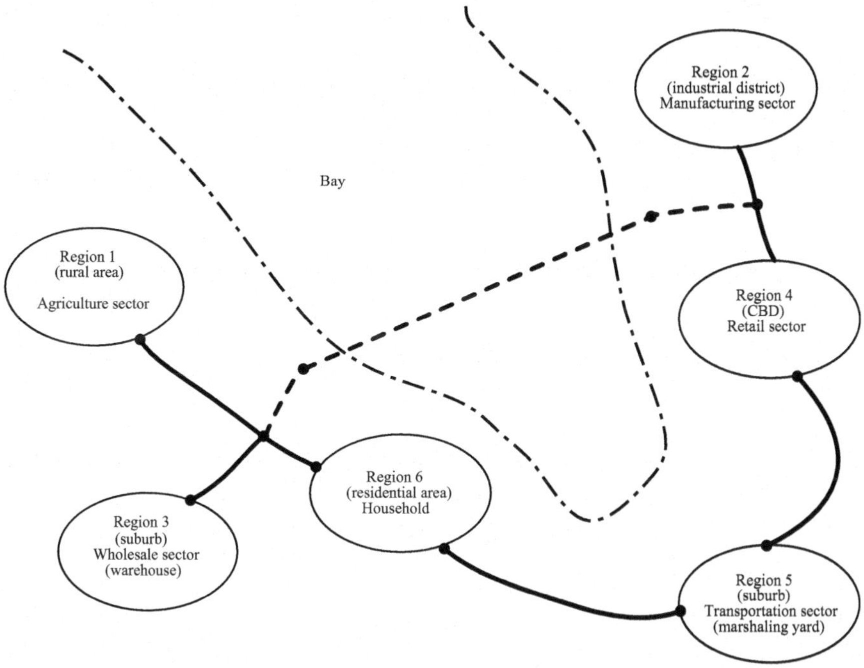

Fig. 4.1 Image of the spatial distribution of sectors

Tables 4.42 and 4.43 and (c) Tables 4.44 and 4.45, which are the Leontief inverse matrix at purchasers' price and producers' prices; respectively.

Image of Spatial Distribution of the Five Sectors and the Final Demand Sector

Figure 4.1 shows an image of the spatial distribution of the five sectors and the final demand sector on a virtual transportation network. Without loss of generality, as far as the explanation is concerned with how to construct shipment activities with the transportation network, we may assume that each region is located at by only one sector and each sector locates at only one region. Namely, agricultural sector is located in region 1, manufacturing sector is in region 2, wholesale sector in region 3, retail sector in region 4, transportation sector in region 5, and final demand sector in region 6.[30]

[30] Precisely speaking, the final demand sector should be composed of a several different sectors, namely household as consumers, private and public sectors as entities of making investments (to increase the physical private capital stock and social infrastructures), wholesale sector which deals international exports and imports, etc. For simplicity of the analysis, we only consider household as an entity which consumes the final demand goods. Substance is not changed by the simplification and any differentiation of the final demand sector has no meaning unless distribution of the value-added mechanism is specified, which beyond the topic in this Appendix.

It may be interpreted that wholesale sector can be located anywhere but the location of, for example, warehouse or logistics center if exist does matter in terms of transportation of physical goods (commodities). Or, even wholesale company can exist, which has neither warehouse nor logistics center. In the former case, the transportation cost paid by wholesale sector and forwarded to retail sector is the costs incurred by the delivery from factory to warehouse or logistics center. In the latter case, it is the cost incurred by the delivery from the factory to retail shop. In this case, the transportation cost can be taken as the sum of: (a) the transportation cost paid by wholesale sector and forwarded to retail sector and (b) the transportation cost paid by retail sector and forwarded to purchaser (production units and household) together with the transportation cost forwarded to by wholesale sector. In the numerical example 2, the ratio of the transportation cost to the cost price between wholesale and retail sector is 0.1:0.07 (figure in the cell of sixth row and fourth column vs. figure in the cell of eighth row and first column in Table 4.39) as for the shipment of manufacturing goods into agricultural sector.

Precisely speaking, shipment activities, which represent trades of goods between sectors and regions, should be decomposed into several shipment activities according to the number of delivery routes from factory to retail warehouse/logistic center/shop because wholesale margin should be subtly or drastically different depending on the dealing process. In this case, distribution parameters should become more minutes depending on which dealing process is used for which trade of goods. With a certain dealing process of certain goods, both margin and transportation costs can be zero with wholesale (retail) sector, which means wholesale (retail) sector does not commit to the said dealing process of the said goods, respectively. Practically, it should be the case in which a company belongs to wholesale (retail) sector in usual sense and the same company does function of retail (wholesale) sector as well, respectively. In this case, the said wholesale (retail) company's activities should be decomposed into wholesale and retail activities and they should be listed in the basic trade table as wholesale and retail activities.

The variety of shipment activities thus categorized is different from the one that is simply due to difference in delivery routes on the transportation network, which categorizes shipment activities in terms of difference in the incurred transportation costs. At this moment, we do not consider such variants of shipment activities due to difference in the dealing process through wholesale and retail sectors, for simplicity of the explanation.

Same story holds as for retail sector and nowadays it is more complicated. Some of goods "purchased" by customers who visited shops are taken home by customers, which mean that goods taken home were delivered into retail shops. Most cases are that customers who visited retail shop make purchasing contracts only and "purchased" goods are delivered from warehouse to customers' house (it is more complicated that sometimes warehouse or logistics center is utilized by wholesale sector as well). With the former case, the transportation cost paid by retail sector and forwarded to purchasers together with the transportation cost forwarded to by wholesale sector is the cost incurred by the delivery from warehouse to retail shop. With the latter case, the transportation cost that purchasers pay is the sum of: (i) transportation cost from factory to warehouse paid by wholesale sector and forwarded by to retail sector and (ii) the transportation cost from warehouse to purchasers' house paid by retail sector and forwarded by to purchasers.

Region 1, where agricultural sector is located, can be taken as the rural area close the city. Region 2, where manufacturing sector is located, is the industrial district in the city. Region 3, where warehouse/logistics center of wholesale sector is located, is the suburb of the city. Region 4, where shop of retail sector is located, is the CBD. If warehouse/logistics center of retail sector is *not* located in region 4, we do not need to specify where it is located on the transportation network. Only we must know the transportation cost from warehouse/logistics center to: (a) retail shop or (b) purchasers of production units or household and we assume the transportation cost is constant irrespective of dealing process for simplicity of the explanation.

Region 5, where transportation sector is located, is the suburb of the city. Actually, it does not matter where transportation sector is located in the sense that the substance of explanation itself is not affected by the location because we have no idea of the shipment of "transportation services." Only the matter is which region the gross value-added of transportation sector should be attributed to. Practically, it should be decided by the reality. It seems consistent with the definition of the FOB term of trades that in each region where sectors other than transportation sector are located should have a sector of transportation, which is consistent with the utilization of the input–output table at purchasers' price. However, it does not necessarily in reality.

Region 5 can be a marshaling yard and out-of-service train, trucks, and so on, can be sent to regions where the demand against transportation services is generated. Considering that most cargo trucks are driven with no cargo on board on the one way, it should be good to simplify the numerical example for the explanation although nowadays the loading ratio is increasing due to several reasons and it becomes possible owing to the logistics center committed by several different companies, which is powered by advanced IT technologies.

Region 6, where household(s) is located, is the residential area of the city. As for the explanation in this section, household can be located anywhere, too. The transportation cost of passenger trip to go for shopping should be taken as the consumption (inputs) of passenger trip services and it is not explicitly treated in the numerical example for simplicity. As for passenger car trips, which may be utilized for shopping and taking purchased goods home, for example, passenger car trips for a shopping mall in the suburb, they should be taken as production and consumption of passenger car trips. It is not explicitly treated in the numerical example due to the same reason.

It should be noted that Table 4.38 is also the basic trade table on which the interregional input–output table can be constructed with the setting of spatial distribution of sectors and non-substantial assumptions for simplicity of the analysis. Therefore, the input–output tables in Tables 4.41 and 4.42 can be taken as interregional input–output tables at purchasers' price and producers' price with the economy of six regions and five sectors. It looks that the example is unusual as an interregional input–output table, not suitable for the explanation of (interregional) shipment activities. However, it represents a rather usual case because the completeness[31] of regional economy in the sense that all the sectors with any classification are located and active in the region does not hold if the specification of regions becomes spatially minute. And, the numerical example is good enough to learn the construction of shipment activities.

Decomposition of the Input–Output Activity into Shipment Activities

[Decomposition rule 1]

Only production activity (in the sense of Leontief system) of *non-service sectors* are decomposed to several shipment activities depending on the difference in input of (logistics) service sectors to non-service sectors, which is due to the difference in logistics costs that may be caused by the difference in distance friction, customs for dealing process through wholesale to retail sector, and so on. However, input coefficients of non-service (non-logistics service) are invariant with the decomposition.

[Decomposition rule 2]

The interregional input–output (we henceforth call it—IRIO) table and the (original) basic trade table on which the IRIO table is constructed should be used for the decomposition.

Rule 1 presumes services are provided anywhere without the friction of distance. In the numerical example for the explanation, each of service (logistics) sectors can survive only in a certain region.

If the original basic trade is not available (nowadays probability is very low), we need to construct (estimate) the basic trade table. It should be a tough job due to Conjecture 2 above to consistently construct the basic trade table based on the results of the IRIO analysis. Anyway, in case the (original) basic trade table is available, it goes smoothly.

[Decomposition rule 3]

IRIO coefficients at purchasers' price should be used.

This is due to a practical reason as we will see later.

[Decomposition rule 4]

[31] In this chapter, it is assumed that each region has transportation sector and the demand against transportation services induced by shipments of goods is made by the transportation sector which is located in the origin region of shipment. This assumption is useful in the sense that we do not need to be bothered by from which region transportation service should be purchased in the model specification. Only one sector which is most effective in production of transportation services, can survive in case we do not make the assumption above in the optimization model and it becomes unusual extreme. Once the transportation sector (service sectors) exists in each region, this assumption is natural one following the FOB terms of trade.

The decomposition procedure must be specified with which the delivery costs shall be calculated depending on the physical amount of traded goods.

As far as the basic trade table is concerned, we need Decomposition rule 4 because the delivery costs are just data based on the survey and estimates on other statistical sources. However, we need a rule in order to decompose the production activity into shipment activities consistently with the basic trade table. As for the numerical example, we simply assume that the delivery costs are linearly dependent on the physical amount of goods (i.e., at the cost price, practically) traded sector by sector and region by region. The parameters are given in Table 4.39. We need the following rule as the basic trade table itself has no idea of "purchasers" price,' explicitly. It is a concrete version of Decomposition rule 4.

[Decomposition rule 5]

The delivery cost parameters shall be specified so that they can be multiplied to the amount of traded goods at purchasers' price.

We need this rule due to Decomposition rule 3.

[Decomposition rule 6]

The intermediate input coefficients of wholesale, retail, and transportation sector in the production activity shall be replaced by the rate of the sum of: (a) the distribution costs of wholesale margin, retail margin, and transportation cost; and (b) intermediate inputs by the distribution sectors of wholesale, retail, and transportation sectors to the amount of goods shipped into the region where the sector that purchases the goods is located.

It should be noted that "the amount of goods shipped into ..." is the amount at purchasers' price due to Decomposition rule 5.

[Decomposition rule 7]

The coefficient of gross value-added should be adjusted so that sum of coefficients of the shipment activity is thus decomposed and the coefficient of gross value-added becomes one.

Owing to this rule, improvements in transportation infrastructures can be evaluated as increases in GDP/NNP that is defined as the sum of GRP/NRP over regions.

Illustration by the Numerical Example: Activities of Agricultural Sector

They are shown with the submatrix of 6×6 in the upper-left corner of Table 4.46. By picking up the first column vector of the sub-matrix, we explain the decomposition procedure (in order to know how to construct shipment activities backward starting with a basic trade table (and logistics (distribution) cost parameters).

$$\begin{bmatrix} v_{11}^{11} \\ v_{21}^{11} \\ v_{31}^{11} \\ v_{41}^{11} \\ v_{51}^{11} \\ va_1^{11} \end{bmatrix} = \begin{bmatrix} 0.0892857142857143 \\ 0.2436185363716040 \\ 0.0887379491673970 \\ 0.2024539877300610 \\ 0.1226993865030670 \\ 0.2532044259421560 \end{bmatrix}$$

$$= \begin{bmatrix} 0 \\ 0 \\ \overline{a}_{31}^{11} \\ \overline{a}_{41}^{11} \\ \overline{a}_{51}^{11} \\ 0 \end{bmatrix} + \begin{bmatrix} a_{11}^{1} \\ a_{21}^{1} \\ a_{31}^{1} \\ a_{41}^{1} \\ a_{51}^{1} \\ va_1^{1} \end{bmatrix}$$

$$= \begin{bmatrix} 0.0892857142857143 \\ 0.2436185363716040 \\ w\_margin(1,4) \times d(9,1)/d(8,1) + T\_basic\_org(7,1)/d(8,7) \\ (1 + w\_margin(1,4)) * r\_margin(3,1)) * d(9,1)/d(8,1) + T\_basic\_org(19,1)/d(8,7) \\ (w\_trans(5,4) + r\_trans(7,1)) * d(9,1)/d(8,1) + T\_basic\_org(20,1)/d(8,7) \\ 1 - \sum_{j=1}^{5} v_{ji}^{11} \end{bmatrix} \tag{4.167}$$

in which: v_{ij}^{pq}: the definition is given in the text in this chapter, namely the coefficient of intermediate input of goods i in region p in order to make a unit shipment of goods j into region q (i = 1, 2, 3, 4, 5; j = 1, 2; p = j; $q = 1, 2, 3, 4, 5, 6$)$\overline{a}_{ij}^{pq}$: input coefficient of ith goods (service) to jth sector in region p in order to ship one unit of jth goods from region p to region q ($i = 3, 4, 5; j = 1, 2; p = j; q = 1, 2, 3, 4, 5, 6$)$a_{ij}^{p}$: input coefficients of ith goods in order to produce one unit jth goods in region p, which are given by input–output coefficients of interregional input–output table at purchasers' price (Table 4.42)

$w\_margin(i,j)$, $r\_margin(i,j)$, $w\_trans(i,j)$, and $r\_trans(i,j)$: the values in the cell of ith row and jth column in Table 4.39

$d(i,j)$: the value in the cell of ith row and jth column in Table 4.46

$T\_basic\_org(i,j)$: the value in the cell of ith row and jth column in Table 4.38

va_j^{pq}: the value-added produced by a unit shipment of goods j (from sector j) in region p to region q.

In the first term of the third element of the last column vector in Eq. (4.167), $w\_margin(1,4) \times d(9,1)$ is inputs of wholesale services incurred by shipment of $d(8,1)$, which is a part of the total products, $d(8,7)$, at purchasers' price. This is the reason why $w\_margin(1,4) \times d(9,1)$ is denominated by $d(8,1)$. In the second term of the third element of the last column vector in Eq. (4.167), $T\_basic\_org(7,1)$ is intermediate input of wholesale service to produce $d(8,7)$. This is the reason why $T\_basic\_org(7,1)$ is denominated by $d(8,7)$. Namely, the third column vector in Eq. (4.167) is a delivery cost vector which is associated to the shipment of agricultural goods to region 1. The fourth column vector in Eq. (4.167) is an input–output coefficient vector which is associated to the production of agricultural goods in region 1. This is a conventional input–output coefficient vector of agricultural sector in region 1 at purchasers' price apart from logistics costs.

We will show another example by picking up the sixth column vector of the sub-matrix. It is calculated as follows:

$$\begin{bmatrix} v_{11}^{16} \\ v_{21}^{16} \\ v_{31}^{16} \\ v_{41}^{16} \\ v_{51}^{16} \\ va_{1}^{16} \end{bmatrix} = \begin{bmatrix} 0.0892857142857143 \\ 0.2436185363716040 \\ 0.0851917241239550 \\ 0.1907514450867050 \\ 0.1734104046242770 \\ 0.2177421755077430 \end{bmatrix}$$

$$= \begin{bmatrix} 0.0892857142857143 \\ 0.2436185363716040 \\ w\_margin(1,4) \times d(9,6)/d(8,6) + T\_basic\_org(7,1)/d(8,7) \\ (1 + w\_margin(1,4)) * r\_margin(3,6)) * d(9,6)/d(8,6) + T\_basic\_org(19,1)/d(8,7) \\ (w\_trans(5,4) + r\_trans(7,6)) * d(9,6)/d(8,6) + T\_basic\_org(20,1)/d(8,7) \\ 1 - \sum_{j=1}^{5} v_{ji}^{16} \end{bmatrix}. \quad (4.168)$$

Illustration by the Numerical Example: Shipment Activities of Manufacturing Sector

They are shown with the submatrix of 6×6 in the upper-left corner of Table 4.47. We also pick up some of the shipment activities to explain the decomposition. The first column vector of the sub-matrix is given as follows:

$$\begin{bmatrix} v_{12}^{21} \\ v_{22}^{21} \\ v_{32}^{21} \\ v_{42}^{21} \\ v_{52}^{21} \\ va_2^{21} \end{bmatrix} = \begin{bmatrix} 0.0678097384079147 \\ 0.2467344998767740 \\ 0.0571985118151209 \\ 0.1770657672849920 \\ 0.1146711635750420 \\ 0.3365203190401570 \end{bmatrix}$$

$$= \begin{bmatrix} 0.067809738407915 \\ 0:246734499876774 \\ w\_margin(2,4) \times d(9,1)/d(8,1) + T\_basic\_org(7,2)/d(8,7) \\ (1 + w\_margin(2,4)) * r\_margin(4,1)) * d(9,1)/d(8,1) + T\_basic\_org(19,2)/d(8,7) \\ (w\_trans(6,4) + r\_trans(8,1)) * d(9,1)/d(8,1) + T\_basic\_org(20,2)/d(8,7) \\ 1 - \sum_{j=1}^{5} v_{ji}^{21} \end{bmatrix}, \tag{4.169}$$

in which all symbols are the same as symbols in section of "Illustration by the Numerical Example: Activities of Agricultural Sector" above except that the reference table, Table 4.46 should be replaced by Table 4.47.

In tenth row of Tables 4.46 and 4.47, the earned gross value-added is calculated with the shipments of goods by agricultural sector and manufacturing sector that are given in first row and second row in Table 4.40 or eighth row in Tables 4.46 and 4.47, respectively.

The gross value-added of shipment is calculated as, for example, $d(6,3) \times d(8,3) = d(10,3)$ with the shipment of agricultural goods (produced in region 1) to wholesale sector (in region 3). The gross value-added of agricultural and manufacturing sectors, which are calculated as $\sum_{j=1}^{6} d(10,j) = 221.125$ in Table 4.46 and $\sum_{j=1}^{6} d(10,j) = 709.950$ in Table 4.46, are shown as $d(10,7)$ in Tables 4.46 and 4.47, respectively. They are equal to the values, IO_table_pur(6,1) and IO_table_pur(6,2) in Table 4.40, the original IRIO table at purchasers' price, which makes it sure that the decomposition is made adequately.

A row vector, for example, $[v_{51}^{11} v_{51}^{12} v_{51}^{13} v_{51}^{14} v_{51}^{15} v_{51}^{16}]$, is called—*transportation vector* of sector 1 (in region 1).

Shipment Activities of Service Sectors

The shipment activities of service sectors are constant between the destination regions because goods of service have no idea of "distribution cost."

$$\begin{bmatrix} v_{1k}^{pq} \\ v_{2k}^{pq} \\ v_{3k}^{pq} \\ v_{4k}^{pq} \\ v_{5k}^{pq} \\ va_{k}^{pq} \end{bmatrix} = \begin{bmatrix} a_{1k}^{p} \\ a_{2k}^{p} \\ a_{3k}^{p} \\ a_{4k}^{p} \\ a_{5k}^{p} \\ va_{k}^{p} \end{bmatrix} \text{ for all } p\ (p = 3, 4, 5), q(q = 1, 2, 3, \ldots, 6), \text{ and } k = p, \tag{4.170}$$

$$va_k^{pq} \equiv 1 - \sum\nolimits_{i=1}^{5} v_{ik}^{pq}; \text{ and}$$

$$va_k^{p} \equiv 1 - \sum\nolimits_{i=1}^{5} a_{ik}^{p}.$$

Shipment activities of wholesale sector are shown as a sub-matrix of 6 × 6 in the upper-left corner in Table 4.48.

A Numerical Example of the Interregional Input–Output Model of Shipment Activities (IRIO-SA)

[Model IRIO-SA]

$$\sum_{q=1}^{6} \delta_{qi}\, x_i^{qp} = \sum\nolimits_{q=1}^{6} \sum\nolimits_{j=1}^{5} \delta_{pj} v_{ij}^{pq} x_j^{pq}$$

$$+ \delta_{p6} F_i^p\ (i = 1, 2, \ldots 5; p = 1, 2, \ldots, 5), \tag{4.171}$$

$$\text{GDP} = \sum_{p=1}^{6} \sum\nolimits_{q=1}^{6} \sum\nolimits_{i=1}^{5} \delta_{pi} va_i^{pq} x_i^{pq}, \tag{4.172}$$

in which:

$$\delta_{ij} \equiv 1 \text{ if } i = j, \text{otherwise } 0; \text{ and}$$

F_i^p: final demand of $i - th$ goods in region p ($p = 1, 2, \ldots, 6$).

The left-hand side of Eq. (4.171) is the supply of goods i in region p. The first term of the right-hand side is the intermediate demand against goods i in region p. The second term is the final demand against goods i in region p. The simple distribution of sectors among regions needs variables δ_{ij} ($i, j = 1, 2, \ldots, 6$).

This can be solved without an optimality condition since it is mathematically a variant of the conventional Leontief model using 'shipment activities.'

Construction and Installment of *New* Shipment Activities

In Fig. 4.1, the broken line represents a "bay bridge" and access roads under consideration of one investment target. It can be expected that the transportation cost can be reduced between regions 1, 4, 5, and 6 because region 4 as CBD area is usually congested.

In this (intentionally) simple example, the impacts on the trade patterns have to be limited to changes in the freight routes: (a) from region 1 to regions 2 and 4; and from region 2 to regions 1 and 6 since each region is specialized in one industry and the regions are exclusive with each other with the specialization. Usually, several or all the industries are located in each region and the trade pattern between the regions and sectors should be changed due to improvements in location advantage thanks to the "bay bridge." However, still it is practically useful to know how new shipment activities can be alternatively installed in simplified model because the substance is the same with the installment of new shipment activities. Using symbols in Eqs. (4.171) and (4.172) mentioned previously, some of δ_{pi} must be replaced by 1 in the equations even if $p \neq i$ and v_i^{pq} must be constructed accordingly as shown subsequently.

Prediction of Reduction in Transportation Cost

In Table 4.39, parameter with wholesale transportation cost is given by assuming that no difference of delivery costs between: (1) shipments of agricultural goods and manufacturing goods; and (2) between from region 1 and region 2 to region 3, where warehouse is located. It just simplifies the numerical example. Here, we assume that figures in Table 4.39 hold before the bridge is placed in service.

For simplicity, we assume that only transportation cost will change after the bridge is placed in service. However, it is still complicated since, for example, it can be assumed that trades between industries are shipped from region 3, once physical goods are shipped into region 3 through wholesale activity. As for the final demand, it can be assumed that goods are taken home from region 4 where shops are located, which means that retail transportation cost is the transportation cost from region 3 to region 4. In case in which some of the goods are directly shipped home from region 3 where warehouse/logistics center is located, calculation of impacts on the reduction in the transportation cost becomes more complicated although the way of installing new shipment activities is the same once the impacts can be specified. We can assume that a same delivery route through warehouse (region 3) holds with the shipment of physical goods from factory (producer) to sectors (purchasers).

Table 4.50 shows, for example, expected impacts of the transportation network improvements (i.e., with bridge) in terms of changes in the transportation cost ratios without bridge. It shows that improvements in delivery routes are assumed only between:

(a) from region 1 to region 2 and regions 4 (the first row in Table 4.50)
(b) from region 2 to region 1 and region 3 (the second row)
(c) from region 3 to region 2 and region 4 (the third row)
(d) from region 4 to region 1 and region 3 (the fourth row).

Namely, it is assumed that transportation costs will not change with routes corresponding to the cells which have zero (0) in Table 4.40. Also, the following are assumed:

(e) agricultural goods and manufacturing goods are once shipped into a warehouse (market), which is located in region 3 from region 1 and region 2, respectively
(f) households purchase agricultural goods in region 4 where shops are located and take home purchased agricultural goods. Therefore, retail transportation cost for retail sector in order to ship agricultural goods to household sector is the transportation cost incurred by the shipment from region 3 to region 4
(g) shipments of agricultural goods to purchasers but for households are made from region 3, where a warehouse is located, to regions where purchasers are located
(h) shipments of manufacturing goods to purchasers are made from region 3, where a warehouse is located, to regions where purchasers are located.

It is assumed that "margin rates" are invariant between with and without bridge. As for purchase of intermediate inputs, it does not matter whether contract of purchase is made through "retail sector" or not. It can be taken that "retail sector" represents any function which incurs additional costs of margin and transportation cost for shipment of goods from warehouse (region 3) to regions where purchasers are located.

For simplicity of explanation, we define symbols as follows:

$ctr(i,j)$: the value of the ith row and jth column in Table 4.50

$$(i = 1, 2, \ldots, 5; j = 1, 2, \ldots, 6);$$

$w\_margin * (i,j)$: the value of the ith row and jth column in Table 4.49

$$(i = 1, 2; j = 5, 6);$$

$r\_margin * (i,j)$: the value of the ith row and jth column in Table 4.49

$$(i = 3, 4; j = 1, 2, \ldots, 6);$$

$w\_trans * (i,j)$: the value of the ith row and jth column in Table 4.49

$$(i = 5, 6; j = 5, 6); \text{and}$$

$r\_trans * (i,j)$: the value of the ith row and jth column in Table 4.49

$$(i = 7, 8; j = 1, 2, \ldots, 6);$$

Due to assumption (e),

$$w\_margin * (i,j) = 0 \text{ for } i = 1, 2 \text{ and } j = 1, 2, 3, 4, \text{and for } i = 1, 2 \text{ and } j = 7, \ldots, 12.$$

Also, due to assumption (e),

$$w\_trans * (i,j) = 0 \text{ for } i = 5, 6 \text{ and } j = 1, 2, 3, 4, \text{and for } i = 5, 6 \text{ and } j = 7, \ldots, 12.$$

Others are calculated as follows:

$w\_margin * (i, (j-1) \times 2 + 1) = w\_margin(i,j)$ as margins are invariant with and without bridge;

$$w\_trans * (i, 6) = w\_trans(i, 4) \times (1 - ctr(4, 3)) \text{ for } i = 5, 6$$

$$r\_trans * (i,j) = r\_trans(i,j) \times (1 - ctr(3,j)) \text{ for } i = 7, 8;\ j = 1, 2, \ldots, 5$$

$$r\_trans * (7, 6) = r\_trans(3, 4) \times (1 - ctr(3, 4))$$

$$r\_trans * (8, 6) = r\_trans(3, 6) \times (1 - ctr(3, 6)).$$

Estimated results are shown in Table 4.49. Once it is obtained, we can calculate new alternative shipment activities. Here the following should be noted:

(a) Usually, the total number of shipment activities will increase drastically if the impacts of improvements in the network are large. In the numerical example, we need to construct new shipment activities due to changes in the trade patterns and the number of new shipment activities is 7
(b) New shipment activities can be additionally installed into Eqs. (4.171) and (4.172) and a new IRIO-SA can be specified. However, it cannot be solved without a normality condition since the model becomes an "IRIO-SA" in its true sense, namely several alternative routes exist for shipment of goods. Usually, the objective function is set GDP (GRP) and it is maximized. However, it is unknown that the maximized GDP would be greater than the maximized objective value of the original model as far as the final demand is unchanged. Actually, such a simulation is not interesting and the model should be combined with the optimization of public investments in the transportation infrastructures by explicitly treating capacity constraints of the transportation network. Or, the model should be changed so that the capacity constraints to the production should be explicitly treated and the final demand is endogenously determined depending on the distribution of value-added. Interesting is that such model treatment will make it a comeback that the freight route is explicitly treated in the model, for example, where wholesale sector stocks the goods and from where the

shipment is made to retail sector' shop or warehouse, where household buys goods, from where household is shipped purchased goods, and so on.

In order to save space, we will not further discuss about this issue and will stop here.

Precise Estimates of Transportation Costs and Shipment Activities

In (i) above, we firstly have Table 4.50 and then we have Table 4.49. It must be tough job to construct Table 4.50. Generally speaking, we must go back to the survey data and statistical sources with which distributional costs are calculated and listed in the basic trade table. Table 4.39 is an example that is taken as an essence of such survey data and statistical sources with the calculation of logistics costs in the basic trade table.

We must check if parameters that were used for the construction of basic trade table would change or not due to the improvements in transportation network. Typical one is decrease in the haul distance of commodities. It saves fuel, labor, insurance costs, and so on. Not only transportation cost but also margin (dealing cost) must be decreased. Next, using new parameters, shipment activities of alternative trade patterns must be constructed. The process must be estimation and estimates should be scrutinized by making reference to changes in distributional costs with current trade patterns since sometimes we have no data with a newly developed trade pattern.

Table 4.50 is taken as a summarized essence of such estimates of changes in Table 4.49.

Installment of Shipment Activities in IRIO Model at Producers' Price

It is logically possible to construct shipment activities at producers' price into IRIO model. However, "shipment activities" at producers' price should be called—*purchase activities* at producers' price.

Input–Output Coefficients at Producers' Price (Again) and Coefficients of the Final Demand Sector: Decomposition

First of all, it can be said that the decomposition of production activities of the conventional IRIO model at purchasers' price into shipment activities at purchasers' price is made with the destination (region) where goods are purchased with purposes of intermediate inputs, final demands such as consumption, investment, international export, and so on. The distribution costs are usually different among destinations since the economy has an idea of space. The production (distribution) cost in terms of the inputs of goods and services is different depending on which region (sector) purchases goods. Owing to improvements in transportation network, transportation costs will change. Shipment activity, of which specification is substantially dependent on transportation network, will change, too. Before considering the installment of shipment activities in IRIO model at producers' price, we will discuss about meaning of "shipment activities."

It seems that the only one shipment activity is selected with each trade (shipment) that has the least cost and the installment of shipment activities has no meaning. The reality does not since there should be capacity constraints on transportation infrastructures as well as on the transportation sectors which produce and provide transportation services. Also, there should be an idea of "congestion" in any sense and the concept of equilibrium makes usually several routes coexist concurrently between regions with shipment of the same goods. Sometimes goods traded are voluminous compared to the economic value and a route less costly in terms of money can be selected even if it makes a detour to the destination. The varieties of routes are increased as the varieties of transportation modes increase. At all, the trade pattern must be determined by taking into account the efficiency of the national economy as a whole. Sectors in each region have production capacities just as distribution sectors have. It cannot be a joke that a sushi shop located in a prefecture where a famous fishery harbor located cannot use locally sourced materials for sushi. Every resource of high value added could be absorbed by Tokyo. This is a reason why alternative shipments activities must be installed in IRIO model in order to estimate and assess the impacts of large-scaled public investments on the regional trade pattern and therefore on the whole national economy.

Technically speaking, IRIO model at producers' price is constructed by attributing all the distribution costs incurred by the deliveries of goods (which are utilized as intermediate goods (materials) or final goods) to the purchasing sector as additions to the *original*[32] intermediate inputs if any. We define notations of $\boldsymbol{a}_j$, $\boldsymbol{f}$, and $\boldsymbol{d}$ as follows for simplicity of the explanation, and explain the construction of shipment (purchasing) activities at producers' price with the numerical example:

[32]The term 'original' means that the goods cannot be produced with no inputs of the said intermediate inputs in the light of the definition of the production activity.

$$
\boldsymbol{a}_j = \begin{bmatrix} a_{1j} \\ a_{2j} \\ a_{3j} \\ \cdot \\ \cdot \\ \cdot \\ a_{kj} \\ a_{k+1,j} \\ a_{k+2,j} \\ \cdot \\ \cdot \\ \cdot \\ a_{n-1,j} \\ a_{nj} \end{bmatrix}, \boldsymbol{f} = \begin{bmatrix} f_1 \\ f_2 \\ f_3 \\ \cdot \\ \cdot \\ \cdot \\ f_k \\ f_{k+1} \\ f_{k+1} \\ \cdot \\ \cdot \\ \cdot \\ f_{n-1} \\ f_n \end{bmatrix}, \boldsymbol{D}^p = \left[d_{ji}^p\right], \boldsymbol{d}_{ji}^F
$$

$$
= \left[d_{ji}^F\right](j = 1, 2, \ldots, n; p = 1, 2, , \ldots, R), \tag{4.173}
$$

in which:

n: the number of sectors ($n = 5$)
k: the number of nondistribution sectors ($k = 2$)
R: the number of regions ($R = 5$)
$\boldsymbol{a}_j$: jth column vector of the input–output coefficient matrix at producers' price ($j = 1, 2, \ldots, n$), which becomes input–output coefficient of jth sector in region j ($j = 1,2, \ldots, R$) with the spatial distribution of sectors (Fig. 4.1);
f_j: the ratio of the final demand of jth goods ($j = 1, 2, \ldots, n$) to the total amount of final demand in region 6 (it is the ratio to the GDP with the illustration example);
d_{ji}^p: the distribution cost that is incurred by the input of jth goods from region j to region p, and shall be attributed to pth sector in region p as input of ith goods (delivery service) in addition to the original intermediate input of ith goods if any in order to produce one unit pth goods ($i = 3, 4, 5; j = 1, 2; p = 1, 2, \ldots, 5$); and

d_{ji}^F: the distribution cost that shall be attributed to the final demand sector in addition to the original consumption/investment of ith goods if any in order to make one unit of final demand of jth goods ($i = 3, 4, 5; j = 1, 2$).

Based on the rule for listing the input–output table at producers' price, we obtain the following equation with the illustration example:

$$a_{ij} = \overline{a}_{ij} \; (i = 1, 2; \, j = 1, \ldots, 5), \tag{4.174}$$

$$a_{ij} = \overline{a}_{ij} + \sum\nolimits_{s=1}^{2} d_{si}^{j} \; (i = 3, 4, 5; \, j = 1, 2, \ldots, 5), \tag{4.175}$$

$$f_i = \overline{f}_i \; (i = 1, 2), \text{ and} \tag{4.176}$$

$$f_i = \overline{f}_i + \sum\nolimits_{s=1}^{2} d_{is}^{F} \; (i = 3, 4, 5), \tag{4.177}$$

in which:

$\overline{a}_{ij}$: the input–output coefficient of jth sector which is calculated using the basic trade table (Table 4.38); and

$\overline{f}_i$: the original final demand ratio of ith goods to the total final demand which is calculated using basic trade table.

The data necessary for calculating $\overline{a}_{pj}, \overline{f}_p, \boldsymbol{D}^i$, and $\boldsymbol{d}_{jp}^F$ should be found in terms of aggregate terms in the basic trade table. For example, as for the agricultural sector and the final demand sector in the numerical example 2, they are calculated as follows:

$$\boldsymbol{D}^1 = \begin{bmatrix} 0.0090909\ldots & 0.03 & 0.0181\ldots \\ 0.01363636\ldots & 0.071590909\ldots & 0.0463636\ldots \end{bmatrix}^{\mathrm{T}}, \tag{4.178}$$

$$\begin{bmatrix} \overline{a}_{31} \\ \overline{a}_{41} \\ \overline{a}_{51} \end{bmatrix} = \begin{bmatrix} 0.04545\ldots \\ 0 \\ 0 \end{bmatrix}, \tag{4.179}$$

$$\begin{bmatrix} \overline{a}_{11} \\ \overline{a}_{21} \end{bmatrix} = \begin{bmatrix} 0.090909\ldots \\ 0.272727\ldots \end{bmatrix}, \tag{4.180}$$

$$\boldsymbol{d}_{jp}^{F}=\begin{bmatrix} 0.02126267582\ldots & 0.0701668302\ldots & 0.063788027\ldots \\ 0.01635590448\ldots & 0.0858684985\ldots & 0.098135426\ldots \end{bmatrix}^{\mathrm{T}}, \tag{4.181}$$

$$\begin{bmatrix} \bar{f}_3 \\ \bar{f}_4 \\ \bar{f}_5 \end{bmatrix}=\begin{bmatrix} 0 \\ 0 \\ 0.104677788681714 \end{bmatrix}, \tag{4.182}$$

$$\begin{bmatrix} \bar{f}_1 \\ \bar{f}_2 \end{bmatrix}=\begin{bmatrix} 0.2126267\ldots \\ 0.3271180\ldots \end{bmatrix}. \tag{4.183}$$

Therefore, $\boldsymbol{a}_1$ and $\boldsymbol{f}$ are calculated as follows:

$$\boldsymbol{a}_1=\begin{bmatrix} a_{11} \\ a_{21} \\ a_{31} \\ a_{41} \\ a_{51} \end{bmatrix}=\begin{bmatrix} a_{11} \\ a_{21} \\ d_{13}^{1}+d_{23}^{1}+\bar{a}_{31} \\ d_{14}^{1}+d_{24}^{1}+\bar{a}_{41} \\ d_{15}^{1}+d_{25}^{1}+\bar{a}_{51} \end{bmatrix}=\begin{bmatrix} 0.0909090909090909 \\ 0.2727272727272730 \\ 0.0681818181818182 \\ 0.1015909090909090 \\ 0.0645454545454545 \end{bmatrix}, \text{and} \tag{4.184}$$

$$\boldsymbol{f}=\begin{bmatrix} f_1 \\ f_2 \\ f_3 \\ f_4 \\ f_5 \end{bmatrix}=\begin{bmatrix} f_1 \\ f_2 \\ d_{13}^{F}+d_{23}^{F}+\bar{f}_3 \\ d_{14}^{F}+d_{24}^{F}+\bar{f}_4 \\ d_{15}^{F}+d_{25}^{F}+\bar{f}_5 \end{bmatrix}=\begin{bmatrix} 0.212626758259732 \\ 0.327118089630357 \\ 0.037618580307491 \\ 0.156035328753680 \\ 0.266601243048741 \end{bmatrix}. \tag{4.185}$$

They are respectively shown in first and sixth column of first to fifth row in Table 4.43. Eq. (4.185) clearly shows that an arbitrary given total final demand (= GDP) (a nonnegative vector) gives solution to the Leontief inverse matrix system due to the solvability condition though it is not interesting.

Shipment Activities at Producers' Price

It looks that the construction of shipment activities at producers' price additionally needs only calculation of the coefficient of the final demand sector. However, the construction of possible alternative shipment activities causes huge amount of calculation in case, for example, we presume improvements in transportation network.

Using symbols above, the impacts of expected improvements in transportation network are realized in terms of changes in the value of parameters, $d^{P}{}_{j3}$ and $d^{F}{}_{j3}$ in the calculation of $\boldsymbol{a}_j$ and $\boldsymbol{f}$. Firstly, $d^{P}{}_{j3}$ and $d^{F}{}_{j3}$ exist as many as the number of possible alternative routes with which jth goods are delivered to pth or final demand sector. If $d^{P}{}_{j3}$ and $d^{F}{}_{j3}$ change with one specific goods (e.g., due to improvements in the cargo handling operation system for certain specific goods, e.g., lumber), the number of alternative shipment activities will increase by the number of alternative routes in all sectors including final demand sector (as far as they use "lumber" as intermediate inputs). However, it should be a rare case. Alternative routes for (some or all of) the other goods must increase as well. Assuming that alternative routes become 3 by adding 2 new routes with a certain pair of regions, the number of, for example, set of d^1_{1i} $(i = 3, 4, 5)$ which have different values, becomes 3 in Eq. (4.184). The same holds for d^1_{2i} $(i = 3, 4, 5)$ and the total shipment activities become 9 (=3 × 3) with a certain pair of regions. This number exponentially increases as the number of alternative routes as well as the number of non-service sectors and regions increase. For example, in case in which the number of non-service goods is 5, the number of alternative shipment activities becomes 243 (3^5). On the other hand, the number of shipment activities at purchasers' price arithmetically increases as the number of routes increases. Of course, the number of routes may increase exponentially with a complicated and minutes network. However, this is the same for the

Table 4.32 Numerical example of I-O table (unit: million JPY)

	Column no. →	1	2	3	4	5
	Output sector →					
Row no. ↓	Input sector ↓	Sector 1	Sector 2	Sector 3	Final demand	Total
1	Sector 1	20	30	20	70	140
2	Sector 2	45	15	50	60	170
3	Sector 3	20	60	40	50	170
4	Gross value added	55	65	60		180
5	Total	140	170	170	180	660

Table 4.33 Numerical example of I-O table: trade table via commercial sectors (unit: million JPY)

		Column no. →	1	2	3	4	5	6	7	8	9	10	11
		Output sector →			Comm 1			Comm 2					
Row no. ↓		Input sector ↓	Agri	Manu	wholesale	Agri Prod	Non-Agri	Retail	Agri Prod	Non-Agri	Transportation	Final demand	Total
1	Agri		–	–	–	300.0	–	–	–	–		–	300.0
2	Manu		–	–	–	–	800.0	–	–	–		–	800.0
3	Comm 1	Agri prod	–	–	–	–	–	–	345.0	–		–	345.0
4		Non-Agri	–	–	–	–	–	–	–	920.0		–	920.0
5		Wholesale	5.0	10.0	0.0	–	–	5.0	–	–	0.0	0.0	20.0
6	Comm 2	Agri prod	76.0	136.8	7.6	–	–	15.2	–	–	30.4	190.0	456.0
7		Non-Agri	121.6	547.2	22.8	–	–	60.8	–	–	76.0	387.6	1216.0
8		Retail	0.0	0.0	10.0	–	–	0.0	–	–	0.0	–	10.0
9	Transportation		0.0	0.0	0.0	15.0	40.0	0.0	45.0	120.0	0.0	60.0	280.0
10	Gross value added		97.4	106.0	89.6	–	–	171.0	–	–	173.6	–	637.6
11	Total		300.0	800.0	1285.0	–	–	1682.0	–	–	280.0	637.6	–
	Total shipment		4347.0										

Table 4.34 Numerical example of I-O table: Basic trade table (unit: million JPY)

		Column no.	1	2	3	4	5	6	7	8	9	10	11
		Output sector →			Comm 1			comm 2					
Row no.		Input sector ↓	Agri	Manu	Wholesale	Agri Prod	Non-Agri	Retail	Agri Prod	Non-Agri	Transportation	Final demand	Total
1	Agri		–	–	–	300.0	–	–	–	–	–	–	300.0
2	Manu		–	–	–	–	800.0	–	–	–	–	–	800.0
3	Comm 1	Agri prod	–	–	–	–	–	–	300.0	–	–	–	300.0
4		Non-Agri	–	–	–	–	–	–	–	800.0	–	–	800.0
5		Margin	–	–	–	–	–	–	30.0	80.0	–	–	110.0
6		Transportation	–	–	–	–	–	–	15.0	40.0	–	–	55.0
7		Wholesale	5.0	10.0	0.0	–	–	5.0	0.0	0.0	0.0	0.0	20.0
8		Subtotal	5.0	10.0	0.0	–	–	5.0	345.0	920.0	–		1285.0
9	Comm 2	Agri prod	50.0	90.0	5.0	–	–	10.0	–	–	20.0	125.0	300.0
10		Non-Agri	80.0	360.0	15.0	–	–	40.0	–	–	50.0	255.0	800.0
11		Margin	41.6	144.0	6.4	–	–	16.0	–	–	22.4	121.6	352.0
12		Retail	0.0	0.0	10.0	–	–	0.0	–	–	0.0	0.0	10.0
13		Transportation	26.0	90.0	4.0	–	–	10.0	–	–	14.0	76.0	220.0
14		Subtotal	197.6	684.0	40.4	–	–	76.0	–	–	106.4	577.6	1682.0
15	Transportation		0.0	0.0	0.0	15.0	40.0	0.0	45.0	120.0	0.0	60.0	280.0
16	Gross value added		97.4	106.0	89.6	–	–	171.0	–	–	173.6	–	637.6
17	Total		300.0	800.0	1285.0	–	–	1682.0	–	–	280.0	637.6	–
	Total shipment		4347.0										

Table 4.35 Numerical example of I-O table: Trade table via commercial sectors aggregated (unit: million JPY)

		Column no.	1	2	3	4	5	6	7	8	9	10	11
		Output sector →			Comm 1			Comm 2					
Row no.		Input sector ↓	Agri	Manu	Wholesale	Agri Prod	Non-Agri	Retail	Agri Prod	Non-Agri	Transportation	Final demand	Total
1	Agri		–	–	300.0	–	–	–	–	–		–	300.0
2	Manu		–	–	800.0	–	–	–	–	–		–	800.0
3	Comm 1	Agri prod	–	–	–	–	–	345.0	–	–		–	345.0
4		Non-Agri	–	–	–	–	–	920.0	–	–		–	920.0
5		Wholesale	5.0	10.0	0.0	–	–	5.0	–	–		–	20.0
6	Comm 2	Agri prod	76.0	136.8	7.6	–	–	15.2	–	–	30.4	190.0	456.0
7		Non-Agri	121.6	547.2	22.8	–	–	60.8	–	–	76.0	387.6	1216.0
8		Retail	0.0	0.0	10.0	–	–	0.0	–	–	0.0	0.0	10.0
9	Transportation		0.0	0.0	55.0	–	–	165.0	–	–	0.0	60.0	280.0
10	Gross value added		97.4	106.0	89.6	–	–	171.0	–	–	173.6	–	637.6
11	Total		300.0	800.0	1285.0	–	–	1682.0	–	–	280.0	637.6	–
	Total shipment		4347.0										

Table 4.36 Numerical example of I-O table: purchasers' price (unit: million JPY)

	Column no.	1	2	3	4	5	6	7
	Output sector →							
Row no.	Input sector ↓	Agri	Manu	Wholesale	Retail	Transportation	Final demand	Total
1	Agri	76.0	136.8	7.6	15.2	30.4	190.0	456.0
2	Manu	121.6	547.2	22.8	60.8	76.0	387.6	1216.0
3	Wholesale	35.0	90.0	0.0	5.0	0.0	0.0	130.0
4	Retail	66.0	176.0	10.0	0.0	0.0	0.0	252.0
5	Transportation	60.0	160.0	0.0	0.0	0.0	60.0	280.0
6	Gross value added	97.4	106.0	89.6	171.0	173.6	–	637.6
7	Total	456.0	1216.0	130.0	252.0	280.0	637.6	–
	Total shipment	2334.0						

Table 4.37 Numerical example of I-O table: producers' price (unit: million JPY)

	Column no.	1	2	3	4	5	6	7
	Output sector →							
Row no.	Input sector ↓	Agri	Manu	Wholesale	Retail	Transportation	Final demand	Total
1	Agri	50.0	90.0	5.0	10.0	20.0	125.0	300.0
2	Manu	80.0	360.0	15.0	40.0	50.0	255.0	800.0
3	Wholesale	18.0	55.0	2.0	10.0	7.0	38.0	130.0
4	Retail	28.6	99.0	14.4	11.0	15.4	83.6	252.0
5	Transportation	26.0	90.0	4.0	10.0	14.0	136.0	280.0
6	Gross value added	97.4	106.0	89.6	171.0	173.6	–	637.6
7	Total	300.0	800.0	130.0	252.0	280.0	637.6	–
	Total shipment	1762.0						

Table 4.38 The basic trade table (T_basic_org) of numerical example 2 (unit: million JPY)

		Column no.	1	2	3	4	5	6	7	8	9	10	11
		Output sector →			Comm 1 (retail)			Comm 2 (retail)					
Row no.		Input sector ↓	Agri	Manu	Wholesale	Agri Prod	Non-Agri	Retail	Agri Prod	Non-Agri	Transportation	Final demand	Total
1	Agricultural sector total sales					550.000							550.000
2	Manufacturing sector total sales						1430.000						1430.000
3	Comm 1 wholesale	Agri prod							550.000				550.000
4		Non-Agri								1430.000			1430.000
5		Margin							55.000	71.500			126.500
6		Trans cost							82.500	143.000			225.500
7	Wholesale total sales		25.000	50.000	15.000			25.000	687.500	1644.500	0.000	0.000	2447.000
8	Comm 2 retail	Agri prod	50.000	90.000	5.000			30.000			50.000	325.000	550.000
9		Wholesale	5.000	9.000	0.500			3.000			5.000	32.500	55.000
10		Retail	16.500	24.750	1.100			6.600			5.500	107.250	161.700
11		Trans cost	10.000	20.700	1.000			6.900			10.000	97.500	146.100
12		Total distri. cost	31.500	54.450	2.600			16.500			20.500	237.250	362.800
13		Non-Agri	150.000	360.000	50.000			120.000			250.000	500.000	1430.000
14		Wholesale	7.500	18.000	2.500			6.000			12.500	25.000	71.500
15		Retail	39.375	75.600	5.250			31.500			26.250	131.250	309.225
16		Trans cost	25.500	72.000	9.000			18.000			45.000	150.000	319.500
17		Total Distri. cost	72.375	165.600	16.750			55.500			83.750	306.250	700.225
18	Retail total sales		303.875	670.050	134.350			242.000			409.250	1368.500	3128.025
19	Intermediate/final demand of retail		0.000	0.000	60.000			20.000			5.000	0.000	85.000
20	Transportation total sales		0.000	0.000	0.000	82.500	143.000	0.000	63.600	176.500	0.000	160.000	625.600
21	Gross value added		221.125	709.950	92.150			288.925			216.350		1528.500
22	Total		550.000	1430.000	2447.000			3128.025			625.600	1528.500	

Total shipment = 8180.6250

Table 4.39 Parameters of distribution costs (rate to the amount traded)

j / *i*	Column no.			1	2	3	4	5	6
		Purchasing sector							
Row no.	Distribution costs	Distribution sector	Goods traded	Agriculture	Manufacturing	Wholesale	Retail	Transportation	Final demand
1	Margin	Wholesale margin w_margin (i,j)	Agri prod	–	–	–	0.10	–	–
2			Non-Agri	–	–	–	0.05	–	–
3		Retail margin r_margin(i,j)	Agri prod	0.30	0.25	0.20	0.20	0.10	0.30
4			Non-Agri	0.25	0.20	0.10	0.25	0.10	0.25
5	Transportation cost	Wholesale w_trans(i,j)	Agri prod	–	–	–	0.15	–	–
6			Non-Agri	–	–	–	0.10	–	–
7		Retail r_trans(i,j)	Agir prod	0.05	0.08	0.05	0.08	0.05	0.15
8			Non-Agri	0.07	0.10	0.08	0.05	0.08	0.20

Table 4.40 I-O table at purchasers' price (IO_table_pur(T_basic_org)) of numerical example 2 (unit: million JPY)

i								
j	Column no.	1	2	3	4	5	6	7
Row no.	Output sector input sector	Agri	Manu	Wholesale	Retale	Transportation	Final demand	Total
1	Agri	81.5	144.45	7.6	46.5	70.5	562.25	912.8
2	Manu	222.375	525.6	66.75	175.5	333.75	806.25	2130.225
3	Wholesale	80	121.5	15	25	0	0	241.5
4	Retail	161.7	309.225	60	20	5	0	555.925
5	Transportation	146.1	319.5	0	0	0	160	625.6
6	Gross value added	221.125	709.95	92.15	288.925	216.35	–	1528.5
7	Total	912.8	2130.225	241.5	555.925	625.6	1528.5	–
Total shipment = 4466.0500								

Table 4.41 I-O table at producers' price (IO_table_pro(T_basic_org)) of numerical example 2 (unit: million JPY)

i								
j	Column no.	1	2	3	4	5	6	7
Row no.	Output sector input sector	Agri	Manu	Wholesale	Retale	Transportation	Final demand	Total
1	Agri	50	90	5	30	50	325	550
2	Manu	150	360	50	120	250	500	1430
3	Wholesale	37.5	77	18	34	17.5	57.5	241.5
4	Retail	55.875	100.35	66.35	58.1	36.75	238.5	555.925
5	Transportation	35.5	92.7	10	24.9	55	407.5	625.6
6	Gross value added	221.125	709.95	92.15	288.925	216.35	–	1528.5
7	Total	550	1430	241.5	555.925	625.6	1528.5	–

Total shipment = 3403.0250

Table 4.42 I-O coefficients matrix with purchasers' price (IO_coeff_pur(T_basic_org)) of numerical example 2

i						
j	Column no.	1	2	3	4	5
Row no.	Output sector input sector	Agri	Manu	Wholesale	Retale	Transportation
1	Agri	0.089285714285714	0.067809738407915	0.031469979296066	0.083644376489634	0.112691815856777
2	Manu	0.243618536371604	0.246734499876774	0.276397515527950	0.315690066106039	0.533487851662404
3	Wholesale	0.087642418930763	0.057036228567405	0.062111801242236	0.044970094886900	0.000000000000000
4	Retail	0.177147239263804	0.145160722458895	0.248447204968944	0.035976075909520	0.007992327365729
5	Transportation	0.160056967572305	0.149984156603176	0.000000000000000	0.000000000000000	0.000000000000000
6	Gross value added	0.242249123575811	0.333274654085836	0.381573498964803	0.519719386607906	0.345828005115090
7	Total	1.000000000000000	1.000000000000000	1.000000000000000	1.000000000000000	1.000000000000000

Table 4.43 I-O coefficients matrix with producers' price (IO_coeff_pro(T_basic_org)) of numerical example 2

i							
j	Column no.	1	2	3	4	5	6
Row no.	Output sector input sector	Agri	Manu	Wholesale	Retale	Transportation	Final demand
1	Agri	0.090909090909091	0.062937062937063	0.020703933747412	0.053964113864280	0.079923273657289	0.212626758259732
2	Manu	0.272727272727273	0.251748251748252	0.207039337474120	0.215856455457121	0.399616368286445	0.327118089630357
3	Wholesale	0.068181818181818	0.053846153846154	0.074534161490683	0.061159329046184	0.027973145780051	0.037618580307491
4	Retail	0.101590909090909	0.070174825174825	0.274741200828157	0.104510500517156	0.058743606138107	0.156035328753680
5	Transportation	0.064545454545455	0.064825174825175	0.041407867494824	0.044790214507353	0.087915601023018	0.266601243048741
6	Gross value added	0.402045454545455	0.496468531468531	0.381573498964803	0.519719386607906	0.345828005115090	–
7	Total	1.000000000000000	1.000000000000000	1.000000000000000	1.000000000000000	1.000000000000000	1.000000000000000

Table 4.44 The Leontief inverse matrix with purchasers' price of numerical example 2

i						
j	Column no.	1	2	3	4	5
Row no.	Output sector input sector	Agri	Manu	Wholesale	Retale	Transportation
1	Agri	1.249569469081640	0.210252882895510	0.152736900304540	0.184396667011376	0.254457369839656
2	Manu	0.883104996442737	1.813435887566400	0.750942781660767	0.705501609635694	1.072603321247890
3	Wholesale	0.190342664124859	0.146809798083883	1.147163026331030	0.118104453242157	0.100715233691671
4	Retail	0.414405820828686	0.352068682643481	0.437924112860296	1.208995712635110	0.244187199111029
5	Transportation	0.332454058075656	0.305639091010168	0.137076124863771	0.135328035255673	1.201601179500090

Table 4.45 Numerical example of the Leontief inverse matrix: producers' price

i						
j	Column no.	1	2	3	4	5
Row no.	Output sector input sector	Agri	Manu	Wholesale	Retale	Transportation
1	Agri	1.172083278609360	0.131485576242867	0.981886262525986	0.117580605408684	0.170898959339948
2	Manu	0.610914562000547	1.538894751193680	0.536062734876227	0.483155316589921	0.775335561940870
3	Wholesale	0.141706165755989	0.115100045937233	1.149849204171050	0.120109821711727	0.105847733601484
4	Retail	0.233784761499206	0.179531613451060	0.413639952889304	1.211819601310350	0.189879444376873
5	Transportation	0.144278655754250	0.132721516377606	0.117563479698388	0.107622795726754	1.177719611846820

Table 4.46 Numerical example of shipment activities: Agricultural sector (region 1)

Shipment activities								
	Column no.	1	2	3	4	5	6	7
Row no.	Input sector	Region 1 to region 1	Region 1 to region 2	Region 1 to region 3	Region 1 to region 4	Region 1 to region 5	Region 1 to region 6	Coefficient of IRIO table
1	Agri	0.0892857142857143	0.0892857142857143	0.0892857142857143	0.0892857142857143	0.0892857142857143	0.0892857142857143	0.0892857142857143
2	Man	0.2436185363716040	0.2436185363716040	0.2436185363716040	0.2436185363716040	0.2436185363716040	0.2436185363716040	0.2436185363716040
3	Wholesale	0.0887379491673970	0.0896935518660190	0.0931777296000738	0.0919043849481213	0.0983102417314661	0.0851917241239558	0.0876424189307625
4	Retail	0.2024539877300610	0.1713395638629280	0.1447368421052630	0.1419354838709680	0.0780141843971631	0.1907514450867050	0.1771472392638040
5	Trans	0.1226993865030670	0.1433021806853580	0.1315789473684210	0.1483870967741940	0.1418439716312060	0.1734104046242770	0.1600569675723050
6	Value-added	0.2532044259421560	0.2627604529283760	0.2976022302689240	0.2848687837493990	0.3489273515828470	0.2177421755077430	0.2422491235758110
7	Total	1.000000000000000	1.000000000000000	1.000000000000000	1.000000000000000	1.000000000000000	1.000000000000000	1.000000000000000
Shipment of agri goods								
8	At purchasers' price	81.5000	144.4500	7.6000	46.5000	70.5000	562.2500	912.8000
9	Atproducers' price	50.0000	90.0000	5.0000	30.0000	50.0000	325.0000	550.0000
10	Gross value-added	20.6361607	37.9557474	2.2617770	13.2463984	24.5993783	122.4255382	221.1250000

Table 4.47 Numerical example of shipment activities: Manufacturing sector (region 2)

Shipment activities								
	Column no.	1	2	3	4	5	6	7
Row no.	Input sector	Region 2 to region 1	Region 2 to region 2	Region 2 to region 3	Region 2 to region 4	Region 2 to region 5	Region 2 to region 6	Coefficient of IRIO table
1	Agri	0.067809738407915	0.067809738407915	0.067809738407915	0.067809738407915	0.067809738407915	0.067809738407915	0.0678097384079147
2	Man	0.246734499876774	0.246734499876774	0.246734499876774	0.246734499876774	0.246734499876774	0.246734499876774	0.2467344998767740
3	Wholesale	0.057198511815121	0.057718274341398	0.060924882519531	0.057659733186966	0.060924882519531	0.054479450936917	0.0570362285674049
4	Retail	0.177065767284992	0.143835616438356	0.078651685393258	0.179487179487179	0.078651685393258	0.162790697674419	0.1451607224588950
5	Trans	0.114671163575042	0.136986301369863	0.134831460674157	0.102564102564103	0.134831460674157	0.186046511627907	0.1499841566031760
6	Value-added	0.336520319040157	0.346915569565695	0.411047733128365	0.345744746477064	0.411047733128365	0.282139101476070	0.3332746540858360
7	Total	1.000000000000000	1.000000000000000	1.000000000000000	1.000000000000000	1.000000000000000	1.000000000000000	1.0000000000000000
Shipment of Man. Goods								
8	At purchasers' price	222.3750000	525.6000000	66.7500000	175.5000000	333.7500000	806.2500000	2130.2250000
9	At producers' price	150.0000000	360.0000000	50.0000000	120.0000000	250.0000000	500.0000000	1430.0000000
10	Gross value-added	74.8337059	182.3388234	27.4374362	60.6782030	137.1871809	227.4746506	709.9500000

Table 4.48 Numerical example of shipment activities: Wholesale sector (region 3)

Shipment activities								
	Column no.	1	2	3	4	5	6	7
Row no.	Input sector	Region 2 to region 1	Region 2 to region 2	Region 2 to region 3	Region 2 to region 4	Region 2 to region 5	Region 2 to region 6	Coefficient of IRIO table
1	Agri	0.031469979296066	0.031469979296066	0.031469979296066	0.031469979296066	0.031469979296066	0.031469979296066	0.0314699792960662
2	Man	0.276397515527950	0.276397515527950	0.276397515527950	0.276397515527950	0.276397515527950	0.276397515527950	0.2763975155279500
3	Wholesale	0.062111801242236	0.062111801242236	0.062111801242236	0.062111801242236	0.062111801242236	0.062111801242236	0.0621118012422360
4	Retail	0.248447204968944	0.248447204968944	0.248447204968944	0.248447204968944	0.248447204968944	0.248447204968944	0.2484472049689440
5	Trans	0.000000000000000	0.000000000000000	0.000000000000000	0.000000000000000	0.000000000000000	0.000000000000000	0.0000000000000000
6	Value-added	0.381573498964803	0.381573498964803	0.381573498964803	0.381573498964803	0.381573498964803	0.381573498964803	0.3815734989648030
7	Total	1.000000000000000	1.000000000000000	1.000000000000000	1.000000000000000	1.000000000000000	1.000000000000000	1.0000000000000000
Shipment of Man. Goods								
8	At purchasers' price	80.0000000	121.5000000	15.0000000	25.0000000	0.0000000	0.0000000	241.5000000
9	At producers' price	37.5000000	77.0000000	18.0000000	34.0000000	17.5000000	57.5000000	241.5000000
10	Gross value-added	30.5258799	46.3611801	5.7236025	9.5393375	0.0000000	0.0000000	92.1500000

Table 4.49 New distributional cost parameters after the bridge is in placed

j	Region (sector)			Region 1 (Agri)		Region 2 (Man)		Region 3 (wholesale)		Region 4 (retail)		Region 5 (trans)		Region 6 (household)	
i	Column no.			1	2	3	4	5	6	7	8	9	10	11	12
	With and without bridge			No	Yes	No	Yes	No	Yes	No	Yes	No	Yes	No	Yes
		Purchasing sector													
Row no.	Distribution costs	Distribution sector	Goods traded (origin region)	Agriculture		Manufacturing		Wholesale		Retail		Transportation		Final demand	
1	Margin	Wholesale margin w_margin*(i, j)	Agri prod (region 1)	–	–	–	–	0.100	0.100	–	–	–	–	–	–
2			Non-agri (region 2)	–	–	–	–	0.050	0.050	–	–	–	–	–	–
3		Retail margin r_margin*(i,j)	Agri prod (region 3)	0.300	0.300	0.250	0.250	0.200	0.200	0.200	0.200	0.100	0.100	0.300	0.300
4			Non-agri (region 3)	0.250	0.250	0.200	0.200	0.100	0.100	0.250	0.250	0.100	0.100	0.250	0.250
5	Transportation cost	Wholesale w_trans*(i,j)	Agri prod (region 1)	–	–	–	–	0.150	0.150	–	–	–	–	–	–
6			Non-agri (region 2)	–	–	–	–	0.100	0.045	–	–	–	–	–	–
7		Retail r_trans* (i,j)	Agri prod (region 3)	0.050	0.050	0.080	0.036	0.050	0.050	0.080	0.044	0.050	0.050	0.150	0.0825
8			Non-agri (region 3)	0.070	0.070	0.100	0.045	0.080	0.080	0.050	0.0275	0.080	0.080	0.200	0.200

Table 4.50 Expected reduction rate to the current transportation cost ratio

ij	1	2	3	4	5	6
1	0.00	0.50	0.00	0.45	0.00	0.00
2	0.50	0.00	0.55	0.00	0.00	0.50
3	0.00	0.55	0.00	0.45	0.00	0.00
4	0.45	0.00	0.45	0.00	0.00	0.00
5	0.00	0.00	0.00	0.00	0.00	0.00

construction of both types of shipment activities. This is a practical reason why we have to construct shipment activities based on the IRIO model at purchasers' price.

Appendix 3: Parameter of $\theta(v, k, q)$

When $v = 1$ and 2, it is given in Table 4.51.

When $v = 1$, it is given in Table 4.52.

Table 4.51 $\theta(v, k, q)$ when $v = 1$ and 2

Destination region →	Hokkaido–Tohoku	Kanto	Chukyo	Kinki	Chugoku–Shikoku–Kyushu
Origin region ↓					
Hokkaido–Tohoku	1	2	2	2	2
Kanto	2	1	3	2	2
Chukyo	2	3	1	2	2
Kinki	2	2	2	1	2
Chugoku–Shikoku–Kyushu	2	2	2	2	1

Table 4.52 $\theta(v, k, q)$ when $v = 3$

Destination region →	Hokkaido–Tohoku	Kanto	Chukyo	Kinki	Chugoku–Shikoku–Kyushu
Origin region ↓					
Hokkaido–Tohoku	1	1	1	1	1
Kanto	1	1	1	1	1
Chukyo	1	1	1	1	1
Kinki	1	1	1	1	1
Chugoku–Shikoku–Kyushu	1	1	1	1	1

Appendix 4: Simplex Criteria

[Standard form of the Linear Programming Problem (LP)]

The following specification of LP is called—standard form of LP (symbols are used within this item only):

$$\left[\begin{array}{l} \max\limits_{\{X\}} .CX \\ \text{subject to} \\ \qquad\qquad \begin{cases} AX = b, \\ X \geq 0, \end{cases} \end{array}\right. \tag{4.186}$$

in which:A : $m \times n$ matrix

C : row vector of n dimension

X : column vector of n dimension

b : column vector of n dimension.

[Basic matrix]

Dividing A into $(A_1|A_2)$, and if A_1^{-1} exist, a square matric A_1 is called—a basic (or basis) matrix of A (the number of basic matrices, A_1, is huge as the number of combinations is huge by selecting m number of column vectors among n number of column vectors of A (in case m and n are big numbers. It is $_nC_m$, maximum). A_2 is called nonbasic matrix. Corresponding to the selection of A_1, the elements of vector X are rearranged and split into $X = (X_1|X_2)$. X_1 is called—a basic vector (activity) and X_2—a nonbasic vector. In the same way, C can be split into $C = (C_1|C_2)$.

[Feasible solution]

The vector X is called—a feasible solution, which satisfies the following constraints:

$$AX = b, X \geq 0. \tag{4.187}$$

[Basic solution]

The vector $X = (X_1|X_2)$ is called—a basic solution (or a vertex), which satisfies the following:

$$X_1 = A_1^{-1}B \text{ and } X_2 = 0. \tag{4.188}$$

[Feasible basic solution]

If a basic solution is feasible solution, then it is called—feasible basic solution. Namely, the following holds as for the basic solution $X = (X_1|X_2)$:

$$X_1 = A_1^{-1}B \geq 0 \text{ and } X_2 = 0. \tag{4.189}$$

[Optimal solution]

Assume that $X = (X_1|X_2)$ is a feasible solution and if there are no other feasible solutions, which give a *larger* value in terms of the objective function, it is called—an optimal solution.

[Optimal feasible basic solution]

If an optimal solution is a feasible basic solution, it is called—optimal feasible basic solution.

[Optimal basic matrix]

If $X = (X_1|X_2)$ such that $X_1 = A_1^{-1}B \geq 0$ and $X_2 = 0$ is an optimal solution, A_1 is called—optimal basic matrix. X_1 is called—optimal basic variables (activities).

There are two important theorems related with the solution algorithm of LP, that is, simplex algorithm.

[Extreme Point Theorem]

A feasible basic solution is, and, only it is an extreme point of the set of all the feasible solutions that is a convex set.

[Basic Theorem]

If an LP has an optimal solution (or optimal solutions),[33] it (one of them if the LP has multiple solutions) is a feasible basic solution.

The basic theorem means that we can find out an optimal solution in the set of all the feasible basic solutions. The number of feasible basic solutions is still huge and bounded. The simplex algorithm is a technical process to find out an optimal solution efficiently and the optimality of the feasible basic solution is confirmed. We will skip it here and only show an important criterion—simplex criterion.

[Simplex criterion]

With a feasible basic solution, $X = (X_1|X_2)$, if the following holds, it is an optimal solution:

$$\boldsymbol{\delta} = C_2 - C_1 A_1^{-1} A_2 \leq \mathbf{0}, \tag{4.190}$$

in which $\boldsymbol{\delta}$ is called—simplex criterion.

[Direct evaluation]

With the simplex criterion $\boldsymbol{\delta}$ above, an element of C_2, the evaluation coefficient, for example, α_k^2, that is associated to the non-basic variable x_k^2 in X_2, is called—direct evaluation of the noninclusion of the variable x_k^2 into the optimal basic variables (activities). Or equivalently, it is called—direct evaluation of the non-inclusion of activity $\boldsymbol{a}_k^2$, that is associated to the nonbasic variable, x_k^2, into the optimal basic matrix A_1.

[Indirect evaluation]

[33] This if clause has no substantial meaning. It just avoids the case in which there are no feasible solution due to, e.g., inconsistency in the constraints.

With the simplex criterion $\boldsymbol{\delta}$ above, an element of a row vector, $C_1A_1^{-1}A_2$, for example, $C_1A_1^{-1}\boldsymbol{a}_k^2$, that is correspond to α_k^2 in the kth element of C_2, is called—indirect evaluation of the *inclusion* of the nonbasic variable x_k^2 into the optimal basic variables (activities) and therefore *exclusion* of one variable from the current basic variables in order to calculate a new feasible basic solution at the next step. Or equivalently, it is called—indirect evaluation of the inclusion of activity $\boldsymbol{a}_k^2$, that is associated to the nonbasic variable, x_k^2, into the optimal basic matrix A_1 and *exclusion* of one basic activity from the current basic matrix in order to calculate a new feasible basic solution at the next step.

We obtain $\boldsymbol{\delta} = C_2 - C_1A_1^{-1}A_2 \leq \mathbf{0}$ with a basic feasible solution, it means the basic matrix is an optimal matrix and the feasible basic solution is an optimal solution owing to Basic Theorem above. Namely, $\boldsymbol{\delta} \leq \mathbf{0}$ means that the direct utilization is not bigger than the indirect utilization, which implies, (i) to keep the current basic activities in the basic matrix is not inferior to (ii) the inclusion of a non-basic activity into the basic matrix by excluding one activity from the current basic activities. In other words, the set of activities in the basic matrix can do more (contribute for the objective function) than (or at least do same contribution as) the activities in the non-basic matrix. We will show more concretely using numerical example in the text.

[Shadow price (imputed price)]

The following p_j is called—shadow price of the resource associated with the j th row:

$$[p_1, p_2, \cdots, p_m] = C_1A_1^{-1}.$$

The shadow price of the p_j is the computed price of jth resource when the basic matrix is A_1. In other words, indirect evaluation is the sum of the valuation of resources consumed (produced) by non-activities. If A_1 is the optimal basic matrix, p_j is called imputed prices (optimal shadow prices).

References

Chenery H (1953) Regional analysis. In: Chenery H, Clark P, Pinna V (eds) The structure and growth of the Italian economy. US Mutual Security Agency, Rome

Dantzig GB (1947) Maximization of a linear function of variables subject to linear inequalities. In: Koopmans (ed) (1951)

Economic Council, Econometric Committee (ECEC) (1967) Econometric Committee: the 1st report: report on the econometric model for the social economic development planning. The Ministry of Finance, Printing Bureau, Tokyo

Economic Council, Econometric Committee (ECEC) (1968) Econometric Committee: the 2nd report—follow-up of econometric model for the social economic development planning. The Ministry of Finance, Printing Bureau, Tokyo

Economic Planning Agency, Composite Planning Bureau (EPA) (1967) Economic planning no. 2: discussion materials on social economic development planning. Economic Planning Association (incorporated body), Tokyo

EPA (1970) Theoretical research on the trunk traffic problems. Economic Planning Association, Tokyo

Higano Y (2020) Genpachiro Konno (1906–1996), Yasuhiko Oishi (1922–2014), and Hirotada Kohno (1932–): The Three Great Fathers of Japanese Regional Science. In: Batey P, Plane D (eds) Great minds in regional science, 1, in Subseries: Great Minds in Regional Science, in Series: (eds. P. Nijkamp, K. Kourtit, K.E. Haynes) Footprints of Regional Science. Springer

Kohno H (1966a) Optimum allocation of public investment. Master Degree Thesis submitted to Graduate School of Economics, University of Tokyo

Kohno H (1966b) The optimum allocation of public investment using an interregional input-output programming model. In: H. Kohno, et al. (1996)

Kohno H (1968) Dynamic Optimum Allocation of Public Investment. Proceedings of Japan Society of Regional Science 6, Japan Society of Regional Science (Japan Section of Regional Science Association)

Kohno H (1969) Optimum allocation of public investment using interregional input-output programming model. Papers and Proceedings of the First Pacific Regional Science Conference of the Regional Science Association, vol 1, p 53–93

Kohno H (1970) Optimum allocation of public investment using interregional industrial input-output programming model. Discussion Paper presented at Annual Conference of Japan Economics and Econometrics Association, University of Hiroshima

Kohno H (1975) Optimum allocation of public investments using interregional industrial input-output programming model. J Econ 41(1):61–82

Kohno H (1991a) Introduction to interregional input-output analysis I: spatial dynamics of economics. Sangyo Renkan, Innov I-O Technique 2(1):65–74

Kohno H (1991b) Introduction to interregional input-output analysis II: tabulation of the competitive import type of interregional input-output structure. Sangyo Renkan, Innovation & I-O Technique 2(2):66–82

Kohno H (1991c) Introduction to interregional input-output analysis III: development of pilot model for comprehensive appraisal of the social overhead capital reinforcement and supply. Sangyo Renkan, Innovation & I-O Technique 2(4):69–84

Kohno H (1992) Introduction to interregional input-output analysis IV: results of quantitative analysis and appraisal. Sangyo Renkan, Innovation & I-O Technique 3(1):56–77

Kohno H (1996) The optimum allocation of public investment using an interregional input-output programming mode. In: Kohno, H., J. Berechman, K. Button, P. Nijkamp (eds) (1996)

Kohno H, Berechman J, Button KJ, Nijkamp P (eds) (1996) Transport and land use (Modern classics in regional science, vol. 2). Edward Elgar

Konno G (1955) Road transportation theory. University of Tokyo Press, Tokyo

Konno G (1959) Development theory of road transportation in USA. University of Tokyo Press, Tokyo

Lefeber L (1958) Allocation in space: production, transport and industrial location. North-Holland, Amsterdam

Maeda K (1961) Optimum ratio between public investment and industrial investment. In: K. Maeda, Treatise on Public Investment, Toyokeizai-shinposha, Tokyo

Marglin SA (1963) Allocation to dynamic investment planning. North-Holland, Amsterdam

Ministry of International Trade and Industry, Ministerial Secretariat, Research and Statistics Division (MITI) (1957) Interregional industrial input-output analysis of Japanese economy. Toyo-Keizai-Shinposha, Tokyo

MITI (1966a) 1960 interregional input-output table, based on interindustry relations study (9 regions, 10 sectors). The Nikkei, Tokyo

MITI (ed) (1966b) Regional Industrial Input-Output Table (9 regions, 43 sectors; producers' price): whole country, Hokkaido, Tohoku, Kanto, Tokai, Hokuriku, Kinki, Chugoku, Shikoku, Kushu. In: MITI (1966a)

MITI (ed) (1966c) 1960 Inverse Matrix Table of Regional Industrial Input-Output (9 regions). In: MITI (1966a)

MITI (ed) (1966d) 1960 Interregional Input-Output Table (25 sectors, 9 regions). In: MITI (1966a)

MITI (ed) (1966e) 1960 Inverse Matrix Table of Interregional Input-Output Table (25 sectors, 9 regions). In: MITI (1966a)

MITI (ed) (1966f) 1968 Input Coefficient Table (60 sectors). In: MITI (1966a)

MITI (ed) (1991) 1985 interregional input-output table (9 regions, 10 industrial sectors). MITI, Tokyo

Ministry of Transport, Bureau of Automobile (MOT) (ed) (1963) Simplified chart of the freight for truck on regular route (Motor Freight no.53, revision approval of Minister of Transport and enforcement in 1963). Japan Truck Association (Incorporated Foundation), Tokyo

MOT (1964) Survey report of nationwide railway transportation structure and condition, and automobile transportation condition (with 306 economic bloc): Edition of rail freight transportation condition (National Development Longitudinal Expressway Economic Survey 11-4). MT, Tokyo

Ministry of Transport Approval (1966) Rate and charges for coastal regular liner of 1966 version of freight and a wide variety of charges. Kotsu-Nippon-sha, Tokyo

Ministry of Transport, Japanese National Railways (MTJNR) (1967) Conspectus of nationwide freight and a wide variety of charges in 1967. Transport Book Press

Ministry of Transport, Ministerial Secretariat, Policy Planner (MTMP) (1972) Composite transport system of Japan. Transport Economic Research Center, Tokyo

Ministry of Transport, Ministerial Secretariat, Distribution Planner (MTMD) (1969) Toward the innovative physical distribution (Record of discussion in the transport economic informal gathering). Transport Economic Research Center, Tokyo

Miyazawa K (ed) (1975) Introduction to the industrial input-output analysis. The Nikkei, Tokyo

Moses L (1955) The stability of interregional trading patterns and input-output analysis. Am Econ Rev 45(5):803–826

Moses L (1960) A general equilibrium model of production, interregional trade and location of industry. Rev Econ Stat 42(4):373–397

Transportation Research Office (incorporated foundation) (TRO) (1965) 1960 Cargo Interregional Flow Survey (Investigation Material no.606: commissioned research by Ministry of Transport). TRO, Tokyo

Watkins RJ (1956) Report on Nagoya-Kobe Expressway Survey (Submitted for Ministry of Construction, Government of Japan). Ministry of Construction, Tokyo

Yasoshima Y (1964) Idea on fundamental transport system in the metropolitan area. Civil Engineering Institute, Faculty of Engineering, University of Tokyo, Tokyo

Chapter 5
Optimal Comprehensive Transport System and Development of the Model

5.1 Principle of the Comprehensive Transport System

It is a historic fact that the railway as *mono-transport* had been so long time the major subject of the national transportation project since the Meiji era. This has been continued till the early 1960s when the Japanese economy had taken off and the motorization was about to start. A paradigm shift had been made and the movement had begun to well place the right shares to right transportation modes including road transport in the market of transportation services based on the general-market-equilibrium-oriented analysis. This is the philosophy and concept of the comprehensive transport system. It is the modern topic in transportation economics in the sense that it must give the right answer with the shares as well as reply to the practical concerns by all related stakeholders in the private sectors and the government ministries or departments under the vertically segmented administrative system.

Typical views of the Japanese government office are summarized in the Ministry of Transport (1972), in which the discussion in the coordination committee is most related to the theme. However, their discussion was on the roles and functions of the transportation modes and competitive conditions in the markets. In the first place, it should have no meaning to discuss the topic qualitatively and the discussion was precisely lead in the opposite direction. It should have been made: (a) first starting to observe what was really happening in the markets, how was the market shares changing among different transportation modes, and what would be requested in the future in the markets; next (b) how the improvements in the transportation infrastructures should be made rightly responding to what would be requested in the markets in future; and eventually (c) the shares would be determined among the transportation modes following what the markets request. The markets should not be conditioned and controlled in any sense, but for the policy which corrects distortions in the markets.

H. Kohno, Y. Higano, *Public Investment Criteria*, New Frontiers in Regional Science: Asian Perspectives 2, https://doi.org/10.1007/978-4-431-55221-5_5

It can be taken that the discussion and analysis in Chaps. 1–3 are made in view of the topic and, in that sense, they are prologues and preliminary examinations. In Chap. 4, we have shown a prototype model, which the basic structures are built-in to reply the right answer with the topics, namely (1) consistent measurement mechanism of direct as well as indirect benefits based on the general equilibrium framework of the national economy and (2) opportunity costs criteria with which the shares can be confirmed optimal in the transportation markets and therefore the shares are optimal between the investments in the transportation infrastructures.

The following chapters will argue possible extension of the model by keeping in mind the concept and philosophy of the comprehensive transport system and pursuing the fields in regional science in which the application of the expanded models come into their own.

5.2 Points of the Development

5.2.1 Practical Usefulness

The topic of the comprehensive transport system has a mission to respond to the diversified requests by practitioners engaged in the fields of transportation. In this sense, the practical usefulness means that the results of the analysis based on the model are informative to policy makers and practitioners in the related fields. One suggested direction is to increase the number of regions, industrial sectors, and transport routes for the shipment of goods. The last necessitate the consideration of routes on virtual future possible transportation network, at least. The practical usefulness further requests inclusion of the routes that take into account modal shifts on the way of shipment. We may call the expansion of the model in this direction – minute specification of the model. The minute specification is "must" with any extension of the model as far as the practical usefulness is pursued.

5.2.2 Comprehensiveness

The loads on transportation infrastructures are basically goods flow (cargo) and person trips. Both must be dealt with in the comprehensive transport system in its true sense. The model in Chap. 4 only focuses on the shipments of goods which cause loads on the transportation infrastructures of railway, marine, and highway. The model is suitable for the treatment of goods flow as it is based on the interregional input–output model. However, person trips are only implicitly treated as a part of the final demand against transportation services. Although it corresponds to commuting, business, and leisure trips, they are not explicitly treated as loads on transportation infrastructures.

When we develop the model in order to analyze the comprehensive transport system in its true sense, explicit treatment of demand and supply of person trips is "must." More precisely, the model must be constructed so that transportation infrastructures are differentiated from transportation services which are provided using transportation infrastructures. Namely, as for railway, cargo trains and passenger trains must be explicitly treated together with railway lines so that demand against cargo trains induced by interregional trades and passenger trains induced by interregional person trips become loads on the transportation infrastructure of railway, the marshaling yards of trains, and so on. Also, as for expressway, demand against cargo trucks induced by interregional trades and demand against intercity buses induced by interregional person trips become loads on the transportation infrastructure of the expressway.

The generalized cost should be incorporated in order to develop the model in the direction above because the competition among modes of transportation in terms of monetary as well as the time cost shall become the decisive factor on investments in transportation infrastructures as far as the comprehensive transport system should respond to the demand of the markets. The development in this direction will necessitate redefinition of the objective function, namely, we need a marginal evaluation coefficient that converts time into monetary value.

Another aspect of comprehensiveness to be completed is the equalization of shadow prices among investment targets of not only transportation infrastructures but also other social overhead capitals such as environmental hygiene; public rental housing; social and medical welfare; education, and so on.

5.3 Possible Development of the Model

It is a natural limitation for the model which is based on the interregional input–output model that the person trips of sightseeing, leisure, commuting, and so on are only treated as the final demand against the transportation service sectors, and the loads are neglected which ought to be induced by the passenger traffics on the transportation infrastructures, since no explicit passenger traffic activities are specified in the interregional input–output model.

A possible development of the model in Chap. 4 can be made by explicitly treating passenger trips as well as cargo shipments so that the demand against not only cargo shipments but also passenger trips will induce loads on the capacity of transportation infrastructures.

The other development is that the targets of public investment are not only the construction and improvements of transportation infrastructures but also the social overhead capitals. This means that the equalization of the opportunity cost of public funds among all the invested targets must hold among the sets of transportation infrastructures and social overhead capitals which get injections by the public funds.

The model expansion is a challenge and there are three agendas: (I) endogenous generation and destination of intra- as well as interregional passenger trips;

(II) optimal assignments of passenger trips for different modes of transportation infrastructures based on the optimality criteria that takes into account the felicity of passenger trips with the objective function; (III) and optimal assignment of the public funds for social overhead capitals by taking into account the equalization of the opportunity cost of the public funds among transportation infrastructures and social overhead capitals which get injections by the public funds.

5.3.1 Incorporation of Leisure Trips and Social Overhead Capitals into the Objective Function

To directly reply to the agendas (I) is very tough. Although the endogenous generation and destination of passenger trips like business trips can be relatively easy to be treated in the developed model as it can be linked to the intra- and interregional cargo shipments, which are originally endogenous in the model. However, the endogeneity of passenger trips like leisure trips which are independent from the cargo shipments needs explicit treatments of: (1) consumer behavior which assigns time between work and leisure as well as disposable income between goods consumption and leisure activities and (2) tourism resources and capital which attract passenger trips of leisure. The capacity of computer and the capability of programming software were limited in order to respond to all the agendas on that day. In Chap. 6, the focus is laid on the agenda (III).

In order to fix agenda (II) and (III), we need to introduce a concept of the marginal rate of substitution (MRS) based on, for example, the multi-attribute utility theory (Keeney, 1974). The MRS with the composite goods can convert the utility of nonmarket goods and services into the value in monetary terms. And, the multi-attribute utility function is assumed to be a separable function in the variables of: (a) goods and services except for leisure activities and public services, to which the access is controlled by pricing, such as hospital services, sewage services, education services, and so on; (b) intra- and interregional leisure activities; and (c) public services, to which the access is not controlled. As a first step, it can be estimated for a representative household through experimental interview on households of different disposable incomes based on Keeney (1974) by taking the expenditure into the consumption of goods and services of composite goods (disposable income minus expenditures for leisure trips that are exogenously given).

The objective function is defined as the utility of the representative household brought by: (A) the aggregate disposable income which is dependent on the GRP; (B) intra- and interregional leisure activities mode by mode and route by route; and (C) the aggregate public goods and services of the above (c) in monetary terms. The conversion of the utility brought by the market and nonmarket goods and services are made using MRSs between (a) and (b), and (a) and (c) which are obtained by totally differentiating the multi-attribute utility function of the representative household.

5.3.2 Assignment of Loads Generated by Passenger Trips

The incorporation of passenger activities and trips into the model in this way can simulate the optimal choice of routes and modes with leisure trips, of which amount of generation and destination are exogenously given, as a first step. The optimality of the choice is, ceteris paribus, pursued in the model with each pair of origin and destination of the leisure trip by maximizing the net utility attained by leisure trip in monetary terms with respect to routes and modes that are alternatively given to the pair of origin and destination of leisure trip. The net utility of leisure trip in monetary terms is the difference between the utility of leisure trip, which is dependent on route and mode, and is converted into monetary terms with the MRS, and the value of demand against the transportation service induced by leisure trip. The transportation service is provided by the transportation sector at the origin region, and it is taken that the cost (price) of transportation service reflects the opportunity cost of goods and services, which are put into the transportation sector depending on the chosen mode and route. In this sense, the selection of route and mode of leisure trips simulates a sort of the cost-consciousness of the representative household, ceteris paribus.

The optimality of assigning leisure trips among routes and modes should be also pursued by taking into account their loads on transportation infrastructures. Leisure trips and cargo shipments are competitive against each other with the usage of transportation infrastructures, and the competition will possibly induce a further assignment of the public funds in order to increase the capacity based on the opportunity cost of the public funds.

5.4 Endogeneity Treatment of Investment

The investment is an important component of the final demand. The amount of the capital funds is exogenously given in our model in Chaps. 3 and 4, which can be allocated for the investments in the private and public sectors. And, the investments are not included in the final demand because the amount of the capital funds are accumulated one during the next 10 years or so by the target year and is too large to be included in the model, a 1-year model. The objective of the analysis is to know ideal shares between investments into the private and public sectors as well as ideal shares among the transportation infrastructure investments. How to realize the ideal comprehensive transport system is another subject in the analysis.

Huge investments cannot be made at once and improvements in transportation infrastructure must be made step-by-step and year-by-year. Priorities among improvements in transportation infrastructures shall be taken into account by corresponding to the growth of the demand against transportation infrastructures. The optimality shall be pursued with all the process of improvements in transportation infrastructures.

It is natural to develop dynamic model in which investment induces input of goods (products of sectors) in the capital formation that are components of the final demand (and therefore, investment is competitive against consumption), and will possibly induce the shipments of goods from other regions into the region where investment is made. Investments are typically composed of investments for improvements in transportation infrastructure in order to fulfill the gap between demand and supply of transportation services and investment for the capital formation in the private sector in order to fulfill the gap between demand and supply of goods. The former can act as a break on the economic growth in the sense that investment into transportation infrastructure is competitive against investment into the production capacity. The latter can break the economic growth in the sense that investment possibly cannot be made into the transportation infrastructures on which passenger trips and cargo shipments are overflowed notwithstanding, such an overflow is induced by the capital formation in industrial sectors. All the kinds of trade-offs between investments targets, utilization of goods among investment and consumption, choice of modes and routes, and so on must be made optimally at various phases and the opportunity cost criteria will effectively work in order to attain the optimal trade-offs if the model is specified as an optimization problem. The dynamic model in its true sense will be shown in Chap. 7.

5.5 Nonlinearity

The model developed in Chap. 3 assumes that the economy is decomposed into five regional economies. Each regional economy is described using input–output structure of five sectors and the regional economies are interdependent with each other through the shipments of goods. The decisive assumptions of the model are: (1) constant returns to scale, (2) divisibility, and (3) additivity.

A most important feature of regional or spatial model should be attributed to the existence of non-convexity in production activities. Typical phenomena are increasing returns to scale, agglomeration economies, economies of scope, congestion costs, and so on.[1] Here, we will not deal with the topics due to space limits.

[1] See Higano and Kohno (1988a, b), which analyzes the acceleration of scale and agglomeration economies in an urban area by a proper management of the urban system based on recursive application of an optimal programming model.

References

Higano Y, Kohno H (1988a) Optimal reorganization of greater Tokyo: an industrial complex of agglomeration and scale economies. Environ Plan A 20(8):1103–1120

Higano Y, Kohno H (1988b) Optimal reorganization of greater Tokyo: an industrial complex of agglomeration and scale economies. Environ Plan A 20(9):1145–1164

Keeney RL (1974) Multiplicative utility function. Operation Res 22(1):22–34

Chapter 6
Optimal Allocation of the Public Funds to the Transportation Infrastructures Using the Interregional Input–Output Programming Model (Part II): Specification with Ten Regions, Ten Industries, and Nine Transport Modes

6.1 Achievements with the Minute Specification of the Model

This chapter analyzes the main topic in Chap. 4 with the expanded model specification in terms of the number of: (1) regions; (2) sectors; (3) transportation infrastructures and modes, which transport cargo as well as passengers; and (d) the targets of public investments, which are extended to include social overhead capitals, based on Kohno and Mitomo (1982).

The model presented in Chap. 4 is useful for the comprehensive measurement of benefits brought by the investments into the private and public sectors as well as for the proof of the optimality of public investments based on the opportunity costs criteria, which is confirmed consistently by the equalization of the imputed prices associated with the selected investment targets. However, it should have been taken as a prototype model from the practical viewpoint of policymakers due to the capability of the computer and software available in that day for the solution of the programming model. In this sense, the results obtained in this chapter would be more informative for the policy makers in charge of the planning of social overhead capitals, especially in the comprehensive transportation planning (Kohno 1995).

6.1.1 Coding of the Expanded Specification

6.1.1.1 Regional Economies and Sector

The Japanese economy is divided into the regional economies of ten regions: Hokkaido, Tohoku, Kanto, Chukyo, Hokuriku, Kinki, Chugoku, Shikoku, Kyushu, and Okinawa (Table 6.1, Fig. 6.1). Each regional economy is divided into ten

H. Kohno, Y. Higano, *Public Investment Criteria*, New Frontiers in Regional Science: Asian Perspectives 2, https://doi.org/10.1007/978-4-431-55221-5_6

Table 6.1 Region and prefecture

Index	Region	Prefecture
1	Hokkaido	Hokkaido
2	Tohoku	Aomori, Iwate, Miyagi, Akita, Yamagata, Fukushima
3	Kanto	Niigata, Ibaraki, Tochigi, Gumma, Saitama, Tokyo, Kanagawa, Chiba, Yamanashi, Nagano, Shizuoka
4	Chukyo	Aichi, Gifu, Mie
5	Hokuriku	Toyama, Ishikawa, Fukui
6	Kinki	Shiga, Kyoto, Osaka, Hyogo, Nara, Wakayama
7	Chugoku	Tottori, Shimane, Okayama, Hiroshima, Yamaguchi
8	Shikoku	Tokushima, Kagawa, Ehime, Kochi
9	Kyushu	Fukuoka, Saga, Nagasaki, Kumamoto, Oita, Miyazaki, Kagoshima
10	Okinawa	Okinawa

sectors: agriculture, forestry, and fisheries; mining; fiber; chemical; metal; machine; other manufacturing; construction; others; and transportation (Table 6.2).

6.1.1.2 Transportation Modes

The number of assumed transportation modes are nine: National Railway (except for Kokuden, which was national trains operated in the suburbs of city for passenger traffic); Kokuden for passenger traffic; local railway; bus; taxi; private automobile; coastal marine and inland water passenger traffic; domestic air for passenger traffic; and other transportation (cargo truck)

6.1.1.3 Transportation Infrastructures

The number of assumed interregional transportation infrastructures is six: railway; Shinkansen; highway; expressway; airport; and harbor. As for intraregional transportation infrastructures, the following five are assumed: railway, Shinkansen, highway, expressway, and Kokuden.

6.1.1.4 Targets of Public Investments

The limited amount of the public funds is assigned for the construction and improvement of transportation infrastructures as well as the construction and improvements of the social overhead capital such as environmental public health, public apartment, welfare and well-being, and education.

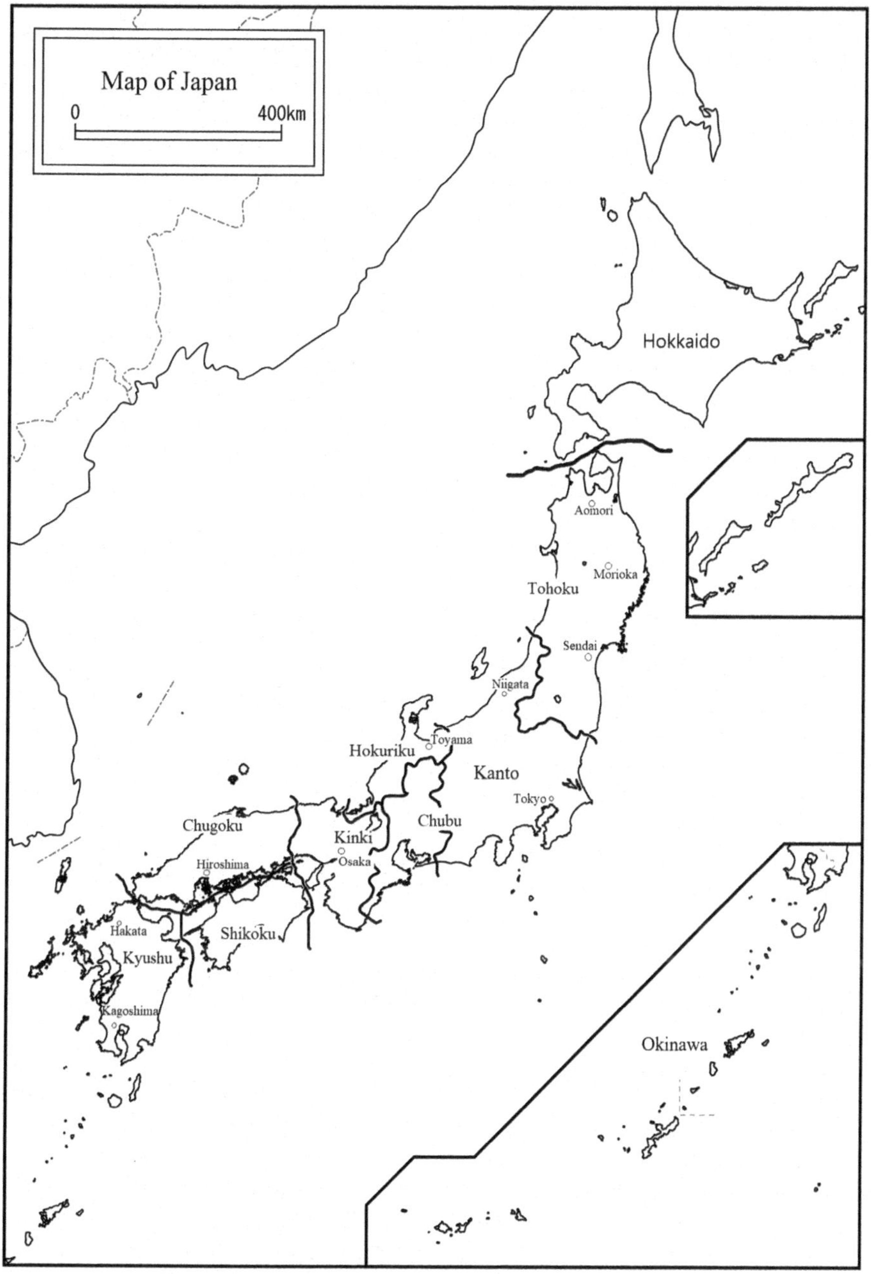

Fig. 6.1 Coding of the regional economies

Table 6.2 Classification of industrial sector

Index	Sector
1	Agriculture, forestry, and fisheries
2	Mining
3	Fiber
4	Chemical
5	Metal
6	Machine
7	Other manufacturing
8	Construction
9	Transportation
Transportation mode	
9-1	National Railway (except for Kokuden)
9-2	Kokuden for passenger traffic
9-3	Local railway
9-4	Bus
9-5	Taxi
9-6	Private automobile
9-7	Coastal marine inland water passenger
9-8	Domestic air for passenger traffic
9-9	Other transportation (cargo truck)
10	Others

6.1.1.5 Import and Export

Trades between the Japanese economy and foreign countries are exogenously given and they are incorporated into the regional final demands that are given exogenously. Therefore, it looks as if the economy is closed.

6.1.2 Model Specification

6.1.2.1 Leisure Trips

In place of directly dealing with the agenda (I) and (II) in Chap. 5, an alternative treatment can be proposed with the following manner in which the generation of leisure trips is exogenously given and their destinations at leisure venues are categorized in terms of the distance of leisure trips into leisure trips of short distance, middle distance, and long distance away from the region where the generation is made. This approach can be taken as the first step to a tourism behavior model, in which the generation and destination of leisure trips are endogenously determined, by presuming it would be developed in the near future and it would be able to be built into the model in order to make endogenous the generation and destination of leisure trips.

Once leisure trips are given with pair by pair of generation and destination, loads of leisure trips on the transportation infrastructures are taken into account jointly with loads of cargo shipments in order to simultaneously make route choice of cargo and leisure trips, which possibly affects the optimal assignment of public funds between improvements in transportation infrastructures and social overhead capitals.

6.1.2.2 The Capital Stock of Private Sectors and Transportation Infrastructures

The year 1990 is the target year of the simulation. For simplicity of the analysis, it is assumed that the production capacity of private sectors in the target year is exogenously given. The initial stock of transportation infrastructures is also given with the values in the year 1975, which is the initial year of simulation. Being different from the analysis in Chap. 4, these assumptions imply that the substantial bottleneck for the economic development is only the shortage in the capacity of transportation infrastructures due to the development of the economy that must meet the exogenously given final demands in 1990.

6.1.2.3 Incorporation of Social Overhead Capitals into the Objective Function

The public investment targets in which the public funds can be assigned are extended to include the social overhead capitals with the following categories: (a) environmental hygiene; (b) public rental housing; (c) social and medical welfare; and (d) education. The assignment of public funds (i.e., investments) into the social overhead capitals in those categories is directly evaluated in monetary terms by the objective function by assuming those social overhead capitals are directly linked to the public services of the category (c) in Sect. 5.3.1 of Chap. 5.

The initial values of the social overhead capitals are given with the values in the year 1975. It is assumed and specified in the model that the social overhead capitals in the categories of (a), (b), (c), and (d) above, only directly contributed to the objective function. The optimality of the assignment of public funds for the social overhead capitals is pursued by making the trade-off between: (1) the relief of the bottleneck of transportation infrastructures that makes possible more effective interregional cargo shipments in order to create a larger value-added, which contributes to increase the value of the objective function; and (2) the direct contribution to increase the value of the objective function by increasing the assignment of public funds to social overhead capitals.

6.1.2.4 The Public Funds and the Interregional Input–Output Table

The amount of the public funds is exogenously given 73.5 trillion JPY (in terms of price in 1975) based on the 7 years of new economic planning (EPA 1979), which is assigned to the new construction of the transportation infrastructures and social overhead capitals. The data used for the specification of cargo shipment activities at purchasers' price is the 1970 interregional input–output table and related materials (MITI 1975).

6.2 Summary of the Main Results

First of all, the main results which are informative for the policy makers who are in charge of the comprehensive transportation system in Japan in the coming 20 years are summarized as follows: (1) road becomes the key transportation infrastructure; (2) the construction and improvements of the expressway network are urgent "must" as it is the main means for the interregional cargo transportation; (3) especially, it is the most important task, from the national economic viewpoint, to construct the Second To-Mei (Tokyo–Nagoya) Expressway and Second Mei-Shin (Nagoya-Kobe) Expressway; (4) it is an indispensably important task to construct and improve the intra-regional highway systems; (5) investments into railway should be limited to the construction and improvements which can be complementary to the highway and expressway with the freight transport; and (6) Shinkansen would be effective with the passenger trips between Tokyo-Osaka.

It still must be said that the study has just taken a first step on the road, as a trial for making up a real practically useful and meaningful model for the planning of the comprehensive transportation system.

6.2.1 Scale of the Linear Programming Model

The constraints of the linear programming model are composed of the following equations/constraints that describe:

1. the market flow conditions region by region and goods by goods,
2. the production capacity constraints of the private sectors region by region,
3. the capacity constraints of the transportation infrastructures mode by mode and route by route,
4. the constraint of the public funds,
5. the constraint of the assignment of the additional labor and,
6. the constraints of the leisure trip origin by origin and destination by destination.

The number of cargo shipment activities is calculated as follows:

$$[10\ (\text{origin regions})] \times [9\ (\text{kinds of commodities})] \times [10\ (\text{destination regions})]$$
$$\times [4\ (\text{transportation modes})] \times [2\ (\text{alternative routes on average})]$$
$$= 7,200.$$

The number of leisure trip activities is calculated as follows:

$$[10\ (\text{origin regions})] \times [10\ (\text{destination regions})] \times [7\ (\text{transportation modes})]$$
$$\times [3\ (\text{alternative routes on average})]$$
$$= 2,100.$$

Therefore, the total number of variables (activities in the sense of linear programming model) must be 9300 which causes loads on the transportation infrastructures. However, due to the capacity of the computer and the applicable software at that time, it is reduced to around 5500, by excluding activities that are unrealistic in terms of routes and modes considering origin and destination and goods transported (with cargo shipment activities).

The number of transportation infrastructure facilities is 197 (Tables 6.1, 6.2, 6.3a, and 6.3b), of which capacity must be equal to or greater than the sum of loads by cargo shipments and leisure trips. The construction costs of social overhead capitals are classified into three categories depending on the values of MRS which converts the utility obtained by social overhead capital into a monetary value. Hence, there are 317 (197 + 40 × 3) variables that define the incremental variables of transportation infrastructure capacities and social overhead capitals. The number of slack variables is 717. The total number of columns (variables) becomes 6731.

As for the number of rows (equations/constraints), the number of the market flow conditions becomes 180:

$$\left\{ \begin{array}{r} [9\ \text{sectors other than transportation}] \\ +[9\ \text{business types in the transportation sector}] \end{array} \right\} \times [10\ \text{regions}] = 180$$

The number of rows that define the production capacity constraints is the same as the number of rows that define the market flow conditions and, therefore, it is 180. The number of rows is 197, which defines the transportation infrastructure capacity constraints. The upper constraints are laid on with the three types of construction costs, with which social overhead capitals having different qualities and different MRSs for the conversion of the utility obtained into monetary values, and the number of the associated rows is 120. The leisure trips are exogenously given and constrained zone by zone depending on the distance, which gives 40 rows. Another row is the assignment constraint of the public funds. Therefore, the total number of rows is, therefore, 718 = 180 + 180 + 197 + 120 + 40 + 1.

The matrix for the linear programming model which is developed with the structural equations of the constraints and the objective function becomes the matrix of 719 × 6,731. It reached almost to the upper limit constrained by the linear

Table 6.3a Optimal allocation of public funds (transportation facilities)

Row no.	Transport facilities	Section	Distance (km)	Optimal investment amounts (million yen)	Imputed price to the constraint row	Row no.	Transport facilities	Section	Distance (km)	Optimal investment amounts (million yen)	Imputed price to the constraint row
	Transport facilities of interregions						Ordinary roads (highway)				
	Rail					51		Sapporo–Kitahiroshima	12.0	512	0.0003
1		Sapporo–Hakodate	286.3	236,088	0.0559	52		Kitahiroshima–Tomakomaihigashi	49.0	0	0
2		Hakodate–Aomori	54.0	41,436	0.0099	53		Tomakomaihigashi–	83.0	3530	0.0023
3		Aomori–Morioka	203.9	122,458	0.0336	54		Toya–Hakodate	153.0	61,840	0.0042
4		Morioka–Sendai	183.5	123,538	0.0336	55		Hakodate–Aomori	113.0	45,806	0.0031
5		Sendai–Fukushima	79.0	31,567	0.0140	56		Aomori–Ikarigaseki	44.0	0	0.0000
6		Fukushima–Ueno	269.3	124,608	0.0559	57		Ikarigaseki–Ashiro	64.0	2738	0.0018
7		Tokyo–Nagoya	366.0	9919	0.0559	58		Ashiro–Sendai	238.0	0	0
8		Aomori–Nagaoka	60.56	47,738	0.0839	59		Sendai–Tokyo	326.0	57,741	0.0090
9		Nagaoka–Toyama	190.8	23,868	0.0419	60		Aomori–Niigata	465.0	0	0
10		Toyama–Kanazawa	59.5	6555	0.0112	61		Sendai–Niigata	229.0	0	0

11		Kanazawa–Tsuruga	130.7	0	0	62		Niigata–Nagaoka	62.0	0	0
12		Tsuruga–Maibara	45.9	0	0	63		Tokyo–Tsukiyono	135.0	20	0.0037
13		Tokyo–Takasaki	105.0	0	0	64		Tsukiyono–Yuzawa	36.0	1498	0.0010
14		Takasaki–Niigata	228.9	0	0	65		Yuzawa–Nagaoka	78.0	12	0.0021
15		Nagoya–Maibara	79.9	1798	0.0140	66		Nagaoka–Kakizaki	47.0	7	0.0013
16		Maibara–Osaka	110.5	2697	0.0210	67		Kakizaki–Asahi	91.0	3780	0.0025
17		Osaka–Okayama	176.5	5795	0.0336	68		Asahi–Kanazawa	102.0	15	0.0028
18		Okayama–Uno	32.9	773	0.0060	69		Kanazawa–Maibara	181.0	0	0
19		Uno–Takamatsu	18.0	352	0.0033	70		Tokyo–Nagoya	347.0	0	0
20		Takamatsu–Ikeda	76.5	1801	0.0140	71		Nagoya–Maibara	59.0	0	0
21		Okayama–Hiroshima	161.9	2189	0.0280	72		Maibara–Osaka	110.0	0	0
22		Hiroshima–Hakata	281.7	0	0	73		Osaka–Himeji	85.0	28,700	0.0023
23		Hakata–Tosu	28.6	0	0	74		Himeji–Bizen	53.0	0	0
24		Tosu–Nagasaki	125.3	0	0	75		Bizen–Okayama	36.0	12,180	0.0010
25		Tosu–Kumamoto	89.8	0	0	76		Ochiai–Okayama	60.0	10,711	0.0016

(continued)

Table 6.3a (continued)

Row no.	Transport facilities	Section	Distance (km)	Optimal investment amounts (million yen)	Imputed price to the constraint row	Row no.	Transport facilities	Section	Distance (km)	Optimal investment amounts (million yen)	Imputed price to the constraint row
26		Kumamoto–kagoshima	201.9	0	0	77		Okayama–Kurashiki	25.0	4464	0.0007
	New trunk line					78		Kurashiki–Kojima	23.9	6299	0.0007
						79		Kojima–Sakaide	18.4	4826	0.0005
27		Sapporo–Hakodate	316.0	20,948	0.0117	80		Sakaide–Kawanoe	47.0	12,400	0.0013
28		Hakodate–Aomori	54.0	3572	0.0020	81		Kurashiki–Fukuyama	48.0	4075	0.0013
29		Aomori–Morioka	170.0	8990	0.0063	82		Fukuyama–Shiwa	65.0	33,760	0.0018
30		Morioka–Sendai	171.0	0	0						
31		Sendai–Fukushima	70.0	0	0	83		Shiwa–Hiroshima	37.0	3138	0.0010
32		Fukushima–Ueno	255.0	0	0	84		Hiroshima–Hatsukaichi	25.0	2126	0.0007
33		Tokyo–Nagoya	342.0	865,188	0.0126	85		Hatsukaichi–Iwakuni	20.0	7126	0.0006
34		Niigata–Toyama	230.2	0	0	86		Iwakuni–Yuda	87.0	7422	0.0024
35		Toyama–Kanazawa	53.9	0	0	87		Yuda–Kitakyusyu	72.0	6136	0.0020

36		Kanazawa–Tsuruga	118.4	0	0	88		Kitakyusyu–Wakamiya	44.0	3739	0.0014
37		Tsuruga–Osaka	110.0	0	0	89		Wakamiya–Tosu	52.0	4428	0.0014
38		Tokyo–Takasaki	108.0	0	0	90		Tosu–Kanzaki	13.0	0	0
39		Takasaki–Toyama	302.1	0	0	91		Kanzaki–Oomura	80.0	0	0
40		Nagoya–Maibara	66.2	105,231	0.0043	92		Oomura–Nagasaki	18.0	0	0
41		Maibara–Osaka	107.1	172,516	0.0070	93		Tosu–Kumamoto	128.0	10,824	0.0035
42		Osaka–Okayama	161.0	0	0	94		Kumamoto–Yashiro	43.0	303	0.0012
43		Okayama–Sakaide	49.2	0	0	95		Yashiro–Ebino	63.0	17,575	0.0017
44		Sakaide–Ikeda	56.9	0	0	96		Ebino–Kagoshimakita	71.0	499	0.0020
45		Okayama–Hiroshima	145.0	0	0	97		Kagoshimakita–Kagoshima	5.0	6625	0.0007
46		Hiroshima–Hakata	248.0	0	0		expressway				
47		Hakata–Tosu	28.6	0	0	98		Sapporo–Kitahiroshima	12.0	4381	0.0003
48		Tosu–Kumamoto	71.0	0	0	99		Kitahiroshima–Tomakomaihigashi	49.0	18,669	0.0014
49		Tosu–Nagasaki	120.0	0	0	100		Tomakomaihigashi–Toya	83.0	30,238	0.0023
50		Kumamoto–kagoshima	170.0	0	0	101		Aomori–Ikarigaseki	44.0	11,773	0.0008

Note: For convenience's sake, a section of the ordinary road and that of the expressway are supposed to be the same programming software available in that day though the scale of the matrix could be fairly extended compared to the time when we constructed the model in Chap. 4.

6.2.2 Simulation Results

6.2.2.1 The Objective Function and the Optimal Basic Activities

The maximized value of the objective function is 5888.2 trillion JPY. The objective function is composed of the monetary values of the cargo shipment activities, leisure trip activities, and the social overhead capital stocks. The cargo shipment activities and leisure trip activities are evaluated with the value-added ratios and the MRSs, respectively, as well as the monetary evaluation coefficients of the (reduced) required time for transportation. The latter coefficients evaluate not only the canceling of the bottleneck to the economic development but also the time saved for transportation. In this sense, a sort of generalized cost is taken into account when the optimal choice is made with routes and modes for the shipment and trip as well as investments into transportation infrastructure improvements. Although the maximized value of the objective function apparently differs quite a lot from any predicted values of the GDP in the target year 1990, which was actually 281.9 trillion JPY (in terms of price in 1975), it is a natural result and it does not make sense if the value was compared with any predicted value of GDP in 1990. The objective function should be taken as a kind of the social welfare function for the decision on the investments into the comprehensive transportation system and social overhead capitals.

6.2.2.2 The Assignment of the Public Funds

Tables 6.3a and 6.3b show the assignment of the public funds, of which amount is exogenously given, to the transportation infrastructures and the imputed prices, which are associated with the transportation infrastructures section by section. In terms of the model specification developed in subsection 3 of Sect. 5 in Chap. 4, the tables show the values of ΔT^k, which satisfies the following equations (cf. Eq. (4. 130) and Eq. (4.136)):

Table 6.3b Optimal allocation of public funds (transportation facilities)

Row no.	Transport facilities	Section	Distance (km)	Optimal investment amounts (million yen)	Imputed price to the constraint row	Row no.	Transport facilities	Section	Distance (km)	Optimal investment amounts (million yen)	Imputed price to the constraint row
102		Ikarigaseki–Ajiro	64.0	16,568	0.0012	152		Cyukyo		2,509,791	0.5557
103		Ajiro–Sendai	238.0	63,074	0.0043	153		Hokuriku		0	0
104		Sendai–Tokyo	326.0	602,318	0.0060	154		Kinki		2,485,973	0.0556
105		Niigata–Nagaoka	62.0	0	0	155		Cyugoku		0	0
106		Tokyo–Tsukiyono	135.0	296,289	0.0062	156		Shikoku		0	0
107		Tsukiyono–Yuzawa	36.0	78,344	0.0016	157		Kyusyu		946,345	0.0556
108		Yuzawa–Nagaoka	78.0	170,722	0.0036	158		Okinawa		260,171	0.0556
109		Nagaoka–Kakizaki	47.0	103,334	0.0022		Intra-regional facilities				
110		Kakizaki–Asahi	91.0	182,140	0.0033		rail				
111		Asahi–Kanazawa	102.0	204,395	0.0037	159		Hokkaido		0	0
112		Kanazawa–Maibara	181.0	13,130	0.0066	160		Tohoku		38,058	0.0052
113		Tokyo–Nagoya	347.0	880,316	0.0161	161		Kanto		81,660	0.0056
114		Nagoya–Maibara	59.0	991,838	0.0027	162		Cyukyo		69,173	0.0034
115		Maibara–Osaka	110.0	1,018,248	0.0051	163		Hokuriku		69,470	0.0060

(continued)

Table 6.3b (continued)

Row no.	Transport facilities	Section	Distance (km)	Optimal investment amounts (million yen)	Imputed price to the constraint row	Row no.	Transport facilities	Section	Distance (km)	Optimal investment amounts (million yen)	Imputed price to the constraint row
116		Osaka–Ochiai	151.0	1,172,776	0.0055	164		Kinki		9219	0.0047
117		Ochiai–Hiroshima	181.0	1,401,245	0.0066	165		Cyugoku		15,295	0.0056
118		Hiroshima–Yuda	149.0	894,361	0.0054	166		Shikoku		42,919	0.0052
119		Himeji–Bizen	53.0	9105	0.0019	167		Kyusyu		19,641	0.0056
120		Okayama–Kurashiki	25.0	4301	0.0009		New trunk line				
121		Kurashiki–Kojima	23.9	6337	0.0009	168		Hokkaido		0	0
122		Kojima–Sakaide	18.4	4878	0.0007	169		Tohoku		51,700	0.0033
123		Sakaide–Kawanoe	47.0	12,609	0.0017	170		Cyukyo		0	0
124		Kurashiki–Fukuyama	48.0	14,636	0.0018	171		Hokuriku		0	0
125		Shiwa–Hiroshima	37.0	11,275	0.0014	172		Kinki		0	0
126		Hiroshima–Hatsukaichi	25.0	2939	0.0009	173		Cyugoku		0	0
127		Iwakuni–Yuda	87.0	10,751	0.0032	174		Shikoku		0	0
128		Yuda–Kitakyusyu	72.0	851,445	0.0026	175		Kyusyu		16,585	0.0036

129		Kitakyusyu–Wakamiya	44.0	519,873	0.0016		Ordinary roads (highway)				
130		Wakamiya–Tosu	52.0	610,110	0.0047	176		Hokkaido		856,404	0.0015
131		Tosu–Kannzaki	13.0	662	0.0001	177		Tohoku		784,964	0.0016
132		Kannzaki–Oomura	80.0	4074	0.0004	178		Kanto		2,106,160	0.0016
133		Oomura–Nagasaki	18.0	916	0.0001	179		Cyukyo		341,290	0.0016
134		Tosu–Kumamoto	128.0	1,491,899	0.0054	180		Hokuriku		88,846	0.0016
135		Kumamoto–Yashiro	43.0	8224	0.0016	181		Kinki		929,691	0.0016
136		Yashiro–Ebino	63.0	4519	0.0023	182		Cyugoku		265,674	0.0017
137		Ebino–Kagoshimakita	71.0	13,602	0.0026	183		Shikoku		302,482	0.0015
138		Kagoshimakita–Kagoshima	5.0	353	0.0002	184		Kyusyu		927,791	0.0016
	Airport					185		Okinawa		167,547	0.0018
139		Hokkaido		51,357	0.0671		Expressway				
140		Tohoku		47,224	0.0671	186		Hokkaido		26,954	0.0001
141		Kanto		339,959	0.0671	187		Tohoku		92,300	0.0003
142		Cyukyo		40,266	0.0671	188		Kanto		980,705	0.0011
143		Hokuriku		9334	0.0671	189		Cyukyo		98,382	0.0008
144		Kinki		279,109	0.0671	190		Hokuriku		40,799	0.0011
145		Cyugoku		2054	0.0671	191		Kinki		385,934	0.0009
146		Shikoku		5042	0.0671	192		Cyugoku		154,698	0.0011
147		Kyusyu		65,102	0.0671	193		Shikoku		23,082	0.0003

(continued)

Table 6.3b (continued)

Row no.	Transport facilities	Section	Distance (km)	Optimal investment amounts (million yen)	Imputed price to the constraint row	Row no.	Transport facilities	Section	Distance (km)	Optimal investment amounts (million yen)	Imputed price to the constraint row
148		Okinawa		99,185	0.0671	194		Kyusyu		253,651	0.0007
	Harbor					195		Okinawa		0	0
149		Hokkaido		1,491,670	0.00556		Kokuden				
150		Tohoku		2,188,787	0.5557	196		Kanto		499,092	0.0280
151		Kanto		0	0	197		Kiniki		97,648	0.0280

$$\sum_{j=1}^{n-1}\sum_{s=1}^{r}\sum_{t=1}^{r}\sum_{h=1}^{m}\sum_{\tau=1}^{\theta(h,s,t)} {}^{h\tau}\delta^{st}(k)\cdot {}^{h}\xi_j^k \cdot {}^{h\tau}x_j^{st}$$

$$+\sum_{j=1}^{n^L}\sum_{s=1}^{r}\sum_{t=1}^{r}\sum_{h=1}^{m}\sum_{\tau=1}^{\phi(h,s,t)} {}^{h\tau}\psi^{st}(k)\cdot {}^{h}\varphi_j^k \cdot {}^{h\tau}P_j^{st} - \Delta T^k$$

$$= \overline{T}^k \ (k = 1, 2, \ldots, n^T) \tag{6.1}$$

$$\sum_{k=1}^{n^T}\mu^k \Delta T^k + \sum_{p=1}^{r}\sum_{j=1}^{n^G}\gamma_j^p \Delta G_j^p \le \overline{C}, \tag{6.2}$$

$$\sum_{t\epsilon R(s,j)}\sum_{h=1}^{m}\sum_{\tau=1}^{\phi(h,s,t)} {}^{h\tau}P_j^{st} = \overline{P}_j^s \ (j = 1, 2, \ldots, n^L; s = 1, 2, \ldots, r). \tag{6.3}$$

in which $R(s,j)$: set of indices of regions which possibly attract passenger trips of leisure type j from region s ($j = 1, 2, \ldots, n^L; s = 1, 2, \ldots, r$); ${}^{h\tau}P_j^{st}$: passenger trips of leisure type j from region s to region t using route τ of transportation mode h($j = 1$, 2, …, n^L; τ = 1, 2, …, $\phi(h, s, t)$; s = 1, 2, …, r; t = 1, 2, …, r; h = 1, 2, …, m); ${}^{h\tau}\psi^{st}(k)$: if passenger trips of ${}^{h\tau}P_j^{st}$ use the transportation infrastructure k, it is 1 (one). If not, it is 0 (zero) (τ = 1, 2, …, $\phi(h, s, t)$; s = 1, 2, …, r; t = 1, 2, …, r; h = 1, 2, …, m); ${}^{h}\varphi_j^k$: coefficient that converts the passenger trips of ${}^{h\tau}P_j^{st}$ into loads on the transportation infrastructure k; ΔG_j^p: increase in the social overhead capital of type j (environmental hygiene (j = 1); public rental housing (j = 2); social and medical welfare (j = 3); education (j = 4)) in region p; γ_j^p: investment cost per increase in the social overhead capital of type j in region p; n^L: number of types of leisure trips ($n^L = 4$); and other symbols are the same as those use in Chap. 4.

The tables also show the values of λ_k ($k = 1, 2, \ldots, n^T$), which are imputed prices associated to Eq. (6.1) (($k = 1, 2, \ldots, n^T$), respectively. The imputed price, $\widehat{\lambda}$, which shall be associated to Eq. (6.2), represents the opportunity cost of an additional increase/decrease in the limited public funds in terms of increase/decrease in the objective function value.

Equation (6.1) is originally the balance between: (a) the k-th section of transportation infrastructure capacity (supply), $\overline{T}^k$; and (b) the demand against the k-th section of transportation infrastructure that is the sum of demands by transportation modes which provide transportation services for commodity flows and passenger trips (cf. Eq. (4.130) in Chap. 4). When $\overline{T}^k$, the initial stock of the k-th section of transportation infrastructure (= capacity) is not enough to meet the demand (the sum of the first and second terms in the left-hand side of k-th equation in Eq. (6.1), the shortage in the capacity can be a bottleneck for the development of the economy.

Taking into account the consistency[1] between the imputed prices (opportunity cost) of the public funds, $\widehat{\lambda}$, and the k-th section of transportation infrastructure, λ_k,

[1]Minute explanation is given later on.

the assignment of public funds will be made to an increase in the capacity of the k-th transportation infrastructure, which is called—public investment into k-th section of transportation infrastructure. If the assignment is not made (and the capacity is fully utilized), the bottleneck if any must be resolved by changing the route and mode of commodity shipments and passenger trips, interregional trade patterns, and so on.

Table 6.4 shows the assignment of public funds to the social overhead capital, which is called—investment into the social overhead capital. Tables 6.5 and 6.6 summarize shares between the total investment into transportation infrastructures and the total investment into social overhead capitals as well as they summarize shares among transportation modes and shares among types of social overhead capitals, respectively.

First, the investment share between the transportation infrastructures and the social overhead capitals is almost 50:50. This is a plausible result according to the public investment shares in the 7 Years New Economic Planning by the Economic Planning Agency (EPA, 1979), which is summarized in Table 6.7. The total budget is 146,650,000 million JPY and it is assumed that around half of the total budget (trillion JPY) is utilized for the maintenance and repair of existing stocks.

The simulation results show that the share of highway and expressway in the planning is plausible and the share of railway and Shinkansen should be reduced to one-quarter. The share of marine in the planning should be almost triplicated. It can be said that an emphasis was still laid on "railway" in the planning in the late 1970s.

6.2.2.3 Opportunity Cost of the Public Funds

The imputed price of the public funds, $\widehat{\lambda}$, is calculated as 0.08387, which means an increase of one million JPY in the budget for public investment (the public funds) results in an increase of 83,870 JPY in the social welfare in monetary terms per year. The efficiency of the public investment implies that it takes around 12 years to get a return on the public investment without maintenance and repair. It can be said that the Japanese economy in the late 1970s was still efficient even considering the costs of maintenance and repair because the assumed durability of social overhead capitals is around 20–70 years depending on their types. For example, it is 20–40 years as for roads and it is 30–70 years as for public rental housing.

As it is shown in Chap. 4, the equalization of imputed prices must hold among the sections of transportation infrastructures to which the public funds are injected. Examples are shown in Table 6.8, which picks up the transportation infrastructures of Highway (row no. 51 in the linear programming specification), Expressway (row no. 98), Airport (row no. 146), and Intra-expressway (row no. 194).

As once both sides of each inequality of the linear programming model specification are divided by the maximum absolute value among the coefficients of variables in its left-hand side in order to minimize possible calculation errors, the following equation must hold:

Table 6.4 Optimal allocation of public funds (social overhead capitals)

Row no.	Region	Facilities	Optimal investment amounts (million yen)
201	Hokkaido	Environmental hygiene	747,760
202		Public lease house	396,800
203		Social and medical welfare	230,368
204		Education	410,839
205	Tohoku	Environmental hygiene	477,479
206		Public lease house	732,840
207		Social and medical welfare	397,992
208		Education	774,741
209	Kanto	Environmental hygiene	3,517,351
210		Public lease house	2,589,740
211		Social and medical welfare	8,903,644
212		Education	319,308
213	Chukyo	Environmental hygiene	1,222,629
214		Public lease house	671,770
215		Social and medical welfare	278,208
216		Education	766,277
217	Hokuriku	Environmental hygiene	144,595
218		Public lease house	207,080
219		Social and medical welfare	123,464
220		Education	441,694
221	Kinki	Environmental hygiene	2,291,066
222		Public lease house	4,322,640
223		Social and medical welfare	602,976
224		Education	983,994
225	Chugoku	Environmental hygiene	329,338
226		Public lease house	537,540
227		Social and medical welfare	278,024
228		Education	623,832
229	Shikoku	Environmental hygiene	146,423
230		Public lease house	286,440
231		Social and medical welfare	186,760
232		Education	839,169
233	Kyushu	Environmental hygiene	696,016
234		Public lease house	777,480
235		Social and medical welfare	539,856
236		Education	802,791
237	Okinawa	Environmental hygiene	93,470
238		Public lease house	166,600
239		Social and medical welfare	21,896
240		Education	32,538

Imputed prices are not calculated as no constraints on the allocation but for the total public funds

Table 6.5 Investment shares among transportation facilities. Unit: million JPY

	Interregional investment	Percentage	Intra-regional investment	Percentage	Total	%	% (against the total public funds)
Railway	783,180	3.04	345,435	3.51	1,128,615	3.17	1.54
Shinkansen	1,176,445	4.57	68,285	0.69	1,244,730	3.50	1.69
Highway	364,855	1.42	6,770,849	68.82	7,135,704	20.05	9.71
Expressway	12,602,909	48.95	2,056,505	20.90	14,659,414	41.19	19.94
Airport	938,632	3.65	0	0.00	938,632	2.64	1.28
Marine	9,882,737	38.38	0	0.00	9,882,737	27.77	13.45
Kokuden	0	0.00	596,740	6.07	596,740	1.68	0.81
	25,748,758	100.00	9,837,814	100.00	35,586,572	100.00	48.42

Table 6.6 Investment shares among social overhead capitals. Unit: million JPY

Social overhead capitals	Environmental hygiene	Public rental housing	Social and medical welfare	Education	Total
Investments	9,666,127	10,688,930	11,563,188	5,995,183	37,913,428
%	25.50	28.19	30.50	15.81	100
% (against the total public funds)	13.15	14.54	15.73	8.16	51.58

Table 6.7 Public investment share of the 7 years new economic plan by EPA. Unit: million JPY

	Transportation infrastructures				
	Highway + Expressway	Railway	Marine	Airport	Subtotal
Assignment of the public funds	46,000,000	17,750,000	6,850,000	2,750,000	73,350,000
Share among transportation infrastructures	31.37	12.10	4.67	1.88	50.02
	Social overhead capitals				
	Environmental hygiene	Public rental housing	Social and medical welfare	Education	Subtotal
Assignment of the public funds	33,580,000	13,500,000	5,420,000	20,800,000	73,300,000
Share among social overhead capitals	22.90	9.21	3.70	14.18	49.98
		Public investment fund total			146,650,000

Source: EPA (1979).

Table 6.8 Equalization of imputed prices

Row no.	Calculated imputed price (λ_i)	$\frac{\text{Construction costs}}{\text{Increment in facility}}$ (μ^i)	Scale for decreasing calculation errors (m_i)	Imputed price in terms of the public funds ($\widehat{\lambda}_i$)
51	0.00033	0.00032	12.29	0.0839
98	0.00033	0.00034	11.59	0.0839
146	0.06710	0.80000	1.00	0.0839
194	0.00067	0.00037	21.58	0.0839

$$\frac{\lambda_1}{\mu^1 m_1} = \frac{\lambda_2}{\mu^2 m_2} = \ldots = \frac{\lambda_{n^T}}{\mu^T m_{n^T}} = \widehat{\lambda} \tag{6.4}$$

in which λ_i = the calculated imputed price associate with the i-th inequality (row); m_i = the scale used for dividing both sides of the i-th inequality (row) in order to minimize calculation errors; μ^i = the coefficient which converts one unit increase in the capacity of i-th transportation infrastructure into the necessary outlay of the public funds; and $\widehat{\lambda}=$ the imputed price of the public funds and it is 0.08387.

There are no calculated imputed prices with investments into the social overhead capitals since there are no inequalities in which the demand must be equal to or less than the supply of social overhead capital. The public funds are injected into the social overhead capitals of which MRSs are equal to or greater than $\widehat{\lambda}$. Three kinds of social overhead capital are assumed, which are classified by the construction costs. Each has the upper limit beyond which the public fund cannot be assigned.

6.2.2.4 Goods Flow

Tables 6.9 and 6.10 show the results of commodity flows with two sectors (agriculture, forestry, and fisheries; mining) in the primary industry. Tables 6.11, 6.12, and 6.13 show the results of commodity flows with the typical three sectors (chemical; metal; and others) in the manufacturing industry.

The intra- and interregional commodity flows are calculated on the following equation:

$$CF_j^{st} \equiv \sum\nolimits_{h=1}^{m} \sum_{\tau=1}^{\theta(h,s,t)} {}^{h\tau}\delta^{st}(k) \cdot {}^{h\tau}x_j^{st} \quad (j=1,2,\ldots,8,\text{and }10; s,t=1,2,\ldots,r), \tag{6.5}$$

in which: CF_j^{st}: intra- and interregional commodity flow of goods j from region s to region t.

The total products are calculated as follows:

$$XX_j^s \equiv \sum_{t=1}^{r} CF_j^{st} \quad (j=1,2,\ldots 8,\ \text{and } 10; s=1,2,\ldots,r), \tag{6.6}$$

in which XX_j^s: the total of the intra- and interregional shipment of goods j from region s to region t and it is the total product of goods j in region s ($j=1,2,\ldots,8$, and 10; $s=1,2,\ldots,r$).

Therefore, the total production of the sector j, XX_j, is defined as follows:

$$XX_j = \sum_{s=1}^{r} XX_j^s. \tag{6.7}$$

The values of XX_j^s are shown in the last column of Tables 6.9, 6.10, 6.11, 6.12, and 6.13 with $j=1$, 2, 4, 5, and 7. The values of XX_j are shown in the cells at the lower right corner of the tables.

Table 6.9 Optimal goods flow pattern (agriculture, forestry, and fisheries). Unit: million JPY/year

	Hokkaido	Tohoku	Kanto	Chukyo	Hokuriku	Kinki	Chugoku	Shikoku	Kyushu	Okinawa	Total
Hokkaido	1,898,022	0	0	0	0	0	0	0	0	0	1,898,022
Tohoku	0	3,224,607	0	0	0	0	0	0	0	0	3,224,607
Kanto	0	0	4,090,685	0	0	0	0	0	0	0	4,090,685
Chukyo	0	0	0	1,146,659	0	0	0	0	0	0	1,146,659
Hokuriku	0	0	0	0	380,556	0	0	0	0	0	380,556
Kinki	0	0	0	0	0	1,694,503	0	0	0	0	1,694,503
Chugoku	0	0	0	0	0	0	1,266,241	0	0	0	1,266,241
Shikoku	0	0	0	0	0	0	0	1,071,566	0	0	1,071,566
Kyushu	0	0	0	0	0	0	0	0	3,569,679	0	3,569,679
Okinawa	0	0	0	0	0	0	0	0	0	134,897	134,897
Total	1,898,022	3,224,607	4,090,685	1,146,659	380,556	1,694,503	1,266,241	1,071,566	3,569,679	134,897	18,477,415

Table 6.10 Optimal goods flow pattern (mining). Unit: million JPY/year

	Hokkaido	Tohoku	Kanto	Chukyo	Hokuriku	Kinki	Chugoku	Shikoku	Kyushu	Okinawa	Total
Hokkaido	212,802	0	0	7768	0	0	0	0	0	0	220,570
Tohoku	0	281,242	5053	0	40,942	0	0	0	0	0	327,237
Kanto	0	0	813,379	0	0	0	0	0	0	0	813,379
Chukyo	0	0	0	104,397	0	194,126	0	0	0	0	298,523
Hokuriku	0	0	0	0	45,383	0	0	0	0	0	45,383
Kinki	0	0	0	0	0	324,336	0	0	0	0	324,336
Chugoku	0	0	0	0	0	183,313	15,977	0	0	0	199,290
Shikoku	0	0	0	0	0	0	0	138,587	0	0	138,587
Kyushu	0	0	0	0	0	0	278,049	0	236,843	0	514,892
Okinawa	0	0	0	0	0	0	0	0	0	8970	8970
Total	212,802	281,242	818,432	112,165	86,325	701,775	294,026	138,587	236,843	8970	2,891,167

Table 6.11 Optimal goods flow pattern (chemical). Unit: million JPY/year

	Hokkaido	Tohoku	Kanto	Chukyo	Hokuriku	Kinki	Chugoku	Shikoku	Kyushu	Okinawa	Total
Hokkaido	1,767,864	1,204,974	0	0	0	0	0	0	0	0	2,972,838
Tohoku	0	3,381,330	0	0	0	0	0	0	0	0	3,381,330
Kanto	0	0	10,610,829	0	0	0	0	0	0	0	10,610,829
Chukyo	0	567,813	2,376,777	2,160,197	0	0	0	0	0	0	5,104,787
Hokuriku	0	542,730	0	0	1,397,080	0	0	0	0	0	1,939,810
Kinki	0	0	0	0	0	6,023,925	0	98,879	919,251	0	7,042,055
Chugoku	0	0	0	0	0	0	3,638,859	0	320,066	0	3,958,925
Shikoku	0	0	0	0	0	0	0	1,765,888	0	0	1,765,888
Kyushu	0	0	0	0	0	0	0	0	4,522,026	262,430	4,784,456
Okinawa	0	0	0	0	0	0	0	0	0	84,984	84,984
Total	1,767,864	5,696,847	12,987,606	2,160,197	1,397,080	6,023,925	3,638,859	1,864,767	5,761,343	347,414	41,645,902

Table 6.12 Optimal goods flow pattern (metal). Unit: million JPY/year

	Hokkaido	Tohoku	Kanto	Chukyo	Hokuriku	Kinki	Chugoku	Shikoku	Kyushu	Okinawa	Total
Hokkaido	2,371,313	1,357,778	0	0	0	0	0	0	0	0	3,729,091
Tohoku	0	4,218,322	0	0	0	0	0	0	0	0	4,218,322
Kanto	0	0	21,169,443	0	0	0	0	0	0	0	21,169,443
Chukyo	0	0	0	0	0	7,975,758	0	0	0	0	7,975,758
Hokuriku	0	0	0	0	1,923,642	0	0	0	0	0	1,923,642
Kinki	0	3,732,870	12,032,062	0	1,072,638	3,387,042	0	0	0	0	20,224,612
Chugoku	0	0	2,555,607	1,166,825	0	0	9,224,102	2,436,874	0	0	15,383,408
Shikoku	0	0	0	0	0	0	0	1,590,505	0	0	1,590,505
Kyushu	0	2,173,607	125,000	0	0	0	0	0	5,922,190	85,919	8,306,716
Okinawa	0	0	0	0	0	0	0	0	0	86,140	86,140
Total	2,371,313	11,482,577	35,882,112	1,166,825	2,996,280	11,362,800	9,224,102	4,027,379	5,922,190	172,059	84,607,637

Table 6.13 Optimal goods flow pattern (other manufacturing). Unit: million JPY/year

	Hokkaido	Tohoku	Kanto	Chukyo	Hokuriku	Kinki	Chugoku	Shikoku	Kyushu	Okinawa	Total
Hokkaido	86,713	0	0	0	0	0	0	0	0	0	86,713
Tohoku	0	1,294,974	0	0	0	0	0	0	0	0	1,294,974
Kanto	126,694	0	3,104,872	0	0	0	0	0	0	0	3,231,566
Chukyo	0	0	0	501,595	0	0	0	0	0	0	501,595
Hokuriku	0	0	0	0	172,991	0	0	0	0	0	172,991
Kinki	0	0	0	0	0	849,149	0	0	0	0	849,149
Chugoku	0	0	0	0	0	0	0	0	0	0	0
Shikoku	0	0	0	0	0	0	104,463	420,896	0	0	525,359
Kyushu	0	0	0	0	0	0	133,629	0	861,584	8154	1,003,367
Okinawa	0	0	0	0	0	0	0	0	0	70,822	70,822
Total	213,407	1,294,974	3,104,872	501,595	172,991	849,149	238,092	420,896	861,584	78,976	7,736,536

Basic Data of Shipment Activities

We had constructed inter-regional input-output table based on MITI 1975. Having written this chapter, we have used data of MITI 1990 in order to examine estimated results of the simulation (Kohno 1979, 1994; MITI 1975, 1990).

Agriculture, Forestry, and Fisheries

Table 6.9 shows that so-called local production for local consumption holds with the products of the agriculture, forestry, and fisheries sector. However, observing that the shipment distance of agricultural products has been lengthened by the construction of highway and improvement in the cargo air services, the interregional shipments with and longer distance should be made. In that sense, there is still space for improvements in the model specification, especially with the specification of distribution margin which accrues to logistics sectors in the origin region. The evaluation of shipment of goods with long distance in terms of the objective function is negative against making longer distance shipment and it must be canceled by a larger distribution margin if a longer distance shipment must be made.

According to the 1990 Input–Output Table of Japan at producer's price, the total production of the agriculture, forestry, and fisheries was 17.8 trillion JPY, which means that the total production of the agriculture, forestry, and fisheries at purchaser's price can be estimated as 19.8 trillion JPY. The simulation result shows 18.5 trillion JPY (Table 6.9) and it is fairly overestimated considering the difference in the price levels in 1975 (GDP deflator is 71.6) and 1990 (108.7). (The model specification assumes the price level of 1975). It is considered that the overestimation reflects the optimization neglects realities such as variety of subsidizing policies against agricultural sectors, some of which presume closed markets.

Mining

Interregional trade patterns can be observed in the mining sector (Table 6.10). Considering the value per weight of product, the pattern should be limited to an intra-regional one. However, the mining sector has an aspect of the site-specific industry. So, the result looks plausible. According to the 1990 I-O Table of Japan, the total production of the mining sector was 2.2 (2.4) trillion JPY at producer's (purchaser's) prices, respectively. The calculated value at purchaser's price is 2.9 trillion JPY in 1975 price and it is 4.4 trillion JPY in 1990 price. It is overestimated since the mining sector was declining during 1970s and 1980s.

Chemical

The total production of the chemical sector (including pottery, soil, and stone engineering) was 47.6 (52.9) trillion JPY according to the 1990 I-O Table of Japan at producer's (purchaser's) price. The calculated value, 41.6 (63.2) trillion JPY in the 1975 (1990) price, respectively, is a little bit overestimate considering the difference in the price level (Table 6.11).

Metal

The total production of the metal sector (including nonferrous metal, metallic products) was 51.0 (56.7) trillion JPY, which is observed by the 1990 I-O Table of Japan at producer's (purchaser's). The calculated result, 84.6 (128.4) trillion JPY in 1975 (1990) price, is far larger than it. The sector of metal is a typical large-scale and site-specific industry, which causes more diversified inter-regional trade patterns (Table 6.12).

Other Manufacturing

The total production of the other manufacturing sector was 32.4 (21.3) trillion JPY according to the 1990 I-O Table of Japan in 1990 (1975) price, respectively. The calculated result, 7.7 (8.6) trillion JPY in the 1975 (1990) price, is underestimate (Table 6.13). It is plausible that the trade pattern is basically of the so-called local production for local consumption.

6.2.2.5 Leisure Trip Pattern

Tables 6.14, 6.15, and 6.16 show results of passenger intra- and interregional trip patterns with typical three transportation modes (private automobile; domestic air for passenger traffic; and national railway (except for Kokuden)). The figures in the tables are expressed in terms of the value of products (transportation services) in million JPY. Therefore, the figures are dependent on the number of trips, the distance traveled per trip, and the travel cost per distance of the said transportation mode.

Table 6.14 Optimal leisure trip pattern (private automobile). Unit: million JPY/year

	Hokkaido	Tohoku	Kanto	Chukyo	Hokuriku	Kinki	Chugoku	Shikoku	Kyushu	Okinawa	Total
Hokkaido	253,799	0	0	0	0	92,926	0	0	0	0	346,725
Tohoku	0	79,664	63,887	1,214,750	0	0	0	0	0	0	1,358,301
Kanto	0	46,531	1,808,578	0	599	0	0	0	0	0	1,855,708
Chukyo	0	1,016,828	0	56,565	0	0	0	0	0	0	1,073,393
Hokuriku	0	18,995	0	0	88,135	72,400	0	0	0	0	179,530
Kinki	0	0	306,742	0	0	602,847	0	0	55,455	0	965,044
Chugoku	0	0	0	17,867	0	0	304,420	0	238,980	0	561,267
Shikoku	0	0	0	6702	0	0	0	104,603	234,360	0	345,665
Kyushu	0	403,324	0	0	0	168,149	11,869	323,914	492,996	0	1,400,252
Okinawa	0	0	0	0	0	35,731	0	0	0	114,083	149,814
Total	253,799	1,565,342	2,179,207	1,295,884	88,734	972,053	316,289	428,517	1,021,791	114,083	8,235,699

The figure in each cell means the input by (sales of) the transportation service sector in the origin region in order to transport leisure trips generated at the origin region and reaching the destination region. Therefore, the amount is dependent on: (1) the number of leisure trips per year and distance in kilometers between the origin and destination and (2) transportation fees per kilometer to use the transportation infrastructures

Table 6.15 Optimal leisure trip pattern (domestic air for passenger traffic). Unit: million JPY/year

	Hokkaido	Tohoku	Kanto	Chukyo	Hokuriku	Kinki	Chugoku	Shikoku	Kyushu	Okinawa	Total
Hokkaido	0	0	72,788	0	0	0	0	0	0	0	72,788
Tohoku	0	0	28,143	0	0	0	0	0	0	0	28,143
Kanto	18,711	0	0	56,862	23,769	190,459	0	0	0	0	289,801
Chukyo	0	0	29,328	0	0	0	0	0	0	0	29,328
Hokuriku	0	0	0	0	0	0	0	4595	4419	0	9014
Kinki	0	0	239,126	0	0	0	0	0	88,653	0	327,779
Chugoku	0	0	0	0	0	0	0	0	0	0	0
Shikoku	0	0	0	0	0	0	0	0	0	0	0
Kyushu	0	0	0	0	0	0	22,184	19,382	0	49,958	91,524
Okinawa	52,343	89,101	0	0	0	0	0	0	0	0	141,444
Total	71,054	89,101	369,385	56,862	23,769	190,459	22,184	23,977	93,072	49,958	989,821

The figure in each cell means the input by (sales of) the transportation service sector in the origin region in order to transport leisure trips generated at the origin region and reaching the destination region. Therefore, the amount is dependent on: (1) the number of leisure trips per year and distance in kilometers between the origin and destination and (2) transportation fees per kilometer to use the transportation infrastructures

Table 6.16 Optimal leisure trip pattern (Railway except for Kokuden). Unit: million JPY/year

	Hokkaido	Tohoku	Kanto	Chukyo	Hokuriku	Kinki	Chugoku	Shikoku	Kyushu	Okinawa	Total
Hokkaido					587,473	200,920					788,393
Tohoku		1,302,832									1,302,832
Kanto						1,387,594					1,387,594
Chukyo			1,289,638	1,307,071							2,596,709
Hokuriku	551,091										551,091
Kinki			2,276,713								2,276,713
Chugoku							282,837				282,837
Shikoku								723,277			723,277
Kyushu									643,099		643,099
Okinawa											0
Total	551,091	1,302,832	3,566,351	1,307,071	587,473	1,588,514	282,837	723,277	643,099	0	10,552,545

The figure in each cell means the input by (sales of) the transportation service sector in the origin region in order to transport leisure trips generated at the origin region and reaching the destination region. Therefore, the amount is dependent on: (1) the number of leisure trips per year and distance in kilometers between the origin and destination and (2) transportation fees per kilometer to use the transportation infrastructures.

The Final Demand of Leisure Trips Against the Transportation Sector

The sum of figures in the lower right corner of Tables 6.14, 6.15, and 6.16, which show the purchased amount of transportation services induced by leisure trips, is 19.8 (39.1) trillion JPY in 1975 (1990) price. The services must be provided by the transportation sector, of which the total product was 42.6 (28.1) trillion JPY according to the 1990 I-O Table of Japan in 1990 (1975) price. From another viewpoint, the sum of the total purchased domestic air services for passenger traffic and railway services except for Kokuden is 11.5 (17.5) trillion JPY in 1975 (1990) price, respectively. The services must be provided by the said transportation sector directly or through agents. The amount was 14.9 trillion JPY according to the 1990 I-O Table of Japan. This is also a little bit overestimate considering that services of other transportation modes such as marine, bus, and taxi, which are used for leisure trips, as well as other types of passenger trips such as business trips, commuting trips, and so on, which use domestic air services and railway services, are all not included in the estimate.

Private Automobile

Leisure trips with private automobiles distribute in local, short-, middle-, and long-distant area with almost all the origin regions but for Chukyo and Okinawa (Table 6.14). With these regions, leisure trips are realized with the transportation modes of marine, domestic air (Table 6.15), railway (Table 6.16), and bus. However, it can be said that the evaluation coefficients of time preference with transportation modes are relatively too much advantageous for the leisure trip of passenger automobile with the longer distance travel considering other passenger trips are too small.

Domestic Air for Passenger Traffic

On the contrary, Table 6.15 shows that the calculated results are a little bit underestimated considering that the scale of the market size was around 1.5–2.0 trillion JPY for passenger air traffic in 1990 even if other types of passenger trips such as business trips are excluded and the GDP deflator is taken into account.

Railway (Except for Kokuden)

As a result of too many passenger trips are absorbed by the mode of private automobile, the distribution of passenger trips between regions is small even taking into account Kokuden excluded from the table. However, the calculated total production, 10.6 trillion JPY, in 1975 price is also an overestimate considering that: the total product of railway sector in 1975 price is estimated as

4.2 ($42.6 \times 0.15 \times 71.6 \div 108.7$) trillion JPY based on the 1990 I-O and by assuming railway share is 15%; and railway services are utilized for cargo shipments.

6.2.2.6 Optimal Allocation of the Public Funds to the Arterial Transportation Network

Conventional Railway

Figures 6.2a shows the current network of the conventional railway (excluding Shinkansen) on that day and Fig. 6.2b shows the optimal assignment of the public funds in order to improve the current network of the conventional railway. Since the amount of public funds allocated for improvements in the inter- and intra-regional railway network is least among the five transportation infrastructure types, clearer characteristics could not be found. However, it can be said that there should be two keynotes for the improvements, namely (1) the traversal route longitudinally cutting through the main island starting from Sapporo in Hokkaido, going through Aomori in Tohoku, Tokyo in Kanto, Nagoya in Chubu, Osaka in Kansai and ending at Hiroshima in Chugoku; and (2) the Sea of Japan side route starting from Aomori, going through Niigata in Kanto, Toyama in Hokuriku and ending at Kanazawa in Hokuriku. As for the latter investment of public funds, it is considered that leisure trips of passenger car induce the investments into the Sea of Japan route of the conventional railway because there is no allocation of public funds for Shinkansen although the number of inter-regional leisure trips is big between Hokkaido, Hokuriku, and Kinki (Table 6.16); and there is no improvement plan with Shinkansen which goes through the Sea of Japan route (Fig. 6.3b). This means that the conventional railway should be only the transportation mode for passenger trips for a while.

Shinkansen

As for improvements in the arterial network of Shinkansen (Fig. 6.3a), two allocations of public funds are made: (1) the new route starting from Sapporo, going through Hakodate in Hokkaido, Aomori and ending at Morioka in Tohoku; and (2) existing route of Tokaido Shinkansen from Tokyo in Kanto going through Nagoya in Chukyo and ending at Osaka in Kinki (Fig. 6.3b). The former is to be positioned as an extension of Tohoku Shinkansen, which was scheduled to be placed in service in 1982, into Hokkaido, a Northern Island. The extension was long-desired by people living in Hokkaido and the total amount of public funds allocated for the extension is less than 100 million JPY, which is almost nothing. It should have been too early in the day to break ground for the extension of Tohoku Shinkansen into Hokkaido.

a

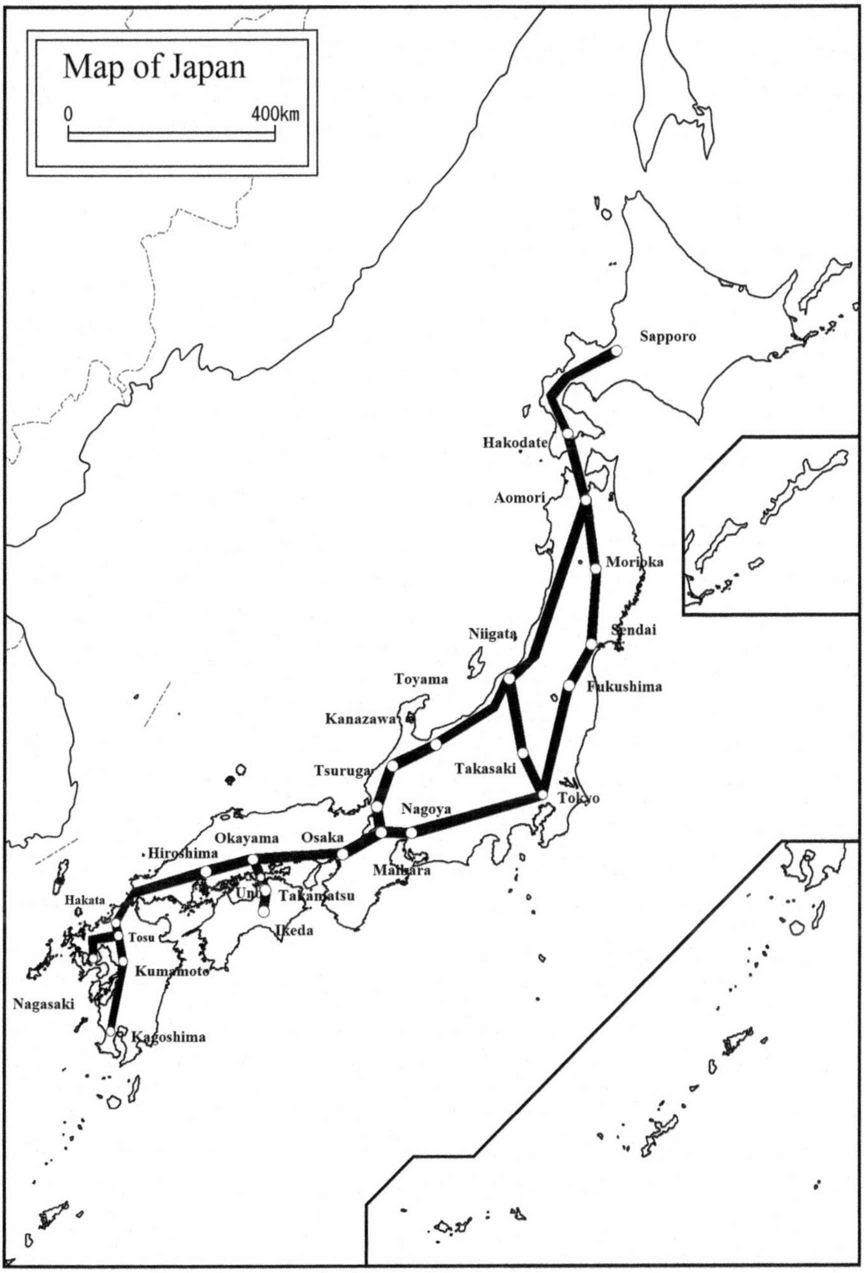

Fig. 6.2 (**a**) Current network of railway. (**b**) Optimal assignment of the public funds for railway improvements

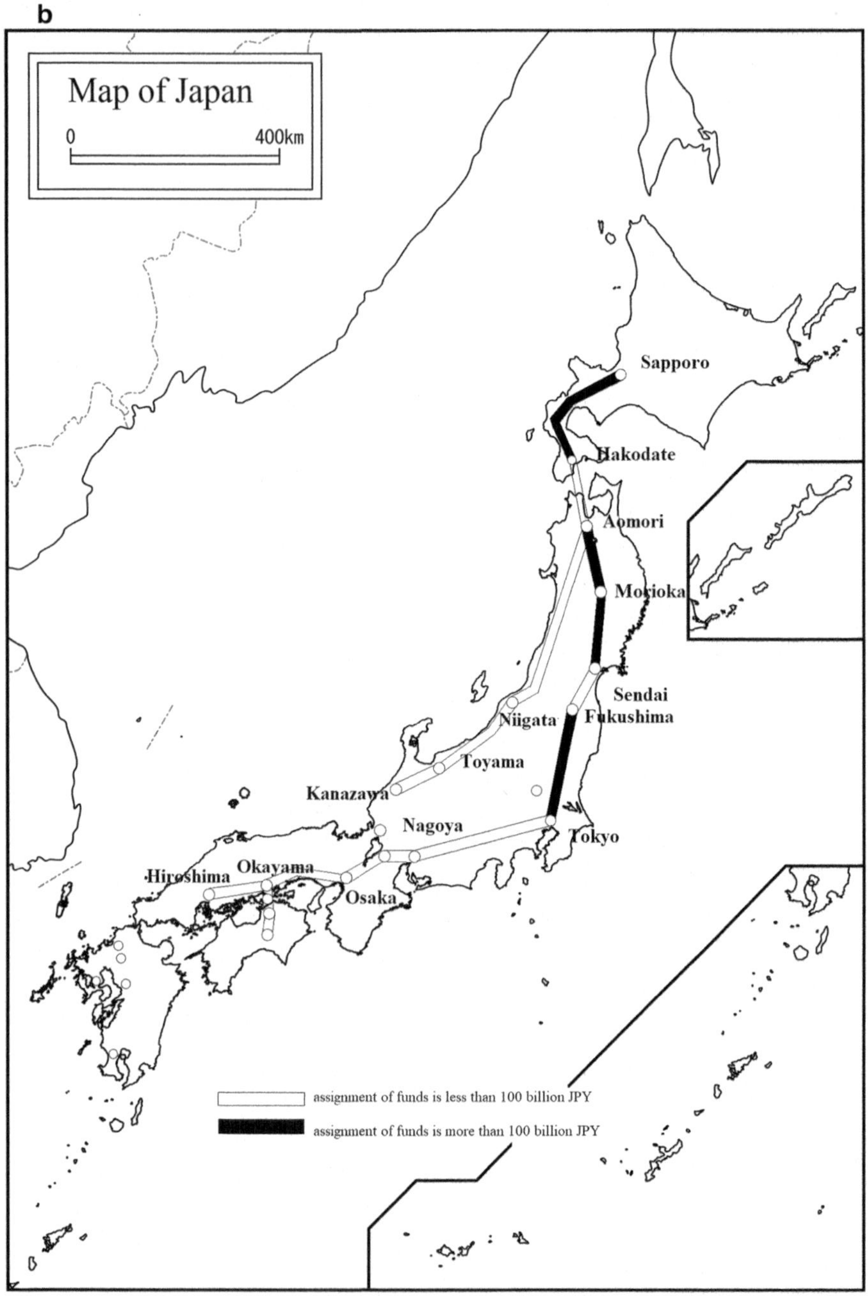

Fig. 6.2 (continued)

a

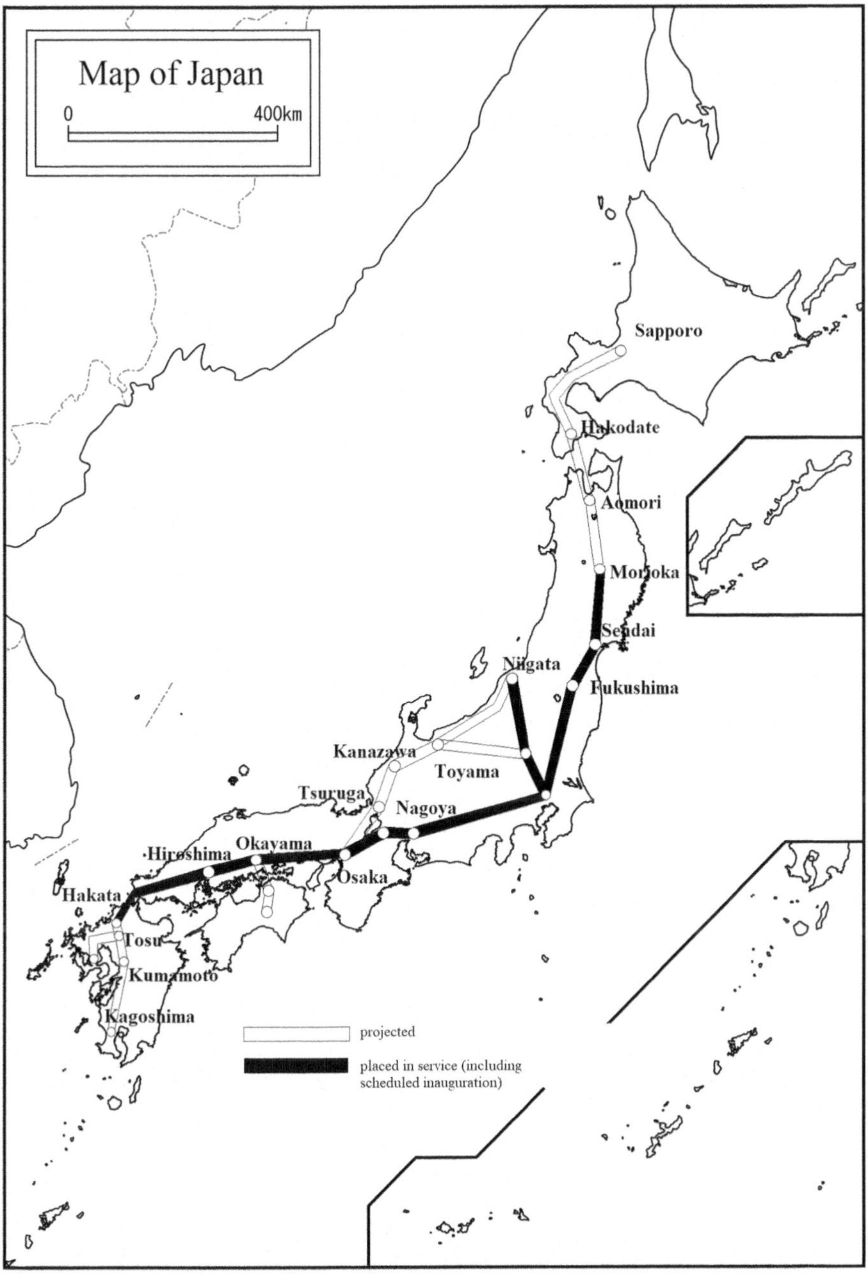

Fig. 6.3 (**a**) Current arterial network of Shinkansen. (**b**) Optimal assignment of the public funds for Shinkansen improvements

b

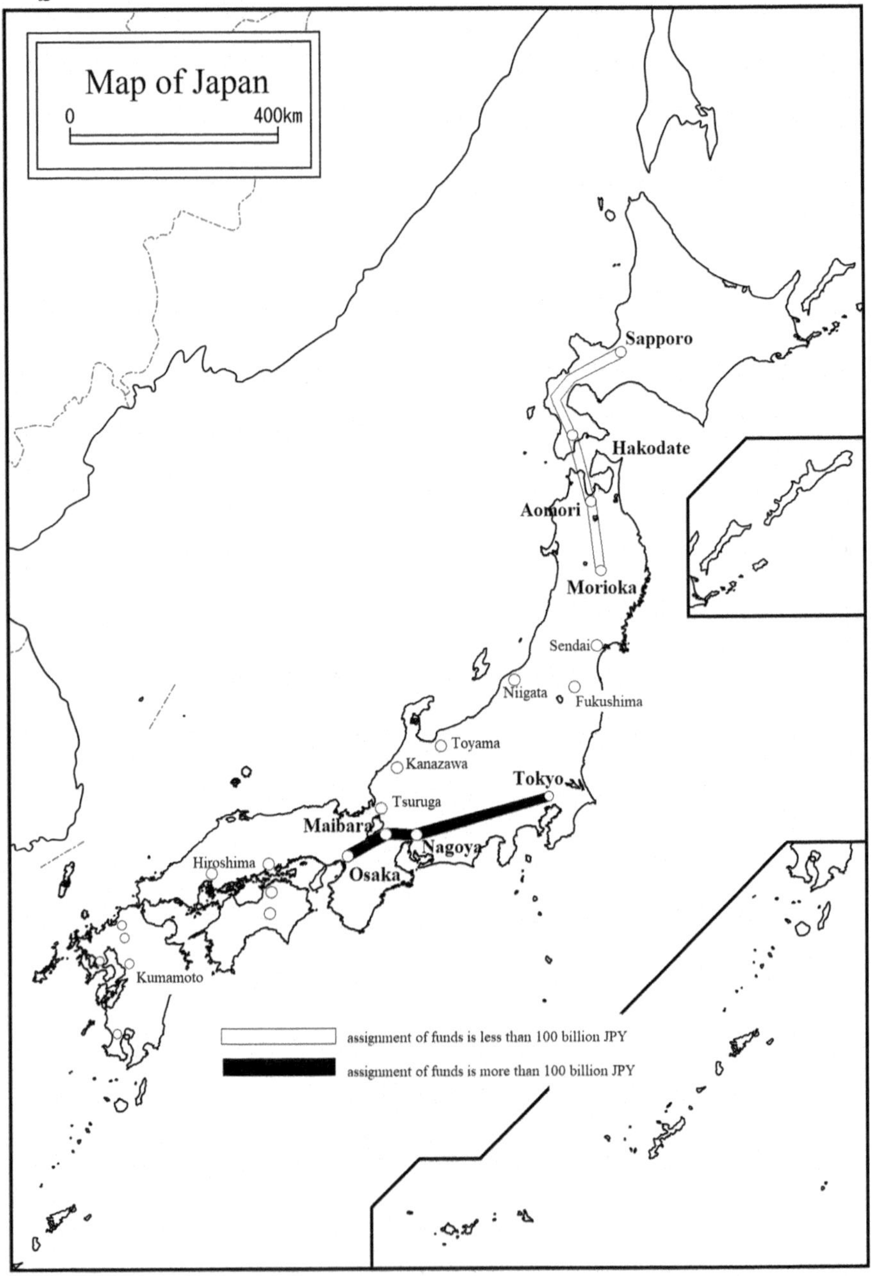

Fig. 6.3 (continued)

Tokaido Shinkansen was one of the cash-cow routes of JNR in that days and Shinkansen were already operated with an overcrowded train schedule. It can be said that the necessity of measures to be taken against the currently overcrowded train scheduled Tokaido Shinkansen is proved based on the rational and consistent criteria. However, the allocation of funds is not enough to the so-called project Second Tokaido Shinkansen considering that the average construction cost already became 3.5–4.0 billion JPY per kilometer with the five Projected Shinkansen in that day.

Highway

The current arterial highway network is shown in Fig. 6.4a. Highway links are specified so that they correspond to expressway links for simplicity of analysis. It can be said that the emphasis of assignments is laid on highway improvements in the northern districts of Japan, Hokkaido and Tohoku, the central districts, Kanto and Hokuriku, and the western districts, Chugoku, Shikoku, and Kyushu (Fig. 6.4b). Especially, taking a close look (Tables 6.3a and 6.3b), fairly good amounts of public funds are assigned to highway links between Toya (in Hokkaido) and Aomori (in Tohoku), Osaka and Himeji (in Kinki), Bizen and Okayama (in Chugoku), Fukuyama and Shiwa (in Chugoku), Hatsukaichi and Iwakuni (in Chugoku), and Kagoshimakita and Kagoshima (in Kyushu) in terms of the public fund assignment per kilometer. The reason why the assignments of public funds are concentrated on improvements of those highway links can be well explained by analyzing the assignments of public funds into improvements of the expressway.

Expressway

The current arterial expressway network is shown in Fig. 6.5a. Figure 6.5b shows optimal assignments of public funds to the expressway network improvements. First of all, it can be said that assignments of the public funds are made with almost all the expressway links which are projected or currently placed in service. Especially, the assignment is concentrated on two routes: the traversal route longitudinally cutting through the Japanese islands, starting from Sendai (in Tohoku), going through Tokyo (in Kanto), Nagoya (in Chukyo), Osaka (in Kinki), Hiroshima (Miyoshi) (in Chugoku), Kitakyushu and ending at Kumamoto (in Kyushu); and the route which connects Kanto and Hokuriku, starting from Tokyo, going through Tsukiyono, Yuzawa, Nagaoka, Kashiwazaki (in Kanto), Asahi, and ending at Kanazawa (in Hokuriku). The former route is an arterial expressway of the lifeline network of Japan and it is natural to look for further improvements and expansions of the route. Especially, in order to maximize the national welfare, it should be taken as an issue of high priority to construct a new route between Nagoya and Osaka, namely the so-called Second Meishin Expressway, since more than 10 billion JPY per kilometer is assigned for expressway links between Nagoya and Osaka. The

a

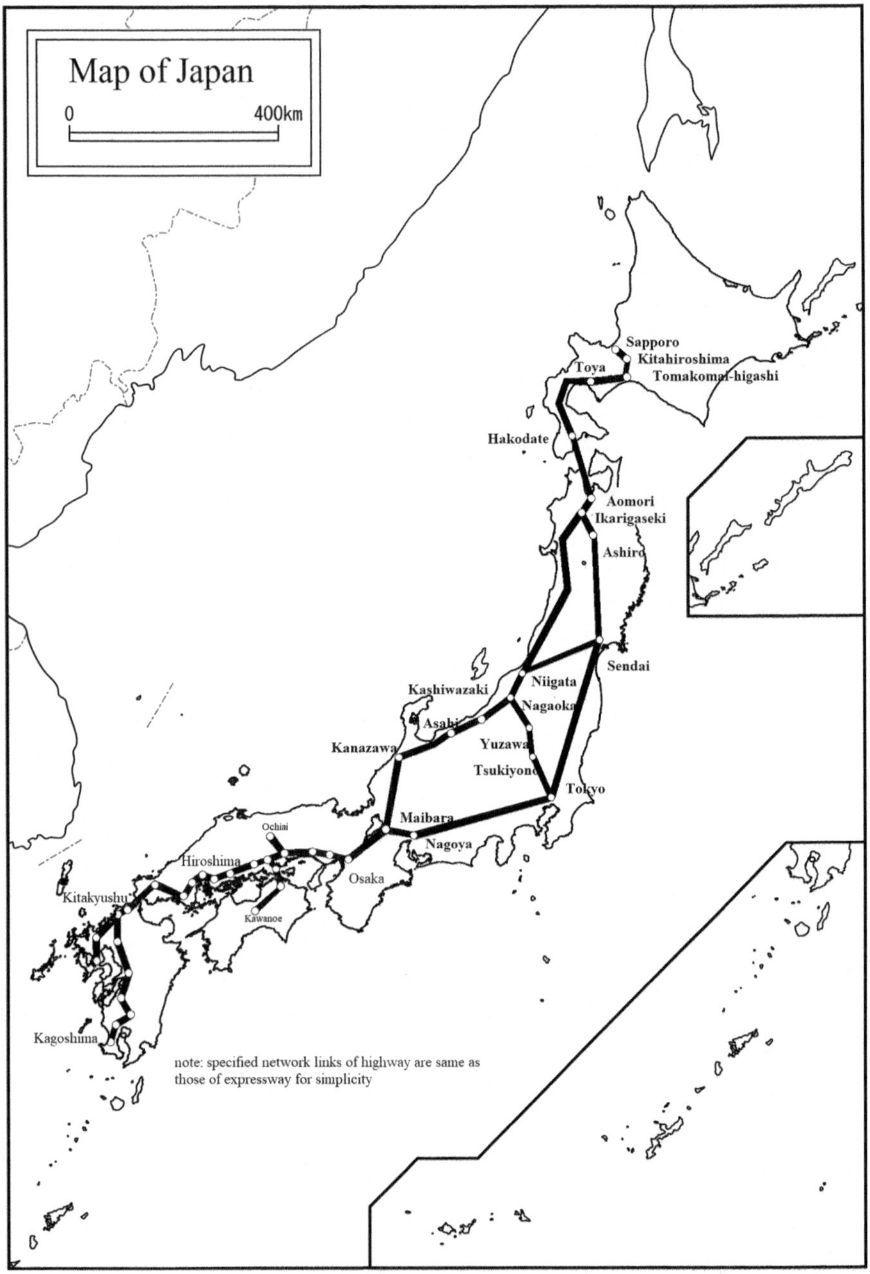

Fig. 6.4 (**a**) Current arterial highway network. (**b**) Optimal assignment of the public funds for highway improvements

b

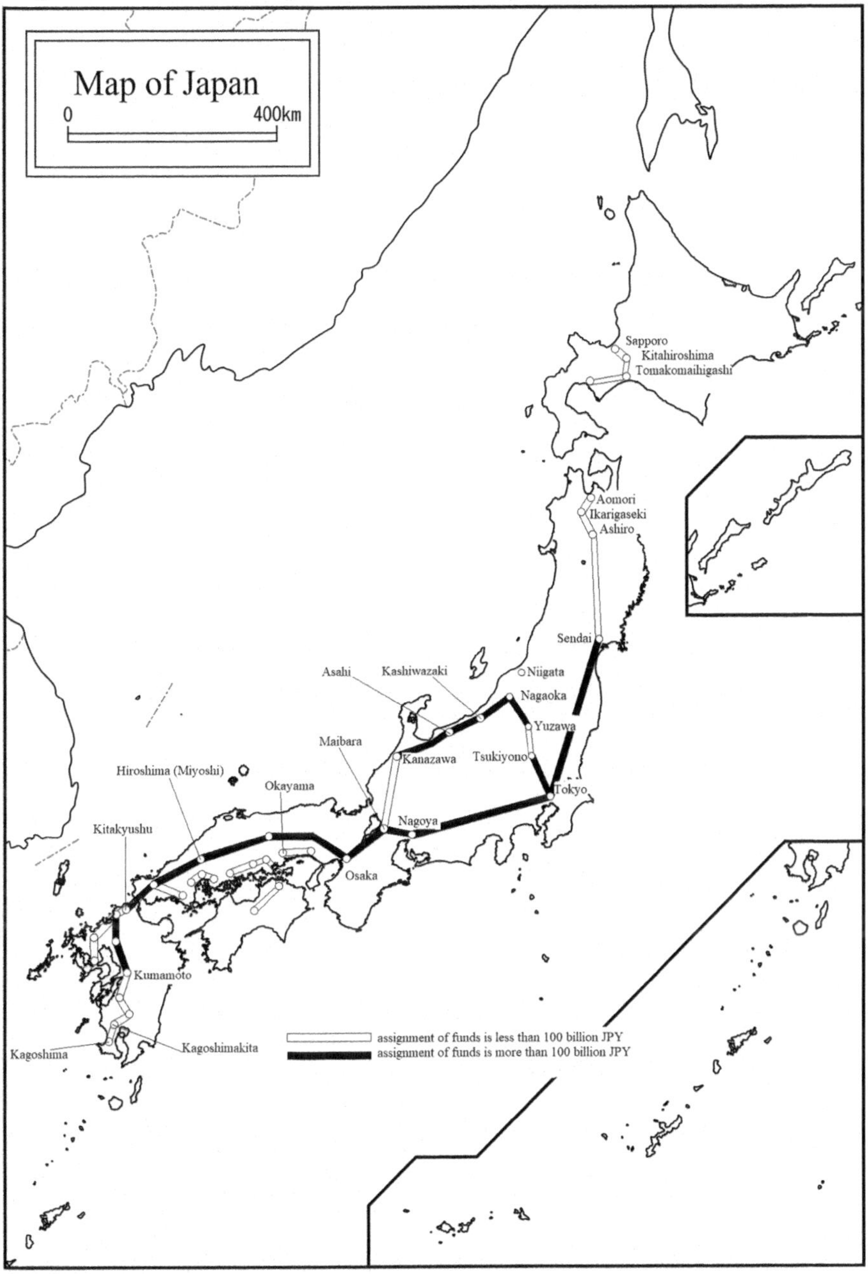

Fig. 6.4 (continued)

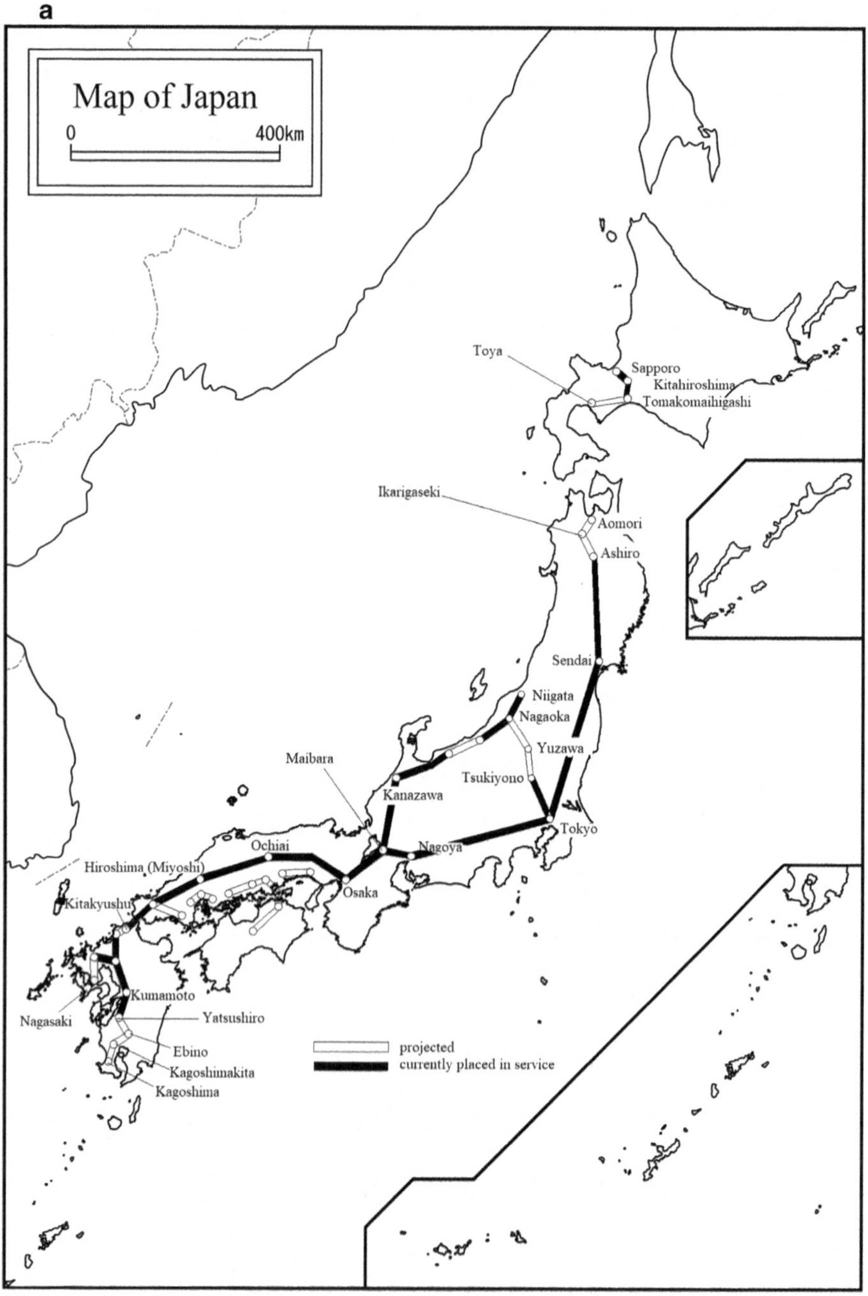

Fig. 6.5 (**a**) Current arterial network of expressway. (**b**) Optimal assignment of the public funds to expressway improvements

b

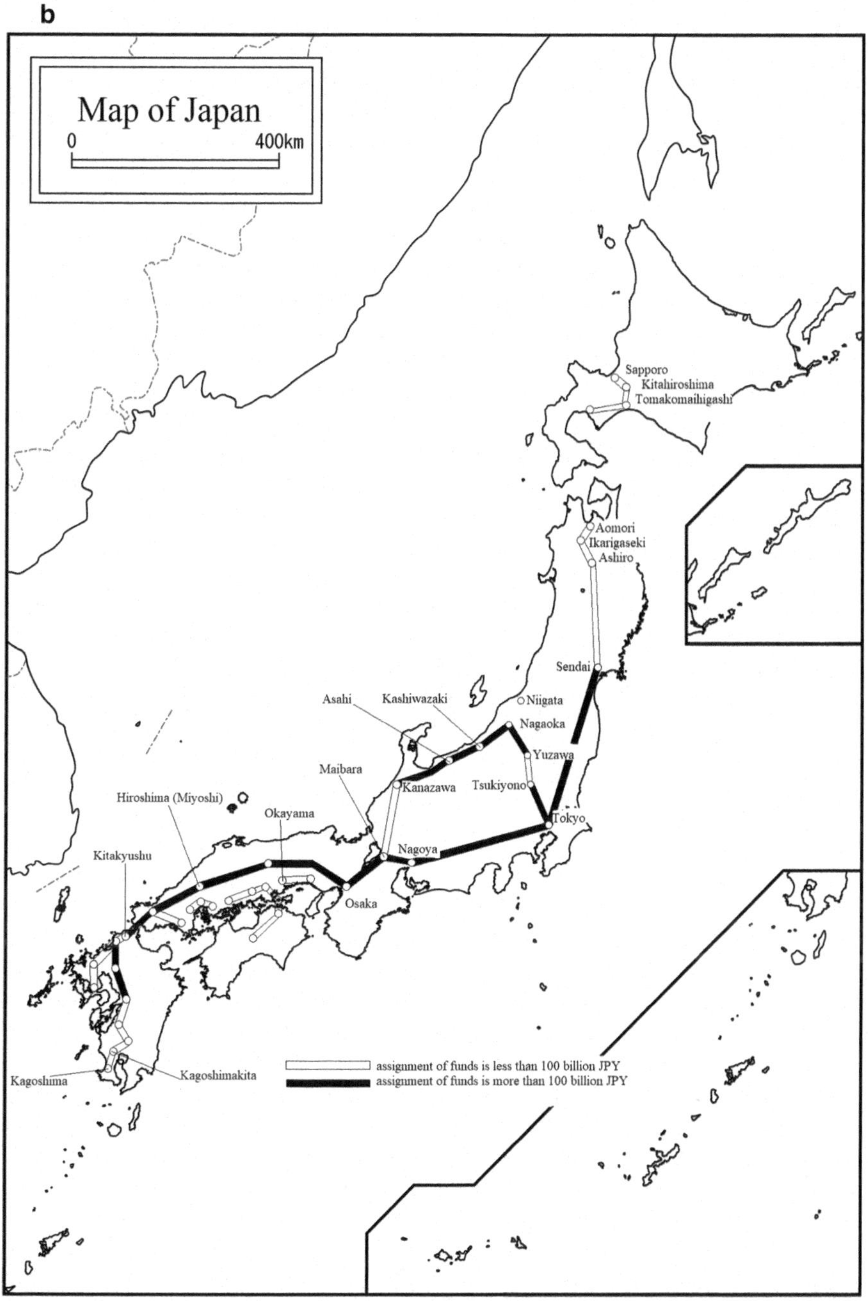

Fig. 6.5 (continued)

assignment of the public funds for expressway links between Tokyo and Osaka almost meets the construction cost requirement that is 2.5 billion JPY per kilometer with the four-lane (two-lane for one side) expressway. It is considered that the necessity of the construction of Second Tomei (between Tokyo and Nagoya) and Meishin Expressway will be further increased as the demand for transportation will further increase between Tokyo and Osaka.

On the other hand, it should be a sensitive matter to confirm that a fairly good amount of public funds is assigned for Chugoku Jidoshado Expressway (traversal route across the mountainous area lying off the coastal area of Kinki and Chugoku regions from Osaka to Shimonoseki) (Tables 6.3a and 6.3b). There exists another route in the Chugoku region which goes Kinki and Chugoku regions along the coastal area of Seto Inland Sea, which is called—Sanyo Jidoushado and starts at Kobe (located between Osaka and Himeji) and going through Himeji, Bizen, Okayama, Kurashiki, Fukuyama, Shiwa, Hiroshima, Hatsukaichi, Iwakuni (in Chugoku), and ending at Kitakyushu (in Kyushu). It was partially placed in service on that day as shown in Fig. 6.5a. With the model construction, the interchange of Miyoshi (that is shown by "Hiroshima (Miyoshi)" on the maps), which is located on Chugoku Jidoshado Expressway, is specified as the *zone node* of the Chugoku region in the sense of the traffic engineering. Due to the specification as well as the partial service of Sanyo Jidoshado, it can be said that the effectiveness of Sanyo Jidoshado from the view of the whole national economy is relatively under-evaluated against Chugoku Jidoshado although the former goes through most of the important cities including Kobe, Okayama, Kurashiki, Hiroshima, Fukuyama, and Shimonoseki along the coastal area of Chugoku region. If the zone node were laid on Okayama, we could expect different results which would highlight the necessity of placing in service the entire route of Sanyo Jidoshado at an earlier stage.

6.2.2.7 Consistency and Complementarity Among Transportation Infrastructure Investments

As Figs. 6.2b and 6.3b show, the assignment of the public funds is consistently made between the railway and Shinkansen. For example, however strong the demand by the people living in Hokkaido in that day against the extension of Tohoku Shinkansen from Morioka to Hokkaido (the route between Tokyo (Omiya) and Morioka was about to be placed in service when the study was done), the model consistently clarified the assignment of public funds for the extension project would not meet the opportunity cost criterion that is represented by the equalization among imputed prices with the invested targets. Alternatively, the model has given a basement for the assignment of public funds to the railway improvements between Sapporo and Morioka in order to meet the demand by the Hokkaido region against the transportation service based on the opportunity cost criterion. However, the amount of public funds allocated is not enough to construct a new route of the railway (Fig. 6.6a) and it should be spent on improvements to the current railway line, especially for Shinkansen (Fig. 6.6b). Also, a fairly good amount of public

a

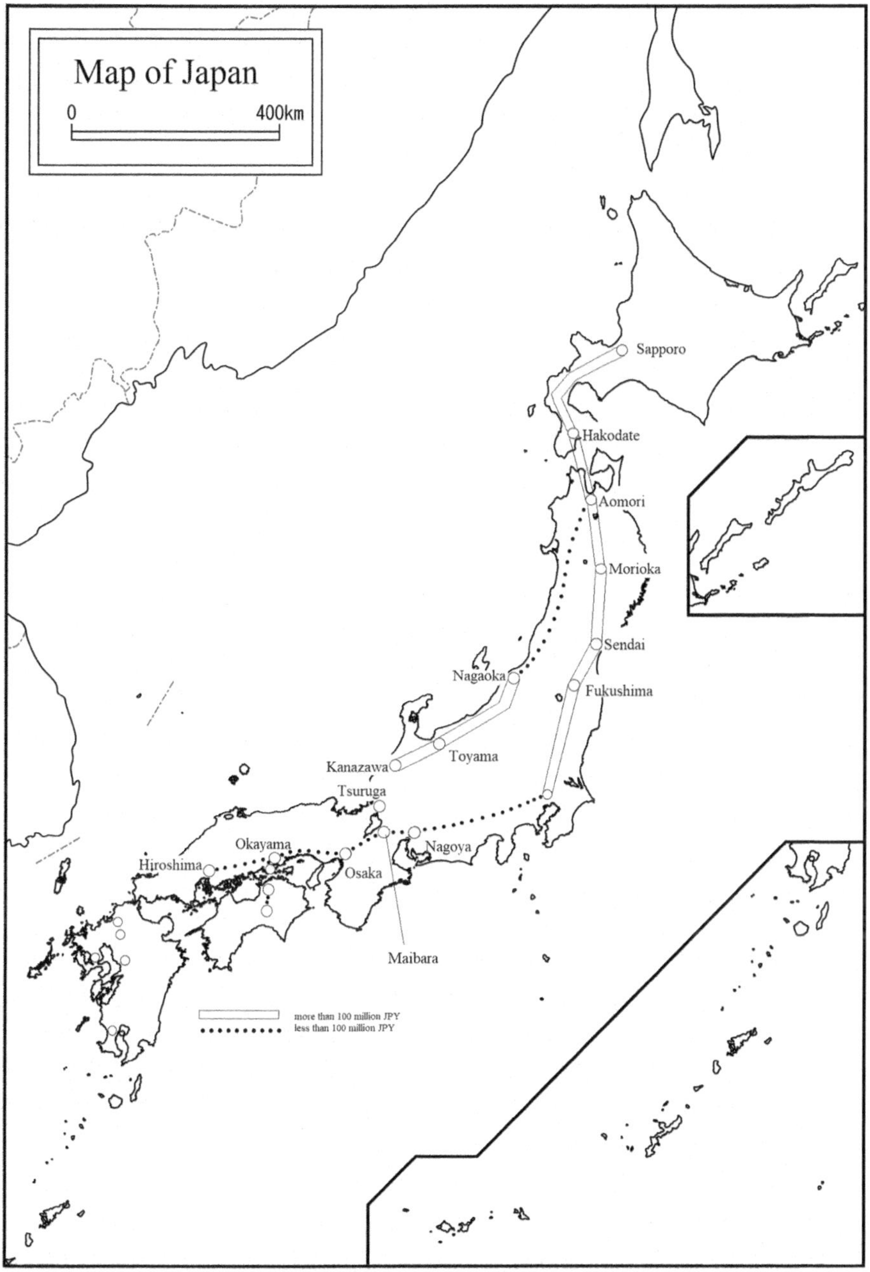

Fig. 6.6 (**a**) The public fund assignment for Railway per kilometer. (**b**) The public fund assignment for Shinkansen per kilometer. (**c**) The public fund assignment for highway per kilometer. (**d**) The public fund assignment for expressway per kilometer

b

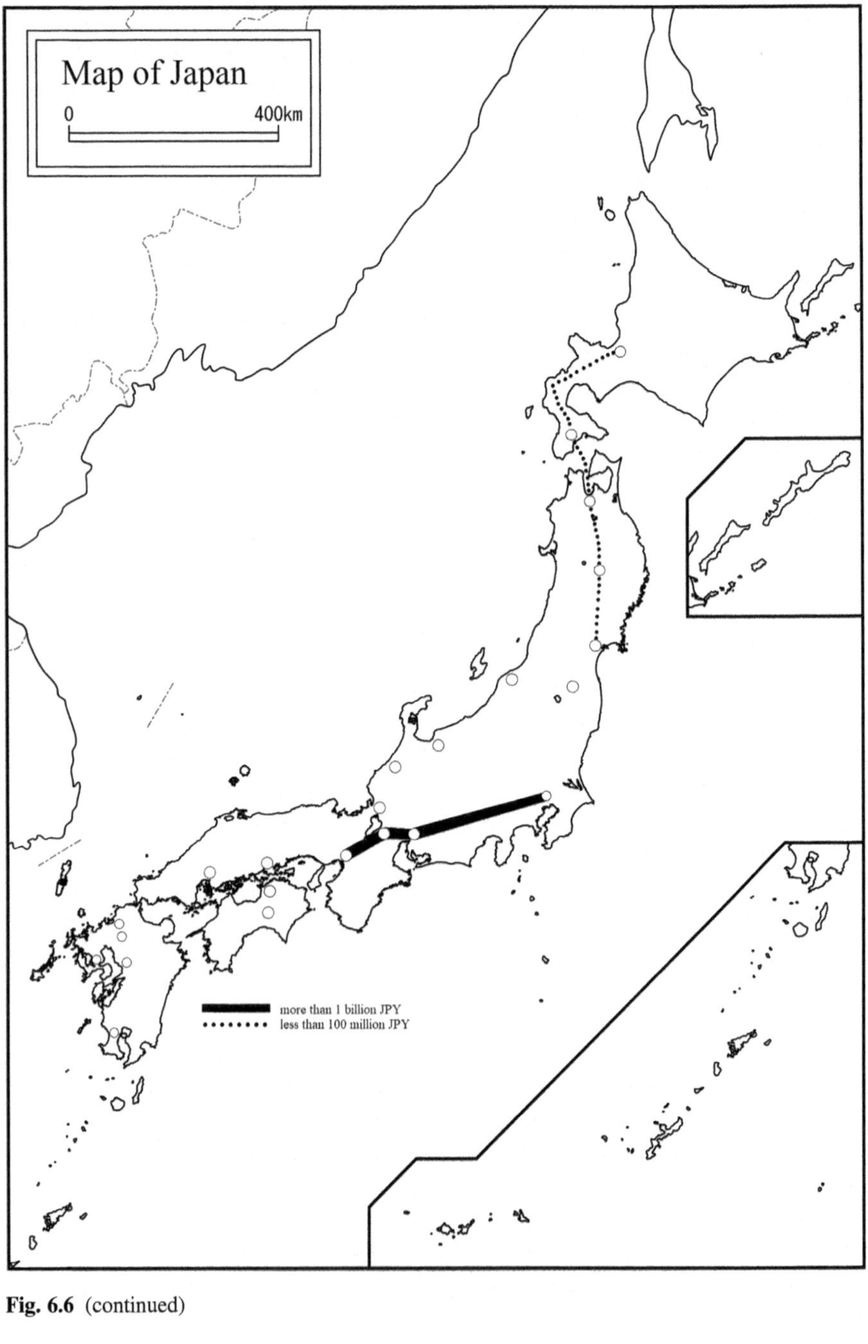

Fig. 6.6 (continued)

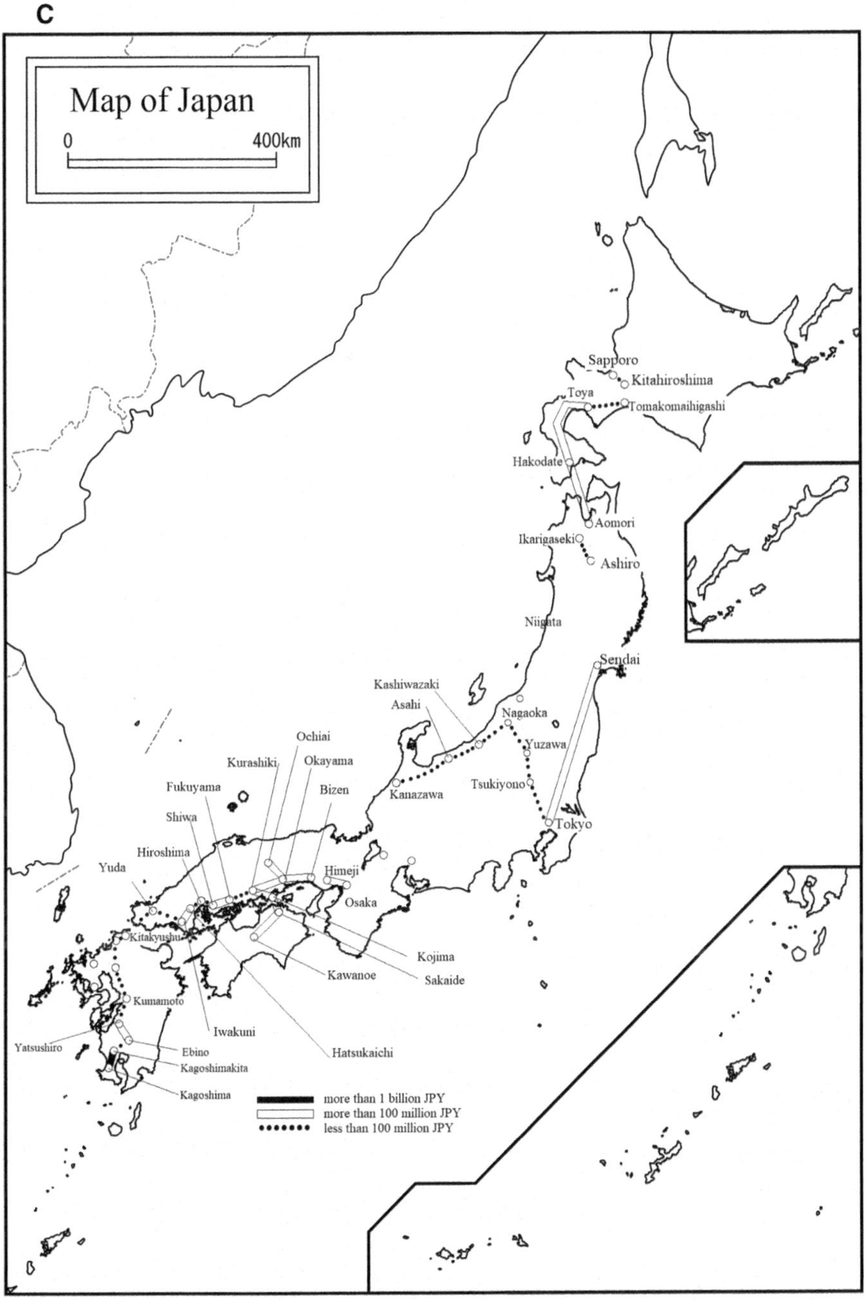

Fig. 6.6 (continued)

d

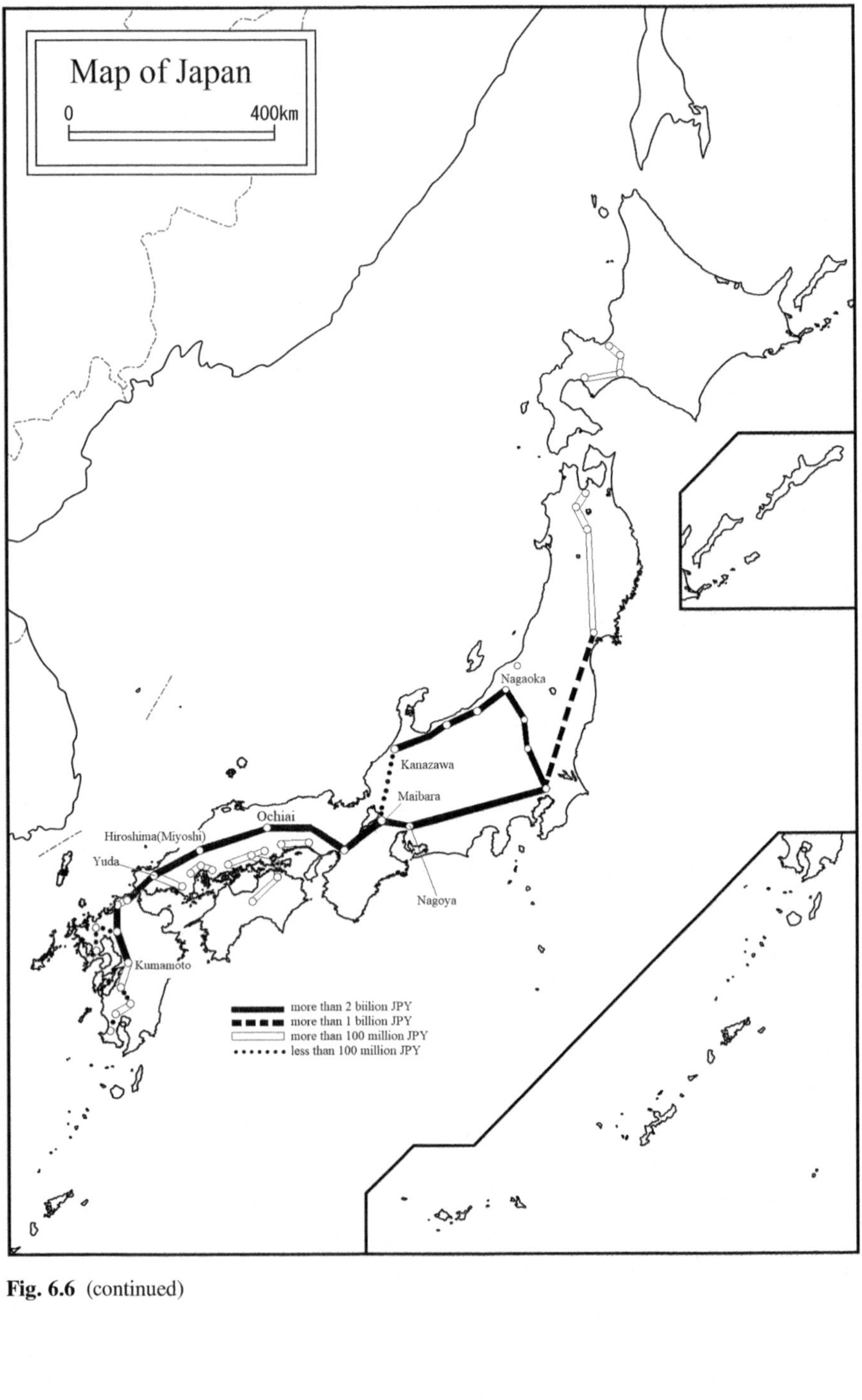

Fig. 6.6 (continued)

funds is assigned for improvements in the airport and harbor in Hokkaido and Tohoku (Table 6.3b).

As Fig. 6.6c, d show, it can be said that fairly good amount of public funds are assigned to highway links, of which alternative expressway links are not assigned enough amount of public funds. Examples are highway links between Toya and Aomori; Himeji and Osaka; Bizen and Okayama; Ochiai and Okayama; Fukuyama and Shiwa; Hatsukaichi and Iwakuni; Yatsushiro and Ebino; and Kagoshimakita and Kagoshima. On the contrary, almost no assignments of public funds are made to highway links, of which alternative expressway links are given assignments of a fairly good amount of public funds. Examples are expressway links between Tokyo, Nagoya, and Osaka; and Yuda, Kitakyushu, and Kumamoto.

It can be said that the assignments of public funds are made by consistently keeping complementarity and competitiveness between the highway and expressway links. A fairly good amount of public funds should be made to improve and construct expressway links in the regions where the demand pressure is strong against road transportation infrastructure even if the construction and improvements of highway links are put on ice in that region. On the other hand, the construction and improvements of highway links should be appropriate and enough for the regions where the demand pressure against road transportation infrastructure is not so strong to construct and improve expressway links of which construction cost is more expensive than that of the highway.

The clear complementarity and competitiveness between highway and expressway links in terms of the assignment of public funds prove that the model is well specified, and is capable of analyzing: optimal investments into the transportation infrastructures; and optimal shares of investments among different transportation modes from the viewpoint of the comprehensive transport system. Any models are not suitable and not capable of analyzing the comprehensive transport system if they eventually show results that contradict with each other in that: investments are made into the construction of transportation infrastructures and the improved traffic capacities are far beyond the demand against thus constructed transportation infrastructures; or investments into improvements in the capacity of transportation infrastructures are concentrated on a specific region and eventually, the improved traffic capacities are far beyond the demand against thus improved transportation infrastructures in that region; and due to this misappropriation of the public funds, the transportation infrastructure links on which the transportation demand is far beyond the traffic capacities are left without assignment of the public funds, and so on. The opportunity cost criterion—equality of imputed prices of the assigned public funds among the investment targets which are assigned to a positive amount of public funds makes it sure that such inconsistency will not occur (though it may occur in reality) with the assignment of public funds between different transportation infrastructures as well as between regions.

6.3 Conclusion

Major results of the perspectives for the comprehensive transport system of Japan are summarized as follows:

1. the road transportation will become more of importance as the major transportation mode,
2. it is an urgent need to improve the expressway network in order to meet increasing demand against inter-regional transportation services,
3. especially, the construction of the second To-Mei and the second Mei-Shin are most important agendas from viewpoints of the whole national economy,
4. the comprehensive transport system cannot be completed without improvements and construction of the highway which meets the local demand of transportation services,
5. railway exists as complements for road and air transportation and,
6. the demand against Shinkansen services will concentrate on the route between Tokyo and Osaka.

The model presented in this chapter is an extension of the model presented in Chap. 4 in the sense that:

1. the coding of the model is minute and practically useful in the specification of regions, sectors, and transportation infrastructures and modes,
2. the optimality of public fund assignments is obtained based on the opportunity cost criteria and,
3. the optimality of investments is pursued and obtained by expanding the investment targets to include the social overhead capitals which should be complements as well as substitutes against the transportation infrastructures in order to increases the welfare of the whole national economy directly and indirectly.

The model is, however, still a prototype. The regional micro-behavior model of the demand against social overhead capitals should be endogenously incorporated in the model. The optimality of public investments should be pursued based on the dynamic opportunity cost criteria. These have remained as topics in future.

References

EPA (1979) New 7 years socio-economic plan. EPA, Tokyo, 181p

Kohno H (1979) Research on the comprehensive valuation-pilot model for social overhead capital construction· maintenance. (Incorporated Foundation) International Science Promotion Foundation, Tsukuba

Kohno H (1994) Lecture on transport economics. Socio-Economic Planning Office, Tsukuba

Kohno H (1995) Public investment criteria for a comprehensive transport system using an interregional input-output programing model. In: van den Berch JCJM, Nikamp P, Reitveld P (eds) Recent advances in spatial equilibrium modelling: methodology and applications. Springer, Berlin

Kohno H, Mitomo H (1982) Optimal allocation of public investment to the trunk highway network. Highway Transp Econ 19:36–56

Ministry of International Trade and Industry (MITI) (1975) 1970 interregional input-output table: report on prepared results, Ministerial Secretariat, Research and Statistics Division of MITI, Tokyo, pp 1–177

MITI (1990) 1985 interregional input-output table: report on prepared results, Ministerial Secretariat, Research and Statistics Division of MITI, Tokyo, pp 1–156

Chapter 7
Optimal Planning of Asian Expressway Network Without Dynamic Interregional Input–Output Programming Model

7.1 Introduction

7.1.1 Characteristics of the Model

7.1.1.1 Dynamic Optimality of Roundabout Production Through Both Time and Space

The optimal assignments of the exogenously given amount of capital funds for transportation infrastructures and social overhead capitals are treated in Chap. 6. The themes are serious agendas in that day and analyzed with an empirical application of the interregional input–output programming model. As an extension of the shipment activities initiated by Moses in order to include the transportation sector explicitly, shipment activities among the regions and sectors are specified based on the interregional input–output table of competitive-import type. Namely, interregional trades are endogenously determined responding to the relative advantage of regional economies that are mainly dependent on the accessibility to the markets. Usually, the trade patterns which are endogenously and therefore optimally determined should be critically different from the presupposed trade pattern inherent to, for example, Isard-type model. The optimality of the assignment of capital funds for potential investment targets is obtained thanks to the opportunity cost criteria that is intrinsically built into the algorithm for solving the linear programming model. However, the optimality obtained is a static one (Hirschman 1968; Kohno 1991a, b, c, 1992, 1994; Kohno et al. 1987).

In this chapter, a dynamic version of the interregional input–output model will be treated (Kohno et al. 1987; Kohno 1988). This is, in a sense, a practical application of the so-called turnpike theorem initiated by DOSSO model (Dorfman et al. 1958; Kohno 1993). In DOSSO model, the turnpike theorem is shown by assuming that goods are all malleable in the sense that goods once utilized by a sector as a capital stock at a certain period of time can be utilized by another sector as a capital at a different period. The assumption makes the turnpike theorem most effective, namely

H. Kohno, Y. Higano, *Public Investment Criteria*, New Frontiers in Regional Science: Asian Perspectives 2, https://doi.org/10.1007/978-4-431-55221-5_7

the highest growth rate of the economy can be attained with the growth on the optimal path. However, in reality, goods once utilized for capital formation of a certain sector has no value than a stock for the said sector. It may be utilized for the same sector in another region in the content of spatial economy although transportation costs may be huge and it should not be a good idea to transport capital stocks. Although the malleability assumption is not so strong once the economy is on the optimal path particular to it, as a practical matter, the difference among initial capital stocks and ideal capital stocks (with the highest growth rate) on the earlier stage must be adjusted step by step by consuming time (as well as on the final stage, if the planning period is finite and the target of the economy is set away from the optimal path. This could happen especially with a spatial model). A surplus capital stock if any will be neglected if free disposability can be assumed. If not, it must be destructed with demolition cost (by spending services and goods).

It can be said that the turnpike theorem proves the rationality of a kind of roundabout production over time. The essence of a dynamic model is pursuing optimality of the roundabout production over time by adjusting capital stock formation. In this sense, it can be said that dynamic optimality means optimality of the roundabout production over time. In a spatial economy, which is always a default for our study, the adjustment should be made over space as well (see Appendix 2). In DOSSO model, in which regions may exist since even same sectors if located in different regions can be taken as different sectors, the highest growth path of the economy was termed as "turnpike." In our spatial model, the turnpike effectively works in order to attain dynamic optimality of the roundabout production over not only the time but also space as exactly imagined by the terminology.

7.1.2 Public Investment Criteria Endogenously Built in the Model

Asian highway network dealt within this chapter is to be mostly located in China. In that sense, the dynamic optimality of the planning was focused on accelerating effects on the taking-off of the Chinese economy on that day. The model deals with the following aspects which are partially or incompletely subjects for the static model in previous chapters:

1. optimal benefit–cost criteria for public investments into transportation infrastructures in the dynamic as well as spatial content,
2. optimal shares between public and private investments in the dynamic as well as spatial content,
3. optimal shares between transportation modes in the dynamic as well as spatial content,
4. optimal private investment shares among regional economies in the dynamic content,
5. optimal interregional trade pattern and regional specialization of production, and so on.

All those subjects are simultaneously and endogenously solved based on the dynamic optimality criteria that are built in the solution algorithm for the optimal planning model that is formulated as a linear programing model. In order to solve subject (1), the model must measure economic effects and (opportunity) costs of public investments considering their alternative utilization (and reproduction) process in the dynamic and spatial content. In order to solve the optimal benefit–cost criteria totally, the alternative utilization and reproduction process must be expanded to include the utilization not only in public but also in private sectors. Eventually, subject (2) can be solved through pursuing optimal benefit–cost criteria in the dynamic as well as spatial content. To pursue the optimality through space eventually solves subjects (3), (4), (5), and so on. (See Appendix 2) Subjects (1), (2), (3), (4), (5), and so on are eventually solved through pursuing optimality of investments into the public as well as private sectors in the dynamic as well as spatial content. In a word, the model can be taken as a comprehensive model for the evaluation of public as well as private investments. Of course, the model is comprehensive to be able to evaluate the economic effects of the investments in the dynamic and spatial content based on the opportunity cost criteria (Kohno 1975).

7.1.3 Subjects to be Solved

Taking construction of the Asian Expressway Network in China, which is connected to Japan through Korea and expanded to Europe through Central Asia and Eurasia, as a major strategy for making takeoff Chinese economy, it is a tough subject how to construct it by keeping a maximum economic growth rate of the Chinese economy. On that day, the transportation that connects provinces in China was mainly railway although coastal and canal shipping had higher potential than other countries, and not high-standard roads existed to connect provinces with each other. This means that the construction of the highway network in China must start from zero. It takes huge costs, which may damage the economic development in China considering that China was not yet an automobile society at that time. Therefore, first of all, the above subject (2) and (3) must be solved considering the economic development stages of the Chinese regional economy and the capability of existing transportation infrastructures in China at that time. The start from zero means that an optimal schedule must be identified with construction priority among highways which connect provinces with each other. This subject must be solved together with the above subjects (4), (5), and so on.

In relation to the arguments mentioned previously, it must be pointed out that a balanced economic growth among countries in Asia was not intended and it was beyond the scope of the study. Rather, it was a wide perspective that making taken-off Chinese economy is strategically the key for neighborhood countries (regions) in order to stably grow and to be prosperous in the future by enhancing trades with China in the future. It was a view and hypothesis taken by the authors that the Chinese economy has a huge potential for accelerating the economic growth by utilizing its spacious national land, abundant natural resources, the scale of the population and markets, and so on if regional economies are well linked and connected with each other systematically and functionally. Thus, China would be a powerful traction engine for the stable growth of the whole of countries (regions) in Asia. In this sense, the work in this chapter is taken as a practical application of the turnpike theory in order to identify the most efficient growth path in terms of not only focused sectors as traction engines in the dynamic content but also focused regional economies in the spatial content. Eventually, the most efficient construction path of transportation infrastructures can be identified which enhances systematic and well functionally connected regional economies, and, thus, accelerates economic growth of the whole national economy.

Seeing it from another perspective, the work has identified so-called bottlenecks for the Chinese economy to stably and effectively grow, which means that what sectors and regions would be barriers as well as what transportation infrastructures are to be proved inadequate, and so on, in the sense that the highest gross domestic products (GDP) can be attained with a fixed time of planning horizon; or the targeted GDP can be attained with the shortest time, and so on.

Of course, viewing China as a key country for the whole countries in Asia to stably and prosperously grow presumed that they will be cooperative with each other in a harmonious way to enjoy a similar living standard of developed countries, for example, Japan at that time by transcending political heavy walls focusing on fruitful results of economic exchange among them. More precisely speaking, the view presumed that China would reconstruct its economic structure into Asia such as Japan and NIES (newly industrializing economies) on that day by transforming the vertical integration-oriented economy, which was mainly dependent on the export of primary products in order to import final products, into a global economy. It would be realized through horizontal integration of regional economies not only in China but also in other Asian countries, which results in the division of labor and specialization in order to enjoy the merits of international as well as interregional trades. Interdependence among sectors in different regions and countries would be strengthened in parallel to improvements in transportation infrastructures between regions and countries. Eventually, it was highly expected that the livelihood of people in countries and regions involved in the Asian Highway Network would be drastically improved, which is of course the essence of the comparative advantage of international trade.

How to finance such a huge project was a big issue as a practical matter. It was reported that a big syndicate of banks had been established in order to finance the project of Channel Tunnel between UK and France, and was going on line. It was composed of 200 banks across the world including 39 banks in Japan (The Nikkei, Oct.25, 1987: on p. 1, ed. 14). Namely, we could say that it was rather easy to finance such a big dream project once its social as well as private profitability had been proved. In this sense, it was expected that the study would contribute to the proof of profitability and social meaningfulness of the Asian Highway Network, a huge social infrastructure construction project, through the measurement of its social benefits. Namely, it would be helpful for stakeholders to know if investments into the Asian

Highway Network project, a dream project for all involved people in that day, was economically feasible from the viewpoints of the whole national economies of involved countries in the long run, or not. Our investigation view was that we cannot know social meaningfulness and profitability at all without calculation based on actual data (Moriguchi 1972; Cohen 1971; Kinoshita 1978).

7.1.4 *Economic Philosophy of Regional Development in Asia*

Asian Expressway Network project, which intended to prime the Asian economy, had the longest time horizon among economic policies. In other words, it was a full-scale economic planning and it should be implemented having the economic philosophy, that is the realization of longer term prosperity and lasting peace.

Supposing 10 years of preparatory period, 20 years of construction period, and 20 years of payback period for generated social–economic effects, during the total 50 years of the planning horizon how Asian countries and regions would grow by allocating resources optimally to keep full employment, fairness in income distribution—namely resolution of income disparities among involved countries and regions, and so on were very difficult agendas as a practical matter. Policy prescriptions for the economic planning based on the economic philosophy of Asian Highway Network should give answers to the questions: in which timing, with what transportation modes, with what capacity, and in and between which regions transportation infrastructures including Asian Highway Network should be constructed and provided to the public use in order to attain the maximized accumulated discounted sum of the total welfare of countries and regions involved in the network over the time horizon of 50 years. The maximization must be obtained through efficient utilization of existing natural, human, and physical resources by enjoying scale merits, technical externalities, and Marshallian type of externalities to a maximum degree, which can be generated by shifting the growth of the economy onto the growth path made possible by indirectly controlling the economy through investments of the public funds into transportation infrastructures and social overhead capitals, and eventually to stop lagging behind, catch up, and possibly overtake United States, Japan, and European countries. In this chapter, we will analyze and discuss about the agenda based on the discrete dynamic multi-region multi-sector multi-transportation mode planning model, which was developed as one of the effective planning support systems in order to be able to give answers to the above questions.

7.1.5 *Shipment Activities and Transportation Infrastructures*

The model in this chapter has several distinctive characteristics than the models presented in previous chapters and it is an expanded version of the so-called DOSSO model that has been the soul for the researchers who deal with the discrete dynamic multi-sector optimal growth model.

7.1.5.1 Explicit Treatment of Regions (Countries)

It is a default for the models in this book that the economy is composed of several regional economies (subeconomies). On the other hand, the DOSSO model assumes that the economy is located at a point, namely, the economy has no idea of space. DOSSO-type model may be expanded to a multiregional model by differentiating sectors located in different regions and additionally creating special sectors which make possible interregional trades among sectors located in different regions. However, as we have already seen in previous chapters, the number of such additional special sectors becomes huge as increases of the number of regions, transportation modes, alternative transportation routes including those which will be constructed in the future, and so on. With the conceptual and theoretical analysis, it would cause no problem. However, as a practical matter, the specification of an empirical model based on such extension needs the same energy as the model specified in this chapter needs or more than that. Apart from the practical issues, more fatal character as an optimal regional growth model is such a model has to assume a noncompetitive import type of input–output structure. In other words, the model specified in this chapter was proposed as a practical and empirical model while keeping the essence of the analysis of the DOSSO model, namely the maximum growth path and turnpike theory.

7.1.5.2 Malleability of Goods (Again)

In the DOSSO model, goods accumulated is taken as capital stock and it is malleable, namely, stock once utilized for a certain sector at a certain period can be diverted to other sectors at the next period (this would mean as for a regional model version of DOSSO model that capital stocks are mobile among regions). This assumption is not critical for the economy that is on the maximum growth path (a steady-state path) but for the periods while the economy reaches the golden path as close as possible since it starts to grow with given initial stock and resources which are not necessarily on the optimal path. In case the time horizon is finite and the targeted economy is not on the golden path, the assumption becomes strong even we may assume free disposability, too.

7.1.5.3 Shipment Activities

The input–output table adopted in Chaps. 4 and 6 was calculated in terms of purchasers' price. On the contrary, the input–output table adopted by the model in this chapter was partially calculated with the formula of an input–output table in terms of producers' price. However, the construction of an optimal planning model using input–output table at producers' price will not cause a practical issue, which is pointed out using Eq.(4.184) in Appendix 2 in Chap. 4, because neither shipment activities of Moses type nor the extended version is not adopted in this chapter. The commodity flows are explicitly defined as activities that substitute ingenious but a little bit complicated ideas of shipment activities initiated by Moses. By using the figures of Table 4.38 in Appendix 2 in Chap. 4, we will explain the essence of the treatment of the input–output structure of the model in this chapter.

7.1.5.4 Input–Output Coefficients

We again assume sectors are located in regions and each region has one sector. Also, we assume final demand (consumption) only occurs in region 6. Using figures in Table 4.38, the input–output activity of the agriculture sector in region 1 at producers' price is decomposed into as follows:

$$\boldsymbol{\alpha}^{11} = \begin{bmatrix} T\_basic\_org(8,1) \\ T\_basic\_org(13,1) \\ T\_basic\_org(7,1) \\ T\_basic\_org(19,1) \\ T\_basic\_org(20,1) \end{bmatrix} / T\_basic\_org(22,1) = \begin{bmatrix} 0.09090909 \\ 0.27272727 \\ 0.04545454 \\ 0 \\ 0 \end{bmatrix}, \tag{7.1}$$

in which α^{11}: vector of coefficients of intermediate inputs into the agriculture sector in region 1 at producers' price.

Analogically, the following vector variables can be specified using Table 4.38:

$\boldsymbol{\alpha}^{ij}$: vector of coefficients of intermediate inputs into sector i in region j at producers' price.

Although the above definition presumes the usual interregional input–output table, as for the numerical example of Table 4.38, only $\boldsymbol{\alpha}^{ii}$ $(i = 1,2,3,4,5)$ have meanings due to the above simple assumption. The definition of coefficients only related to intermediate inputs that are essentially necessary for the production by neglecting logistics costs for the shipments of intermediate inputs into and shipment of products from the site. Thus, the first two elements are only input coefficients at producers' price and this is why the input–output table adopted by the model in this chapter is partially calculated in terms of producers' price.

$$\boldsymbol{\alpha}^{22} = \begin{bmatrix} T\_basic\_org(8,2) \\ T\_basic\_org(13,2) \\ T\_basic\_org(7,2) \\ T\_basic\_org(19,2) \\ T\_basic\_org(20,2) \end{bmatrix} / T\_basic\_org(22,2) = \begin{bmatrix} 0.062937062 \\ 0.251748251 \\ 0.034965034 \\ 0 \\ 0 \end{bmatrix}, \quad (7.2)$$

$$\boldsymbol{\alpha}^{33} = \begin{bmatrix} T\_basic\_org(8,3) \\ T\_basic\_org(13,3) \\ T\_basic\_org(7,3) \\ T\_basic\_org(19,3) \\ T\_basic\_org(20,3) \end{bmatrix} / TTT3 = \begin{bmatrix} 0.020703933 \\ 0.207039337 \\ 0.062111801 \\ 0.248447204 \\ 0 \end{bmatrix}, \quad (7.3)$$

$$\boldsymbol{\alpha}^{44} = \begin{bmatrix} T\_basic\_org(8,6) \\ T\_basic\_org(13,6) \\ T\_basic\_org(7,6) \\ T\_basic\_org(19,6) \\ T\_basic\_org(20,6) \end{bmatrix} / TTT4 = \begin{bmatrix} 0.053964113 \\ 0.215856455 \\ 0.044970094 \\ 0.035976075 \\ 0 \end{bmatrix}, \quad (7.4)$$

$$\boldsymbol{\alpha}^{55} = \begin{bmatrix} T\_basic\_org(8,9) \\ T\_basic\_org(13,9) \\ T\_basic\_org(7,9) \\ T\_basic\_org(19,9) \\ T\_basic\_org(20,9) \end{bmatrix} / TTT5 = \begin{bmatrix} 0.0799232736 \\ 0.3996163682 \\ 0 \\ 0.0079923273 \\ 0 \end{bmatrix}, \quad (7.5)$$

in which:

$$\begin{aligned} TTT3 = {} & T\_basic\_data(7,1) + T\_basic\_data(7,2) + T\_basic\_data(7,3) \\ & + T\_basic\_data(7,6) + T\_basic\_data(7,9) \\ & + T\_basic\_data(7,10) + T\_basic\_data(9,11) \\ & + T\_basic\_data(14,11) \end{aligned} \quad (7.6)$$

$$\begin{aligned} TTT4 = T\_basic\_data(19,1) + T\_basic\_data(19,2) \\ + T\_basic\_data(19,3) + T\_basic\_data(19,6) \\ + T\_basic\_data(19,9) + T\_basic\_data(19,10) \\ + T\_basic\_data(10,11) + T\_basic\_data(15,11) \end{aligned} \quad (7.7)$$

$$\begin{aligned} TTT5 = T\_basic\_data(20,1) + T\_basic\_data(20,2) \\ + T\_basic\_data(20,3) + T\_basic\_data(20,6) \\ + T\_basic\_data(20,9) + T\_basic\_data(20,10) \\ + T\_basic\_data(11,11) + T\_basic\_data(16,11). \end{aligned} \quad (7.8)$$

As readers may see:

$$TTTj = IO\_table\_pur(7,j) = IO\_table\_pro(7,j), \quad (7.9)$$

in Tables 4.40 and 4.41 with j such that $j = 3$, 4, and 5.

7.1.5.5 Commodity Flow Variables

The following commodities flow variables are defined, which substitute shipment activities of Moses type (Moses 1955, 1960; Chenery 1953):

CF_{ij}^{kl}: amount of the commodity flow of goods k from region i to region j using the transportation route l.

Though the above definition also presumes general interregional commodity flows, as for the simple numerical example of Table 4.38, only CF_{ij}^{kl} $(i = 1, 2, .., 5; j = 1, 2, \ldots, 6; i = k, l = 1)$ have meanings. Next, production activities are defined as follows:

Y_{ij}: total product of sector i in region j $(i, j = 1, 2, 3, 4, 5)$.
Again, only Y_{ii} have meanings as for the numerical example due to the simplicity assumption. Final demand variables are defined as follows:
C_{kj}: final demand of goods k in region j ($k = 1,2,3,4,5$; $j = 1,2,3,4,5,6$).
Due to the same reason, only C_{k6} ($k = 1$, 2, 3, 4, and 5) have meanings.

7.1.5.6 Input Coefficients of Logistics Services into Commodity Flow

The following coefficients are defined which generate demand against logistics services depending on the amount of commodity flows between regions:

${}^{p}a_{ij}^{kl}$: demand against service p that is induced by one unit commodity flow of goods k from region i to region j through the transportation route l ($p = 3, 4, 5$; $k = 1, 2; i = 1, 2, 3, 4, 5; j = 1, 2, 3, 4, 5, 6;$ and $i = k$). With the simplicity assumption, $l = 1$ for all p, k, i and j.

With the numerical example of Table 4.38, we can calculate

$$^{p}a_{ij}^{kl}\ (p = 3,4,5; k = 1,2; i = 1,2,3,4,5; j = 1,2,3,4,5,6; \text{and } i = k)$$

as follows:

$$\begin{bmatrix} {}^{3}a_{11}^{11} \\ {}^{4}a_{11}^{11} \\ {}^{5}a_{11}^{11} \end{bmatrix} = \begin{bmatrix} T\_basic\_org(9,1)/T\_basic\_org(8,1) \\ T\_basic\_org(10,1)/T\_basic\_org(8,1) \\ T\_basic\_org(11,1)/T\_basic\_org(8,1) \end{bmatrix} = \begin{bmatrix} 0.1 \\ 0.33 \\ 0.2 \end{bmatrix}$$

$$\begin{bmatrix} {}^{3}a_{12}^{11} \\ {}^{4}a_{12}^{11} \\ {}^{5}a_{12}^{11} \end{bmatrix} = \begin{bmatrix} 0.1 \\ 0.275 \\ 0.23 \end{bmatrix}, \begin{bmatrix} {}^{3}a_{13}^{11} \\ {}^{4}a_{13}^{11} \\ {}^{5}a_{13}^{11} \end{bmatrix} = \begin{bmatrix} 0.1 \\ 0.22 \\ 0.2 \end{bmatrix}, \begin{bmatrix} {}^{3}a_{14}^{11} \\ {}^{4}a_{14}^{11} \\ {}^{5}a_{14}^{11} \end{bmatrix} = \begin{bmatrix} 0.1 \\ 0.22 \\ 0.23 \end{bmatrix},$$

$$\begin{bmatrix} {}^{3}a_{15}^{11} \\ {}^{4}a_{15}^{11} \\ {}^{5}a_{15}^{11} \end{bmatrix} = \begin{bmatrix} 0.1 \\ 0.11 \\ 0.2 \end{bmatrix}, \begin{bmatrix} {}^{3}a_{16}^{11} \\ {}^{4}a_{16}^{11} \\ {}^{5}a_{16}^{11} \end{bmatrix} = \begin{bmatrix} 0.1 \\ 0.33 \\ 0.3 \end{bmatrix},$$

$$\begin{bmatrix} {}^{3}a_{21}^{21} \\ {}^{4}a_{21}^{21} \\ {}^{5}a_{21}^{21} \end{bmatrix} = \begin{bmatrix} T\_basic\_org(14,1)/T\_basic\_org(13,1) \\ T\_basic\_org(15,1)/T\_basic\_org(13,1) \\ T\_basic\_org(16,1)/T\_basic\_org(13,1) \end{bmatrix} = \begin{bmatrix} 0.05 \\ 0.2625 \\ 0.17 \end{bmatrix},$$

$$\begin{bmatrix} {}^{3}a_{22}^{21} \\ {}^{4}a_{22}^{21} \\ {}^{5}a_{22}^{21} \end{bmatrix} = \begin{bmatrix} 0.05 \\ 0.21 \\ 0.2 \end{bmatrix}, \begin{bmatrix} {}^{3}a_{23}^{21} \\ {}^{4}a_{23}^{21} \\ {}^{5}a_{23}^{21} \end{bmatrix} = \begin{bmatrix} 0.05 \\ 0.105 \\ 0.18 \end{bmatrix}, \begin{bmatrix} {}^{3}a_{24}^{21} \\ {}^{4}a_{24}^{21} \\ {}^{5}a_{24}^{21} \end{bmatrix} = \begin{bmatrix} 0.05 \\ 0.2625 \\ 0.15 \end{bmatrix},$$

$$\begin{bmatrix} {}^{3}a_{25}^{21} \\ {}^{4}a_{25}^{21} \\ {}^{5}a_{25}^{21} \end{bmatrix} = \begin{bmatrix} 0.05 \\ 0.105 \\ 0.18 \end{bmatrix}, \begin{bmatrix} {}^{3}a_{26}^{21} \\ {}^{4}a_{26}^{21} \\ {}^{5}a_{26}^{21} \end{bmatrix} = \begin{bmatrix} 0.05 \\ 0.2625 \\ 0.3 \end{bmatrix}.$$

7.1.5.7 Market Flow Condition

The market flow condition is specified with the numerical example as follows in a little bit general form:

$$\alpha^{ii}Y_{ii} + \begin{bmatrix} 0 \\ 0 \\ \sum_{j=1}^{6}\sum_{l=1}^{MT(i,j)}\sum_{k=1}^{2} {}^{3}a_{ij}^{kl}CF_{ij}^{kl} \\ \sum_{j=1}^{6}\sum_{l=1}^{MT(i,j)}\sum_{k=1}^{2} {}^{4}a_{ij}^{kl}CF_{ij}^{kl} \\ \sum_{j=1}^{6}\sum_{l=1}^{MT(i,j)}\sum_{k=1}^{2} {}^{5}a_{ij}^{kl}CF_{ij}^{kl} \end{bmatrix}$$

$$= \begin{bmatrix} \sum_{j=1}^{5}\sum_{l=1}^{MT(j,i)} CF_{ji}^{1l} \\ \sum_{j=1}^{5}\sum_{l=1}^{MT(j,i)} CF_{ji}^{2l} \\ \sum_{j=1}^{5}\sum_{l=1}^{MT(j,i)} CF_{ji}^{3l} \\ \sum_{j=1}^{5}\sum_{l=1}^{MT(j,i)} CF_{ji}^{4l} \\ \sum_{j=1}^{5}\sum_{l=1}^{MT(j,i)} CF_{ji}^{5l} \end{bmatrix} \quad (i = 1, 2), \tag{7.10a}$$

$$\alpha^{ii}Y_{ii} = \begin{bmatrix} \sum_{j=1}^{5}\sum_{l=1}^{MT(j,i)} CF_{ji}^{1l} \\ \sum_{j=1}^{5}\sum_{l=1}^{MT(j,i)} CF_{ji}^{2l} \\ \sum_{j=1}^{5}\sum_{l=1}^{MT(j,i)} CF_{ji}^{3l} \\ \sum_{j=1}^{5}\sum_{l=1}^{MT(j,i)} CF_{ji}^{4l} \\ \sum_{j=1}^{5}\sum_{l=1}^{MT(j,i)} CF_{ji}^{5l} \end{bmatrix} \quad (i = 3, 4, 5), \tag{7.10b}$$

$$\begin{bmatrix} C_{16} \\ C_{26} \\ C_{36} \\ C_{46} \\ C_{56} \end{bmatrix} = \begin{bmatrix} \sum_{j=1}^{5}\sum_{l=1}^{MT(j,i)} CF_{j6}^{1l} \\ \sum_{j=1}^{5}\sum_{l=1}^{MT(j,i)} CF_{j6}^{2l} \\ \sum_{j=1}^{5}\sum_{l=1}^{MT(j,i)} CF_{j6}^{3l} \\ \sum_{j=1}^{5}\sum_{l=1}^{MT(j,i)} CF_{j6}^{4l} \\ \sum_{j=1}^{5}\sum_{l=1}^{MT(j,i)} CF_{j6}^{5l} \end{bmatrix}, \tag{7.11}$$

in which $MT(j, i)$: number of transportation routes on which commodities can be shipped from region j to region i ($i = 1, 2, 3, 4, 5, 6; j = 1, 2, 3, 4, 5$). With the numerical example, $MT(j, i) = 1$ for all i and j.

More specifically with the numerical example, Eqs. (7.10a) and (7.10b) become as follows:

$$\alpha^{ii}Y_{ii} + \begin{bmatrix} 0 \\ 0 \\ \sum_{j=1}^{6}\sum_{k=1}^{2} {}^{3}a_{ij}^{kl}CF_{ij}^{k1} \\ \sum_{j=1}^{6}\sum_{k=1}^{2} {}^{4}a_{ij}^{kl}CF_{ij}^{k1} \\ \sum_{j=1}^{6}\sum_{k=1}^{2} {}^{5}a_{ij}^{kl}CF_{ij}^{k1} \end{bmatrix} = \begin{bmatrix} CF_{1i}^{11} \\ CF_{2i}^{21} \\ CF_{3i}^{31} \\ CF_{4i}^{41} \\ CF_{5i}^{51} \end{bmatrix} \quad (i = 1, 2), \tag{7.12a}$$

$$\alpha^{ii}Y_{ii} = \begin{bmatrix} CF_{1i}^{11} \\ CF_{2i}^{21} \\ CF_{3i}^{31} \\ CF_{4i}^{41} \\ CF_{5i}^{51} \end{bmatrix} \quad (i = 3, 4, 5), \tag{7.12b}$$

$$\begin{bmatrix} C_{16} \\ C_{26} \\ C_{36} \\ C_{46} \\ C_{56} \end{bmatrix} = \begin{bmatrix} T\_basic\_org(8, 10) \\ T\_basic\_org(13, 10) \\ T\_basic\_org(7, 10) \\ T\_basic\_org(19, 10) \\ T\_basic\_org(20, 10) \end{bmatrix} = \begin{bmatrix} CF_{16}^{11} \\ CF_{26}^{21} \\ CF_{36}^{31} \\ CF_{46}^{41} \\ CF_{56}^{51} \end{bmatrix}. \tag{7.13}$$

7.1.5.8 Total Supply Condition

Because of explicit specification of goods flow variables, CF_{ij}^{kl}, we additionally need the following equations, which complete the so-called market flow condition together with Eqs. (7.10a) and (7.10b), and Eq. (7.11):

$$Y_{ii} = \sum_{j=1}^{6}\sum_{l=1}^{MT(i,j)} CF_{ij}^{il} \; (i = 1, 2, 3, 4, 5). \tag{7.14}$$

Again, it is simplified:

$$Y_{ii} = \sum_{j=1}^{6} CF_{ij}^{i1} \; (i = 1, 2, 3, 4, 5). \tag{7.15}$$

With the following final demand:

$$\begin{bmatrix} C_{16} \\ C_{26} \\ C_{36} \\ C_{46} \\ C_{56} \end{bmatrix} = \begin{bmatrix} T\_basic\_org(8,10) \\ T\_basic\_org(13,10) \\ T\_basic\_org(7,10) \\ T\_basic\_org(19,10) \\ T\_basic\_org(20,10) \end{bmatrix} = \begin{bmatrix} 325 \\ 500 \\ 0 \\ 0 \\ 160 \end{bmatrix}, \tag{7.16}$$

the system of Eqs., (7.12a), (7.12b), and (7.15) gives solution of Y_{ii} ($i = 1,2,3,4,5$) as follows:

$$\begin{bmatrix} Y_{11} \\ Y_{22} \\ Y_{33} \\ Y_{44} \\ Y_{55} \end{bmatrix} = \begin{bmatrix} 550 \\ 1,430 \\ 241.5 \\ 555.925 \\ 625.6 \end{bmatrix}, \tag{7.17}$$

in which

$Y_{11} = T\_basic\_org(8,11) = 550,$

$Y_{22} = T\_basic\_org(13,11) = 1430,$

$Y_{33} = T\_basic\_org(7,11) - T\_basic\_org(7,7) - T\_basic\_org(7,8) + T\_basic\_org(9,11) + T\_basic\_org(14,11) = 241.5,$

$Y_{44} = T\_basic\_org(19,11) + T\_basic\_org(10,11) + T\_basic\_org(15,11) = 555.925,$

$Y_{55} = T\_basic\_org(20,11) - Table\_basic\_org(20,4) - T\_basic\_org(20,5) - T\_basic\_org(20,7) - T\_basic\_org(20,8) + T\_basic\_org(11,11) + T\_basic\_org(16,11) = 625.6.$

The solution is unique as routes for commodity flows between regions (sectors) are unique.

It has been often overlooked or neglected that it is more difficult than someone thinks to give final demand at purchasers' or producers' price because a typical utilization of (interregional) input–output table is to forecast the total production of sectors with given final demand when a big exogenous impact is made on the economy. A good example is the construction of bridges of railway and highway/expressway, which connects a big island and the main island via three routes. Due to improvements in the transportation infrastructures thanks to the construction of such substantially critical transportation infrastructures, interregional trade patterns must be changed. Logistics costs of interregional commodity flow definitely change with all interregional commodity flows that use bridges and changes in the logistics costs must be estimated in order to exogenously give final demand in all the regions. In reality, the estimation is tough and it is almost equivalent to forecast the total production of sectors even if we can assume interregional trade patterns are unchanged since we cannot calculate logistics costs which must be paid by the final demand sector (consumers) without knowing the amounts of commodity flows into the final demand sectors which are made using the bridges.

7.1.5.9 Gross Regional Product and Gross Domestic Product

The gross domestic product is calculated as follows:

$$\mathrm{GDP} = \sum_{i=1}^{5} Y_{ii} - \sum_{i=1}^{5}\sum_{j=1}^{5} \alpha_{ji}^{ii} Y_{ii} - \sum_{p=3}^{5}\sum\nolimits_{j=1}^{6}\sum\nolimits_{k=1}^{2} {}^{p}a_{kj}^{k1} CF_{kj}^{k1}, \tag{7.18}$$

in which: α_{ji}^{ii} is the *j-th* element of α^{ii} $(i = 1, 2, \ldots, 5)$. With the numerical example,

$$\begin{aligned}\mathrm{GDP} = & \sum_{i=1}^{5} Y_{ii} \\ & -\sum\nolimits_{j=1,2,3,6,9} (T\_basic\_org(8,j) + T\_basic\_org(13,j) + T\_basic\_org(7,j)) \\ & + T\_basic\_org(19,j) + T\_basic\_org(20,j)) \\ & - (T\_basic\_org(12,11) + T\_basic\_org(17.11)) \\ = & 3{,}403.025 - (225 + 930 + 115 + 85 + 0) - (362.8 + 700.225) = 985,\end{aligned}$$

which is equal to the total final demand:

$$\begin{aligned}& T\_basic\_org(8,10) + T\_basic\_org(13,10) + T\_basic\_org(7,10) \\ & \quad + T\_basic\_org(19,10) + T\_basic\_org(20,10) \\ & \quad = 325 + 500 + 0 + 0 + 160 = 985,\end{aligned}$$

which creates the welfare of consumers at the cost (producers') price.

The gross regional product of the region i is given as follows:

$$\mathrm{GRP}_i = Y_{ii} - \sum_{j=1}^{5} \alpha_{ji}^{ii} Y_{ii} - \sum_{j=1}^{2} \alpha_{ji}^{ii} \left(\sum_{q=3}^{5} {}^{q}a_{ji}^{j1} \right) Y_{ii} \; (i = 1, 2, \ldots, 5). \tag{7.19}$$

The definition of GDP in Eq. (7.18) presumes logistics costs are born by sellers. The definition of GRP in Eq. (7.19) presumes logistics costs are born by purchasers (GRP which presumes sellers pay for logistics costs can be defined, too, as follows:

$GRP_i = Y_{ii} - \sum_{j=1}^{5} \alpha_{ji}^{ii} Y_{ii} - \sum_{p=3}^{5} \sum_{j=1}^{6} {}^{p}a_{ij}^{i1} CF_{ij}^{i1}$ (i = 1,2); $GRP_i = Y_{ii} - \sum_{j=1}^{5} \alpha_{ji}^{ii} Y_{ii}$ (i = 3,4,5) GRP of region 1 becomes negative (– 37.8) (due to specified figures of ${}^{q}a_{ji}^{j1}$), although it could often happen in reality with a region (sector), e. g., which can survive depending on transfers from the central government). With the numerical example, $GRP_1 = T\_basic\_org(21,1) = 221.125$, $GRP_2 = T\_basic\_org(21,2) = 709.95$, $GRP_3 = T\_basic\_org(21,3) = 92.15$, $GRP_4 = T\_basic\_org(21,6) = 288.925$, and $GRP_5 = T_{basic_{org(21,9)}} = 216.35$. The sum of GRP_i $(i = 1, 2, \ldots, 5)$ is 1528.5, which is equivalent to the GDP obtained in I-O tables at purchasers' and producers' prices (Tables 4.40 and 4.41). The difference in GDP calculated and the sum of *GRP* s is the difference in the assumption of who pays for logistics costs and the difference is logistics costs associated with commodity flows into region 6 for the final demand. It is calculated as follows: $\sum_{j=1}^{2} \sum_{q=3}^{5} {}^{q}a_{j6}^{j1} C_j = T\_basic\_org(12,10) + T\_basic\_org(17,10) = 237.25 + 306.25 = 543.5$.

7.1.5.10 Which Region Provides Logistics Services

It can be considered that shipment activities, CF_{ij}^{kl}, are taken as sort of production activities which induce demand against logistics services as intermediate inputs. In the numerical example, since logistics sectors are located in regions 3, 4, and 5, logistics services must be provided from those regions to regions 1 and 2 where demand against logistics services are created. With usual interregional input–output tables, sectors of logistics services exist in each region. So, several types of models can be constructed depending on whether demands against logistics services are provided by logistics sectors located at the departure region of commodity shipment or by those at the address region of the delivery or any other region (this should be taken as a kind of specification of the model which should reflect the reality and it is not an assumption who (sellers, purchasers, etc.) would pay for logistics costs). Actually, it has no meaning to specify which region provides logistics services and the point is which region provides intermediate inputs for the production of logistics services which are located wherever. When a truck transports goods for long distances across several regions, it needs to feed at several gas stations in different regions.

7.1.5.11 A departure from the Conventional Interregional Input–Output Analysis

The system of equations, Eqs. (7.10a), (7.10b), (7.11), and (7.14), gives the solution of Y_{ii} $(i = 1, 2, 3, 4, \text{ and } 5)$ with an exogenously given final demand, C_{j6} $(j = 1, 2, 3, \ldots, 6)$ and it departs from the conventional analysis that is based on an interregional input–output table at purchasers' price or producers' price. The system of equations, Eqs. (7.10a), (7.10b), (7.11), and (7.14) is a basic system in a static content without any capacity constraints. It is easy to expand it in a dynamic model in which, for example, bottlenecks of transportation infrastructures for the economic growth are resolved by making investments in order to improve existing transportation infrastructures or construct new expressway routes of a high standard, and so on. The formulation of such a model must be an optimization model. The model in this chapter can be taken as a typical example in this sense.

7.2 Skeleton of the Planning and Framework of the Model

In order to construct a simulation model systematically, so-called coding is very important. Coding is setting parameters with which non-digital information (i.e., geographic, network, socio-economic, etc.) configuration characters into digital information with which the model can be specified in terms of mathematical expressions and, eventually, in the language of a software applied to the simulation. Here, we show important parts of the coding and readers may guess how coding is made for the model construction to see Appendix 1 in this chapter.

7.2.1 Target Area, Planning Horizon, Industrial Classification, and Network of Expressway

7.2.1.1 Zone Classification of the Target Area, Link Node, and Zone Node

The target area, with which economic effects of the construction of Asian Expressway Network are measured and its optimal construction schedule is identified, is the main land China, which is divided into seven regions (zone codes are 1–7), and surrounding countries and regions such as Japan (zone code is 11), Korea (12), Europe–Former Soviet Union (13), South-East Asia–Australia (14), and United States–Canada–Latin America (15) (see Table 7.1). Surrounding countries and regions are specified for the inclusion of international trades between China and those countries into the model. Also, as for countries/regions 11, 13, and 14, they are specified presuming possible expansion of the expressway network into surrounding regions, and conversion of commodity flows onto Asian Expressway Network from commodity flows of trades between countries/regions 11 and 13, 11 and 14, and 13 and 14. It was highly expected that such conversion of commodity flows from the existing logistics routes onto Asian Express Network will generate toll revenues, which would be an important factor for profitability of the network.

Transportation infrastructures that connect regions and countries are aggregated into virtual transportation infrastructures. Transportation infrastructures are divided into "links" in order to explicitly specify the construction and/or improvement schedule of transportation infrastructures. The division is made mainly dependent

Table 7.1 Zone division of the target area, zone code, city code, etc

Zone code	Zone name	Zone node code	Name of zone node (city)	Number of links
1	Northeast China	1	Harbin	4
		2	Changchun	
		3	Shenyang	
2	North China	4	Tianjin	8
		5	Jinan	
		6	Zhengzhou	
		7	Xuzhou	
3	Northwest China	8	Xian	10
		9	Lanzhou	
		10	Urumqi	
4	Middle China	11	Wuhan	9
		12	Nanchang	
		13	Changsha	
5	East China	14	Hangzhou	10
6	West China	15	Chengdu	5
		16	Guiyang	
7	South China	17	Hengyang	11
		18	Canton (Guangzhou)	
		19	Nanning	
		20	Mon Cai (Beihai)	
11	Japan	21	Kitakyushu	1
12	Korea (Peninsula)	22	P'yongyang (Pyomgyang)	3
		23	Seoul	
		24	Pusan (Busan)	
13	Soviet–Europe	25	Roma	1
14	Southeast Asia ·	26	Singapore	1
15	USA–Canada ·	27	New York	1

on geographical distribution of relatively major cities over surrounding regions/countries. A node of two different links is called link node and it virtually represents an important city around there. As shown in Table 7.1, virtual cities are 57 in China, among which 20 cities are zone nodes—a zone node is a link node through which commodities are shipped from the zone where the said zone node is located or shipped into the zone using the transportation infrastructures.

Using notation defined in Appendix 1, Table 7.1 means $J = \{1, 2, 3, \ldots, 7\}$, and $\widehat{J} = \{11, 12, 13, 14, 15\}$. Also, $JCT(1) = 4$, $JCT(2) = 8$, $JCT(3) = 10$, and so on.

Table 7.2 Classification of industries

Sector code	Industries
1	Agriculture
2	Mining
3	Light industry
4	Heavy industry
5	Services industry
6	Freight truck transport industry
7	Railway transport industry
8	Coastal shipping and water route transport industry
9	Harbor distribution industry

7.2.1.2 Classification of the Economy

The economy of China is divided into nine sectors (Table 7.2).[1] The first four sectors induce demand against the transportation services when they are traded within regions and between regions/countries. The fourth sector is a sector of service other than transportation services. The last four sectors provide transportation services. It looks that the division of sector is not minute and it was the limit of the model specification considering the capacity of the computer and software on that day.

Using notations defined in Appendix 1, Table 7.2 means $I = \{1, 2, 3, \ldots, 9\}$, $I_s = \{5, 6, 7, 8, 9\}$, $I_o = \{5\}$, $I_I = \{1, 2, 3, 4\}$, $I_v = \{6, 7, 8, 9\}$, $v_1 = \{6\}$, $v_2 = \{7\}$, $v_3 = \{8\}$, and $v_4 = \{9\}$.

7.2.1.3 Planning Horizon

The planning horizon was set 25 years from 1985 to 2009, which is divided into five periods (Table 7.3). The fifth period was taken as a tentative goal, during which the proposed Asian Expressway Network would be about to be completed.

7.2.1.4 Specification of Proposed Asian Expressway Network

Asian Expressway Network was proposed as transport infrastructure, which improves and strengthens the capacity of road transportation not only between regions in China but also between China and European countries or South-East

[1] At that time, the most issue was a lack of data available. Only source at hand was Chinese National Statistics Bureau (1983). Even with input–output data (at national level), we had no data available. Data of Japan (e.g., Administrative Management Agency 1979; MITI 1980) were referenced and the estimation of input–output coefficients were made through calibration based on the development stages of provinces.

Table 7.3 Planning horizon

Period	t	Years
First period (Period 1)	0	1985–1989
Second period (Period 2)	1	1990–1994
Third period (Period 3)	2	1995–1999
Fourth period (Period 4)	3	2000–2004
Fifth period (Period 5)	4	2005–2009

Asian countries. Eventually, mobilities would be increased between European countries, Former Soviet (Central Asia), China, and South-East Asian countries including Japan, and it was expected that international and interregional trades between those countries and regions would be invigorated once free-trade agreement, smoother trade management and cooperation, and so on, are progressed in the future. Focus of the analysis was of course laid on the impacts of the proposed Asian Expressway Network on China and an interesting concern was how to schedule investments to construct the expressway network links following the endogenously identified priority.

Looking at length of expressway link in Table 7.4, readers realize that distance of most links (distance from a link node (city) to another link node) is around 500 km. It is too long, even considering that one planning period is 5 years. In order to capture the impacts of the expressway network, more minute specifications should have been appropriate. However, considering the computer and software capacity limit on that day and appropriate minuteness of other specifications of the model, total 30 expressway links were structured into the model, which are possible investments targets in order to increase transportation capacity between countries and regions (Table 7.4 and Fig. 7.1). Of course, the initial capacity is set zero (0) with all the specified expressway links. (Specification of other transportation infrastructures is skipped.)

7.2.1.5 Specification of Routes by Origin–Destination

As a basic and starting framework of the model, seven zones and five zones are specified in China and outside China, respectively. The next essential step is how to structure into the model transportation infrastructures through which commodities are transported as a result of interregional and international trades that would be more created by strengthening interregional and international mutual dependence among sectors. As shown in Table 7.2, four transportation sectors are specified and it is plausible to presume that shipment of commodity uses several different transportation services because haul distance is relatively longer than that of the economy assumed in Chaps. 4 and 6. As readers will see later on, the specification of shipment activity in 7.1.5.5 is also a useful device for specification of transportation networks that are consisted of different transportation modes. Here, a concept of (transportation) route between regions is important. The route is specified with interregional as well as intra-regional commodity flows just as intra-regional shipment activities are defined in Chaps. 4 and 6.

Table 7.4 Asian Expressway Network link

Expressway link code	Expressway link nodes	Length of expressway link (km)	Expressway link capacity at the initial period (10,000 tons/day)
101	Harbin–Changchun	240	0.0
102	Changchun–Shenyang	310	0.0
103	Shenyang–Tianjin	650	0.0
104	Tianjin–Jinan	270	0.0
105	Tianjin–Zhengzhou	630	0.0
106	Jinan–Xuzhou	310	0.0
107	Zhengzhou–Xuzhou	300	0.0
108	Xuzhou–Hangzhou	660	0.0
109	Zhengzhou–Wuhan	600	0.0
110	Hangzhou–Nanchang	570	0.0
111	Wuhan–Changsha	370	0.0
112	Nanchang–Changsha	380	0.0
113	Changsha–Hengyang	150	0.0
114	Hengyang–Guangzhou	500	0.0
115	Hengyang–Nanning	770	0.0
116	Guangzhou–Beihai	860	0.0
117	Nanning–Beihai	190	0.0
118	Zhengzhou–Xian	530	0.0
119	Xian–Chungdu	880	0.0
120	Chungdu–Guiyang	640	0.0
121	Guiyang–Changsha	780	0.0
122	Xian–Changsha	660	0.0
123	Lanzhou–Urumqi	2100	0.0
151	Shenyang–P'yongyang	420	0.0
152	Pyongyang–Seoul	240	0.0

(continued)

Table 7.4 (continued)

Expressway link code	Expressway link nodes	Length of expressway link (km)	Expressway link capacity at the initial period (10,000 tons/day)
153	Seoul–Busan	420	0.0
154	Seoul–Busan[a]	540	0.0
155	Busan–Japan	250	0.0
161	Urumqi–Europe·Soviet	6570	0.0
162	Guangzhou–South East Asia	3750	0.0

[a]West route

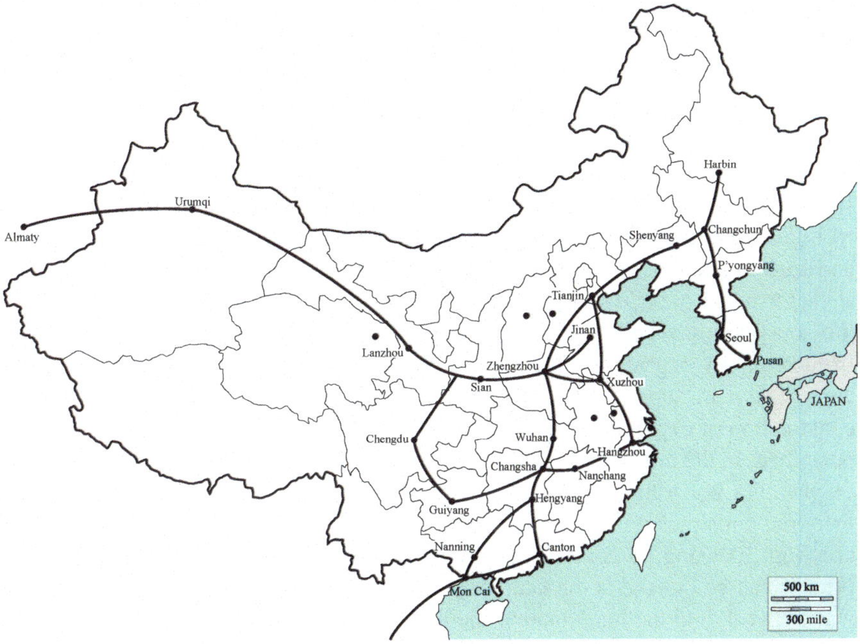

Fig. 7.1 Expressway network

Table 7.5 shows the number of routes which specified within and between regions and countries. Indices *i* and *j* represent zone code in Table 7.1. For example, from zone 1 (North East China) to zone 7 (South China), it is specified that 14 alternative routes exist on the transportation network, which can be consisted of a several different transportation modes.

The transport routes from origin zone to destination zone are set up based on the transport networks consisting of different transportation modes (that of Asian Expressway is shown in Fig. 7.1). Table 7.5 shows, for example, the number of

Table 7.5 Number of routes by pair of origin and destination zones (rank 1)

j												
i	1	2	3	4	5	6	7	11	12	13	14	15
1	2	3	16	14	8	15	14	3	2	3	3	2
2	3	2	7	7	8	13	18	4	3	4	5	3
3	16	7	2	4	6	2	5	2	0	1	2	0
4	14	7	4	2	6	5	2	2	0	1	1	0
5	8	8	6	6	2	6	5	4	3	4	4	3
6	15	13	2	5	6	1	6	2	0	1	1	0
7	14	18	5	2	5	6	2	2	1	2	2	1
11	3	4	2	2	4	2	2	0	0	2	6	0
12	2	3	0	0	3	0	1	0	0	0	0	0
13	3	4	1	1	4	1	2	2	0	0	2	0
14	3	5	2	1	4	1	2	6	0	2	0	0
15	2	3	0	0	3	0	1	0	0	0	0	0

routes of rank 1. With ranks 2, and 3, they are set so that the number of possible routes will increase (not decrease).

Considering that the trip length of China would be very long compared to that of Japan (due to the transportation network specification) and the existing transport facilities are in full operation to the limit of capacity, it is presumed that the construction of the expressway must be concentrated on a specific line step-by-step as a matter of reality. "Rank" is a device with which a kind of priority is given to the construction schedule of expressway network links. As the expressway starts from zero, any expressway link can be constructed if the economic impacts of the construction are superior to the construction of other links. However, a concentrated construction of expressway network would be more effective and politically it must be argued. In the model specification, the rank is set till "rank 4." At the earlier stage of planning horizon, only routes of the higher priority rank can be utilized (and therefore constructed if the construction is right in the light of the opportunity cost criterion) focusing on coastal regions around Beijing and Shanghai and the lower priority can be utilized at the later stage of planning horizon to expand the expressway network into the inner land to the west and to the south.

7.3 Structural Equations

Actually, the model presented in this chapter was huge at that time, even considering the capacity of the main frame computer and the cutting-edge software available at that time. The whole system of equations is shown in Appendix 1 in this chapter. In order to save space, we here focus on the substance of structural equations, which characterizes the general applicability of the model as well as highlights the advantage of the model so far developed in this book.

7.3.1 *Flow Conditions*

7.3.1.1 Market Flow Condition 1: Non-Service Industry

For almost all the economic models, which utilize input–output table, the most important structural equation is the so-called market flow condition. This is the equation with which the supply and demand of goods must be equated goods by goods, region (zone or subeconomy) by region, and period by period. The demand is composed of intermediate demand and final demand. The latter is composed of consumption demand and investment demand, which are both endogenously determined. Note that it is a little bit different specification that demand does not explicitly include "exports" to other regions and countries. The following Eq. (7.20) completes the specification of the market flow condition together with Eq. (7.23) that is defined later on and corresponds to Eq. (7.14).

$$\left\{\begin{array}{r}\text{intermediate}\\ \text{demand}\end{array}\right\} + \left\{\begin{array}{r}\text{investment demand (formation of}\\ \text{industrial capital, housing capital,}\\ \text{transport infrastructures, and other social}\\ \text{overhead capital)}\end{array}\right\} + \left\{\begin{array}{r}\text{consumption}\\ \text{demand}\end{array}\right\} - \left\{\begin{array}{r}\text{total commodity inflow}\\ \text{(inflow from all the regions}\\ \text{and countries including}\\ \text{commodity flow from own}\\ \text{region)}\end{array}\right\} \leq 0 \tag{7.20}$$

The last term in Eq. (7.20) is the total supply to the said region.

7.3.1.2 Market Flow Condition 2: Other Service

As for goods of other service industry, the last term in Eq. (7.20) becomes only the production ($\equiv$ supply) in the said region because it is presumed that services cannot be exported and imported.

7.3.1.3 Market Flow Condition 3: Transportation Service

It is assumed that demand against transportation services shall be met by the supply of transportation services zone by zone and transportation mode by mode. This implies that, for example, the demand against transportation services which are induced by the commodity flow from region i to region j using one of the routes, which are specified having priorities (ranks), shall be provided at each of the zones through which the said route goes. In case railway is utilized by the said route in zone k, the demand against railway transportation services that is induced by the commodity flow which uses the said route shall be met by the provision of railway transportation services which are produced in zone k (and of course, the commodity flow causes loads on the railway transportation infrastructure capacity). As already mentioned previously, the specification matters which region will provide intermediate inputs for transportation services and it does not matter which region will pay for the transportation costs. We can eventually construct interregional input–output table at producers' or purchasers' prices and the construction of interregional input–output table is a different matter because we use neither the table at producers' nor purchasers' price.

Truck (Freight) Transportation Service

$$\left\{\begin{array}{r}\text{demand against freight}\\ \text{transportation services in}\\ \text{zone } k \text{ that are induced by}\\ \text{all the commodity flows}\\ \text{which use expressway}\\ \text{highway links located}\\ \text{in zone } k\end{array}\right\} + \left\{\begin{array}{r}\text{demand against freight}\\ \text{transportation services}\\ \text{in zone } k \text{ that are induced by}\\ \text{all the commodity flows}\\ \text{which use ordinary road links}\\ \text{located in zone } k\end{array}\right\} - \left\{\begin{array}{r}\text{production}\\ \text{of freight}\\ \text{transportation}\\ \text{services in zone } k\end{array}\right\} \leq 0 \tag{7.21}$$

Railway Transportation Service

$$\left\{\begin{array}{r}\text{demand against railway}\\ \text{transportation services in}\\ \text{zone } k \text{ that are induced by}\\ \text{all the commodity flows}\\ \text{which use railway links}\\ \text{located in zone } k\end{array}\right\} - \left\{\begin{array}{r}\text{production of railway}\\ \text{transportation services}\\ \text{in zone } k\end{array}\right\} \leq 0 \tag{7.22}$$

Coastal/Water Shipment Service

It is specified in an analogous way above and skipped.

Harbor Distribution Service

It is specified in an analogous way above and skipped.

7.3.1.4 Shipment Balance Equations

The market flow conditions defined in the above are completed together with the following shipment balance equations.

Shipment Balance Equation 1: Shipment from a Region in China (Including Exports to Other Countries)

$$\left\{\begin{array}{r}\text{total commodity outflow of} \\ \text{goods } k \text{ from zone } i \\ \text{in China to all zones}\end{array}\right\} - \left\{\begin{array}{r}\text{total production of goods } k \\ \text{in zone } i \text{ in China}\end{array}\right\} \leq 0 \quad (7.23)$$

The first term of Eq. (7.23) includes intra-regional commodity flow and exports to other countries. Eq. (7.23) implies that the total outflow from a region cannot be more than the total production in the said region.

Shipment Balance Equation 2: Definition of Export from China to Other Countries

$$\left\{\begin{array}{r}\text{total outflow of} \\ \text{all commodity (goods } k\ (k = 1, 2, 3, 4)) \\ \text{from all zones (zone } j (= 1, 2, 3, \ldots, 7)) \\ \text{in China to zone } i \\ \text{outside China}\end{array}\right\} - \left\{\begin{array}{r}\text{export from China} \\ \text{to country (region) } i\end{array}\right\}$$
$$\leq 0 \quad (7.24)$$

Since the economy of other countries than China is not endogenously structured into the model, which means the economy of other countries are black boxes, the following constraints are specified in order to avoid uninteresting solutions:

$$\left\{\begin{array}{r}\text{the lowest amount}\\ \text{of export to country } i\\ \text{estimated from}\\ \text{the past trend}\end{array}\right\} \leq \left\{\begin{array}{r}\text{export from China}\\ \text{to country } i\end{array}\right\}$$
$$\leq \left\{\begin{array}{r}\text{the largest amount}\\ \text{of export to country } i\\ \text{estimated from the past trend}\end{array}\right\} \quad (7.25)$$

Shipment Balance Equation 3: Definition of Imports from Other Countries to China

$$\left\{\begin{array}{r}\text{total inflow}\\ \text{of all commodity (goods } k\ (k=1,2,3,4))\\ \text{into all zones (zone } j(=1,2,3,\ldots,7))\\ \text{in China from zone } i \text{ outside China}\end{array}\right\}$$
$$-\left\{\begin{array}{r}\text{import}\\ \text{from country (region)} i\\ \text{to China}\end{array}\right\} \leq 0 \quad (7.26)$$

Because of the same reason in the definition of exports from China, the following constraints are specified:

$$\left\{\begin{array}{r}\text{the lowest amount}\\ \text{of import from country } i\\ \text{to China estimated from}\\ \text{the past trend}\end{array}\right\} \leq \left\{\begin{array}{r}\text{import}\\ \text{from country } i\\ \text{to China}\end{array}\right\}$$
$$\leq \left\{\begin{array}{r}\text{the largest amount}\\ \text{of import from country } i\\ \text{to China estimated from}\\ \text{the past trend}\end{array}\right\} \quad (7.27)$$

7.3.1.5 Balance of International Payments: Cumulative Deficit Constraint

Although "money" is not explicitly treated in the model, the international balance of payments of China should be controlled so that deficit if any shall be within a tolerable limit.

Definition of Accumulated International Deficit at Period t

$$\left\{\begin{array}{r}\text{discounted summation}\\ \text{of the total import}\\ \text{from all other countries}\\ \text{(regions) } i\ (i=11,12,13,14,15)\\ \text{to China over periods 0}\\ \text{to } t \text{ to the value at period 0}\end{array}\right\}$$

$$-\left\{\begin{array}{r}\text{discounted summation}\\ \text{of the total revenue of expressway toll}\\ \text{charged on the commodity flows}\\ \text{which are induced by}\\ \text{international (regional)trades}\\ \text{among other countries (regions)}\\ \text{outside China}\\ \text{and go through expressway links}\\ \text{inside China over periods 0 to } t\\ \text{to the value at period 0}\end{array}\right\}$$

$$-\left\{\begin{array}{r}\text{discounted summation}\\ \text{of the total export}\\ \text{from China to}\\ \text{all other regions } i\ (i=11,12,13,14,15)\\ \text{over periods 0}\\ \text{to } t \text{ to the value at period 0}\end{array}\right\}$$

$$-\left\{\begin{array}{r}\text{accumulated}\\ \text{international deficit}\\ \text{at period } t\\ \text{in the value at period 0}\end{array}\right\}=0 \qquad (7.28)$$

In the previous definition, the expressway toll revenues charged on the commodity flows which are induced by international (–regional) trades among other countries (regions) outside China and go through the expressway links inside China are taken as exports of China to countries committed to the commodity flows. The expressway toll charged on such a commodity flow must be greater than the total costs which are incurred by the intermediate inputs to freight truck transport sectors in all the regions in China in order to supply freight transportation services to the said commodity flow. Eq. (7.28) is the definition of accumulated international deficit at period *t*. If it is negative (black ink) at period t, it means that the sum of exports from period 0 to *t* is more than the sum of imports from period 0 to *t* in terms of the value at period 0. However, such a case usually never occurs since the simulation is made with the maximization of, for example, GDP of China. If positive, it means a deficit trade balance. The economy outside China is a kind of black box and the deficit balance must be within a plausible limit. Ideally, at the final period, it should be the same level of the deficit balance before the planning starts. Also, from period 0 to t − 1, it must be within a tolerable and realistic level since it is unrealistic that China economy can borrow an infinity amount from abroad if there is no constraint on a deficit balance. Therefore, the following equation completes the equation of international trade balance.

Control of Deficit Balance

$$\left\{\begin{array}{r}\text{accumulated}\\ \text{international deficit}\\ \text{at period } t\end{array}\right\} - \left\{\begin{array}{r}\text{tolerable deficit balance level}\\ \text{at period } t\end{array}\right\} \leq 0 \tag{7.29}$$

The second term is exogenously given.

7.3.2 *Conditions of Stock Variables*

The model in this chapter is a full-scale dynamic model that is applicable to real policy issues related to public investment and optimal regional development planning.

7.3.2.1 Balance Between Demand and Supply Against Capital Stock, Labor, and Housing Stock

One of the important features of dynamic model is that activities (production, transportation, daily life, etc.) are bound by capacity constraints of stocks such as industrial capital, labor, housing stock, transportation infrastructure.

Balance Between Demand and Supply of Industrial Capital

$$\left\{\begin{array}{c}\text{total production of sector } i\\ \text{in region } j \text{ in China at period } t\end{array}\right\} \leq \left\{\begin{array}{r}\text{the maximum total production}\\ \text{limited by the amount of industrial capital}\\ \text{which is available for sector } i \text{ in zone } j\\ \text{in China at period } t\end{array}\right\} \tag{7.30}$$

Equation (7.30) is the definition of production function and it is assumed of the Harrod-Domar-Leontief type together with Eq. (7.31).

Balance Between Demand and Supply of Labor

$$\left\{\begin{array}{c}\text{total production of sector } i\\ \text{in region } j \text{ in China at period } t\end{array}\right\} \leq \left\{\begin{array}{r}\text{the maximum total production}\\ \text{limited by the amount of labor}\\ \text{which is available for sector } i \text{ in zone } j\\ \text{in China at period } t\end{array}\right\} \tag{7.31}$$

Balance Between Demand and Supply of Housing Stock

$$\left\{\begin{array}{r}\text{total demand}\\ \text{against housing stock in region } j\\ \text{in China at period } t\\ \text{that is induced by all workers (labor)}\\ \text{who are living in zone } j \text{ in China}\\ \text{and available for all sector } i\ (i = 1, 2, \ldots, 9)\\ \text{in zone } j \text{ in China}\end{array}\right\}$$

$$\leq \left\{\begin{array}{r}\text{summation of housing stock}\\ \text{available in zone } j \text{ in China}\\ \text{over all varieties}\\ \text{of housing quality } i\\ (i = 1, 2, \ldots, n_H)\end{array}\right\} \tag{7.32}$$

Parameter n_H is the number of varieties of housing (quality).

7.3.2.2 Balance Between Demand Against and Supply of Transportation Infrastructure

Improvement in transportation infrastructures is a typical target of public investment and it is taken as one of the most effective and powerful policy instruments for regional development planning because poor quality of transportation infrastructures become serious bottleneck to the economic growth of the whole national economy as R. Watkins had pointed out. In order to structure the seriousness of the bottleneck and put rational priority on the resolution of the bottleneck, the following constraint is specified.

$$\left\{\begin{array}{r}\text{total load to link } p\\ \text{of the transportation network}\\ \text{(transportation infrastructures)}\\ \text{placed by all the commodity flows}\\ \text{which use link } p \text{ at period } t\end{array}\right\} - \left\{\begin{array}{r}\text{one period capacity}\\ \text{of link } p\end{array}\right\} \leq 0 \quad (7.33)$$

7.3.2.3 Balance Between Demand and Supply of Social (Overhead) Capital (Other Social Capitals)

$$\left\{\begin{array}{r}\text{demand against}\\ \text{minimum permissible}\\ \text{level of social services}\\ \text{in zone } j \text{ in China,}\\ \text{which is calculated}\\ \text{based on workers}\\ \text{in zone } j \text{ in China}\end{array}\right\} - \left\{\begin{array}{r}\text{supply}\\ \text{of social services,}\\ \text{which is calculated}\\ \text{based on stock}\\ \text{of social capital}\\ \text{in zone } j \text{ in China}\end{array}\right\}$$

$$+ \left\{\begin{array}{r}\text{supply}\\ \text{of social services}\\ \text{exceeding}\\ \text{the minimum}\\ \text{permissible level}\\ \text{of demand in zone } j\\ \text{in China}\end{array}\right\} \leq 0 \quad (7.34)$$

7.3.2.4 Formation of Industrial Capital

$$\left\{\begin{array}{r}\text{amount of capital}\\ \text{that is available}\\ \text{for sector } i \text{ in zone } j\\ \text{in China}\\ \text{at period } (t+1)\end{array}\right\} - \left(1-\widehat{\delta}_i^{k}\right)\left\{\begin{array}{r}\text{amount of capital}\\ \text{that is available}\\ \text{for sector } i \text{ in zone } j\\ \text{in China}\\ \text{at period } t\end{array}\right\}$$

$$-\left\{\begin{array}{r}\text{formation of capital}\\ \text{at period } t\\ \text{that is available}\\ \text{for sector } i \text{ in zone } j\\ \text{in China}\end{array}\right\} = 0 \qquad (7.35)$$

Parameter $\widehat{\delta}_i^{k}$ is a depreciation rate for industrial capital in sector i (in 5 years). The last term is the capital formation in sector i in zone j in China, which induces final demand of investment in zone j in China at period t.

7.3.2.5 Formation of Housing Capital

$$\left\{\begin{array}{r}\text{amount of housing capital}\\ \text{of quality } i\\ \text{in zone } j \text{ in China}\\ \text{at period } (t+1)\end{array}\right\} - \left(1-\widehat{\delta}_i^{H}\right)$$

$$\times\left\{\begin{array}{r}\text{amount of housing capital}\\ \text{of quality } i\\ \text{in zone } j \text{ in China}\\ \text{at period } t\end{array}\right\}$$

$$-\left\{\begin{array}{r}\text{formation of housing capital}\\ \text{of quality } i\\ \text{in zone } j \text{ in China}\\ \text{at period } t\end{array}\right\} = 0 \qquad (7.36)$$

Parameter $\widehat{\delta}_i^{H}$ is a depreciation rate for housing capital of quality i (in 5 years). The last term is the housing capital formation of quality i in zone j in China, which induces final demand of investment in zone j in China at period t.

7.3.2.6 Formation of Social Capital (Other Capitals)

$$\left\{\begin{array}{r}\text{amount of social capital}\\ \text{available in zone } j\\ \text{in China}\\ \text{at period } (t+1)\end{array}\right\} - \left(1-\widehat{\delta}^{S}\right)\left\{\begin{array}{r}\text{amount of social capital}\\ \text{available in zone } j\\ \text{in China}\\ \text{at period } t\end{array}\right\}$$

$$-\left\{\begin{array}{r}\text{formation of social capital}\\ \text{in zone } j\\ \text{in China}\\ \text{at period } t\end{array}\right\} = 0 \tag{7.37}$$

Parameter $\widehat{\delta}^{S}$ is a depreciation rate for social capital (in 5 years). The last term is the social capital formation in zone j in China, which induces the final demand of investment in zone j in China at period t.

7.3.2.7 Formation of Transportation Infrastructure

$$\left\{\begin{array}{r}\text{amount of}\\ \text{transportation infrastructure } j\\ \text{(ordinary road, expressway, or railway link, port logistics facility, etc.)}\\ \text{at period } (t+1)\end{array}\right\}$$

$$-\left(1-\widehat{\delta}^{R}_{MS(j)}\right)\left\{\begin{array}{r}\text{amount of}\\ \text{transportation infrastructure } j\\ \text{at period } t\end{array}\right\}$$

$$-\left\{\begin{array}{r}\text{formation}\\ \text{(construction or improvement)of}\\ \text{transportation infrastructure } j\\ \text{in China}\\ \text{at period } t\end{array}\right\} = 0 \tag{7.38}$$

Parameter $\widehat{\delta}^{S}_{MS(j)}$ is a depreciation rate for transportation infrastructure of type *MS* (j) (in 5 years). $MS(\cdot)$ is a function in transportation infrastructure link code j, which maps transportation infrastructure link j to 1 (expressway), 2 (ordinary road), 3 (railway), 4 (coastal/water shipment), or 5 (port logistics facility). The last term is the improvement (or construction) of link j at period t and it induces final demand of investment in zones that are associated to transportation infrastructure j.

7.3.2.8 Population Growth and Migration

Natural Growth

$$\left\{\begin{array}{r}\text{summation of}\\ \text{natural increase}\\ \text{in workers (labor)}\\ \text{over all sectors } i(i=1,2,\ldots,9)\\ \text{and all zones } j(\,j=1,2,3,\ldots,7)\\ \text{in China}\\ \text{at period } t\end{array}\right\} - \widehat{n}^{h}\cdot\left\{\begin{array}{r}\text{summation of}\\ \text{workers (labor)}\\ \text{over all sectors } i(i=1,2,3,\ldots,9)\\ \text{and all zones } j(\,j=1,2,3,\ldots,7)\\ \text{in China}\\ \text{at period } t\end{array}\right\}=0 \tag{7.39}$$

Parameter $\widehat{n}^{h}$ is a natural growth rate of workers (in 5 years). The first term is the total natural increase in workers, which is proportional to the total workers.

Migration: Social Population Growth

$$\left\{\begin{array}{r}\text{summation of}\\ \text{inflow of workers}\\ \text{over all sectors } i(i=1,2,3,\ldots,9)\\ \text{and all zones } j(\ j=1,2,3,\ldots,7)\\ \text{in China}\\ \text{at period } t\end{array}\right\} - \left\{\begin{array}{r}\text{summation of}\\ \text{outflow of workers}\\ \text{over all sector } i(i=1,2,3,\ldots,9)\\ \text{and all zones } j(\ j=1,2,3,\ldots,7)\\ \text{in China}\\ \text{at period } t\end{array}\right\} = 0 \qquad (7.40)$$

$$\left\{\begin{array}{r}\text{summation of}\\ \text{outflow of workers over}\\ \text{all sectors } i(i=1,2,,3,\ldots,9)\\ \text{and}\\ \text{all zones } j(\ j=1,2,3,\ldots,7)\\ \text{in China}\\ \text{at period } t\end{array}\right\} - r^{IS}\cdot\left\{\begin{array}{r}\text{summation of}\\ \text{workers (labor) over}\\ \text{all sectors } i(i=1,2,3,\ldots,9)\\ \text{and}\\ \text{all zones } j(\ j=1,2,3,\ldots,7)\\ \text{in China}\\ \text{at period } t\end{array}\right\} \leq 0 \qquad (7.41)$$

Parameter r^{IS} defines the upper rate of mobility of workers between sectors and zones in China to the total workers in China. Eq. (7.41) defines the maximum amount of the total movement of workers among sectors in China (the first term). Eq. (7.40) binds that the total inflow of workers into and outflow from all sectors in all zones in China must be equated with each other.

Population Growth: Natural Plus Social Growth

$$\left\{\begin{array}{r}\text{workers (labor)}\\\text{employable}\\\text{in sector } i \text{ in zone } j\\\text{in China}\\\text{at period } (t+1)\end{array}\right\}-\left\{\begin{array}{r}\text{workers employable}\\\text{in sector } i \text{ in zone } j\\\text{in China}\\\text{at period } t\end{array}\right\}$$

$$-\left\{\begin{array}{r}\text{increase in workers}\\\text{in sector } i \text{ in zone } j\\\text{in China at period } t\\\text{due to natural growth}\end{array}\right\}-\left\{\begin{array}{r}\text{inflow of workers}\\\text{in sector } i\\\text{in zone } j\\\text{in China}\\\text{at period } t\end{array}\right\}$$

$$+\left\{\begin{array}{r}\text{outflow of workers}\\\text{from sector } i\\\text{in zone } j\\\text{in China}\\\text{at period } t\end{array}\right\}=0 \tag{7.42}$$

In Eq. (7.42), it is assumed that a natural increase in workers in China can move any zone in China if they can find jobs, irrespective of their birth place (location of their graduated schools).

7.3.3 National Income Accounting of China

7.3.3.1 Gross National Income (GNP/GNI)

$$\left\{\begin{array}{r}\text{summation of}\\ \text{total product over}\\ \text{all sectors } i(\text{i} = 1, 2, 3, \ldots, 9)\\ \text{and}\\ \text{all zones } j(\ j = 1, 2, 3, \ldots, 7)\\ \text{in China at period } t\end{array}\right\} - \left\{\begin{array}{r}\text{summation of}\\ \text{intermediate input}\\ \text{over all sectors}\\ i\ (i = 1, 2, 3, \ldots, 9)\\ \text{and all zones}\\ j\ (\ j = 1, 2, 3, \ldots, 7)\\ \text{in China at period } t\end{array}\right\}$$

$$- \left\{\begin{array}{r}\text{summation of losses}\\ \text{due to capital formation}\\ \text{(intermediate inputs to}\\ \text{the capital formation activity)}\\ \text{over all capital stocks, housing stocks,}\\ \text{social overhead capitals}\\ \text{and transportation infrastructures,}\\ \text{and all zones } j\ (\ j = 1, 2, 3, \ldots, 7)\\ \text{in China at period } t\end{array}\right\}$$

$$+ \left\{\begin{array}{r}\text{total revenue}\\ \text{of expressway toll}\\ \text{charged on commodity flows}\\ \text{between}\\ \text{countries (regions) outside China}\\ \text{which use expressway links}\\ \text{in China at period } t\end{array}\right\}$$

$$= \left\{\begin{array}{r}\text{Gross National Product}\\ \text{(GNP)}\\ \text{of China}\\ \text{at period } t\end{array}\right\} \tag{7.43}$$

The first two terms of the left-hand side of Eq. (7.43) are usual definition of the gross domestic product (GDP). The third term takes capital formation as a kind of *implicit* production activity. A kind of loss related to the capital formation process due to any reason is also taken as a kind of intermediate inputs to the capital formation activity. The addition of this term is to put emphasis on the consistency in utilization of value (US dollar) unit that can be applied to the valuation of "capital." Another way of capital valuation is of course the total value incurred by the formation of capital becomes the value of capital. The difference among the two becomes a difference among the way of calculation of output-capital ratios. Alternatively, the third term can be taken as a sort of capital depreciation at the beginning of the period in which capital formation is made although the third term is deducted from "usual GNP/GNI definition" in Eq. (7.43). The difference between gross investment and net investment is the sum of the third term and the total capital depreciation cost. In case this interpretation is adopted, GNP is defined by Eq. (7.43) is increased by the third term. The fourth term is a kind of payment from abroad and this is a reason why the right-hand side of Eq. (7.43) is defined as GNP/GNI.

7.3.3.2 Net National Product (NNP)

$$\left\{\begin{array}{r}\text{GNP}\\ \text{at}\\ \text{period } t\end{array}\right\} - \left\{\begin{array}{r}\text{summation of}\\ \text{industrial capital}\\ \text{depreciated over}\\ \text{all sectors } i\ (i = 1, 2, 3, \ldots, 9)\\ \text{and all zones } j\ (\ j = 1, 2, 3, \ldots, 7)\\ \text{in China}\\ \text{at period } t\end{array}\right\}$$

$$- \left\{\begin{array}{r}\text{summation of}\\ \text{housing capital}\\ \text{depreciated over}\\ \text{all varieties of}\\ \text{housing quality } i\ (i = 1, 2, \ldots, n_H)\\ \text{and all zones } j\ (\ j = 1, 2, 3, \ldots, 7)\\ \text{in China at period } t\end{array}\right\}$$

$$
-\left\{\begin{array}{r}
\text{summation of}\\
\text{social capital depreciated over}\\
\text{all zones } j\ (\ j=1,2,3,\ \ldots,7)\\
\text{in China}\\
\text{at period } t
\end{array}\right\}
$$

$$
-\left\{\begin{array}{r}
\text{summation of}\\
\text{transportation infrastructure capital}\\
\text{depreciated over all links } l\ (\epsilon\ MLC)\\
\text{in China}\\
\text{at period } t
\end{array}\right\}
$$

$$
=\left\{\begin{array}{r}
\text{NNP}\\
\text{at}\\
\text{period } t
\end{array}\right\} \tag{7.44}
$$

MLC is a set of link codes of transportation infrastructures that are located in China.

7.3.3.3 Gross Investment (INV)

$$
\left\{\begin{array}{r}
\text{summation of}\\
\text{inputs to}\\
\text{industrial capital formation}\\
\text{over all sectors}\\
i\ (i=1,2,3,\ \ldots,9)\\
\text{and all zones}\\
j\ (\ j=1,2,3,\ \ldots,7)\\
\text{in China at period } t
\end{array}\right\}
+
\left\{\begin{array}{r}
\text{summation of inputs}\\
\text{to housing capital formation}\\
\text{over all varieties}\\
\text{of housing quality}\\
i\ (i=1,2,3\ldots,\ n_H)\\
\text{and all zones}\\
j\ (\ j=1,2,3,\ \ldots,7)\\
\text{in China at period } t
\end{array}\right\}
$$

$$+\left\{\begin{array}{r}\text{summation of}\\ \text{inputs to}\\ \text{social capital formation}\\ \text{over all zones}\\ j\ (\ j=1,2,3,\ \ldots,7)\\ \text{in China at period } t\end{array}\right\}+\left\{\begin{array}{r}\text{summation of inputs}\\ \text{to transportation}\\ \text{infrastructure formation}\\ \text{over all links } l\ (\epsilon\ MLC)\\ \text{in China}\\ \text{at period } t\end{array}\right\}$$

$$=\left\{\begin{array}{r}\text{gross investment}\\ \text{(INV)}\\ \text{at period } t\\ \text{in China}\end{array}\right\}\leq 0 \tag{7.45}$$

7.3.3.4 Net Investment (NI)

$$\left\{\begin{array}{r}\text{summation of}\\ \text{difference in industrial capital}\\ \text{available at periods } (t+1)\text{and } t\\ \text{over all sectors } i\ (i=1,2,3,\ \ldots,9)\\ \text{and all zones } j\ (\ j=1,2,3,\ \ldots,7)\\ \text{in China}\end{array}\right\}$$

$$+\left\{\begin{array}{r}\text{summation of}\\ \text{difference in housing capital}\\ \text{available at periods } (t+1)\text{and } t\\ \text{over all varieties of}\\ \text{housing quality } i\ (i=1,2,\ \ldots,n_H)\\ \text{and all zones } j\ (\ j=1,2,3,\ \ldots,7)\\ \text{in China}\end{array}\right\}$$

$$
+\left\{\begin{array}{r}\text{summation of}\\ \text{difference in social capital}\\ \text{available at periods } (t+1) \text{ and } t\\ \text{over all zones } j\ (j=1,2,3,\ \ldots,7)\\ \text{in China}\end{array}\right\}
$$

$$
+\left\{\begin{array}{r}\text{summation of difference}\\ \text{in transportation infrastructure}\\ \text{available at periods } (t+1)\text{and } t\\ \text{over all links } l\ (\epsilon\ MLC)\\ \text{in China}\end{array}\right\}
$$

$$
=\left\{\begin{array}{c}\text{net investment}\\ \text{(NI) at period } t\end{array}\right\} \tag{7.46}
$$

7.3.3.5 Consumption

$$
\left\{\begin{array}{r}\text{summation of}\\ \text{minimum permissible}\\ \text{amount of goods } k\\ \text{consumed by worker}\\ \text{employed in sector } i \text{ in zone } j\\ \text{over all goods } k\ (k=1,2,3,\ \ldots,5),\\ \text{all sectors } i\ (i=1,2,3,\ \ldots,9),\\ \text{and all zones } j\ (j=1,2,3,\ \ldots,7)\\ \text{in China at period } t\end{array}\right\}
$$

$$
+\left\{\begin{array}{r}
\text{summation of consumption} \\
\text{exceeding} \\
\text{minimum permissible} \\
\text{amount of goods } k \\
\text{consumed by worker employed} \\
\text{in zone } j \\
\text{over all goods } k\ (k=1,2,3,\ldots,5), \\
\text{and all zones } j \\
(j=1,2,3,\ldots,7) \\
\text{in China at period } t
\end{array}\right\}=\left\{\begin{array}{r}
\text{Consumption} \\
\text{at} \\
\text{period } t \\
\text{in China}
\end{array}\right\} \qquad (7.47)
$$

7.3.4 Objective Function

In order to complete the model, we need to specify the scope of spatial area, in which the regional development planning must be controlled and optimized. The scope of the time horizon for planning is already specified as five periods (25 years). Considering not only the Chinese geographical as well as geopolitical "must" for Asian Expressway Network but also (regional) economic development stage of China and other surrounding countries at that time, it was essential to make China economy taken-off and catch up with developed countries as soon as possible for the project to be successful. The model itself is generally applicable and extendable to cover a wider scope and here it is confined to China as one of the experimental applications.

Related with thus specified scope of spatial area, several explanations are made together with the specification of objective functions. First, it is assumed that Asian Expressway outside China will be improved from period 1 to period 5 at the costs of countries and regions through which the expressway goes. This means that no explicit investments into the expressway outside China are treated in the model. Any amount of commodity flows, which meet other structural equations, can be transported from and into regions/countries outside China into and from regions in China, respectively, as far as those commodity flows together with the commodity flows between regions in China meet the capacity constraints of transportation infrastructures inside China.

Second, it is assumed that improvements in transportation infrastructures outside China are made by countries/regions on which the said transportation infrastructures are located at their costs. The regional planning outside China together with investment planning to transportation infrastructures formulate a simulation model analogous to the model in this chapter. In case an overall optimal regional development planning with the scope of Asia and Eurasia is to be designed, we need to construct an overall model which is consisted of the models of China and other countries/

regions. At that time, this was just a dream considering the capacity of computer and now it has a reality. The optimization with an overall model pursues a kind of *optimum optimorum*.

Hereafter, the model in this chapter is explicitly characterized and specified as China Model. Once the scope of the area is specified, the following four types of objective function can be formulated. They each embodies the economic principle, on which the regional development planning shall be based by making schedule of investments into Asian Expressway Network construction as one of major policy instrumental variables.

7.3.4.1 Maximization of GNP of China

This is the first approximation to the regional development plan in which the economic growth of the whole national economy of China is maximized as much as possible being subject to the minimum permissible level of consumption and social capitals. The development planning eventually causes an issue of disparities among regions and the resolution is beyond the scope of the optimization with this objective function.

7.3.4.2 Maximization of NNP

This will have the same story as the maximization of GNP.

7.3.4.3 Welfare Maximization with Lower Constraint on the Accumulation of Industrial Capital Stock at the End of Period

In case the planning has a finite horizon, the amount of accumulated capital stocks at the end of period should be controlled since the economy and the welfare of the people (future generation), who live in the future after the end of period, must be dependent on it. In case the objective function is specified in terms of welfare (or satisfactions of consumption, living style, etc.) in any definition which accrues to people living within the time horizon (current generation), a kind of trade-off, which should be made with the welfare between current and future generations, is essentially important issues. As the target of accumulated amount of capital stock at the end of period increases, the welfare enjoyed by the current generation must be decreased. The accumulated amount of capital stock has an upper limit depending on the initial capital stock and the target must be set within an upper limit, of course.

7.3.4.4 Consumption Maximization with Lower Constraint on the Accumulation of Industrial Capital Stock at the End Period

It neglects spatial distribution of the consumption of goods that exceeds the minimum permissible level while other welfare variables such as social overhead capitals and housing capitals are bind to the minimum permissible level.

7.3.5 Boundary Conditions for the Differential Equations

Equations (7.35) to (7.38) and Eq. (7.42) constitute so-called equations of motion with the system of linear differential equation. In order to give a unique optimal solution, boundary conditions must be given. In this case, they are initial value for stock variables such as industrial capital, social capital, housing capital, transportation infrastructure, and workers, which specify the amount of stock variables available at the initial year.

7.4 Simulation Cases

7.4.1 Presumptions

7.4.1.1 Scope of the Spatial Area for Planning

As it is already mentioned related to the objective function, the scope of spatial area for planning is confined to China by exogenously specifying the construction schedule of Asian Expressway links outside China such as Changchun – (P'yong-yang)Pyongyang – Seoul – Pusan (Busan), Mon Cai (Bohai)–Hanoi – East Asia – Australia, and Urmqi – Almaty – Central Asia (Former Soviet Union) – Istanbul – Eastern Europe. It is expected that Asian Expressway itself contributes not only to the development in China but also surrounding countries and regions. However, the necessity of the network in China should be firstly argued by proving if the network will critically contribute to the development of China. The model becomes the China model and the investment demand against the Asian Expressway network inside China will be able to be analyzed by presuming that the Chinese economy must bear the construction costs. The investment demand is a kind of derivative demand induced by: not only (1) activated interregional commodities flows inside China in parallel with the take-off of the Chinese economy, which is to be synergetically accelerated by the construction of the Asian Expressway, but also (2) international commodity flows between regions and countries in Europe and Asia which are diverted onto Asian Expressway Network from currently utilized existing transportation routes and modes.

7.4.1.2 Borrowing from Abroad

Currency is not explicitly structured in the model as it is a material (goods) model though goods are measured in terms of monetary unit (US dollar-value unit). It is assumed that the deficit of international payments defined by Eq. (7.28) is borrowing from abroad and balance of other recurring items (non-trade business transaction, capital transfer, etc.) are stable. Domestic saving and borrowing money from abroad are *competitively* invested into improvements in social infrastructures including Asian Expressway Network as well as industrial capitals.

7.4.1.3 Disposition of Person Trip

Person trips such as leisure trips and business trips are not explicitly dealt with in the model. As it is mentioned in Chap. 5, we need a person trip generation and distribution model and it must be combined with the model in this chapter in order to explicitly analyze the competitively induced demand against transportation infrastructures. Here, it is assumed that around 20% of the capacity is to be utilized for person trips as a first approximation to such an integrated model (Kohno et al. 1987, p. 35, 100).

7.4.1.4 Capital and Labor Productivity

With a developing country where labor is relatively abundant like China in that day, it is usually observed that labor productivity increases and capital productivity decreases as the capital is accumulated as the economy develops. However, here it is assumed that the productivity is stable over the planning horizon. This can be interpreted in several ways. One possible way is that China's economy will be able to fully enjoy the advantage of the least developed country, namely, the economy can install capitals which embody most advanced technologies every time when it makes investments and usually it does not need to be stick to the capitals which embody out-of-date technologies. On the other hand, it was unofficially said that a fairly large amount of unemployment (concealed unemployment) substantially exists in China's economy as all workers should be employed due to institutional reasons (Mao et al. 1998). The former can save a decrease in capital productivity while keeping labor productivity stable thanks to the background of the labor market in China.

7.4.1.5 Load on Transportation Infrastructure Capacity

In the model specification, the sum of commodity flows in both directions become loads on the sum of capacities of transportation infrastructure in both directions.

Although the direction of transportation infrastructures (links) should be identified with the model specification because the identification will possibly confine spatial development patterns, it was neglected as a first step due to the computer capacity limit at that time.

7.4.1.6 Population Movement

It is assumed that population (labor) movement between regions and sectors occurs at once at the end of each period (except for the last period) and new distribution of population (labor) is realized at the start of the next period. As it is already mentioned in the above 7.3.2.8, the initial distribution of graduates between regions and sectors is not bound by their graduation departments (specialism) and places of schools/colleges/universities.

7.4.1.7 Commodity Flows Induced by International and Interregional Trade

Commodity flows between regions in China and those between countries including China, which possibly use Asian Expressway, are structured into the model with the following categories from 1. to 4.:

1. Endogenous specification with no constraints.
   The commodity flows that are induced by interregional trades between seven regions in China are endogenously determined in the model.
2. Endogenous specification within an exogenously given range
   The commodity flows that are induced by international trades between regions in China and countries/regions are endogenously determined subject to the balance of the international trade of China is within a prespecified range of exogenously given upper and lower limits.
3. Endogenous specification as far as the commodity flow induces demand against Asian Expressway Network.
4. No specification in the model.
   Trades between North Korea (Democratic People's Republic of Korea: DPRK) and other countries are not explicitly structured into the model.

Table 7.5 shows possible alternative routes of transportation infrastructure for commodity shipment by pair of origin and destination. The table shows alternative routes of rank 1 which are available from period 1 ($t = 0$) to period 3 ($t = 2$) in the sense that: (i) alternative routes are prespecified assuming that some Asian Expressway Network links will not be constructed in the periods even if the investment to the construction were efficient and (ii) some of the prespecified alternative routes, on which commodity flows are induced by interregional and international trades, are able to use links of Asian Expressway Network as far as investments against the said Asian Expressway Network links are made because the investment is proved to be efficient in terms of the investment criteria endogenously built in the model based on the social opportunity cost criteria. This is a device in order to exclude too many routes that are structured into the model, which will be theoretically possible alternative routes, and in reality, or as a result of political decision, apparently will not be constructed in the periods. The alternative routes of rank 2 (a table is omitted), which is applied to commodity flows in periods of 4 ($t = 3$) and 5 ($t = 4$), are constituted using all links of the Asian Expressway Network (therefore rank 1 is inclusive to rank 2). Of course, capacities of some links belonging to rank 2 including those firstly constitute the alternative routes of rank 1, can be zero (if links, which constitute routes belonging to rank 1, are not constructed till period 3).

7.4.2 *Variants for Cases of Analysis*

Cases originally should be set up with the combinations of the following three items:

1. borrowing rate from abroad,
2. allowable upper limit on accumulating external debt and,
3. specification of the objective function with variation in social discount rate.

7.4.2.1 Supposed Interest Rate of Borrowing from Abroad

The weighted average of interest rates for the credit grants given for China (the total is around 20 billion US dollars) based on government guarantees from March 1979 to November 1982 is 6.65% and the weighted average of loan periods is 10.21 years. On the other hand, the weighted average of interest rates for the loan to China (the total is 4 billion US dollars) on nongovernment bases is 2.27% and the weighted average of their loan periods is 5.61 years. Considering these figures, two variants are assumed with borrowing rates of 4% and 6%. The former is favorite for borrowing compared to the past trend.

7.4.2.2 Upper Limit on Accumulating External Debt

At the end of 1984, the accumulating middle/long external debt of China is 20 billion US dollars. On the other hand, the accumulating external debt of short period is around 4 billion US dollars. It is assumed that the accumulating short period external debt is constant after period 1 (1985–1989) and the payments of interest to the short period external debt will be canceled by the receipts of interests to short-period overseas loan. Three variants with upper limit on the accumulating middle/long period external debt are specified in Table 7.6, which are intentional to mainly aim at enhancement of construction of the Asian Expressway Network at an earlier stage and debt payments at a later stage thanks to enhanced regional developments in China.

Variant 1 presumes natural transitional debt growth pattern till period 3 ($t = 2$) based on trends in the past and it shall be declined since periods 4–5 owing to regional economic development in China.

Variants 2 and 3 presume external debts in addition to variant 1 that is equivalent to the construction patterns of Asian Expressway Network in China shown in Table 7.7. It shows links in kilometer four lanes standard to be constructed within the period with variants 2 and 3 which respectively expect that Asian Expressway Network in China (total length 13,350 km) will be completed by the end of period 5 ($t = 4$) with four lanes and two lanes. The construction patterns are tentatively presumed for specifying the upper limits on accumulating middle/long period external debts and have no authority. Furthermore, simulation results will not necessarily show that in cases of variants 2 and 3, respectively, the Asian Expressway Network in China will be completed by the end of period 5 with four and two lanes because the borrowing may be utilized for more effective investment targets such as improvements in other transportation infrastructures and/or capital formations in private sectors for the whole of the Chinese economy to develop with higher growth rate. On the contrary, it can be an optimal solution in which the construction of Asian Expressway Network has progressed with higher pace than presumed in Table 7.7 and completed earlier than period 5 (and with more capacity in case of variant 3) following the turnpike theory because Asian Expressway Network is to be proved extremely efficient and effective for the Chinese economy as a whole to grow rapidly.

If the production of agricultural and manufacturing sectors become four times by 2000 (the start of period 4) compare to 1984, which means the GDP of China becomes around 1100 billion US dollars, interest payments to the presumed external debt of 110 billion US dollars or more with variant 2 might be a fairly heavy load to the Chinese economy although the rate of external debt to GDP is far less than Brazil, Mexico, Korea, Indonesia (around 20–30%) at that time.

Table 7.6 Allowable upper limit on accumulating middle/long period external debt (Unit:100 million US dollar)

	$t = 0$	$t = 1$	$t = 2$	$t = 3$	$t = 4$
Variant 1	236	489	885	825	735
Variant 2	266	578	1102	1141	1129
Variant 3	251	533	992	986	931

Table 7.7 Construction patterns of Asian Expressway Network links (Unit: kilometer·four lanes standard)

	$t = 0$	$t = 1$	$t = 2$	$t = 3$	$t = 4$	Total
Variant 2	1000	2000	4350	3000	3000	13,350
Variant 3	500	1000	2125	1500	1500	6625

7.4.2.3 Objective Function

Considering that Asian Expressway Network construction must be dependent on the huge amount of external debt till the end of the time horizon and it must be decreased as earlier as possible, the objective function to be maximized in order to derive optimal regional development and investment policies should be the maximization of GDP (GDI) of China. It is presumed that the social discounting rate is 4% in cases in which Asian Expressway Network is a target of investment because the project put more weight on the future generation and the discount rate should be lower than the current interest rate from the political viewpoint. In case where the economic development in regions in China is simulated based on the past trend, the social discount rate and borrowing rate from abroad are 6%.

7.4.2.4 Case (Scenario) for Simulation

Presumed four cases are specified with simulation analysis, which is basically composed of "variants of upper limit on accumulating external debt" (Table 7.8).

Cases 1, 2, and 3 presume that the construction of the Asian Expressway Network (and provision of expressway services to the public) is within the scope of targets, in which the fund available (saving + borrowing from abroad) should be invested if the investment is effective in order to enhance regional economic development in China taking into the account opportunity cost of the capital fund. This never means that Asian Expressway Network exists at the start of the planning horizon, or shall come into existence as time elapses. Therefore, "with" means "investment opportunity exists for." Case 4 presumes "without Asian Expressway," which means that Asian Expressway Network is forcibly out of the scope of investment targets.

The upper limit on accumulating external debt specifies fund-raising conditions from abroad. Case 1 presumes that international funds are tight and/or the risk of the Asian Expressway Network project is evaluated high by overseas investors. On the other hand, Case 2 presumes that financial conditions are favorite and/or the risk taken is low.

In Case 4, it is presumed that the financial condition for borrowing from abroad is the same as Case 2, that is, investment funds are excessive (variant 2) but the borrowing rate (6%) is the same as the trend in the past since no big special project, which may be attractive for foreign investors, is not planned for the time horizon. We can evaluate the potential impacts of the Asian Expressway Network on the regional

Table 7.8 Case (scenario) for simulation

Case	Borrowing rate	Asian Expressway Network	Upper limit on accumulating external debt
1	4%	With	Variant 1
2	4%	With	Variant 2
3	4%	With	Variant 3
4	6%	Without	Variant 2

economic development in China by comparing simulation results of other cases with Case 4.

7.5 Simulation Results

7.5.1 Optimal Allocation of Funds to Expressway Links by Period[2]

7.5.1.1 Period 2 ($t = 1$; 1990–1994)

With all cases, investments (at period 1)[3] into the expressway line that connects from Wuhan to Canton (Guangzhou) through Changsha and Hengyang, that is, expressway links of Wuhan–Changsha–Hengyang–Canton, which includes a bottleneck of transportation from Wuhan to Xujiadong, are made with the spot traffic volumes of 6000 trucks in both ways per day, which can transport commodities of 60,000 tons per day. Also, investments in the construction of the link between Xian and Lanzhou are made with spot traffic volumes of 75,000 tons (7500 trucks) per day. With links of Tianjin – Jinan–Xuzhou–Hangzhou, it is wholly provided to the public in Cases 1 and 3 although the investment is not so big and the capacity of the link of Jinan–Xuzhou is around 10,000–20,000 tons per day more or less. On the other hand, fairly good amounts of investment are made in both cases and the link capacities of Tianjin–Jinan and Xuzhou–Hangzhou are 120,000 and 190,000 tons per day, respectively (Fig. 7.2).

In Case 2, no investment is made to the link of Jinan–Xuzhou. Fairly good amounts of investment are made to the links of Tianjin–Jinan and Xuzhou–Hangzhou and the link capacities are 130,000 and 190,000 tons per day, respectively.

Discriminating differences among cases are not observed with investment patterns to the expressway links at period 2, it can be seen that priorities should be first given to the two routes of Wuhan to Canto through Xujiadong and Tianjin to Hangzhou. Especially, links from Wuhan to Canton and links of Tianjin–Jinan and Xuzhou–Hangzhou are all critically important considering the whole national economy of China since investments are made in Case 2 in which the borrowing rate is higher than Case 1 and accumulating external borrowing is limited lower than Case 3. Also, it can be seen that expressway links, to which fairly good amounts of investments are made, are confirmed as bottlenecks of the existing transportation

[2] In order to save space, maps are drawn with expressway investments in Case 3 only as it typically shows necessity of the construction of expressway network for regional development in China as readers may see later on.

[3] It is specified in the model that capital (infrastructure) formation made at period t is realized as an increase in capacity of capital in the next period. Therefore, logically Asian Expressway Network at first period ($t = 0$) does not exist at all. Investments (capital formation) at period 5 ($t = 4$) must be zero, too

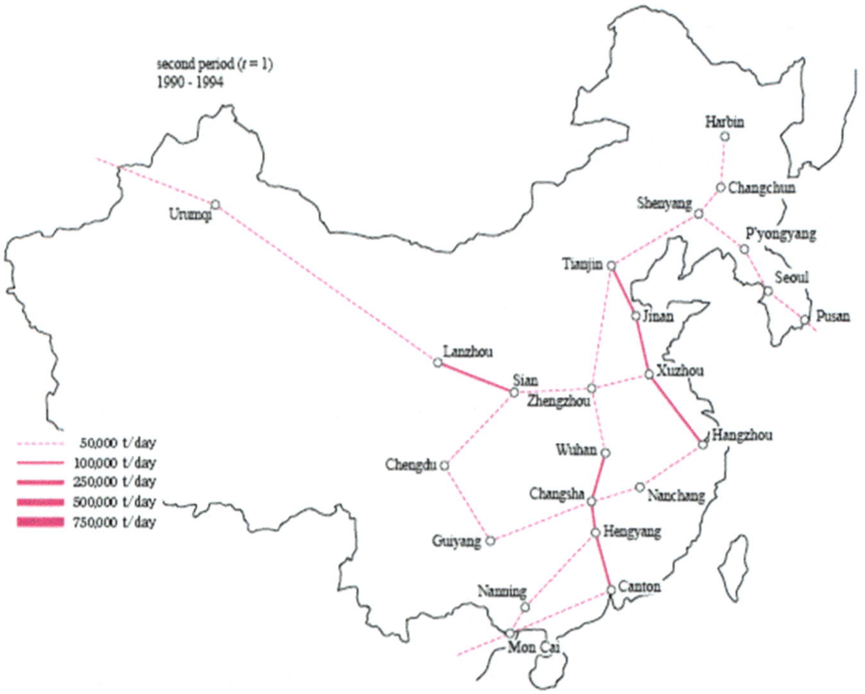

Fig. 7.2 Asian Expressway Network at period 2 ($t = 1$): 1990–1994 (Case 3)

network. This implies that the construction of the Asian Expressway Network is also an effective strategy in order to enhance regional development in China by resolving bottlenecks of the existing transportation network.

7.5.1.2 Period 3 ($t = 2$)

Differences are a little bit observed with simulation results among the three cases at period 3. The link capacity between Jinan—Xuzhou is small compared to that of Jinan—Tianjin and Xuzhou—Hangzhou. Further investments (at period 2) are made to the link of Tianjin—Jinan in Cases 1, 2, and 3, and its capacities are increased to 340,000, 370,000, and 360,000 tons per day, respectively. With Cases 1, 2, and 3, the link capacities of Xuzhou—Hangzhou are increased to 22,000, 22,500, and 22,500 tons per day, respectively, too (Fig. 7.3).

With all the cases, the link capacity between Xian and Lanzhou increases to 100,000 tons per day. Although the capacity provided is around 10,000 tons per day, investment demand is first observed against the construction of links from Xian to Wuhan through Zhengzhou in Case 2. The link capacities of Wuhan–Changsha–Hengyang–Canton are increased to 130,000, 100,000, and 110,000 tons per day, respectively (Fig. 7.3).

Fig. 7.3 Asian Expressway Network at period 3 ($t = 2$): 1995–1999 (Case 3)

The results indicate that higher priority should be put on the construction of the link between Tianjin—Jinan.

7.5.1.3 Period 4 ($t = 3$)

With Cases 2 and 3, the expressway line from Changchun to Canton through Tianjin and Wuhan is wholly provided to the public (thanks to the investment made at period 3) although the link capacities from Changchun to Wuhan through Tianjin and Zhengzhou are only 10,000 tons per day. With Case 1, no investment is made to the link of Tianjin—Zhengzhou. The expressway line from Lanzhou to Xuzhou through Xian and Zhengzhou is wholly provided to the public in Case 2 though the link capacities from Xian to Xuzhou are just 10,000 tons per day. Fairly good amounts of investment are added to improvements in the link between Lanzhou and Xian and the link capacities become 580,000, 630,000, and 570,000 tons per day with Cases 1, 2, and 3, respectively (Fig. 7.4).

In all cases, the link capacities of Tianjin-Jinan and Xuzhou-Hangzhou are increased to with a range of 350,000–500,000 tons per day although the link capacity of Jinan–Xuzhou is still around 100,000 tons per day. The link capacity of the

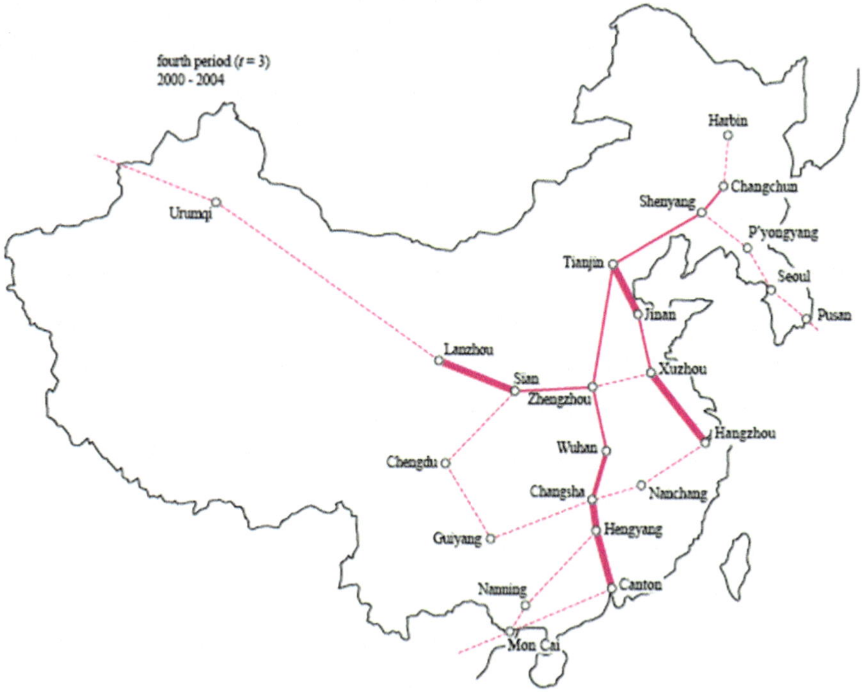

Fig. 7.4 Asian Expressway Network at period 4 ($t = 3$): 2000–2004 (Case 3)

expressway line between Wuhan and Canton through Hengyang becomes around 500,000 tons per day with all cases. At this stage, it becomes clear that the expressway network is improved at the earliest stage in Case 2, next in Case 3, and at latest stage in Case 1 as it is expected.

7.5.1.4 Period 5 ($t = 4$)

At this stage, investments are made (at period 4) to expressway links which connect the Asian Expressway Network in China to other countries and regions with all cases (Fig. 7.5). The capacities of expressway line to Europe through the Former Soviet Union (Central Asia) and to Japan through Korea are expanded to around 10,000 tons per day. The expressway line to South Asia starting from Mon Cai (Vietnam) located in the border to China is expanded almost 10,000 tons per day and it is connected to Nanning through Hengyang in China with the same capacities with all Cases.

It can be said that the expressway investments at periods 1, 2, and 3 are intensively made to the construction of the main transportation artery connecting between North China and East China with links of Tianjin–Hangzhou, and to the resolution of the transportation bottlenecks of Wuhan–Canton and Lanzhou–Xian. At period

Fig. 7.5 Asian Expressway Network at period 5 ($t = 4$): 2005–3009 (Case 3)

4, presumed investments are made by related countries to the expressway links which connect the Asian Expressway Network in China to other regions and countries corresponding to drastic increases in international trade between regions and countries other than China. At period 5, then, the expressway links constructed through periods 1–4 indicate the whole Asian Expressway Network under construction as a phase of "network" but only vaguely. The degree of completion is highest in Case 2, the next is in Case 3, and last in Case 1, as expected by the combinations of borrowing rate and upper limit to the accumulating external debts which are presumed with the specification of cases.

7.5.2 Commodity Flow

7.5.2.1 Overview

Period 1 ($t = 0$)

The total of commodity flows between zones (regions) in China is around 300 billion US dollars per year with all cases, which is equivalently converted to commodities of

5.52 billion tons using a conversion coefficient of 0.01841 billion tons/billion US dollar (Tables 7.9 and 7.10). As trades between countries (regions) outside China are zero which use the Asian Expressway Network, the grand total of commodity flows between countries in the world (excluding Korea and North Korea (DPRK)) which use the Asian Expressway Network is around 337 billion US dollar (6.21 billion tons).

Commodity flows in China are intensively made between North China, Middle China, and East China. The total commodity flow between these regions is around 169 billion US dollars (3.12 billion tons), which is around 56% of the total commodity flows in China, in all cases. The total commodity flows into those regions are around 61% of the total of China and the total commodity flows originated by those regions are around 66% of the total of China.

Tables 7.9 and 7.10 can be named as an O.D. table (in terms of commodity flows between zones (regions)). However, tables are completely different from, for example, Table 2.22 in Chap. 2, which are results of a road survey of traffic volumes, and are the sacrosanct data exogenously given to the analysis. Tables 7.9 and 7.10 are results of the simulation with which analysis is developed, and endogenously determined the responding to Cases which are specified presuming different decisive policy parameters. Therefore, investments to improvements in transportation network are endogenously (and optimally) determined, which means transportation network is endogenously determined in the dynamic content.

By the way, it is natural that there exists almost no difference in the total commodity flows shipped into and from regions in China at period 1 ($t = 0$) between cases because the initial conditions of the stock variable are the same among cases and there is little space for optimization with production except for investment that may induce a little bit different commodity flows between regions.

Period 2 ($t = 1$)

The total commodity flows between regions in China becomes 422 billion US dollars (7.77 billion tons) per year and the annual growth rate is 7.1% in Case 1. As for Case 2, those figures are 429 billion US dollars (7.89 billion tons) and 7.4%, respectively. As the total commodity flow shipped from and into North East China remarkably increase with the annual growth rates of 30.0% and 29.9%, respectively, the share of the commodity flows which are intensively made between North China, Middle China, and East China is rather relatively decreased to around 53% of the total in Case 1. With Case 2, a same pattern of changes can be observed.

Period 5 ($t = 4$)

The total commodity flows between regions in China are 929 billion US dollars (17.1 billion tons) and 932 billion US dollars (17.2 billion tons) per year with Cases 1 and 2, respectively. This means that the total commodity flow in China at the end of the time horizon (2009) is around three times of the commodity flow that can be

Table 7.9 Total commodity flows between zones (regions): Case 1

Period 1 ($t = 0$)													Unit: 100 million US dollar	
	1 North East China	2 North China	3 North West China	4 Middle China	5 East China	6 West China	7 South China	Total of China	11 Japan	12 Korea	13 Soviet–Europe	14 South East Asia–Australia	15 USA––Canada–South America	Total
1 North East China	1,969	22	103	0	0	82	0	2,176	0	0	119	0	0	2,295
2 North China	0	1,009	273	703	530	29	12	2,556	0	0	38	66	0	2,660
3 North West China	0	116	115	0	0	0	16	247	0	0	4	0	0	251
4 Middle China	0	197	0	990	2,528	0	104	3,819	0	0	0	0	0	3,819
5 East China	0	755	610	1,484	266	461	0	3,576	326	0	0	339	0	4,241
6 West China	0	0	0	127	6	852	25	1,010	0	0	0	0	0	1,010
7 South China	1	186	0	160	0	163	1,087	1,597	11	0	0	0	0	1,608
Total of China	1,970	2,285	1,101	3,464	3,330	1,587	1,244	14,981	337	0	161	405	0	15,884
11 Japan	100	0	0	0	82	0	255	437	0	0	0	0	0	437
12 Korea	0	0	0	0	0	0	0	0	0	0	0	0	0	0
13 Soviet–Europe	48	0	0	0	0	0	96	144	0	0	0	0	0	144
14 South East Asia–Australia	0	0	0	0	343	0	0	343	0	0	0	0	0	343
15 USA–Canada–South America	0	0	0	0	54	0	0	54	0	0	0	0	0	54
Total	2,118	2,285	1,101	3,464	3,809	1,587	1,595	15,959	337	0	161	405	0	16,862

(continued)

Table 7.9 (continued)

Period 2 ($t = 1$) Unit: 100 million US dollar

	1 North East China	2 North China	3 North West China	4 Middle China	5 East China	6 West China	7 South China	Total of China	11 Japan	12 Korea	13 Soviet–Europe	14 South East Asia–Australia	15 USA–Canada–South America	Total
1 North East China	5,416	1,214	0	0	0	0	0	6,630	0	0	0	0	0	6,630
2 North China	0	1,009	475	862	2,360	0	227	4,933	0	0	576	112	0	5,621
3 North West China	0	190	628	0	0	72	0	890	0	0	0	0	0	890
4 Middle China	0	618	0	204	445	440	0	1,707	0	0	0	0	0	1,707
5 East China	0	920	344	1,181	1,181	886	0	4,512	43	0	0	695	0	5,250
6 West China	0	551	0	69	25	218	0	863	0	0	0	0	0	863
7 South China	0	0	0	386	0	89	1,081	1,556	433	0	63	0	0	2,052
Total of China	5,416	4,502	1,447	2,702	4,011	1,705	1,308	21,091	476	0	639	807	0	23,013
11 Japan	105	0	0	0	92	0	264	461	0	0	0	0	0	461
12 Korea	0	0	0	0	0	0	0	0	0	0	0	0	0	0
13 Soviet–Europe	0	19	0	0	0	0	466	485	0	0	0	0	0	485
14 South East Asia–Australia	0	0	0	0	469	0	0	469	0	0	0	0	0	469
15 USA–Canada–South America	0	456	0	0	239	0	0	695	0	0	0	0	0	695
Total	5,521	4,977	1,447	2,702	4,811	1,705	2,038	23,201	476	0	639	807	0	25,123

Period 5 ($t = 4$)													Unit: 100 million US dollar
	1 North East China	2 North China	3 North West China	4 Middle China	5 East China	6 West China	7 South China	Total of China	11 Japan	12 Korea	13 Soviet–Europe	14 South East Asia–Australia	15 USA–Canada–South America	Total
1 North East China	13,888	0	0	0	0	0	0	13,888	0	0	0	0	0	13,888
2 North China	618	2,096	72	2,663	3,855	0	0	9,304	586	0	446	2,262	0	12,598
3 North West China	0	596	880	0	313	3	8	1,800	0	0	0	0	0	1,800
4 Middle China	0	2,065	0	1,397	2,665	1	347	6,475	0	0	0	0	0	6,475
5 East China	0	2,018	657	3,513	5,076	251	0	11,515	0	0	0	0	0	11,515
6 West China	0	276	0	0	133	345	0	754	0	0	0	0	0	754
7 South China	0	191	0	619	0	0	1,914	2,724	28	0	0	0	0	2,752
Total of China	14,506	7,242	1,609	8,192	12,042	600	2,269	46,460	614	0	446	2,262	0	49,782
11 Japan	0	0	0	0	421	0	757	1,178	0	0	60	19	0	1,257
12 Korea	0	0	0	0	0	0	0	0	0	0	0	0	0	0
13 Soviet–Europe	0	0	0	0	0	0	1,192	1,192	0	0	0	0	0	1,192
14 South East Asia–Australia	0	585	0	0	614	0	0	1,199	0	0	0	0	0	1,199
15 USA–Canada–South America	0	0	0	0	0	0	0	0	0	0	0	0	0	0
Total	14,506	7,827	1,609	8,192	13,077	600	4,218	50,029	614	0	506	2,281	0	53,430

Note: Tables of periods 3 and 4 are omitted
Source: Kohno1998

Table 7.10 Total commodity flows between zones (regions): Case 2

Period 5 ($t = 4$)				Unit: 100 million dollar				Unit: 100 million dollar					
	1 North East China	2 North China	3 North West China	4 Middle China	5 East China	6 West China	7 South China	Total of China	11 Japan	12 Korea	13 Soviet–Europe	14 South East Asia–Australia	15 USA–Canada–South America	Total
1 North East China	1970	6	101	0	21	82	0	2180	0	0	120	0	0	2300
2 North China	0	1002	274	164	1054	30	12	2536	0	0	40	66	0	2642
3 North West China	0	114	114	0	0	0	16	244	0	0	5	0	0	249
4 Middle China	0	740	0	1008	1980	0	104	3832	0	0	0	0	0	3832
5 East China	0	230	611	2023	265	461	0	3590	329	0	0	316	0	4235
6 West China	0	0	0	127	5	852	26	1010	0	0	0	0	0	1010
7 South China	1	186	0	161	0	162	1088	1598	9	0	0	0	0	1607
Total of China	1971	2278	1100	3483	3325	1587	1246	14,990	338	0	165	382	0	15,875
11 Japan	100	0	0	0	82	0	255	437	0	0	0	0	0	437
12 Korea	0	0	0	0	0	0	0	0	0	0	0	0	0	0
13 Soviet–Europe	48	0	0	0	0	0	96	144	0	0	0	0	0	144
14 South East Asia–Australia	0	0	0	0	343	0	0	343	0	0	0	0	0	343
15 USA–Canada–South America	0	0	0	0	61	0	0	61	0	0	0	0	0	61
Total	2119	2278	1100	3483	3811	1587	1597	15,975	338	0	165	382	0	16,860

Period 2 ($t = 1$)												unit: 100 million dollar		
	1 North East China	2 North China	3 North West China	4 Middle China	5 East China	6 West China	7 South China	Total of China	11 Japan	12 Korea	13 Soviet–Europe	14 South East Asia–Australia	15 USA–Canada–South America	Total
1 North East China	5382	1234	0	0	0	0	0	6616	0	0	0	0	0	6616
2 North China	0	1021	477	365	2446	498	219	5026	0	0	591	3	0	5620
3 North West China	0	189	632	0	0	68	0	889	0	0	0	0	0	889
4 Middle China	0	1160	0	223	412	0	3	1798	0	0	0	0	0	1798
5 East China	0	960	349	1348	1162	819	0	4638	47	0	0	804	6	5495
6 West China	0	0	0	509	180	221	0	910	0	0	0	0	0	910
7 South China	0	0	0	387	0	89	1079	1555	429	0	63	0	0	2047
Total of China	5382	4564	1458	2832	4200	1695	1301	21,432	476	0	654	807	6	23,375
11 Japan	110	0	0	0	90	0	261	461	0	0	0	0	0	461
12 Korea	0	0	0	0	0	0	0	0	0	0	0	0	0	0
13 Soviet–Europe	0	23	0	0	0	0	463	486	0	0	0	0	0	486
14 South East Asia–Australia	0	0	0	0	469	0	0	469	0	0	0	0	0	469
15 USA–Canada–South America	0	470	0	0	291	0	0	761	0	0	0	0	0	761
Total	5492	5057	1458	2832	5050	1695	2025	23,609	476	0	654	807	6	25,552

(continued)

Table 7.10 (continued)

Period 5 ($t = 4$)					Unit: 100 million dollar				Unit: 100 million dollar					
	1 North East China	2 North China	3 North West China	4 Mid-dle China	5 East China	6 West China	7 South China	Total of China	11 Japan	12 Korea	13 Soviet–Europe	14 South East Asia–Australia	15 USA–Canada–South America	Total
1 North East China	13,430	0	0	0	0	0	0	13,430	0	0	0	0	0	13,430
2 North China	1105	2030	9	2980	4236	0	0	10,360	651	0	398	1662	0	13,071
3 North West China	0	339	589	0	856	0	0	1784	0	0	0	0	0	1784
4 Middle China	0	2378	0	531	2258	4	253	5424	0	0	0	0	0	5424
5 East China	0	2078	618	3515	5822	196	0	12,229	0	0	0	0	0	12,229
6 West China	0	61	0	0	237	232	79	609	0	0	0	0	0	609
7 South China	0	175	0	693	0	0	1914	2782	0	0	0	0	0	2782
Total of China	14,535	7061	1216	7719	13,409	432	2246	46,618	651	0	398	1662	0	49,329
11 Japan	0	0	0	0	0	0	1178	1178	0	0	81	43	0	1302
12 Korea	0	0	0	0	0	0	0	0	0	0	0	0	0	0
13 Soviet–Europe	0	498	0	0	0	0	238	736	0	0	0	0	0	736
14 South East Asia–Australia	0	415	0	0	784	0	0	1199	0	0	0	0	0	1199
15 USA–Canada–South America	0	0	0	0	0	0	0	0	0	0	0	0	0	0
Total	14,535	7974	1216	7719	14,193	432	3662	49,731	651	0	479	1705	0	52,566

Note: Tables of periods 3 and 4 are omitted
Source: Kohno 1998

taken as the amount limited by the transportation capacity at the initial year (1985). The average annual growth rate is around 4.6%.

The total commodity flow which possibly uses expressway links between Changsha and Canton (Guangzhou) can be estimated based on the total commodity flows shipped into and from South China. It is around 120 US billion dollars per day (2.20 billion tons per year and 6.03 million tons per day) with Case 2 presuming that around 60% of the commodity flow from Japan to South China induced by export from Japan to China is diverted to utilize the Asian Expressway Network (trades with other regions and countries are not necessarily all diverted to the expressway and the estimation neglects the trades in case they are small figures). With Case 1, the figures become 123.8 billion US dollars per year (2.28 billion tons per year and 6.30 million tons per day) presuming that around 60% of the trades with the Former Soviet Union and Europe induce diversion of commodity flow to utilize the expressway network.

The link capacity between Wuhan and Canton through Changsha and Hengyang, which is one of the critical transportation bottlenecks, is around 420,000 tons per day with Case 2. It is around 7% of the commodity flow which is estimated as possible potential demand against transportation infrastructures between Changsha and Hengyang.

With Case 1, in which investment funds are most tight, the commodity flow which may use expressway link of Xian – Lanzhou is estimated based on the commodity flows shipped into and from West China and the Former Soviet Union and Europe presuming 60% of the latter commodity flows will be possibly diverted to utilize the expressway. It is around 68.8 billion US dollars per year (1.27 billion tons per year and 3,470,000 tons per day), which is around 16.7% of the capacity of the expressway link between Lanzhou and Xian in terms of the spot volume traffic capacities. With other Cases, almost the same figures are observed.

7.5.2.2 Minute Discussion with Visual Flow

In order to visually show and confirm the analysis in the above, Figs. 7.6, 7.7, 7.8 are drawn based on commodity flows on links. For example, the commodity flow between East China (EC: zone code 5) and Middle China (MC: zone code 4) is the sum of commodity flows which uses transportation links of the expressway, railway, water shipment if any, and the ordinary road that connects EC and MC. In Case 1 at period 1 (Fig. 7.6), it is 447.3 billion US dollars per year. The commodity flow between EC and North China (NC: zone code 2) is 197.7 billion US dollars. With the commodity flow between EC and South China (SC: zone code 7), it is 68.2 billion US dollars. Figures 7.6, 7.7, 7.8 more clearly show why a certain transportation link (i.e., expressway link) must be improved by making transportation investment at period τ ($\tau = 1, 2, 3, 4$) in order to meet the increase in demand against the capacity in terms of spot traffic volume at period t ($t = 2, 3, 4, 5$) based on optimized commodity flows between zones and countries shown in Tables 7.9 and 7.10.

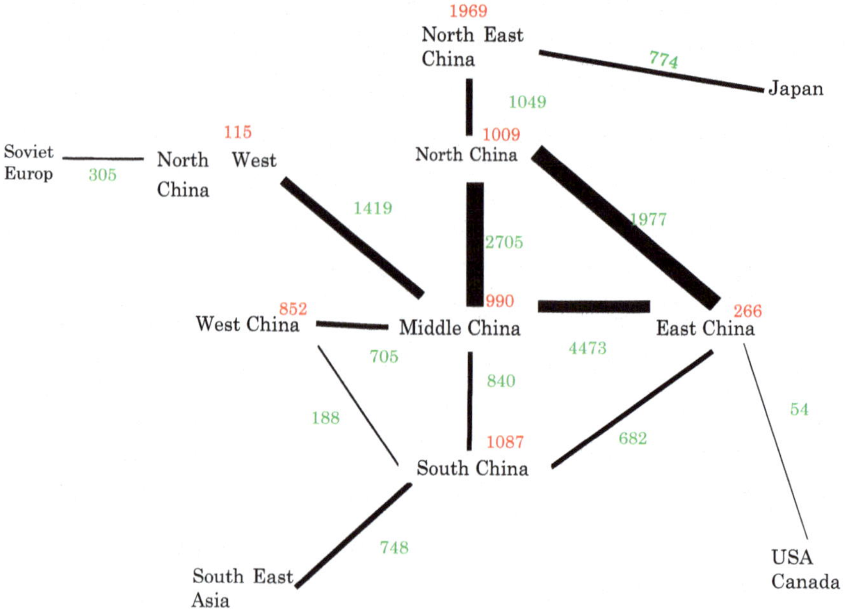

Fig. 7.6 Commodity flows on transportation link (Case 1): Period 1 ($t = 0$)
Unit: 100 million US dollar

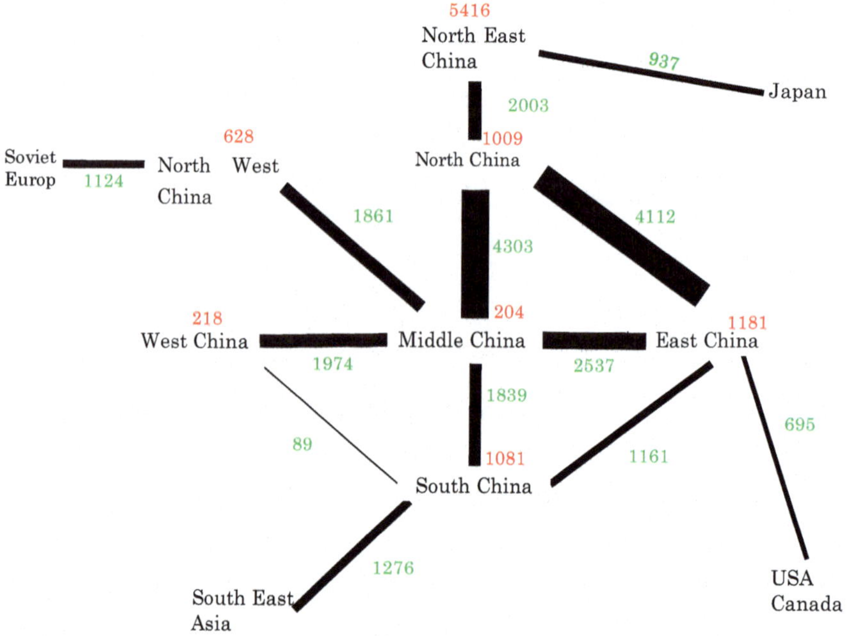

Fig. 7.7 Commodity flows on transportation link (Case 1): Period 2 ($t = 1$)
Unit: 100 million US dollar

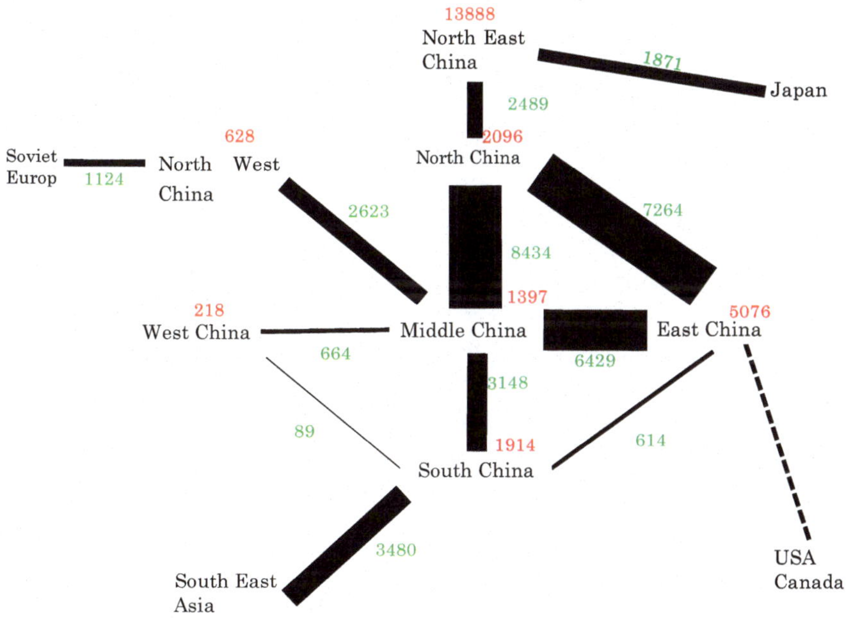

Fig. 7.8 Commodity flows on transportation link (Case 1): Period 5 ($t = 4$)
Unit: 100 million US dollar

Figures 7.6, 7.7, 7.8 have consistent relations to Tables 7.9 and 7.10. The tables show commodity flows between zones and countries. Namely, these tables show commodity flows at origin-destination (O-D) basis and the commodity flows represented indexed by pairs of origin zone and destination zone create traffic flows (commodity flows) on the network of transportation links that connect the said zones with each other.

Representing commodity flow from zone i to j in Tables 7.9 and 7.10 as $OD(i,j)$, intra-regional commodity flow of North-East China (NEC) (zone 1) is $OD(1,1) = 1{,}969$ (100 million US dollars) in Case 1 at period 1 (see Table 7.1 as for zone code), which is written in Fig. 7.6 in red color.

Commodity flow between NEC and Japan (zone code 11) in Case 1 at period 1 is calculated as follows:

$$
\begin{aligned}
&\sum\nolimits_{i=1}^{15} OD(i,11) + \sum_{i=1}^{15} OD(i,12) \\
&\quad - 2\{OD(11,11) + OD(12,12) + OD(11,12) + OD(12,11)\} \\
&\quad + \sum\nolimits_{j=1}^{15} OD(11,j) + \sum_{j=1}^{15} OD(12,j) - OD(11,15) - OD(12,15) - OD(15,11) \\
&\quad - OD(15,12) \\
&= 337 + 0 - 2 \times (0+0+0+0) + 437 + 0 - 0 - 0 - 0 - 0 = 774.
\end{aligned}
$$

This means that all the commodity flows between Japan and regions in China utilize the expressway network[4].

The commodity flows between NEC and NC are calculated as follows:

$$
\begin{aligned}
&\sum\nolimits_{j=1}^{15} OD(1,j) - OD(1,1) - OD(1,11) - OD(1,12) + \sum\nolimits_{i=1}^{15} OD(i,1) \\
&\quad - OD(1,1) - OD(11,1) - OD(12,1) + \sum\nolimits_{i=1}^{15} OD(i,11) - OD(1,11) \\
&\quad - OD(11,11) - OD(12,11) - OD(15,11) + \sum_{1=1}^{15} OD(i,12) - OD(1,12) \\
&\quad - OD(11,12) - OD(12,12) - OD(15,12) + \sum\nolimits_{j=1}^{15} OD(11,j) - OD(11,1) \\
&\quad - OD(11,11) - OD(11,12) - OD(11,15) + \sum\nolimits_{j=1}^{15} OD(12,j) - OD(12,1) \\
&\quad - OD(12,11) - OD(12,12) - OD(12,15) \\
&= 2,295 - 1,969 - 0 - 0 + 2,118 - 1,969 - 100 - 0 + 337 - 0 - 0 - 0 - 0 \\
&\quad + 0 - 0 - 0 - 0 - 0 + 437 - 100 - 0 - 0 - 0 + 0 - 0 - 0 - 0 - 0 \\
&= 1049
\end{aligned}
$$

This means (a) all the commodity flows between NEC and regions/countries outside China except for Japan, Korea use land transportation in China; and (b) all the commodity flows between regions in China and other countries except for NEC, United States – Canada – South America use land transportation in China.

On the other hand, the commodity flows which uses links between: (a) EC and NC (it is defined as F_{EN}); (b) EC and MC (F_{EM}); (c) EC and SC (F_{ES}); and (d) intra-regional links in EC (F_{EE}), must satisfy the following equation if all commodity flows between regions and countries utilize land transportation networks in China:

---

[4]Operation $\sum\nolimits_{j=1}^{15}$ means $\sum\nolimits_{j=1}^{7} + \sum\nolimits_{j=11}^{15}$, etc., as region codes jump from 7 to 11

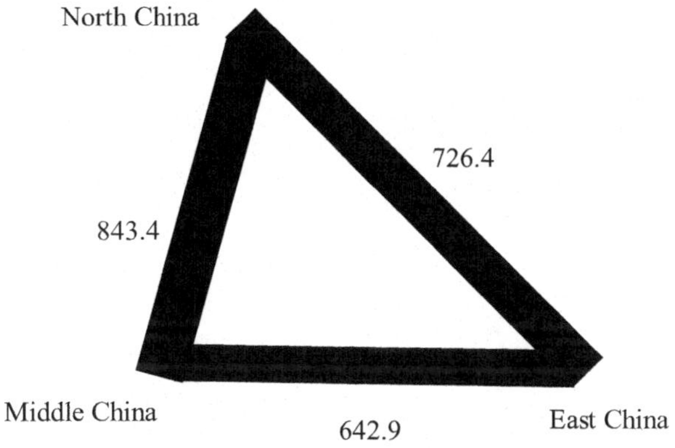

Fig. 7.9 Triangular circumferential commodity flows in Eastern Coastal Development Area (Case 1: period 5 ($t = 4$)). unit: billion tons/period (5 years)

$$F_{EN} + F_{EM} + F_{ES} = \sum_{j=1}^{15} OD(5,j) + \sum_{i=1}^{15} OD(i,5) - 2 \times OD(5,5) \quad (7.48)$$

However, $F_{EN} + F_{EM} + F_{ES} = 1977 + 4473 + 682 = 7132$ and $\sum_{j=1}^{15} OD(5,j) + \sum_{i=1}^{15} OD(i,5) - 2 \times OD(5,5) = 4241 + 3809 - 2 \times 266 = 7518$. Therefore, Eq. (7.48) does not hold. This result is plausible since all the trades between EC and regions in China and the trades between other regions/countries outside China do not necessarily use transportation network links in China. Some of the commodity flows between EC and regions/countries outside China may be diverted to use transportation network links other than in China.

One of the conspicuously strong and amazing results obtained by looking at these commodity flows at periods 1, 2, and 5 (Figs. 7.6, 7.7, 7.8), which are able to be sustained by improvements in transportation infrastructures, is that the appearance of massive triangular flows in Central China (or, Zhong-yuang) and the Eastern Coastal Development Area as shown in Fig. 7.9. China is a big country and she should have strategically several development stages. The simulation results had clearly shown that the regional economic development in China should be intensively made in the North China, Middle China, and Eastern China regions, where the economic development potential was relatively higher than other districts. Of course, this strategy may increase the disparity between those regions and other regions, especially in Western China. At the start of the twenty-first century, the Western Development Planning has officially started at a full scale and the simulation results have clearly shown that the expressway network is one of the important social infrastructures in parallel to the railway network, which could sustain such a big scale national policy, has been almost completed by period 4 ($t = 5$; 2000–2004). The simulation results conform with historical facts.

Another one is the massive commodity flows from North-East China to South China as shown in Fig. 7.10. It can be sustained by the formation of the north–south arterial transportation infrastructures, which is to be constructed along with one of the strategically important national land development axes, that is, the north–south axis, in parallel to the east–west axis (Fig. 7.11).

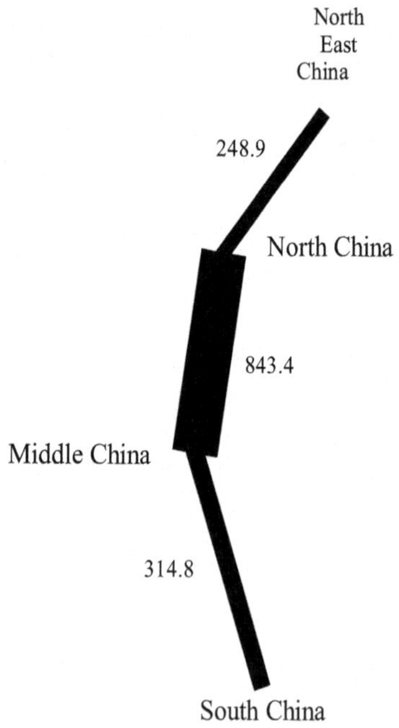

Fig. 7.10 Commodity flows along the north-south development axis (case 1: period 5 ($t = 4$)). unit: billion tons/period (5 years)

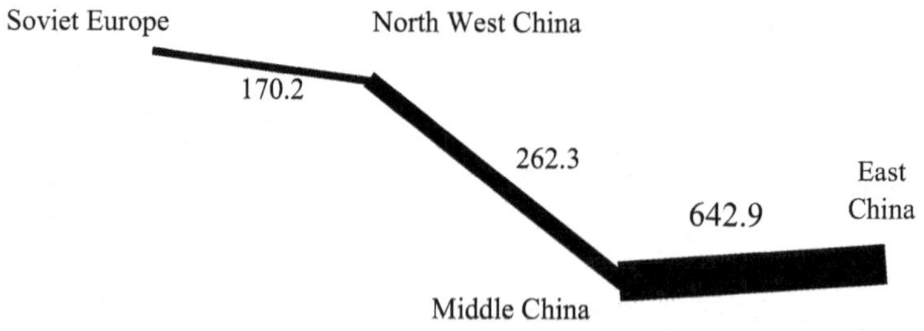

Fig. 7.11 Commodity flows along the east–west development axis (Case 1: period 5 ($t = 0$)). unit: billion tons/period (5 years)

The development along the north–south axis has an important meaning in the sense that industrial core districts in North East, East, Middle, and South China regions could be effectively and efficiently restructured into the whole of the national economy by strengthening inter-industrial dependence on each other. Of course, the core of the axis is the above-mentioned triangular circumferential zones centering on Beijing, Tianjin, Shanghai, Hangzhou, Zhengzhou, and Wuhan.

On the other hand, the east–west development axis is not yet completed by 2009 although it should be important development axis in order to resolve the disparity between the coastal zones and Western China regions. Also, the completion of east–west axis development is important for East and Southeast Asian countries as well as Central and European countries in order to complete Asian Expressway Network truly to be an international expressway network.

Table 7.11 GNP/GNI (results of simulation + statistic data). Unit: trillion US dollar

Case	Period 1	Period 2	Period 3	Period 4	Period 5
1	1.50	2.28	3.04	4.38	6.56
2	1.70	2.30	3.32	4.75	6.71
3	1.70	2.29	3.23	4.40	6.68
4	1.53	2.58	2.60	3.57	4.33
Statistic of GDP in 1985 price	1.57	1.42	1.71	2.60	4.93

7.5.3 Macroeconomic Indicators

7.5.3.1 GNP/GNI

Simulation results of GNP case by case are shown in Table 7.11. The last row shows statistic data of GDP, which is calculated using annual data from 1885 to 2009 (Table 7.12) as follows:

1. using GDP deflator, calculate GDP in terms of 1985 price and
2. sum up annual real GDP over every 5 years which corresponds to periods 1–5.

First of all, the sum of annual real GDP over the first 5 years in the first period well corresponds to simulation results of GNP. Second, variations between Cases 1, 2, and 3 are not so distinctive (Fig. 7.12). This means that the China economy has already sufficient potential (investment funds) to effectively enjoy the merits of the expressway network being not necessarily dependent on external finance. This is a plausible result since the estimated construction cost of the expressway with the total 13,350 km of four lanes is 0.1046 trillion US dollars and it is around 2.8% of the sum of net investment over periods 1 to 4. However, there exist a slightly critical differences among Cases 1, 2, and 3. This can be shown in Fig. 7.13, on which cumulative discounted GNP are drawn. As expected, the sum of GDP discounted at the initial period is the greatest with Case 2, the second is with Case 3, and the last is with Case 1 consistently over the time horizon.

On the other hand, the difference between those three cases and Case 4 is distinctive. Though it seems that GDP at period 2 in Case 4 is greater than all the other three cases (Fig. 7.12), it is less than or almost the same as GDP at period 2 of all the three cases in terms of the accumulated discounted sum of GDP (Fig. 7.13). The discounted sum of GDP in Case 4 is less than all the other three cases at period 3 and the difference is increasing till period 5. This means that the advantage of investments into the construction of the Asian Expressway Network is apparently highest among opportunities for transportation infrastructure investments (mainly for improvements of so-called bottlenecks) and capital formation investments into private sectors. Although external financial condition (allowance for external borrowing) is favorite for investments in Case 4, it is not sufficient for an acceleration of regional economic development since Case 1, in which external financial condition is inferior to Case 4 but the expressway is a target of investments, is finally superior to Case 4 in terms of both GDP at period 5 and discounted sum of GDP.

Table 7.12 Statistic data of GDP and GDP deflator. Unit trillion US dollar

Statistical data of GDP and deflator							Simulation result of GNP in 1985 year's price			
Period	Calendar year	Nominal GDP	5-Year sum	Real GDP	5-Year sum	GDP deflator	Case 1	Case 2	Case 3	Case 4
	1984	0.31		0.34		18.79				
1 ($t = 0$)	1985	0.31	1.81	0.31	1.57	20.68	1.50	1.70	1.70	1.53
	1986	0.30		0.29		21.66				
	1987	0.33		0.30		22.77				
	1988	0.41		0.33		25.53				
	1989	0.46		0.34		27.79				
2 ($t = 1$)	1990	0.40	2.48	0.28	1.43	29.42	2.28	2.30	2.29	2.58
	1991	0.41		0.27		31.47				
	1992	0.49		0.30		33.99				
	1993	0.62		0.33		39.07				
	1994	0.56		0.25		47.04				
3 ($t = 2$)	1995	0.73	4.66	0.28	1.70	53.43	3.04	3.32	3.23	2.60
	1996	0.86		0.31		56.93				
	1997	0.96		0.34		57.90				
	1998	1.02		0.37		57.30				
	1999	1.09		0.40		56.40				
4 ($t = 3$)	2000	1.21	7.61	0.43	2.59	57.58	4.38	4.75	4.40	3.57
	2001	1.33		0.47		58.77				
	2002	1.47		0.51		59.23				
	2003	1.66		0.56		60.79				
	2004	1.95		0.62		64.93				
5($t = 4$)	2005	2.29	18.27	0.70	4.93	67.83	6.56	6.71	6.68	4.33
	2006	2.75		0.81		70.41				
	2007	3.56		0.97		76.02				
	2008	4.58		1.16		81.52				
	2009	5.09		1.29		81.50				

Source of statistical data: https://ecodb.net/country/CN/imf_gdp.html (accessed date: 2021/04/16) (in Japanese)

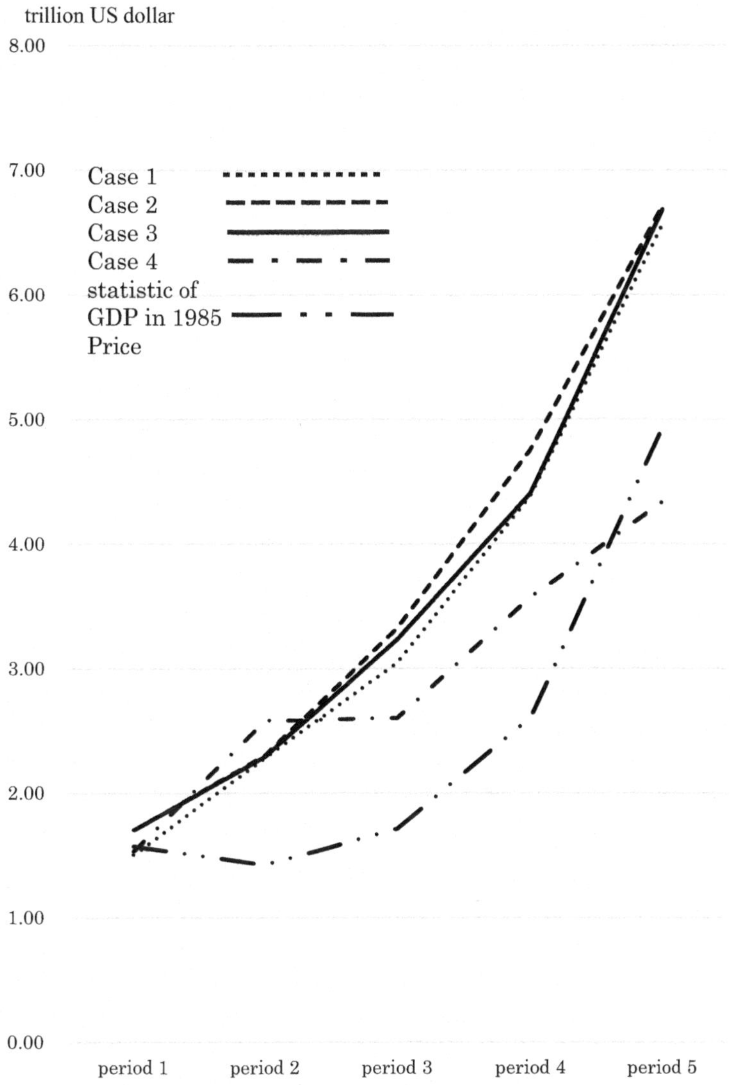

Fig. 7.12 GNP and statistic of GDP in 1985 price

7.5.3.2 NNP

Here only table of NNP is shown because the trend and patterns are almost same as GDP (Table 7.13).

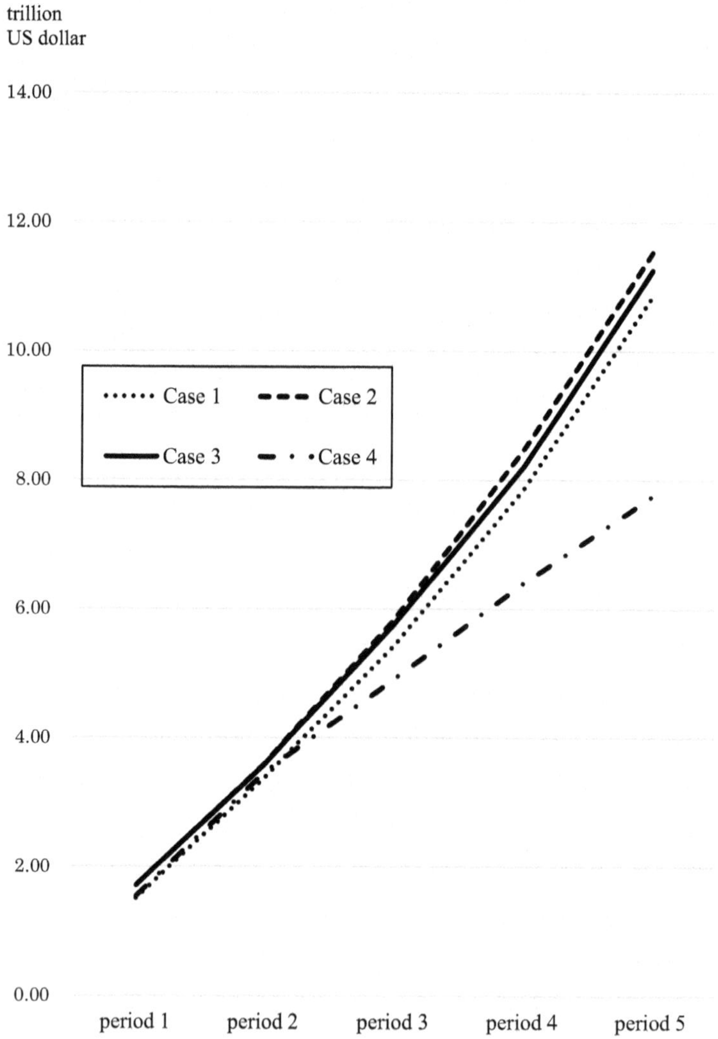

Fig. 7.13 Cumulative discounted sum of GNP

Table 7.13 NNP. Unit: trillion US dollar

Case	Period 1	Period 2	Period 3	Period 4	Period 5
1	1.27	1.82	2.53	3.77	5.78
2	1.27	1.84	2.81	4.14	5.93
3	1.27	1.83	2.72	3.79	5.91
4	1.19	2.00	2.43	2.76	3.78

7.5.3.3 Net Investment

Net investment is shown in Table 7.14 and Figs. 7.14 and 7.15. It is interesting that the net investment is the largest with Case 4 from periods 1 to 3 and it is the least with Case 4 in period 4. This means that more investment must be made for the China economy to develop with a top growth rate without the expressway, which

Table 7.14 Net investment. Unit: trillion US dollar

Case	Period 1	Period 2	Period 3	Period 4	Period 5	Total
1	0.49	0.60	0.98	1.68	0.00	3.75
2	0.49	0.62	1.04	1.68	0.00	3.83
3	0.49	0.61	1.01	1.69	0.00	3.80
4	0.57	0.70	1.41	1.03	0.00	3.71

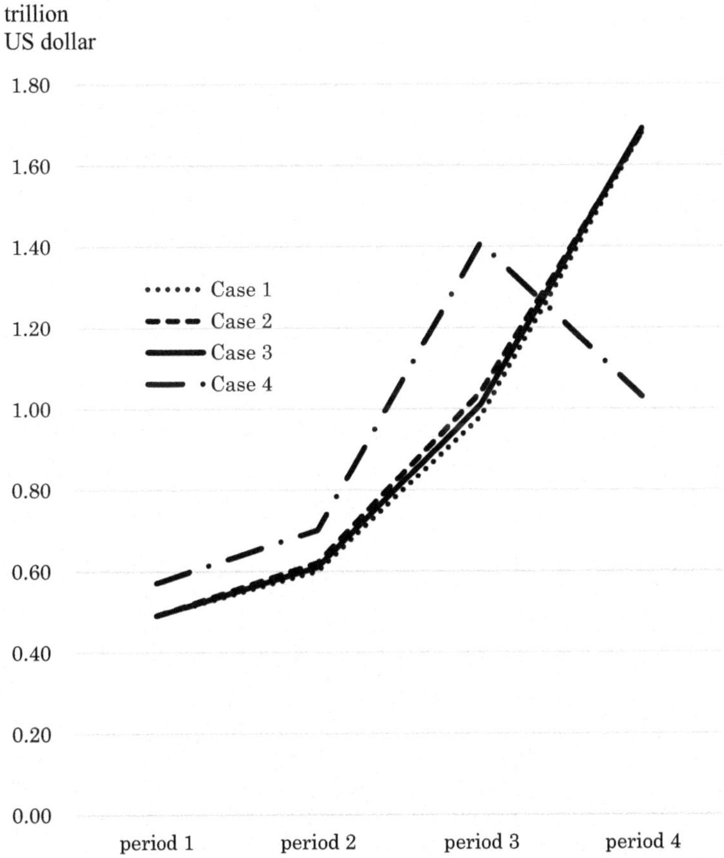

Fig. 7.14 Net investment

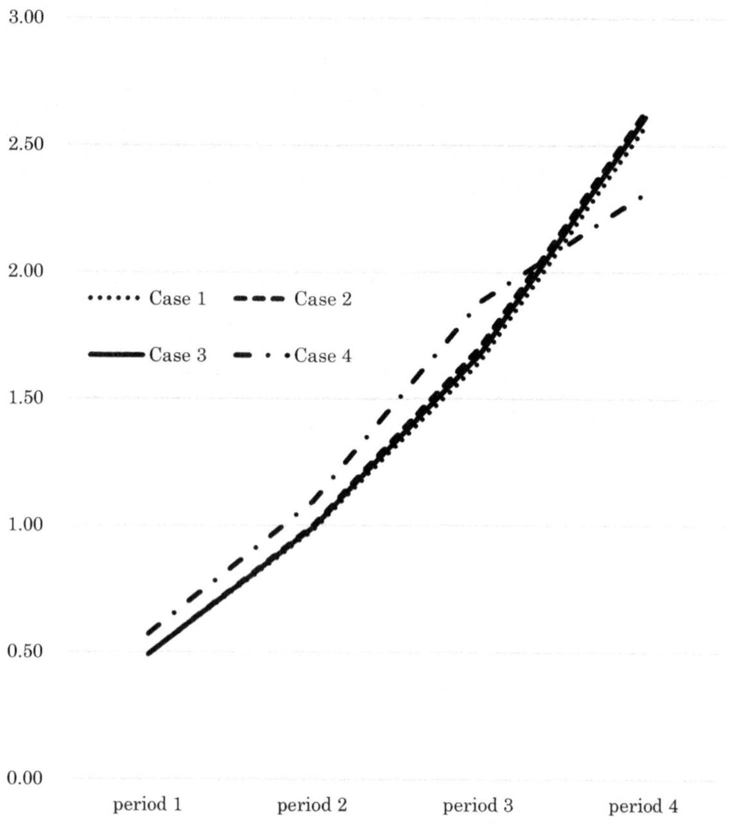

Fig. 7.15 Cumulative discounted sum of net investment

means that more investment must be made in a split way to various sectors in various regions because commodity flows must be mostly limited intra-regions. And, GDP attained is the smallest among cases. There are no big differences between Cases 1, 2, and 3. Delicate differences among the cases just reflect differences between the upper limits on the accumulated external debt. This means that cases with and without expressway critically make difference in the investment patterns and eventually in the economic growth in the long run. China's economy has the potential to grow except for missing effective transportation infrastructures, otherwise that would sustain massive commodity flows between regions if investments are made into industrial sectors considering the relative advantage of sectors between regions. It can be said that the construction of the Asian Expressway Network restructures the Chinese regional economies, which are so weakly interrelated with each other before the construction, into a whole national economy in which regional economies are interrelated and dependent on each other based on their relative advantage. It eventually induces economic growth based on the turn-pike theory.

7.5.3.4 Value of the Objective Function

As expected, the discounted sum of GNP over the time horizon is the largest in Case 2, secondly, it is in Case 3, third in Case 1, and finally in Case 4. Differences between Cases 1, 2, and 3 are small and differences between the three cases and Case 4 are distinctive. For example, the difference in Case 2 and Case 4 is 3.78 trillion US dollars, which can be taken as benefits attributable to the construction of the expressway. Since the sum of calculated construction costs of the whole expressway is around 0.090 trillion US dollars, the benefit–cost ratio becomes 42 although the whole expressway is not yet constructed at period 5 (Fig. 7.16 and Table 7.15).

7.6 Takeoff Accelerating Effects of Asian Expressway Network on the Chinese Economy

Figure 7.17 shows typical growth patterns of GDP in cases with and without expressway and planning. In Case A, which corresponds to Cases 1, 2, and 3 in Fig. 7.12, the economy is controlled and the construction of the expressway is one of the control (policy) variables. In Case B, which corresponds to Case 4, the economy is controlled but the construction of the expressway is not planned. In Case C, which corresponds to statistical GDP data in the past, expressway construction is in the scope of policies but the economy is partially controlled basically dependent on the

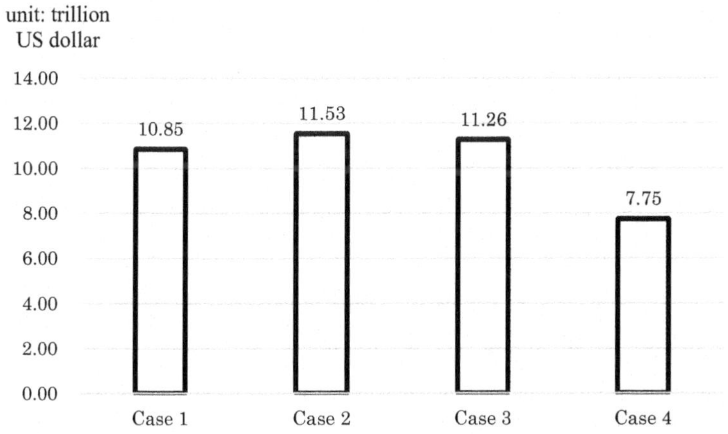

Fig. 7.16 Value of objective function

Table 7.15 Value of objective function (Unit: trillion US dollar)

Case 1	Case 2	Case 3	Case 4
10.85	11.53	11.26	7.75

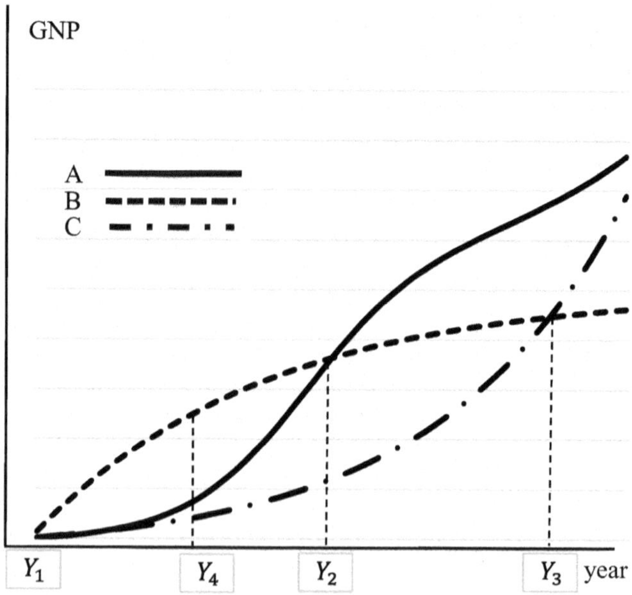

Fig. 7.17 Accelerating takeoff effect of expressway. (**a**) planning economy with expressway, (**b**) planning economy without expressway, (**c**) trend with expressway

past trend except for the construction of expressway is in the scope of policies (cf. McKenzie 1963; Dorfman et al. 1958).

Comparison between Case A and Case B clearly shows that the construction of expressway pushes up the trajectory of economic growth upward. That is possible by sacrificing the economic growth in the earlier stage (from years of Y_1 to Y_2), which is caused by diverting investment funds to the construction of expressway from into industrial sectors. After a year of Y_2, bigger rewards can be obtained as the trajectory of economic growth is far above that of Case B. In both Cases A and B, the economy is controlled in order to maximize the sum of discounted GDP/GNI. To save investments that ought to be made in order to improve the capacity of interregional as well as intra-regional transportation infrastructures if commodity flows between regions were increased, investments pattern into private sectors should be made evenly into all the sectors in each region. This may save larger investments into transportation infrastructures that cover commodity flows at long range, and, owing to this, investments can be made intensively into private sectors. However, balanced growth realized in Case B should have a limit compared to Case A, in which regional specialization is realized by absorbing merits of the relative advantage of certain sectors in certain regions and the whole national economy is restructured by making investments intensively into certain sectors in certain regions so that interregional commodity flows become massive. Simulation results show that the expressway can meet the demand induced by such huge interregional commodity flows.

Case C, which corresponds to the historically realized trajectory of China economy, is interesting since it clearly shows that: (1) a planned economy (Case A), irrespective of it is real or virtual, could accelerate the economic growth in the earlier stage than the real existing economy (Case C); and (2) it can catch up with a planned economy in the later stage. We can say that this is possible wholly owing to the construction of expressway through China because a controlled economy (Case B) without the construction of expressway cannot compete against Case C, which is not controlled but with construction of the expressway. In a sense, a controlled economy accelerates economic growth in the earlier stage which can be seen by the comparison between Case B and Case C from years of Y_1 to Y_2 in Fig. 7.17. However, after Y_2 the economic growth rate of Case C is larger than Case B and GDP becomes far larger after Y_3. The accelerated economic growth after Y_2 is owing to the construction of the expressway because it can be considered that the economy was not (totally or adequately) controlled in Case C due to several reasons. Logically, it is a natural conclusion that: (a) a planned economy generates effects of accelerating economic growth (till Y_2 in Fig. 7.17 with the comparison between Cases B and C); (b) a planned economy combined with construction of expressway generates effects of accelerating economic growth in the earlier stage (after Y_4 with comparison between Case A and Case B); and (c) eventually it generates a far larger amount of GDP after Y_2.

Appendix 1: Mathematical Expression of the Model

Index, Set of Indices, and Index Function

$I \equiv$ a set of sector codes (indices).
$Q \equiv$ a set of indices for varieties of housing quality.
$J \equiv$ a set of zone/region codes in China.
$\widehat{J} \equiv$ a set of zone codes outside China.
$JJ \equiv$ a set of all zone codes $\equiv J \cup \widehat{J}$.
$I_S \equiv$ a set of service sector codes.
$I_o \equiv$ a set of other service sector codes.
$I_I \equiv$ a set of non-service sector codes.
$I_\nu \equiv$ a set of transport sector codes.
$\nu_1 \equiv$ a set of truck transport sector codes.
$\nu_2 \equiv$ a set of railway transport sector codes.
$\nu_3 \equiv$ a set of coastal/water shipment sector codes.
$\nu_4 \equiv$ a set of harbor distribution sector codes.
$I \equiv I_I \cup I_o \cup I_\nu \equiv I_I \cup I_S$.
$I_S \equiv I_o \cup I_\nu$.
$MT(i,j,r) \equiv$ a set of (network) route codes, each of which connects regions i and j using transportation infrastructure links of rank 1 to rank r ($i,j \in JJ, 1 \leq r \leq 4$).

ML≡ a set of transportation infrastructure codes.

MM≡ a set of indices of transportation infrastructure facility $\equiv\{1,2,3,4,5\}$; 1: expressway; 2: railway; 3: infrastructure for coastal and water shipment; 4: ordinary road infrastructure; 5: harbor infrastructure.

$JCT(j)$≡ a set of transportation infrastructure (link) codes which (partially or totally) belong to zone *j*.

MS(j)≡ an index function that converts transportation infrastructure (link) code into 1, 2, 3, 4, or 5 as follows:

$MS(j)$	=	1	if	$101 \leq j \leq 199$;
		2	if	$201 \leq j \leq 299$;
		3	if	$301 \leq j \leq 399$;
		4	if	$401 \leq j \leq 499$; and
		5	if	$501 \leq j \leq 599$.

$NR(t)$ ≡ a rank index that specifies transportation infrastructures (links) available at period *t*.

$JH(k,r) \equiv \{(i,j,l)|$ expressway link in zone k constitutes routes *l* which connect zones *i* and *j* using transportation infrastructures (links) of rank 1 to rank $r\}$.

$JRL(k,r) \equiv \{(i,j,l)|$ railway link in zone k constitutes routes *l* which connect zones *i* and *j* using transportation infrastructures (links) of rank 1 to rank $r\}$.

$JS(k,r) \equiv \{(i,j,l)|$ coastal/water shipment infrastructure (link) in zone k constitutes routes *l* which connect zones *i* and *j* using transportation infrastructures (links) of rank 1 to rank $r\}$.

$JR(k,r) \equiv \{(i,j,l)|$ ordinary road infrastructure (link) in zone k constitutes routes *l* which connect zones *i* and *j* using transportation infrastructures (links) of rank 1 to rank $r\}$.

$JP(j)$≡ a set of harbor codes which is located in zone *j*.

$MOOD(k,r) \equiv \{(i,j,l)|$ transportation infrastructure (link) k constitutes routes *l* which connect zones *i* and *j* using transportation infrastructures (links) of rank 1 to rank $r\}$.

$JTH \equiv \{(i,j)|$ routes that connect between zones (regions/countries) i and j use expressway link $(i, j \epsilon \widehat{J})\}$.

MLC≡ a set of codes of transportation infrastructures (link) which (totally or partially) belong to China.

Variables

$Y_{ij}(t)$: total production of sector *i* in zone *j* at period *t* ($i \epsilon I$, $j \epsilon J$, $0 \leq t \leq N_h$).

$\Delta K_{ij}(t)$: industrial capital formation of sector *i* in zone *j* at period *t* ($i \epsilon I$, $j \epsilon J$, $0 \leq t \leq N_h$).

$\Delta H_{ij}(t)$: housing capital formation of housing quality type *i* in zone *j* at period *t*

$(i \epsilon Q, j \epsilon J, 0 \leq t \leq N_h)$.

$\Delta SK_j(t)$: social (overhead) capital formation in zone j at period t $(j \epsilon J, 0 \leq t \leq N_h)$.

$DW_{ij}(t)$: workers employed by (employable for) sector i in zone j at period t $(i \epsilon I, j \epsilon J, 0 \leq t \leq N_h)$.

$CF_{ij}^{kl}(t)$: shipment of commodity k from zones i to j using route l at period t $(i, j \epsilon JJ, k \epsilon I_I, l \epsilon MT(i,j,NR(t)), 0 \leq t \leq N_h)$.

$C_{kj}(t)$: consumption of goods k in zone j which exceeds the minimum permissible level at period t $(j \epsilon J, k \epsilon I_I \cup I_o, 0 \leq t \leq N_h)$.

$\Delta R_p(t)$: capital formation of transportation infrastructure (link) p at period t

$(p \epsilon ML, 0 \leq t \leq N_h)$.

$EX_i^k(t)$: export of goods k from China to zone i outside China at period t $(i \epsilon \widehat{J}, k \epsilon I_I, 0 \leq t \leq N_h)$.

$IM_i^k(t)$: import of goods k from zone i outside China into China at period t

$(i \epsilon \widehat{J}, k \epsilon I_I, 0 \leq t \leq N_h)$.

$BEX(t)$: international balance of payments of China at period t $(0 \leq t \leq N_h)$.

$K_{ij}(t)$: industrial capital stock for sector i in zone j at period t $(i \epsilon I, j \epsilon J, 0 \leq t \leq N_h)$.

$H_{ij}(t)$: stock of housing capital of quality i in zone j at period t $(i \epsilon Q, j \epsilon J, 0 \leq t \leq N_h)$.

$R_P(t)$: stock of transportation infrastructure (link) p at period t $(p \epsilon ML, 0 \leq t \leq N_h)$.

$SK_j(t)$: stock of social (overhead) capital in zone j at period t $(j \epsilon J, 0 \leq t \leq N_h)$.

$GH_{ij}(t)$: natural growth of workers employable by sector i in zone j at period $(t + 1)$ $(i \epsilon I, j \epsilon J, 0 \leq t \leq N_h - 1)$.

$ISH_{ij}(t)$: social increase in workers employable by sector i in zone j at period $(t + 1)$ $(i \epsilon I, j \epsilon J, 0 \leq t \leq N_h - 1)$.

$OSH_{ij}(t)$: social decrease in workers employable in sector i in zone j at period $(t + 1)$ $(i \epsilon I, j \epsilon J, 0 \leq t \leq N_h - 1)$.

$SSK_j(t)$: stock of social (overhead) capital available in zone j at period t exceeding the minimum permissible level $(j \epsilon J, 0 \leq t \leq N_h)$.

$GNP(t)$:gross national product (income) of China at period t $(0 \leq t \leq N_h)$.

$NNP(t)$: net national product of China at period t $(0 \leq t \leq N_h)$.

$INV(t)$: gross investment of China at period t $(0 \leq t \leq N_h)$.

$NI(t)$: net investment of China at period t $(0 \leq t \leq N_h)$.

$CC(t)$: total consumption of China at period t $(0 \leq t \leq N_h)$.

Parameters

(a_{ki}^j): input–output coefficient matrix in zone j $(j \epsilon J, k \varepsilon I_I \cup I_o, i \epsilon I)$.

(μ_{ki}): industrial capital formation coefficient matrix $(k \epsilon I_I \cup I_o, i \epsilon I)$.

(λ_{ki}): housing capital formation coefficient matrix $(k \epsilon I_I \cup I_o, i \epsilon Q)$.

(ψ_k): social overhead capital formation coefficient matrix $(k\epsilon I_I \cup I_o)$.
$\sigma_k(t)$: minimum permissible consumption level of goods k per worker at period $t\ (k\epsilon I_I \cup I_{o,}\ 0 \le t \le N_h)$.
Y^d: coefficient for conversion from variable per day to variable per period.
(τ_i^k) : capital formation matrix of transportation infrastructure mode i $(i\epsilon MM, k\epsilon I_I \cup I_o)$.
$\omega_p(j)$: ratio of the part of transportation infrastructure (link) p which belongs to zone j to the total length of link p $(p\epsilon ML, j\epsilon JJ)$.
$DDR(p)$: geographical length of transportation infrastructure (link) p $(p\epsilon ML)$.
a_i^k : coefficient of production of transport/distribution sector i per one unit distance transportation of goods k $(k\epsilon I_I,\ i\epsilon I_\nu)$.
$DH(p,q,k,l)$: economic distance of expressway links located in zone k if any that constitute route l from zone p to zone q $(k\epsilon J,\ p,\ q\epsilon JJ,\ l\epsilon MT(p,q,4))$.
$DRL(p,q,k,l)$: economic distance of railway links located in zone k if any that constitute route l from zone p to zone q $(k\epsilon J,\ p,\ q\epsilon JJ,\ l\epsilon MT(p,q,4))$.
$DS(p,q,k,l)$: economic distance of coastal/water shipment links located in zone k if any that constitute route l from zone p to zone q $(k\epsilon J,\ p,\ q\epsilon JJ,\ l\epsilon MT(p,q,4))$.
$DR(p,q,k,l)$: economic distance of ordinary road links located in zone k if any that constitute route l from zone p to zone q $(k\epsilon J,\ p,\ q\epsilon JJ,\ l\epsilon MT(p,q,4))$.
ρ: social discount rate.
$\widehat{\rho}$: borrowing interest rate.
$\widetilde{\rho}$: growth rate of the permissible level of consumption.
ρ^S: growth rate of the permissible level of social overhead capital stock.
m^k: markup ratio in order to add expressway toll onto charge for utilization of truck (freight) transport service which is used for the transportation of goods k in China in case shipment of goods k from foreign zone to foreign zone uses Asian Expressway in China.
$\overline{UEX}_k(t)$: upper limit to export of China to zone (country) k at period $t\ (k\epsilon\widehat{J}, 0 \le t \le N_h)$.
$\overline{LEX}_k(t)$: lower limit to export of China to zone (country) k at period $t\ (k\epsilon\widehat{J}, 0 \le t \le N_h)$.
$\overline{UIM}_k(t)$: upper limit to import of China from zone (country) k at period $t\ (k\epsilon\widehat{J}, 0 \le t \le N_h)$.
$\overline{LIM}_k(t)$: lower limit to import of China from zone (country) k at period $t\ (k\epsilon\widehat{J}, 0 \le t \le N_h)$.
$\overline{LBEX}$ (t): upper limit to the accumulated international deficit from period 0 to $t\ (0 \le t \le N_h)$.
$\overline{THEX}_{pq}$(t): upper limit to the total export from zones p to q using expressway in China at period t $(pq\epsilon JTH,\ 0 \le t \le N_h)$.
α_{ij}: output-capital ratio of sector i in zone j $(i\epsilon I, j\epsilon J)$.
β_{ij}: output-labor ratio of sector i in zone j $(i\epsilon I, j\epsilon J)$.
d^H: reciprocal of the number of workers per household.

g_i^k: coefficient which converts transportation of goods k to load to transport infrastructure of mode i ($k\epsilon I_I$, $i\epsilon MM$).

$d^s(t)$: minimum permissible level of social overhead capital per worker at period t ($0 \leq t \leq N_h$).

$\widehat{\delta}_i^K$: depreciation rate for industrial capital stock of sector i ($i\epsilon I$).

$\widehat{\delta}_i^H$: depreciation rate for housing capital of quality i ($i\epsilon Q$).

$\widehat{\delta}^S$: depreciation rate for social overhead capital.

$\widehat{\delta}_i^R$: depreciation rate for transport infrastructure of mode i ($i\epsilon MM$).

$\widehat{n}^h$: natural growth rate of worker.

r^{IS}: ratio of the upper limit on the total movement of workers between sectors to the total worker.

N_h: planning horizon

$WC(j)$: ratio of the part of transportation infrastructure (link) j which belongs to China to the total length of link j ($j\epsilon MLC$).

ν_i^R: coefficient which converts transportation infrastructure (link) stock in terms of [capacity $\times$ (link length in km)] into monetary value ($i\epsilon MM$).

$\delta^{NH}(t)$:it is 1 if $0 \leq t \leq N_h - 1$, otherwise it is 0.

α_{kj}^C: valuation coefficient of consumption of goods k, of which amount exceeds the minimum permissible level.

α_j^S: valuation coefficient of consumption of social overhead capital, of which amount exceeds the minimum permissible level.

Structural Equation and Objective Function

Market Flow Condition 1: Non-service

$$\begin{aligned}
&\sum\nolimits_{i\epsilon I}\alpha_{ki}^j \cdot Y_{ij}(t) + \sum\nolimits_{i\epsilon I}\mu_{ki} \cdot \Delta K_{ij}(t) + \sum\nolimits_{i\epsilon Q}\lambda_{ki} \cdot \Delta H_{ij}(t) + \psi_k \cdot \Delta SK_j(t) \\
&\quad + \sum_{i\epsilon I}\sigma_k(t) \cdot DW_{ij}(t) \\
&\qquad + C_{kj}(t) + \sum_{s\epsilon JCT(j)} \tau_{MS(s)}^k \cdot \omega_s(j) \cdot DDR(s) \cdot \nu_{MS(s)}^R \cdot \Delta R_s(t) \\
&\qquad - \sum_{i\epsilon JJ}\sum\nolimits_{l\epsilon MT(i,j,NR(t))} CF_{ij}^{kl}(t) \leq 0 \; (k\epsilon I_I, j\epsilon J, 0 \leq t \leq N_h)
\end{aligned} \tag{7.49}$$

Market Flow Condition 2: Other Service

$$\sum\nolimits_{i\epsilon I} \alpha_{ki}^{j} \cdot Y_{ij}(t) + \sum\nolimits_{i\epsilon I} \mu_{ki} \cdot \Delta K_{ij}(t) + \sum\nolimits_{i\epsilon Q} \lambda_{ki} \cdot \Delta H_{ij}(t) + \psi_{k} \cdot \Delta SK_{j}(t)$$
$$+ \sum_{i\epsilon I} \sigma_{k}(t) \cdot DW_{ij}(t)$$
$$+ C_{kj}(t) + \sum_{s\epsilon JCT(j)} \tau_{MS(s)}^{k} \cdot \omega_{s}(j) \cdot DDR(s) \cdot \nu_{MS(s)}^{R} \cdot \Delta R_{s}(t) - Y_{kj}(t)$$
$$\leq 0 \; (k\epsilon I_{o}, \;\; j\epsilon J, \;\; 0 \leq t \leq N_{h}) \tag{7.50}$$

Market Flow Condition 3: Transport/Distribution Service

Truck (Freight) Transportation Service

$$\sum_{s\epsilon I_{I}} a_{k}^{s} \{ \sum_{(p,q,l)\epsilon JH(j,NR(t))} DH(p,q,j,l) \cdot CF_{pq}^{sl}(t)$$

$$+ \sum_{(p,q,l)\epsilon JR(j,NR(t))} DR(p,q,j,l) \cdot CF_{pq}^{sl}(t) \} - Y_{kj}(t)$$
$$\leq 0 \; (k\epsilon \nu_{1}, j\epsilon J, 0 \leq t \leq N_{h}) \tag{7.51}$$

Railway Transportation Service

$$\sum_{s\epsilon I_{I}} \sum_{(p,q,l)\epsilon JRL(j,NR(t))} a_{k}^{s} DRL(p,q,j,l) \; CF_{pq}^{sl}(t) - Y_{kj}(t)$$
$$\leq 0 \; (k\epsilon \nu_{2}, j\epsilon J, 0 \leq t \leq N_{h}) \tag{7.52}$$

Coastal/Water Shipment Service

$$\sum_{s\epsilon I_{I}} \sum_{(p,q,l)\epsilon JS(j,NR(t))} a_{k}^{s} DS(p,q,j,l) \; CF_{pq}^{sl}(t) - Y_{kj}(t)$$
$$\leq 0 \; (k\epsilon \nu_{3}, j\epsilon J, 0 \leq t \leq N_{h}) \tag{7.53}$$

Harbor Distribution Service

$$\sum_{s\epsilon I_I}\sum\nolimits_{i\epsilon JP(j)}\sum\nolimits_{(p,q,l)\epsilon MOOD(i,NR(t))} a_k^s\, CF_{pq}^{sl}(t) - Y_{kj}(t) \le 0 \ (k\epsilon\nu_4, j\epsilon J, 0 \le t \le N_h) \tag{7.54}$$

Shipment Balance Equation 1: Shipment from Zones in China

$$\sum_{j\epsilon JJ}\ \sum_{l\epsilon MT(i,j,NR(t))} CF_{ij}^{kl}(t) - Y_{ki}(t) \le 0 \ (k\epsilon I_I, i\epsilon J, 0 \le t \le N_h) \tag{7.55}$$

Shipment Balance Equation 2

Export of China

$$\sum_{k\epsilon I_I}\sum_{j\epsilon J}\ \sum_{l\epsilon MT(j,p,NR(t))} CF_{jp}^{kl}(t) - EX_p(t) = 0,$$

$$\overline{LEX_p}(t) \le \overline{EX_p}(t) \le \overline{UEX_p}\ (\mathrm{t})\ \left(p\epsilon\widehat{J}, 0 \le t \le N_h\right) \tag{7.56}$$

Import of China

$$\sum_{k\epsilon I_I}\sum_{j\epsilon J}\ \sum_{l\epsilon MT(p,j,NR(t))} CF_{pj}^{kl}(t) - IM_p(t) = 0,$$

$$\overline{LIM_p}(t) \le \overline{IM_p}(t) \le \overline{UIM_p}\ (\mathrm{t})\ \left(p\epsilon\widehat{J}, 0 \le t \le N_h\right) \tag{7.57}$$

Balance of International Payments: Cumulative Deficit Constraint

$$\sum_{\tau=1}^{t+1}(1+\widehat{\rho})^{\tau-1}\ \{\sum_{k\epsilon I_I}\sum\nolimits_{i\epsilon\widehat{J}}\sum\nolimits_{j\epsilon J}\sum\nolimits_{l\epsilon MT(i,j,NR(\tau-1))} CF_{ij}^{kl}(\tau-1)$$

$$-\sum_{p\epsilon J}\sum_{k\epsilon I_I}\sum_{ij\epsilon JTH}\ \sum_{l\epsilon MT(i,j,NR(\tau-1))}\left(1+m^k\right)\cdot a_1^k\cdot DH(i,j,p,l)\cdot CF_{ij}^{kl}(\tau-1)$$

$$-\sum_{k\epsilon I_I}\sum_{i\epsilon J}\sum_{j\epsilon\hat{J}}\ \sum_{l\epsilon MT(i,j,NR(\tau-1))} CF_{ij}^{kl}(\tau-1)\} - BEX(t) = 0$$

$$\mathrm{BEX(t)} \leq \overline{LBEX}\ (t)\ (\ 0 \leq t \leq N_h) \tag{7.58}$$

Shipment Balance Equation 3: Between Foreign Countries (Regions)

$$\sum_{k\epsilon I_I} \sum_{l\epsilon MT(i,j,NR(t))} CF_{ij}^{kl}(t) \leq TH\bar{E}X_{ij}(t)\ (\ ij\epsilon JTH, 0 \leq t \leq N_h) \tag{7.59}$$

Balance Between Demand and Supply of Industrial Capital

$$Y_{ij}(t) - \alpha_{ij}K_{ij}(t) \leq 0\ (\ j\epsilon J, i\epsilon I, 0 \leq t \leq N_h) \tag{7.60}$$

Balance Between Demand and Supply of Labor

$$Y_{ij}(t) - \beta_{ij}DW_{ij}(t) \leq 0\ (\ j\epsilon J, i\epsilon I, 0 \leq t \leq N_h) \tag{7.61}$$

Balance Between Demand and Supply of Housing Stock

$$d^H \sum_{i\epsilon I} DW_{ij}(t) - \sum_{i\epsilon Q} H_{ij}(t) \leq 0\ (\ j\epsilon J, 0 \leq t \leq N_h) \tag{7.62}$$

Balance Between Demand Against and Supply of Transportation Infrastructure

$$\sum_{k\epsilon I_I} \sum_{(i,j,l)\epsilon MOOD(p,NR(t))} g_{MS(p)}^k\ CF_{ij}^{kl}(t) - Y^d\ R_p(t) \leq 0\ (\ p\epsilon ML, 0 \leq t \leq N_h) \tag{7.63}$$

Balance Between Demand and Supply of Social (Overhead) Capital (Other Social Capitals)

$$d^S(t) \sum_{i\epsilon I} DW_{ij}(t) - SK_j(t) + SSK_j(t) = 0\ (\ j\epsilon J, 0 \leq t \leq N_h) \tag{7.64}$$

Formation of Capital Stock

Formation of Industrial Capital

$$K_{ij}(t+1) - \left\{1 - \widehat{\delta}_i^k\right\} K_{ij}(t) - \Delta K_{ij}(t) = 0\ (i\epsilon I, j\epsilon J, 0 \leq t \leq N_h - 1) \tag{7.65}$$

Formation of Housing Capital

$$H_{ij}(t+1) - \left\{1 - \widehat{\delta}_i^H\right\} H_{ij}(t) - \Delta H_{ij}(t) = 0 \; (i\epsilon Q, j\epsilon J, 0 \le t \le N_h - 1) \tag{7.66}$$

Formation of Social Capital (Other Capitals)

$$SK_j(t+1) - \left\{1 - \widehat{\delta}^S\right\} SK_j(t) - \Delta SK_j(t) = 0 \; (j\epsilon J, 0 \le t \le N_h - 1) \tag{7.67}$$

Formation of Transportation Infrastructure

$$R_j(t+1) - \left\{1 - \widehat{\delta}_{MS(j)}^R\right\} R_j(t) - \Delta R_j(t) = 0 \; (j\epsilon MLC, 0 \le t \le N_h - 1) \tag{7.68}$$

Population Growth and Migration

Natural Growth

$$\sum_{i\epsilon I}\sum_{j\epsilon J} GH_{ij}(t) - \widehat{n}^h \cdot \sum_{i\epsilon I}\sum_{j\epsilon J} DW_{ij}(t) = 0 \; (0 \le t \le N_h - 1) \tag{7.69}$$

Migration: Social Population Growth

$$\sum_{i\epsilon I}\sum_{j\epsilon J} ISH_{ij}(t) - \sum_{i\epsilon I}\sum_{j\epsilon J} OSH_{ij}(t) = 0 \; (0 \le t \le N_h - 1) \tag{7.70}$$

$$\sum_{i\epsilon I}\sum_{j\epsilon J} OSH_{ij}(t) - r^{IS} \cdot \sum_{i\epsilon I}\sum_{j\epsilon J} DW_{ij}(t) = 0 \; (0 \le t \le N_h - 1) \tag{7.71}$$

Population Growth: Natural Plus Social Growth

$$\begin{aligned} &DW_{ij}(t+1) - DW_{ij}(t) - GH_{ij}(t) - ISH_{ij}(t) + OSH_{ij}(t) \\ &\quad = 0 \;\; (i\epsilon I, j\epsilon J, 0 \le t \le N_h - 1) \end{aligned} \tag{7.72}$$

National Income Accounting of China

Gross National Income (GNP/GNI)

$$\sum\nolimits_{j\epsilon J}\sum\nolimits_{i\epsilon I} Y_{ij}(t) - \sum\nolimits_{j\epsilon J}\sum\nolimits_{i\epsilon I}\sum\nolimits_{k\epsilon I_I \cup I_o} a_{ki}^j \cdot Y_{ij}(t)$$

$$+\sum\nolimits_{p\epsilon J}\sum\nolimits_{k\epsilon I_I}\sum\nolimits_{ij\epsilon JTH}\sum\nolimits_{l\epsilon MT(i,j,NR(t))} m^k \cdot a_1^k \cdot DH(i,j,p,l) \cdot CF_{ij}^{kl}(t)$$

$$
\begin{aligned}
&-\sum_{j\epsilon J}\sum_{i\epsilon I}\left(\sum_{k\epsilon I_I\cup I_o}\mu_{ki}-1\right)\cdot \Delta K_{ij}(t)\\
&-\sum_{j\epsilon J}\sum_{i\epsilon Q}\left(\sum_{k\epsilon I_I\cup I_o}\lambda_{ki}-1\right)\cdot \Delta H_{ij}(t)\\
&-\sum_{j\epsilon J}\left(\sum_{k\epsilon I_I\cup I_o}\psi_k-1\right)\cdot \Delta SK_j(t)\\
&-\sum_{s\epsilon MLC}\left(\sum_{k\epsilon I_I\cup I_o}\tau^k_{MS(s)}-1\right)\cdot WC(s)\cdot DDR(s)\cdot \nu^R_{MS(s)}\Delta R_s(t)\\
&-GNP(t)\\
&=0\ (0\le t\le N_h)
\end{aligned}
\tag{7.73}
$$

Net National Product (NNP)

$$
\begin{aligned}
&GNP(t)-\sum_{j\epsilon J}\sum_{i\epsilon I}\widehat{\delta}^K_i\cdot K_{ij}(t)-\sum_{j\epsilon J}\sum_{i\epsilon Q}\widehat{\delta}^H\cdot H_{ij}(t)-\sum_{j\epsilon J}\widehat{\delta}^S\cdot SK_j(t)\\
&-\sum_{j\epsilon MLC}WC(j)\cdot\widehat{\delta}^R_{MS(j)}\cdot DDR(j)\cdot \nu^R_{MS(j)}\cdot R_j(t)-NNP(t)\\
&=0\ (0\le t\le N_h)
\end{aligned}
\tag{7.74}
$$

Gross Investment (INV)

$$
\begin{aligned}
&\sum_{j\epsilon J}\sum_{i\epsilon I}\left(\sum_{k\epsilon I_I\cup I_o}\mu_{ki}\right)\cdot \Delta K_{ij}(t)+\sum_{j\epsilon J}\sum_{i\epsilon Q}\left(\sum_{k\epsilon I_I\cup I_o}\lambda_{ki}\right)\cdot \Delta H_{ij}(t)\\
&+\sum_{j\epsilon J}\left(\sum_{k\epsilon I_I\cup I_o}\psi_k\right)\cdot \Delta SK_j(t)\\
&+\sum_{s\epsilon MLC}\left(\sum_{k\epsilon I_I\cup I_o}\tau^k_{MS(s)}\right)\cdot WC(s)\cdot DDR(s)\cdot \nu^R_{MS(s)}\cdot \Delta R_s(t)\\
&-INV(t)=0\ (0\le t\le N_h-1)
\end{aligned}
\tag{7.75}
$$

Net Investment (NI)

$$
\sum_{i\epsilon I}\sum_{j\epsilon J}\{K_{ij}(t+1)-K_{ij}(t)\}+\sum_{i\epsilon Q}\sum_{j\epsilon J}\{H_{ij}(t+1)-H_{ij}(t)\}
$$

$$+\sum_{j\epsilon J}\{SK_j(t+1)-SK_j(t)\}+\sum_{s\epsilon MLC}WC(s)\cdot DDR(s)\cdot \nu^R_{MS(s)}\cdot\{R_s(T+1)-R_s(t)\}$$

$$-NI(t)=0\ (0\leq t\leq N_h-1) \tag{7.76}$$

Consumption (CC)

$$\sum_{j\epsilon J}\sum_{i\epsilon I}\sum_{k\epsilon I_I\cup I_o}\sigma_k(t)\cdot DW_{ij}(t)+\sum_{j\epsilon J}\sum_{k\epsilon I_I\cup I_o}C_{kj}(t)-CC(t)=0$$

$$(0\leq t\leq N_h) \tag{7.77}$$

Objective Function

GNP(GNI) to Be Maximized

$$\max .FV=\sum_{t=0}^{N_h}\left(\frac{1}{1+\rho}\right)^t \mathrm{GNP}(t) \tag{7.78}$$

NNP to Be Maximized

$$\max .FV=\sum_{t=0}^{N_h}\left(\frac{1}{1+\rho}\right)^t \mathrm{NNP}(t) \tag{7.79}$$

Welfare Maximization with Lower Constraint on the Accumulation of Industrial Capital Stock at the End of Period

$$max .FV=\sum_{j\epsilon J}\sum_{k\epsilon I_I\cup I_O}\alpha^c_{kj}(t)\cdot C_{kj}(t)+\sum_{j\epsilon J}\alpha^S_j(t)\cdot SSK_j(t)$$
$$+\sum_{j\epsilon Q}\sum_{j\epsilon J}\alpha^H_{ij}(t)H_{ij}(t), \tag{7.80}$$

$$\textbf{st.}\sum_{i\epsilon I}\sum_{j\epsilon J}K_{ij}(N_h)\geqq \bar{K} \tag{7.81}$$

Consumption Maximization with Lower Constraint on the Accumulation of Industrial Capital Stock at the End of Period

$$\max .FV = \sum_{t=0}^{N_h} \left(\frac{1}{1+\rho}\right)^t CC(t) \tag{7.82}$$

$$\text{st.} \sum_{i \epsilon I} \sum_{j \epsilon J} K_{ij}(N_h) \geqq \bar{K} \tag{7.83}$$

Initial Conditions

$K_{ij}(0)$, $H_{ij}(0)$, $R_p(0)$, $SK_j(0)$, and $DW_{ij}(0)$ are exogenously given with non-negative values.

Appendix 2: Dynamic Programming Model and Roundabout Production Through Space and Time

In order to explain the two concepts—roundabout production through space and time, we construct the following simple closed economy model: (1) only one kind of goods (e.g., composite goods) is produced[5]; (2) the economy is consisting of two regions, which are called—region 1 and region 2; (3) goods are produced in each region; (4) the production of goods is dependent on the capital stock and intermediate input of goods; (5) goods can be used for consumption, intermediate input, and capital stock formation in the region in which the goods are produced as well as in another region; (6) two regions are connected with each other through highway (transportation infrastructure) that is used for the shipment of goods to another region; (7) highway has the capacity that limits the shipment of goods between two regions.

The following equation system shows the essence of the roundabout production. Of course, all variables are nonnegative.

Production Function

$$Y_t^i = f^i\left(K_t^i, X_t^{ii} + X_t^{ji}\right) \; (i, j = 1, 2; i \neq j, t = 0, 1, 2, \ldots, N), \tag{7.84}$$

in which: Y_t^i: production of goods in region i at period t; K_t^i: amount of capital stock in region i at period t; X_t^{ij}: intermediate input (shipment) of goods from region i to

[5]The essence of the explanation will not change if multiple goods are assumed.

region j at period t ($i, j = 1, 2$; $t = 0, 1, 2, \ldots, N$); $f^i(\cdot)$: production function of goods in region i at period t, and N: the time horizon for the planning

Flow Condition of the Markets[6]

$$Y_t^i = X_t^{i1} + X_t^{i2} + I_t^{i1} + I_t^{i2} + C_t^{i1} + C_t^{i2} + IR_t^{i1} + IR_t^{i2} \; (i = 1, 2; t = 0, 1, 2, \ldots, N), \tag{7.85}$$

in which: I_t^{ij}: investment (shipment) of goods from region i for the capital stock formation in region j at period t ($i, j = 1, 2$; $t = 0, 1, 2, \ldots, N$); C_t^{ij}: shipment of goods from region i for the consumption in region j at period t ($i, j = 1, 2$; $t = 0, 1, 2, \ldots, N$); and IR_t^{ij}: investment (shipment) of goods from region i for the improvements in the highway capacity in region j at period t ($i, j = 1, 2$; $t = 0, 1, 2, \ldots, N$).

Stock Formation

$$\Delta K_t^1 = h^1\left(I_t^{11} + I_t^{21}\right) \; (t = 0, 1, 2, \ldots, N), \tag{7.86a}$$

$$\Delta K_t^2 = h^2\left(I_t^{12} + I_t^{22}\right) \; (t = 0, 1, 2, \ldots, N), \tag{7.86b}$$

$$\Delta R_t^{12} = g^{12}\left(IR_t^{11} + IR_t^{21}\right) \; (t = 0, 1, 2, \ldots, N), \tag{7.86c}$$

$$\Delta R_t^{21} = g^{21}\left(IR_t^{12} + IR_t^{22}\right) \; (t = 0, 1, 2, \ldots, N), \tag{7.86d}$$

in which: $h^i(\cdot)$: function that converts investment of goods into increase in the capital stock in region i ($i = 1, 2$); $g^{ij}(\cdot)$: function that converts investment of goods into increase in the stock of highway that can be only used for the shipment of goods from region i to region j ($i, j = 1, 2; i \neq j$); and it is assumed that: (a) the capacity of lanes is differentiated between the lanes from region 1 to region 2 and from region 2 to region 1; (b) namely, the shipment of goods from region i to region j becomes loads on the highway capacity of the lane from region i to region j, and (c) increase in the capacity of highway lane from region i to region j can be made only by the investment of goods for the highway stock formation in region i ($i, j = 1, 2; i \neq j$).

---

[6]The definition of an export variable such that $E^{12}(t) = X_t^{12} + I_t^{12} + C_t^{12} + IR_t^{12}$ may make simple the market flow condition. However, Eq. (7.85) is better for the explanation of the roundabout production.

Dynamic Equation

$$K_t^i = K_{t-1}^i + \Delta K_{t-1}^i \ (i = 1,2; t = 1,2,3, \ldots, N) \tag{7.87}$$

$$R_t^{12} = R_{t-1}^{12} + \Delta R_{t-1}^{12} \ (t = 1,2,3, \ldots, N), \tag{7.88a}$$

$$R_t^{21} = R_{t-1}^{21} + \Delta R_{t-1}^{21} \ (t = 1,2,3, \ldots, N), \tag{7.88b}$$

$$K_0^i \equiv \overline{K}^i \ (i = 1,2), \tag{7.89}$$

$$R_0^{ij} \equiv \overline{R}^{ij} \ (i, j = 1,2; i \neq j), \tag{7.90}$$

in which: $\overline{K}^i$: initial capital stocks in region i ($i = 1,2$), which are nonnegative constants; and $\overline{R}^i$: initial highway stocks in region i ($i = 1,2$),which are nonnegative constants.

Highway Capacity Constraint

$$X_t^{ij} + I_t^{ij} + C_t^{ij} + IR_t^{ij} \leq q^i\left(R_t^{ij}\right) \ (i, j = 1,2; i \neq j), \tag{7.91}$$

in which: $q^i(\cdot)$: function that converts the amount of highway stock into the highway capacity in terms of the shipment of goods; and it is assumed that the intra-regional shipment can be made with no highway capacity limit for simplicity of the explanation.

Definition of Vector Variable

We define the following vector variables for the simplicity of notation:

$$Y^i \equiv \left(Y_0^i, Y_1^i, Y_2^i, \cdots, Y_N^i\right) \ (i = 1,2),$$

$$X^{ij} \equiv \left(X_0^{ij}, X_1^{ij}, X_2^{ij}, \cdots, X_N^{ij}\right) \ (i, j = 1,2; i \neq j),$$

$$I^{ij} \equiv \left(I_0^{ij}, I_1^{ij}, I_2^{ij}, \cdots, I_N^{ij}\right) \ (i, j = 1,2; i \neq j),$$

$$IR^{ij} \equiv \left(IR_0^{ij}, IR_1^{ij}, IR_2^{ij}, \cdots, IR_N^{ij}\right) \ (i, j = 1,2; i \neq j),$$

$$C^{ij} \equiv \left(C_0^{ij}, C_1^{ij}, C_2^{ij}, \cdots, C_N^{ij}\right) \ (i, j = 1,2; i \neq j),$$

$$C^i \equiv C^{ii} + C^{ji} \ (i, j = 1,2; i \neq j)$$

$$X^i = X^{ii} + X^{ji}\ (i, j = 1, 2; i \neq j)$$

$$K^i \equiv \left(K_0^i, K_1^i, K_2^i, \cdots, K_N^i\right)\ (i = 1, 2),$$

$$R^{ij} \equiv \left(R_0^{ij}, R_1^{ij}, R_2^{ij}, \cdots, R_N^{ij}\right)\ (i, j = 1, 2; i \neq j),$$

$$\Delta K^i \equiv \left(\Delta K_0^i, \Delta K_1^i, \Delta K_2^i, \cdots, \Delta K_N^i\right)\ (i = 1, 2), \text{and}$$

$$\Delta R^i \equiv \left(\Delta R_0^i, \Delta R_1^i, \Delta R_2^i, \cdots, \Delta R_N^i\right)\ (i = 1, 2).$$

A bundle, Y^i,is called—trajectory of the production in region i ($i = 1, 2$), a bundle, X^{12}, is called—trajectory of the shipment of goods from region 1 to region 2, and so on.

Feasible Trajectory of the Economy

We define bundles of vector variables, T^i (i = 1, 2), as follow:

$$T^1 \equiv \left(Y^1, X^{11}, X^{21}, I^{11}, I^{21}, IR^{11}, IR^{21}, C^{11}, C^{21}, K^1, R^{12}, \Delta K^1, \Delta R^1\right), \text{and}$$

$$T^2 \equiv \left(Y^2, X^{12}, X^{22}, I^{12}, I^{22}, IR^{12}, IR^{22}, C^{12}, C^{22}, K^2, R^{21}, \Delta K^2, \Delta R^2\right).$$

A bundle, T^i, is called—trajectory of the economy of region i ($i = 1, 2$) and a bundle, $T \equiv (T^1, T^2)$, is called—a trajectory of the economy.

Suppose that the trajectory of consumption in each region is exogenously given as follows:

$$C^i = \overline{C}^i\ (i = 1, 2), \tag{7.92}$$

in which: $C^i \equiv \left(C_0^i, C_1^i, C_2^i, \cdots, C_N^i\right)$ (i = 1,2) (namely, $C_t^i = C_t^{ii} + C_t^{ji}\ (i, j = 1, 2; i \neq j; t = 0, 1, 2, \cdots, N)$ by definition of C^i above); $\overline{C}^i \equiv \left(\overline{C}_0^i, \overline{C}_1^i, \overline{C}_2^i, \cdots, \overline{C}_N^i\right)$ (i = 1,2); and $\overline{C}_t^i$: given level of the consumption in region i at period t, which are nonnegative constants.

We symbolize a given trajectory of the consumption as follows:

$$\overline{C} = \left(\overline{C}^1, \overline{C}^2\right).$$

A trajectory of the economy, T, which meets all the Eqs. (7.84)–(7.92), is called—a feasible trajectory of the economy with $\overline{C}$.

The Objective of the Planning

A set of feasible trajectories of the economy, $\widetilde{T}$, which satisfy the system of Eqs, (7.84)—(7.92), is the correspondence (a set of feasible trajectories of the economy) to $\overline{C}$ and it can be symbolized as $\widetilde{T}(\overline{C})$. A possible and most plausible objective of the planning is to find out an optimal consumption trajectory, $\widehat{C} \equiv \left(\widehat{C}^1, \widehat{C}^2\right)$, by solving the system of Eqs. (7.84)—(7.92), by changing components of $\overline{C}$ in terms of a given valuation function. A typical valuation function is given as follows:

$$W\left(\widehat{C}\right) = W\left(\widehat{C}^1, \widehat{C}^2\right) = \max_{\left\{\widetilde{T}(\overline{C}), \overline{C}\right\}} \sum_{t=0}^{N} U_t\left(\overline{C}_t^1, \overline{C}_t^2\right) \tag{7.93}$$

in which: $W(\cdot)$: valuation function of the consumption trajectories of region 1 and region 2; $U_t(\cdot)$: evaluation function of the consumption of goods in region 1 and region 2 at period t; and $\widehat{C}^i$: (optimal) consumption trajectory of region i ($i = 1, 2$), which is a component of the optimal consumption trajectory, $\widehat{C}$.

Specifically, $U_t(\cdot)$ can be defined as follows:

$$U_t(\cdot) \equiv \frac{1}{(1+\rho)^t} U(\cdot) \quad (t = 0, 1, 2, \cdots, N) \tag{7.94}$$

in which: ρ: given discount rate ($\rho > 0$); and $U(\cdot)$: evaluation function of the consumption of goods in region 1 and region 2, of which functional form is constant over the time horizon.

The function, $\sum_{t=0}^{N} U_t\left(\overline{C}_t^1, \overline{C}_t^2\right)$, is called—objective function. Though it is empirically or practically tough work to give a concrete functional form of $U_t(\cdot)$ or $U(\cdot)$, we do not need to explicitly specify it as far as the substance of the roundabout production is concerned.

A set of trajectories of the economy which maximize the objective function is called—optimal set of trajectories of the economy and it can be represented as $\widehat{T}\left(\widehat{C}\right)$, which is a subset of $\{\widetilde{T}(\overline{C}) |$ trajectory of the economy which meets the system of Eqs. (7.84)–(7.91) for any $\overline{C} \geq 0\}$, by definition.

Necessary Conditions for the Optimality

Roundabout Production Through Time

Hereafter we consider only feasible trajectories of the economy. Namely, without specific notation of overline, "$\overline{\square}$," tilde, $\widetilde{\square}$, and hat, "$\widehat{\square}$," we use notation of $T = (T^1$,

T^2), representing a feasible trajectory of the economy that corresponds to the consumption trajectory, $C = (C^1, C^2)$.

Consider a perturbation, ε (>0), with, for example, X_τ^{11} and I_τ^{11} in the market flow condition of region 1 with a given feasible trajectory T at a certain period τ ($0 \leq \tau \leq N - 1$) such that[7]:

$$Y_\tau^1 - \omega = \left(X_\tau^{11} - \varepsilon\right) + X_\tau^{12} + \left(I_\tau^{11} + \varepsilon\right) + I_\tau^{12} + \left(C_\tau^{11} - \omega\right) + C_\tau^{12} \\ + IR_\tau^{11} + IR_\tau^{12} \tag{7.95}$$

The perturbation causes a decrease in the production of goods in region 1 at period τ as the intermediate input of goods in region 1 at period τ is decreased by ε:

$$Y_\tau^1 - \omega = f^1\left(K_\tau^1, X_\tau^1 - \varepsilon\right) \tag{7.96}$$

in which: ω: decrease in the production of goods in region 1 at period τ, which is caused by a decrease, ε, in the intermediate input of goods into the production, compared to the given trajectory.

A decrease, ω, in the production can be borne by any term other than X_τ^{11} and I_τ^{11} in Eq. (7.85), it is supposed that a decrease in the production of goods, ω, is all borne by a decrease in C_τ^1 by ω, which results in a decrease in the valuation of the consumption by γ:

$$U\left(C_\tau^1, C_\tau^2\right) - \gamma = U\left(C_\tau^1 - \omega, C_\tau^2\right). \tag{7.97}$$

On the other hand, the perturbation causes an increase in the investment by ε for the capital formation in region 1, which will result in an increase in the capital stock by δ, and will increase the production of goods by $\alpha_{\tau+1}$ in region 1 at period $\tau + 1$ compared to the given feasible trajectory of the economy, T:

$$\Delta K_\tau^1 + \delta = h^1\left(I_\tau^{11} + \varepsilon + I_\tau^{21}\right), \tag{7.98}$$

$$K_{\tau+1}^1 + \delta = K_\tau^1 + \Delta K_\tau^1 + \delta, \tag{7.99}$$

[7] It has no meaning to consider the perturbation at period N as far as N is a given constant and/or the objective function does not include valuation of the capital and highway stock at the terminal period of the planning horizon. If not, the perturbation is related to the transversality condition as well.

$$Y^1_{\tau+1} + \alpha_{\tau+1} = f^1\left(K^1_\tau + \delta, X^1_{\tau+1}\right). \tag{7.100}$$

An increase in the production in region 1 at period $\tau + 1$, $\alpha_{\tau + 1}$, can be again used for the perturbation with any term in the market flow condition at period $\tau + 1$. This means that there could be many (infinite number of) trajectories of the economy which could be different from the given feasible trajectory, *T*, with its components at period τ and later till period *N*. However, for a while, suppose that an increase in the production, $\alpha_{\tau + 1}$, is all used to increase the consumption in region 1, which results in an increase in the evaluation of the consumption by $\beta_{\tau + 1}$ in region 1 at period $\tau + 1$:

$$U\left(C^1_{\tau+1}, C^2_{\tau+1}\right) + \beta_{\tau+1} = U\left(C^1_{\tau+1} + \alpha_{\tau+1}, C^2_{\tau+1}\right). \tag{7.101}$$

We suppose that a perturbation of Eq. (7.95) is made only once at period τ and adjustments to the perturbation are made following Eq. (7.97) and Eq. (7.98). The supposition means that the triggered trajectory, which is generated by the perturbation in Eq. (7.95) and adjustments of Eq. (7.96)–(7.101), is different from the given feasible trajectory, ***T***, with respect to its (*T* 's) components, X^{11}_τ, I^{11}_τ, C^{11}_τ (C^1_τ), Y^1_τ, K^1_t $(t = \tau + 1, \tau + 2, \cdots, N)$, and Y^1_t $(t = \tau + 1, \tau + 2, \cdots, N)$ by $-\varepsilon$, ε, ε (ε), $-\omega$, δ $(t = \tau + 1, \tau + 2, \cdots, N)$, and α_t $(t = \tau + 1, \tau + 2, \cdots, N)$, respectively. We may symbolize it as T^b and call it—perturbed trajectory of the economy. We now examine a necessary condition for the optimality of trajectory of the economy and we may put aside another perturbed trajectory of the economy with T^b for a while because we may apply a set of obtained necessary conditions to T^b, recursively. Of course, as we see previously, the triggered trajectory is a feasible trajectory with the following trajectory of the consumption:

$$C' = \left(C^{1\prime}, C^2\right), \tag{7.102}$$

in which:

$$C^{1\prime} = \left(C^1_0, C^1_1, C^1_2, \cdots, C^1_{\tau-1}, C^1_\tau - \omega, C^1_{\tau+1} + \alpha_{\tau+1}, C^1_{\tau+2} + \alpha_{\tau+2}, \cdots, \right.$$
$$\left. C^1_{N-1} + \alpha_{N-1}, C^1_N + \alpha_N\right) \tag{7.103}$$

The trajectory of the difference in the evaluation of the consumption trajectory between C' and C can be calculated as follows:

$$\Delta W(C') = W\left(C^{1\prime}, C^2\right) - W\left(C^1, C^2\right)$$

$$= \frac{1}{(1+\rho)^{\tau}} \left\{ -\gamma + \sum_{t=1}^{N-\tau} \frac{1}{(1+\rho)^{t}} \beta_{\tau+t} \right\}. \tag{7.104}$$

Since $f^{i}(\cdot)$ $(i = 1, 2)$ and $U(\cdot)$ are usually concave functions and α_t and β_t $(t = \tau + 1, \tau + 2, \cdots, N)$ decrease (not increase) as t increases. Therefore, ΔW (C') has an finite value in case N is infinite because $\frac{1}{(1+\rho)^t}$ will vanish as t increases to the infinity.

We can say that C' is superior to C if $\Delta W(C') > 0$. The perturbation of ε in Eq. (7.95) is taken as an example of the roundabout production *through time* in that a saving of consumption at a certain period results in the possibility of more consumption *later on* (namely, as time elapses). The roundabout production through time is possible by further accumulating the capital stock compared to the case in which the said saving in the consumption was not made. If $\Delta W(C') > 0$, we can say that the roundabout production which generates the consumption trajectory, C', is successful and $T(C)$ is not an optimal trajectory of the economy or we can say that $T'(C')$ is superior to $T(C)$.

As already mentioned previously, there are many trajectories which can be generated and triggered by the perturbation of ε in Eq. (7.85): (i) to change timing from $\tau + 1$ to $\tau + n$ $(1 < n \ll N)$, namely to postpone the timing of joy of the merit of the roundabout production of $\boldsymbol{\varepsilon}$ that is made at period $\boldsymbol{\tau}$ while keeping the increasing merits to be used for the capital stock accumulation in region 1 till the merits are enjoyed as a further increase in the consumption in region 1, (ii) by changing the period τ, at which the perturbation itself is made, and so on. Also, (iii) a similar and different perturbation from that of Eq. (7.95) can be made by alternating region 1 and region 2 with region indices, and so on. Further, so many different trajectories of the economy can be generated and triggered with the combination and nesting of (i) and (ii) above with each other as well as the combination and nesting with the alternation (iii) above, and so on. We call these generated and triggered trajectories of the economy—perturbed trajectories of the economy *through time.*

We can obtain the following:

[Necessary condition-1 for the optimality through time[8]].

A necessary condition for a feasible trajectory of the economy, $T(C)$, to be optimal is that there exists no perturbed trajectory of the economy *through time*, $T^T(C^T)$, which is superior to $T(C)$, namely there exists no $T^T(C^T)$ that gives a larger value to the function, $W(\cdot)$,than $T(C)$.

[8]This is a necessary condition for the local optimality.

Roundabout Production Through 'Space'

Analogically with Eq. (7.85), we suppose the following perturbation of ε_t ($\varepsilon_t > 0$, $t = \tau, \tau + 1, \cdots, N$) at period τ and all the periods that follow with the market flow condition:

$$Y_t^1 - \omega_t^1 = \left(X_t^{11} - \varepsilon_t\right) + \left(X_t^{12} + \varepsilon_t\right) + I_t^{11} + I_t^{12}$$

$$+\left(C_t^{11} - \omega_t^1\right) + C_t^{12} + IR_t^{11} + IR_t^{12} \ (t = \tau, \tau + 1, \cdots, N), \tag{7.105}$$

in which:

ω_t^1 is defined as a solution to the following equation:

$$Y_t^1 - \omega_t^1 = f^1\left(K_t^1, X_t^1 - \varepsilon_t\right) \ (t = \tau, \tau + 1, \cdots, N). \tag{7.106}$$

The perturbation will trigger the following adjustments:

(1) decrease in the valuation of the consumption in region 1 at period t ($t = \tau, \tau + 1, \cdots, N$):

$$U\left(C_t^1, C_t^2\right) - \gamma_t^1 = U\left(C_t^1 - \omega_t^1, C_t^2\right) \ (t = \tau, \tau + 1, \cdots, N); \tag{7.107}$$

(2) as the shipment of the goods from region 1 to region 2 increases by ε_t and the capacity of highway from region 1 to region 2 needs to be increased in advanced, the following adjustments are further triggered:

$$Y_{\tau-1}^1 - \omega_{\tau-1}^1 = \left(X_{\tau-1}^{11} - \varepsilon_{\tau-1}\right) + X_{\tau-1}^{12} + I_{\tau-1}^{11} + I_{\tau-1}^{12}$$

$$+\left(C_{\tau-1}^{11} - \omega_{\tau-1}^1\right) + C_{\tau-1}^{12} + \left(IR_{\tau-1}^{11} + \varepsilon_{\tau-1}\right) + IR_{\tau-1}^{12}, \tag{7.108}$$

$$Y_{\tau-1}^1 - \omega_{\tau-1}^1 = f^1\left(K_{\tau-1}^1, X_{\tau-1}^1 - \varepsilon_{\tau-1}\right), \tag{7.109}$$

$$U\left(C_{\tau-1}^1, C_{\tau-1}^2\right) - \gamma_{\tau-1}^1 = U\left(C_{\tau-1}^1 - \omega_{\tau-1}^1, C_{\tau-1}^2\right), \tag{7.110}$$

$$\Delta R_{\tau-1}^{12} + \delta = g^{12}\left(IR_{\tau-1}^{11} + \varepsilon_{\tau-1} + IR_\tau^{21}\right), \tag{7.111}$$

$$R_\tau^{12} + \delta = R_{\tau-1}^{12} + \Delta R_{\tau-1}^{12} + \delta, \tag{7.112a}$$

$$R_{t+1}^{12} = R_t^{12} + \Delta R_t^{12} + \delta \ (t = \tau, \tau + 1, \ldots, N), \tag{7.112b}$$

$$X_t^{12} + \varepsilon_t + I_t^{12} + C_t^{12} + IR_t^{12} = q^1\left(R_t^{12} + \delta\right) \; (t = \tau, \tau + 1, \cdots, N), \quad (7.113)$$

in which: we may assume that the highway capacity constraint, Eq. (7.91), holds with equality by period τ with a given trajectory of the economy, *T*(*C*), as the (composite) goods must be a superior goods (as far as τ is enough large compared to given initial stock conditions);

(3) in region 2, the following adjustments are made supposing an increase in the product is all used for an increase in the consumption at period τ and all the subsequent periods:

$$Y_t^2 + \alpha_t^2 = f^2\left(K_t^2, X_t^2 + \varepsilon_t\right) \; (t = \tau, \tau + 1, \tau + 2, \ldots, N), \quad (7.114)$$

$$U\left(C_t^1, C_t^2\right) + \beta_t^2 = U\left(C_t^1, C_t^2 + \alpha_t^2\right) \; (t = \tau, \tau + 1, \tau + 2, \ldots, N). \quad (7.115)$$

The triggered trajectory, which is generated by the perturbation of Eq. (7.105) and adjustments of Eqs. (7.106)–(7.115), is different from the given feasible trajectory, ***T***, with respect to its (***T***'s) components, X_t^{11} $(t = \tau - 1, \tau, \tau + 1, \tau + 2, \cdots, N)$, $IR_{\tau-1}^{11}$, X_t^{12} $(t = \tau, \tau + 1, \tau + 2, \cdots, N)$, Y_t^1 $(t = \tau - 1, \tau, \tau + 1, \tau + 2, \cdots, N)$, $C_t^{11}(C_t^1)$ $(t = \tau - 1, \tau, \tau + 1, \tau + 2, \cdots, N)$, Y_t^2 $(t = \tau, \tau + 1, \tau + 2, \cdots, N)$, $C_t^{12}(C_t^2)$ $(t = \tau, \tau + 1, \tau + 2, \cdots, N)$, and R_t^{12} $(t = \tau, \tau + 1, \tau + 2, \cdots, N)$ by $-\varepsilon_t$ $(t = \tau - 1, \tau, \tau + 1, \tau + 2, \cdots, N)$, $\varepsilon_{\tau-1}$, ε_t $(t = \tau, \tau + 1, \tau + 2, \cdots, N)$, $-\omega_t^1$ $\left(-\omega_t^1\right)$ $(t = \tau - 1, \tau, \tau + 1, \tau + 2, \cdots, N)$, $-\omega_t^1$ $\left(-\omega_t^1\right)$ $(t = \tau - 1, \tau, \tau + 1, \tau + 2, \cdots, N)$, α_t^2 $(t = \tau, \tau + 1, \tau + 2, \cdots, N)$, α_t^2 (α_t) $(t = \tau, \tau + 1, \tau + 2, \cdots, N)$, and δ $(t = \tau, \tau + 1, \tau + 2, \cdots, N)$, respectively. We may assume that a shortage in the capacity, R_t^{12} $(t = \tau + 1, \tau + 2, \cdots, N)$, due to growth of the economy and concavity of the function, $q^1(\cdot)$, can be neglected as δ is small and $U\left(C_t^1 - \omega_t^1, C_t^2 + \alpha_t^2\right) = \beta_t^2 - \gamma_t^1$ $(t = \tau, \tau + 1, \cdots, N)$. We may put aside another perturbed trajectory with thus obtained perturbed trajectory by the same reason above, too. Of course, as we see previously, the triggered trajectory is a feasible trajectory with the following trajectory of the consumption:

$$C'' = \left(C^{1''}, C^{2''}\right), \quad (7.116)$$

$$C^{1''} \equiv \left(C_0^1, C_1^1, \cdots, C_{\tau-1}^1 - \omega_{\tau-1}, C_\tau^1 - \omega_\tau, C_{\tau+1}^1 - \omega_{\tau+1}, \cdots, C_{N-1}^1 - \omega_{N-1}, C_N^1 - \omega_N\right), \quad (7.117)$$

$$C^{2''} \equiv \left(C_0^2, C_1^2, \cdots, C_{\tau-1}^2, C_\tau^2 + \alpha_\tau, C_{\tau+1}^1 + \alpha_{\tau+1}, \cdots, C_{N-1}^1 + \alpha_{N-1}, C_N^1 + \alpha_N\right). \quad (7.118)$$

$$\Delta W \equiv W(C'') - W(C)$$
$$= \frac{1}{(1+\rho)^{\tau-1}}\left\{-\gamma^1_{\tau-1} + \sum_{t=1}^{N-\tau}\frac{1}{(1+\rho)^t}\left(\beta^2_t - \gamma^1_t\right)\right\}. \tag{7.119}$$

If $\Delta W > 0$, the perturbed and triggered trajectory, $T(C'')$, is superior to a given trajectory of the economy, $T(C)$.

The perturbation of Eq. (7.105) and triggered adjustments can be taken as an example of the roundabout production *through space*, namely it aims to increase the total welfare of the economy through reallocation of resources from region 1 to region 2. However, due to the highway capacity constraint of Eq. (7.91), which usually holds with equality, an investment to the highway stock formation must be made in advance in order to enjoy merits of the roundabout production through space. This means that a roundabout production through time is necessary for the roundabout production through space and vice versa. With the supposed model, the main reason why a roundabout production through space can be a superior trajectory of the economy is that there possibly exists difference in the productivity between region 1 and region 2. If we assume traffic congestion on the highway, and specify a kind of traffic congestion function into the left-hand side of Eq. (7.91), the superiority of roundabout production must be examined in a complicated way. Increase or decrease in the congestion costs for all the traffic on the highway must be taken into the calculation of opportunity costs of diverting goods from region 1 to region 2 and investment into highway capital formation.

The triggered trajectories by the perturbation through space are many, too: (1) the timing of the perturbation can be changed over the time horizon for the planning (most probably in the early phase); (2) the timing of the investment into highway construction prior to the timing for the perturbation can be changed; (3) at a certain period τ' ($\tau < \tau' < N$)), the perturbation (reallocation of resource) over space can be stopped, namely $\varepsilon_{\tau'} = 0$; and (4) a similar and different perturbation from that of Eqs. (7.105) and (7.108) can be made by alternating region 1 and region 2 with region indices, and so on. Further, so many different trajectories of the economy can be generated and triggered with the combination and nesting of (1), (2), (3), and so on above with each other as well as the combination and nesting with the alternation (4) above, and so on. We call these generated and triggered trajectories of the economy—perturbed trajectories of the economy through space.

[Necessary condition-2 for the optimality *through "space"*[9]].

A necessary condition for a feasible trajectory of the economy, $T(C)$, to be optimal is that there exists no perturbed trajectory of the economy *through* "space," $T^S(C^S)$, which is superior to $T(C)$, namely there exists no $T^S(C^S)$ that gives a larger value to the function, $W(\cdot)$,than $T(C)$.

[9] See ibid.

Roundabout Production Through Space and Time

In the last two subsubsections, various ways of the perturbation and adjustment with the roundabout production through time and the roundabout production through "space" are separately illustrated in order to highlight the two concepts of the roundabout production. As readers may see, the merits of the roundabout production can be strengthened if the perturbation and triggered adjustments are made through space and time in the nested and combined ways. For example, a saving of the consumption at period τ in region 1 through saving of the intermediate input in region 1 can be shipped into region 2 for further capital stock formation in region 2. At a certain period τ' ($\tau < \tau' < N$), some of the products in region 2 can be shipped back into region 1 for the capital formation. In case of the multiple kinds of goods and therefore in case of multiple sectors, which is a more realistic case, if region 1 is less advantageous with the production of a certain goods that is the key for the capital formation and region 2 is relatively advantageous with the production of the key goods, such a return of the products from region 2 to region 1 for the capital formation in region 1 can be advantageous as far as region 1 is relatively advantageous in the production of other goods using the capital stock. This is the essential background of the so-called Turnpike Theorem by taking regions as sectors. We call all these perturbed and triggered trajectories—perturbed trajectories through space and time.

[Necessary condition-3 for the optimality *through space and time*[10]].

A necessary condition for a feasible trajectory of the economy, $T(C)$, to be optimal is that there exists no perturbed trajectory of the economy through space and time, $T^{ST}(C^{ST})$, which is superior to $T(C)$, namely there exists no $T^{ST}(C^{ST})$ that gives a larger value to the function, $W(\cdot)$,than $T(C)$.

Dynamic Optimality and Dynamic Model

Dynamic optimality should be dependent on the definition of "dynamic model." The dynamic model in this book implies that the optimality of the state of the economy over the time horizon can be pursued using the said model by meeting the necessary conditions-3 for the optimality through space and time as far as the dynamic model has the spatial dimension in any sense. The optimality, thus obtained, is called—dynamic optimality. In order to pursue the dynamic optimality, the mechanism must be specified into the said model with which the (re-)allocation of resources over time as well as space can be made, that is, the equation for the capital accumulation, the network for the shipment of the goods which connects spatially dispersed economies, and so on. However, usually the specification of such mechanisms is not enough for the model alone to pursue the dynamic optimality.

[10]See ibid.

An algorithm such as the optimal control theory, the simplex algorithm, and so on is also required to pursue the dynamic optimality. In this sense, the dynamic model involves such an algorithm.

Dynamic Programming (Optimization) Model

The optimal trajectory of consumption, $\overline{\boldsymbol{C}}$, which maximizes the valuation (objective) function, Eq. (7.93), with the specific valuation function, Eq. (7.94), is substantially the solution to the following programming (optimization) problem:

$$\max_{\{T(C),C\}} \sum_{t=0}^{N} \frac{1}{(1+\rho)^t} U(C_t^1, C_t^2), \tag{7.120}$$

in which: $T(C)$ is a feasible trajectory of the economy with C, namely $T(C)$ is $T = (T^1, T^2)$ which satisfies Eqs. (7.84)–(7.91) with a given constant non-negative vector, $\boldsymbol{C}$. We shall call the programming model of Eq. (7.120)—dynamic programming (optimization) model and we shall call the optimal trajectory of the economy[11] which maximizes the objective function of Eq. (7.120)—optimal solution.

Bang-Bang Solution

The dynamic programming model has a defect in the sense that it sometimes gives an optimal solution in which the variables drastically change through time, which describes the state of the economy. For example, a feasible trajectory of the economy can be an optimal solution to the dynamic programming model in which the consumption is almost zero while the most of the products are devoted for the stock formation and intermediate inputs and the most or all the products are devoted to the consumption at several last periods of the time horizon. It could happen if the productivity of the capital stock in terms of the production function is higher than the discount rate and the roundabout production through time is much advantageous than the devotion of the produced goods to the instance consumption at each period till the period approaches to the end of time horizon. This has a kind of collateral

---

[11]Basically, the optimal trajectory can be described by only using stock variables, K^i $(i = 1, 2)$,R^{ij} $(i, j = 1, 2; i \neq j)$ once $\overline{K}^i$ $(i = 1, 2)$ and $\overline{R}^{ij}$ $(i, j = 1, 2; i \neq j)$ are given as far as the goods is superior goods. However, we keep to use the definition of the trajectory of the economy made in previous subsection, The objective of the planning.

effect such that the people belong to the current aged generation may relatively have disadvantage than the younger people who also may belong to the future generations to be able to enjoy a lavish consumption thanks to the roundabout production through time. The time horizon is the longer, the bigger is the inequity among the current and future generations.

The roundabout production through space (and time) has the same adverse effect such that, for example, the consumption of the people in region 1 is less or almost zero compared to the amount of the goods produced in region 1 as some or most of the products in region 1 are shipped into region 2 for the capital stock formation except for several last periods of the time horizon. It will cause an inequality among people who belongs to the same generations, and lives in different regions (inequality between region 1 and region 2) as well as an inequality between generations in the sense above. This type of inequality could happen irrespective of whether the valuation function takes into account the equality principle in any sense since it could happen due to differences in the technical condition such as the productivity with capital stock, efficiency in the capital stock formation, discount rate, and so on.

One possible way to eliminate and relieve the inequality between generations and regions is to set the lower constraints to the trajectory of consumption of the economy, which is typically given as follows:

$$C_t^i \geq \overset{=i}{C_t} \; (i = 1, 2; t = 0, 1, 2, 3, \ldots, N), \tag{7.121}$$

in which: $\overset{=i}{C_t}$: exogenously given minimum level of the consumption in region i at period t ($i = 1, 2; t = 0, 1, 2, 3..., N$).

The possible inequality with the optimal trajectory of consumption to the dynamic model which has no constraint of Eq. (7.121) (which shall be called—original dynamic model) can be eliminated in the optimal trajectory of consumption to the dynamic model which has the constraint of Eq. (7.121) (which shall be called—dynamic model of constrained consumption). However, as far as the original dynamic model gives the optimal trajectory of consumption that is inequal among generations and/or regions, the dynamic model of constrained consumption will still give an inequal trajectory of consumption to be a solution analogically as the technical condition that causes the inequality is not at all eliminated by the constrained consumption. With the example mentioned previously, the consumption will be kept minimum by making it as much as close to the lower constraint while the saved products will be invested for the capital formation for the most periods. Actually, it can be taken that the consumption variables of the original dynamic model have the lower constraints which are zero due to the non-negativity constraints. The degree of inequality in any sense can be relieved by increasing the values of $\overset{=i}{C_t}$ from zero (0) to positive values. Dissatisfaction with inequality in any sense will exist till a perfect equality is realized forcibly.

It is tough to agree on the exogenously given values of $\overset{=i}{C}_t$ $(i = 1, 2;$ $t = 0, 1, 2, 3..., N)$ and it cannot be totally neglected that: (a) the region having the more population will be assigned the higher values of $\overset{=i}{C}_t$; and (b) the region having more products will be assigned the higher values of $\overset{=i}{C}_t$. A compromise must be made between the former, which is based on a kind of the equality principle, and the latter, which is based on a kind of market principle.

Expanding the Production Possibility Frontier

It is tough at all to specify the functional form, $U(\cdot)$, which is necessary for the practical planning because it should be directly linked with the compromise between the value judgment of (a) and (b) discussed in the previous subsection. To change the view, it can be another approach to pursue the maximized economic growth in terms of the gross domestic products (GDP) while the consumption is kept at an exogenously given level. The consumption level is still must be dependent on a value judgment. However, it can be calibrated to show a difference in the optimal trajectories of the economy to the stakeholders in order to smoothly obtain an agreement among them. The information given by the calibration would be useful for policy process. The dynamic model based on such approach is specified as follows:

$$\max_{\{T(C)\}} \sum_{t=0}^{N} \frac{1}{(1+\rho)^t} \sum\nolimits_{i=1}^{2} V_t^i, \tag{7.122}$$

$$\text{subject to}: C_t^i = \overset{=i}{C}_t \; (i = 1, 2; t = 0, 1, 2, 3, \ldots, N), \tag{7.123}$$

in which: V_t^i : gross value-added in region i at period t and $V_t^i \equiv Y_t^i - \left(X_t^{ii} + X_t^{ji}\right)$ $(i, j = 1, 2; i \neq j)$.

Balanced Development

The dynamic model of Eqs. (7.122) and (7.123) will pursue the roundabout production through space and time, which will cause the same issue with the inequality between generations and regions. The issue of inequality in terms of the consumption is relieved due to Eq. (7.123) and the inequality between regions in terms of the capital stock accumulation may be raised. This is another issue of the balanced development of national land. Analogically, the following constraint can be added in order to relieve the issue:

$$F^k\left(K_t^1, K_t^2\right) \geq 0 \; \left(t = 0, 1, 2, 3, \ldots, N; k = 1, 2, \ldots, n^F\right), \tag{7.124}$$

in which: n^F is the number of additional constraints.

An example of the specification of $F^k(\cdot)$ is the following:

$$\theta_t \leq \frac{K_t^2}{K_t^1} \leq \varphi_t \; \left(K_0^i \neq 0 \; (i = 1, 2), 0 < \theta_t \leq 1, \varphi_t \geq 1 \; (t = 0, 1, 2, 3, \ldots, N)\right). \tag{7.125}$$

Although it is tough to specify values of θ_t and φ_t, too, according to the genuine balanced development of national land, θ_t and φ_t should converge to the ratio of $\frac{A^2}{A^1}$ (A^i is the inhabitable land area in region i ($i = 1, 2$)) as the period reaches to the end of the time horizon. The calibration with θ_t and/or φ_t could be informative for the policy and political process related with the balanced development of national land. The addition of constraints, Eq. (7.125), is a compromise between the efficient trajectory of the economy and the less efficient trajectory which takes into account the balanced development of national land. Starting with a very small (large) value with θ_t (φ_t), an additional increase (decrease) in θ_t (φ_t) causes a decrease in the maximized value of the objective function, Eq. (7.122), respectively. A decrease in the maximized objective function is an indicator of the cost in terms of the present value of the gross value added in order to pursue a further balanced development of national land. The indicator is linked to the imputed prices associated with the constraints, Eq. (7.125), for example, the imputed price associated with the first (left) inequality in Eq. (7.125) is a decrease in the maximized objective function due to a unit increase in the value of θ_t, and so on.

Positioning of the Dynamic Programming Model

Generally speaking, it is very tough to specify constraints or functional form explicitly in the model as the specification substantially should be dependent on a value judgment and the specification itself has been an important policy agenda on which decision should be made through a policy and political process using different terms and phrases. However, it should be rather taken that the dynamic programming model provides useful information for such a policy and political argument process to efficiently and effectively converge to an agreeable decision by openly presenting not only results of the simulation case by case but also adopted functional forms as well as value judgments presumed by the adoption of a specific functional form if any, and so on. We will stop here the explanation about the usefulness of the dynamic programming model due to the limited space.

References

Administrative Management Agency (1979) 1975 industrial input-output tables. Administrative Management Agency, Tokyo

Chenery H (1953) Regional analysis. In: Chenery H, Clark P, Cao-Pinna V (eds) The structure and growth of the Italian economy. US Mutual Security Agency, Rome

Chinese National Statistics Bureau (1983) China statistical year book:1983. China Statistics, Beijing

Cohen JA (1971) Chinese law and Sino-American trade. In: Eckstein A (ed) China Trade Prospects and U.S. Policy. Prager Publishers, New York

Dorfman R, Samuelson PA, Solow RM (1958) Inter-temporal efficiency in Leontief Models. In: Linear programming and economic analysis. McGraw-Hill, New York, pp 335–339

Hirschman AO (1968) The strategy of economic development. Yale University Press, New Haven

Kinoshita T (1978) Survey on the New 10 Years Planning of China and the Japan-China Trade. Modern Econ Quarter 31:118–133

Kohno H (1975) The optimal allocation of public investment using an interregional input-output programming model. Treatise Econ 41(1):61–82

Kohno H (1988) Economic effects measurement method for the appraisal of optimal investment planning of Asian Expressway Network: a summary. Report of Self-Research Project of 1988 fiscal year in the Institute of Socio-Economic Planning. The University of Tsukuba, Tsukuba

Kohno H (1991a) Introduction to interregional input-output analysis I: spatial dynamics of economics. Sangyo Renkan Innov I-O Tech 2(1):65–74

Kohno H (1991b) Introduction to interregional input-output analysis II: tabulation of the competitive import type of interregional input-output structure. Sangyo Renkan Innov I-O Tech 2 (2):66–82

Kohno H (1991c) Introduction to interregional input-output analysis III: development of pilot model for comprehensive appraisal of the social overhead capital reinforcement and supply. Sangyo Renkan Innov I-O Tech 2(4):69–84

Kohno H (1992) Introduction to interregional input-output analysis IV: results of quantitative analysis and appraisal. Sangyo Renkan Innov I-O Tech 3(1):56–77

Kohno H (1993) Introduction to interregional input-output analysis V-1: dynamic interregional input-output programming model. Sangyo Renkan Innov I-O Tech 4(2):67–92

Kohno H (1994) Introduction to interregional input-output analysis V-2: optimal redevelopment model of the Greater Tokyo. Sangyo Renkan Innov I-O Tech 5(2):60–95

Kohno H, Higano Y, Matsumura Y (1987) Dynamic appraisal of the Asian Expressway Network benefits on China. Report of Self-Research Project of 1987 fiscal year in the Institute of Socio-Economic Planning. The University of Tsukuba, Tsukuba

Mao G, Higano Y (1998) Measurement of concealed unemployment in Shanghai. Int Reg Sci Rev 21(1):59–78

McKenzie LW (1963) The Dorfman-Samuelson-Solow Turnpike Theorem. Int Econ Rev 4(1)

MITI (1980) 1975 interregional input-output table: report on prepared results, ministerial secretariat, research and statistics division of MITI, Tokyo, pp 1–156

Moriguchi S (1972) JIS FORTRAN: introduction. The University of Tokyo Press, Tokyo

Moses L (1955) The stability of interregional trading patterns and input-output analysis. Am Econ Rev 45(5):803–826

Moses L (1960) A general equilibrium model of production, interregional trade and location of industry. Rev Econ Stat 42(4):373–397

Postscripts

Connection with the Monograph by Leon N. Moses

Having moved to Tokyo, one of the authors (H. Kohno) had been attached to the incorporated foundation, Express Highway Research Foundation of Japan, which had tentatively dispatched him to the Institute of Production, Waseda University, "in the form of lending human resources to another organization," in order to assist those who were doing research in the Institute on the theme: if some area (of Japan) was attacked by a hypothetical enemy and stroked a deadly blow, how should Japan cope with it? The area was wide, for example, Nagoya, Tokyo, and Sendai.

The research staffs were Prof. and Head Susumu Kobe, Prof. Yoshiji Nishino, lecturer Masaki Oota (at that time), et al. The research had started with a kind of coursed work to thoroughly digest the innovative idea of the article by Leon N. Moses (1960) in order to prescribe practical countermeasures and plans with the theme.

The research results were brought together in *Regional economic analysis of Japan* as the interim report (Kohbe 1962). At that time, Kohno was only a staff of computation branch. Once the project was over, the research team was dissolved. However, he himself continued studying.

Moses model was originally presumed the analysis of American industrial economy by sector, that is, it is suitable for the study of private industry sectors, which are the territory of the Ministry of International Trade and Industry of Japan and her policy is oriented to. On the contrary, there was a feeling that something is wrong with the study of Japan and the Ministry of Construction. It was conspicuous that the public sector is greatly delayed and the reinforcement of infrastructural facilities is the urgent pressing need.

What were created in such a tendency is the very futuristic and beneficial idea that the private industrial organization and public investment allocation can be jointly dealt with by incorporating the public investment allocation mechanism into the Moses's type of interregional input–output programming model. Technically

H. Kohno, Y. Higano, *Public Investment Criteria*, New Frontiers in Regional Science: Asian Perspectives 2, https://doi.org/10.1007/978-4-431-55221-5

speaking, the model can firstly simulate optimal shares between the allocation of investment funds to the private sectors and the public sectors based on the economic rationality and, therefore, consistently. Though it was realized later on, one of the critical mechanisms specified in the model is also a little bit same as Lefeber (1958).

Our model was born heuristically from the policy-oriented need of "How should public investment be allocated optimally (rationally)?" in the periphery of policy government agencies such as the Ministry of Construction and Japan Highway Public Corporation. It is not too much to say that such studies in Japan had begun from the study of Moses (1960). So, it was more than 60 years ago. Kohno still has fond memories of the study session in the Institute of Production, Waseda University, and pays his respects anew to the existence and clear-sightedness of Dr. Susumu Kohbe.

Argument for Optimal Composite (Comprehensive) Transport System

Topics of the composite transport system had been boisterously discussed at the deliberative assemblies of the Ministry of Transport, Ministry of Construction, Economic Planning Agency, and so on, which were set up by the necessity to meet non-negligible demand for improvements in the poor transportation infrastructures, facing the exponentially advancing motorization in the high-speed economic growth period (Dec. 1954–46 Nov. 1973) of the Japanese economy. In a sense, it was an eye-opening fact that the necessity was advocated by a person who was not affiliated with the government, a leader of a business association (Maeda 1961). He was enlightened by epoch-making Watkins Report (Watkins 1956), which had harshly pointed out the chaotic situation in the transport fields in that day as written in the text. The report should have been recognized as the major views of influential experts in the field of transportation policy. However, foresighted scholars were quite few and most pathologically stick to a kind of dogma, namely railway-oriented policy with assistance of coastal shipment transportation infrastructures although the report must have been taken as a grievous blow by the related transport infrastructure investment bureaus, of course.

In the early stage, Prof. Yoshinosuke Yasoshima published *Idea on Fundamental Transport System in the Metropolitan Area* (Yasoshima 1964). *Toward the Innovative Physical Distribution* (MOTDP 1969); *Composite Transport System of Japan* (MOTPP 1972); *Limits of Megalopolis* (Kawagoe 1974); *Interim Report on Composite Transport System* (Shintani 1974), etc. had followed.

It can be said that the composite transport system in Japan was firstly advocated and argued with the terminology of 'comprehensive transport system' as it is mentioned in the text. However, in whichever of these ideas and arguments, objective basements were not found at all, on which economic rationality of, for example, the claim for modal shares can be proved and sustained based on quantitative materials.

In such a chaotic situation, the work presented in Chap. 4 had firstly shown that shares of capital allocation between the public and private sectors should be 0.333:0.667 and those among transport modes of road, railway, and marine (port) should be 0.7629:0.2034:0337. In this sense, the work in Chap. 4 had made cutting-edge achievements in the field of the composite transport system in Japan. It was owing to the DNA which Kohno was injected while he was engaged in the Economic Research Office of Japan Highway Public Corporation under the mentorship of Mr. Tsuneichi Sasaki, and has been succeeded by his disciples till now.

In Chap. 5, several topics are discussed which still leave vast space for further development and improvements in the models presented in this book. To sum up, there are three directions: (a) practically useful minute specification of regions, sectors, transport modes, etc.; (b) dynamic model in its true sense; and (c) incorporation of the demand by person against the transportation infrastructures. The theme of (a) is dealt with in Chap. 6 and nowadays it can be said that it is substantially solved considering the amazing development of computer architecture, data collection, and processing technologies. The trial of topic (b) is shown in Chap. 7. Possible extension in the direction of theme (c) is only discussed and it is left unresolved. In this sense, it can be said that the optimization of the composite transport system is still unresolved.

Relationship with PPBS

The PPBS (Planning, Programming, and Budgeting System) is the management system which unites planning and budgeting. It was firstly introduced by Robert S. McNamara[1], Secretary of National Defense, The United States Department of Defense, in 1961. The introduction to all the Ministries/Agencies of the Federal Government was directed by Vice President Lyndon B. Johnson in 1965, by which the new era would be constructed in the history of reorganization of the federal budgetary system (Miyagawa 1971).

Responding to the movement in the United States, the terminology of PPBS and the tendency to adopt PPBS grew in popularity during 1961–65 in Japan. Kohno studied PPBS from Kato (1965), who was, at that time, Accountant Assistant, the Budget Bureau, the Ministry of Finance, and he was persuaded to cope with PPBS (Schultz 1968). In such a different phase of age, what had made a major progress was the formulation of Steiner=Marglin type of optimization model which was applied to a practical policy agenda for the improvements in the expressway network in Japan.

It can be inferred that equalization of imputed prices, incompatibility location, service constraints, etc. on the economic rationality while pre-empted allocation of budget constraint with the authority concerned on the political and policy argument

[1]He was the high official serving as President of The World Bank (1968–1980).

are the very idea of PPBS with which it was intended that budgetary allocation process in departments of the federal government is made effectively and efficiently without sterile arguments and debates. However, having reread and examined again, e.g., Miyagawa (1971), it is my impression that a concept of optimization or imputed price cannot be found with the assignment of budget though the subdivided vast budget items are enumerated.

In the meantime, it may be said that this PPBS had rapidly been declined without seeing the light of day in the United States and Japan. It is just guessed that a welcome was not given to the new proposal which would entail additional obligations to the regular works. Historically, the PPBS had died down relatively earlier. It can be understood that the failure to introduce PPBS in the government budgetary process and planning was due to the denial reaction to the alteration of traditional structure in the government authorities concerned. This is the very unamazing joke. The elite (persons in high-rank office in the government) have enrolled in the top universities through extraordinarily tough examinations, and have mastered difficult principles and theories. However, once they graduate, and are attached to the central government departments, they start to work for their office (department), and then they do all the work based on the four simple fundamental operations of arithmetic (addition, subtraction, multiplication, and division), an average growth rate, for example, on a ceiling system or the past trend, plus a proportional rate on, for example, vested rights. This is a kind of tease heard in both the Occident and the Orient.

The model in Chap. 3 has suggested a possible direction for the introduction of PPBS successfully. However, as readers might have seen, the introduction of PPBS would have resulted in a miserable failure if it had been welcomed by the officers involved at that time. In a word, PPBS was too early to be proposed. The implementation of PPBS needs vast amount of data (some of them must be top secrets, usage of them can be incompatible with privacy) with which there was not established an overall data collection system in any sense. Even if a vast data could be obtained successfully thanks to cooperative citizens, organizations, communities, municipalities, states, etc., there were no computers and software which can process huge data collected and provide practically useful quantitative materials of budgetary assignment and planning on the rational basement, with which stakeholders would come to an agreeable decision on the implementation of budgetary assignment and planning.

If PPBS were adopted at the present day, what would happen? Data collection even on a real-time base, data mining, model specification, and installing of parameters, simulation, human-friendly display, even analysis of simulation results, etc. can be systemized nowadays thanks to the amazing development of information-related technologies software, which are still developing with critically high speed. The right answer should be simple like there is no problem technically and PPBS shall be able to work. We are afraid that a system once established becomes outdated at once. It can be said that the failure of introducing PPBS into the government administrative system was totally due to technical affairs of the computer engineering around 55 years ago, which was a fortune for bureaucratic officers who should like to keep their established interests. So, it might become again a nightmare if someone tries to implement it. However, it should be recognized that different merits owing to miracle development of information science have been already enjoyed by government officers with all the line of their own posts of duties related to the budget assignment and planning although the realization of merits is not made systematically, and, therefore, attained merits must be limited compared to the potential merits. I other words, computer and software do the calculation with the four operations that has been done manually. Reality has an inevitable meaning and it is sometimes irrational.

By the way, let us cast a glance on how the practical execution has been made related to the public investment criteria, namely a decisive allocation of budget to a proposed project. Spoken directly, it has been done through assessment by budget examiners, the Budget Bureau. Of course, for example, in the way of process to the final stage, there existed many proposals and materials prepared by experts in the fields, who were not necessarily engaged in the department which has made the budget appropriation request. Kohno had come, a few times, to the Budget Bureau in order to wait for his turn to make an assessment of the Japan Highway Public Corporation project on behalf of our Chief of Department. He had learned a great deal about the process of assessment to the determination of budget assignment, which ought to have been done based on the public investment criteria, and that was done before his very eyes.

Shipment Activities Initiated by Moses

We have thought highly of and have with a sense of reverence placed a high value on Leon N. Moses's work, *A general equilibrium model of production, interregional trade and location of industry* (Moses 1960). It is very epoch-making and has unparalleled valuable achievements. It is a kind of Bible for us.

The application of interregional input–output model of noncompetitive import type to the measurement of economic effects seems to be suitable for the analysis of regional economies or in the regional content whatsoever because the table expresses regional interdependency directly by assuming fixed interregional trade patterns. However, we have been suspicious about whether we can measure economic effects in the right way which ought to be generated by a big public investment project such as a composite bridge which connects two big isolated islands and would diffuse into regions via shipment of commodities through the bridge by using an interregional input–output model of Leontief–Isard type, namely, which assumes input–output coefficients of the noncompetitive import type. In reality, why can we expect a fairly good amount of economic effects which could cover the initial investment costs of the bridge? The economic effects are composed of not only time savings in monetary value which are obtainable by using the bridge but also profits and consumers' surplus which are created by new business through changing interregional trade patters among pairs of different regions than those before the bridge is constructed.

The latter effects are far larger than the former, especially in case of public investment projects of large scale. So, there exists self-contradiction with the application of interregional input–output model of the noncompetitive import type to the measurement of economic effects which are generated by a big public investment project, with which we must presume interregional trade patterns possibly.

Even now, the difference between input–output model of the competitive and noncompetitive import types are explained by the difference in the treatment of (net) imports in the input–output tables. For the most usual people who study input–output table, the difference has no substantial meaning other than the difference in the cells where the operation of subtracting/adding imports is made. However, the difference is critical in the content of interregional input–output model, especially its application to the measurement of economic effects which ought to be created by a big public investment project.

Why it must be the noncompetitive import type? The non-substitution theorem is the critical principle with which we can claim we do not need to install alternative production activities. The interregional input–output model of the noncompetitive import type is the embodiment, thanks to the non-substitution theorem. However, it does not hold if the economy faces two or more constraints. Again, backing to the example of bridge, why is the bridge a prosperous project? It can be expected that it will resolve bottlenecks in the economic development such as shortage in supply of transportation services based on transportation infrastructures which connect regions with each other more efficiently and effectively. The situation which makes the project prosperous presumes that there are constraints on the economy from region to region and on the adoption of the method, which cannot be allowed to assume such a situation, to the appraisal of project must be a self-contradiction. However, the model of noncompetitive import type has still been utilized as a reality. We just guess so because a solution, which should be simply called—solution, is obtained by a simple calculation of the inverse matrix and it is unique. Therefore, of course, there is no room for discussion if it is optimal, if it will be realized on what logic with which we can argue, etc. In other words, the reason why the interregional input–output model of the noncompetitive import type has been utilized is that there was no operational interregional input–output model of the competitive import type.

Reasons why the input output model of the noncompetitive import type has been utilized so far, in a sense, become defects of the interregional input–output analysis although it does not matter whether the reasons are true or not. As far as we are able to judge, Moses's desert to be praised is that he has firstly developed the idea of 'shipment activity' and formulates an operational interregional input–output model of the competitive import type, which is the right specification of I-O model suitable for the appraisal of large-scale public investment, and far saves necessary data for the composition of inter-regional I-O model. However, apart from no explicit specification of sectors of transportation or transportation infrastructures, Moses's idea was a little bit confusing. The shipment activity of Moses's definition should be named as—production activity of goods. It can be defined related with production and logistics technologies available for the origin region only, with goods by goods and delivered region by delivered region. This was unfamiliar for those who have firstly mastered the inter-regional I-O model of Isard type, of which specification needs technology and logistics data with all pairs of regions. We just guess this is a reason why his work has been under-evaluated for so long. However, his model has substantial features, with which most of the defects inherent to the *conceptual* and *non-operational* interregional input–output model of competitive-import type although, of course, it was a proto-type model.

In Chap. 4, the model is presented in which transportation sectors and infrastructures constraints are explicitly specified. It is an extension of Moses's model in the sense that we reconstruct his original model into the model which is suitable for the appraisal of economic effects by highlighting his innovative idea of shipment activity. The model is a maximization model of the gross (or net) value added contrary to Moses's model in which the transportation cost is minimized in order to obtain a finite solution without constraints. The formulation of the model as an optimization model jointly solves the installment of optimal investment criteria into the model that is the essential subject to any model for the appraisal of public investment projects which must be implemented under the scarce public funds. It is explained how parameters of shipment activities are calculated based on input–output table at purchasers' price and basic trade table. A practical reason is clarified why shipment activities must be constructed based on input–output table at purchasers' price and not producers' price although it is said the latter is superior to the former and the latter is used for usual analysis.

In Chap. 7, the main subject was construction of a dynamic model in its true sense; we have defined "shipment activities" which are different from the ones used by Moses in Chaps. 4 and 6. Owing to the definition, we are able to avoid a sterile discussion among experts about utilization of data from I-O table at producer's price or I-O table at purchaser's price for the specification of an interregional trade model although we need data in the basic trade table on which both I-O tables are constructed.

Tokyo, Japan Hirotada Kohno

References

Kato T (1965) Public investment and finance. (mimeograph)

Kawagoe A (1974) Limits of megalopolis (record of the informal gathering for discussion on greater city problem), T.E.R.C., Tokyo, Japan

Kohbe S (1962) Regional economic analysis of Japan, Interim Report of 1961, Waseda University, Production Institute, Tokyo, Japan

Lefeber L (1958) Allocation in space: production, transport and industrial location. Amsterdam, North-Holland

Maeda K (1961) Treatise on public investment, Toyokeizai-shinposha, Tokyo, Japan

Miyagawa K (1971) Research of PPBS: emphasis on program system and output index, Research series 24, The Economic Planning Agency of The Economic Research Institute, The Ministry of Finance, The Printing Bureau, Tokyo, Japan

Moses LN (1960) A general equilibrium model of production, interregional trade and location of industry. Rev Econ Stat 42(4):373–397

Schultz CL (1968) The politics and economics of public spending, Brookings Institution, Washington, DC

Shintani Y, Yohji Shintani, Mitsugu Nakamura Composite Transport Research Meeting et al. (1974) Interim Report on Composite Transport System (Direction oriented under the new constraints) C.T.R.M., Tokyo, Japan

The Ministry of Transport (MOTDP), The Ministerial Secretariat, Distribution Planner (1969) Toward the Innovative Physical Distribution (Record of transport economic informal gathering for discussions), T.E.R.C., Tokyo, Japan

The Ministry of Transport (MOTPP), The Ministerial Secretariat, Policy Planner (1972) Composite Transport System of Japan, Transport Economic Research Center, Tokyo, Japan

Yasoshima Y (1964) Idea on Fundamental Transport System in the Metropolitan Area, The University of Tokyo, the Faculty of Engineering, Civil Engineering Institute, Tokyo, Japan

Acknowledgments

Colleagues with Whom We Had Broken Bread

We would like to express our sincere gratitude to Prof. Hitoshi Mitomo, Prof. Yuji Matsumura, and Prof. Takaharu Morishima, who assisted laborious works related to the works dealt with in this book at the University of Tsukuba. They were our colleagues in the true sense with whom we had broken bread, for some years. Especially, Prof. H. Mitomo had taken charge of simulation in Chap. 6. Prof. Y. Matsumura was in charge of computer simulation related to the work in Chap. 7. His program coding skill to convert a complicated mathematical equation system into a digital data without mistake adaptable to the software available at that time was excellent. He had punctually responded to our complicated and esoteric directions and requests, which were sometimes big orders, of course. In the evening, we gathered and used to go to any restaurant; most frequently, we visited *TonQ restaurant* to take a fried cutlet set meal. It was a very pleasant time.

Gratitude to My Family

I would like to express my sincere gratitude to my spouse, Yukiko, who has devoted herself modestly and silently to cooking, washing, cleaning, etc. She has good friends of a parent association, one of whom lives in a great residence which is so grand that she can't see the entrance from the gate. On the other hand, our poor condominium is comparable to its verandah yet being short of one meter. However, regardless of such a thing, she faces anything positively and faithfully based on firm belief.

Her friend at a meeting of daughter/son's parent association said, "My husband said, Yukiko need not feel so small, rather to be proud of more because she has induced both her son and daughter to enter The Faculty of Law, Tokyo University, the highest seat of learning. It is very tough for usual people through my experience through the major bank."

Two Teachers to Whom I have Been Greatly Indebted

One of them is late Mr. Tsuneichi Sasaki, Chief of the Economic Research Office (ERO), the Japan Highway Public Corporation (JHPC) (Sasaki 1961; Kohno 2012). ERO had established a kind of sister research institute relationship with the Expressway Highway Foundation of Japan, which I was engaged in as a researcher when I first came up to Tokyo. Fortunately, we both are from the same province (30–40 km between Mitoyo City of my home village and Niihama City). He sometimes bantered me saying that I had come to Tokyo with great ambitions. He sometimes bantered me by saying that Kohno had come to Tokyo with great ambitions. I just thought he recalled it with fondness that he himself had gone to Manchuria (the Northeast China) before the last Second War just after graduation from the Law School of the Imperial University of Tokyo in order to obtain a researcher position in the Research Department of the South Manchuria Railway Company, which had been established as a national policy concern and recognized as the top level research institute in Japan.

After my place of work was moved formally to ERO of JHPC on October, 1960, I had been trained by him as a quantitative economic researcher. During my service in JHPC, I had mainly engaged in the preparation of economic documents, which were submitted to the World Bank in order to receive the loan funds for the Mei-Shin and To-Mei Expressway construction projects (focusing on the measurement of economic effects of expressway and investment criteria).

Chief T. Sasaki had retired and moved to the Institute of Behavioral Science as Executive Director. At that time, I entered the Graduate School of Economics, The University of Tokyo. Subsequently, I was lucky to be hired by his new institute as an investigating researcher. Fortunately, I could support my wife and children thanks to Chief T. Sasaki. I shall never forget what he has done for me.

Another teacher to whom I had been greatly indebted is late Dr. Yasuhiko Oishi, Professor Emeritus, Faculty of Economics, at the University of Tokyo. Since I had attended at the Graduate School of Economics, I had been receiving his guidance. An oracle delivered by Prof. Oishi "if the student of economics has conquered only *General Theory* by Keynes and *Value and Capital* by Hicks, he/she would be able to have foresight for the future prospect" was very famous. It had a positive effect on me (Oishi 1953; Higano 2020; Kohno 2021).

During the graduate school, I was lucky enough to be given a chance to translate Klein (1962) under the editorial supervision of Professor Oishi. I am much obliged to his teachings given in different circumstances, among which the most influential and, therefore, greatest one for me considering my long research life is "Without going with the current of the times, pursuit research of your favorite target." At that time, in the graduate school, my seniors and colleagues were pursuing achievement in various fields like neo-classical school model of economic growth, two-sector model of economic growth, etc. So, I had concentrated my energy on the large-scale computing measurement work, which was done by using a big computer named mainframe. It was a programming model shown in Chap. 4.

I would like to dedicate this book to Professor Oishi as a token of my sincere gratitude for the valuable advice and guidance given to me.

Tokyo, Japan Hirotada Kohno

References

Higano Y (2020) Genpachiro Konno (1906–1996), Yasuhiko Oishi (1922–2014), and Hirotada Kohno (1932–): The three great fathers of Japanese regional science. In: Batey P, Plane D (eds) Great minds in regional science, Springer, Cham

Kohno H (2012) The State of the Japan Section of the Regional Science Association International in the Early Years: The first 50 years of the JSRSAI. In: JSRSAI (ed) The fifty years of the JSRSAI and Prospects, Sasaki-Shuppan, Tokyo, Japan

Kohno H (2021) Presentation of my books to library and the memories of The Faculty of Economics. Yushin (Alumni Association Bulletin of The Faculty of Economics, Kagawa University), Takamatsu, p 4

Klein LR (1962) An introduction to econometrics, Prentice-Hall, Englewood Cliffs, NJ.

Oishi S (1953) Modern economics: from marginal revolution to J. M. Keynes: Introduction to the study of economics. Nihon Hyoron-shinsha, Tokyo, Japan

Sasaki T (1961) Treatise on economic effects of road: classification and measurement of economic effects (mimeograph)

Watkins RJ (1956) Report on Nagoya-Kobe Expressway Survey (Submitted for Ministry of Construction, Government of Japan). Ministry of Construction, Tokyo

Printed by Printforce, the Netherlands